THE SOUL
OF BATTLE

From Ancient Times to the Present Day,

How Three Great Liberators

Vanquished Tyranny

VICTOR DAVIS HANSON

The Free Press

THE FREE PRESS
A Division of Simon & Schuster Inc.
1230 Avenue of the Americas
New York, NY 10020

Designed by Carla Bolte

Manufactured in the United States of America

10 9 8 7 6 5 4 3 2 1

Library of Congress Cataloging-in-Publication Data

Hanson, Victor Davis.
    The soul of battle : from ancient times to the present day, how
three great liberators vanquished tyranny / Victor Davis Hanson.
        p. cm.
    Includes bibliographical references and index.
    1. Military history.   2. Epaminondas, b. ca. 420 B.C.—Military
leadership.   3. Sherman, William T. (William Tecumseh), 1820–1891—
Military leadership.   4. Patton, George S. (George Smith),
1885–1945—Military leadership.   5. Motivation (Psychology)
I. Title.
D25.5.H26   1999   99-23853   CIP
355'.009—dc21

ISBN 0–684–84502–4   (alk. paper)

IN MEMORIAM

Sergeant William F. Hanson (1921–1998), U.S. Army Air Corps

504th Bombing Group, 313th Bomber Wing, 398th Squadron, Tinian

Coporal Victor Hanson (1922–1945), U.S. Marine Corps

29th Marines, 6th Marine Division, Okinawa

CONTENTS

PART II
THE ARMY OF THE WEST

SHERMAN'S MARCH TO THE SEA

NOVEMBER 16–DECEMBER 21, 1864

PART III
THE THIRD ARMY

PATTON'S RACE INTO GERMANY

AUGUST 1, 1944–MAY 8, 1945

LIST OF MAPS AND ILLUSTRATIONS

There is a soul to an army as well as to the individual man, and no general can accomplish the full work of his army unless he commands the soul of his men, as well as their bodies and legs.

William Tecumseh Sherman

The secret of victory lies not wholly in knowledge. It lurks invisible in that vitalizing spark, intangible, yet evident as lightning—the warrior soul.

George S. Patton

PROLOGUE

I

My father, who helped in a small way to kill thousands, was not a violent man. Curtis LeMay, who led him into battle, surely was. The former, two years off a small farm in the central San Joaquin Valley, left a quiet college campus in California in early 1943, and at twenty-one joined the American armed forces. For much of the Great Depression, a decade prior, millions in the Imperial Japanese Army had been plundering China and Southeast Asia, and they were now engaged in a murderous fight to the death against an assorted host of enemies. In contrast, William Hanson had fired a small rifle only at birds and rabbits, in the countryside five miles outside the backwater farming town of Kingsburg, California. In his two decades he had never ventured much more than a few miles from his parents' farmhouse. He had never been in an airplane and had never seen a bomb. When he enlisted in the United States Army, his future plane, the B-29, did not even exist as a combat-tested bomber.

When William Hanson joined the American army, imperial Japan was still largely unscathed. The closest American land forces to Japan were well over 2,000 miles away. Only a few planners like Curtis LeMay knew that thousands of enlisted civilians like my father in a few months of training could kill both brutally and efficiently, if given the proper equipment and leadership—and backed by the vast industrial capacity of the American nation. My grandfather, a farmer who twenty-seven years earlier had left the same forty acres, also served in a democratic army. Frank Hanson ended up as a corporal in the 91st Infantry Division and was gassed in the Argonne. He told my father that he should quickly get used to killing—and that he probably would either not come back, or would return crippled. Americans, my grandfather added, had to learn to fight fast.

1

A little more than a year after his enlistment, on March 9, 1945, a 400-mile-long trail of 334 B-29s left their Marianas bases, 3,500 newly trained airmen crammed in among the napalm. The gigantic planes each carried ten tons of the newly invented jellied gasoline incendiaries. Preliminary pathfinders had seeded flares over Tokyo in the shape of an enormous fiery X to mark the locus of the target. Planes flew over in small groups of three, a minute apart. Most were flying not much over 5,000 feet above Japan. Five-hundred-pound incendiary clusters fell every 50 feet. Within thirty minutes, a 28-mile-per-hour ground wind sent the flames roaring out of control. Temperatures approached 1,800 degrees Fahrenheit. The Americans flew in without guns, and LeMay was not interested in shooting down enemy airplanes. He instead filled the planes with napalm well over their theoretical maximum loads. He wished to destroy completely the material and psychological capital of the Japanese people, on the brutal theory that once civilians had tasted what their soldiers had done to others, only then might their murderous armies crack. Advocacy for a savage militarism from the rear, he thought, might dissipate when one's house was in flames. People would not show up to work to fabricate artillery shells that killed Americans when there was no work to show up to. Soldiers who kill, rape, and torture do so less confidently when their own families are at risk at home.

The planes returned with their undercarriages seared and the smell of human flesh among the crews. Over 80,000 Japanese died outright; 40,918 were injured; 267,171 buildings were destroyed. One million Japanese were homeless. Air currents from the intense heat sent B-29s spiraling thousands of feet upward. Gunners like my father could see the glow of the inferno from as far away as 150 miles as they headed home. The fire lasted four days. My father said he could smell burned flesh for miles on the way back to Tinian. Yet, only 42 bombers were damaged, and 14 shot down. *No single air attack in the history of conflict had been so devastating.*

Unfortunately for the Japanese, the March 9 raid was the beginning, not the end, of LeMay's incendiary campaign. He sensed that his moment—a truly deadly man in charge of a huge democratic force free of government constraint—had at last arrived, as the imperial Japanese command was stunned and helpless. All the old problems—the weather, the enemy fighters, the jet stream, the high-altitude wear on the engines, political limitations on bombing civilians—were now irrelevant. There was to be no public objection to LeMay's burning down the industrial and residential center of the Japanese empire—too many stories about Japanese atrocities toward subjugated peoples and prisoners of war had filtered back to the American people. To a democratic nation in arms, an enemy's unwarranted aggression and murder is everything, the abject savagery of its own retaliatory response apparently nothing.

Suddenly, all of Japan lay defenseless before LeMay's new and unforeseen plan of low-level napalm attack. To paraphrase General Sherman, he had pierced the shell of the Japanese empire and had found it hollow. LeMay had thousands of recruits, deadly new planes, and a blank check to do whatever his bombers could accomplish. Over 10,000 young Americans were now eager to work to exhaustion to inflict even more destruction. Quickly, he upped the frequency of missions, sending his airmen out at the unheard-of rate of 120 hours per month—the Eighth Air Force based in England had usually flown a maximum of 30 hours per month—as they methodically burned down within ten days Tokyo, Nagoya, Kobe, and Osaka before turning to smaller cities. His ground crews simply unloaded the bombs at the dock and drove them right over to the bombers, without storing them in arms depots. Between 300 and 400 planes roared out almost every other day, their crews in the air 30 hours and more each week. Missions over Japan, including preliminary briefings and later debriefings, often meant 24 consecutive hours of duty. Benzedrine and coffee kept the flyers awake.

In revenge for the unprovoked but feeble attack at Pearl Harbor on their country, American farmers, college students, welders, and mechanics of a year past were now prepared—and quite able—to ignite the entire island of Japan. Their gigantic bombers often flew in faster than did the sleek Japanese fighters sent up to shoot them down. Japanese military leaders could scarcely grasp that in a matter of months colossal runways had appeared out of nowhere in the Pacific to launch horrendous novel bombers more deadly than any aircraft in history, commanded by a general as fanatical as themselves, and manned by teenagers and men in their early twenties more eager to kill even than Japan's own feared veterans. So much for the Japanese myth that decadent pampered Westerners were ill equipped for the savagery of all-out war. Even in the wildest dreams of the most ardent Japanese imperialists, there was no such plan of destroying the entire social fabric of the American nation.

When the war ended, William Hanson had become a seasoned central fire control gunner on a B-29, with thirty-four raids over Japan. His plane and nearly a thousand others had materialized out of nowhere on the former coral rock of the Mariana Islands, burned the major cities of Japan to the ground—and in about twelve months were gone for good. Yet for the rest of their lives these amateurs were fiercely loyal to the brutal architect of their lethal work, who announced after the inferno was over, "I suppose if I had lost the war, I would have been tried as a war criminal." LeMay was absolutely right—he would have. My father occasionally ridiculed LeMay's bluster and his cigar, but it was LeMay nonetheless whom he ridiculed—and LeMay whom he was proud that he had served under.

For much of my life I have wondered where such a murderous force of a season came from. And how a democracy made a willing killer out of my father and other farm boys, putting their lives into the hands of an unhinged zealot like LeMay, who ostensibly was neither emblematic of a democratic citizenry nor representative of the values that we purportedly cherish. Or was he? How can a democratic leader brag of such destruction, take pride in his force's ability to destroy thousands—in short, how can he be so utterly uncouth? How in less than a year after being assembled can a motley group of young recruits fly the most lethal bombers in history to incinerate a feared imperial militaristic culture six thousand miles from their own home? And how can that most murderous air force in the world nearly disappear into the anonymity and amnesia of democracy six months after its victory?

Those thoughts are the easy anxieties of the desk-bound class. I have come to realize that both Curtis LeMay and my father are stock types, not aberrations, of the democratic society that produced them. Democracy, and its twin of market capitalism, alone can instantaneously create lethal armies out of civilians, equip them with horrific engines of war, imbue them with a near-messianic zeal within a set time and place to exterminate what they understand as evil, have them follow to their deaths the most ruthless of men, and then melt anonymously back into the culture that produced them. It is democracies, which in the right circumstances, can be imbued with the soul of battle, and thus turn the horror of killing to a higher purpose of saving lives and freeing the enslaved.

My father knew of that soul long ago, which explains why during these last fifty years he was proud to have served under LeMay—an authentic military genius notwithstanding his extremism. Despite his horrific stories of B-29s overloaded with napalm blowing up on takeoff, of low-flying bombers shredded by flak and their crews of eleven sent spiraling into their self-generated inferno over Tokyo, of the smell of burning Japanese flesh wafting through the bomb-bay doors, of parachuting flyers beheaded on landing, he never equated that barbarity with either LeMay or himself.

On the contrary, he seemed to think the carnage below his plane and the sacrifice of his friends in the air—twelve of sixteen B-29s in his 398th Squadron, 132 of 176 men, were shot down, crashed, or never heard from again—had been necessary to win the war against a racist imperial power, and to save, not expend, both Asian and American lives. Despite his lifelong Democratic party credentials, my father spoke highly of "Old Iron Pants" even in the midst of the general's subsequent entry into controversial right-wing politics. The bastard shortened the war against evil, my father told me. You were all lucky, he went on, once to have had angry men like LeMay and us in the air. We flew into the fire, he said, because we believed that we were saving more lives than we took. As he aged, all memories—childhood, job, family— receded as the recollection of those nights over Tokyo grew sharper; parties, vacations, and familial holiday festivities were to become sideshows compared to annual reunions with his 313th Bomber Wing and 398th Squadron. His last hallucinatory gasps of July 1998 in death's throes were a foreign vocabulary of B-29 operations and frantic calls to crew members, most of whom were long since dead.

Democracies, I think—if the cause, if the commanding general, if the conditions of time and space take on their proper meaning—for a season can produce the most murderous armies from the most unlikely of men, and do so in the pursuit of something spiritual rather than the mere material. This book, devoted to infantry, not airpower, tries to learn why all that is so.

II

What, then, is the soul of battle? A rare thing indeed that arises only when free men march unabashedly toward the heartland of their enemy in hopes of saving the doomed, when their vast armies are aimed at salvation and liberation, not conquest and enslavement. Only then does battle take on a spiritual dimension, one that defines a culture, teaches it what civic militarism is and how it is properly used. Alexander, Hannibal, Caesar, Napoleon, and other great marshals used their tactical and strategic genius to alter history through the brutality of their armies. None led democratic soldiers. They freed no slaves nor liberated the oppressed. They were all aggressors, who created their matchless forces to kill rather than to preserve. As was true of most great captains of history, they fought for years on end, without democratic audit, and sought absolute rule as the prize of their victories. None were great men, and praise of their military prowess is forever tainted by the evil they wrought and the innocent they killed. They and their armies were without a moral sense and purpose, and thus their battles, tactically brilliant though they were, were soulless.

In contrast, three lesser-known generals were as great in battle and far greater in war; the killing they did and the magnificent armies they led were to save not take lives, to free not enslave, and to liberate not annex ground. We military historians, if we claim a morality in our dark craft, must always ask not merely what armies do, but rather what they are for.

In the winter of 370–369 the obscure Theban general Epaminondas marched his army of democratic yeomen and their allies about 180 miles south into Laconia, the legendary home of the Spartan army and a region inviolate from invasion for more than six hundred years. In a little over four months, the Theban-led invasion dismantled the system of Spartan apartheid—the enslavement of 200,000 Messenian serfs—and permanently weakened the military culture which had rested upon the principle that elite warriors should not work. The culture of classical Greece was never again the same.

Sparta, which had fielded the predominant infantry in Greece for three centuries, ceased to be a major military power in that single winter. Yet it was not merely their Helot servants across the mountains in the region of Messenia who were to be emancipated in the winter of 370–369. Epaminondas's Thebans also drove into the very suburbs of Sparta, caused near revolution among the Spartiate overlords themselves, ravaged the farms of Laconia, humiliated the plantation class, liberated the subject states of the Spartans' Peloponnesian alliance, and ensured that three vast cities—Messenê in Messenia, and Mantinea and Megalopolis in Arcadia—would be independent and fortified to ensure that their men and property would stay home, free from Spartan expropriation. Within a few weeks, Sparta's allies were gone, the majority of her Helots liberated, and her army humiliated.

Epaminondas killed more Spartan hoplites in a single day at the battle of Leuctra than had the entire Persian army that once invaded Greece over a century earlier, more than Athens had in twenty-seven years of the Peloponnesian War. He destroyed the Spartan state in one season—something imperial Athens could not do in nearly three decades of warring. In 370 during Epaminondas's invasion, the Spartan women themselves came out of their homes to witness the terror in their midst—and the strange revolutionary who had shown the entire "Spartan mystique" to be a sham. Is it any surprise that the Spartans after the battle of Mantinea (362) erected a monument to the soldier who finally killed the hated Epaminondas?

This was a general, after all, who when told of Athenian opposition, promised to turn the Athenian countryside into nothing more than a pasture for sheep. At one point the Theban upstart even bragged to his peers that he would lead his phalanx right onto the Athenian acropolis, pull down their hallowed marble propylaeum, gateway to the Parthenon, and resurrect it in

6

the Theban agora!—the equivalent of an Emiliano Zapata boasting that he would cart off the Washington Monument to plant it in the Plaza de Armas. Epaminondas, not Zapata, really could have. How this man and his army in the winter of 370–369 freed thousands of serfs, ended the power of the Spartan military state in Greece, created killers out of farmers, and lost scarcely a soldier in battle—and accomplished that feat in a few months—should tell us something about the deadliness of a particular brand of democratic militias, which run amuck murderously for a season behind a great leader for a just cause and then suddenly disappear back to their homes.

More than twenty-two hundred years later William Tecumseh Sherman marched a similar-sized army of over 60,000 Westerners—like Thebans mostly rural, agrarian, and voting citizens—into the heart of the Confederacy—like Sparta the warden of sorts of an entire enslaved race. Sherman's Federal army rent the fabric of Georgian society. It freed rural black slaves, and left the opposing Rebels impotent and discredited before their helpless women and children. In less than forty days from November 16 to December 21, 1864, when he entered Savannah on the coast, Sherman's three-hundred-mile march had changed the entire psychological and material course of the Civil War.

My maternal grandmother, Georgia Johnston Davis, whose family— Johnstons from the South who claimed Albert Sidney Johnston as one of their own—had migrated to California from the ex-Confederacy, told me at ten that Sherman was a satanic "monster." Over a century after he died, many Southerners would still agree. In spring 1998, wire services reported the curious story of a wealthy Southerner who sought to write into the deed of his recently restored South Carolina plantation a restriction of future sale to anyone named "Sherman." In fact, the owner, Henry Ingram, Jr., told the Associated Press that his plantation, five miles north of Savannah and destroyed by Sherman in January 1865, should never fall into the hands of anyone of the "Yankee race" who was born above the Mason-Dixon line. Anyone with the name Sherman, Ingram promised, would not be allowed even to set foot on the property.

Very few of Sherman's Yankees were professional soldiers. The majority of his officers—most promoted from the enlisted ranks—were not raised in a hallowed tradition of military academies and genteel chivalry. Sherman, a West Point man, knew this and understood that the very tenets of free yeomanry lent a natural distaste for the binary world of the serf and plantation, giving his recruits a moral impetus to wreck Georgia. They marched out of Atlanta singing "John Brown's Body," and ravaged plantations to "The Battle

Hymn of the Republic." Northerners from the Midwest and West, like the Thebans of old—no strangers to physical work, and eager rather than reluctant to march, camp outdoors, and live off the land—were to become lethal destroyers when given an ethical imperative, free rein, and a leader to drive them on. From November 1864 until it vanished in June 1865 just as abruptly as it was formed, Sherman's Army of the West was quite literally the most impressive and deadly body in the history of armed conflict—a truly ideological army that reflected the soul of its creator, Uncle Billy Sherman.

As in the advance of Epaminondas into the Peloponnese, Sherman fought few decisive engagements, but in a matter of weeks left a military culture in ruins, as no Georgian army dared meet him in pitched battle—as no Spartan phalanx had braved Epaminondas. To paraphrase Napoleon, Sherman, like Epaminondas, had "destroyed the enemy merely by marches" in a classical display of the indirect approach around rather than directly against the enemy's armies.

Sherman was well connected politically but was entirely democratic in his personal demeanor—without money, without title, or much desire to profit from his military glory. And like Epaminondas, this creature of democracy, indistinguishable to the eye from his men, had an innate disdain for the masses, a near loathing which in the abstract can only be seen as elitist: a few gifted men, a natural not an aristocratic elite, devoted to order were alone to be trusted to lead a mostly undereducated and easily swayed rabble whose natural proclivity was always to anarchy. Only educated, self-restrained, and rather fatalistic men like Sherman could govern soldiers like Americans, just as only a rare man like Epaminondas could manage his Thebans.

That this asthmatic and often sickly man suffered from occasional manic depression may be true. He threatened to hang reporters and shoot insubordinate enlisted men and was not afraid to match Confederate execution for execution or burn down entire cities that harbored terrorists. Admirer of the agrarian yeomen who had built his country, he had no real confidence in the intellect and culture of the American black, Indian, and Mexican. In short, like Epaminondas, he often seemed a dangerous, opinionated, and in some sense antidemocratic ascetic in charge of a murderous democratic militia whose deadliness derived in large part from his own tactical and strategic genius. His army's legacy, like the Thebans', is that his mob of burners and ravagers saved far more lives than they took, helped to free an enslaved people when others more liberal could not, and in a few months disgraced the notion of militarism without fighting a major battle.

The war for the Union ended a few months after Sherman reached Savannah on the coast and turned northward into the Carolinas. Within a year of burning Atlanta most of his bluecoats were back again farming in the Midwest. Almost to the man they were never to muster under arms again—at the time the most rapid demobilization of the most accomplished army in history. It is difficult to determine whether Georgians hated Sherman and his army as much as the Spartans despised Epaminondas and the Thebans. Both men had wrecked their centuries-old practice of apartheid in a matter of weeks. It is a dangerous and foolhardy thing for a slaveholding society to arouse a democracy of such men.

Eighty years after Sherman reached Savannah, General George S. Patton officially took command of the newly formed Third Army on August 1, 1944, a few weeks after the Allied invasion of Normandy. When Patton arrived in Normandy, the Allied armies of General Eisenhower were just beginning to break out from nearly six weeks in the hedgerows of western France. The German army in Western Europe was still a formidable occupying force of over a million men. General Montgomery was calling for a slow American sweep, as he requested the lion's share of Allied supplies to thrust through Holland. Only with ever more men and supplies that would at last ensure material superiority could the Allies, Montgomery thought, press on a single narrow front into Germany, perhaps crossing the Rhine in winter or spring 1946. Eisenhower and his lieutenants, Generals Bradley and Hodges, although no fans of this British modern-day McClellan—similarly a genius at methodical organization and training—were apparently unable to offer a successful strategic alternative, in constant worry over supply lines, flanks, and the reputation of the German army.

Patton, recently disgraced from two slapping incidents in Sicily, considered unbalanced, the object of both envy and disdain, like Epaminondas and Sherman was lucky to obtain the command that he was born for. In the past he had been a superior to Eisenhower and Bradley and now was fortunate to serve under both. Just as Epaminondas was reduced to carrying a shield as an ordinary hoplite in the phalanx, just as Sherman was once declared insane and sent away to recuperate, so too Patton by early 1944 was a general without an army, an acknowledged military genius considered too unstable to command a brigade—many wondered whether his many past head injuries had resulted in permanent brain damage.

Ten months after Patton took over the Third Army, the German forces in the West were wrecked, Patton's GIs were across the Rhine into central Europe, and Germany itself was in ruins. Patton came late to Normandy; but in August 1944, during the first thirty days of the Third Army's operations, Patton pushed his Americans five times as far to the east as the entire Allied army had progressed during the prior seven-week period after D-Day. Most

Americans of the Third Army had been in combat less than a year when they reached the death camps of Germany and helped to put an end to German military power and its entire pseudo-science of an overclass of genetic supermen. Patton's chief of staff, Hobart Gay, concluded of their march:

> Not since 1806 has an army conquered Germany or crossed any large portion of it. I question if anyone a few years ago even as late at the beginning of this war or as late as last year, felt the war would end with American forces having completely over-run Germany and passed into other countries. This time the Germans know what war at home means. The German nation has completely disintegrated, and even though they are an enemy nation, it is a saddening sight to witness.

Unlike the First World War, this time Americans would be in Germany; the German landscape would experience what the German army had done to others elsewhere; and there would be no question that anyone had stabbed the Wehrmacht in the back.

George S. Patton, who insisted on hot food and clean socks for his men, who led by example, a wounded World War One veteran who braved gunfire as a display of heroic leadership, was also no fan of democracy in the abstract. His diary entries at times can elicit disgust. Like Epaminondas, he fought continuously with his fellow generals and was nearly court-martialed for his altercations with his superiors—like Epaminondas he was relieved of command after his greatest victories. Like the Theban, he could be brutal to his men and, as some crazed modern-day Pythagorean, believed in reincarnation and his own appointed destiny. He fought democratically, but thought aristocratically, and did not believe the men whom he led and loved were themselves capable of governing themselves.

"Old Blood and Guts" may have been admired by his soldiers, but like "Iron Gut" Epaminondas and "Uncle Billy" Sherman, he possessed a certain distance and at times contempt for the very masses he led. While he fought, he hated the Nazis, and yet was relieved of command in part for expressing sympathy with ex–German officials—not unlike Sherman's latter admiration for Southern veterans, or Theban charges that Epaminondas had ruined Sparta but was soft on Spartans.

All three, who followed some arcane code of honor, were poorly suited for peace; and thus in some sense all three admired the very warrior culture that they helped to destroy. All three were at the most basic level intellectuals, widely read in literature and the scholarship of war, and with a keen interest in questions metaphysical and philosophical—which suggests that most of their tirades and crudity were efforts to mask the embarrassment of such an aesthetic sense, and to project to their men and the public an image of a general who was a warrior always, not a keen student of the arts and sciences.

Patton, severely wounded in World War One, could not refrain, even as general of hundreds of thousands, from stalking the front lines like Epaminondas, who perished at the van under a hail of Spartan spear thrusts, and like the wounded Sherman at Shiloh, who had three mounts shot out from under him in a few hours. No wonder that of all American generals, Patton was most impressed with Sherman and his daring march into the interior of Georgia. It was not the drunken Alexander the Great nor the megalomaniac Hannibal whom Patton saw as the great general of antiquity, but Epaminondas, who, in his words, was alone worthy of emulation due to his "great genius, great goodness, and great patriotism."

Within months all three forces developed from an untrained amateur muster into a deadly, fast-moving horde of predators, who traveled continuously and left fire and ruin in their wake. All three armies and their commanders upset conventional wisdom about the role of mobility, logistics, and amateur militias, proving that the most lethal, the most disciplined, and the most organized armies can emerge from the chaos of democracy. Such armies do not linger after they are finished. They are not used to further the personal ambitions of their beloved generals, or to change public policy—much less as instruments to overturn the constitutional governments they serve. Epaminondas's 70,000, who marched in midwinter into Sparta, by May the next season were farming. The greatest army in the history of conflict until the late nineteenth century was Sherman's, and yet it disappeared literally within a few days of the armistice; in May 1945, Patton's Third Army numbered over a half million, but by Christmas both its veterans and its general were gone.

These marchers of a season must be led by ruthless and gifted men who are often of little use in a peacetime democracy but find their proper authoritarian and aristocratic calling only as absolute rulers of an armed citizenry. Yet much of their bluster and avowals to make the enemy "howl," to turn the countryside into a "sheep-walk," to kill the "bastards," was the necessary veneer to their more subtle strategy of indirect approaches—marches to destroy the enemy's spiritual and material resources rather than the annihilation of his armies in the field per se—a strategy so suited to a democracy that is fickle and wary of costs and casualties, yet so misunderstood by fellow commanders and politicians weaned on the parallel Western tradition of brutal frontal assault on the fighting forces of the enemy.

All three forces had not started the war and did not wish it to begin. All three armies wrought a terrible vengeance on those who had once felt them poor soldiers. These generals who so believed in a code of military gallantry and order destroyed utterly the paradoxical notion of "honor" among a society of slaveholders, by marching into the enemy's native land and daring these gaudy warriors in their red cloaks, plumed hats, and *Feldgrau* to come out and fight fairly before their women and children. The legacies of these epic marches for freedom are one with democracy itself, proof positive of the ability of a free society rapidly to muster, invade, conquer, and then disband—a tradition that so often in the eleventh hour has kept the democracies of the West free and one that we abandon only at our peril.

Democracies, of course, can change military policy precipitously and without reason. We know that they can sometimes curtail needed military action out of the terror of human and material losses. Assemblies tend to find scapegoats for defeats and deify the lucky rather than reward the talented. In times of peace and prosperity they relax their guard with often disastrous subsequent consequences—all that is the well-chronicled military liability that arises from a volatile democratic culture. But the great military strength of such open and free societies is less well known: the dramatic manner in which we can mobilize people in a tremendous retaliatory crusade for a just cause to be led by men whom we otherwise do not appreciate—an asset greater even than the excellence of our technology or the sheer superabundance of our military equipment.

Too often military historians, armed with postbellum sociological profiles of the combat soldier, attuned to the cynicism of the modern age that has witnessed the slaughter of the trenches and the holocaust of the death camps, and cognizant of the twentieth-century propensity to admit openly to naked self-interest, tend to believe that soldiers fight only instinctually—largely to preserve their battle comrades, not for some wider abstract and ethical idea. Do soldiers, in mud and cold, maimed and terrified, really march forward for an abstraction to free the oppressed? Similarly, we are told, their commanders push men onward for their own promotions, for the satisfaction of some inner psychological compulsion, or out of blind duty and unthinking adherence to professional training.

Yet, Messenian helotage did not survive Epaminondas, African slavery Sherman, nor Nazism Patton; and we should, it seems to me, admit without reservation or qualificiation that the salvation of these millions were good things and certainly not accidents. The best indication of the achievement of each of these generals is not to read the accounts of modern historians but rather to ask whom did the contemporary supporters of helotage, African slavery, and genocide especially hate and whom did they most fear. The Spartans built a statue to the man who killed Epaminondas. Supporters of the

Confederacy have despised Sherman for over a century. German generals talked in feared and hushed tones of some nonexistent "Army Group Patton" that might alone wreck their Panzers. "Patton," German Field Marshal von Rundstedt concluded simply after his capture, "he is your best."

Theban hoplites, Union troops, and American GIs, this book argues, were ideological armies foremost, composed of citizen-soldiers who burst into their enemies' heartland because they believed it was a just and very necessary thing to do. The commanders who led them encouraged that ethical zeal, made them believe there was a real moral difference between Theban democracy and Spartan helotage, between a free Union and a slave-owning South, and between a democratic Europe and a nightmarish Nazi continent. This study is more an essay on the ethical nature of democracies at war than a purely military history of three epic marches for freedom, for it claims that on rare occasions throughout the ages there can be a soul, not merely a spirit, in the way men battle.

PART I
YEOMEN OF THEBES

EPAMINONDAS'S DESCENT INTO THE PELOPONNESE

WINTER–SPRING, 370–369 B.C.

1

"THE DANCING FLOOR OF WAR"

THEBES—the present-day community is built right atop the ancient—
is a pleasant but little-visited Greek provincial town. No one travels to
Greece to experience either ancient or modern Thebes. A pity. There
are indeed certain things worth seeing there. A farmer, unconcerned about the
absence of good beaches, the paucity of impressive archaeological remains, or
the dearth of majestic landscape, immediately feels at home among the rolling
plains of the surrounding Boeotian landscape—over 250,000 acres of rich
wheat fields, row crops, olive orchards, and vineyards, a larger area even than
the Attic countryside that surrounds Athens. From the Theban acropolis a
keen agrarian eye notices that things grow wonderfully on this good ground—
both food and people.

The ancients knew that. The Theban soil, all Greeks conceded, could
fuel a prosperity that would be manifested in ways other than the mere production of food. The poets Hesiod, Pindar, and Corinna were Boeotians; so
was Plutarch and a host of lesser-known philosophers, artists, and politicians
who inhabit the pages of Greek literature and remark on the fertility of their
native ground. The Boeotian Pythagorean philosophers, Philolaus, Simmias,
and Cebes, are prominent in Plato's dialogue *Phaedo*, suggesting that the out-
of-the-way wheat fields and vineyards of Thebes may have in fact served as a
refuge for an enclave of that vanishing philosophical sect. Boeotia means
"cow pastures" in Greek, but despite its ancient reputation for rusticity, this

rich farmland developed a peculiar rural culture all its own; one that was always inseparable from the land.

The mountains in the distance—the verdant Mts. Cithaeron and Helicon on the west flank, snow-capped Parnassus looming to the north, eastward the barren Messapion and Ptoön, and wooded Parnes separating Attica to the south—rise in all directions to provide good watershed. The summer heat—nearly unbearable for tourists—ensures bountiful vegetables and fruits; the soil is heavy and black in its fertility, the present-day population skilled and healthy.

Water, heat, soil, and independent farmers combine to create a real agrarianism, successful enough to produce food to feed other Greeks not so fortunate, both ancient and modern. Such climate, agriculture, and terrain instantly explain the prominent place of ancient Thebes in Greek history—the site of an important Mycenaean citadel (still unexcavated beneath the modern streets and shops); the seven-gated city of myth and home to Cadmus, Herakles, Oedipus, and Antigone; and the capital city of the surrounding classical Boeotian federation.

Foreigners—from the mythical Seven Against Thebes to Roman Republican generals—have always wanted this land, their megalomania usually resulting in a brutal confrontation since its tough farmers have always been just as determined not to give it up. For those Greeks in Boeotia who perished fighting the Macedonians at the battle of Chaeronea, their stark epitaph simply ended with "We died on the famed plains of Boeotia." The Greeks, we must remember, often calibrated the quality of a region's soil by the number and nature of the infantrymen it might produce.

Today in these famed but seldom visited plains, in the midst of tractors and spray rigs, there is still the stale scent of war. To the east of Thebes, less than twenty miles away, lie the rolling plains of Tanagra, Oinophyta, and Delium, sites of decisive and often glorious pitched hoplite battles against Thebes's hated rival Athens—presently mere cotton and wheat fields covering the long-dead whose exploits are entirely unknown to the thousands who whizz by on the national freeway. How many Greeks, who have recently ripped the soil around the small resort of Delesi for the foundations of their imposing vacation homes, know that Socrates once, after the battle of Delium, bravely retreated through their backyards?

To the south of Thebes about ten miles distant is the countryside of Plataea, where the grand Greek alliance of 479 destroyed the Persian army of invasion. A new road has cut right through the site and nearly ruined appreciation of the ancient town and environs—right where Theban attackers for generations tried to storm the city and likewise tear down the walls of their sometimes confederate ally. Things change and do not change on the farm-land of Boeotia.

On the way from Thebes to Plataea, a brief detour of a few minutes takes you to Leuctra. Out in a remote grainfield, by a small irrigation aqueduct, rises the Theban trophy of 371, a stark white marble column ringed with sculpted shields, commemorating the day Epaminondas and his Thebans demolished the Spartan elite. Not a soul will be there. Not one of the thousands of tourists who cram into Delphi each morning has visited this lonely pillar, a hallowed spot where the history of Greece was changed far more radically than by any event which occurred at that ostentatious though venerable mountain shrine thirty miles to the northwest.

The killing fields of Chaeronea—where the Theban Sacred Band in 338 went down before the cavalry charge of the murderous eighteen-year-old Alexander—lie farther to the northwest in the shadow of Mt. Helicon, near the shores of the now drained Copaic basin. A proud limestone lion, erected over the remains of those illustrious 300 warriors, after twenty-three centuries still guards the old highway. Not far away are the little-visited ancient re-mains of Haliartus. There the Thebans once overwhelmed a Spartan corps and killed their maverick general Lysander, the brilliant Spartan commoner who fancied himself king.

The little-known, hard-to-find battlefield of Tegyra also looms across the way from this northern plain of Boeotia. The Theban Pelopidas stopped cold a Spartan army there in 375 in what Plutarch called a "prelude to Leuctra." And Coronea—"a battle like none other of our time," the historian and eye-witness Xenophon wrote—is roughly between Chaeronea and Haliartus; in that tiny valley the Thebans slammed head-on into the phalanx of King Ages-ilaus and nearly killed him. Not one of these battles was brought on by the Thebans; but in nearly all of them the presence of their hoplites ensured may-hem and death for those involved. To walk the fields of Boeotia is to trample unknowingly over the bones and ashes of thousands of long-forgotten and anonymous farmers who died in their mud to keep others off of it.

In a single afternoon one can drive through the farmland to nearly every major battlefield in the history of ancient Greece—Plataea, Tanagra, Oino-phyta, Coronea, Delium, Haliartus, Tegyra, Leuctra, and Chaeronea. They are all in Boeotia. Mass graves, stone lions, marble columns, and funerary in-scriptions dot the Boeotian landscape and fill the museums. These battles' un-canny proximity to each other reveal the real history and character of the Boeotians. For Persian and Macedonian autocrats marching south, and for Spartan professionals pushing north, the rich plains of Boeotia always were ahead, full of tough farmers who were eager to bar the way. It is a good place to farm, and for heavy infantry an even better place to fight—and Thebes is in the very center of it all. No wonder their general Epaminondas dubbed his flat and accessible countryside "the dancing floor of war," a black-earthen land that only tough men "who kept a grip on their shield straps" could hold on to. The corpses of thousands of Spartans and Athenians in the muck of Boeotia proved that in fact they usually could.[1]

Or at least die trying. That glorious millennium of the city's existence came to an abrupt end in September 335. Alexander the Great, the "Savior of the Greeks," simply destroyed it. Utterly. The birthplace of Herakles—the people, the buildings, the farmsteads about, everything and everybody—vanished. Gone was everything Theban in a matter of days. Alexander obliterated Epaminondas's legacy of a democratic *polis* when Thebes (much of its crack infantry had been demolished or demoralized three years earlier at the Greek defeat at Chaeronea) chose not to join his puppet league of Greek subservient states, and instead opted for independence from Macedon on false rumors of Alexander's demise. The agrarians of Thebes always had an unfortunate tendency to be obstinate—or rather politically inept in the baffling cosmology of shifting Greek alliance and counteralliance: fighting alongside the Persians at Plataea when the momentum had clearly swung over to the Greeks; turning on Sparta at the very conclusion of their successful joint twenty-seven-year war against Athens; parting with Alexander when the latter's quest for Greek hegemony was nearly complete. Farmers are good fighters but poor politicians.

Our ancient sources, Arrian, Plutarch, and Diodorus, agree that nearly thirty years after the Theban general Epaminondas died, Alexander butchered over 6,000 Theban men, women, and children in the streets of the city in a few hours. The rest—over 30,000 in number—were sold into slavery, the profits invested in preparations for his own upcoming march through Asia Minor to "liberate" the Greek cities from the "oppressive" Persian yoke. Arrian editorialized that the wholesale disappearance of Thebes was a novel event in Greek history—no prior disaster had instilled such horror, as the houses and walls themselves were razed, and the land parceled out to neighboring communities who had joined in the slaughter.[2]

To mask his own culpability in the genocide, Alexander, a current favorite now once again of modern encomiastic scholars, unloosed jealous Boeotian neighbors to run amuck in the city. Like present-day Serbians, Bosnians, and Croatians, a few fellow Boeotians had long nursed private grudges and old ethnic hatreds, and so made useful murderers for Alexander to employ once his army stormed the city and formal resistance was quashed. Diodorus adds that "Greeks were mercilessly slain by Greeks, relatives were butchered by their own relatives, houses plundered, and children and women and aged persons who fled into the temples were torn from sanctuary and subjected to outrage without limit." He sums up: "Every corner of the city was piled high with corpses."

Epaminondas had once instilled a love of liberty and autonomy in Thebes, and a democratic alliance among the towns of Boeotia. But by 335 he had been dead now for almost three decades. His legacy of resistance against tyranny would result in an Armageddon for the entire recalcitrant culture of Thebes. When Alexander sacked Thebes, the remains of Pelopidas's once daunted Sacred Band were rotting in their third year under a limestone lion twenty-five miles to the north at the battlefield of Chaeronea. Few of the now slaughtered revolutionaries at Thebes had remembered Epaminondas's final orders to his Theban comrades as he lay dying on the battlefield of Mantinea in 362—make peace, since there was no general left to lead them. And there was not. Now the grandchildren of his hoplites who had marched into the Peloponnese to give freedom to others lay dead in the streets of their own city, unable to save their own. In their defense, perhaps the brave but foolhardy who attacked the Macedonian constabulary on the Theban acropolis—causing the present retaliation of Alexander—remembered how a half century earlier a prior generation of liberators had once routed Spartan interlopers from the very same Cadmea.[3]

So Alexander's holocaust was an inglorious finish to a glorious people, as the history of classical Thebes came to an abrupt end in 335. Modern historians publish endlessly on the eminence of Alexander the Great, the greatest thug that the ancient world produced, a man who in his sheer propensity for killing the innocent—over a million were to die in his swath to the Indus—was a kindred spirit to Hitler. Yet, few write of the Boeotians and the democratic culture fostered by Epaminondas, by ancient accounts the most energetic statesman and champion of liberty of the classical era, about whom not a single modern biography exists in English. When he died, Epaminondas was lauded for the next century by all Greeks; in contrast, when "the Great" perished, few noticed—and then mostly to rejoice—his demise. We moderns, with different tastes, values, and aspirations from the ancients', still fawn over the destroyer of Greek liberty, completely ignorant of or uninterested in the creator of freedom. There will never be some gaudy museum extravaganza entitled "The Search for Epaminondas"; and even the Greek government will probably never put his head on a coin.

Pre-Epaminondan Thebes had not always been so heroic. A century and a half before its devastation it had joined the enemies of Greece, fought *not* to liberate Hellas from northern invaders, but to aid the Persians in the conquest of their own countrymen. Later Greeks were aware of this vast change of fortune. They told a tale that King Leonidas, who held the pass at Thermopylae in 480 against the Persians, purportedly had a dream in which Thebes was in convulsion, but at last towered above all the other Greek cities—and then disappeared abruptly. The vision was taken to mean a panorama of the Theban decline after the Persian Wars (480–479), its resurrection under Epaminondas (371–362), and its sudden destruction by Alexander (335). So to understand the achievement of Epaminondas and his great march of democratic yeoman in 370–369, we must first recall the prior checkered history of this most peculiar, often misunderstood, and usually despised region of Greece.

2

"THE BOEOTIAN PIG"

B Y THE fifth century the ancient assessment of Boeotians as *hues*— "pigs"—and as stupid and unfeeling was well entrenched—a reflection mostly of the agrarian nature of Boeotian culture and its general physical and spiritual distance from maritime intellectual centers like Athens, Corinth, Syracuse, and the coastal cities of Asia Minor. The porcine national epithet was long-standing and even antedated the celebrated Boeotian failure to resist the Persian invasion of 480. By the later fifth century, Aristophanes, in his comedy *Acharnians* (ca. 425), could expect the Athenian audience to laugh at a Boeotian lumbering in from the fields, a coarse rustic smelling of eels and nearly incomprehensible with his rural twang—a dullard easily snookered out of his repulsive though tasty catch by a wily smooth Athenian. Most of the darkest of classical Athenian tragedies—*Seven Against Thebes*, *Oedipus*, *Antigone*, *Bacchae*—are situated at Thebes, as if to reassure the Attic audience viewing the barbarity unfolding on stage that Athenians are not really like those macabre wild folk on the other side the mountains. In Boeotia, after all, did not brothers kill each other? Sons married their mothers after slaying their fathers. Were not children beheaded by their mothers, and did not sisters commit suicide in dank caves?

The Boeotian plain was, in short, the San Joaquin Valley of ancient Greece, a violent, backward, and maligned place of extraordinary energy and unrealized natural and human potential. Even in Roman times the historian

Nepos could still remark that Thebans "possessed more physical strength than intellect." Travelers passed through Boeotia either on their way northward to the oracle and sanctuary at Delphi, or southward to Athens and the Peloponnese—they rarely visited Thebes or its surrounding satellite hamlets. If a few other Greeks sought mystical experiences up in the mountains of Boeotia—the legendary Maenads on Cithaeron, the Muses about Helicon, the oracle on the slopes of Mt. Ptoön and the eerie ravine of the seer Trophonius above Levadia—they avoided the rural drudgery and the summer swelter down on the plains. Despite producing poets such as Hesiod, Pindar, and Corinna, most Greeks saw Boeotia as a queer place where rustics spoke a funny dialect, dined on slimy delicious things fished from the oozy Copaic marshes, had atrocious table manners, and never developed a real unified state as had Athens from the roughly equal-sized countryside of Attica. Pericles purportedly called the uncouth internecine Boeotians "holm-oaks," tough trees that have a tendency to crash together in the wind and thus instinctively destroy each other endlessly.

The ancient fascination with the miraculous achievement of Epaminondas in 370–369 can be understood only through this prior century-and-a-half history of Theban disrepute. By 525 most of the towns of the surrounding Boeotian countryside were only loosely federated and constantly at odds with Thebes's efforts to acquire the natural spiritual and political leadership of the region's smaller villages. A relatively flat land united in a single political entity meant political tranquility, a large military, and steady material progress—Athens had proved as much with the democratic unification of her own hinterland of Attica, Sparta's oligarchy with the brutal subjugation of surrounding Laconia and Messenia. But a relatively flat land beset with constant fighting among its over twenty independent communities was a recipe for disaster. Such was the history of Boeotia for 150 years, the promise of rich soil and a large hardworking populace largely unfulfilled. It was as if the states of North America were allied under the Articles of Confederation led by an oligarchal elite, with a weak federal government occasionally mounting ad hoc posses to the south and northwest to put down recalcitrant local militias.

Conditions did not improve with the onslaught of the Persian invasion of 480, when most of Boeotia "Medized," or joined the Persians, before the invading army of a quarter-million Easterners. At the defining moment of Greek destiny, the farmers of Boeotia were shown sadly wanting in Panhellenic spirit. But had they any real choice? Absent a fleet that might have offered refuge overseas, and without safe mountain redoubts or substantial fortifications, the country folk of Boeotia were alone—*and alone right in the path of 250,000 Persians*. The option for the flatlanders was between absolute destruction or accommodation. To the everlasting infamy of the Thebans—seven centuries later the Boeotian Plutarch could still feel the sting of the age-old disgrace in his formal defense of their behavior—they chose absolute accommodation and thus an ignominious survival.

In the aftermath of the Persian defeat and withdrawal, a humbled Thebes was overrun and plundered by vengeful fellow Greeks. A century later at Hellenic conferences their treachery was still a hackneyed theme in every long-winded peroration, the inevitable wages of an inbred region that had produced Oedipus and his rebellious, querulous, and self-destructive offspring. So, alone and isolated, Thebes and her Boeotian satellites essentially disappeared from Greek history for a quarter century. No scholar even today asks—or cares—where the Boeotians were between 480 and 465. They were nowhere other than at home, in shame and obscurity, working their small plots—giving collective credence to Emerson's dictum that a farm is a perfect sanctuary in which to hide failure. Thebes in the early fifth century was to be neither a member of the Athenian-led Delian league nor a part of the Spartans' Peloponnesian counteralliance. The Classical Age in Greece had begun with the magnificent Hellenic victories over the Persians at the battles of Plataea and Salamis—fights where Boeotians were either absent or actively aiding the enemy. For an entire decade (457–447) most of Boeotia came under Athenian domination, until at last the Thebans defeated the Athenians at the first battle of Coronea (447) and reclaimed their autonomy.

The subsequent Peloponnesian War (431–404) brought permanent relief from the hated Athenians. Indeed, the Thebans joined with the Spartans to invade Attica five times between 431 and 425. On their own initiative, the Theban-led Boeotians shattered the Athenian phalanx at the dramatic battle of Delium (424). Later they helped to plunder the Athenian countryside continuously from their joint fortified base at Decelea (413–404), just fifteen miles from the Athenian walls. An anonymous fourth-century historian claims that the rustic Theban plunderers were so thorough—or so practical?—that they took even the woodwork and roof tiles from the nearby farmhouses of Attica—estates that were stocked with plunder from the imperial subjects of the Athenian Maritime Confederacy. In the Peloponnesian war, the Thebans— who a half century later would soon change the entire political organization of the Peloponnese—could not build a large fleet, did not invade Attica on their own, and rarely sent their manhood to die on foreign expeditions. But when it was a question of joining in to plunder and ravage Attica across the mountains, or fighting any Athenians who had crossed their borders, they were, as agrarian conservatives traditionally are, suddenly quite ferocious.[4]

In the aftermath of the Peloponnesians' victory (404), landed government in Boeotia continued to be dominated by aristocrats rather than yeomen. These elites sought to intensify the old favorable accords with Sparta and confine office-holding to the larger landowners. Although propertied government had always been remarkably broad-based and stable in Boeotia—perhaps 20 percent of some 70,000 adult men and women residents could vote by the mid fifth century—the steady gravitation toward Sparta among the wealthier classes had tended de facto to concentrate offices in the hands of reactionary Laconiaphiles. The city-states of Boeotia were thus still querulous, and there was no unification in either the legal or spiritual sense.

Without maritime trade, and traditionally at odds with Athens—the orator Demosthenes once shrugged that, given the blanket hatred of Thebans in his city, his Athenian listeners were incapable of believing anything good said about them. Indeed, most Boeotians knew of the outside world through either Spartan adventurers or Thessalians to the north. Yet neither backwater was representative of the political and cultural potential of the Greek city-state—the high culture of Athens, Ionia, and southern Italy and Sicily. In a parochial and rural society such as Thebes, conservatism is but a small step from real oligarchy, as farmers traditionally excuse the privilege of the aristocrat in exchange for the shared avowal of an inflexible cultural continuity. Rarely do agrarians tolerate social change as part of a larger cultural egalitarianism, even when it serves their own economic interests. As a youth my grandfather, a crusty viticulturalist, perhaps in the kindred spirit of some failed Theban democrat, admonished me never to forget that blinkered, impoverished American farmers "vote Republican as they go broke and hate the Democrats who make them money."

In reaction to continued oligarchic control, more popular Boeotian factions arose in the 390s and 380s, openly calling for resistance to the Spartan policy of hindering popular governments and fragmenting the towns of Boeotia. Their dream—a nightmare to Sparta's new Panhellenic Confederacy—was to be a truly democratic Boeotia, where the traditional eleven local districts of the region's federation were reformulated into seven larger democratic canons, with officials now to be elected by the entire citizenry *regardless* of property or census qualification. Under this new plan the free peoples of Boeotia were to be ethnically and linguistically one. It made sense that all residents should unify under a democratic federation, in which property per se was not a criterion for political participation. It was as if the Articles of Confederation had passed into the Constitution of the United States; or as if independent republics in Texas, California, and other Western states at last decided to join the Union.

Such classless democracy in the Greek hinterlands was a bold idea. Usually, radical democracy in classical Greece had appeared on the coast. There
its cargo was an array of taxes, public works, navies, and the ascendancy of the
urban poor—an Athenian or Syracusan maritime concept in which the landless engaged in crafts, day labor, government service, and trade. Such radical
governments found no sympathy from aristocrats and their sometimes allied
reactionary farmers—the tough infantrymen who felt, like Aristotle, that
agriculture alone made the "best" citizen. Democracy in the Greek paradigm
was supposedly antiagrarian, anti-infantry, and usually commercial and naval,
in which class hatred simmered beneath the surface.

In contrast, the idea that middling farmers, joined by wealthier horsemen,
might voluntarily share power with the poor to create a real democratic culture
in the rural backwaters was without parallel in the history of Greece—and yet
perhaps that development was the logical culmination to the entire evolving
notion of the traditional, stable Greek *polis*. The city-state, outside the anomalous Sparta and Athens, had enjoyed an illustrious three-century tradition
under exclusive constitutions of small yeomen hoplites. In short, the Boeotian
democratic ideal as envisioned by Epaminondas for a brief time united two in-
congruities that have baffled Western populists for two-and-a-half millennia:
how to forge economic egalitarianism while retaining freedom and cultural
conservatism. When Boeotian farmers dropped the property qualification for
political participation, without resorting to imperialism or massive entitlement,
the promise of the Greek *polis* was in its eleventh hour realized—and the stage
was set for the grand army of Epaminondas.

Common hatred of Sparta, of course, was the immediate catalyst for this
bold experiment in agrarian democracy. By 394, Thebes was at open war with
its old ally Sparta to preserve the fragmenting Boeotian federation under its
own control and to prevent Sparta from dominating the other Greek city-
states. But after its hard-fought defeats at the battles of Nemea and Coronea
in the same year (394), and the intervention of Persia to impose a common
peace, Thebes was further marginalized by Sparta and would remain impotent
for another quarter century (394–371). An established democracy free from
invaders apparently would have to wait.

The idea that a tiny Theban army of a few thousand could win its own independence, much less that of 100,000 others in Boeotia—and still much
less, nearly an additional quarter million more in the Peloponnese!—seemed
lunatic. Faced with a pro-Spartan oligarchic upsurge throughout the towns of
its Boeotian Confederacy, a wary alliance with democratic Athens across the
border was about all Theban democratic leaders could hope for. And so by
382 a Spartan garrison of occupation was perched on the Theban acropolis;

unpopular local right-wing pro-Spartan toadies were again ascendant in most of the Boeotian cities.

The Spartan takeover of the sacred Theban Cadmea (382)—the city's spiritual and political center—was the most foolhardy foreign enterprise in the entire history of Spartan foreign policy. Even some Spartans were aghast at the nerve. Such a flagrant attack on an autonomous Greek city in times of peace energized the people of Thebes as nothing had before. It shocked the rest of the Greek world—and would not be forgotten by a group of Theban democratic fanatics who would dedicate their lives to paying their oppressors back in kind. In the eyes of Theban reformers, the issue of whether Boeotia was to be controlled by larger landowners as a Spartan satellite, or become an agrarian democracy of independent infantrymen with an autonomous foreign policy, had been only momentarily settled in Sparta's favor.[5]

Three years later, in winter 379, a remarkable revolution altered the entire political climate of Boeotia and changed the course of Greek history forever. A group of Boeotian insurrectionists—seven wealthy exiles led by the previously obscure Pelopidas and Melon—overthrew the Spartan garrison and assassinated some of their quisling Theban sympathizers. The Boeotian conspirators had earlier sought refuge at Athens, and they may have been favorably impressed with, and so learned from, the strengths and weaknesses of Athenian-style democracy. With the help of the nationalists Epaminondas and Gorgidas, the Thebans now expelled the Spartan occupational forces, inaugurated real democracy in Thebes and most of the nearby towns of Boeotia—and prepared for open war with Sparta.

Thanks to the recent years of Spartan repression, landed government of the past was seen by most Boeotians as indistinguishable from narrow oligarchy and thus both were now discredited. For the first time in the long history of Boeotia, the poorer were given the vote, along with the right to serve on courts and conduct democratic audits of elected officials. That democracy could take root among rural conservatives, with their history of open hostility to Athens, and a traditional allegiance to property qualifications, was unheard of in classical Greece. Athenian thinkers remarked of this change that when Thebes began to be governed by philosophers—a reference to the Pythagorean training of Epaminondas—the city reached its greatest level of happiness and prosperity. In those rare moments in history, when conservatives encourage economic egalitarianism, and liberals remain cultural traditionalists, a country like Boeotia can indeed unite, thrive, and field a murderous army of a season. Some pigs!

This democratic renaissance in Boeotia also had three far more important *military* ramifications that would echo throughout Greece for the next three decades, explaining why in less than eight years the Thebans alone of the more than one thousand Greek city-states would feel strong and reckless enough to lead a march against Sparta itself. First, since surrounding local councils would now be free to elect their own governments and representatives, the towns of Boeotia were much more willing to give up sovereign power to a truly federated government under leaders of a democratic Thebes. Under proportional representation it obtained the greatest block of seats in the confederate council, and usually four of seven executive officers—the so called Boeotarchs. Thebes would now lead *not* as in the past through coercion, nor even due to its greater population and wealth. It would instead guide by the moral example of men like Epaminondas and Pelopidas, who had ended foreign interference and domestic aristocratic monopoly for *all* of Boeotia. For the first time, Thebes would be indistinguishable from the surrounding countryside of Boeotia—in fact, the two terms were now to be used as near equivalents, with apparent approval of both urban Thebans and rural Boeotians. Even on coins and inscriptions from Thebes proper, "Boeotian," not "Theban," was usually employed, even as contemporary Greeks in turn might call rural Boeotians "Thebans."

The democratic Athenians were wary of what a vast agrarian basin of over one thousand square miles might accomplish if it were to be both federated and democratic—and right across their border. When the Theban army marched, it would now be an equal partner with and in service to the thousands of citizens of Boeotia. The rise of democratic federalism along the Boeotian model later would be followed elsewhere in Arcadia and Achaea, and for a while would keep even the Macedonian successors and Roman legions at bay. Had such democratic regional leagues themselves united and given all of Greece a truly national state—not realized until the early nineteenth century—the values of the *polis* might have survived both Philip of Macedon and perhaps even the later Roman onslaught.

Second, the diminution of traditional Greek property qualifications meant that even the poorer natives of the Boeotian countryside could now vote and hold office. This expansion of the franchise reduced the possibility of revolution and increased the manpower reserves of the national army, which drew on the *entire* native population of Boeotia—perhaps upward of 200,000 to 250,000 total residents—to field some 10,000 to 12,000 heavy infantry and at least that number of light-armed troops, in addition to 1,000 to 2,000 horsemen. A nation in arms of 20,000 Boeotian heavy infantrymen was now foreseeable, composed mostly of farmers, but also of previously ignored craftsmen and day laborers. At the battle of Delium in 424 under the more narrow government of the past, the Boeotians had still fielded some 7,000

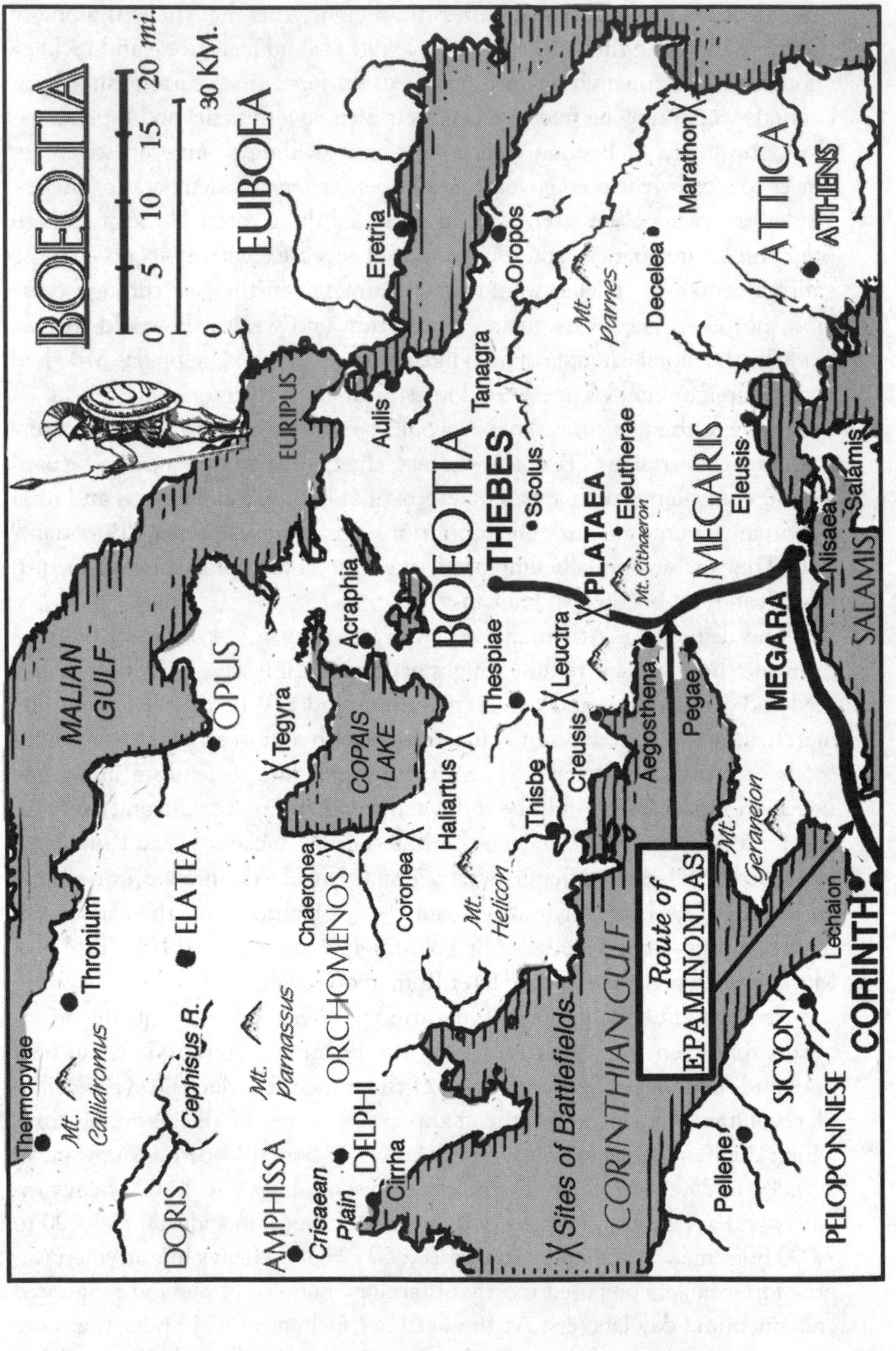

Epaminondas's Boeotia

hoplites, which scholars suggest may have represented about two-thirds of a total heavy-infantry force of 11,000. But there were also at Delium 10,000 light-armed troops and another 500 peltasts, targeteers, and javelin-throwers. A half century later, under the subsequent new democratic federation led by Epaminondas and Pelopidas, those formerly disenfranchised would now enjoy full citizenship. *All* free males would be eligible for hoplite service—if military exigency called for a greater preponderance of heavy infantry. In one stroke the needs of the battlefield, not class, determined whether a man lined up in the phalanx as a hoplite or skirmished as a light-armed trooper. Like the army of the modern liberal state, Epaminondas mustered his columns from the entire manhood of his country, and infused them with a fervor not matched among other rival city-states.

In any case, there was the frightening potential for a levy of 20,000 infantrymen, although such an entire force could never *in toto* leave Boeotia empty of defenders with potential enemies at Athens and in Thessaly to the north. A modern archaeological survey has suggested an ancient Boeotian countryside of 10,000 homestead farms, and it would not be inconceivable that such plots could produce at least two able-bodied hoplites between the ages of twenty-one and sixty. This renewed Theban vigor in traditional land forces came at precisely the time when Athens and Sparta were short of heavy infantry—the former still suffering from the three-decade effects of the Peloponnesian War and the plague, the latter from the intrinsic problems of a declining birthrate among a Spartiate overclass. When other Greek states were turning away from armies of heavy infantry, Thebes was crafting the most deadly hoplite force in Greece.[6]

Third, there was now a growing and near-fanatical hatred of Sparta instilled in the Boeotian populace. True, the former allies had long ago experienced a falling out after the defeat of Athens in the Peloponnesian War and the division of its spoils. Thebes had fought Sparta off and on for nearly a quarter century in at least five open engagements and nearly as many invasions. But the creation of democracy now vented in a much more dramatic way the old underlying enmity for Spartan arrogance—Spartans, after all, had marched into Boeotia, never vice versa—even as the new federation offered the promise of concrete retribution. Many of the new citizens of Boeotia must have attributed their previous political nonexistence either to the power of local oligarchs or to the presence of foreign troops—and in their eyes Sparta was responsible for both. One story relates that to build morale on the eve of the battle of Leuctra, Epaminondas told his hoplites that if they lost, the Spartans had planned to kill all the males, enslave their women and children, and raze the city to the ground—something Alexander, not the Spartans, would in fact bring about three decades later. That his army purportedly believed such propaganda should tell us something about their terror and loathing of all things Spartan.

Add a readily identifiable philosophical idealism on the part of generals like Epaminondas and Pelopidas, and a natural empathy of the former dispossessed Boeotians with the Helot serfs to the south at Sparta, and the idea of a future great crusade of vengeance against Sparta began to take root. In general, there is to free men something odious about an apartheid state—as Sherman confirmed in Georgia, and Patton in Germany—that sends its elite killers away from its interior, always in the seemingly smug assurance that no enemy would dare march onto its own sacrosanct soil to bring fire and ruin home to the perpetrators of misery. For men like Epaminondas, Sherman, and Patton, the best way to stop such thuggish bullies was to crash into their home ground and quite publicly vitiate their claims to ethnic, regional, or racial superiority, to give them a taste of a total war that transcended the battlefield.[7]

To nip in the bud this nascent federated Boeotian democracy, Sparta invaded four times between 378 and 371. All such attempts at destroying the democratic confederacy through military conquest and fostering oligarchal revolution in the villages of Boeotia failed utterly. Finally, the Thebans under Epaminondas and Pelopidas had had enough and saw the emperor unclothed: Sparta's repeated failure to overturn Theban democracy made them weaker, not stronger, each season. Epaminondas's colleague, Pelopidas, when surprised and outnumbered by Spartans at the battle of Tegyra (375), and told by a scout that "we have fallen into the enemy hands," replied, "Why not they into ours?" He then led his men right through their vaunted phalanx.

On their fourth and final invasion, the Spartans and their allies—now over 20,000 strong—at last met the new Boeotian army at the small plain of Leuctra, not far from Thebes. There the much larger Spartan phalanx was nearly annihilated and the cohesion of the Peloponnesian coalition destroyed, largely through the personal magnetism of Epaminondas and the combat skill of 6,000 Boeotian farmers. The vastly outnumbered Theban democrats had not so much pushed the Spartan phalanx off the battlefield as obliterated the very core of their military elite.[8]

Without a premier hoplite vanguard, Sparta was now seen as vulnerable: she had no walls, a restive class of oppressed and indentured serfs, a declining population of Spartiate warriors, internal dissension among the baffling array of classes and orders, factious allies in the Peloponnese—and a now discredited and hobbled military. All that was needed was a man of courage and vision to lift the veil of Spartan invincibility and to think the unthinkable—an invasion into the heartland of Sparta itself. As architect of the victory at Leuctra, and newly elected Boeotarch from Thebes, Epaminondas made plans to convince his Boeotian generals to muster the army and march south. Had he not been persuaded to delay, he would have preferred to destroy the enemy survivors of Leuctra who were still lingering in Boeotia—a move that would have essentially ended all claims of Spartan military power in a few hours. This was a man who now envisioned not just defeating the Spartan army but demolishing the enemy's ability to make war itself.

Epaminondas, at least for a brief season in 371–370, now had the best infantry in the Mediterranean world, a unified population, and the moral imperative to ensure that Spartans never again set foot in Boeotia. His vision of something grand for the Thebans in the Peloponnese beyond the mere defeat of the Spartan army seems to have been his alone. For six centuries Sparta stood inviolate. Sparta ravaged Attica, not vice versa. Sparta marched down into Boeotia, not Boeotians into Sparta. Epaminondas the military innovator and philosopher now simply asked why must this be so. He was surely tired of the Spartans' Napoleonic boast that they buried their dead in the land of others, while no enemy ever fell in their own. If Boeotians were to die in battle, why not for a change alongside Spartans on Spartan soil?

Yet, after he ensured the survival of Boeotian democracy, Epaminondas's chief problem would now be convincing his rustics to ignore the prevailing opinion of the majority and to follow the vision of a single man. Epaminondas alone fathomed that the Spartan catastrophe at Leuctra was the beginning, not the end, of the war, and understood that fighting in Greece was becoming for better or worse far more than a traditional pitched battle of hoplites, closer to the modern Western concept of total warfare as a collision of cultures rather than merely a decisive battle between fighters. What made the Spartan army march was not just the Spartiate hoplites themselves, but the entire supporting structure of Spartan helotage. Unlike other military revolutionaries of the times who looked to mercenaries and the use of fortifications to kill greater numbers of people, Epaminondas in a larger strategic sense saw that a nation of hoplites in arms could still form a deadly army—if the army wished to destroy the spirit rather than the bodies of the enemy, and if it fought for the old soul of the *polis*.

Epaminondas, not King Philip, not Divine Alexander, not wild-eyed Pyrrhus, and not one-eyed Hannibal, who all led hired thugs, was the real modern military thinker of the ancient world, the sole constitutional general who realized that a democratic nation in arms must make the entire society of the enemy pay for the aggression of its army, must convince his own democratic army that they are morally superior to the enemy.

An invading phalanx of Boeotian hoplites could be economical in the old sense of winning wars without losing men, by threatening to use overwhelming force in head-on battles even as it marched to the rear to plunder and liberate the unfree. The key, again, was the size of the muster: small armies must fight their way in; huge armies might walk in unopposed. Moreover, Epaminondas had the keen, almost uncanny ability, shared with both Sherman and Patton, to sense that the interior of a slave society is not strong, but weak. Its offensive presence abroad is not always a reflection of greater power at home, but just as often proof positive that the core is rotten and decaying from within. It was into the dreaded vale of this almost legendary realm of helotage—Laconia seldom visited, and never invaded—that Epaminondas now proposed to let his parochial yeomen of Thebes run wild. It is one of the great losses of ancient history that we do not know any of the names of these brave infantrymen—indeed, we have not a scrap of evidence about any of these many thousand individuals who were to change the very nature of the Greek world.[9]

3

"THE FAIREST AND MOST LEVEL GROUND"

THUS THE historian Herodotus makes the Persian invader Mardonius describe the arena of traditional Greek battle: a head-on collision "in a most irrational manner through senselessness and stupidity." But what was this usual Greek way of warfare like, and who were these hoplites who charged on "the most level ground"? To answer those questions is to learn of the very origins of Hellenic culture itself—and to learn of this curious Theban attempt under Epaminondas, after four centuries of *polis* history, to reformulate at the eleventh hour the ideal of a hoplite republic.

By 700 the Greek recovery from more than four centuries of cultural ob-scurity during the Greek Dark Ages was well under way. Nearly a thousand small, autonomous communities like the cities of Boeotia now dotted the Greek-speaking world from southern Italy to the Black Sea. Population growth was the catalyst, reaching 2 to 3 percent per annum in some years. To feed the greater numbers, Greeks began to associate freely and confidently without restriction on economic activity, as Greek colonies and trading posts sprouted throughout the Mediterranean. Written constitutions appeared in the great majority of city-states and their colonies, ensuring the spread of gov-ernment by consensus of landed peers—the first truly constitutional states in the history of civilization.

By the sixth century the Greek countryside itself was no longer a sparse pastureland for sheep, goats, and horses, but now more often a teeming patch-

35

work of small ten-acre farms of trees, vines, and grain, often with an isolated homestead to house its ever vigilant and independent owner, a new citizen who alone in the Mediterranean had clear legal rights to land tenure, property inheritance, and his own arms. All that we hold dear in the West—the separation of religion and state, the civilian control of the military, the creation of an empowered middle class, the open exchange of ideas among a free citizenry—had their origins not in the eighteenth-century Enlightenment, not in the Renaissance, not in the Republic of Rome, not even in the urban fervor of classical Athens, but among these backwater communities of often forgotten yeomen that emerged in this spectacular renaissance of the eighth and seventh centuries.[10]

Just as Greek city-states and their surrounding satellite villages grew to service the burgeoning agricultural population and to facilitate expanding trade, so too the hills outside the *polis* were gradually reclaimed and terraced. Eventually, there may have been ten thousand small farms in Boeotia alone. The seventh-century farmer-poet Hesiod, who lived near Ascra, on the slopes of Boeotian Mt. Helicon, wrote of a growing agrarian consciousness and dislike of aristocratic grandees—those elites who would populate the odes of the other famous Boeotian poet, Pindar.

Farmers like Hesiod's father, who had immigrated to Boeotia from Asia Minor, sought empty land wherever they could, whether on the hillsides near a new city-state or through external colonization in pristine territory across the Aegean and Mediterranean. Just as land and property were dispersed to this new class beyond the control of aristocratic horsemen, just as landed councils replaced aristocratic cabals, just as livestock raising was overshadowed by intensive agriculture, just as metalworking was redirected from the tripods of the wealthy to the arms and farming implements of small agrarians, so too was the practice of Greek warfare made anew.[11]

Consequently, in the seventh and sixth centuries most decisive battles that put an end to disputes between developing Greek city-states were fought by heavy hoplite infantry (*hoplitai*) composed of farmers outfitted in bronze armor (*hopla*) with thrusting spears. Moreover, intensively worked vineyards, orchards, and grainfields were now privately held, increasingly valued, and served an ever growing population. If a community was self-supporting through, and governed by, its surrounding private landowners, then hoplite warfare, far better than fortifications or garrisoning passes, made perfect sense: muster the largest, best-armed group of farmers to protect land in the quickest, cheapest, and most decisive way possible. It was far easier and more economical for farmers to defend farmland on farmland against other farmers, than to tax and hire the landless endlessly to guard passes—the sheer ubiquity of which in mountainous Greece ensured that they could usually be forced by enterprising invaders anyway. The choice of military response to win or protect territory was now a civic matter, an issue to be voted on by free landowning infantrymen themselves. Such men had little patience in raising taxes to pay professionals to sit behind expensive fortifications.

These militias and their assemblies were not yet real democracy. Indeed, the Greeks called their invention timocracy, "rule by those who held honor," or simply polity, "*polis* government"—the idea that not wealth, not birth, but the possession of a small plot of farmland gave one political freedom and responsibility. To the Greeks land was everything; those who had it voted and fought; those who did not, did not.

As such, hoplite militia fighting by means of shock collision marks the true beginning of Western warfare, a formal idea of decisive confrontation now fraught with legal, ethical, and political implications. Almost all these wars of a day between rugged and impatient yeomen were infantry encounters over land, usually disputed border strips involving agrarian prestige more than prized fertility. Customarily, the army of one city-state, an Argos, Thebes, or Sparta, met its adversary in daylight in formal columnar formation—the word "phalanx" means "rows" or "stacks" of men—according to a recognized and often quasi-ritualistic sequence of events.

After divination a general gave a brief exhortation, and then the assembled infantry prepared to charge the enemy. In minutes the respective armies packed together to achieve a greater density of armed men, who sought to crash together, sometimes trotting the last two hundred yards between the two phalanxes. It was just such a collision that the army of Sparta relished and mastered, and its very repute often sent enemy hoplites running even before battle commenced. Behind the entire invasion of Epaminondas, its flying columns of plunderers, its rapid descent from the mountains into Laconia, lay the specter of the Theban phalanx and its ability to charge through any column of spearmen in Greece.

For the defenders in a hoplite war the action often occurred on the same soil they and their neighbors had worked a few days before. For the invaders, the farmhouses, orchards, vineyards, and stone field walls were largely identical to their own plots back home. Once a neighboring Greek community had fashioned a force of armored columns to take or hold flatland, there was very little a like-minded rival could do other than to meet the challenge in about the same manner—or exit the battlefield and give up claim to the disputed ground. Thus the Boeotian small towns around Thebes, like other rural communities in Greece, for nearly two centuries before the Classical Age had decided almost all their quarrels by a conventional collision of infantry columns.

After the meeting of phalanxes, farmers, blinded by the dust and their own cumbersome helmets, stabbed away with their spears, screamed the war cry—*Eleleu!* or, *Alala!*—pushed on ahead with their shields, and, failing that, grabbed, kicked, and bit, desperately hoping to make some inroad into the enemy's phalanx. Usually, they had little idea whom, if any, they had killed or wounded. It was bloody, dirty, and mostly blind work. Success was at first gauged by the degree of motion achieved by the pushing of the ranks—the literal confused thrusting of a man's shield upon the shoulders, side, or back of his comrade ahead. There were few feints, reserves, encircling maneuvers, or sophisticated tactics in hoplite battle before the latter fifth century—just the frightful knowledge that a man must plow through the spears across the plain. Short, bloody, and ideal this fighting was for farmers who wanted to do things cheaply and in person: vote, arm, muster, fight, and then march right back to their land.

The terrain as well as the political culture of Greece explains this "fairest and most level ground" of killing. Anyone who has farmed exclusively on flat ground for his entire life grows uneasy in mountainous or rugged country; he feels his line of vision interrupted, his realm of movement curtailed by obstacles suddenly much too near. No wonder the impatient Greeks of the small plains preferred to do their fighting where they could see and target and run at their enemy. Flatland grew heavy tough infantry, the Greeks said—the mountains only queer folk who fought as cowardly archers, slingers, and skirmishers.

The first three ranks of the eight rows of the classical phalanx alone reached the enemy in the first assault with their spears. If the shafts broke—and we see that often in Boeotian art—they went hand-to-hand with swords and their butt spikes. A bloodbath, to be sure, for those at the front, but bloody mayhem was not unusual for rustics who butchered their own animals and saw enough of savagery on their upland farms. Later Greek tactical writers stress just how important such front-line fighters were in achieving an initial inroad. Once the phalanx ripped and stormed through the ranks of its adversary, the opponent often collapsed *in toto* through panic and fright, perhaps not more than a half hour after the initial collision. The short duration and sudden disintegration of battle is understandable if we keep in mind that combatants were squeezed together in column, trapped in heavy bronze under the summer sun, mostly robbed of sight and hearing, in a sea of dust and blood—the captives, as the historian Thucydides reminds us, of rumor and their own fears.

One line soon cracked, and hoplites turned, scattered, and lumbered away to prevent encirclement and probable annihilation. Heavy infantrymen made poor—and sometimes vulnerable—pursuers, especially when the defeated threw away their equipment, became more mobile, and headed to the hills. Under the protocols of early city-state warfare, there was not much desire anyway to exterminate an adversary who spoke the same language, worshiped identical gods, observed common festivals, and enjoyed similar types of government by landowning citizens. Again, the primary purpose of hoplite warfare was to acquire or take back border real estate and gain prestige, not to risk time and money in annihilating a neighboring society of like-armored farmers over the hill; not even to attack those noncombatants who did not wear the bronze panoply.[12]

Such fighting between Greek city-states could be frequent but *not* necessarily catastrophic, once cavalry and missile men were largely excluded from any integrated role in the fighting and the infantry combatants were uniformly encased in bronze. The early Greeks invented decisive infantry battle; but total war was another, later Western invention of the fourth century. In the first two centuries of hoplite fighting (700–490), it was enough, as the philosophers and orators noted, every so often to kill a small portion of the enemy in an afternoon clash, crack his morale, and send him scurrying in defeat and shame whence he came. The set battle piece with its myriad protocols both prevented nascent agrarian communities from exhausting each other in ruinous wars, and yet ensured that their respective farmers would alone fight and so keep a tight rein on political power within their own communities. That economy meant few taxes for capital expenditure outside of agriculture—and a clear chauvinism against mounted grandees and landless skirmishers. To understand the miraculous explosion of the Greeks in the seventh through the fifth centuries is to appreciate the manner in which the Greeks fought battles without waging wars.

The early Greek city-state had hit upon a rare mechanism to limit defense expenditure, keep religion outside of both war and politics, and make military policy hinge on the majority vote of the citizens—all that saved lives, property, and money. If, as the Persians thought, hoplite fighting appeared absurd—decisive battle, the choice of level battlefields rather than defensible mountain passes, heavy bronze armament under the Mediterranean sun, the diminution of both the poor and the very wealthy—at least brutality worked for a purpose: the preservation and expansion of an agrarian middle class that was not enervated by constant military expense, service, and loss.

Both Athens and Sparta, however, were to grow increasingly uncomfortable with war defined as battle by rural amateurs. It was, after all, a very poor way to create and maintain an empire: agrarian warfare led not to Athenian fleets in Egypt and Sicily or Spartan raiders in Asia Minor, but simply to farmers like Epaminondas's Boeotians working in peace and alone, who would neither go overseas nor be invaded. A state with imperial or hegemonic ambitions either had to turn these rustics into professional infantry who could fight away from their farms at will, or abandon infantry exclusivity entirely and seek naval supremacy or a multifaceted army of horseman, archers, and artillery men.

For all the hoplite monopoly of Greek warfare, there were intrinsic paradoxes in such infantry military practice that would eventually undermine the entire system, causing the understood protocols to become increasingly irrelevant as warfare evolved beyond set infantry collisions. As the Greek city-states prospered throughout the Aegean and Adriatic in the fifth and fourth centuries, capital was created outside of agriculture, mostly from maritime trade. In most places near the coast, this growing flexibility and expansion of the ancient economy had disastrous results for the general practice of Greek warfare defined as a few hoplite battles. Great cities like Athens, Syracuse, and Corinth fielded only moderate-sized hoplite forces and usually of inferior quality. Hoplite warfare had once worked not because of some conspiracy of small farmers, but because it was a practical and effective way of protecting the agricultural property that was the exclusive lifeblood of the small *polis*.

Once small property owners lost their economic—and soon their political—dominance within the city-state, pitched battle became but one of many "roads of war," and was free to evolve according to the marketplace of Western science, technology, and materialism. Wars were soon to be fought over not just grazing land and border strips, but hegemony, natural resources, and tribute. Athenian maritime and imperial democracy, fueled by the capital of tribute and the manpower of egalitarianism, quickly revealed the military dynamism—and sheer barbarity—that resulted when a state raised revenue, manned a navy, and avoided pitched battle. By 431 B.C. and the outbreak of the Peloponnesian War, few Greeks believed that any major conflict could any longer be solved by a magnificent collision of glorious men in bronze. Patton would have lamented the passing of the heroic hoplite code; Sherman, in contrast, would have felt that it was an absurdity to kill men while their property and means to make further war were spared.

The very practice of equating landholding with exclusive citizenship rights and military service was always tenuous, as holders of ten-acre plots never made up much more than half of the resident male population of the *polis*. Others—the landless poor, resident aliens, even the unfree—were intrinsically no less capable in war, if the theater of Greek warfare ever migrated from the farmland around the *polis* to the sea, mountains, and overseas territory where horsemen, archers, and sailors were essential. If democracy or sheer economic growth gave the landless clout, they surely would expect to fight for things other than farmland, and to be paid well in the process. Indeed, democracy—the extension of the franchise and office-holding to the propertyless, the political supremacy of the assembly, and the selection of officeholders by lot—led to a radical increase in the frequency and general destructiveness of Greek warfare.[13]

The Peloponnesian War (431–404) between Athens and Sparta destroyed forever the notion that war was simply hoplite battle over borderland. A single year of Athenian-style fighting by land and sea would bankrupt the majority of the Greek city-states—expending as much as the twenty-year construction cost of the Athenian acropolis temples alone. Of course, on the purely tactical level, shock battle was proven to be still a dramatic way to obliterate the infantry of an opponent, as both the fights at Delium (424) and Mantinea (418) had shown. Still, few states any longer were ready to entrust under any circumstances their entire defense to heavy infantry.

By the time of Epaminondas's generalship (371–362), if hoplites could win pitched battles, material resources and preparedness won wars—and the two were no longer always the same thing. Once the connection between citizenship and military service was eroded, many Greek armies now preferred to augment infantry with more flexible hired light-armed troops and missile-throwers. Cultural and social concerns were secondary to killing the enemy as efficiently as possible. Apparently, the old Greek idea that the military was to serve society rather than society the military was by the end of the fifth century lost, especially at imperial Athens and the Spartan apartheid state—lost almost everywhere but in the reactionary enclave of Epaminondan Thebes.

Yet for all their inventiveness, the other Greek states had no solutions for the new paradoxes raised by the Peloponnesian War—that is, if they still wished to be traditional city-states. Hired troops, the growing science of logistics, and the technology of siegecraft and fortification cost far more than did a column of hoplites—and meant taxes, the old anathema to the agrarian city-state. But those freeholding farmers eligible for public infantry service were now an increasing minority of the resident population and not eager to fight beyond the border without pay, and most of the general population felt that the muster of hoplites in itself could no longer ensure the safety of the city-state anyway. A city-state was now a physical structure with people in and around it, no longer an idea of an autonomous and uniform citizenry who fought, voted, and worked as an integrated whole.

A brutal cycle was to be newly inaugurated in most of Greece by the age of Epaminondas: income, property, and excise taxes would be raised to pay for military expenditures. This in turn further weakened the agrarian fabric of the *polis*, which meant even fewer yeomen hoplites for military service.

Armies then grew still more mercenary—requiring yet more money from a dwindling pool of hardworking farmers. Farmers left the countryside for the army, since they would prefer to receive wages than pay property and income taxes. Land would continue to be farmed, but under radically different economic and social circumstances—a cycle also to be repeated in the last two centuries of the Roman Republic when warfare beyond local borders similarly evolved into service to less than egalitarian interests. Because of this dramatic revolution in warfare, Greek society throughout the fourth century gradually moved to a culture of two, not three, classes: the few who owned the land and the many who worked it and protected it for others. A good way to understand the changing nature of Greek warfare is to examine the evidence from some of the recent archaeological surveys of the Greek countryside: from the mid to the late fourth century there begins a gradual drop-off in finds from the rural hinterlands surrounding ancient city-states. And by time of the Hellenistic Age (323–146 B.C.), fields appear almost uninhabited, as workers commuted from town, the size of farms exploded, and homesteads and agrarian settlements disappeared altogether.[14]

In the larger background of contemporary fourth-century Greek political and military evolution, the Theban hoplite rebirth must be seen as a striking incongruity! The reforms started by the Theban generals Epaminondas and Pelopidas were at once both a revolutionary *and* a reactionary movement: there was a continued emphasis on hoplite infantry, and yet hoplite infantry was a source of tactical and strategic innovation in service to a democractic idea. All citizens of Boeotia—not just farmers, not just Thebans—were to be the new nation in arms of a Federal state. No Greek general had ever freely mustered the entire male population of the countryside into one large national army. Philip and Alexander would do so in the next half century to come; but they would employ coercion and offer booty, not the freedom of others, as the incentive to march.

Fourth-century Greeks knew that hoplite battle in itself was no longer warfare. Most acknowledged that light-armed troops and skirmishers were absolutely critical in order to harass the enemy and plunder the countryside. In contrast, only Epaminondas saw that the old infantry—and the old infantry alone—would now not bother the enemy or loot his land so much as march openly into his homeland and attack his culture. If Sparta chose to have no walls other than the shields of her hoplites, then Theban hoplites would batter down those walls and thereby free her unfree.

If an *entire* Greek state could march together as heavy infantrymen, then all the innovations in tactics and armament still meant little. Skirmishers and artillery might harass armies or besiege cities, but to overrun an entire countryside, humiliate its army, and march unimpeded through its farmland—and to do all that for an idea rather than in pursuit of lucre—heavy infantry was still necessary. Again, hoplite battle may have no longer constituted war, but to make war really destructive hoplite soldiers were critical—and the Thebans now determined to muster their entire citizenry to do just that. If Epaminondas's ranks were not filled exclusively with property-owning farmers, nevertheless they were to arm, fight, and feel as if they were. He had divorced hoplite service from farm-owning and thereby made his agrarian hoplite state more powerful than ever.

In short, Epaminondas's military revolution was not merely a means to preserve the democracy and the Boeotian Confederacy, or even to end the stain of Spartan helotage. In a much larger sense, his invasion represented an attempt to salvage through battle the very soul of the Greek *polis* itself. When his men trekked southward against Sparta, he demonstrated that a free militia could still muster, campaign, and fight under consensual government, could still battle as infantrymen without sophisticated technology or mercenaries, and for a cause other than mere aggrandizement. It was precisely under those conditions that the Greek city-state had once arisen—and just those conditions it was now everywhere else but in Thebes in the process of repudiating. Greek warfare in its eleventh hour was to see once more an ideological army, composed of hoplite infantrymen, and led by a philosopher-general. Sparta would never be the same again.

4

"THE THEBANS ARE
MIGHTIER IN WAR"

T HE THEBAN phalanx that shattered the Spartans at Leuctra (371) had
evolved unlike any other: a conservative reliance on hoplites, and yet
subtle refinements in the tactics and strategy of phalanx warfare that
might lend the old army a new deadly power if used under careful strategic
considerations of time and space—and under a new-style government that
was not confined solely to landowning farmers. Epaminondas, in short, was to
create a land army more democratic than the Athenian, and yet more deadly
than the Spartan.

True, Epaminondas proved at the battle of Leuctra that Theban hoplites
could destroy any other infantry in Greece. But an hour of hard fighting in
sight of one's farm was not the same as marching for weeks on end through
the winter cold into the very heart of the most dangerous military culture in
Greece. Boeotian hoplites could push, spear, and trample ferociously on their
home turf. But never in their centuries-long history had they—or any other
Greeks—marched en masse deep into the Peloponnese. Yet now they were
asked by their philosopher general to conduct a multitheater war, not merely
fight a one-hour battle. Epaminondas asked his farmers to keep faith in the
phalanx, but to use the phalanx for purposes beyond mere battle.

This Theban die-hard faith in traditional hoplites had a certain logic.
Navies, fortifications, siegecraft, mercenaries, and missile troops were expensive and largely necessary for campaigning outside the protective plains of

mainland Greece. Yet, if a state's strategic vision was largely defensive—fighting in and around its own inland territory—or at least confined to a march on land in strength, traditional hoplite armies still remained invincible and extremely cheap. Even if other city-states did not play by the old rules, all potential invaders would eventually have to cross the plain of Boeotia and thereupon meet the Theban phalanx on flat ground—under the old rules. In an accessible flatland like Boeotia, massed infantry still made sense. It was sensible, of course, for farmers to defend their farms. But to destroy others' property far from home, to liberate serfs, to terrify an entire people? That was another dilemma altogether.[15]

The trick now was to protect the old phalanx while on the move from new challenges of combined forces, and to ensure that the old civic faith in public military service remained strong when it was eroding just about everywhere else. The Thebans under the leadership of two of its elected generals, Epaminondas and Pelopidas, accomplished both brilliantly. First, Boeotia still remained largely agrarian, without large numbers of urban poor, resident aliens, or chattel slaves; once all Boeotian natives were given equal rights, there were few resident adult males without the franchise. Thebes discovered that a full-fledged democracy was no longer antithetical to a traditional army of hoplite infantrymen—if the army could be reinvented to include more than just property owners.

Without a navy (a small fleet of twelve triremes was expanded to nearly a hundred, but then largely abandoned after a couple of years), dock works, fortifications, mercenaries, and taxes remained largely nonexistent. Thus there was no constituency of poor rowers—what some Athenians called the "naval mob"—to demand maritime imperialism to secure jobs and income. Heretofore, in most Greek city-states the lack of a property qualification inevitably meant Athenian-style democracy, where docks, a navy, port and urban fortifications, and public donatives were the norm. The poor would vote in the assembly for entitlements and military aggression out of concern for their own livelihood. But in the newly constituted democratic Boeotian Confederacy, all natives participated on a more or less equal basis while retaining the conservative rural values that had been traditionally associated with the old hoplite governments. Democracy, therefore, could achieve real egalitarianism without becoming sectarian, extremist, or imperial. There was almost a naïve idealism in Boeotia about this new concept of democracy, free of Athenian cynicism, that Epaminondas would draw on to spread freedom and democracy to hundreds of thousands of others in the Peloponnese. Battle would not be for mere land, much less for conquest, but now for the soul of peoples miles away to the south.

The Boeotian federated system of representative and constitutional government curtailed infighting, and thus most surrounding agrarian communities willingly contributed their hoplites to the Boeotian cause. In essence, the Boeotians developed democracy with rights granted to all native-born citizens of their great plain, quite apart from the Athenian paradigm where military expenditure and adventure were tied to the welfare of a large block of poor but politically astute voters in the Assembly. Thus arose the comic poet Aristophanes' caricatures of whiney Athenian urbanites and loungers who wished to expropriate capital—foreign and domestic—to ensure that their own public entitlements were secure.[16]

Second, Epaminondas's novel tactical innovations enhanced the inherent strengths of Boeotian infantry, which in antiquity had a reputation for muscular strength and combative ferocity. From the battle of Delium (424) onward, the Thebans had always massed more deeply than the hoplite standard of eight shields. In most battles, their columns ranged from sixteen to twenty-five, and at Leuctra fifty men deep. True, the flanks of such a massed phalanx were more exposed by the ensuing deeper column. The initial killing power of offensive weaponry was reduced as more spearmen were taken out of the first three ranks (which alone could reach the enemy in the inaugural onslaught) and stacked to the rear. Cannae and in some sense Waterloo are testaments to what happens to columns when they approach lines, when firepower is decreased in the failed hope of using the resulting depth to break a shallower linear formation.

But the Thebans took that chance and thereby gained enormous penetrating power, as accumulated shields created greater thrust—the ideal was that the sheer physicality of Boeotian yeomen might punch a hole and then push right on through the enemy before they were overwhelmed on the flanks. In classical tactical parlance, Epaminondas has refined the tradition of applying equal pressure along the battle line into a concentration of force on the left wing, realizing that in past battles victory was achieved on the horns anyway. His men need not become professional drillers and maneuverers like the Spartans or light-clad skirmishers like Athenian expeditionary forces, but rather would wrestle, work their farms, and then line up deep to push and stab ahead.

A deeper phalanx also reinforced the notion of revolutionary élan, and in our sources there is a definite sense that the Thebans en masse—like later Swiss pikemen of the democratic cantons or Napoleonic columns—often broke through the enemy because they thought they could do so. Unlike the more skilled Spartans, who walked to the music of flutes, and whose drilling might allow complicated reversals of direction and flanking movements, the amateurishness of Boeotian farmers found a natural outlet in sheer brute strength and the rolling momentum of mass attack. The best veterans of the lot would both man the blade of the phalanx and hold the rear tight, while those strong but less experienced might push from the middle. When the Spartan redcloaks approached at a walk to the eerie music of flutes, they were to be met by a column at least four times deeper of screaming rustics on the run.

Epaminondas added a couple of vital ancillary tactical touches. The Theban mass and fighting elite would be placed on the left, *not* the right, of the Boeotian battle line, in order to smash the opposite elite royal right of the Spartan phalanx (the history of Boeotian pitched battle in the first half of the fourth century is mostly a story of fighting Spartans) destroying the morale of the entire Peloponnesian army, and preempting the known Spartan tendency to roll up the enemy by initiating a flanking movement from its right.

There were other more pragmatic reasons for the Theban mass to fight on the left, not the traditional right wing of honor. At the earlier battles of Nemea and Coronea (394) under the old more oligarchal confederation, the Thebans had massed deep, rendering their hapless Boeotian allies vulnerable to outflanking moves by the longer enemy across the battlefield. Sacrificing fellow yeomen of the Boeotian rustic hamlets to Spartan killers was no way to lead a newly founded democratic federation into battle. But now since the Theban mass faced the Spartiate elite head-on, there was no objection by the allied Boeotian villagers who were to be pitted against the *weakest* of the enemy. True, the allied battle line was made shorter to cover the Thebans' mass on the left, but these Boeotian regiments were now more or less ensured of easy victory over the inferior contingents across the way.

Military historians praise Epaminondas for his desire to concentrate his deep column on the left and to decide the issue dramatically against the royal guard of Sparta. It is almost always forgotten it may have been just as likely that, given the new communitarian spirit of the confederation, Epaminondas did not wish to leave the shallower lines of his fellow Boeotians naked before the enemy elite. Of course, he did concentrate Thebans where they could do the most damage, but in doing so he made sure his confederate Boeotians were not left vulnerable as a result. He took considerable risks in placing his Thebans—and himself—right in the inferno of battle. A decade after Leuctra, at the battle of Mantinea (362), his death on the left against what was left of the Spartan elite meant an end to the Theban renaissance itself.

There was one final consequence of Epaminondas's fighting on the left wing. He would not only pulverize the hated Spartiate elite, but in the process also spare the purported enemy Peloponnesian allies. They were on the enemy left wing facing his own weaker Boeotian allied right. Once the

Spartiates were crushed, there was no reason for them to fight and die for a cause that was not their own. At Leuctra, Epaminondas simultaneously wrecked the Spartiate master class, saved his own Boeotian allies from being outflanked, *and* allowed the Peloponnesians to flee relatively unhurt. It was no accident that many of these same Peloponnesian troops in a few months would welcome Epaminondas into their own homeland to finish the job against their hated Spartan overlords. In short, Epaminondas did away with the sham of coalition armies, and demonstrated on the battlefield that the real struggle was always between all his Thebans and the Spartiate overclass in particular.[17]

In addition, specialized contingents—the famous Sacred Band (*hieros lochos*) of 150 pairs of best "friends" is the most well known—and the use of integrated cavalry tactics ensured that the Boeotians themselves could protect their new ponderous and unwieldy columns from enemy light-armed skirmishers and peltasts. Tradition has it that Pelopidas led the Sacred Band at "the cutting edge" of the battle line—apparently, these crack troops would be the wedge that prepared the way for the mass behind. Usually, specialized troops were aristocratic in nature. But the 300 of the Sacred Band, almost uniquely so, seem to have served the democracy faithfully and in fact to have been led by a succession of populists and revolutionaries. The Boeotian wealthy, rather than hatching plots to reclaim power, would now, in exchange for military glory, help to form the basis for a crack unit that would spearhead the attack of the democratic mass. Similar elite and specialized *hamippoi*, or light-armed troops trained to fight alongside cavalry, also protected the flanks and added flexibility to the charge of horsemen. The old aristocratic, formidable Boeotian cavalry took on a more aggressive role to confuse the enemy before battle and to follow any victory with deadly pursuit.

Traditionally, elite units and cavalry in Greek history were suspected of being potential right-wing insurrectionists, unhappy over their reduced or underappreciated role under democratic government. At Athens and Argos, for example, mounted troops and elite corps were instrumental in overthrowing democratic governments. Thus neither corps ever really fulfilled its military potential on the classical Greek battlefield, as they were used sparingly and with occasional reluctance by suspicious hoplite pikemen and radical democratic governments alike. The Boeotian cavalry and the Sacred Band, in marked contrast, were fully integrated into the democratic militia of Boeotia, and thus were vital in protecting and enhancing the phalanx of their massed hoplite comrades.[18]

The result was the creation of the most deadly infantry in the history of classical Greek warfare, a true nation at arms without either the brutal system of helotage at Sparta or the often insidious class jealousies at Athens that at times so divided hoplite, cavalryman, and rower. At Leuctra (371), the Theban phalanx led its vastly outnumbered Boeotian allies right through the Spartans, killing King Cleombrotus himself, annihilating 400 of the elite and increasingly scarce Spartiates, and hundreds more of their allies nearby who unfortunately were sucked into the carnage. Nearly every one of the elite Similars on the Spartan right wing who faced directly the Theban steamroller—eighty shields in breadth, fifty in depth—was slaughtered. The Spartan army that had once held the pass at Thermopylae, that had broken the Persian charge at Plataea and had smashed enemy columns at first Mantinea, Nemea, and Coronea, now littered with its dead the small Boeotian plain around Leuctra.

Leuctra demonstrated that Epaminondas's ideas—if they were in fact his alone, as his other generals quickly claimed equal credit for the victory—were magically suited for a particular time and place in Theban history. Highly motivated agrarian troops on the defensive, rallying behind a popular democratic leader and fired by a new sense of political community, were natural ingredients for forming a revolutionary column of brawlers. As Epaminondas would learn when he marched southward, the reputation of his men would precede him. Their repute would ensure that no Peloponnesian army would face his hoplites in battle, thus allowing them the opportunity instead to march and plunder at will—and to seek wider strategic and humanitarian goals than the mere defeat of the hated Spartan hoplites. The historian Diodorus once made a moral point in connecting ethics to political success when he remarked how odd it was that the Thebans, for so long exploited, could reverse their fortunes instantaneously, whereas the Spartans, for so long the exploiter, could never again regain their lost hegemony. But to the *polis* Greeks, it made perfect sense that the gods would eventually punish hubris and reward the just. The Thebans marched southward with the confidence that most Greeks welcomed their crusade to liberate the unfree; Sparta waited their arrival in dread, with the suspicion that the Hellenic world wished their serfs free and their strange culture at last emasculated.

By 371 the Thebans had established battle superiority over all armies in Greece. But it was left to a single individual to use that tactical excellence for a larger *strategic* purpose. If Greek armies would now avoid pitched battle with the newly energized Theban phalanx, then it was high time to use its formidable reputation for the greater goal of a new total warfare. Fighting would involve not merely battle, but the annihilation of an oligarchal society's means to conduct war itself and the spread of terror among the enemy's civilian population. Most military thinkers in Greece had operated on the principle that such novel wars of attrition required diverse and flexible troops, mercenaries, large fleets, missile troops, and siege engines—the capital-consuming nightmare that would finally bankrupt the classical city-state. Epaminondas, the revolutionary reactionary, thought it simply required enough good hoplites, level ground, a moral incentive—and an audacious leader. Like Sherman, he had no inclination to occupy, garrison, and hold enemy territory; rather, he preferred to sweep in, destroy, terrorize—and move on. In the detritus, slave might leave master, aristocrat blame aristocrat, and the entire absurdity of an apartheid society might be revealed.

Thebes was a country of rough farmers who appeared in battle as they did behind the plow. In contrast, Sparta was a labyrinth of oppression and exploitation whose psychological capital accrued from fear, terror, and intimidation of the weak. To maintain the illusion of an overlord class, it could *not* afford to allow rustics from the north to intimidate its warriors and burn its houses. But that was precisely Epaminondas's idea: he would now march the dreaded Theban phalanx in the general direction of the enemy, call them out to fight, and then with his allied contingents and auxiliaries plunder the Spartan countryside. The Spartans could either have a second Leuctra, or watch their homesteads and villages go up in flames—either way, thousands of their oppressed Helots would at last learn that free men and democracy, not a tiny clique, were the real warriors. What is usually forgotten about Epaminondas's novel strategy is that in theory he would ruin Sparta, free the Helots, and lead 70,000 men without much more than a few hundred people being killed on all sides during the entire operation. Many great generals can defeat the enemy by incurring massive losses of their own—Grant's methodical approach to Richmond and the American repulse of the Germans during the Ardennes offensive are good examples. But only a few of genius—an Epaminondas, a Sherman, or a Patton—can waste an entire culture without ruining their own army in the process.

Such democratic armies are both fragile and volatile, reaching a peak of battle excellence that is hard to calibrate and difficult to maintain. We do not know at what point the restless Theban army was confident enough to meet and then to demolish the Spartan army. At Tegyra (375) on the plains of northern Boeotia, it had defeated a small Spartan contingent, and yet until Leuctra (371) the Boeotians subsequently chose *not* to meet the invading Spartans in battle on their home turf for most of the ensuing decade of the 370s. For two years the Boeotians had timidly ringed their rich farmland with an enormous wooden stockade, in a failed effort to keep the Spartans off their grainfields.

But then inexplicably under Epaminondas the army chose to fight, and destroyed, the best of the Spartan troops in 371, and within months drove into the heart of Sparta itself. Yet by 362 at the battle of Mantinea the Boeotian army collapsed and retreated the moment Epaminondas perished at the front of the phalanx, never to mount a serious invasion southward again. The great democratic militias are by definition armies of a season and of a particular spirit, and it may be that the Boeotians' training, élan, and sheer anger was never quite again what they were during that miraculous year after Leuctra. Just as there was not an army in the world that could have stopped Sherman as he neared Savannah, or Patton as he dashed eastward in August 1944, so too in the winter of 370 no force in Greece could have withstood Epaminondas's descent into Sparta.

Ancient commentators remarked that Epaminondas's Thebans were "swelled with pride," "increasingly renowned for their martial courage," and "sky-high in their spirits"—in short, under Epaminondas they were a *polis full of confidence,*" with men who "were by nature fond of fighting," just like "young dogs." Such ancient editorializing does not describe soldiers who fight merely for self-preservation, or for the immediate safety of their particular group, but rather reflects a real sense that the hoplites of Thebes, at least for a moment, felt that their army was on a moral crusade to change the very map of Greece. Epaminondas had turned a fierce group of farmers into ideological warriors. Within days after Leuctra, contemporaries raised an epigram commemorating the victory of these "young dogs" over Sparta and the newfound chauvinism of the Theban army. "The Thebans," the stone inscription proclaimed simply, "are mightier in war."[19]

5

"PRINCEPS GRAECIAE"

"THE FIRST man of Greece," proclaimed the Roman essayist and orator Cicero three centuries subsequent to Epaminondas's death, after collating the deeds of the most renowned Greeks of the past and coming to the conclusion that none had rivaled the Theban liberator. Would that we today had the same rich sources that Cicero had read! Unfortunately, the contemporary fourth-century histories of Ephorus and Callisthenes are lost and often poorly excerpted by later extant accounts. Plutarch's life of Epaminondas has not survived. Xenophon, the Athenian Spartophile, mentions him only rarely in his history of fourth-century Greece—and apparently made sure that Epaminondas played no real prominent role until late in his narrative. What little we know of Epaminondas instead is gathered from the secondhand account of the Theban hegemony in the first-century B.C. historian Diodorus, anecdotes in Plutarch's extant *Lives* and *Moralia*, adages in the military compendia of Frontinus and Polyaenus, and a few biographical scraps in Nepos and Pausanias, also both of the Roman era.[20]

Still, the outlines of his brief career of some eighteen years from his small role in the revolutionary ouster of the Spartans (379) from the Theban acropolis to his death at Mantinea (362) are fairly clear. From the late 390s to 371 he may well have fought at all of the Theban engagements with and against the Spartans; Pausanias and Plutarch mention him as rescuing his colleague Pelopidas at an obscure fight near Mantineia in 385. Yet he must have been almost forty—about the same age as Sherman at the dawn of the Civil War and like him an unknown before the conflict, and like Patton from an old and respected family—when we first receive any full account of him, in 379, as part of a general effort to expel the Spartan garrison at Thebes. By 371, as one of seven elected Boeotarchs, he crushed the Spartan army at Leuctra. Our sources suggest that much of the tactical plan of the battle, indeed the very decision to face the much larger Spartan army, may have been his alone.

From that moment on, Epaminondas was apparently annually elected Boeotarch, serving as a general of the confederation—save in 368 when in the aftermath of his second historic invasion of Sparta he was again tried on capital charges for treason. He led the Thebans on two more invasions of the Peloponnese before dying at the moment of victory in the battle against the Spartan alliance at Mantinea (362). He may have been in his late forties to mid-fifties when he led the Theban left wing one final time into the horde of Spartan redcloaks. Epaminondas is usually regarded as the architect of the entire strategy to isolate Sparta by freeing the serfs and creating citadels in Arcadia, to create a Theban naval presence, and along with Pelopidas to keep the Thessalian tyrants away from the northern borders of Boeotia.[21]

At that point the man ends and the myth begins. In addition to what we do know with certainty about his life—apparent noble lineage but general impoverishment, a follower of the teachings of the mathematician-philosopher-mystic Pythagoras, proponent of democracy, tactical innovator and strategic thinker, unmarried and without children, elected general of the army for at least nine years, incorrigible Spartaphobe—an entire mystique arose shortly after his death to account for two inexplicable phenomena: (1) the rise of Boeotian power had seemingly coincided with Epaminondas's ascension to Boeotarch and ended with his death; and (2) to the cynical fourth-century Greeks, the nature of his conquests was unusually ethical, resulting in giving democracy to his fellow Boeotians, autonomy to the city-states of the Peloponnese, and freedom to the Helots of Messenia—all without gratuitous killing, personal lucre for himself, or political exploitation by his Boeotians (in that regard the contrast with the earlier fifth-century Athenians and the later Philip and Alexander is remarkable). When, for example, Epaminondas captured Boeotian right-wing refugees and exiled traitors on his marches through the Peloponnese, he always found ways of saving them from the mandated death penalty, and usually took pains simply to let them go without punishment.

Anecdotes about his Shermanesque temper and disdain for tyrants also read larger than life. Plutarch says that even Alexander, the tyrant of Thessaly, quivered at his approach, and "though a warrior bird, like a slave drooped his wings" in fear of the Theban. At various times he shouted back at the venerable King Agesilaus of Sparta in a Panhellenic peace conference in the monarch's own council hall—declaring bluntly in front of the cringing delegates that "the prior war had made Sparta powerful at the expense of the sufferings of the rest of the other Greeks."

After that veiled warning, the oppressed states of Greece looked to Thebes, not Athens, for their liberation. Twenty days later Epaminondas would add injury to insult by demolishing the Spartan army at Leuctra and teaching his old rival and moral inferior Agesilaus just who in fact could and could not lead an army into an enemy's heartland. Later stripped of his generalship, Epaminondas simply marched as a regular hoplite soldier. On trial for his life, he dared his compatriots to find him guilty of treason. He had even saved the life of Pelopidas in battle and once left the ranks to take over the army when it was in a tactical quandary. He was uniformly praised by all contemporary sources, and there exists in the ancient record no "hostile" tradition at all, which marks most historical assessments of Greek generals from Pericles to Alexander.[22]

There is no reason to doubt any of the encomia per se—even Xenophon, for all his apparent neglect of Epaminondas in his *Hellenica*, provides little outright criticism and some occasional praise. Rather, the key is to detect beneath the sometimes unctuous adages and laudation an astute, rather fanatical man, whose ascetic life of Pythagoreanism was devoted to the employment of the Theban army for his own particular political vision of roughly equal and free states throughout Greece. In that regard, as we shall see, under the rules of Hellenic warfare and for his own understanding of a higher good, he could plunder and devastate the land of his enemies as easily as any other Greek.

Epaminondas rebuked pacifists at Thebes with the warning that they wanted slavery, not peace. "Those who wish to enjoy peace must be ready for war," he lectured them, seven hundred years before Vegetius's more famous Roman dictum, *Qui desiderat pacem, praeparet bellum*. No wonder later critics dubbed him "Iron Gut" when he ordered his men to march around the Peloponnese on sparse rations. From what we can derive from ancient sources, Epaminondas was born to fight, and lived solely to destroy Sparta. To the philosophical Epaminondas, to paraphrase Heraclitus and Plato, "war was the father of all things," and "peace but a parenthesis."[23]

Contemporaries were even more impressed with his character—his philosophical distance and sometimes fatalism—than with his political or military brilliance. A small sampling from the commendatory tradition gives some indication of the effect that he had on others. Plutarch tells us that

Epaminondas never executed any person of a captured city, nor ever sold any Greek captive into slavery—a policy that should have been nearly impossible for any victorious Greek general to carry out, given the moral landscape of the times. Only in his absence on campaign did the Thebans attack the nearby hamlet of Orchomenos and destroy their citadel for not joining the Boeotian Confederacy and for openly abetting Sparta—an expedition against a Boeotian neighbor that Epaminondas vehemently opposed. Once when invited to dinner, finding a sumptuous feast, he got up and left, remarking, "I thought you were going to eat, not show off"—an asceticism not unlike Sherman's expressed preference for hardtack while on campaign. He purportedly owned one cloak only—on days that he had it cleaned, he stayed indoors naked. Again, like Sherman, he was dressed drably and indistinguishably from his men.

Any signs of megalomania after his great victory at Leuctra? The battle made the dutiful, middle-aged son happiest simply because his mother and father were still alive and so he could bask in their pride. His "daughters," he said at his death, "were his victories at Leuctra and Mantinea." Ancient accounts add that he usually lectured others on their lapses in marriage when he was criticized for having neither a wife nor children. He seems to have been immune to female flattery and had little if any interest in the opposite sex. An occasional anecdote suggests that he was more relaxed in the company of men in the field. His mettle in battle? We hear that in the midst of the mass shoving at Leuctra, Homeric-like he yelled to his men, "Grant me one step further and we will have the victory." They did and so they won.

Plutarch and Pausanias contain an entire litany of such random Epaminondisms, attesting to his selfless character and stark, Pythagorean-inspired personal regimen—what nineteenth-century German classical scholars in obvious admiration called his "philosophisch-asketische Richtung." In similar approval ancient biographers relate how the general sacked the obese, himself achieved a master command of arms, insisted on wrestling and gymnastic training for his men, shunned money, and ridiculed the allure of materialism among weaker spirits. "When all the Thebans were at festival," Plutarch records, "he alone patrolled their arms depot and walls, announcing that he was both sober and awake so that others might be free to drink and sleep."

Epaminondas appears in our laudatory sources as forever the enigmatic philosopher, immune from more worldly enticements, who voluntarily spurned wealth, women, rich food, and wine—the four ancient sins that biographers of the Neoplatonic tradition customarily cite as the standard causes of self-inflicted tragedy. In the eyes of Pythagoreans like Epaminondas, philosophy was not abstract contemplation, but "a way of life" that was to be quasi-religious and to affect the daily behavior of the initiate—silence and constant self-examination were vital to resist the appetitive urges and prepare the soul to migrate after death to a higher plane. So Epaminondas fired his attendant when he heard he had taken a bribe: "Give me back my shield," he told the servant, "and go buy yourself a dining club to live in, since you won't be willing to face danger any longer once you've made yourself rich." Such zealous men and women nursed on Pythagorean thought could make this world better and ensure their own tranquility hereafter. To his fellow general Pelopidas, he advised that each time he went to the marketplace he was not to leave until he had made at least one new friend. The two themselves came to symbolize the idealized notion of a balanced Greek friendship—Epaminondas the more philosophical warrior; Pelopidas always eager to improve his physical prowess.[24]

In the absence of either an extant biography or a sustained ancient historical narrative of Epaminondas, what are military historians to make of all these scattered details of his life? Military genius, of course, including the tactical rediscovery of the entire notion of concentration of force and the strategic novelty of indirect approach to attack the infrastructure, not merely the army, of the enemy. But there is also a mysticism that is often connected with Pythagorean thought—ancients associated the sect with the worship of Orpheus—which helps to explain much of Epaminondas's puritanism, selfless devotion to a cause, fascination in city-founding and fortification, friendship with Pelopidas—and hatred of Sparta. As we shall see, Epaminondas, like Sherman and Patton, had fanatical ideas about his own destiny and a real sense of fatalism, that living audaciously was far preferable to a lengthy life in obscurity.

By the early fourth century, the followers of the long-dead Pythagoras had been expelled from Italy, the few surviving adherents wandering the Adriatic and Aegean. Diodorus says that in the time of Epaminondas they were in their "last generation." Prominent devotees like Lysis and a few others had earlier settled in Thebes, perhaps drawn to the safety of its backwater isolation, the richness of its religious traditions and ubiquitous sanctuaries, and its old aristocratic sympathy for educated thinkers. Tradition has it that the young Epaminondas was devoted to the teacher Lysis, who sought refuge in his father's house; the boy followed the Pythagorean about Thebes, soaking up his precepts. Diodorus remarks that he became the old man's adopted son, and because of his Pythagorean training and innate virtue "became the first citizen not only of Thebes but of all Greece."

In the most unlikely of places, amid the farms of a parochial and isolated countryside, the future general was absorbing the most holistic, all-encompassing, and in some ways radical of Greek philosophical systems, a creed that had more naturally been at home among the sophistication of the cosmopolitan Greeks of southern Italy. Even other Greek rationalists thought Pythagoreans dangerous: they practiced an open disdain for material gain and an apparent communism, under which private property was not to exist among friends. Followers led an ascetic existence, yet were devoted to music and flute-playing. They sought to bring a rigid code of personal behavior into politics—an inflexibility and severity that may have been their downfall in Italy—practiced vegetarianism, treated women as social and cultural equals, felt animals too had spirits, favored silence, and believed in the transmigration of souls: the continual reincarnation of the spirit back into a corporeal existence—human, plant, or animal—until the human essence was purified and free from the temptations of the material world. No surprise that much of Socratic asceticism and Platonic metaphysics may have been inspired by earlier and mostly lost Pythagorean teachings. No surprise either that they incurred outright hostility. More than three centuries after Epaminondas's death Cicero also wrote that he would rather be wrong with Plato in philosophical speculation than find himself right but in agreement with the Pythagoreans.

The Theban revolutionaries of 379 initially left Epaminondas out of their conspiracy because of his general reputation as a philosophical recluse and his strong reluctance for killing other Thebans. Cornelius Nepos's life of Epaminondas is mostly a litany of Pythagorean *exempla*—Epaminondas the impoverished but generous benefactor, who is incorruptible by money, power, food, or sex, and obsessed with his singular goal of liberating both serfs and free men from the autocracy of Sparta. When told that a fine Theban citizen had died about the time of his victory at Leuctra, Epaminondas reportedly scoffed, "By Heracles! How did this man find the time to die when there were so many great things going on?" Plutarch remarks that his dress, conduct, language, and life were constant, absolutely unaffected by the changing surroundings about him. When out at dinner, he customarily drank only a cheap vinegary wine—the only way to remind himself what his ordinary fare at home was like.

We know of Pythagoras from his celebrated investigations into the relationships between numbers, most famously his theorem concerning the area relationships between the lengths of the sides of a right triangle—$a^2 + b^2 = c^2$. But we forget that Pythagoreans saw such research not in the modern sense as purely mathematical inquiry, or even necessarily as practical science to be applied to engineering or construction, but originally as a metaphysical tool to unlock divine and absolute truths of the universe. Pythagoras had not "discovered" a law, as much as uncovered a passage into the divine world of absolute symmetry—a mathematical revelation not subject to human perception or interpretation, but one the philosopher should emulate in uncovering similar divine truths hidden in the world about.

The sect applied a scientific, rationalist investigation of higher mathematics as part of an overall effort to discover proportion, balance, and ultimately a spiritual plan perceptible to the devotee who had undergone sufficient religious, scientific, and personal indoctrination. If Epaminondas would found the new city Messenê on a grid, and parcel the surrounding countryside into equal allotments, it was because this was not just a practical and fair solution to creating a society *ex nihilo*, but rather also a humane policy that logically followed from a belief in the divinity of mathematical proportion and harmony. Epaminondas would apply the order of the universe to the disorder in his own world; people would act justly when presented with a divinely just social and political plan.[25]

In more practical terms, the efforts of Pythagoreans to ignore the traditional Olympian gods, overturn conventional prejudice, postulate a heliocentric solar system, censor the luxury and decadence of the more wealthy and powerful, and apply a radical equality to fellows both female and male could only ensure animosity and eventual hostility. The enemies of all Pythagoreans were superstition, blinkered tradition, conventional religion and custom—anything handed down through ignorance that might impede unfettered examination of natural phenomena and hence man's proper role in the universe. Their utopia, similar in this regard to Plato's, was not democracy, but rather a commune of the ascetic and educated, a sect of natural and trained elites, whose own exemplary behavior would allow them to bring justice and enlightenment to the ignorant other.

Naturally, most have attributed Epaminondas's selfless character and stark personal regime to his Pythagoreanism, as well as his impatience with the unfit, his ideal of shared property among friends, and rough material equality as the model for others. We can go much further and see—as did contemporaries—his political idealism, occasional impatience with democracy, and sense of missionary zeal as a natural dividend of Pythagorean education. Before Leuctra, when the timid clamored that the omens of the Olympians were unfavorable, Epaminondas simply led his army forward, offering the wavering and superstitious in the ranks only a line from Homer's *Iliad:* "Only one omen is best: to fight on behalf of the fatherland."

The historian Diodorus remarks that because of his Pythagorean training and reliance "on the reason of his education," Epaminondas thought that "cognizance of virtue and care for justice" were more important than mere "signs." Before Leuctra, his chair suddenly collapsed, to the sudden dismay of his superstitious hoplites. Unlucky? "No," he told his men, "we are just forbidden to sit." About the only portents the rationalist Epaminondas did pay attention to were those that he faked to induce the more ignorant to fight at Leuctra when the situation looked bleak and "the Spartans covered the entire plain." Some scholars—if understandably so—have gone perhaps too far in attributing Pythagoreanism even to the nuts and bolts of Epaminondas's tactical planning, arguing that his idea of placing troops on the left, not the right, wing was the logical result of Pythagorean assault on traditional Hellenic superstition prejudices against the left hand.[26]

In any case, we can at least say that Epaminondas's bold experimentation in altering the point of attack of the phalanx, his disdain for military oracles and divine portents, his increasing the phalanx to new depths, insisting on democracy and equality for all citizens of Boeotia and those far distant, reflect a mind not bound by tradition, but convinced that his own record of behavior in the here and now would radically alter the condition of his eternal soul in the hereafter—a self-righteousness shared with Sherman, a spiritual fanaticism that Patton, another devout believer in reincarnation, could easily appreciate. To a man of Epaminondas's education and belief, then, the world was subject to canons that operated on divine mathematical principles, where logic and virtue—not money, power, or even class, status, or gender—brought harmony. The evil in this life was not a mysterious or even inexplicable phenomenon, but a clearly identifiable lapse of human character and reason, and thus a sin that could be rectified through investigation, criticism—and force.

The hubris of Sparta could be countered by an army that was in prime physical condition, guided by selfless principles, and led by a philosopher who would not distort its ethical mission even in the face of political and legal opposition. The winding, chaotic streets of the Spartan Helot state should be demolished in order that a new society in Messenia of its former serfs, established on egalitarian principles and laid out afresh on a symmetrical grid, might further human aspirations for harmony and tranquility.

As we shall see, both Sherman and Patton shared a similar zeal, and felt their own personal regimen, wide reading, and eagerness to undergo both hardship and danger made them uniquely fit to lead men who otherwise would not or could not do what they themselves had. If one had asked contemporary observers of the Civil War which senior Union general was the most unusual, learned—and sometimes terrifying—the answer surely would have been William Tecumseh Sherman; the same general consensus of peers would be true of George S. Patton. We should not be surprised about either the fervor or eccentricity of Epaminondas the Theban, for the very idea of cutting loose thousands of marchers from supply lines to destroy the heartland of a slave state *is* an eccentric, terrifying, and arrogant proposal. All three men in varying degrees were in a sense possessed, not especially worried about their own safety, and arrogantly convinced that they were not merely warriors, but prophets of larger cultural and political causes.

There is ancient support for the prominence of philosophical training at the foundation of Epaminondas's military acumen. The philosopher and rhetorician Alcidamas of Elaea remarked that Thebes rose when it was run by philosophers. In regard to Epaminondas's record, Aelian points out that philosophers could also be skilled in war. A late passage from Nonnus implies that Epaminondas won at Leuctra because of his training by Philolaus the Pythagorean. All generals have messianic visions of their roles on earth. Even those who feel in touch with divine spirits are not rare—the lawless such as Alexander, Napoleon, and Hitler all believed in their own fate and their almost divine mission, and, as half-educated dilettantes, could quote a line or two of the great thinkers to impress their intellectual inferiors. But generals who combine such egoism and superficial mysticism with real erudition, wide reading, a rigid personal regimen, and devotion to constitutional government are quite unusual.[27]

To understand his almost mystical hold on his men and obsession with reaching Sparta, we must see his career-long philosophical antipathy to the entire culture of the Spartan state and the apartheid it represented. He habitually pardoned wavering allies, even traitorous Boeotians, but sought to destroy the very buildings of Sparta—the hodgepodge nature of the town must have bothered his Pythagorean sense of proportion, and thus logically helped explain to him Sparta's moral confusion—a brutal system ironically praised by Athenian rightists for its "order" and "good government."

By sheer force of personality Epaminondas convinced his fellow generals to make a stand at Leuctra, and only with difficulty was he dissuaded from attacking and killing the enemy survivors the next day. We see a little of the moral absolutism of Stonewall Jackson in Epaminondas, who also applied his religious zeal to killing the enemy. Xenophon, the Spartan apologist, finally conceded to Epaminondas and his Thebans that "he had brought his army to such a degree of preparation that his men flinched from no toil, whether by night or day, and never avoided any danger, always being eager to obey him even when their provisions were scanty." At the battle of Mantinea he plunged head-on against the royal elite, this time ensuring his death under a sea of enemies. So great was the fear and hatred of Epaminondas that at Sparta for the next half a millennium Anticrates would be praised as his slayer. To the Athenians the honored killer was supposedly their own native, Gryllus, the son of Xenophon himself. The Mantineans argued that the "honor" was due their own citizen, Machairion, "the little knife" who had stabbed the leader in the melee.[28]

It is no accident that he grabbed a snake and knocked out its brains to symbolize his plan to kill the Spartan royal elite at Leuctra—a class that to his mind was aptly symbolized by a fanged reptile. Two anecdotes reveal his instinctual dislike of Spartans and things Spartan. When in conference he heard a long list of accusations against his countrymen from the normally succinct Spartans, he replied abruptly, "At least these Thebans put an end to your habit of brief speaking." When told by the Spartan King Agesilaus that his Thebans had no business speaking for the other hamlets of the newly comprised Boeotian Confederacy, he shot back that neither did the Spartans for the other Peloponnesians—a subtle threat of what was very shortly to come in a matter of days. The Spartans would soon discover that the only way to keep the Thebans out of Sparta's world was to kill this very strange and most murderous philosopher. The very next time Agesilaus would see the mad Theban would be in the suburbs of his own Sparta at the head of a huge invading army.[29]

6

"AN ALTOGETHER CRUEL
AND BITTER CONDITION"

"AN ALTOGETHER cruel and bitter condition," the historian Theopompus concluded of the general plight of the Messenian Helots, the thousands of agricultural serfs who put the food on the tables of the Spartan messes. First, it is important to keep in mind just how unique the institution of helotage was; the majority of Greek city-states, like those of Boeotia—well over a thousand in number—developed from a free society of small landowners, who formed militias and often used chattel slaves to work on their small plots and as arms carriers during campaigns. The spread of personal slavery corresponds to the ascension of the Greek *polis* itself in the eighth century B.C. Small farmers and craftsmen might own outright another human being—of any race, gender, or nationality, including Greek—as part of an overall effort of the household to increase productivity and clearly delineate the new conception of a free citizen, who was now to be defined as someone who was not owned by someone else. Race, in most cases, was not a factor in chattel slavery; the conditions of one's birth, bad luck, or the aftermath of military conquest were.

Sparta, in contrast, sought to solve her problems of a growing population and finite land neither by overseas colonization nor by intensive servile labor in agriculture and small crafts, but rather by annexing in the eighth and seventh centuries the entire territory and people of surrounding Laconia and neighboring Messenia across the mountains—perhaps a combined population of 250,000—in a series of brutal wars and insurrections that lasted nearly three centuries. But these Messenians and Laconians were not—in the normal Greek pattern of conquest and exploitation—simply to be rounded up in order to be sold off piecemeal throughout the Greek world. Nor were they to be claimed as individual property by Spartan farmers. Instead, the Spartans kept them working en masse on their ancestral plots as serfs. These clearly identifiable second- and third-class peoples—the term *Heilôtai* may have been derived from the verb "those taken"—contributed large portions of their agricultural produce to the warrior communal messes of Sparta. Consequently, their treatment was often harsher and surely more humiliating than that experienced by chattels elsewhere in the Greek city-states. Entire communities of Messenia, not mere individuals, were relegated to inferior status, obviating all chance of a close paternal relationship between warrior and personal attendant. The seventh-century poet Tyrtaeus, encomiast of Spartan military virtue, himself admitted of the Messenian Helots that they were "like asses exhausted under great loads; under dire necessity to give their masters half of the fruit that their cultivated land produced."[30]

Slavery in general in Greece was an insidious institution and largely unquestioned precisely because it was *not* constructed on some pseudo-theory of racial inferiority. After all, some chattel slaves were educated, possessed skills, and were intimate with the members of a household. Thus the institution never incurred the type of widespread opprobrium that would have occurred if all slaves of a clearly identifiable race were relegated to drudgery or mine work, or arbitrarily killed. For example, the capture and enslavement of a learned Greek in a siege did not question either the morality or logic of this reprehensible institution—if the captive was confused why he, a clearly smarter, more moral man than his master, was now a slave, he would have inevitably been told that he was in the wrong place at the wrong time. Period. As Plato and Aristotle lamented, all Greeks were a defeat away from bondage. Slavery was an equal-opportunity nightmare.

In contrast, helotage as practiced in Messenia was relatively unique in the Greek world—"the most discussed and controversial subject in Greece," Plato said—and resembled more the nightmare of racial exploitation in the American South: an entire culture enslaved, with an identifiable heritage, dialect, and shared experience of laboring hard in order to enrich a completely alien group, their occupation almost exclusively farmwork. Scarcely any Helots were educated. None were tutors, bankers, accountants, or craftsmen as was true of chattel slaves elsewhere in the Greek world. They could not be freed; they did not live with their owners. What bothered the Greeks about helotage was not so much the physical circumstances of servitude—the chattel slaves in the Athenian silver mines surely must have endured worse conditions—but the sheer labyrinth of laws and customs necessary in maintaining an entire race of fellow Greeks in bondage, and subjecting them to eternal forced service based on their ethnicity, not the unfortunate circumstances of war or birth. Greek city-states were supposed to be free and autonomous, but most of the southern Peloponnese was kept as an agrarian backwater in service to a single *polis*.

Add that Messenia was an immense and rich land, that Helots vastly outnumbered Spartiates, and that such serfs had a long history of national chauvinism and constant rebellion, and the danger to Sparta's militaristic system becomes understandable. In the hardheaded pragmatist Aristotle's characteristically understated parlance, Helot surveillance had been a "troublesome matter." Serfdom as practiced at Sparta and in parts of Thessaly, the Black Sea region, and the island of Crete was generally associated by the Greeks with economic and political stagnation. It was an institution, the Greeks felt, that retarded the city-state, was antithetical to urbanism and trade, was often found with a monarchy and aristocratic hierarchies, and hampered the development of a truly free hoplite citizenry.[31]

Messenians were not servants working alongside their masters pruning vines, nor women weaving near their mistresses. Much less were they loyal attendants who accompanied boys to school or customarily carried arms next to their owners on campaign. Nor were they extended members of particular families, living, eating, and sleeping in proximity to their masters. There were no stories of Messenian philosophers who had been enslaved—no clever, smart-talking slaves or unfree bankers whom we see at other city-states. Rather, Helots were anonymous families of like kind, enjoying a shared nonexistence, who toiled exclusively in agriculture to give away food to distant professional warriors—overseers who patrolled visibly and sent agents secretly to monitor compliance. Manumission by individual Spartans, sale abroad, or adoption into the home of a Spartiate were illegal, crimes against the Spartan state itself. Helots were, in the topographer Pausanias's words, "slaves of the community," property as it were of the entire Spartan Soviet. To the Helot, nursed on a rich oral tradition of past Messenian freedom, and working outdoors in "the black earth" of his forefathers, outright mass rebellion and war against Sparta—not flight from a particularly cruel master—was the reigning ideology. Aristotle summed it up best: the Helots were "an enemy constantly sitting in wait for the disasters of the Spartans."

Nor should we forget these effects of Messenian helotage upon the larger Hellenic culture. Many Greeks did not hold slaves. A few thinkers, we can fairly assume from literature and philosophy, either had reservations about the institution itself or sought to ameliorate its material conditions. Aristotle, at least, acknowledged a body of critics who did not agree with him that certain people were natural slaves. The status of chattel slavery in a free society of Greeks, like the position of women on the Athenian stage, or the nature of non-Greeks in philosophical treatises, was open for discussion without state censure or danger of incurring charges of treason from fellow citizens. The insidious ubiquity of chattel servants in most states of Greece did not lead to the rise of militarism; Greek soldiers outside of Sparta did not drill and march regularly because someone else produced all their food.

In contrast, the Messenians were owned by the Spartan state, and in theory and practice *every* Spartan citizen was their owner. We have no surviving text from Sparta or public decree suggesting that Helots were anything other than inferiors; abolition existed only as a quid pro quo during the crises of Spartan power—in the case of the Messenian Helots a promise rarely offered and even more rarely honored. The yeomen free militias of the other Greek city-states existed in spite of chattel slavery, not entirely because of it. In contrast, the entire idea of Spartan group messes, barracks life, collectivized property-holding, secret police, and constant military training were directly attributable to the Helots of Laconia and Messenia. Without Helots, there was essentially no Spartan power.

The fact that such Messenian serfs lived and worked together on ancestral plots, along with their linguistic and ethnic cohesion, raised constantly the specter of insurrection and rebellion. This ingrained paranoia helps to explain in large part the militaristic nature of Spartan society itself. Sparta evolved into an elite colony of warriors who did not farm, but as state police trained constantly for war, foreign and domestic, each year ritualistically declaring war on their own enslaved. Almost alone of the city-states, they created a Gestapo-like secret police (*krupteia*). So great was their dread that Spartans feared even to leave their armbands on their shields at home, on the chance a Helot uprising might find readily usable weapons. The glue that held such allegiance to apartness together was a queer notion of Spartan honor, an increasingly unworkable and preposterous idea of military regimentation and duty passed down by the mythical lawgiver "Lycurgus" that put military prowess and gallantry in battle for the state above economic success, education, artistic or literary accomplishment, even purportedly ahead of family relationships and personal ambition.[32]

In addition to the Helots of Messenia on the other side of Mt. Taygetos, the Spartans also had conquered the entire indigenous population of their own environs of Laconia, relegating their immediate neighbors to a similar serflike existence. Controversy rages about their status, but in general, given the proximity to Sparta and claims of linguistic and ethnic affinity, the Laconian Helots received easier treatment than the Messenians and were more often allowed to serve in the Spartan army in exchange for freedom. Besides this additional pool of Laconian Helots, a few satellite villages near Sparta proper were allowed to retain their own familial and civic structures, but otherwise were absolutely subjugated to the economic and political dictates of the Spartan state.

Nor did these so-called Perioikoi ("the dwellers around") exhaust the Spartan labyrinth of socially subordinate categories. There were also gradations within the Spartiate class itself of dispossessed and inferior groups who had lost property, had proven cowardly in battle, or were in some sense at odds with the Spartan state. Among all these subordinate classes, there was admiration, both covert and open, for Epaminondas's democratic revolution, and a recognition that on the battlefield—to the Greeks, the ultimate arbiter of relative political and moral success—free Theban farmers had once run right over professional Spartan elites. While the Laconian Helots were clearly considered inferiors, it was in Messenia, across the mountains and in a land of another race, where suspicion of and brutality against Helots were the most severe.[33]

To grasp some sense of the powder keg these Spartiates sat atop we must look also at the demography of the southern Peloponnese. Because of a declining birthrate and the constant warring of the fifth and fourth centuries, by Epaminondas's time the Spartiate Similars—the elites who enjoyed full rights and fought in the phalanx—had dwindled from 8,000 warriors in 480 to little more than 1,500 to 2,000. Four hundred of those, remember, were killed in a single day by Epaminondas's massed army at Leuctra in 371. Adult Helots of Messenia, in contrast, may have numbered 50,000 to 60,000, with a total resident population over 200,000. Even in Laconia in the immediate environs of Sparta there were probably another 100,000 to 150,000 serfs, Perioikoi, and other assorted inferior groups.

The great danger of any apartheid state is always demography—not merely the existing lopsided ratios of free and slave, but the constant, inescapable demographical laws that govern relative population growth in the future. The psychological and material conditions of constant surveillance and enforcement eventually enervate a tiny elite, called on both to put down domestic insurrection and alone to wage war against foreigners—even as the protected enslaved are encouraged to populate and multiply to ensure more production and to increase the capital of their masters. More insidiously still, the privilege given to the few often discourages fertility. The narcotic of privilege works on the elite, as child-raising is seen as bothersome and an impediment to the aristocratic lifestyle—even as the slave caste finds in its offspring one of the few true enjoyments in an otherwise brutal life. Confederate slave owners and Nazi purists alike were fearful that they were drowning in a rising tide of fertile inferiors—even as they counted on just those *Untermenschen* to work their farms and factories.

Messenian Helots were eager to form their own state; Perioikoi and Laconian Helots wished either outright autonomy or rough equality with the Similars; and renegade Spartiates tired of barracks life, the absence of coined money, or the centuries-long domination of politics by a few aristocratic or royal families, plotted mechanisms to encourage insurrection wherever they could find it. To face the Spartan army "was a fearful thing," but that state's entire substructure by the fourth century was morally bankrupt, increasingly unworkable, and rife with a maze of cultural, political, and economic contradictions.[34]

To understand classical Sparta, its power in Greece as a whole, its distinctive military culture, its lordship of the entire Peloponnese, is—as the historian Thucydides noted—to understand the plight of the Helots. To weaken or strengthen Sparta was to aid or harm Helot aspirations for freedom. Athens in the fifth century at times did both, marching to quell Messenian insurrection when Sparta was friendly (462), then again creating a safe zone of Helot liberation at Pylos in the southwestern Peloponnese to encourage flight in mass during the Peloponnesian War (425). In short, the entire Spartan military machine rested on a chain of circumstances that inevitably went back to its original enslavement of thousands of serfs to the west in Messenia. The work of Helots and the need to police this underclass of thousands led to a professional army that drilled constantly, freed from farming but obliged to enforce helotage. The Athenian right-wing revolutionary Critias thus called the Spartan state—where some farmed all the time and others not at all—at once the home of the most enslaved and free peoples of Greece.

This ensuing Spartiate professionalism predictably led to a warrior class that was soon not just a domestic police force but also a proficient hoplite corps unmatched in Greece, one that ensured that the surrounding free Dorian peoples of the Peloponnese—the Arcadians, Elaeans, Achaeans, Megarians, and Corinthians—must join Sparta's Peloponnesian League. When that confederation marched, it numbered 30,000 heavy infantry and more, a force that for most of the fifth century not an army in Greece could stop. That grand confederacy had marched into Attica five times during the first decade of the Peloponnesian War alone (431–421), and had met no opposition. It had defeated the Thebans twice in 394, at Nemea and Coronea, and invaded Boeotia four times before Epaminondas wrecked its Spartan core at Leuctra. Apparently, Epaminondas alone of the Theban high command thoroughly understood the intricate links of Spartan power. Free the Helots, and the Spartan hoplite was forced to work, not free to drill. Free the Peloponnese from a weakened Sparta, and thousands of satellite Dorian Greeks would find their independence and political autonomy. And free Greece from that grand Peloponnesian army, and in theory regions like Thebes would be free of invasion forever.[35]

The Helot connection was not merely linear, leading to subjugation of Laconia, lordship of Messenia, leadership of the Peloponnese, and hegemony of Greece, but circular as well. To police the other—by Epaminondas's time Helots may have outnumbered Spartiates twenty to one—Spartan males trained in the arts of war under a brutal age-class regime from age seven until thirty, the notorious *agôgê*, or life, of the barracks. Helot harvests daily supplied the group messes of the Spartan warriors, who could then better oppress Helots by devoting attention to drill and arms mastery.[36]

Yet the mirror opposite of Sparta was Athens, not Thebes. Both Athens and Sparta were immune from hoplite war, the former because of its fleet and array of maritime subjects, the latter because of the Helots. The one evolved beyond the norms of Greek constitutions into a radical democracy, the other was frozen in time as a narrow reactionary oligarchy. The Athenians increasingly came to disdain pitched infantry battle in favor of sea power, becoming the first large subhoplite state in Greece, largely immune from the agrarian protocols of Greek infantry battle.

In contrast, the Spartans were a hyperhoplite culture, whose professional soldiers drilled year-round and welcomed constant pitched battle as much as Athens avoided it. The former sought empire using more than hoplites; the latter by using them all the time. Both cultures by the early fourth century had repudiated the amateur and seasonal warfare of the Greek city-state, based on an ad hoc heavy-infantry militia and a culture of small farm-owning citizens, which Thebes more than any other *polis* now sought to restore. Whatever Athens and Sparta had become, it was not exactly a Greek city-state in the traditional sense of the word.

For many, it is unsettling to suggest that the rise of radical Athenian democracy and maritime imperialism led to the gratuitous slaughter of thousands of innocent Greeks and the loss of freedom for thousands more. It is also equally controversial to offer a blanket condemnation of Sparta as the mirror-image of Athens and a society equally deviant from the old ideals of the *polis*. In the history of classical scholarship, Sparta holds an ambiguous position—its socialist egalitarianism among a tiny warrior elite was praised by the Nazis for its military fervor, and championed by Communists for its diminution of money, frequent public ownership of property, and redistribution of agricul-

MACEDONIA

CHALKIDIKE

Amphipolis

Olynthos

Mt. Olympus

Mt. Ossa

THESSALY

MAGNESIA

EPIRUS

Pharsalos

SKIATHOS

ACARNANIA

Lamia

Artemision

Thermopylae

EUBOEA

SKYROS

AITOLIA

LOCRIS

Cephisus R.

Amphissa

Chaeronea

Orchomenos

Chalkis

Delphi

Coronea

Copais L. Tanagra

Delium

Eretria

Thespiae

ITHACA

Leuctra

THEBES

Decelea

KEPHALLENIA

Gulf of Corinth

Plataea

Aegosthena

ACHAEA

Megara

ATHENS

ELIS

Sicyon

CORINTH

SALAMIS

Olympia

Orchomenos

Mycenae

ANDROS

Heraia

ZAKYNTHOS

MANTINEA

Argos

Epidaurus

AEGINA

KEOS

Hysiai

Nauplion

MEGALOPOLIS

Tegea

Eurotas R.

Hermione

MESSENÊ

Sellasia

Prasiai

MESSENIA

SPARTA

0   40 MI

Pylos

Amyclae

Methone

Asine

HELOTS

Gythium

KYTHERA

MELOS

N

FOURTH-CENTURY GREECE

tural produce. Other scholars without either strong political views or much interest in ideology have found an understandable fascination with sheer Spartan mettle when it was employed in a noble cause—the 300 at Thermopylae or the rugged hoplites who held firm against the Persian cavalry charge at Plataea.

There is, of course, something ostensibly admirable in a society that deliberately eschews material progress and an open economy in the professed pursuit of virtue. In this regard, the Spartans are somewhat similar to the confederate elites, who put such a premium on honor, and were often proud rather than ashamed that they had not industrialized their economy. I have even known professors who have lectured eloquently either about the retreating German graycoats in Russia in 1944 or the retreating Red Army in 1941. In these respective views, both Germans and Russians were armies of unusually brave draftees who sought to stop either a murderous Bolshevism or ascendant Nazism—and who were the natural products of societies that put a high premium on duty, public service, and the idea that life is more than materialism and leisure. But even such superficial admiration is, in the end, of course misguided and disturbing: the "virtue" that is the by-product of such militarized societies is always the dividend of privilege for the few and comes at the expense of enslaving thousands of others. It is always based on the lie that the free men of a consensual society are not up to their standard of courage.

Epaminondas had visited Sparta probably only once before his invasion, to discuss general peace terms a few weeks before the battle of Leuctra—indeed, most of his Thebans probably had never set foot off their farms. But he knew the Spartan system and thus now was about to craft the perfect strategy to destroy it. Spartan prestige rested on three mutually connected principles. The Helots supplied the material foundation for the elite corps of Spartiate warriors. The Peloponnesian allies provided the manpower for the Spartan-led army when it marched northward, and in addition served as a ring of buffer states blocking foreign invasion into the interior of a flat and unwalled Laconia. Finally, the long-haired, red-cloaked Spartiate phalanx instilled fear into the militias of Greece, keeping their culture of the barracks functioning as long as their military honor was unblemished. To Epaminondas the liberation of Messenia, the fortification of Peloponnesian cities, and the humiliation of the Spartan army in the field—preferably before the very eyes of Spartiate women and children—were interconnected strategies that would end forever the presence of Spartan hoplites on the soil of others.

Not all of Epaminondas's plans were purely self-interested or narrowly strategic. His revolutionary decision to enter Messenia seems to have arisen from a real repugnance for Spartan helotage and a desire to end the gratuitous cruelty toward a subjugated race—a view shared by a few philosophers and orators but by no statesmen whom we know of. Helots as a class were worked constantly. Secret police infiltrated Messenia, rooting out possible insurrectionists. On occasion, Sparta could announce a program of liberation in exchange for military service—only to execute the more daring Messenians who stepped forward for the opportunity. Thucydides relates that 2,000 were garlanded and paraded around in freedom—the better to be identified and slaughtered subsequently in secret.

This ancient Gestapo often preferred to kill anonymously at night. Helots might be gratuitously murdered without consequence of trial. Humiliation even reached the absurd: each year Spartans dressed some of them in dog-skin caps and hides to suffer the lash "to remind them that they were slaves." Even their physical condition was monitored—the too hardy and industrious often taken out and killed as potential adversaries, the obese punished as slothful and unproductive. At group messes Helots were forced to drink undiluted wine, to dance in risqué skits, and to sing ribald songs to show young Spartiates how embarrassing the inebriated appeared.

The conspirator Cinadon, an "inferior" who may have in fact been treated far better than the Messenians, when asked why he had forfeited his life in the hope of rebellion, purportedly answered that "he wished to be second to no man." Xenophon noted that when the topic of Spartiates was brought up among Helots, the universal wish was "to eat them raw." Is it any surprise that after the Theban victory at Leuctra they flocked in from all over the Greek world to follow this strange Theban back to their ancestral homeland?[37]

7

"AN UNRAVAGED
AND INVIOLATE LAND"

THE BRUTAL defeat of the Spartans at Leuctra in the summer of 371
unleashed to the south a democratic firestorm in Sparta's once loyal
Peloponnesian enclave. Megarians, Corinthians, and Argives now all
agitated for local democratic councils and federated leagues independent of
Sparta patterned after the Boeotians' apparently successful experiment. If the
Athenian empire in the fifth century had once introduced democracy to a
host of tributary subjects in the Aegean through the threat of a massive fleet,
the Thebans in the fourth did it with an idea—any Greek state was now free
to declare itself an autonomous democracy and to band together with other
like communities to form leagues of mutual protection. The Theban army
would march with them against all those who would object. In the past, Pericles' entire democratic ideology had been inseparable from Athenian imperialism—"For what you hold is, to speak somewhat plainly, a tyranny; to take it
perhaps was wrong, but to let it go is unsafe," he once told the wavering
Athenians in the assembly—an admission also shared by his archrival, the
demagogue Cleon. At Athens demagogues and statesmen both professed that
their maritime empire was probably amoral and yet essential for the material
well-being of the classical Athenian state.

In contrast, Epaminondas asked for no tribute. He made no precondi-
tions on the terms of his assistance. He executed no Greek who chose to resist
his overtures. How odd that the former, whose sophisticated culture enslaved

or killed thousands of freedom-fighters at Euboea, Aegina, Samos, Scione, and Melos, we venerate as the icon of democracy; whereas the latter, who mobilized rustics to allow communities hundreds of miles distant to decide their own affairs, we largely ignore. More puzzling still, that in the pivotal hour of democracy in Greece, Athens would work to undo the efforts of Thebes, joining Sparta to put down autonomous democratic federations and giving aid to the efforts to maintain the subjugation of the Helots. The ninety-year-old Athenian orator Isocrates, who had once so eloquently decried Persian autocracy, in 366 composed a speech on behalf of Spartan apartheid, arguing how unjust it was that the Thebans had made former slaves stronger than their masters! Had Epaminondas had his way and reconstructed an impressive propylaeum in the center of Thebes to give a veneer of art and culture to the Boeotian capital, later historians might have been more laudatory of his efforts.[38]

Within months of the victory at Leuctra newly proclaimed democratic states from Argos to Elis were spanning the entire northern border of the Peloponnese, effectively shutting Sparta off from the rest of the mainland of Greece. If left unchecked, this new democratic belt effectively meant that the Spartan army could no longer march north—an intolerable condition that Spartan hegemonists could not let stand. At the town of Mantinea in central Arcadia, an immense new fortress rose from the valley, its mud-brick circuit walls and moat running for over five miles to unify and enclose the previously unfortified villages of the plain. Newly elected Mantinean magistrates, given no help from Athens, now called the Thebans to come to their aid in anticipation of the inevitable counterresponse of the Spartan army that would sweep into Arcadia to quell the outbreaks. In the last century, Greek states had learned that it was one thing to proclaim freedom from Spartan hoplites, quite another to win it in the field.

There was also talk in the air of uniting the other rebellious Arcadians at an entirely new, even bigger stronghold of Megalopolis ("the great city"), an envisioned capital whose massive fortifications would ensure safety from Sparta in perpetuity. Even centuries later the words of Epaminondas were still remembered by Greek historians: the key to autonomy from Sparta and freedom in the Peloponnese was to keep this federated city of Megalopolis in constant alliance with the Helots' free city of Messenê—the two urban cultures that Epaminondas would make possible through direct intervention during the winter of 370–369. But to create democracy, found cities, and build walls, it was first necessary either to keep the Spartan army bottled inside Laconia or to humiliate the entire culture of Sparta to such an extent that it felt impotent to interfere with the radical political and urban renaissance occurring in the northern Peloponnese. Apparently, the only way to do that was to muster the farmers of Boeotia for a trek southward.

Almost no one in Boeotia in the year after Leuctra had any plans for further war. They were agrarians, not imperialists. After spending most of the decade before 370 cementing their northern flank against the Thessalians, and fighting the Spartans inside their own country, the Boeotians at last felt that they were safe and that the Spartans would be kept south of the Isthmus of Corinth for another generation. The prior decade they had fought invaders and built stockades around their cropland; it was now time to enjoy farming in solitude at last. After all, they had not wanted to fight the Spartans at Leuctra in the first place—and when they did, they had killed over 1,000 of the Peloponnesians with little more than a few dozen lost of their own, proof enough that they had done their share to repel autocracy in Greece. The Boeotian way—at the brutal battles of Tanagra (457), Delium (424), Coronea (394), Tegyra (375), and Leuctra (371)—had always been to stay put and let the enemy come to them.[39]

Only a few rare times in their entire history had any Boeotian hoplites mustered to fight abroad. In 418 a contingent of 5,000 infantrymen had marched along with Spartans against the Argives for a few days; a few hundred had joined the Sicilians to help thwart the Athenian invasion of 415–413. After the Peloponnesian War in 394 they had engaged the Spartans in a horrific fight right across the gulf near Corinth at the Nemea River. In 385 a few Boeotians—perhaps both Epaminondas and Pelopidas among them—fought near Mantinea. But it is fair to conclude that by 370 there were very few Boeotians of military age who had ever been out of Boeotia, and fewer still who even knew what the Peloponnese looked like, and perhaps none—except a few diplomats and the hated clique of aristocratic quislings—who had ever looked upon the hamlet of Sparta. Besides, it was now December, and the annual tenure for confederate officials was nearly over. By the first of the year, elections would have to be held to choose new Boeotian generals. Many of the Arcadians could logically assume that the Thebans would not come south after all.

Yet two of the Boeotarchs, Epaminondas and Pelopidas, thought intervention on behalf of these newly egalitarian buffer states in Arcadia to be vital if democracy was to spread and the enemy kept out of northern Greece for good. Time was of the essence. On the eve of the anticipated Spartan invasion against the Peloponnesian city of Mantinea in late fall 370, the call went out for Theban help. Who else was there in Greece who had either the will or the ability to ensure the freedom of these new Arcadian democratic states? Athens, the first and oldest democracy in Greece, had already turned down a request to aid the fledgling Peloponnesian democracies—indeed, she was beginning to rethink her former support of Thebes altogether, given the sudden rise of Boeotian power. Balance of power, not ideological affinity, was the reigning foreign policy in most of the city-states, especially in fourth-century Athens, which lacked the old dogmatic zeal of the past.

Yet these Arcadian revolutionaries of the high plains showed some signs that they could fight. Their citizens historically were prized mercenaries throughout the Mediterranean world—the core of the hired Ten Thousand whom Xenophon accompanied through Asia was Arcadian; and for years they had anchored the center and left of the allied Spartan battle line. If the Spartans were kept at bay, and these brave Peloponnesians given time to consolidate and fortify new urban strongholds at Mantinea and Megalopolis, then it was highly unlikely that a foreign army from the south would ever reach Thebes again. In fact, from the battle of Leuctra (371) to Chaeronea (338), the Boeotians enjoyed a generation in which not a single major battle was fought on their farmland—in dire contrast to the land's reputation during the fifth and early fourth centuries as the dancing floor of war. In 338, when pikemen at last returned to Boeotia, it was from the north, not the south—and they were *not* Peloponnesians.

Although Epaminondas had spent his life furthering the establishment of democracy, had he given way this winter to the majority of his elected colleagues—who mostly reflected the general sentiment of the Boeotians—the army would have stayed put. Had he not marched, the Arcadians would have gradually come to terms with a resurgent Spartan army. The Messenians would have remained as slaves for another two centuries. Other than Pelopidas, none of the other six officers of the Boeotian Confederacy at first wished to plunge into the quagmire of Peloponnesian politics and thus ultimately to deal with the Spartan army on its home ground. Epaminondas had about as much support from his colleagues for his crusade as Sherman received for his initial proposal to march to Savannah or Patton for his request to be given enough supplies to plunge into Germany in September 1944. There were enemies enough of Thebes on the northern border with the states of Locris and Phocis, and the Athenians were now jealous of Theban success—and could be counted on to intervene somewhere against their army in transit. Strategic interest, logistical considerations, and tactical reality made the idea of a December invasion southward unwise. Most ancient armies stayed put in winter, since there was no chance to augment supplies by stripping produce from the fields.

On both the outward and return trek, Epaminondas would have to lead his men along a difficult journey right along the border of Attica, through

Megaris across the isthmus, and then over the mountains into the high plains of Arcadia. Whatever the Peloponnesians' present democratic protestations and professed allegiance to Thebes, these were still all Dorian states—in dialect and custom far more akin to Sparta than to Thebes. Most Boeotians did not favor the idea of intervening into the shifting alliances of the kindred Peloponnese only to be caught as outsiders when ethnic and regional solidarity overrode ostensible devotion to the abstraction of democracy.

The Eleans in the western Peloponnese, the newfound allies of the Arcadians, promised to lend Epaminondas ten talents to get the army into the Peloponnese—or about enough money to purchase supplies for 6,000 Theban hoplites for ten days of marching. Given the monetary subsidy and the looming figure of the hero of Leuctra, the other Boeotian generals now ceased opposition, washed their hands of the enterprise, and turned over their command to Epaminondas and Pelopidas alone. What Epaminondas's full and ultimate plans for the expedition at this moment were we do not know—other than his immediate stated intention to keep the Spartans out of the northern Peloponnese and in some way to protect the states of Arcadia as they fortified new citadels against Spartan invasion. The biographer Nepos remarks of Epaminondas that "he was excellent in keeping secrets—a quality that is of no less advantage than the ability to speak well." For a man who our sources say thought more and kept silent longer than any man in Greece, it was wiser *not* to disclose to either his own army or the Boeotian assembly exactly what he intended to do once he had the army in the Peloponnese. His associates knew about as much of Epaminondas's ultimate plans of marching as did Sherman's staff about his precise ideas on leaving Atlanta. Of the latter, a contemporary reporter remarked, "Above all the men I have met, that strange face of his is the hardest to read. It is a sealed book even to his friends." Great marches that challenge orthodoxy and defy military tradition, it seems, spring from the deep recesses of a single military mind, and—if they are to go forth—are not to be discussed and debated openly with either superiors or staff.

Many Boeotian hoplites, though, would have remembered that after Leuctra, Epaminondas had to be convinced to allow the Spartan survivors to leave the battlefield. Then he gave in, but cryptically remarked that it was better to "move the war from Boeotia into Sparta"—a sentiment long expressed by other Greeks who realized that in the future someone might fathom that the way to stop Sparta was to march on her homeland. Over twenty years earlier Timolaus the Corinthian had tried to make that very point to his Peloponnesian allies, comparing the Spartans in Laconia now to a river that is smallest and easiest to be dammed at its source, then again to wasps: "All who want to get rid of wasps, if they try to get them as the wasps dart out, are stung by many of them; but if they will apply the fire to them while they're in their nests, they can destroy the wasps without harm to themselves."[40]

Still, to burn out the Spartan nests, it was not an easy thing to move an army of such vast proportions in the ancient Greek world without reliable maps, logistics, and accessible roads. Even more difficult was to march a column of several thousand farmers in midwinter southward through the choke point of less than six miles at the isthmus at Corinth, and then to continue over the mountains and passes of the Peloponnese. The meandering route from Thebes to Sparta via the Arcadian cities was 160 to 180 miles long, often on rough ground and in hostile territory. The men would not only be responsible for some seventy pounds each of arms and armor and assorted gear, but also enough rations to keep them alive until they reached friendly Mantinea.

December, when Epaminondas set out southward, is the worst time to march in Greece. It is untrue that farmers are not busy in winter. The dormant period of Mediterranean agriculture is nearly over as quickly as it begins—from November leaf fall to spring bud break is but ninety days, and there is a frantic race to plant wheat and barley in late fall or even early winter. Farmers are then at their busiest during the cold months—pruning vines and fruit trees, sowing cereals, pressing olives, manuring, fixing equipment, staking vines, repairing terraces—in a breakneck preparation for the nine-month-long growing season. There is a reason why Hesiod, the yeoman poet of Boeotia, devotes so much advice to the winter building of wagons and plows, and to keeping warm during the numerous tasks of the harried dormant season. To march on some great crusade to the south was to entrust all those vital farm tasks to the elderly, women, children, and occasional family slaves and to hope they were finished before spring bloom and leaf break.[41]

Worse yet, a winter march from Boeotia meant there was no chance for the army to live off the crops in the fields—in dire contrast to Sherman's postharvest autumn swath through Georgia where grains, rice, and sweet potatoes were often still in the field. Logistics, even in the age of mass production and mechanized transport, would stop Patton cold, and he would be reduced to relying on inadequate caches of captured gas and food. The usual paradigm of aggression is that the invader finds it harder to bring up supplies for his extended lines, even as the defender gains strength as his own perimeter shrinks around his home base.

By December, wheat and barley in Laconia were long-harvested and hidden away in storage. There were no grapes on the vine, few if any olives left on the trees. To feed an army of several thousand meant one of two things: either

77

bringing along massive stores of barley, wheat, onions, dried fruits, and fish—a talent's worth of food a day for 6,000 to 7,000 men—all to be carried by servile attendants, donkeys, and mules, or to plunder the countryside of the enemy by rifling unevacuated, stored grains from small homesteads and villages.

During these three months the winter can be severe in the countryside, especially over the mountain passes of Boeotia and Arcadia, where temperatures drop well below freezing; snow is common; and paths are obstructed by mud, debris, and ice. The Greek climate is not tropical; its superb vintages, olives, and tree fruit are not so much the dividends of long hot summers and mild springs, as due to the short, chilly winters, where frosts are frequent but not lethal, ensuring the necessary number of chilly nights—a cumulative total of five hundred to eight hundred hours of below fifty degrees—to ensure full dormancy for—but not damage to—trees and vines.[42]

Tourists today pitch tents ubiquitously in summer on the beaches of Greece. They are almost never found in midwinter sleeping in the hinterlands. In March—not December, when Epaminondas's men camped in Laconia—I once slept out on the battlefield of Chaeronea near the mass grave of the fallen Macedonians. The ground around the *polyandrion* was wet and muddy, and the nighttime temperature dipped below thirty degrees—a terrible sleepless experience despite a down bag, vinyl tarps, insulated clothing, and the assorted paraphernalia of the modern backpacking student. That thousands of middle-aged hoplites with leather jerkins and wool capes slept outside on similar muddy ground in midwinter, after marching ten to fifteen miles a day over rugged terrain, drinking out of muddy streams, and foraging for food, seems almost beyond comprehension.

Consequently, Epaminondas's decision to march south immediately demanded of the rustics of Boeotia that they quickly finish their late fall sowing, leave their olive presses, cease pruning their vines, pull down their ancestral and sooty armor from above the hearth, and assemble in the thousands at Thebes with their slaves and mules. And for what? And for whom? An abstract idea of democracy for someone else? To repel a Spartan army from the far-off new city of Mantinea? None of these yeomen had any comprehension that it was much worse than all that—they were to follow their Pythagorean general on an initial march of several days, almost all through enemy land, to a place they had never seen, against an army they still dreaded, for an ultimate end of which they were not fully aware, and for a time that was left unstated—and behind a general who was "excellent in keeping secrets."

Had these farmers known that in reality for the next *several months* they would march into Arcadia, join thousands more hoplites there, sweep into Sparta, plunder Laconia, march down to the very tip of the Peloponnese to burn the harbor of Sparta, and then reverse course, head first north, and then west into Messenia, free nearly a quarter-million Helots, supervise the construction of a vast new fortified city at Messenê, promise on the return to protect the new Arcadian idea of federated states anchored by a fortified Mantinea and soon-to-rise Megalopolis, and then on the way back home burst through an Athenian guard at the Corinthian isthmus—if they had known all this, surely they never would have left.

To leave a sufficient guard at home in Boeotia against northern intrusions and an increasingly hostile Athens across the border, Epaminondas and Pelopidas could safely take only about half the army, perhaps no more than 6,000 to 7,000 hoplites accompanied by a few hundred horsemen. But on this winding and difficult march southward from Thebes to Mantinea, a number of allied northern Greeks were eager to follow Epaminondas, perhaps an additional 9,000 to 10,000 Euboeans, Locrians, Phocians, Thessalians, and Acarnanians, and an untold number of camp followers and hangers-on who had their own grudges against the Spartans.[43]

Not since the Persian War of more than a century earlier had such a large Greek army mustered, under democratic auspices, to ensure rather than extinguish liberty. Such an expedition of this size and spirit would *never* again occur in classical Greek history. The earlier Spartan-led treks into Attica during the 420s were professedly aimed at protecting oligarchy from Athenian democratic imperialism. Athens's 40,000-strong armada that sailed for Sicily in 415 was nakedly imperialistic, bent on plunder and the subjugation of Syracuse—a similar democratic city-state. The Ten Thousand hired by Cyrus in 401 to give him the Persian throne were mercenaries who wanted gold, not freedom, and were far smaller in number than the present Greek muster. Even Epaminondas's last great assemblage eight years later (362) would find many of his present allies squabbling, jealous—and on the side of Sparta. Little need be said about either Philip's march south into Greece (338) or his son's decade-long swath through Persia (334–323). Both invasions were little more than efforts at naked and brutal conquest, the latter involving plundering and killing on a theretofore unimagined continental scale. After the demise of the old agrarian warfare, fourth- and third-century Greek armies were usually motivated by gold or the desire for hegemony. Epaminondas's march, in contrast, was a strangely reactionary event in the best sense. It was a throwback to an age of a century and more in the past, when Greeks had once united to destroy tyranny, envisioned good and evil as separate from power and profit, and saw nothing odd with having a philosopher, not a bandit, in command.

Visually, this odd muster must have presented an eerie spectacle, as farmers trudged into Thebes through the winter mud in small groups attended by motley groups of livestock and servants. These troops had none of the pretensions of Spartan professionals, whose red cloaks, polished bronze armor, long oily hair, careful drill, wooden dog tags, and slow steady walk to the music of pipes were designed to instill terror and display years of brutal training.

Not that Boeotian hoplites in their own way were not frightening to behold; Diodorus says that the Spartans themselves were wary of such men who were "bold and reckless" in battle. These "young dogs" had abandoned the cumbersome though reliably safe Corinthian heavy helmet—a Darth Vader–like headgear that encased the face and neck and was topped off with a gaudy crest. Instead, they were comfortable with an elongated version of what the Greeks knew as the *pilos,* a simple, cheap bronze and crestless cone which left the face, neck and back of the head completely unprotected. The Boeotian version of this odd-looking cap left the warrior terribly vulnerable to head and neck, wounds but allowed a much greater sense of perception and thus the ability to pass and receive commands in the melee. It was also far cheaper, and Boeotia was without the financial capital of Attica or the Peloponnesian allies. In addition, massive three-foot round "Boeotian" shields were notched, with small half-circle cutouts on each side—more a stylistic device echoing a military tradition that went back centuries than a utilitarian mechanism to guide the spear. So characteristic were these shields of local hoplites that at one time or another they adorned most of the coinages of Boeotia—symbolic confirmation that what Boeotia did best was to fight in the phalanx. On the bronze veneers of the Boeotians' shields was not riveted the letter beta in the traditional Greek manner of identifying hoplites by the first letter of their city or league's name—e.g., β for "Boeotians"—but rather simply the image of the dreaded *ropalon,* or notched club, of Herakles—the uncouth brawling brute born at Thebes, whose sons had reclaimed the Peloponnese. Sherman's Westerners of the 15th Corps, whose insignia was the equally martial cartridge box, would have approved.

All our sources suggest that these men appeared bigger and stronger than other Greek hoplites—emblematic of their status as tough outdoorsmen and agrarians. Whether or not Epaminondas, like Sherman, went further to exclude the unfit for his marches we are not sure. But it is true that anecdotal evidence emphasizes his Pattonesque harangue on physical fitness—and the Boeotian army usually marched out in numbers quite smaller than what the manpower reservoirs of Boeotia might have otherwise fielded.

Boeotian art often displays muscular hoplites advancing with drawn swords, spears broken in the foreground. For infantrymen who excelled in wrestling and whose mass depended on weight and thrust, the majority of the first rank must have had their spears splintered on the first collision and relied on brute strength and swordplay to cut through the enemy. Plutarch, Diodorus, and Xenophon remark on the sheer physical strength of the Boeotians, whose wrestling skill overmatched the drill and order of the Spartans. It is not surprising that their peculiar garb, their distinctive accent, their reputation as fierce rustic infantrymen, their propensity to yell as they charged, and their fondness for insularity naturally has sometimes given rise to comparisons with Scottish highlanders or Dutchmen.[44]

Thousands of such farmers with pack animals and servants headed out over the mountains of Boeotia to the Megarian plain, followed by a horde of assorted other Greeks, who felt safe only when following the mass that had destroyed the Spartans at Leuctra. In the lowlands of Megaris their broad columns might have stretched out nearly five miles and more. But much of the way would be through mountain passes—first over their own forested Mt. Cithaeron and then later the rocky heights of the Peloponnese—where at times men could climb not more than two or three abreast and the attenuated column might stretch for nearly twenty-five miles or more. The Corinthians, allies of the Spartans, would complain to the Athenians that when this hungry and angry pack passed through their territory "the Thebans cut down fruit trees, burned houses, seized property, and drove off cattle."

No Corinthians were willing or able to contest the passage of their isthmus, and they now bore the wages of their years of support for the Spartan armies that had passed through their land on their way to ravage Boeotia. The Spartans had plenty of advance warning that a vast army was heading into the Peloponnese, but as yet they had no real proof that its ultimate destination was in fact themselves.

On this initial leg of the march, perhaps 10,000 servants followed, who, along with over a thousand pack animals, carried shields, spears, body armor, helmets, greaves, camping equipment, dried fruits, fish, and vegetables, stretching the line of march even farther for miles on end. An army of 20,000 hoplites might bring along over 500 tons of iron, bronze, and wooden arms and armor alone. When this strange, cumbersome band of Northerners arrived in the Peloponnese, even Xenophon—whose Spartan prejudices in his history are rarely disguised and who himself had either seen or marched in a number of both Spartan and mercenary armies—conceded that the élan of the Boeotians had a near-magical quality: "For all of the Boeotians were now engaged in training in the practice of arms, and they were still basking in their victory at Leuctra." Later he called them "fire-breathers." To the Arcadians, Argives, and Eleans, tough veterans who had fought side by side with the Spartans, the Thebans were "puffed up" in their eagerness to fight. On later marches the allies were so impressed with the martial prowess of their deliverers that they too painted the Theban club of Herakles on their shields right over their own insignia.[45]

There was a sense of urgency in the winter muster of 369—rumor had it that the Spartans were marching on Mantinea—and the army of northerners must have reached the isthmus at Corinth in little over three or four days out of Boeotia, well before the Corinthians and Athenians could bottle up the passage. Even if the Athenians had manned the heights or built stockades—they would attempt just that in the subsequent invasions of the years to come—there was not an army in Greece that could hold back a force of such size and skill. From Corinth to Mantinea the columns continued on over the high mountain passes—only to arrive in Arcadian territory just after the Spartan army had left for home.

Twenty thousand northern Greeks at last filed into central Arcadia with the ostensible purpose of their expedition *already fulfilled*. The Spartan army was in retreat, soon to be disbanded and with no desire for a replay of Leuctra. Old King Agesilaus had lit out for home on the rumor of the Theban muster, lest in disgrace he be caught fleeing openly on their arrival. The Arcadians were safe. They could finish their fortifications of Mantinea in peace. The year was about over; the legal tenure of the Boeotarchs was in a few days to expire. Most of the Thebans felt satisfied that their quick march had ended the crisis to the south. It was time to get this huge and hungry army back home. To retain this militia in the field, Epaminondas, the protector of democracy, would have to press on in violation of the laws of the Boeotian democratic federation, relying on the personal allegiance of his men alone. Apparently, only his colleague Pelopidas wished to march farther into the Peloponnese.

But numbers do not lie. Epaminondas had safely led 20,000 men from the farmland of northern Greece into the Peloponnese—no mean feat in midwinter through hostile territory. And 6,000 of them were veterans of Leuctra who had the year before given him "one more step" in crushing the Spartan serpent. Moreover, the new Peloponnesian confederates at Mantinea could add nearly another 20,000 seasoned hoplite troops, some of the best fighters in Greece. Our ancient sources confirm that his combined Greek muster at Mantinea now numbered 40,000 heavy infantrymen. There were another 30,000 light-armed troops, camp followers, and curiosity-seekers who were eager to follow the main army southward to engage in the plunder of Spartan farms. Sparta itself was unwalled and little more than two days' march away. The Arcadians, Argives, and Eleans were now clamoring to follow in the wake of this monstrous army and go south.[46]

Epaminondas, from what we can gather, cared little that his own generals opposed the dare—that it was cold and midwinter, that his use of the army far into the new year was a clear capital offense against the Boeotian state, that the southern Peloponnese was ringed with mountains and its passes guarded, that no foreign army had risked entering Laconia in over six hundred years, that the Spartans could be expected to fight ferociously for their families and property, that he would have to leave his supply lines behind and forage in the countryside, and that a loss in the field would throw away the spiritual capital earned at Leuctra and endanger the new fortified city of Mantinea and the soon-to-rise Megalopolis.

Epaminondas had come south to destroy the system of helotage, not to play an endless game of strategic chess against the Spartan army, which could muster and disband in the Peloponnese far easier than he could march down from Boeotia. Like Sherman's disgust with the fleeing General Hood, he too had no patience for following the Spartan army, waiting for it to reappear and then only to dissolve; like Patton, he was tired of the cautionary tales of timid men, whose advice to halt would let the enemy off unscathed and get his men killed in the process.

In contrast, these newfound allies, the Arcadians and their friends, now made a better argument: there were plenty of discontented Helots and Peri-oikoi in Laconia who would revolt and join his army; the troops were eager to move and take vengeance on the Spartans; local villagers knew the passes and would guide them over. Sparta was an emperor with no clothes; all that was needed was someone with enough courage to tell the world that she was inept in her nakedness. Quickly, Epaminondas, with the strong support of Pelopidas, convinced his colleagues in the field to allow him to redirect the combined army of southern and northern Greeks, and made plans to take the 70,000 over the narrow crossings that led down into the Eurotas Valley and the plains that surround Sparta.

As Epaminondas reasoned, the Boeotians had made the law of a one-year limitation on the tenure of Boeotarchs solely to circumvent tyranny—the specter of a dangerous man at the head of an army who wished to set himself up as lord of Boeotia. But he was no tyrant. The farmers in the assembly had never envisioned that their army might march for months beyond the borders, much less that it would, in midwinter, be in the Peloponnese on the brink of invading Sparta and spreading democracy. As Epaminondas figured, he would press on and let the orators in the assembly haggle over the legality of his command when he returned triumphantly. To give up command now or to turn his muster over to newly elected incompetents was, in short, "to destroy the army itself." His was the largest infantry force Greece had seen since the Persian Wars—larger than all of Sherman's columns that went through

Georgia—and it was the first army in six centuries to march into "an unravaged and inviolate land." His detractors, as he said later, could try killing him for freeing Messenia, isolating Sparta, and plundering Laconia. In contrast to the worries of his own officers, his newfound Peloponnesian allies required no formal treaty alliance, but simply agreed to follow and gave over command of their own native forces to Epaminondas and Pelopidas. As far as Epaminondas was concerned, the one-year tenure of command was a stipulation, in his words, already "out of date."[47]

It was always difficult to enter the land of Sparta, more so to take thousands over the narrow and fortified mountain defiles in midwinter. Even the modern visitor driving between Arcadia and Sparta, in an underpowered rental car, can find the modest climb and winding descent over the high plain more taxing than anticipated—about thirty miles of curving road rising and falling between 2,000 and 3,000 feet. An army of over 40,000 hoplites and thousands of servants and plunderers could be thwarted up there for days. A few hundred bowmen and javelin-throwers on the higher peaks, aided by December rain and occasional light snow, might even destroy outright a serpentine column of hoplites.

Consequently, Epaminondas, like both Sherman and Patton, divided his huge allied army into separate corps, a tactic that often had fatal consequences in Greek military history. Given the poor state of communications and reconnaissance, the problem of reliable logistics, and the absence of good maps and sure knowledge of local topography, Greek armies when divided tended to become lost or to lose cohesion for good. In 424 the Athenian generals Demosthenes and Hippocrates had tried a dual land and sea invasion of Boeotia—only to see their plans betrayed to the enemy, their agreed-on dates of arrival confused, and their widely dispersed forces easily countered by the Boeotians. On Sicily in 413, the retreating Athenian army split in two, only to have both columns under Demosthenes and Nicias become lost, nearly wiped out, and forced to surrender.

Moreover, just to supply provisions for 70,000 men for a month, and to pay commensurate wages to the 40,000 civic hoplites in the army, would traditionally have required over 500 talents—in a few weeks matching well over half the cost of the twenty-year expense of building the Athenian Parthenon alone. Clearly, neither the Boeotians nor the Arcadians had anywhere near such capital. Unlike Alexander the Great's rampage into Asia, there were no provincial capitals of stores of imperial specie to plunder—and no desire gratuitously to murder and terrorize innocent local populations. An army that kills as it marches can sometimes find quicker and easier passage than a force of liberation, which leaves an emancipated—and alive—though vulnerable populace in its wake. Instead of coined money, Epaminondas and his confederate generals would rely on the stored food of Laconian farms and the democratic fervor of their own troops. The Pythagorean asceticism of "Iron Gut" would set the example for his men of how to march on low rations.

To Epaminondas the greatest consideration was neither political nor financial, nor even logistical, but rather simply spiritual—at all costs not to lose the momentum of the attack and the cohesion of such a rare muster. His army was huge, the single greatest example of Greek infantry prowess in over a century, a real monstrosity that taxed the nascent Greek science of troop maneuver and sheer logistics, one that could not stay still, but either had to move and feed itself as it plundered, or to disband immediately.

Again, in relative terms of the mobilization of available manpower, the Boeotian grand coalition was large beyond modern comparison. Sherman's army of November 1864—62,000 men left Atlanta—was considered immense by observers of the time; but the population of the North and the sympathetic border states at the time was over 23,000,000. Epaminondas's 70,000, in contrast, represented a far greater relative mobilization, given that the entire population of Greece proper excluding Italy, Sicily, and Asia Minor in the fourth century was probably not much over 2,000,000. Sherman led a force of about a quarter of 1 percent the size of the entire northern populace; Epaminondas's larger army comprised almost 4 *percent of the entire population of the Greek mainland*. In other words, that winter almost one out of every twenty Greeks—man, woman, young, old, free, slave—was involved directly fighting with or against Epaminondas. When we add the over 200,000 Messenian Helots who were to be liberated, the Spartan Helots, the thousands of Perioikoi, and assorted loyal allies of Sparta who took part one way or another in the fighting, to the sum of Epaminondas's invading army and the Spartan defenders, then we learn that *one out of every six Greeks* on the mainland was in some way to be affected by the march—as invader, defender, or liberated. One man in a matter of days had convulsed the entire Greek world in his plans of retribution and liberation. A volcano like none other in the last century had erupted in the Peloponnese.

Through the tactic of dividing his army into four wings, and attempting four approaches at once, any one successful foray might allow thousands to double back behind enemy garrisons and relieve pressure for the other three columns from the rear. As Sherman and Patton would know, there was economy in motion within such division, as hoplites might march strung out for only a few miles. Perhaps 15,000 to 20,000, not 70,000, would file through each of the respective four approaches. They would be entering Laconia at four different points, making it impossible for the Spartans to anticipate exactly at which one spot in their plain they would all reunite. If skillfully divided for a time and well coordinated, even a large army can be unpredictable in its movement, leaving defenders baffled as to where and when it will concentrate and strike—leaving them with the dilemma of defending everything and thus nothing.

Once Epaminondas left Arcadia, the key was to get over the passes immediately and descend into the plain of Laconia, where the insatiable material appetite of the army could be sustained. It was winter on the barren peaks, and the yeomen in the ranks could not count on sure supplies of food and forage or even potable water. They would have to bring along their own initial provisions from Arcadia, since there were few upland farms or villages to plunder. For an army of 70,000, even if there was only one pack animal for every fifty soldiers, more than 1,300 mules, donkeys, or horses would be necessary to accompany the expedition. In theory the weight of the army's *daily* grain, forage, and water requirements was nearly a million and a half pounds—in addition to another million pounds of bronze armor that had to be carted along. Thus there was a real incentive to move this voracious drain on local resources away from friendly Arcadia, over the mountains, and into farmland where it could forage and destroy simultaneously.

While still in Arcadia, Epaminondas had worried about wearing thin the hospitality of his host, and losing through even brief intimacy with the locals the mystique of his rustic Boeotian brawlers. He went so far as to forbid his men even to go into town: "The Arcadians admire you now well enough as you practice in arms and wrestle. But once they see you sitting beside the fire sipping bean soup they will think you are no better men than they are."[48]

The Elean allies, who resided near the sanctuary at Olympia, now were mustering on the western flank. They had the easiest approach and simply marched unimpeded along the old Sparta–Olympia road. That way they would come up from behind the frontier Spartan garrison at Sellasia—the entryway from the north into Laconia. The Argives to the east also had little trouble going over the hills of Parnon and soon joined the Thebans and Arcadians, who were marching in between along two separate routes to link up at Sellasia. Some of our sources speak of a Thermopylae-like glorious last stand of the enemy, as the Spartan mountain garrison was annihilated. The four converging armies then reunited, destroyed the outpost, and slowly descended into the vale of Laconia; off in the distance between Parnon and Taygetos lay the unwalled city of the Spartans.[49]

Epaminondas's men were the *first* invading army in the age of the city-state that had ever marched inside Laconia. That they came to wreck the Spartan caste system in enormous numbers, led by a philosopher, and sanctioned by the vote of democratic assemblies, showed that there was still for a while yet an ethical imperative at the heart of the Greek city-state, that the *polis* was more than just economic dynamism, literary genius, and intellectual sophistication. That it took Theban farmers, not Athenian intellectuals, to lead such an army, should remind us all that the source of the moral sense is not always in the theater or in bookstalls. Athens had once fought Sparta for nearly three decades not so much for the principle of democracy versus oligarchy as for the preservation of the Athenian system of imperial tributary allies against the aims of Spartan hegemony. Scholars too often forget that on this expedition Thebes now battled for neither money nor power, but for the idea of allowing all Greek states to be autonomous. Indeed, at the moment Epaminondas entered Laconia, Spartan delegates were convincing the Athenians to send help to save them from this new type of agrarian democracy. But to the Spartans at home, Xenophon relates, there was the realization that "there was the utmost danger to their wives, children, and the entire *polis*." Centuries later Arrian wrote that the mere *idea* of seeing Thebans and Arcadians descending into Laconia was as terrifying to the Spartans as the actual enemy armies marching in the field—a striking confirmation of Sherman's dictum that his army's mere passage through the plantation belt of Georgia did as much damage to the Confederacy as an attack on its army.

Not that there was not plenty of booty to be found in the process for the Peloponnesian allies. Thousands of cold and hungry soldiers now fanned out widely over the Laconian plain, looting and ravaging, even as Epaminondas and his Thebans slowly followed the Eurotas River on toward Sparta proper. Would he storm the city or march on by, plundering the country—or both? Laconia is one of the richest valleys in Greece—its citrus and vegetables today are unexcelled—and the troops must have busied themselves rifling isolated farmhouses at will. Our sources call Laconia of the time *aporthêtos* ("unplundered"), a rare term used to describe a rich countryside untouched by war. A mournful Xenophon, author himself of a treatise on household management, says that there were "houses full of many valuable things." Freebooters in small groups took off from the main columns, aided by fugitive Helots and sympathetic Perioikoi, to ransack the estates of the entire Eurotas Valley. Servile field hands, as Sherman's bummers discovered in Georgia, usually knew exactly where their masters' stores and valuables were hidden.

In January there was no standing grain either to harvest, trample, or burn. It is a difficult proposition at any season, even without rain and damp fog, to systematically burn or cut down olive and fruit trees with any great success. Most orchards that were chopped down were used as palisades for the camps and perhaps added as fuel to the roaring nightly fires—the eerie glow that would soon so terrify the grande dames of Sparta. The invaders' efforts instead were directed at rounding up livestock, plundering grain bins and wine vats, and generally stealing everything movable away from the farms of Laconia, bringing the booty inside ad hoc palisaded camps to be consumed, packed away, or ruined. When Epaminondas, the destroyer of Laconia, once threatened to turn Attica into a sheep walk, he knew whence he spoke. Plutarch, quoting the historian Theopompus, rightly called the Theban-led onslaught that swept forth from the mountains over the Laconian plain "a tidal wave of war." The 70,000 must have seemed to the amazed Spartans like the end of all things, a final *Götterdämmerung* of avenging Thebans now storming into their inner sanctum, freeing serfs, spreading fire and ruin over the countryside, and scarcely stopping to notice the Spartans' bewildered presence as they made their way through Laconia—all a small prelude for the outright liberation of Messenia to come.[50]

But Epaminondas had Spartan hoplites on his mind, who in the general flood of invasion now retreated to the small atoll of the city where thousands of civilians huddled about in fear. He and his Thebans stalked slowly along the east bank of the Eurotas River, which marked the boundary of the city proper. It was not at this stage feasible to cross the river, since a few Spartan hoplites manned the banks opposite and the river was swollen from winter rains and mountain runoff, its current dangerous, its waters ice-cold. Today in summer the Eurotas River is a mere creek bed, but in some winters it can still reach a roaring torrent that is impassable. I have seen it well over twelve feet deep in January and February, little more than a foot by July. January storms in Sparta present an eerie scene—snow-capped Mt. Taygetos rising immediately to the west, a wintry Parnon more distant in the east, the plain itself muddy and water-soaked, as small rivulets run into a now roaring Eurotas, with fog hugging the lower hills. We should imagine, then, a frightening scene as tough leather-clad armored soldiers, their breath visible in the cold, emerged out of the fog and gloom to take apart the city.

Elders in the city restrained the younger Spartan hoplites from marching out to certain death—the aristocratic hotbloods so typical of a militaristic culture, so similar to the 300,000 Confederate zealots whom Sherman once said had to die for there to be lasting peace. Luckily for them, Spartan veterans knew the mettle of these angry Boeotians all too well. The aged surely recalled that they had lost their general, Lysander, and many of their best hoplites to the Thebans at the battle of Haliartus (395). And King Agesilaus had nearly been killed the next year at the battle of Coronea (394)—terrible collisions of a quarter century past when the Spartan army itself barely made it out alive. Other veterans would remind their inexperienced Spartan hotbloods of what had happened at Tegyra (375) and at that awful afternoon the year before at Leuctra (371), when a similar cohort of proud Spartans had marched into the Theban mass and had not come out alive. Everyone at Sparta, young and old, remembered what had occurred eight years earlier (379) to the Spartan zealots who once occupied the Theban Cadmea—most were eventually killed or driven out of town. The wisdom gained from a prior generation of catastrophe was used to hold the Spartan youth inside the town safely away from these deadly Theban farmers.

With allies, some of the more loyal Perioikoi, and the remaining Spartiates, Sparta might have still fielded an impressive phalanx of 6,000 to 8,000 hoplites—a fearsome thought to most Greeks, but man-to-man hardly a match for Epaminondas's Thebans. Yet the largest force the Spartans could field would still be vastly inferior, outnumbered ten to one by the enemy invasion force. Like Southerners who gazed at Sherman's blue columns, which seemed as though they would never end, so too the residents of Laconia had never seen so many soldiers in their very midst—no Greeks anywhere had in the generations since the Persian invasion. The genius of Epaminondas was not merely tactical, but logistical as well; somehow in midwinter he had organized an army of 70,000 and marched it right through the most dreaded countryside in Greece.

Epaminondas passed the city by, marched to a point farther south, about five miles away, and then suddenly found a ford and crossed near the hamlet of Amyclae. He was now on the Spartan side of the river—Diodorus says here that he fought off the expected sharp Spartan foray—and immediately swung around to approach the city from the southwest.

As the other thousands of plunderers continued to span out for miles throughout Laconia, Epaminondas kept his eye on the Spartan army in town, slowly approaching the outskirts where now neither river nor walls barred his entry, notching up the pressure among the terrified population and the confused classes of various inferiors inside. All our ancient sources note the pandemonium: 6,000 Helots in town rushed to fight for their masters in exchange for a rare grant of manumission. But their sudden and collective presence in the city frightened the Spartiates as much as the terror of the Thebans did in the suburbs. The offer of freedom was apparently withdrawn.

In contrast, many others of the Perioikoi and Helots in the countryside—to the shock of their Spartan overseers—now openly joined the invaders in plundering their masters' estates. Two conspiracies among the Spartiates in town were uncovered and their ringleaders were executed without trial, a sure sign of savage desperation—full-fledged Spartiates summarily killed without consent of their peers. Seventy-four-year-old, lame King Agesilaus, who himself had habitually led his Spartans on plundering expeditions throughout Asia Minor, northern Greece, the Peloponnese—and Boeotia—now hobbled to and fro through the city, fashioning a last-ditch defense and rooting out possible traitors and defectors. But about the only hoplites his men managed to kill were a few of his own Spartans, whom they rightly suspected of insurrection.

Sparta, in short, was feeling the heat of a democracy aroused, and was now in the process of unraveling: serfs sought their freedom from either their Spartan overlords or Theban liberators even as various Spartiates simultaneously planned revolution, attempted feeble resistance to the Thebans, or tried to prevent, not incite, a march of their more hotblooded youths. The strategist B. H. Liddell Hart once wrote of such chaos that "psychological dislocation fundamentally springs from the sense of being trapped"—and argued such collapse occurs when an enemy is attacked suddenly, and at their least-expected, most vulnerable spot. So it was now.

Agesilaus withdrew to the center and highest part of town, and abandoned the suburbs, claiming an oracle had promised "victory" if he kept his men on high ground—that is, if they wisely did *not* fight. The Spartan grandee Antalcidas—a chief Spartan diplomat of the last quarter century—was so terrified of the invaders that he secretly sent his own children off to Cythera, an island sanctuary off the southern coast of Laconia. Even as former serfs were proudly flocking back to join Epaminondas, Spartan elites were secretly making arrangements for their own safety. There is a sense of noble desperation in the collapse of free cities—Paris in 1940, Singapore in 1941, or Seoul in 1950—before the onslaught of tyrannical armies. In contrast, predictably there is little shared public sympathy for an enclave of apartheid in its eleventh hour, as those besieged in Atlanta in 1864 or Berlin of 1945 can attest. The pandemonium, rumor, and mutual recrimination in Sparta this winter was comparable to Georgia in the fall of 1864, when Sherman's arrival ripped apart, rather than united, the various classes of Confederate society.

The women of Sparta, who under the peculiar practice of Spartan land tenure owned much of the property that was now going up in flames, were terrified at the approach of the Thebans—unsure whether the greater sacrilege was a foreign army running loose on their parents' farms or their own husbands and sons now huddled inside the city both unwilling to fight this matchless army and unable to protect their own patrimony. The matriarchs of Sparta, remember, were a wealthy class famous for bravado, admonishing their sons as they departed for battle with a Laconic, "With it or on it"—their hoplite offspring were either to keep a grip on their shields in battle or be carried back on them dead.

But now the problem was not men losing their shields or having them used as biers, but simply getting men to pick them up in the first place. Neither the defeats at Thermopylae (480) nor Leuctra (371), both battles in which a Spartan king and royal guard were wiped out, matched the present calamity among the womenfolk—the earlier defeats were glorious occasions where far to the north Spartiates in mass fell spearing and stabbing, not inactive, surrounded, and terrified at their birthplace in front of their womenfolk. Yet the shrieking matrons of Sparta made about as much impression on Epaminondas as the aristocratic belles of the South did on Sherman. Neither general cared that aristocratic matriarchs were terrified by a marauding enemy whom in the past they had so arrogantly dismissed.[51]

All that prevented Epaminondas from burning down their city was the specter of being bogged in a dirty war inside the winding streets of Sparta, since women and children might oppose him from the rooftops, and Spartan hoplites from the houses might engage in guerrilla attacks. Seven years later when he tried to break through a second time, that was precisely what happened—the picture of flying roof tiles is a *topos* in every ancient description of a siege, and the general Pyrrhus, in fact, perished when knocked senseless by one in the streets of Argos. Surely Aristotle, writing in the late fourth century, was thinking of the Theban experience in Sparta when he said that the new Hippodamian grid cities of his own age were less secure than the old traditional Greek towns with their haphazard and winding streets, which "for enemy troops are difficult both to enter, and to find their direction when they are attacking."

Sparta bragged that she had no walls and that her defense had always rested with her men in battle. The truth was that the city atop six hills was protected by its height, a river below, and its sheer maze of structures—and Agesilaus had now withdrawn to the very center of that elevated labyrinth and hence would be almost impossible to pry out. In any case, a few thousand of the remaining diehard Peloponnesian allies had now arrived by sea and sneaked into the town around the Theban columns. Furthermore, Epaminondas's army was swollen with deserting Helots and Perioikoi, and bogged down further with tons of plunder. At this point it must have resembled both in size and comportment Sherman's army in mid-Georgia a few days out of Atlanta, wagons full of loot and followed by thousands of freed slaves, who were ill equipped to capitalize on the fruits of their liberation. A few of Epaminondas's army who rashly made their way inside the town were caught and slain, and the intensity of that street fighting convinced Epaminondas that there was no need to engage in urban brawling when the city was now surrounded and its entire rural infrastructure in his hands. Better, he thought, to back out, turn around, spread the terror, and head farther south to the Spartan seaport at Gytheum twenty-seven miles away—and perhaps later ever further afar to the west.

At this point Epaminondas was more interested in property damage, psychological terror, and mobility than besieging cities, inciting pitched battle, or assaulting fixed positions. The confusion on the Spartan acropolis proved that a society like Sparta was more likely to fall apart rather than unite when its property was ruined. Sherman wrote of the same phenomenon about the Confederacy: "It is nonsense to suppose that the people of the South are enraged or united by such movements. They reason very differently. They see in them the sure and irresistible destruction of all their property. They realize that the Confederate armies cannot protect them and they see in such raids the inevitable result of starvation & misery."

As Epaminondas left, his Thebans marched defiantly along the edge of the city, boisterously calling out to the Spartans to fight in pitched battle or "to acknowledge that they were lesser men than their enemies." A few Thebans spotted elderly King Agesilaus himself, and immediately dared him personally to come out, shouting that the old man's machinations were responsible for "igniting the flames of war." The aged king stayed put. Stunned at the abuse and humiliation, the septuagenarian could only rage back at Epaminondas, "Oh, the ambitious man." This was the silly monarch, remember, who had once boasted that no Spartan woman "would ever see smoke of an enemy campfire"—braggadocio not much different from Jefferson Davis's inane declaration that Sherman would never reach the Atlantic coast, but perish like Napoleon in Russia, and similar to Hitler's idle boast that a single crack Panzer division would send the Americans back into the Channel. Whatever the actual extent of the enemy inroads into the Spartan municipal center, later tradition had it that Epaminondas's Thebans had entered the very streets of Sparta—and their campfires, fueled from the brush of Laconia, must have roared at night and lit up the suburbs.

We should imagine Epaminondas as a man not much over five feet in height, burdened by fifty to seventy pounds of bronze and wood armament, holding an unwieldy oak shield, three feet in diameter, a nine-foot spear in his right hand, on foot, dressed identically to thousands of other hoplites, marching through his ranks, ordering his men onward, a democratic leader no different from a rough-looking Uncle Billy riding alongside his men in Georgia, a Patton in his Jeep cruising back and forth to the front line, hoarse from screaming at his GIs to head eastward, all three intent personally to lead thousands of men in their attack.

Epaminondas now wisely saw that his troops were in almost no danger—

he had lost only a few hundred or so out of over 70,000 men to small Spartan sorties—and that he could accomplish even more than a successful siege by continuing to humiliate the enemy huddled inside the walls and carting off its rural infrastructure, all the while tearing apart the psychological fabric of Spartan helotage and torching every town in the vale of Laconia. The pro-Spartan Xenophon laments that some of the Perioikoi "not only joined in the attacks but also marched right alongside the troops that followed the Thebans." No surprise—unfree men and women sometimes are not so docile when a liberator is in their midst. After three days Epaminondas left the Spartan seaport at Gytheum, after wrecking the dockyards. He now headed back through the middle of Laconia, bypassed Sparta, and made his way north over the mountains back into Arcadia. In a few weeks this Boeotian-led force had discovered that its rapid advance, superb command, and crack Theban hoplites made their army unassailable. Greece had never seen anything quite like it.

Ancient accounts point out that the winter weather had turned worse; Epaminondas's Peloponnesian plunderers were drifting away, laden with pillage and driving livestock, and the Laconian countryside itself was now almost denuded of supplies. Midwinter or not, Epaminondas still did not plan to linger in Arcadia, much less head home to Boeotia—he was technically now without legal command of his matchless army and likely to be indicted for keeping his hoplites in the field past the first of the new year.

Epaminondas had learned a great lesson in Laconia about the Spartans. At Leuctra the year before, he had nearly demolished their army, yet in but a few months Spartan infantrymen were back once more terrorizing their neighbors. In contrast, now that same military hid in the streets with their sobbing women and children—like the females who were left to beg from Sherman on the plantations, and the once proud German citizens who took down their portraits of Adolf Hitler and approached Patton's army with white flags.[52]

The only way to end Spartan aggression was to fight it far beyond the battlefield, destroy the material and spiritual capital that fueled the army in the first place: plunder its farmland, free its castes of inferiors, and exhibit how shallow was the entire "Spartan mystique." The elite of all militaristic slave states, with elaborate pseudo-scientific claims to ethnic and racial superiority, must fight and fight well when invaded. To huddle in town, to avoid the army of the enemy, to flee his onslaught in prima facie evidence of the lie that permeates such societies, as terror quickly gives way to humiliation. No Spartan, like no Confederate, like no German could ever claim that "a stab in the back" had brought the enemy among his women and children; it was now plain to see that only the failure of a militaristic society's military was to blame.

Laconia was the beginning, not the end, of this winter of Spartan discontent. Across the mountains to the west thousands of serfs in Messenia were already praying for the arrival of Epaminondas. If the Thebans had nearly put an end to a bankrupt culture in Laconia, their thoughts were now on raising up a humane one in Messenia. An oracle had told the rationalist Epaminondas that his own fate was tied up with the serfs of Messenia across the mountains—for the first and only time the skeptical general agreed with the "signs" and so now went westward, following the voice of the divine.

8

"NATURE HAS MADE
NO MAN A SLAVE"

A FEW WEEKS earlier in mid-December when the Thebans had arrived to save the city of Mantinea, the Arcadians and their allies had to convince the Boeotarchs not to turn around for home, but instead stay to ravage Laconia. Now in January, after the astounding success at plundering Laconia, when the army returned to the upland plain of Arcadia, it was Epaminondas who took the initiative in organizing yet a third new ambitious phase to this historic expedition—no less than the liberation of Messenia itself. "His nature," the historian Diodorus says of Epaminondas and his abrupt decision to free Messenia, "was to seek after great enterprises and to seek everlasting renown." There is no evidence that the army even stopped, and we should imagine that it left Laconia, marched into Arcadia, and then quickly turned southwest into Messenia. Like Sherman who paused in Savannah before heading north into the Carolinas, Epaminondas had learned that the morale and efficacy of an army increased after a successful march, as his own men wanted more of the same, the enemy less.

The devastation of the Spartan countryside, for all its theater, had done little permanent economic damage to Laconia. After the departure of the Thebans, and without a permanent fortified base to coordinate ongoing plundering, Spartan farms could be repaired, thousands of Laconian Helots run down and punished, and in a few seasons rural life put back on a road to recovery. Few orchards or vineyards—always difficult to burn or chop down—were permanently lost. The real effect of those weeks outside Sparta had been to weaken the entire psychological structure of Helot servitude in Laconia, and to show the Greek world that a police state that could not police its environs was little threat to their own freedom. In that spiritual sense Plutarch was right in saying that Sparta—like the South after Sherman's march—never quite recovered, comparing it to a seemingly sound body that had in fact overextended itself, and thus was brought to utter ruin by a single setback.[53]

The liberation of Messenia on the other side of Mt. Taygetos was a different proposition altogether, involving the very material foundation of the entire slave state. Most Spartan warriors were fed by Helot farms in Messenia—or through more indirect exploitation of Messenian hamlets that were given status similar to the Perioikoi of Laconia. No adult men, women, or children at Sparta had really worked on the land for centuries, and the food necessary for their maintenance was beyond the resources of surrounding Laconia, which had to support its own subservient laborers and assorted inferior classes. Moreover, the Helots of Messenia provided valuable manpower—they were the oxen and mules of the Spartan army and on occasion functioned as irregulars to engage in guerrilla activity and skirmishing. Even more important, an occupied Messenia ensured that the entire southern half of the Peloponnese, from the Mediterranean on the west to the Aegean Sea on the east, was free of foreign enemies, allowing Sparta to worry only about land attack from the north. No longer.

To liberate Messenia—the centuries-old dream of every Helot was to live in a free capital of Messenê—was to make the Spartans work for their own food in Laconia. It was to rob their vaunted army of thousands of support troops. It was to create instantaneously a fierce enemy for Sparta a mere thirty miles on the other side of the mountain. To Epaminondas the philosopher, it was to right a wrong of two-and-a-half centuries—and to send an example to the other city-states of Greece that he could build a democratic society as well as destroy an oligarchic culture. Finally, unlike the temporary occupation of Laconia, Messenia on the other side of the mountains could be unhinged from Sparta for good—there were hundreds of thousands of Helots whose ancestors had lived there for centuries and who now welcomed the chance to create their promised state in perpetual hostility to Sparta. Plundering Laconia and surrounding Sparta were not ends in themselves, but a means of ensuring that no enemy garrison would be present in their vast breadbasket to the west. The postwar period of Epaminondas's Spartan "Reconstruction" was to be nothing other than creation of a new culture of the once Other. It was as if Sherman had taken the entire state of Georgia, evicted the whites, settled it with 4,000,000 freed black slaves, armed them, created fortified points of resistance, and remained with his army until they had fashioned adequate defenses—that way racial discrimination, much less slavery, would never return to the central South, and the land south of the Mason-Dixon line would be a perpetual cauldron of mutual enmity between master and former slave.

Unlike the Laconian serfs, Messenians had nothing in common with Spartiates—not a common ancestry, ethnic background, or manner of life, nothing other than a shared three centuries of mutual hatred and a slightly similar Dorian brogue. Their enmity may have gone back centuries through the Dark Ages to the fall of the Mycenaean palaces. Epaminondas might have to spend months organizing the initial resistance, creating the democratic charter of the city, even overseeing the building of the walls, but when he left Messenia, he would leave it free forever—a natural ally to another soon-to-be-founded Peloponnesian fortress to the north at Megalopolis. The ex-serfs were, after all, an enterprising people who had previously waged three unsuccessful wars to destroy the Spartan army. They now were to own the richest ground in Greece—a deep loam that still today produces wines and olives found in gourmet shops around the world. Messenian soil is even better than good Laconian dirt. That such people were made free by Boeotian yeomen had a certain logic to it.

Many of the 30,000 allied irregulars had tagged along to Sparta simply for plunder, and so now on returning to Arcadia they dispersed with their booty to their own farms. Other Peloponnesians had once worried only about the Spartan threat on their southern borders; with the looting of Laconia they too saw their mission accomplished and thus also disbanded. No matter. Epaminondas and his Thebans, along with the more diehard Peloponnesians, northern Greek allies, and an increasing number of free Messenian patriots who had heard his call, for the third time that winter formed up the army and set out from Arcadia to march even farther from Thebes, once again into the depths of the Peloponnese and the inner sanctum of the Spartan slave state where no Boeotian army had ever visited. Sparta was weakened, but not destroyed. Allies were free—for a time. It was time now to ensure the permanence of Epaminondas's prior two feats of this winter.

None of our sources suggest that there were any Spartan overlords there when they arrived. Like worried Georgian Confederate soldiers who deserted home when they heard of Sherman's presence at their backs, Spartiates on frontier duty in Messenia must have fled to Sparta to defend their wives and children. The Thebans swept unimpeded through the Helot farms of the countryside, declaring all free, and headed for Mt. Ithômê the conical hill that was the spiritual home of the Messenians and the past locus of insurrections. There Epaminondas would found the sprawling city of Messenê, aptly named for the new capital of a free and democratic Messenia of over 200,000 persons, a state larger, more populous, and richer than Laconia itself.

The final card of Epaminondas was at last on the table: in the past, Helot insurrections had failed not out of a shortage of manpower or martial gallantry but simply because there was no initial window of protection for the revolutions to consolidate their toehold. Now his Thebans would provide that critical breathing space, and the walls of a citadel would prevent attack after he left. Epaminondas had absolute confidence in the plan, believing a priest who had recently come into his dreams and apprised him that his des-

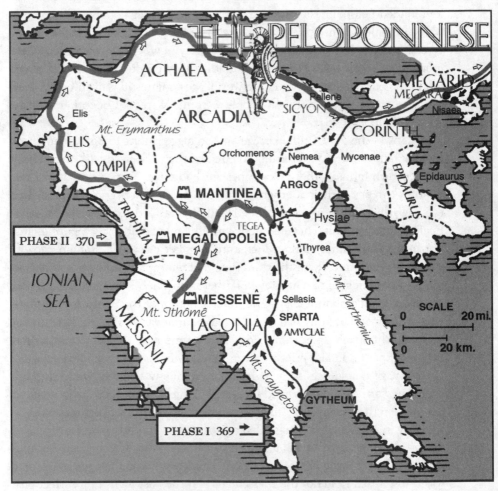

EPAMINONDAS'S INVASION OF LACONIA AND MESSENIA

tiny rested with liberation of the serfs: "My gift for you is to overcome any enemy you attack and when you have left the company of men, O Theban, I shall ensure that your name is never forgotten and your glory undiminished. But you are to restore to Messenians their ancestral land for now the old wrath of the Dioscuri against them has come to a close."

Two things amaze about Messenê: the sheer beauty and size of the walls and the utopian ideals that surround its founding. It was probably rainy and cold in late January or early February when Epaminondas and his army arrived and began hauling stones around the spurs of Mt. Ithômê. Unlike Laconia, Messenia was now instantaneously transformed from a rich source of potential enemy plunder to an allied democratic state whose resources had to be protected and enhanced, not stolen. Thus problems of logistics in a friendly country were worse than among the hated enemy in Laconia. The immediate worry was to find sufficient food and to begin quarrying stone to build enough of a circuit wall around Mt. Ithômê to ensure the Messenians safety in their new city, should Spartan hoplites under old King Agesilaus return when the Thebans left. As February led into March and April, grain stores were at their lowest level of the entire year, and the Spartan army would soon recover and begin to mobilize against this other, far greater Helot insurrection.

Epaminondas earlier had announced that all exiled Messenians were to assemble on his arrival in their country to rebuild their society around an enormous fortress. Another oracle—useful devices for a rationalist philosopher to persuade a religious people that their appointed hour was at hand—had advised him to look toward Mt. Ithômê. There on its sloping shoulders Epaminondas chose the site of the new city and laid out a five-mile circuit, anchored by an acropolis astride the mountain itself. His architects planned the city on a Hippodamian grid and divided up the environs in equal parcels, to be distributed in the spirit of democratic egalitarianism. Anyone who visits the site today and spends hours lumbering over the walls and tracing the ancient circuit, comes away with two distinct impressions: How could an impoverished people construct such beautiful, massive fortifications in the dead of winter? And how much more elegant and impressive are the ruins of Messenê than the scattered blocks and rubble that litter the classical Spartan acropolis!

Thousands of Messenians from as far away as Sicily, southern Italy, and northern Africa, displaced for nearly three centuries, now flocked in to join the undertaking with freed Helots, as Epaminondas and his Thebans and the remaining Peloponnesians supervised the construction and guarded the surrounding countryside. Although Messenê clearly was to be the home of the freed Helots, our sources suggest a utopian Panhellenic charter. It was to be an enclave open, as Diodorus put it, to "any others who wished" to be citizens. Pausanias, the topographer of the Roman age, tells us, "the Messenians returned back into the Peloponnese and recovered their own land two hundred and eighty years after the capture of Eira, in the archonship of Dyscinetus at Athens and in the third year of the hundred and second Olympiad." Well over four centuries after most Greek city-states had arisen from the chaos of the Dark Ages, now thanks to the initiative of a single Theban, Messenê belatedly joined the brotherhood of the more than a thousand Greek *poleis*. Pausanias perhaps in some exaggeration says that the exiles had not forgotten their local Messenian customs and spoke the purest Doric Greek in the Peloponnese.

The sheer rapidity and scale of the fortifications suggest centuries of pent-up energy that democracy had now unleashed. Diodorus also notes the general Greek amazement, remarking that Epaminondas's founding of Messenê "was received with great approval by all men." Yet we hear of no Spartan-style witch-hunts, no ethnic cleansing of Spartan sympathizers—and there must have been considerable numbers of these in such a huge enclave—no creation of a *krupteia* to monitor internal security. Some measure of both the morality and popularity of Messenê can be found in the shrill denunciation of the ninety-year-old right-wing Isocrates, the old doyen of Athenian letters, who grumbled that it was not enough that Thebes had freed Messenia, but had gone on to the further outrage of settling there freed Helots, of "making slaves the masters" of the land. Like some pathetic Southern pro-slavery barrister of the antebellum age, he claimed that the emancipation of the Helots had been "illegal" and constituted theft from Sparta of its "property."

In the spirit of the Panhellenic enterprise Epaminondas appointed the Argive Epiteles as "oikist" or official founder and overseer of the enterprise. The remains of a monument commemorating this role of Argos in founding Messenê is one of the first sites the modern visitor sees today as he enters the sanctuary at Delphi—deliberately erected near the Spartan offering. Perhaps over 200,000 men, women, and children joined in on erecting the fortifications, raising over thirty towers, along walls that were often over eight feet thick and fourteen feet in height, all composed of unmortared squared blocks—a spectacle of free people at work not seen in Greece since Themistocles had organized thousands of Athenians to join in the rapid building of their Long Walls to the Piraeus right after the end of the Persian Wars. For tough Helots who plowed for Spartans, hard labor for their own freedom was invigorating, not drudgery. A vast fortress—still the most impressive extant classical walls in mainland Greece—slowly arose, protecting a new city and hundreds of intramural acres of farmland that might keep alive thousands during a protracted siege. Tourists to Greece should realize that the Parthenon in the heart of bustling Athens is testament to a maritime imperial power that looted its subjects, whereas the grandiose walls of Messenê in the rural hinterlands of the Peloponnese tower as a monument to freedom.

Workers cut stone and hoisted blocks—as the Pythagorean Epaminondas had them labor to the music of Theban and Argive pipes. Food was supplied from Helot stores and the money to hire stonecutters, day laborers, and teamsters came from the plunder of Laconia—Spartans who disdained walls as unmanly now had their own property sold off to pay for the most magnificent fortifications in Greece to house their most hated enemy. During the entire enterprise an army of 6,000 Thebans provided security and morale as well as material support. Still, we should imagine that the conditions in midwinter must have been miserable. Thousands of hoplites were camping in the open, far too many to be housed in the Helot hovels of Messenia. Most simply kept warm in tents and lean-tos as the life-sustaining walls went up first, houses and public buildings later.[54]

The workers were no tyros, and shared a mutual determination to wall themselves off forever from the hated Spartan army. The Arcadians back at home were selling off their plunder to finish their own massive fortifications of Mantinea, itself a vast ellipse of several miles in circumference, protected by dozens of square towers and ten gates, all ringed with a moat with girdling walls thirteen feet thick. As they finished work on Mantinea, fifty miles to the southwest other Arcadians were already breaking ground at Megalopolis, destined to be an even larger Arcadian fortress, enclosing a vast interior space ringed by massive walls to house the consolidated population of forty surrounding villages. The Thebans, who had sent their experts to help rebuild the Athenian Long Walls (394) and had themselves erected massive wooden stockades to keep out the Spartans during 379–378, must have dispatched their own engineers and architects throughout the Peloponnese. Both Arcadian citadels in design, scale, and construction technique show close affinity with Messenê, suggesting perhaps that the Theban liberators had offered some general master plan of fortification for all three citadels. The wall-building citizens of the Peloponnese were almost Pavlovian in their response to Spartan weaknesses, and needed no apparent encouragement to build while they had the chance.

Again, modern students of Greek history, to gain full insight into the real contemporary Greek view of Spartan culture, must visit the remains of Messenê, Megalopolis, and Mantinea. That such vast circuits could arise so quickly after the Spartan defeat at Leuctra and subsequent invasion of Laconia should tell us exactly what Sparta's neighbors thought about Spartan society. Battlements—the Berlin Wall and the current fieldworks arising on the American-Mexican border are good examples—often provide more honest testimony than literary sources and government proclamation about the respective apprehensions, fears, and ideologies of the cultures on either side of the ramparts. Just as tremors in the Soviet Union caused walls to crash in Germany, so too the check on Sparta offered by Epaminondas immediately prompted thousands to go out into the Peloponnesian countryside to cut and raise stone while they still had the chance.

Due to the silence of the Spartaphile Xenophon and the loss of contemporary accounts, the later narratives in Pausanias, Plutarch, and Diodorus cannot fully capture the emotional tide that was sweeping across the Peloponnese, and the utopian assumptions that underlay creating *ex nihilo* Megalopolis and Messenê, two of the largest fortified cities in the contemporary Greek world, whose new citizenry, constitution, and physical infrastructure would be burdened with none of the pathologies inherent in the gradual evolution of other city-states. Aristotle long ago remarked about the early Greek colonization movements of the eighth and seventh centuries that the principles of egalitarianism were much easier to enact by simply drawing out new equitable parcels of land for the citizens without the baggage of the past: new colonies did not have to contend with old families, simmering land disputes, and crusty reactionaries. And over a hundred years ago the great historian of Greece George Grote similarly observed:

> In describing societies already established and ancient, we find the force of traditional routine almost omnipotent in its influence both on men's actions and on their feelings; bad as well as good is preserved in concrete, since the dead weight of the past stifles all constructive intelligence, and leaves little room even for improving aspirations. But the forty small communities which coalesced into Megalopolis, and the Messenians and other settlers who came for the first time together on the hill of Ithômê, were in a state in which new exigencies of every kind pressed for immediate attention.

Recent archaeological survey confirms the agrarian idealism of Epaminondas's reforms. Before the Thebans' arrival in the Peloponnese, the Messenian countryside as a part of Spartan helotage shows little sign of dispersed habitation or small farming. But in the latter part of the fourth century, there is evidence that farms and farmhouses began to appear in place of absentee estates, suggesting the rise of an ex-Helot populace now free in the countryside. The Greeks' discovery of agrarianism—the notion of a countryside of roughly equal parcels, lived on and worked by free citizens—had at last come with a vengeance to Messenia, three centuries *after* its appearance in the rest of Greece. As the agrarian ideal aged and declined elsewhere in fourth-century Greece, it had a rebirth among the once enslaved Helots, explaining in large part the remarkable growth of Messenian wealth and culture in general during the next two centuries. It was as if Epaminondas sought to infuse the tenets of three centuries of *polis* culture within a matter of weeks.

The impatient Epaminondas's ideas of democratic egalitarianism were now to be rushed into actuality with the same force and spirit that he had destroyed "in a single day" the Spartan army at Leuctra, overrun the valley of Laconia, and earlier spread democracy in Boeotia. Plutarch remarks that the Spartans, after Epaminondas's invasion of their homeland, had neither the courage to attack Messenê nor the ability to hinder its founding. All they could do was blame their seventy-four-year-old King Agesilaus for losing their food-producing dependents. Later, when they made a probing attack against Messenê, the entire Messenian population—men, women, and children—issued forth from the walls to give battle. Polyaenus preserves a story that the Spartans retreated in depression, realizing that the Messenians were prepared to "give up hopes of living and thereby fight all the more gallantly." The contrast was unmistakable: former slaves would eagerly leave their massive and impenetrable fortifications for the chance of meeting the hated Spartans head-to-head—their onetime overlords who had huddled earlier in their own unwalled streets to escape pitched battle with their "inferiors."

In less than three months at Messenê, Epaminondas the Pythagorean laid out a beautiful municipal grid, turned over thousands of acres of the richest soil in Greece to a collection of ex-Helots, Messenian exiles from all over the Hellenic world, Laconian fugitives, and any other interested Greeks. Then he abruptly gathered beside his Thebans his force of Argives, Eleans, and Arcadians to oversee the work and keep the enterprise safe. His supplies were low, his men were tired, and he had been in Arcadia and Laconia perhaps for a month and now nearly another three in Messenia. Yet when he marched northward from Messenê in early April 369, there was a huge city rising at his back and a free people of thousands inside its walls.

Epaminondas made his way back through the Peloponnese expecting the democracy of Athens to hinder the crossing of his democratic liberators at the Isthmus of Corinth. He was not disappointed. The adventuresome captain Iphicrates and a large Athenian and Corinthian force—perhaps upward of 12,000 men—occupied the passes around Corinth. Iphicrates and his feared light-armed skirmishers had been the terror of Greece for years, obliterating a small corps of Spartan elite hoplites before Corinth years earlier. But when told that the Athenians now came with "new equipment," Epaminondas scoffed, "Why should a maestro care if some tyro had brought along a new flute?" Despite their considerable numbers, Iphicrates and his men were in no mood to take on the Theban phalanx of Epaminondas's hoplites, fresh from plundering Laconia and humiliating the best army in Greece. The latter marched on through a conveniently unguarded route near Cenchreae and made the last eighty miles home in undisturbed safety.

In this strange winter of 370–369 Epaminondas had earned the everlasting hatred of thousands of Spartans and the enmity of the entire state of Athens. He would now come home to worried relatives and a host of jealous rivals in the Boeotian Assembly eager to try him for his life—this firebrand who, along with thousands of his fellow Boeotians, had been incommunicado for months deep in the bowels of the Peloponnese. The Greek world was stunned that after three unsuccessful and bloody Helot wars of liberation and despite nearly three centuries of subjugation, Epaminondas and his Thebans had freed the Helots in three months.

When it came to extending formal recognition to Messenê as a free and autonomous Greek *polis*, the rhetorician and philosopher Alcidamas remarked of the liberation simply that "nature has made no man a slave"— quite appropriately one of the few unambiguously abolitionist sentiments in the entire corpus of ancient Greek literature.[55]

9

"AND ALL OF GREECE BECAME INDEPENDENT AND FREE"

E PAMINONDAS received about the same thanks from his government that greeted Sherman and Patton once their marches were over—threatened demotions and accusations of everything from insubordination to collusion with the enemy. Such are the jealousies that arise in a democratic society when one man alone has crafted an army in his own image. But unlike the other two generals, there were to be formal capital charges lodged against the Theban. Immediately on his return Epaminondas was put on trial by his rivals in the Boeotian assembly for retaining an illegal command. Besides keeping the army in the field beyond the appointed mandate and after his own tenure as Boeotarch had expired in late December, the more lunatic of his enemies later brought additional charges of treason on the grounds that he had allowed the Spartans to escape destruction by not burning down their city. No wonder that when he got back to Thebes, and his tiny Maltese terrier greeted him with a wag of the tail, he shrugged, "While this dog gives me thanks for my favors to him, the Thebans in contrast for all that I have done for them try to execute me."

His formal defense? Simply that he would gladly suffer execution if the Thebans would publicly inscribe their sentence on his tombstone so that the Greeks would know his crimes. He told them to write the following:

> Epaminondas had forced the Thebans against their will to torch Laconia, which had been heretofore untouched for 500 years; he resettled Messenê

after two hundred and thirty years; he had united and organized the Arcadians into a league; and he gave back to the Greeks their autonomy.

He then walked out of the court chamber; all charges were dismissed without even a vote of the jurors.

In the aftermath of the great winter march of 370–369, Epaminondas would go on to muster his Thebans three more times for marches southward—in summer 369 to punish any Peloponnesians who had aided Sparta; again in 366 to establish autonomy for the Achaeans along the northwestern coast of the Peloponnese; and for the fourth and last time in 362 either to destroy Sparta itself or obliterate the reconstituted Spartan army in battle. Had he not died in his moment of victory on the battlefield of Mantinea, he likely would have done both.

Yet none of the later three invasions rivaled the great trek southward of 370–369 either in the size of the muster, the spirit of the endeavor, or the results achieved. In some sense, there was simply little left to do once the Peloponnese was free of Spartan hegemony, the serfs of Messenia were liberated and Messenê founded, Mantinea now completely fortified, the idea for a new city of Megalopolis about to become reality, and Sparta emasculated. The great *raison d'être* for any democratic muster—moral outrage over being unjustly attacked—became more problematic as Sparta was further weakened and kept within her ancestral borders, as Thebes was in turn energized and more eager to march abroad.

In 370–369 the Boeotians had marched out as a great defensive army, bent on revenge for centuries of Spartan transgression. But during their subsequent three musters of the ensuing decade, there were less concrete, more abstract justifications for entry into the Peloponnese—punishing Spartan sympathizers, maintaining a balance of power, or protecting Theban long-term interests. Like the Americans after World War Two, the Thebans learned that former beneficiaries quickly chafe—whether through righteous grievance or petty envy—at the continued armed presence and power of their liberators. Like the experience of Federal troops in the reconstructed South, it is a difficult, messy proposition for an army to return to the theater of war when the great clear-cut work of battle and liberation is largely complete. Patton learned that during his disastrous tenure as proconsul of Bavaria. So the Athenian Demosthenes concluded of these later Theban marches that "the Thebans had overplayed their trumps."

After that great winter of triumph, a series of personal and public reversals plagued the Thebans. Pelopidas was killed at the battle of Cynoscephalae in northern Greece in 364. His loss robbed Epaminondas of his fellow visionary—and the only other Theban whose moral capital could persuade the Boeotian assembly to fight tyranny abroad. Efforts during the years 367–364 to become a naval power were largely an expensive failure. Soon the Arcadians themselves, the beneficiaries of so much Theban largess, began to resent the growing power of Thebes, as factional strife engulfed the Peloponnese. At his death Epaminondas was fighting against, not alongside, the Mantineans who had so desperately called on his help in 370 and precipitated the entire crusade in the first place.

Athens and Sparta, radical democracy and extreme oligarchy par excellence, formally entered an unholy partnership to thwart the egalitarian liberation movements of the Thebans—both at various times tried to bar the Isthmus of Corinth from Thebans marching southward. Finally, in the ensuing decade, other Greeks outside the Peloponnese began to resent the success of the Thebans; the old Athenian Isocrates summed it up best that "they were into everything." Their requests for Persian subsidies and insistence on marching abroad each year began to take on the appearance of aggression, not liberation, more so when Athenian and Spartan propagandists presented the humiliating image of a rustic people now in charge of the most deadly army in Greece. The sheer idealism and revolutionary fervor of the Theban army that set out in midwinter 370 were never to be captured again.

Another problem was the very indifference to domination shown on the part of Epaminondas. Scholars call his great decade (371–362) between Leuctra and Mantinea "the Theban hegemony," but it was really a hegemony of nothing—no tribute, no taxes, no sworn fealty, no politically correct line for allies to toe. If anything, the decade was simply ten years of Theban military omnipotence, a rare time in Greek history when an army chose not to do all that it easily might have. When Epaminondas invaded the Peloponnese and liberated cities from Spartan control, he seems to have cared little whether the beneficiaries adopted constitutions according to his own democratic taste. He chose not to round up opponents and have them exiled or murdered, and in general cherished the utopian ideal that his army was sent to free city-states, not to bind them in some allegiance to Thebes.

While he was a brilliant general and a rare man of character, Epaminondas made a lousy imperialist: he could show little profit back home for all his campaigning abroad. For someone so gifted, Epaminondas's political instincts were as inept as both Sherman's and Patton's, both of whom likewise failed to realize just how tired a population can become of war, and just how suspect a successful general can become to his peers. No newfound allies—save the noble Messenians—saw any need to repay past beneficence with any pretense of loyalty or succor. Unless Epaminondas was willing to kill large numbers of fellow Greeks, there would always be local aristocrats of the northern Pelo-ponnese who would arise in the newly established democratic assemblies to proclaim that subservience to Sparta had not been so bad after all—to the nods of bought toadies and timid fence-sitters alike. His own Boeotian Con-federacy was hard enough to maintain, and Epaminondas made no real efforts elsewhere to wean Greek city-states from their centuries-old ideal of *autono-mia*—complete political independence—to adopt a Panhellenic federated al-liance. The Boeotians' general repute for rusticity and dullness made the very idea of them as political, military, and moral exemplars particularly hard to swallow for maritime cities whose superior intellectual and artistic reputa-tions had been entrenched for centuries.

As the 360s wore on, most Boeotians themselves became increasingly tired of the expense and costs of interference in the Peloponnese. In the fu-ture they would vote to enforce strict time limits on any expedition to the south—no one wished to repeat the great five-month heroic trek of 370–369. Recalcitrant Boeotian city-states, like Thespiae, Plataea, and Orchomenos, past centers of both pro-Athenian and Spartan sympathizers, had been razed and their populations exiled or spread among smaller villages—not a proud accomplishment for a confederacy dedicated to democracy abroad.

Remember also that Boeotia was an agricultural state, without much commerce, manufacturing, shipping, mining, or any real income other than that from farming. For all their selfless campaigning abroad, the Thebans—so unlike the Spartans, Athenians, and Macedonians—brought very little ex-propriated wealth home, very little other than the Epaminondan satisfaction of freeing serfs and subjects. It is likely that even during the great march of 370–369 the Arcadians took away almost all the plunder of Laconia to their own farms; the rest was sold to pay for the construction of Messenê. Not much Spartan infrastructure made its way back to Boeotia. When Pelopidas began to organize marches into northern Greece, and Epaminondas contin-ued intervention both to the south and at sea, it was obvious that the limits of local Boeotian military manpower were at hand: there never again could be enough hoplites for a great muster like that of the winter of 370–369. Time away from farms also hit the countryside hard. There were no substantial ports, mines, or craft industries to supply capital to replace the labor lost from the fields.

When Epaminondas fell at Mantinea in 362, nearly all of the old zealots who had stormed the Theban Cadmea in 379 were at last dead, and thus the so-called Theban hegemony formally ended with the demise of the last and best of that so gifted revolutionary generation. Ancient observers all con-firmed this modern assessment that the so-called decade of Thebes began and ended with Epaminondas's rise and death—or rather his victory at Leuctra and his last charge into oblivion at the battle of Mantinea. Most noted further that without such a general the natural Boeotian tendency for rural parochialism and isolation naturally reasserted itself. After Epaminondas, the historian Ephorus concluded that the Thebans had indeed returned to mediocrity. Without the philosopher, "they down played the value of learning and close associations with outsiders," as if the ideological warriors of old could now predominate "through concentrating on military virtue alone."[56]

The final score card of that winter of 370–369, however, was unquestioned, and the ripples of Epaminondas's plunge into the Peloponnese would spread for centuries hence. Over 200,000 people in Messenia were now free—and were to remain free for the duration of Greek freedom itself. For the next twenty years Sparta, both indirectly and more flagrantly, would try to overturn the verdict of Epaminondas—to no avail, thanks to the massive fortifications of Messenê and its growing consolidation of the Messenian countryside and alliances with the northern Peloponnesians. Thousands more runaway Helots in Laconia would now have a secure place of refuge, and rights to citizenship in a free Messenian state that would welcome the dispossessed of Greece. The small farmers of Messenia would now live on and work their own land, and their produce would fuel a Messenian renaissance that ensured the Spartan army would never again confiscate their harvests.

There was now at least a structure of leagues and confederacies in the Peloponnese under the auspices of democratic assemblies, thanks to Epaminondas's Kantian notion that war was avoidable only through a voluntary combination of democratic states. Whatever their political sympathies and shifting alliances, the Peloponnesian city-states of Messenia, Megalopolis, and Mantinea would be autonomous, and the decision to march for or against Sparta, to battle one another—or to turn on Thebes herself—would now rest solely with their own democratically elected assemblies. That too was the direct result of Epaminondas's march of winter 370–369. For better or for worse, after Epaminondas's great invasion the free citizens of the entire Peloponnese would now vote when and when not to go to war.

The Spartan army, after a tactically brilliant but strategically insignificant victory in Arcadia, would never again march forth from the Peloponnese, playing little if any role in the Panhellenic resistance in the coming decades against Philip (352–338). Those Spartans who did battle abroad did so as hired mercenaries or military consultants. Sparta's victory over the Arcadians after the Thebans returned home—the so-called Tearless Battle of 368—restored little to Spartan wounded pride, but showed clearly just how much the Arcadians and all the other Peloponnesian states owed their entire military success to Epaminondas and his phalanx of dour farmers, who alone of the Greeks welcomed battle with Spartan redcloaks. Later the Arcadians confessed that they had been terrified by the martial prowess of the Thebans and the mere presence of Epaminondas.

The Theban enervation of Spartan hegemony, if anything, increased each year after the great invasion, as the loss of Messenia and the Peloponnesian allies slowly sapped the entire ideological and material basis for Spartan servitude. A shrunken and increasingly paranoid Sparta had little aid to offer the Greeks at their last stand at Chaeronea three decades later (338), where the defense of a free and autonomous Hellenic culture rested largely in the hands of the Athenians and Thebans alone. Sparta's fate was to become a provincial backwater where for the next few centuries tourists flocked to observe her quaint customs of military training among a tiny and impotent elite.

If the power to instill democracy elsewhere was over, nevertheless Epaminondas had given his own Boeotia a democratic government that would last for another three decades until the army was overwhelmed by Philip and the city destroyed by his son Alexander (335). When idealists like the Athenian Demosthenes *in extremis* looked for concrete support for resistance to Philip, they looked first to the old yeomen of Thebes, the offspring of Epaminondas. The irony is that when Epaminondas returned from the Peloponnese after his great crusade of 370–369, the real serpent was not beheaded but was being hatched in his own courtyard: a young Philip II of Macedon was a hostage in Thebes, absorbing the very tactical manifesto of the Theban army that Epaminondas had created to destroy autocracy. But whereas the Macedonian youth during his brief internment would learn of Epaminondas's massed phalanxes and the proper way to invade Laconia, he had very different ideas of ultimately what such military power was for.

The final military verdict on the great Boeotian army of 370–369? Militarily, *no* force produced by Athens or Sparta in either the fifth or fourth century was its rival. Athens, it is true, had earlier mustered militias of some magnitude but used them solely to destroy the countryside of its poorer neighbor Megara or to try to enslave—quite disastrously for themselves—democratic Sicily. None of Sparta's great invasions in Attica during the Peloponnesian War were especially successful or public-spirited, even if we accept the dubious notion that its Peloponnesian alliance marched to dethrone an imperialistic Athens from the hegemony of Greece. The forays of Sparta into Asia Minor and central Greece in the 390s and 380s were without much support from any but its own coerced allies. The Spartans' victories of the early fourth century against Persia, Athens, and Thebes proved nothing other than that their battlefield prowess would never translate into strategic competence or political acumen—and surely would never be seen as a moral exemplar for a Greece weary of parochialism and a century of Athenian imperialism. All of the above were either marches smaller in magnitude or of shorter duration than Epaminondas's—and most likely both.

Epaminondas's advance was not fueled by stored gold or captured treasuries; the Theban army left poor and returned poor, and had a hard time of it on the march. There was no Persepolis waiting to frolic in, loot, and burn. The Theban founding of cities in the Peloponnese was not, like Alexander's municipal creations, a megalomaniac enterprise to reward a small cadre of loyal brigands—there was not to be a series of new cities called "Epaminondiases" founded in Arcadia or Messenia, where one day an ambitious lieutenant might put on display the conqueror's embalmed corpse. No cities were to be named after Epaminondas's horse—most accounts suggest he had no mount, but instead that he walked alongside his men and fought with them on foot. Like Sherman, Epaminondas was an infantry commander who in the spirit of the times had only disdain for aristocratic cavalrymen. Those soldiers who set out with Alexander—and they were less numerous than Epaminondas's allied army of 370–369—did so either under coercion or in hope of lucre. When their drunken and diseased commander died a decade later, the few of his original Macedonian followers who were still alive scarcely lamented his passing. It is a true enough generalization that Alexander never really led a single free, voting citizen into battle, whereas Epaminondas never led any who were not; the former commanded 30,000 obsequious subjects, the latter in 369 twice that number of free citizens. In short, the army of Epaminondas in size, conduct, spirit, and achievement was like none other in Greek history and surely demands an explanation for its remarkable winter of 370–369.

Moral purpose characterized the march in an age of increasing amorality and political duplicity—whatever the theatrical invective and exaggeration within surviving Greek rhetoric of the fourth century, to read the Athenian orators is still to read of ubiquitous pusillanimity, bribery, and treason. In contrast, all combatants who followed Epaminondas did so with the clear notion that they were battling an apartheid state that had steadily tried to destroy them for a decade. The entire Epaminondan laudatory tradition is rooted in contemporary observations of his zeal (at the time shared by almost no other Greek states) to free the unfree.

All democratic armies of a season, which march under the prerogative of elected assemblies that monitor the course of military conduct daily, must have at least the appearance of an ethical imperative; they must be ostensible avengers, not perpetrators of evil, and thus inevitably must be a muster of retaliation, not aggrandizement. That is the essence of maintaining public support in a civil society under consensual government. The absence of even the pretense of a moral sense, after all, in large part led to the material and spiritual dissolution of the Athenian empire and the subsequent decline of Spartan hegemony. If we can believe Thucydides, few of the 40,000 Athenians and their allies who marched into disaster on faraway Sicily (415 B.C.) believed they were fighting for the liberty of the Greeks. The Spartan hoplites that marched north into Boeotia in the 370s saw their work clearly for what it was: the effort to destroy the democracy of a people who had done them no harm. The proper question, then, is not "Why did the Boeotians become prominent for a mere decade?" but rather "How did a rustic, rural society for ten years determine events in Greece?"—an answer impossible to ascertain without some consideration of the ethical agenda and character of Epaminondas himself.

Still, the notion of defense, and spirit, and confidence in the inherent righteousness of a cause, together with the idea of retaliation for past Spartan transgressions in Boeotia, *do not* in themselves explain the great *success* of 370–369: avenging armies with excellent intentions can march out triumphantly and come back ruined, as Americans, French, and English learned in the dark early days of World War Two, and as the North learned after Bull Run and Chancellorsville. Just as important as the cause, there was also the implicit assurance to the marching farmers of Boeotia that the great expedition was seasonal, of a limited duration, with a clear agenda and an acknowledged manner of operation. Epaminondas was to lead the army for a season to free Peloponnesians from Spartan subjugation, in a linear march with a clear sense of direction. Later, auditors and critics could harangue Epaminondas that he had exceeded authority in prolonging the invasion. He did. Rivals would add that he had no authorization to head into Laconia, much less Messenia. He did not. Many must have complained that his actual plans and even the direction of his march were known only to a very few. That too is true. George Patton would have approved.

Such critics were not among the 70,000 who marched south. To his own men there was never any question that their general had led them to harm Sparta, whether that meant freeing allied cities, plundering Laconia, or liberating Messenia—all were but elements in a widely shared purpose. Epaminondas's Thebans, like Sherman's bluecoats and Patton's GIs, must have had little idea of their day-to-day itinerary or even the exact targets of their onslaught. All three armies knew that they were marching in a straight direction—and why. And when they were done, they could go home.

Besides moral purpose, we should not forget the constant specter of demobilization. The Thebans that left in 370 were not, as was increasingly the case elsewhere in Greece, professional troops. Rather, the army was the last purely citizen muster in the history of Greece until the final stand at Chaeronea, in which an entire culture marched out to war. There was surely a sense of adventure, if not naïveté, among the troops. Most Boeotians, as Sherman discovered of many of his men in Georgia, and as Patton learned of his GIs in Germany, had not been on such a campaign before, and literally had no idea of the nature of the countryside that they now destroyed. Instead, the prevailing spirit was one of great excitement among thousands who were abroad for a set mission and would be quickly sent back home to their farms when the job was ended.

For democratic armies on the march to be successful, they should have a sense that military experience is ephemeral, with the assurance that after their march they will be summarily demobilized and sent back to their homes. If Epaminondas's army proved anything, it was that a citizen militia was every bit as ferocious as a professional military elite, when the parameters of its existence are clearly marked; armies of a season must be just that—able to dissolve as quickly as they arise. Confederate general Joe Johnston remarked of Sherman's army that there had been nothing like it since Caesar's legions—an understandable if flawed comparison when we remember the mercenary, illegal, and checkered careers of those lethal veteran Roman legionaries who crossed the Rubicon. In fact, there had been only *one* army of the past, which in mobility, battlefield ferocity, and size was Sherman's match, and it is no accident that Epaminondas, like Sherman, used such a rare force as part of a democratic mandate to dismantle an entire slave state in a single season.[57]

Idealism, a prescribed tenure, a clear agenda, constant motion, and seasoned yeomen explain much of the success of Epaminondas's remarkable army. To these factors we can add more critical and more generic characteristics of democratic musters. The Theban army, for all its purported destructive capability, for all the horror stories of Spartan devastation, was not a gratuitous killing machine. We hear of no rapes, murders, executions, or unnecessary brutality. The real aim was the destruction of Laconian property and Spartiate morale as part of a larger strategy of altering the political map of the Peloponnese—all in accordance with a democratic mandate. Unlike Alexander's Macedonians, who conducted a war of murder among the civilians of Afghanistan and India, Epaminondas's Thebans killed no one other than Spartan soldiers.

The effect on the troops of this deliberate strategy of attacking the enemy's material and spiritual will to resist? From all accounts they must have enjoyed immensely those "houses full of many valuable things." The plundering of farms, the burning of structures, the carting away of food and wine were tangible events, often proof of real accomplishment if not enjoyment by thousands of soldiers let loose and on the move. The sheer exuberance of 70,000 in motion and the moral challenge of creating a new society from the ground up in Messenia were far preferable to stationary camps and direct frontal charges. Most young men, ancient and modern, would choose to burn down a house rather than to spear a man in his face, more so when they felt the former accomplished greater damage to the enemy cause than the latter. The attack on property is an easier, quicker, more emotionally gratifying task than colliding into an enemy army and killing and being killed. It is disheartening to add that the same in the inverse holds true of the enemy. Epaminondas knew, as did Sherman, that the loss of property, not a state's manhood, is considered the most traumatic of losses—confirming Machiavelli's dictum that "men more quickly forget the death of their father than the loss of their patrimony."

More important, the strategy of attacking assets and prying away allies preserves rather than erodes an army on the move—critical in a democracy where popular will does not for long tolerate high casualties without clear evidence of tangible results. If anything, throughout Epaminondas's five-month march there is no indication that the army shrank, and much to suggest that it was constantly in flux if not growing—Arcadians leaving as they departed from Laconia, Messenians joining as they turned toward Messenia. During the entire expedition it is likely that not more than a few hundred men were killed in an army of thousands, and those were mostly the careless picked off by Spartans in the process of either plundering or attempting to enter unaided Sparta itself. While the army paused in Arcadia, encircled Sparta, and oversaw the building of Messenê, it was ultimately a force on the move that had marched nearly five hundred miles in midwinter over some of the roughest terrain in Greece, most of it hostile territory manned by Spartan or Athenian garrisons.

In strategic terms, what are we to call the march of Epaminondas? For over a century scholars have argued whether his was a revolutionary effort to annihilate the enemy by striking directly at his military forces in the field—the so-called strategy of annihilation—or rather the first true mastery of the mechanism of indirect approach, a preference for attrition and exhaustion by lightning-quick marches in lieu of direct conflict, in order to detach an adversary from a base of support and allied succor, and thus to win a war without casualties.

Is Epaminondas the forerunner of Alexander the Great and his strategy of a total, destructive warfare against his enemy in the field (what the Germans call *Niederwerfungsstrategie*)? Or is the Theban the strategic successor to Pericles, who sought to avoid decisive battle and casualties in a longer war of economic exhaustion (*Ermattungsstrategie*), whose aim was to destroy enemy coalitions, remove sources of supply, and shake the spiritual will of the enemy without the expenditure of one's own precious men or matériel?

Such arbitrary distinctions do not really apply to Epaminondas, the victor of Leuctra and invader of Laconia. Like both Sherman and Patton, he was at once an economic and military thinker, strategist and tactician alike, who sought simultaneously to engage the enemy *and* to destroy his infrastructure, all in the process of marching in a path through *and* around enemy lines. The Thebans set out in 370, as they had at Leuctra and would again at Mantinea, ready and eager to meet the Spartan phalanx—but on their terms only. They were not particularly interested in either chasing or waiting for its appearance. Rather, like Sherman in Georgia, the strategy of the army was to march through enemy territory, destroying property and humiliating its citizenry, displaying to subject states and underlings alike the impotence of their masters, with the confidence that if the enemy chose to fight, it would lose even more dramatically.

Epaminondas's Thebans were not a light army of plunderers or skirmishers, nor a plodding phalanx that existed for battle alone, but rather both. He is neither predecessor to Alexander nor successor of Pericles, but rather innovator of this new balance of movement in force against the human and material capital of the enemy—a paradigm that other democratic musters would follow in the centuries to come. At any point, Epaminondas was prepared either to meet the Spartan phalanx in battle or to continue his march at its periphery and to its rear—thereby in Sherman's words putting the enemy "on the horns of a dilemma."

The point was that the mastery of events was preordained—as in the case of Sherman and Patton—and entirely in the hands of the invading army. Should the Spartans choose battle, Epaminondas's Thebans had the tactical means to end the war decisively and immediately by killing them outright. Should the enemy lay back, he was equally prepared to continue with his strategy of indirect approach that would yield the same dividend as battle victory, albeit more slowly and through economic rather than purely military means. Whether he destroyed the enemy phalanx in the field or left it alone at his rear was irrelevant, once he could freely destroy the property of Sparta's citizens and teach them that the pride of their society—their vaunted army—was hollow.

Patton likewise sought to trap armies as he marched, to let them come to him to save their land from being gobbled up by his fast-moving, flanking columns. Similarly, when Germans took the bait, he preferred to cut off salients at their source, as far into enemy territory as possible, so that tactical victory might extend to the strategic loss of men, matériel, civilians, and territory in an ongoing war of attrition. This was a strategy that King Agesilaus, Grant, and the other British and American generals in Normandy, with their preference for direct frontal assaults, single thrusts, and clearly defined targets, never fully understood.

Epaminondas was probably an even better tactician than either Sherman or Patton; neither of the latter ever sought out a battle like Leuctra or Mantinea. During the Atlanta approach and against the Siegfried Line, Sherman and Patton both displayed a real frustration with the idea of sending men against either entrenched positions or large armies similar to their own. Not so Epaminondas, whose massed phalanx on the left wing could itself shatter Spartan hoplites. Still, Epaminondas's tactical goals were not designed to deliver the enemy to his battlefield steamroller, but rather to achieve victory without need of those very dramatic encounters at which he so excelled. Very rarely in military history do great tacticians, in charge of murderous armies, use that battlefield prowess in an ancillary role, subordinate to larger strategic aims of winning the war without losing men. Epaminondas was ready and willing to be Grant, but he preferred to play Sherman. And like Sherman's March to the Sea, Epaminondas's plunge into Laconia resulted in much enemy hatred, an enormous amount of plunder, the complete demoralization of the opposing army—and very few killed on either side.

The strategic legacy of Epaminondas is thus an entirely new mobile army at all times capable of direct annihilation and indirect attrition. Its trademark is overwhelming numerical superiority mustered for a short time, a brilliant burst of democratic frenzy that drives right to the heart of the enemy reservoirs of matériel and human wealth, with every intent of meeting and smashing tactically any enemy army that stands in its way. The enemy, unsure of the exact aim of the invasion—Sparta herself? her port at Gytheum? the Laconian countryside? Messenia?—is unable to marshal at any given point. When it does mass in force and seek resistance (i.e., at Sparta itself), it can be easily bypassed and outflanked to pursue other easier targets (e.g., Laconian farms and harbors). Sherman and Patton both were masters of just that flexibility in attack. The Spartans knew about as much of Epaminondas's real intention as those Confederate troops holed up in Augusta and Macon, waiting in terror of Sherman as he simply marched on by.[58]

Finally, there is the general himself, and the idea that one man out of 70,000 was the difference between victory and defeat. Nepos closed his life of Epaminondas with the remark that the career of Epaminondas proved that "one man was worth more than the entire citizen body." It was an unfortunate truth, not an idle boast, when in his dying breadth Epaminondas purportedly

116

told his men to make peace since there was now "not a general left among them." Sherman by 1864 was worth far more to the Union cause than an entire corps; Patton's value was incalculable to the Allied cause. Individuals do count—often a difficult concept to grasp in a democracy, when the reigning ideology is that we all are more or less of the same caliber, or insignificant agents in a larger inevitable predetermined structure of consensual government, personal freedom, and market capitalism. Just as it is inconceivable to imagine a march through Georgia led by anyone but Sherman—even Grant and perhaps Sheridan would have lacked the audacity and expertise—or the Third Army breaking out and racing through Normandy in August under another American general like Mark Clark, so too it was with Epaminondas, the only man alive in Greece who could have assembled, led, and brought back intact such a huge force.

There was one key ingredient to Epaminondas's military career that perhaps stands as an exemplar of democratic leadership. Such generals must not be timid or afraid, must not lead their army in the very manner in which they themselves are audited and held accountable by a democratic consensus. Epaminondas by all accounts was a zealot and a fanatic—Sherman and Patton perhaps even more so. The worst generals in the ancient and modern worlds were those with a constant feel for the pulse of the assembly or board of overseers—a Nicias in Sicily or Cleombrotus of Sparta, the worrisome politico, a McClellan always fearful of losing the wonderful army that he is entrusted with, or a Halleck careful not to offend his fellow generals and superiors who monitor his command.

Armies are not assemblies. The conduct of war is not a discussion over taxes or public expenditures. The very qualities that make a poor democratic statesman in peacetime—audacity, fatalism, truthfulness, fearlessness, initiative, hatred of compromise, fanaticism, even recklessness—are critical for command of a great egalitarian army, just as the strengths of a politician—affability, consensus-building, retrospection, manners, inactivity even—can prove lethal on campaign. Other Boeotians may have been better statesmen than Epaminondas; all of them would have ruined the army of 370–369. Bradley and Hodges were more circumspect, kinder, maybe even better men than Patton; McClellan, Halleck, and Hooker likewise more politically savvy and accommodating than Sherman—and all of them far less successful in keeping a large army always fed, arrogant, murderous, and on the move against the enemy. In that context we can understand that Epaminondas's plunge into the Spartan line at Mantinea, Sherman's front-line rallying at Shiloh, and Patton's constant presence amid gunfire were not examples of mock-heroic leadership, nor the antics of a youthful, demented, and often drunken beserker like Alexander, but the logical personal expression of the command of a democratic muster on the move.

I think it is almost axiomatic that if a general of a great democratic march is not hated, is not sacked, tried, or relieved of command by his auditors after his tenure is over, or if he has not been killed or wounded at the van, he has *not* utilized the full potential of his men, has not accomplished his strategic goals—in short, he is too representative of the very culture that produced him, too democratic to lead a democratic army of marchers and plunderers. Would that the American generals Schwarzkopf or Powell had risked resigning for insisting that American troops march onto Baghdad to liquidate the Hussein regime!

Finally, we of the academic class are sometimes reluctant to equate mastery of military command with sheer intellectual brilliance. But to lead an army of thousands into enemy territory requires mental skills far beyond that of the professor, historian, or journalist—far beyond too the accounting and managerial skill of the deskbound and peacetime officer corps. From Epaminondas's philosophical training, the corpus of his adages and sayings that have survived, and his singular idea to take 70,000 men into Laconia and Messenia, it is clear that, like both Sherman and Patton, he had a first-class mind and was adept in public speaking and knowledge of human behavior. Perhaps with the exception of Pericles and Scipio, it is hard to find any military leader in some twelve centuries of Graeco-Roman antiquity who had the natural intelligence, philosophical training, broad knowledge, and recognition of the critical tension between military morale and national ethics as Epaminondas the Theban. In his range of political and strategic thought, he towered over his Greek contemporaries—an Iphicrates, Chabrias, or Agesilaus—in precisely the way that Sherman did over all generals of the Civil War, precisely as Patton dwarfed his British and American superiors. In short, Epaminondas, the philosopher, may have been the best-educated man of action of the ancient world—an education that stressed logic, mathematics, rhetoric, memorization, philosophy, and literature, an education far more valuable to the leadership of great democratic armies than what is offered in most universities today.

The leader of such a march surely must be politician and anthropologist alike—his army by design changes the entire social structure of the land he enters, making slaves free, and the once wealthy and exploitive now poor. He must understand what war is and is for, a social phenomenon that is moral only when killing at the front and individual ruin to the rear are the synonymous wages of aggression and evil, when the moral ledger can place thousands of dead against thousands more freed and saved. If we are not to see again a great democratic march in our time, it may be that we have lost the ability simply to produce military leaders with the broad education and sense of history of an Epaminondas, Sherman, or Patton. When we do produce such men of strong views, it is likely that they will be considered failures or worse—at least until war's darkest hour. Let us hope it is not because we have lost the ability in an age of moral relativity to distinguish between largely evil and largely good.

Epaminondas's proper legacy is no less than the beginning of the great tradition of self-appraisal and military self-critique in the West—which at the core is the very struggle for the Western heritage itself. Discipline, order, separation of politics from religion and superstition, rationalism, science, and free inquiry can result in a military dynamism unseen anywhere else in the world—Spartan hoplites; Southern generalship, cotton gins, and majestic plantations; and Nazi Panzers are proof of the frightening wages of Hellenic and later European science and enlightenment.

But from that same culture also arises the more liberal tradition of civil rights, democracy, and consensual government that must fight to reclaim the Hellenic legacy from its fringe elements and rival claimants, who craft a labyrinth of hierarchies and supporting intellectual architecture to reward the naturally "gifted" who see the West as a racial rather than a cultural entity— an elite whose courage and audacity sometimes elicits a natural admiration and secret approbation among even the best of us. But when Epaminondas destroyed Sparta as a military power, he helped to reassert the humanity of the West, and so established a precedent for centuries to come: when there arose a distortion of the main evolutionary course of Western civilization— Spartan helotage, Southern slave society, National Socialism—there would often be an eventual terrible response from more liberal societies in order to reclaim the Western legacy that was properly theirs alone.

It is no accident that Epaminondas, Sherman, and Patton in the end turned out to be better war-makers than their purportedly ferocious enemy counterparts—the engine of the Western military dynamism is ultimately fueled best by an ethical agenda. The great march of 370–369, then, is a repudiation of a strain of Western culture—Plato and the Germanic tradition of Hegel, Nietzsche, and Spengler are good examples—that is always impatient with egalitarianism and democracy, ever eager to place us all for our own benefit in our proper places, to see race as the prerequisite of excellence.

In the end, the undeniable strength of Epaminondas was his sense of tragedy, so rare in modern democratic culture. His role was a Sophoclean one, that of an Ajax or Philoctetes keen to the growing realization that his was a struggle for an autonomous and yet federated Greece that Greeks themselves either no longer wanted or no longer were willing to sacrifice for. Faced with that realization that he was a better man than those Peloponnesians he aided, it was inevitable that he would come to prefer annihilation in battle to a timid complacence. He did not worry whether the destruction of Sparta might interrupt the balance of power; he did not care much whether Mantinea, Megalopolis, and Messenia might themselves later enter into recriminations and hostilities with one another or Thebes itself; he fretted little that his enemies in the assembly would try to execute him on return. Instead, he acted decisively for what he felt was right and let others decide whether it was prudent.

To the Greeks the legacy of Epaminondas and his army of a season was never questioned. Over half a millennium after his death the itinerant traveler Pausanias could still gaze at his statue and read his proud epitaph, which made it clear that Epaminondas felt his life work had been devoted to freeing those in bondage:

> By my plans was Sparta shorn of her glory,
> And holy Messenia at last received back her children.
> By the arms of Thebes was Megalopolis fortified
> And all of Greece, became independent and free.[59]

PART II
THE ARMY OF THE WEST

SHERMAN'S MARCH TO THE SEA

NOVEMBER 16–DECEMBER 21, 1864

1

THE PYTHON'S PARADE

WASHINGTON, D.C.

May 24, 1865

TWENTY-TWO HUNDRED and thirty-four years after Epaminondas's homecoming, a triumphant parade marched through Washington, D.C. By all contemporary accounts the army of William Tecumseh Sherman both delighted—and awed—the Washington crowd. Sherman himself, who rode with his men like a Roman *imperator*, was proud of that dual nature of his soldiers, an army of deadly democratic avengers that had burnt its way through Georgia in wonderful order, ruining for the cause of freedom the rich countryside in its path. The narrative of his memoirs closes with a description of that last ceremonial march of his men:

> It was, in my judgment, the most magnificent army in existence—sixty-five thousand men, in splendid physique, who had just completed a march of nearly two thousand miles in a hostile country. . . . The steadiness and firmness of the tread, the careful dress on the guides, the uniform intervals between the companies, all eyes directly to the front, and the tattered and bullet-riven flags, festooned with flowers, all attracted universal notice. Many good people, up to that time, had looked upon our Western army as a sort of mob; but the world then saw, and recognized the fact, that it was an army in the proper sense, well organized, well commanded and disciplined; and there was no wonder that it had swept through the South like a tornado. For six hours and a half the strong tread of the Army of the West resounded along

123

Pennsylvania Avenue; not a soul of that vast crowd of spectators left his place; and, when the rear of the column had passed by, thousands of the spectators still lingered to express their sense of confidence in the strength of a Government which could claim such an army.

Sherman himself would never have been content had his men simply marched in good order and discipline like Grant's Easterners in the Army of the Potomac. His "tornado," after all, was not exactly an Eastern army. Something else made his veterans, his perceived "mob" different, and he was not about to let the world forget it—many of his men had refused the newly issued blue parade uniforms, but kept on the ragged clothes worn continuously since the march through the woods of Georgia six months earlier. Sherman thus finished his description on a more Roman note:

> Each division was followed by six ambulances, as a representative of its baggage-train. Some of the division commanders had added, by way of variety, goats, milch-cows, and pack-mules, whose loads consisted of game-cocks, poultry, hams, etc., and some of them had the families of freed slaves along, with the women leading their children. Each division was preceded by its corps of black pioneers, armed with picks and spades. These marched abreast in double ranks, keeping perfect dress and step, and added much to the interest of the occasion.

Sherman's was an army that was wilder and more rugged than other Northern corps, and yet still far better equipped, disciplined, organized—and more lethal—than the battle-hardened veterans of the South it opposed in 1864. Just as Epaminondas's rustic Thebans had outshone their purportedly professional Arcadian allies and terrified the crack troops of Sparta, so too Sherman's Westerners, who had routed or bypassed all veteran Southern forces, also made the well-drilled and veteran Army of the Potomac look in comparison somewhat soft. For Sherman's men, the spring parade was just another—simply the last—day on the long march; but for Grant's troopers the ceremonial procession was something quite unlike the months of crawling and digging in the mud of Virginia. Other observers that May afternoon at once perceived the Westerners' army's incongruous ferocity and recklessness beneath its veneer of seeming order and precision. On the following day, May 24, the *New York Times* described Sherman's army as "tall, erect, broad shouldered men, the peasantry of the west, the best material on earth for armies. The brigades move by with an elastic step."

Most contemporaries naturally compared Grant's and Sherman's men, noting that it was much harder to distinguish officers from enlisted men in the Army of the West. Sherman's troops walked, even talked, differently from other corps; they somehow seemed "more intelligent, self-reliant, and determined." Marching through an enemy country and destroying its economic infrastructure and social strata—while losing less than 1 percent of an army—can instill confidence in soldiers in a way that camp life, entrenchment, and even ferocious set battles cannot.

Sherman's enlisted men themselves were aware that the Union's other great army had settled in Virginia and ended there, while they had started in Tennessee, marched through Georgia and the Carolinas, and finished their circle ten months later right beside the sluggish Army of the Potomac. A soldier from the 7th Iowa wrote—perhaps rather unfairly—of Sherman's men and the Army of the Potomac, "The difference in the two armies is this: They have remained in camp and lived well; we have marched, fought and gone hungry and ended the war." A Minnesota recruit scoffed of the Easterners, "The more I see of this Army [Potomac] the more I am disgusted with operations for the last years. If there had been an army worth anything here, Richmond would have fallen three years ago."[1]

Sherman's veterans failed to appreciate that their corps, except for normal furloughs, were one and the same army that had left Atlanta a half a year earlier. In that sense, their esprit de corps was more akin to Epaminondas's hoplites than to Grant's army, which, in contrast, was in reality a continually metamorphosing body. In its revolving-door manner of mustering, thousands of its crack troops were to be killed in a series of harrowing assaults in the Wilderness (May 5–12, 1864), Cold Harbor (June 3, 1864), and outside Petersburg (June–October 1864), always to be replaced by a continual stream of raw and often anonymous human fodder. In a way, the Army of the Potomac was not an army at all, but an abstraction, an organization that facilitated the recruitment of mostly adolescents, their brief training, their charges into battle, ending all too often a few weeks or months later in their deaths or injuries. To Grant and his army, men—in the general and brutal sense of sheer manpower that shot iron into the flesh of the enemy—were the key to Northern victory; in contrast, the Westerners under Sherman believed that their *particular* men alone would both win and survive the war.

All Union troops in both armies sensed that dichotomy: by late summer 1864, those with Sherman felt that in the year to come they would live, while a great many with Grant knew they would probably die. Not one soldier in Sherman's army pinned paper with his name to his back—the nineteenth-century equivalent of dog tags—as he marched toward battle. The Ohioan C. B. Welton wrote home of his general that Sherman "was a great military genius who depends upon his brains to win his victories instead of the lives of his men." An officer on General Thomas's staff agreed that Sherman knew "it is sometimes much easier to fight with the legs and feet than with muskets and cannon."[2]

The outward appearance of invincibility of the Westerners was due in large part to the fact that they had fought and marched together for over a year and had survived the ordeal. When General Peter Osterhaus's 15th Corps marched past the Washington reviewing stand—they had occupied the southern wing during Sherman's March to the Sea—the German ambassador remarked, "An army like that could whip all Europe." Of the 20th Corps— half of Sherman's renamed Army of Georgia—that followed, he added, "An army like that could whip the world." And finally when its sister corps, the 14th under the fiery General Jefferson C. Davis, passed, he concluded, "An army like that could whip the devil."

In the same manner that Epaminondas's Thebans stood apart from their Arcadian allies when they entered Laconia, so too Sherman's men were intimidating even to their own Union comrades. Before they were removed to the opposite bank of the Potomac, the Westerners in camp habitually picked fights with Easterners, drank, were disobedient, and required Sherman himself to ride out into the streets at night to calm his men. Some had no shoes. All were sunburnt from their last leg through the Carolinas. Blacks from Georgia and the Carolinas marched proudly in the ranks, and the men still carried plunder from the plantations of the South.[3]

Why this nearly unanimous verdict on the superiority of Sherman's men? They had fought in few bloodbaths like the Army of the Potomac's against Lee—nothing quite like Gettysburg, the Wilderness, or Cold Harbor. Nearly two-thirds of all Northern casualties in the Civil War came from the Army of the Potomac, which had continuously battled Robert E. Lee's crack Army of Northern Virginia for over three years.

The answer was nevertheless clear to the thousands of onlookers in Washington: Sherman's men had marched, moved hundreds of miles, and survived, whereas too many of Grant's were fixed and had died. The former had sliced through hostile territory and freed slaves, destroyed property, and brought fire and ruin to the enemy; the latter fought not far from home, pitted against like military kind, and had rarely touched the economy that fueled the enemy. The South would hate Sherman, whose troops had killed relatively few Confederates, for a century to come, but come to forgive Grant their future president, whose army butchered its best soldiers—a propensity to value property over life. By April 1865, Grant at horrendous cost had at last overwhelmed the best of the Confederate army; Sherman at little human expenditure defeated the very soul of the Confederate citizenry with a force that was mobile, patently ideological, and without experience of defeat. These facts the crowds in Washington knew, and the rugged appearance of Sherman's army now confirmed their previous belief in his army's singular ability to destroy the enemy without destroying itself.[4]

Yet Americans had not always been so impressed by the Union armies. Less than a year earlier, Northerners were despondent and gradually coming to the realization that winning the war of more than three years' duration required something more than the defeat of Southern soldiers in the field or even the occupation of Confederate state capitals. Even when Sherman arrived on the outskirts of Atlanta in the summer of 1864, there was no guarantee that the war was likely to be won by the North at all—or that Lincoln would be reelected to a second term in the fall. Nothing less, it seemed, than a new mentality of war-making—or an armistice—was needed to conclude this most horrible of American conflicts.

Spectacular Northern battlefield successes in the past had not translated into the collapse of Southern morale or even of the Confederacy's ability to field new armies. The Union string of victories in 1862 along the Mississippi, at Shiloh, Antietam, and Perryville, and the presence of ponderous and plodding Union armies a few miles from Richmond led to vast numbers of Southerners killed, territory lost, and communications disrupted—but *not* to a crippling of the Southern desire or ability to continue war, as the subsequent recoveries by Jackson in the Shenandoah Valley and Lee's stand against McClellan in the encounters during the Seven Days prove. Even the second wave of dramatic and brilliant campaigns in the summer of 1863—at Gettysburg, Vicksburg, and Chattanooga—did not make the South sue for peace. Before those successes, the Confederates had been victorious at Fredericksburg and Chancellorsville. Even after that summer of Northern optimism, the South would rally to stand firm against Union troops at the Wilderness and Spotsylvania (May 5–19, 1864). Cold Harbor (June 3, 1864) was a bloodbath for Grant's men. By June 1864, the Northern armies had lost 90,000 in just the last two months of fighting. The *New York World* asked the question, "Who shall revive the withered hopes that bloomed at the opening of Grant's campaign?"

It was not clear how much longer the Northern public would stand for further catastrophic losses in Grant's trenches and for Lincoln's policy—whether inadvertent or not—of the "terrible arithmetic": trading horrendous fatalities with the South on the premise that the Confederates would exhaust their manpower reserves first. The now accustomed reversal after each promising Union battle success bred cynicism, and soon contempt for Lincoln. By mid-1864 there was the resigned acknowledgment that even a victory in battle was unlikely to end Southern resistance on purely Northern terms.[5]

While it is true that the North enjoyed considerable superiority in human and material resources, by late 1864 the traditional advantages that accrue to the defense in a war of attrition were starting to play an increasingly prominent role. The South need not win, only not lose. As it was stripped of its territory to the west of the Mississippi and south of Tennessee, its shorter interior lines alleviated problems of supply and movement—as the Spartans learned when they were under siege in Laconia and did not venture into Boeotia, and as the Germans discovered during their retreats before the Americans in late 1944 and early 1945. As the Northern armies advanced southward from Tennessee into Alabama and Georgia in 1864, garrisons were left at towns and railroad junctions to occupy and protect territorial gains. So Sherman's army shrunk, even as his opponent's grew from desperate calls to resist the invader of their homes. Moderate Union success did not ensure greater recruitment from a tired and complacent Northern citizenry; greater Southern failure demanded wider participation from the desperate secession-ists to save the homeland.

From now on, brave Confederate soldiers would be fighting not on Northern or Border State ground, but almost always on their own home soil. They would not even be killing any longer for abstractions like states' rights or plantation slavery, but rather battling desperately to repel invading troops from their sacred earth. Fortification and entrenchment—the dirty arena where casualties soared—would now serve as more frequent points of resis-tance, as defenders were given direct aid from civilians and guerrilla bands alike. More and more Northerners conceded that if the Union were to win, they must either annihilate almost all the Confederate zealots in uniform— Sherman's dictum that "We must *kill* those three hundred thousand"—or find some other way of bringing the costs of war home to the Southern populace itself. If the North had mixed results in defeating Confederate soldiers in bat-tle, how could it invade and subdue the entire territory of the South itself?

It is often remarked that the North had a potentially mobilizable popula-tion four times the size of the South; but in actuality the Confederacy had nearly doubled the North's rate of recruitment from their respective man-power pools. In terms of actual men recruited into the army—950,000 for the South, 2,100,000 on the Union side—the Confederacy had an army almost half the size of the North, not a decisive disadvantage for a Southern force that was to repel invaders as it fought on familiar ground with access to local supplies.[6]

Their land southeast of the Mississippi was no small country, but still a gi-gantic region of millions of free citizens and over 4,000,000 black slaves; and even a truncated Confederacy comprised a geographical expanse alone far larger than most nations in Europe. The South's comparatively backward transportation network might now favor the defenders, who knew local terrain and the idiosyncrasies of provincial rail lines, and could move more easily on less well known and traveled roads. Northern forces—blockading the coast, patrolling the Mississippi, occupying the West, responsible for the distant frontier, entrenched between Washington and Richmond—would be even farther afield, spread thinner, harder to supply, and more dependent on long, single, and vulnerable railroad lines.[7]

To all Southerners there was no tomorrow in defeat, and an understandable hysteria about Northern invaders: their entry east of the Mississippi and south of Tennessee threatened a complete end to the entire antebellum way of life, and a surrender to the new, growing—and mostly foreign—culture spreading throughout the North. Not just slavery was to be gone and the South's peculiar notion of states' rights. Defeat also, the planters believed, meant an embrace of laissez-faire capitalism, increased materialism, massive immigration, urbanization—all antithetical to the rural and agrarian hierarchies of the past. Southerners, in short, despite the vast geographical extent of the slaveholding states, were as far removed from the mainstream of North American life as the Spartans were from the other Greek city-states. Whether this blinkered perception was entirely true or not, Southern elites in a newly reconstituted Federal Union feared a crass, egalitarian morass, where a radically heartless and soulless market—not status gained at birth— would govern the opportunity of all citizens in America. Success and status would be found solely in profit, not in inherited reputation. The states, in this often paranoid view, would slowly give up local cultures and rights in exchange for an all-encompassing Federal government that would lead all to a more uniform America through greater taxation, transportation, communication, and national expenditures. As Mr. Lincoln and his Union generals insisted on unconditional surrender, the end of slavery, and the specter of an egalitarian nation where race and class were in theory to be subordinate ideas, so recalcitrant Southerners by the summer of 1864 dug in deeper for their Armageddon to come.

In contrast to the fanaticism of the Lost Cause, there was real opposition in the North to the Union effort of total war. Copperheads and traditional Democrats were agitating at best for different presidential leadership—someone other than Lincoln who might bring about either a return of the Confederacy to the Union with slavery intact, or an agreement to let the South go in peace and become a second kindred American nation on North American soil. At worst, outright Southern sympathizers in the North welcomed an admission of Union defeat. Racial prejudice and self-interest were constant choruses—why send thousands of free whites to die for Southern Negro slaves? Liberating slaves by presidential edict in the abstract was not the same thing as sending thousands of young white Northern boys down South either to die or to kill other white adolescents to ensure that blacks were free to leave their masters. Of course, there were Unionists in the Confederacy and quarrels among the worn fabric of the increasingly self-interested and bickering Southern states, but politics in early 1864 was far more volatile in the North. Opposition there was more likely to change the administration and the very policy of continuing the war unabated. Ironically, Lincoln, not Jefferson Davis, whose economy was in fact on the verge of collapse, was more likely to be run out of office. By the same token, the former would be assassinated, while the latter would live to an honorable old age among recalcitrant secessionists. So too was Epaminondas put on trial in the aftermath of his greatest triumph, even as the defeated King Agesilaus faced no such challenge from within his collapsing society, and would outlive the far younger Theban. In a slave society at war, democracy functions poorly, if at all, and in its eleventh hour has little choice but to trust in the will of its last fanatic.[8]

Then, abruptly, in autumn 1864 one man at the head of more than 60,000 of their soldiers ended for good all the Northern worries. Now there was a general and an army that could march into the heart of the South, free the slaves, destroy the prospects of the enemy where it hurt most, and come through unscathed—and *mirabile dictu* could articulate as no other Union leader except Lincoln why and how the South would lose through an entirely new concept of "total war." So in understandable wonder mixed with trepidation the jubilant crowds this May afternoon cheered their slightly crazy, red-haired general William Tecumseh Sherman and "the most magnificent army in existence"—this rumpled fellow and his boys who had brought them victory when victory was not foreseen.

In November 1864 the citizens of the Confederacy were about to be squeezed precisely in the manner as the Spartans had been by Epaminondas so many centuries earlier. "All sorts of colors, over a wild monotony of columns, began to sway to and fro, up and down," the *New York World* wrote of the May 23 entrance of Sherman and his army into the streets of the nation's capital, "and like the uncoiling of a tremendous python, the Army of Sherman winds into Washington."

2

THE IDEA

ATLANTA, GEORGIA

November 16, 1864—First Day Out

ON SEPTEMBER 2, General Sherman's men had taken Atlanta after a brilliant, though brutal summer of campaigning in Tennessee and northern Georgia. Now it was about time to leave. No soldiers in the army that set out on the morning of November 16 believed that in six months they would complete a circuit through Georgia, the Carolinas, and Virginia, occupy three state capitals, and end up as conquerors marching in the streets of the capital more than a thousand miles away. After all, there were still nearly 200,000 Confederate veterans in uniform on the front lines, and most of the Southern populace had not been greatly hurt by the conflict.

In this third week of November 1864, Northern fortunes already had begun to change for the better. Just two days earlier the recently elected President Lincoln had accepted the formal resignation of General George McClellan from the regular army. The once "drunk" Grant and "insane" Sherman were at the head of rare veteran forces that were larger, better equipped, and more confident than their Confederate counterparts. Since the prior May, Sherman had continuously maneuvered three combined Union armies of over 100,000 men southward until they had cut all rail links with Atlanta, outflanked the Confederate defenses, and forced the defenders to either leave or face capture. Shortly after entry into Atlanta in early September, Sherman had expelled under protest the civilian population and then garrisoned the

131

city. Now after returning from chasing the remaining Confederate armies of John Bell Hood northward, Sherman's force—nursed on victory and increasingly infused with its commander's ideological zeal—was leaving the city afire and its industry in ruins. Sergeant Rice Bull, one of some 60,000 Union infantrymen who were leaving Atlanta, was imbued with his general's lesson that the maker of the bullet was as polemical as the man who shot it. As he marched out from the city, he remarked of the view of the burning city:

> All the public property and store houses, factories and machine shops where materials had been manufactured or stored for the Confederate Army that still remained had been set on fire. Their destruction meant the whole city; for when the blaze started there was no one to prevent its spread to all the business and residential districts. Soon we were out of sight of burning Atlanta but the smoke rose in black columns and was visible all day.

An Indiana sergeant also looked back as the army headed east into the heart of Georgia and observed, "A whole city, as it were, on fire and the smoke and flame ascending and mingling with the clouds. Were I to live a thousand years I never should forget that scene."[9]

All telegraph lines and railroads linking Sherman's army to the North had been cut on November 12. In early morning on November 15, Atlanta was still burning. Sherman was now marching virtually unopposed out into the Georgia countryside beyond. For the first time in his life he had complete freedom of will and the confidence and support of his nation to do what he pleased. General Grant at last had relented and approved his unorthodox plan of departure, conceding on November 2, "I do not see that you can withdraw from where you are to follow Hood, without giving up all we had gained in territory. I say, then, go on as you propose."[10]

Years later Sherman wrote about the morning of his departure:

> We rode out of Atlanta by the Decatur road, filled by the marching troops and wagons of the Fourteenth Corps; and reaching the hill, just outside of the old rebel works, we naturally paused to look back upon the scenes of our past battles. We stood upon the very ground whereon was fought the bloody battle of July 22nd, and could see the copse of wood where McPherson fell. Behind us lay Atlanta, smoldering and in ruins, the black smoke rising high in air, and hanging like a pall over the ruined city. Away off in the distance, on the McDonough road, was the rear of Howard's column, the gun-barrels glistening in the sun, the white-topped wagons stretching away to the south; and right before us the Fourteenth Corps, marching steadily and rapidly, with a cheery look and swinging pace, that made light of the thousand miles that lay be-

tween us and Richmond. Some band, by accident, struck up the anthem of "John Brown's soul goes marching on"; the men caught up the strain, and never before or since have I heard the chorus of "Glory, glory, hallelujah!" done with more spirit, or in better harmony of time and place.

Then we turned our horses' heads to the east; Atlanta was soon lost behind the screen of trees, and became a thing of the past. Around it clings many a thought of desperate battle, of hope and fear, that now seem like the memory of a dream; and I have never seen the place since.[11]

But where exactly was Sherman going with his army of 62,000 men? How was he to move without railroads, telegraphic messages, or supporting corps? And why alone of seasoned Union generals and Northern politicians did he desire to cut loose from safety, and march through the heart of the Georgia countryside unaided? There were reasons, after all, why no Greek army had dared to march into Laconia before Epaminondas—and why no Northern general believed that he could traverse through the heart of the Confederacy without lines of supply, constant communications, and accessible reinforcement.

The orthodox alternative would have been to leave a large Union garrison to hold Atlanta, detail sizable parties to keep all the rail lines northward open, and then gradually move back toward Tennessee to trap and engage the last large Confederate army in the West of some 40,000 commanded by Hood. Military doctrine as taught at West Point emphasized destruction of enemy armies, maintenance of supply corridors, and close correlation and communication with various allied and auxiliary forces. One did not march forward with an enemy army roaming around at one's rear.

By mid-October, Sherman had essentially tried the traditional options. He had backtracked almost a hundred miles into Tennessee, where he had started the prior spring, all in a fruitless search to trap Hood's 40,000 men and force them to fight. And now he was growing increasingly tired of watching Hood and his Confederates play Sherman, as Southerners destroyed railroads and moved freely and unexpectedly to the rear of new advanced Northern lines in northern Georgia and southern Tennessee. Besides, Hood's army seemed to grow and thrive on keeping out of reach as it destroyed property, Sherman's to shrink as he chased and guarded.

Not that this conventional approach advocated by Grant and others did not have merits. As a huge occupation force, Sherman's troops could be based in Atlanta and they could be supplied by rail as they bird-dogged Hood or made regular though limited forays into the countryside of Alabama and Georgia. Land taken in Georgia would be held permanently by troops and protected from insurrectionists and terrorists. The eventual destruction or forced isolation of Hood's forces would leave only Lee's army in Virginia as a major threat to the North, and thus ensure the ongoing liberation of Tennessee. Sherman could become a proconsul of sorts in a vast province in which his Westerners took on the steady and safe role of legions of occupation—with luck ending their service by 1866 or perhaps 1867, not as fighters but as constabularies on a thousand-mile frontier. Just as Benjamin Butler had done in New Orleans in the latter part of 1862, so Sherman might ensconce himself in Atlanta as a virtual military dictator, surrounded by posh quarters and an enormous staff, assuring his superiors that northern Georgia was now pacified as he waited patiently and safely for Grant to grind up Lee.[12]

Sherman disliked the entire idea of stasis. Quartering his army in cities repelled him. He hated even more following an enemy army solely in search of a glorious victory on the field of battle. He would be stripping his own forces continually, leaving garrisons behind until he caught up with Hood—and then possibly to be forced to root him out of fortified positions without much numerical superiority. "Damn him," Sherman remarked to his aides of Hood's evasiveness. "If he will go to the Ohio River, I'll give him rations. . . . Let him go north, my business is down south."

Better, Sherman now thought, to allow Hood to outmaneuver himself from the very territory his Southerners were supposed to defend. Let Hood go north and Sherman go south, and then see which army could and could not survive and do the greater damage. Let Hood try to cut the supply lines of a Union army, while Sherman would cut the supplies lines of the entire Confederate nation. Let Hood in his infinite wisdom get ever more to the rear of Sherman, while Sherman gained in the exchange an ever clearer path into the heart of the Confederacy. Southerners deemed themselves great raiders and marauders, who harassed fixed garrisons and terrorized timid populations. Sherman would now give the Confederacy the raid of its life—"a raid," as he put it, "that will make the South feel the terrible character of our people." So Sherman's plans were now set: "Instead of being on the defensive, I would be on the offensive; instead of guessing at what he means to do, he would have to guess at my plans. The difference in war would be fully twenty-five percent." Both Epaminondas and Patton would have agreed.

Frontal assaults, as Sherman had learned earlier that spring at Kennesaw Mountain, were often lethal to the attacker, who, even if victorious, might lose more men than the defeated. As Grant was beginning to realize in Virginia, horrific casualties were also fatal to the morale of the survivors in an army, and undermined the will to continue the fight in a consensual society at large—the Army of the Potomac would lose more men in any four-week period of that latter part of 1864 than Sherman's Westerners would in six months. If Sherman, present at the very first and last of the major battles of the Civil War, had learned anything from the fighting, it was the importance of keeping recruits alive and turning them into skilled veterans, crack shots who knew how to handle waves of advancing Rebs. His aide, Henry Hitchcock, remarked on the march through Georgia:

> No man in the army is bolder or more rapid and daring than Sherman, whether personally or as a General; but no man is more unwilling to throw away his men. I have repeatedly heard him say that the best way, he thought, to win battles was more by the movement of troops than by fighting. On this campaign in particular he has expressed his determination not to damage this army—"it's too valuable." His men all understand this thing in him, and hence their unbounded confidence in him.[13]

Troops stationed in camps and field fortifications, often near towns, especially in the late fall and winter, were more likely to die of illness and disease than of enemy bullets. To Sherman, of all the generals in the Civil War, goes the credit for understanding that camp life, not travail on the march, was fatal to the health of a huge army. The natural milieu for the Western soldier in the Union army was outdoor living, physical exertion, and constant activity; Sherman, the Ohio native, knew what his men needed because he knew himself—this sickly asthmatic who was free of discomfort only when he was riding through the South at the head of his army.

Even if his cumbersome army survived battle and sickness and then cornered Hood, Sherman would be restrained in his movements by the necessity of basing his logistical lifeline on the railroad—for much of its path a single track. In the past, whereas rail destruction isolated Atlanta, now these same rail lines were critical for keeping his own soldiers fed—his army, after all, was far larger than the prewar population of the city itself. His men in September and October had rebuilt more tracks than they had destroyed the prior summer. He summed up both his frustrations and hopes in a telegraph to Grant:

> It will be a physical impossibility to protect the roads, now that Hood, Forrest, Wheeler, and the whole hatch of devils, are turned loose without home or battalion.... I propose that we break up the railroad from Chattanooga forward, and that we strike out with our wagons for Milledgeville, Millen, and Savannah. Until we can repopulate Georgia, it is useless for us to occupy it; but the utter destruction of its roads, houses, and people, will cripple their military re-

sources. By attempting to hold the roads, we will lose a thousand men a month, and will gain no result. I can make this march, and make Georgia howl![14]

Sherman himself knew that his own military forte had never been battle tactics—he had an innate distaste for losing his men in an endless series of head-on attacks, which might not lead directly to strategic gains. And he was not even a keen pursuer of the defeated; unlike an Alexander or Napoleon, Sherman never cared much for the Cannae-like extermination of a defeated army that ostensibly should be the goal of every great tactician. At Bentonville, the last major battle of the Civil War, he may have more or less let General Johnston's Southerners escape, sacrificing the glory of an encirclement and annihilation of the enemy on the grounds that the fighting would end in a few days and thus killing the doomed was essentially redundant.

For all his bluster Sherman was uncomfortable with the idea of killing thousands in a war he increasingly felt was near to ending—especially when he viewed his enemies as fellow Americans temporarily taken leave of their senses. His mind much preferred to see war beyond battle victories and defeats, in a larger strategic canvas that involved the complex relationship of a free citizenry, its elected officials, and the government's will to maintain the material and spiritual support of armies in the field. In this greater context he was beginning to have a feel for the Confederacy and the vital forces that had led to its secession and survival under the direst of circumstances. War against the secessionists must be in some sense far crueler than practiced thus far, but it need not necessarily mean more deaths. The Confederacy was a treasonous state, Sherman reasoned, but its people were not beyond redemption if someone might show them the true costs of their own impetuosity.

The South's life spirit was not its infantry, but rather the remarkable morale and determination of its civilian population. Thus far in the war, much of the interior of Georgia, Alabama, Mississippi, and the Carolinas was more distant from the ongoing battle inferno than was the United States capital in Washington. Despite occasional Union raiding, millions of Confederate citizens remained unperturbed on well-stocked farms in Mississippi and Alabama; large cities of some industry like Atlanta, Savannah, and Macon were untouched; and small communities with polemical governments and fiery newspapers hitherto had urged their armies onward without suffering the direct consequences of their actions. On the eve of his departure from Atlanta, Sherman wrote Halleck:

This movement is not purely military or strategic, but it will illustrate the vulnerability of the South. They don't know what war means, but when the rich planters of Oconee and Savannah see their fences and corn and hogs and sheep vanish before their eyes they will have something more than a mean opinion of the "Yanks."

To an uncanny degree, Sherman was able to transmit this ideological fervor throughout his army. "It is evident our soldiers are determined to burn, plunder, and destroy everything in their way on this march. Well, that shows they are not afraid of the South at any rate, and that each individual soldier is determined to strike with all his might against the rebellion, whether we ever get through or not."

As for Southern guerrillas, mounted raiders, and sharpshooters who might wage a dirty war against both Sherman's ponderous columns and the small garrisons he would be forced to leave behind, why not reverse the equation? Let the Rebels, not he, worry about protecting territory. He would no longer garrison and protect Southern ground, but destroy it—and then move on. Let the enemy have the parched earth of Georgia in the Army of the West's wake. Any small protective garrisons stripped from a larger army would be Confederate, not Union. The latter army would move in mass, not occupying land, but making the very occupation of ruined territory an absurdity. Armies fight over land with value—either to protect or to acquire it. But land ceases to be of worth to a military force when it is deserted, charred, or robbed clean. Land and its impoverished inhabitants become near liabilities for the other side. Army garrisons must fix supply lines and protect railroads when they plan to occupy cities and towns or retrace their steps; they can abandon, destroy, and forget about infrastructure when they press ahead with no intention or need of returning—and no army, we should remember, is more mobile and reckless than a democratic muster of young recruits.

Negro slaves, the great moral question at the heart of the struggle, were to a large extent still in bondage and in that regard aiding the Confederate material effort. What was now needed was a bold stroke that would accomplish three vital aims at once—employ the act of emancipation as moral counterweight against the necessary brutality of fire and ruin; rob the South of its servile labor—or at least disrupt it—and gain zealous thousands of former slaves as both workers and soldiers in a cause that was their own. In addition, information about the nature of Union troops in the South was stale and inaccurate, as the Confederate populace was fed yesterday's lies. It still nursed the comfortable image of the enemy as a massive but unworkable army of forced conscripts and immigrants off the boat who could not stand up to Southern manhood—the multicultural Army of the Potomac having been stymied for years in Virginia by Lee's smaller but more heroic and ethical defenders. A march into the bowels of the South, Sherman felt, where women, children, and the aged had not before experienced the mayhem at the front, would show the populace the real battle mettle of Union troops and the kind of men it might field. Later, Patton would deem it vital that the German people see that his Third Army was not—as Nazi propaganda said of American GIs—a motley mob of cowboys and gangsters, but a deadly army that had annihilated the very best of the Wehrmacht and roamed freely through the fatherland.

As Captain Daniel Oakley put it, "The march through Georgia has been called a grand military promenade, all novelty and excitement. But its moral effect on friend and foe was immense. It proved our ability to lay open the heart of the Confederacy, and left the question of what we might do next a matter of doubt and terror." Sherman's appearance en masse also would lay to rest the absurd Southern notion that, if given a choice, blacks would prefer to remain on the plantations. A chaplain of an Ohio regiment, George Pepper, gives a picturesque image of the effect of the army as it passed through Georgia:

> Winding columns, glittering muskets, glowing flags, General's cavalcades, wagon trains, stragglers, and thousands of negroes in the rear, stretching over miles, a country of level fields, crossed by streams, broken occasionally by swamps and patches of forest, the distant smoke of fires, ragged villages and ragged hovels by the way; at intervals a woman's head peeping out from a door or a window, quickly closed, at times, a colored family, voluble with questions, thanking God for the advent, and joining in the march with their kind in the rear.[15]

The Confederacy, perhaps the Union too, had thus far failed to understand the new complex relationship between war and morality in the industrial age. To Sherman's modern way of thinking, the family who shipped livestock and wheat to a Confederate quartermaster was a key proponent of war. Without them, the Confederate army would starve and soon quit. The soldier at least realized he was an honest combatant and took full measure of the consequences of his aggression. What a strange morality, Sherman thought! Both sides hitherto had allowed a bloodbath of the nation's youth, in the naïve and illogical assumption that a citizenry's property should survive when its sons would not. "I propose to demonstrate the vulnerability of the South," Sherman, the realist, grimly announced, "and make its inhabitants feel that war and individual ruin are synonymous terms." In Sherman's mind the real immorality was in separating war and personal catastrophe, not in combining them. Implicit in Sherman's plan was to rend the fabric of Southern society, and make it clear that the plantation class which brought on the conflict would at last pay for their folly. If the lesser craftsmen, farmers, and mechanics were ruined by his swath through Georgia, then perhaps they would learn the wages of their blind faith in a selfish elite.[16]

Practically, the idea behind the March to the Sea is easy to grasp, once one understands Sherman's obsession with strategic thinking and his keen sense of what constituted the true moral practice of war. The material losses of the Confederates to his burners and ravagers would be immense—he would later claim at Savannah to have ruined $100,000,000 in property in Georgia alone. This estimate may *not* have been an exaggeration if we figure in declines in labor proficiency, the material ramifications of psychological stress, the loss of slaves, and the decreased productivity of those servants who stayed on the plantation.

Devastation would not be a case of skirmishers in a cool northern countryside trying to torch orchards and vineyards among stone fences and brick houses, but rather ravagers in forests and grainfields of a hot climate, replete with dry fodder, fence rails, wooden houses, all readily combustible after a long arid summer. And the Union army would be traveling through the food belt of the South. The South, like Laconia before, would suffer as it fed its enemies, as black slaves, like Laconian Helots, guided ravagers to caches of food and fodder on their way to freedom.

If his army lived off the land, Sherman would be free of logistical constraint and the enemy unsure of his exact move once he set out cross-country. Would he head for Macon or Augusta? End up in Savannah, or to the north in South Carolina or to the south in Florida? It depended. He would bypass any region heavily defended for the other not so, or might feint at both and go in between. Either horn of the dilemma will be worth a battle. "I would prefer his [Bragg's] holding Augusta (as the probabilities are)," Sherman wrote, "for then, with the Savannah River in our possession, the taking of Augusta will be a mere matter of time." Gone then was the idea of a predictable linear march after an identifiable goal. Sherman in contrast was now "cutting loose," and neither his Union superiors, his own marchers, his Confederate enemies—nor he himself—knew exactly where his serpentine columns would slither next.

"The fact is our army is spread out into so many columns, marching in so many different directions, threatening so many different points, and careering over the country in such *apparent* disorder, yet really good order," Major James Connolly wrote, "that the rebels can't really make up their minds *where* we are going or *what* we intend to do, and fearing that we might just catch them in some trap, are just digging dirt and hiding behind breastworks at Augusta and Savannah." The key to Epaminondas's entry into the supposedly impenetrable frontier of Laconia was the radical division of his huge army into four corps who breached the border separately. When Patton neared Germany, his army was spread along a two-hundred-mile front, heading in three different directions. The success of all such marches into the enemy interior was in having a general who could disperse his forces to such a degree that the enemy had no real idea of either his immediate route or his ultimate destination.

Sherman alone would decide daily the course of 62,000 men in transit, as the enemy resistance unfolded and it became clear where he might do the most material and psychological damage to the Georgian citizenry and lose the fewest men in the process. His huge python might shrink and expand its girth as it wound through the heart of Georgia between the two key cities of Augusta and Macon, threatening to swallow both but besieging neither, instead always destroying the main rail links of the greater Confederacy. More astute Southerners in Richmond remarked at the outset that Sherman sought "to induce the collection of troops at points at which he seemed to be aiming and then he has passed them by, leaving the troops useless and unavailable."[17]

Would he not be bypassing solid Confederate resistance, leaving solid pockets of enemy opposition at his rear? It depended on how one defined "resistance" and "opposition." Once it was known that he "had made Georgia howl," desertion from the Southern front, impassioned letters from the rear, turmoil in the Confederate press, recrimination among the Southern leadership—all this and more would do as much as Union bullets to thin the ranks of the enemy. A Southern garrison army left alone in Augusta was more likely to dissipate as men hurried to protect their families or to be forever blamed and discredited as plantations went up in smoke while healthy soldiers were idle. As one of Sherman's generals, Jacob Cox, saw the march:

> A region isolated from the rest of the Confederacy would not furnish men or money, and could not furnish supplies; while anxiety for their families, who were within the National lines, tempted the soldiers from those States to desert, and weakened the confidence of the whole army. In such a situation credit would be destroyed, the Confederate paper money would become worthless, its foreign assistance would be cut off, and the rebellion must end.

General Pierre Beauregard had seen exactly that peril and already had set the mock-heroic tone of the official Confederate response in his general orders of resistance on October 17 to Sherman's impending onslaught:

> The security of your wives and daughters from the insults and outrages of a brutal foe shall be established soon, and to be followed by a permanent and honorable peace. The claims of home and country, wife and children, united

with the demands of honor and patriotism, summon us to the field. We cannot, dare not, will not fail to respond.[18]

Finally, whatever Sherman's own ambiguous—and often changing—views on slavery, abolition, and civil rights, his march would have the effect of reconfirming the ideological and moral differences between North and South. On the arrival of 62,000 Union troops in plantation country, slaves would desert and thus Southern paternalism would be revealed a lie. Some of the more hale blacks would aid the Union army as hired day laborers and paid service hands, or in small groups head northward to enlist. Others would strike out on their own, flocking to cities and leaving the wealthy of the South either to hire their own labor or do the work themselves. Others still would stay with their masters, but with their owners now unsure of the legality or morality—or the ties of loyalty—of their doomed ownership.

In turn, Northern soldiers in their own ranks would find moral support in the damage they wrought through knowledge of the men they freed. Sherman's march would not, as in Virginia, pit thousands of nearly identical blue and gray soldiers in a death lock against each other over a few thousand yards of earth. Rather, in the grand spirit of the Northern cause, Union troops would now destroy the plantation class of central and northern Georgia, in the flesh proclaiming to slaves that they now were no longer servile. "The Battle Hymn of the Republic" was a marching song, far better to be sung on the lips of mobile columns in the South than on entrenched, dirty troops stuck fast a few miles from Washington. If Epaminondas's men built Messenê to the music of flutes, then it is no exaggeration to say that Sherman's men destroyed the property of a slave state to the chorus of a song.[19]

Moreover, as the men marched on, the esprit de corps would only increase—no slaughters like Cold Harbor or the Seven Days on this campaign: "We're Bill Sherman's raiders—you'd better git," some yelled as they advanced. Sherman's troops, alone of the Northern armies, would receive a bird's-eye view of the plantation elite. No longer would they merely kill the poor of the South, but rather burn the estates of the ruling class—a far safer task with more lasting consequences, which they were to enjoy immensely. Moreover, Sherman himself not only realized that his own troops were precious, but also was increasingly reluctant to kill Southern boys in battle as well. The attack on the property of the more affluent was far preferable to the assault on the bodies of the poor. Sherman's thinking was now evolving beyond battle tactics, beyond even the strategy of destroying Confederate assets, to larger more theoretical questions of what was the South, and what would be the United States when the war closed.

Most important, and most controversially, the entire veneer of a "civilized" war would now be ripped off forever. War was unrefined hell; a more perfect peace the only goal. Men ran or deserted not so much from cowardice or lack of training, but from the realization that the cause for their families and property was lost, their immediate efforts, even if for a time successful, in the end vain. Sherman's march though Georgia would teach North and South alike what war really was for, and how it could be ended. He took occasion to summarize some of his views when he wrote the mayor of Atlanta:

> Now that war comes home to you, you feel very different. You deprecate its horrors, but did not feel them when you sent carloads of soldiers and ammunition, and moulded shells and shot, to carry war into Kentucky and Tennessee, to desolate the homes of hundreds and thousands of good people who only asked to live in peace at their old homes, and under the Government of their inheritance. But these comparisons are idle. I want peace, and believe it can only be reached through union and war, and I will ever conduct war with a view to perfect and early success.[20]

Even if local provisions were low, Sherman's men would still end up somewhere on the Atlantic coast, and thus could be supplied by the Union navy, which had achieved almost complete control of the sea and major Confederate ports. Once refreshed, the Army of the West would not be hundreds of miles away occupying Alabama, Georgia, or Tennessee, but three hundred miles nearer to Richmond—poised to march northward, through the hated Carolinas where the rebellion had started, right up to the rear of Lee's army in Virginia. To Sherman, there really was one enormous circle that would end the war: his army alone, he believed, had the expertise and courage to march all the way from Atlanta through Richmond to Washington, through whose streets it would parade in victory.

In the end, the gambit perhaps could be defended on strategic grounds, but did any one man have the sheer nerve to devise such a revolutionary plan of departure for 62,000 troops? Could any one man—and in this case, an asthmatic with a history of depression—carry in his own head the solutions for the enormous logistical, military, cultural, and political crises that would arise when thousands of reckless adolescents marched through the heart of an enemy apartheid society: burn or spare a particular plantation? enlist or turn away thousands of freed Negroes? execute or make prisoners of bushwhackers? on finding murdered foragers, retaliate with the execution of Southern prisoners or merely threaten to do so? imprison or keep in office minor Confederate officials? torch, consume, or ignore the foodstuffs of the nonelite? bypass or besiege major cities? evacuate or leave behind the Union wounded? True, the march had rational arguments in its favor, but could any one individual, against the original preferences of the commanding officer of the Union army and the president of the United States, take on the sole responsibility of an entire army—the size of which to lead, in the modern age, would have required thousands of hours of academic research, hundreds of staff officers, an array of satellite communications, and volumes of top secret intelligence reports—and then probably fail or be called off at its moment of victory?

Others legitimately worried about the grand vision of this "crazy" general. True, if successful, Sherman would take pressure off Grant, both directly and indirectly. An army coming up from the rear in the Carolinas might accelerate the progress of arms in Virginia. Grant himself, as Sherman's onslaught became unmistakably unstoppable, would come to worry that the Army of the West, not the Army of the Potomac, would be credited with defeating Lee's Army of Northern Virginia. When Lee's men—many from Georgia—learned that an army of over 60,000 was burning their homes, some would leave. All Southerners would find rations scarce and hard to find, as railroads and farms went up in the flames to the rear.

But who would take pressure off Sherman? If he was cut off, Grant was entrenched, and had an enemy army between them—the specter of 50,000 Confederates marching down to trap an unsuspecting Sherman was in the mind of all his marchers. Hood's army was approaching Tennessee. What if General Thomas could not hold him? A spectacular Southern victory to the north, with rebels pouring into Ohio "on their way to Chicago," might soon make Sherman's romp through Georgia appear ridiculous, if not cowardly—thousands of veterans marching *away* from gunfire, as their comrades were overwhelmed near home ground to the north. To advance forward while an enemy was loose in the rear was a violation of rudimentary military science. If Sherman had been in Hood's place with 40,000 veteran marchers, he would certainly have avoided Thomas entirely and circled around to do to Ohio and Illinois what he was now doing to Georgia. Still, Sherman was unfazed:

> As we rode on toward Atlanta that night, I remember the railroad-trains going to the rear with a furious speed, the engineers and the few men about the trains waving us an affectionate adieu. It surely was a strange event—two hostile armies marching in opposite directions, each in the full belief that it was achieving a final and conclusive result in a great war; and I was strongly inspired with the feeling that the movement on our part was a direct attack upon the rebel army and the rebel capital at Richmond, though a full thousand miles of hostile country intervened, and that, for better or worse, it would end the war.

If contemporaries could have asked Epaminondas why he had left Agesilaus and his army alone to posture on the hills of Sparta, and instead headed to Messenia, no doubt he would have remarked, "Damn him, my business is over West." And so Sherman would now head out for the agricultural and servile underbelly of the South, and let the opposing army who would not meet him in battle do what it pleased.[21]

Without rail lines, could the 62,000 be fed? Up until Sherman's march, logistics was primarily the science of feeding large armies that were relatively static, and kept close to major cities, rail lines, or rivers. In contrast, the exact nutritional requirements of men constantly marching over fifteen miles a day, and the capacity of the changing landscape to feed that horde, were generally unknown. Even when Sherman had stayed close to rail lines, more than eighty railcars a day had been needed to supply the needs of over 60,000 men and their animals—what a modern military historian once called "Sherman's logistical monster." On his approach to Atlanta, Sherman had once estimated that he needed a hundred locomotives and a thousand railcars to prevent his army from starving. Now he was simply abandoning that entire base of support, on the assumption that there was food enough in the middle of Georgia to match those thousand railcars of supplies.

Might not so many thousands of men devour the very Georgia countryside that they traversed? Might not his men end up, as fanatical Georgians promised, not 300 miles away in Savannah, but perhaps 150 miles to the east of Atlanta in midwinter in the middle of nowhere—lost and stuck in transit in the red Georgia mud, starving, and picked off by guerrillas—as Grant warned and Jefferson Davis promised—as local militias blocked roads, burned bridges, and destroyed the food supply? What if the Army of the West had to fight for a week or so straight? How could a mere two hundred rounds of cartridges per man suffice, scarcely what an army might fire in a single day of heavy fighting? Were animals that had been collected and stalled in Atlanta fit enough to pull wagons three hundred miles through Georgia? Without communications, how was Sherman to know whether Hood, Longstreet, or even Lee was marching to blindside him near the coast? If Grant and Thomas were defeated while he was incommunicado, how was he to explain that his men were not fighting Rebs but burning plantations? Could the North spare an army of 60,000 out of the theater of battle operations? And if so, for how long?

To the iconoclast B. H. Liddell Hart, Sherman's preference for the indirect approach in ending the war was "a supreme act of moral courage."

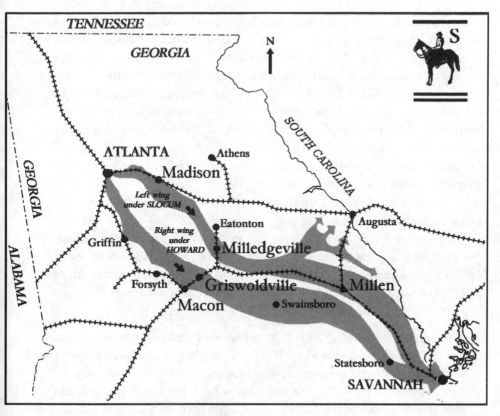

THE SWATH THROUGH GEORGIA

To leave the enemy in his rear, to divide his army, to cut himself adrift from railroad and telegraph, from supplies and reinforcements, and launch not a mere raiding force of cavalry but a great army into the heart of a hostile country—pinning his faith and his fortune on a principle which he had deduced by reasoning contrary to orthodoxy. And with nothing to fortify his spirit beyond that reasoning, for his venture was to be made under the cloud of the dubious permission of his military superior, the anxious fears of his President, and the positive objections of their advisers.[22]

The chorus of doubters was indeed unanimous in their disdain. Neutral observers in Europe wrote, "He has done either one of the most brilliant or one of the most foolish things ever performed by a military leader." General Halleck wavered and General Rawlins, Grant's chief of staff, went to Lincoln to stop him: Sherman, who had suffered one breakdown, was now about to sacrifice his entire army. Even Grant for a time believed that Sherman "would be bushwhacked by all the old men, little boys, and such railroad guards as are still left at home." Lincoln himself later would confess to Sherman, "When you were about leaving Atlanta for the Atlantic coast, I was anxious, if not fearful; but feeling that you were the better judge, and remembering 'nothing risked, nothing gained,' I did not interfere." On Sherman's departure Lincoln had earlier remarked to anxious inquirers, "I know what hole he went in, but I don't know which one he will come out." Later in the afterglow of Sherman's fame the envious would claim that Grant, Halleck, Thomas, or others had planned the March to the Sea. But in November 1864, no one other than Sherman wanted anything to do with the idea of a march through Georgia. "In thus fixing his purpose," wrote Jacob Cox, one of Sherman's generals, "Sherman had no assistance."[23]

Southerners feigned delight with the madman's apparent recklessness. One minister proclaimed that "God has put a hook in Sherman's nose and is leading him to destruction." The old war veteran Jefferson Davis, president of the Confederacy, pompously dismissed the idea of a march through his country in pseudo-historical terms:

> Sherman can not keep up his long line of communications, and must retreat. Soon or later he must, and when that day comes the fate that befell the army of the French Empire in its retreat from Moscow will be re-enacted. Our cavalry and our people will harass and destroy his army, as did the Cossacks that of Napoleon, and the Yankee General, like him, will escape with only a bodyguard.[24]

Sherman in contrast had not a doubt—neither did the majority of his men. As he left Atlanta in flames on November 16, Sherman in fact rejoiced at the thought of leading 62,000 men wherever he wished:

> The day was extremely beautiful, clear sunlight, with bracing air, and an unusual feeling of exhilaration seemed to pervade all minds—a feeling of something to come, vague and undefined, still full of venture and intense interest. Even the common soldiers caught the inspiration, and many a group called out to me as I worked my way past them, "Uncle Billy, I guess Grant is waiting for us at Richmond!"

Sherman continued:

> Indeed the general sentiment was that we were marching for Richmond, and that there we should end the war, but how and when they seemed to care not; nor did they measure the distance, or count the cost of life, or bother their brains about the great rivers to be crossed, and the food required for man and

beast, that had to be gathered by the way. There was a "devil-may-care" feeling pervading officers and men, that made me feel the full load of my responsibility, for success would be accepted as a matter of course, whereas, should we fail, this "march" would be adjudged the wild adventure of a crazy fool.[25]

To his superior, General Halleck, this crazy fool was more sober. "I can take so eccentric a course that no general can guess my objective. Then when you hear I am off have look-outs at Morris Island, S.C., Ossabaw Sound, Ga., Pensacola and Mobile Bay. I will turn up some where."

And so he did, and when he came out of the hole he had entered, the fate of the Confederacy was at last sealed. The Iowa sergeant, Alexander Downing, summed up the army's spirit best as they left Atlanta: "Started early this morning for the Southern coast, somewhere, and we don't care, so long as Sherman is leading us."[26]

3

THE SOUL OF AN ARMY

MADISON, GEORGIA

November 20, 1864—Fifth Day Out

THE CHANGE in the men in just a few days out in the country was miraculous. After five nights and a little less than eighty miles out from Atlanta, General Henry Slocum's 20th Corps of Sherman's immense army now swept absolutely unafraid through the picturesque hamlet of Madison, a planter's paradise of beautiful homes and landscaped yards, untouched by three years of war. Sherman's men were already part of something hitherto unseen in American military history—a mass of 62,000 troops, entirely self-contained, possessed of lethal destructive power unmatched by any other infantry force in the history of conflict, lightning quick, absolutely unstoppable—and but a few days old. Previously, in Atlanta over 100,000 men of Sherman's corps had camped out for over two months, as various divisions passed into and out of the amorphous and motley collection of garrison soldiers. Now, in contrast, they were to be culled and regrouped by Sherman into a deadly instrument of a new mobile warfare, hundreds of miles from the nearest supply depots in Tennessee. Once this new force left the wreckage of Atlanta, few men would now be added to or subtracted from the Army of the West for the duration of the war—until the army disbanded a few days after the victory march in Washington. Sherman's marchers were for all practical purposes an autonomous band, in theory subject to control from Washington, in reality free to do whatever they pleased.

Once the march got underway, the men instinctively knew that some-thing strange, wonderful, even frightening was occurring, transforming them into not just killers of enemy soldiers, but brutal executors of the larger issues of social and political directives that lay behind the war itself. Enlisted sol-diers on this march to Savannah would learn what the war was now for, how the North inherently differed from the South, and why the Confederacy was a pipe dream, not a real nation—"You must first make a government," Sher-man began lecturing the outraged plantation class, "before you can have property. There is no such thing as property without a government." Sherman would show that in the past Southern slavery, in fact, had operated solely under the protective aegis of the United States government, which before 1860 had turned a blind eye to its amorality. Now that planters had foolishly thrown away their allegiance to just that stable Federal government, they must go it alone—and so perish.

The knowledge that the Army of the West's march was a "hard species of war" and yet also more "statesmanship than war" would lend its routine plun-dering almost a messianic zeal. A more contemplative soldier remarked that Northerners back home should "realize that the Sacrifice of our brave and noble comrades who have fallen in the Struggle are every one of them mar-tyrs. Justice demands at our hands that they shall not have fallen in vain, but that Every vestige of the great National sin Shall be washed anyway with their blood." An Ohio officer on Sherman's march concluded with the same ideological fervor, "We could not resist the conviction that a civilization in which a score of lives are impoverished and embittered, are blasted and de-based and damned, in order that one life may be made sweeter, is a system of wrong that no language can properly condemn."[27]

The soldiers were also apprehensive at the huge columns headed into the interior of Georgia. The army was like the great Spanish invasion of Mexico when Cortes cut his supply lines—an apt image in more ways than one, given the destruction of the enemy culture to come and the similar mad genius who led the invaders. George Nichols, another aide-de-camp to Sherman, summed up the mood of apprehension:

> And so we have cut adrift our base of operations, from our line of communica-tions, launching out into uncertainty at the best, on a journey whose projected end only the General in command knows. Its real fate and destination he does not know, since that rests with the goodness of God and the brave hearts and strong limbs of our soldiers. The history of war bears no similar example, except that of Cortes burning his ships. It is a bold, hazardous undertaking. There is no backward step possible here. Thirty days' rations and a new base: that time and

those supplies will be exhausted in the most rapid march ere we can arrive at the nearest sea-coast; when arrived there, what then?

Even the more informed, like Lincoln and Grant, saw the interior of Georgia as a quagmire, entering it was like "going into the hole and pulling the hole in after us." Even Captain Orlando Poe, Sherman's technological brain who taught the troops the mastery of rapid and mass destruction of Southern infrastructure, wrote to his wife, "This may be the last letter you will ever get from me." In the aftermath of the march dozens would take credit for the enterprise, dozens more scoff that it had been an easy inroad. But when Sherman set out, no Union general or politician was eager for him to depart, and the majority of observers thought he would fail.

No wonder—the acknowledgment that thousands were going into the heart of enemy country was both a comforting and foreboding thought. Men took solace from the sheer number of comrades with them, their past expertise in the art of killing, their abundant matériel, and the brilliance of their leadership. Yet the magnitude and isolation of their undertaking sounded also a melancholy note—given the hatred of their adversaries and the realization of just how tragic it all could turn out when they began to attack the very fabric rather than the army of the enemy. Even the ever confident young aide to Sherman, Henry Hitchcock, was no stranger to the fatalism inherent in the undertaking: "This campaign will be no joke in *any* point of view—but if successful, as we believe and expect, a splendid one now and hereafter. Doubtless it will be death to those of us who may fall into their hands—but if so, 'twill cost them dear." Like Epaminondas's Thebans, Sherman's Westerners expected even an apparently doomed enemy to offer continual resistance once its inner sanctum was penetrated.[28]

The Athenian expedition of 40,000 to Sicily during 415–413 B.C. is a good example of how quickly the fortitude of a confident invading armada far away from home after even a moderate setback can degenerate into abject depression, as thousands realize they are not going home, but may well die—together, unknown, miserably far away in foreign territory. The uncertainty rippling through the ranks of a large force grows to billows of fear and then a final tidal wave of panic, even as a previously awed and purportedly pacified countryside smells the blood of a wounded predator and now, suddenly brave, turns out in mass for the final kill. At the end of Thucydides' majestic account of the Syracusan debacle, thousands of once haughty Athenians of its greatest army in its greatest age are left scrambling amid a fouled streambed of mud and blood—fighting with one another to drink the filth as they are shot with missiles by the enemy throng on the banks above. The historian closes his tragedy with the destruction of nearly 40,000 men eight hundred miles from home: "They were beaten at all points and altogether; all that they suffered was great; they were destroyed, as the saying is, with a total destruction, their fleet, their army—everything was destroyed, and few out of many returned home. Such were the events in Sicily." As the once arrogant Romans on the doomed retreat with Crassus from Carrhae (53 B.C.) and as the thousands of trapped legionaries butchered to the man with Varus in Germany (A.D. 9) knew, the shared realization that a once splendid and cocksure entire army is about to perish far from home only magnifies, rather than lessens, the terror of massacre. The idea that thousands will be killed brutally alongside each other is not comforting but only all the more harrowing. No wonder so many of Sherman's men were exhilarated and wary all at once. They realized that the dead must be left in shallow unmarked graves, stragglers would be killed, foragers executed, and the wounded at best imprisoned; and the apparently timid local citizenry would soon be eager for vengeance and increasingly murderous should Union columns falter or individual soldiers become separated.[29]

All the injured and sick of the Union armies had been sent northward on the last trains out of Atlanta; like Epaminondas, Sherman had culled the unfit from his forces to ensure a planned march of ten to fifteen miles per day through Georgia. The Union ambulances started out all empty, as wagons carried only enough rations for about a week of travel out from Atlanta. Sherman's comment even years later still bore a note of apprehension. "The most extraordinary efforts had been made to purge this army of non-combatants and of sick men, for we knew well that there was to be no place of safety save with the army itself."

On this fifth day out, the thousands who now descended on Madison, Georgia, were part of a much greater force of some 55,000 infantry, 5,000 horsemen, and nearly 2,000 artillery men. Sherman had radically reduced his supply train—diminishing the ratio of wagons per thousand men from fifty-two to forty—but nevertheless brought along 14,500 horses, 19,500 mules, 2,500 wagons, and 5,500 head of cattle—and those numbers would grow as his men stripped bare the plantation stables of northern Georgia. Yet Sherman did not intentionally limit the size of his army; indeed, he was perfectly willing to march 100,000 and more out of Atlanta. The 62,000 were all the able-bodied soldiers he could get his hands on, since recruitment tended not to keep up with the natural attrition of his army to sickness, furloughs, and enemy action. A march is not a raid, and what makes both Epaminondas's and Sherman's accomplishments so extraordinary is the sheer magnitude of the undertaking, and the expectation of a decisive battle with the enemy. Finally, we should remember that Sherman's men were not starting out entirely fresh, but for the entire summer of 1864 had marched hundreds of miles continuously from Tennessee under constant enemy attack, and had enjoyed only a brief respite in Atlanta.[30]

Besides the nearly identical size of the two marches, and the similar nature of their foe, there were other eerie similarities of quality. Scholars speak loosely of Sherman's "Westerners"; the general himself knew his forces as the "Army of the West." That generalization of the times was entirely apt for a force made up almost entirely of Midwesterners, who were raised on the then frontier of the nation. Over half the army was from Ohio, Illinois, and Indiana alone. Only 33 of 218 regiments had been sent from the East, little more than 15 percent of the army's total strength.

Given the fact that the Army of the West was to a great extent composed of soldiers twenty-one years old and younger—unlike the middle-aged and elderly that filled out Epaminondas's army—that the ill and unhealthy had been sent home, and that the majority of the men were raised on homestead farms, troopers quickly took on a look far different from either their Southern adversaries or the allied Army of the Potomac. The army, in short, was born to march and to live in the wild—a force that had no tradition of military protocol, no affinity for urban life, no patience for fortification and retrenchment, and no tolerance for hierarchy and manners. No wonder that there was sometimes outright hostility between the few more polished Easterners in Sherman's army and the rowdy, unkempt Westerners. The latter boasted openly that "we are better fighters"; the former worried to loved ones in the East, "We shall get entirely uncivilized in this howling wilderness of Hoosiers, Buckeyes, Suckers, and Wolverines, unless you give us occasional glimpses of our eastern home." After his fight with Secretary of War Edwin Stanton and Chief of Staff Henry Halleck, Sherman would write of his disgust with Easterners in general: "If such be the welcome the East gives the West, we can but let them make war and fight it out themselves. I know where is a land and people that will not treat us thus—the West, the Valley of the Mississippi, the heart and soul and future strength of America, and I for one will go there."

All contemporary observers agreed with the later parade watchers in Washington that Shermans' men were healthier, larger, and better fed than the Confederates who faced them, and also had none of the near-lethargic air of Easterners defending Washington. In short, they "were taller and stronger than the blue coats of the Eastern armies, and were bearded, long-haired and tattered, who marched with a rolling stride. Midwesterners, most of them, sons and grandsons of pioneer settlers of the country from Kentucky to Minnesota, of English, Irish and Scotch descent, with a sprinkling of Germans and Swedes." The combination of Theban yeomen and Arcadian highlanders must have presented a similar spectacle to the invaded of Laconia in 370—rural folk by the thousands descending upon the virgin land of a privileged plantation class. Just as the Thebans had awed their own Peloponnesian allies by their record of warring and the appearance of rural ferocity, so too now the Midwesterners tended to lend a savage look to the Union army in general. Just as Sherman's men would not have endured the inconclusive nightmare of Grant's trench warfare in Virginia, so the Army of the Potomac would have been directionless and confused during the hundreds of miles of trudging through Georgia and the Carolinas. An army on a great march is no army at all if its soldiers have no affinity for either rural hardship or cross-country tramping—perhaps an ominous warning to the modern age, where the vast majority of democratic populations is comfortable and suburban.[31]

Like Epaminondas's veterans of Tegyra, Leuctra, and the earlier fights on Boeotian soil during most of the 370s, many of Sherman's choice 62,000 had seen nearly constant combat and had rarely been beaten. Some had been at battle since at least early 1862, and had fought continuously at Vicksburg, Chattanooga, and during the long summer months prior to the Atlanta campaign. Other transferred regiments had even battled at Bull Run, the Seven Days, Antietam, Fredericksburg, Chancellorsville, and Gettysburg, ensuring that in the Army of the West as a whole there was some collective memory and experience of nearly every engagement of the Civil War thus far. One young veteran summed up best the unique conglomeration of men that now were in Madison: "It is not likely that one equal to it will be seen again in this country in our day and generation."

Nothing the South could now offer as opposition, no surprise attack, cavalry sortie, mass charge, or nighttime flanking movement could surprise this core of veterans. They had seen it all before and lived through it all, and now they were at last all together, the best men the North had to offer—and the sum of those dreadful experiences was about to be unleashed upon the citizens of Georgia. Contemporaries shuddered at the Westerners' élan; his men were, in Sherman's own words, "the bravest and best army that ever trod American soil." Even the Confederates who hated the coming of this host acknowledged it—General Joseph Johnston would later concede that "there had been no such army since the days of Julius Caesar." To an Illinois infantryman, Sherman's army that set out "had been in the service from the beginning and what they did not know about campaigning was not worth inquiring into. Each soldier was practically a picked man. Such had been the ratio of casualties that he may be said to have been the sole survivor of four men who had set out from Cairo in 1861; all but he having succumbed to disease or death."[32]

The term "army" is a generalization. There were a number of armies within an army. The Army of the West was in truth two—each in turn composed again of two large corps. The left wing—the newly christened Army of Georgia—of over 26,000 men that marched on the northern flank through Georgia was commanded by Major General Henry W. Slocum. It was composed of Jefferson Davis's (no relation to the Confederate president) 14th Corps and Alpheus William's 20th—the latter being the only force with a sizable number of Easterners who had come west from Virginia in 1863 from the Army of the Potomac. Sherman usually rode on this northern wing with Davis's 14th Corps, the desperate brawlers who a year earlier had stormed Missionary Ridge and thus ended the Confederates' attack on Chattanooga.

To the south, sometimes as much as fifty to sixty miles disant, marched the right flank of the devout, one-armed General Oliver Howard, the future founder of Howard University, with roughly another 26,000 troops. This Army of Tennessee likewise was broken into two corps, the 15th of Peter J. Osterhaus—Sherman's own battle-hardened division from the Shiloh days—and the 17th of Frank Blair. The mercurial Judson Kilpatrick had two brigades of cavalry and reported directly to Sherman. In theory, each wing would head for their respective targets, Augusta on the north, and Macon to the South, but then bypass these centers of resistance and converge on the state capital of Milledgeville. Each army was a large knife that would determine how large the slice of Georgia pie in between was to be cut—a serving to be utterly consumed, but one whose actual size could change instantaneously, from twenty to nearly sixty miles in breadth depending on the nature of the countryside and the caliber of Southern opposition.[33]

The divisions were necessary, for Sherman faced the same logistical nightmare that Epaminondas did on entry into Laconia—how to bring a huge army of over 60,000 foot soldiers through enemy territory without stretching the columns for twenty to thirty miles, without leaving them vulnerable to Grant's predicted nightmare of bushwhackers, and without being so unwieldy as to make it nearly impossible to quarter and camp the throng with any uniformity of time and space. Had Sherman not divided his army into tetrads, and had he not assigned them separate avenues of transit along an immense front, the force would have taken nearly three days simply to pass any given point.

As the army moved forward, messengers rode back and forth among the four huge columns, and signal fires and rockets were used to keep the army in touch with its components as it cut across forty to sixty miles of countryside. Men spread out in every direction. Cavalry scouted ahead, followed by pioneer regiments—soon to be composed mostly of freed slaves—who cleared the roads and bridged creeks. Infantry followed, marching four abreast. Artillery caissons and wagons were intermixed. Meanwhile, foraging teams searched laterally for provisions and fresh livestock, often meeting up with fleeing Georgians and runaway slaves. In theory, such parties might depart in the morning in groups of a hundred; in reality, they soon broke up into twos and threes to visit more outlying plantations off the main roads. Scholars often suggest that these "bummers" were inefficient provisioners due to their indulgences in petty looting and an unsystematic approach to gathering staples. True, but the sheer number of roaming soldiers lent a sense of chaos to Georgians as well, giving the impression that Sherman's army was even larger than it was, the countryside now seemingly literally alive with Union men in the most unlikely and out-of-way places—proof positive that the entire state was in Northern hands. Amid the confusion, Sherman himself rode everywhere, maps always in hand, saying little, but intent each day on directing his amorphous columns on a general route east. Unlike Epaminondas, Sherman was not headed so much for a particular city as he was for the sea. The sea and the sea alone, not Confederate soldiers, not some glorious siege, would mark the end of his progress.

A liberated slave best captured the thunderous effect of even a fourth of the army as it passed by: "Dar's millions of 'em—millions! Is dere anybody left up north?" A Southern resident of Burke County after the war described the advent of one-half of one wing of Sherman's army: "It was the 14th Corps that came through my place. They looked like a blue cloud coming. They had all kinds of music,—horns, cow-bells, tin-pans, everything they could pick up that would make a hideous noise. It was like Bedlam broke loose. It was enough to frighten the old stumps in the deadenings, say nothing about the people." A Confederate widow agreed: "It seemed to me the whole world was coming. Here came the 'wood-cutters'—clearing the way before the army. Men with axes on their soldiers, men with spades, men with guns." Even with the army divided, each corps of roughly 11,000 to 13,000 men marched in columns five to ten miles in length. In theory, although not in fact because there were also sizable, detached flying parties of foragers, it might take the rear of a corps an entire day to reach its own front-line marchers. The impression of such a trampling, singing horde was like nothing anyone in Georgia had ever seen. To one Southern onlooker, "There was nothing gay about this vast procession, with its rambling soldiers, the clattering horsemen, and its lumbering wagons, except the temper of the men. They splashed through the mud, cracking their jokes and singing snatches of song." Southern revolutionaries were now to learn of the vast size and power of the Union they so hated, when thousands of deadly Midwestern yeomen marched unmolested into their very front yards and demanded food, destroyed their property, and ended their way of life.[34]

Sherman's marchers shared most of the same reliance as the ancients on wagons for food and supplies, cavalry for reconnaissance, and personal aides and servants to tend livestock and carry equipment. Yet Sherman's thousands were free of the absolute dependence of Patton's mechanized divisions upon petroleum, whose absence could stop cold a motorized army's advance at the moment of its greatest independence and success. But the Army of the West as it left the railheads was just as vulnerable to the absence of fuel of a different sort—fodder for thousands of pack animals and rations for even more men, whose caloric intake was prodigious since they walked, rather than rode, each mile of the march. Most soldiers were not just marchers or fighters, but day laborers who fanned out to destroy rails and to take apart factories—and needed plentiful food to continue. Remember that for all Sherman's efforts at economy, at various points throughout the march the army was not so lean. The number of cattle gathered, wagons and carts stolen, horses collected and ex-slaves brought along on the march ensured that the supply train grew, not shrank, as the army neared the Atlantic coast.

Although Sherman's army left behind almost two hundred artillery pieces, it still towed nearly sixty-five cannon, each on an eight-horse team—about one gun for every thousand men. Each soldier in addition carried 40 rounds for his rifle and could get access to another 150 cartridges or so each in the wagons—about enough for four or five days of good sporadic fighting, but hardly sufficient should the army have to shoot its way through Georgia for a month or two, or engage even in a substantial set battle of a few hours.

Given the army's tremendous size, the tons of matériel it carried, the growing number of camp followers who joined his horde, and the vast work of destruction his men undertook, Sherman's chief worry was that his force might simply eat itself into oblivion, finding its human and material hunger greater than its own mobility—the nightmare of every great march that cannot move fast enough to reach new forage before its own daily appetite denudes the surrounding countryside and so brings progress to a permanent halt. Sherman was not just slicing through Georgia at a rapid ten-to-fifteen-mile-a-day clip to confuse the enemy, outmaneuver enemy troops, and advance ever nearer to the rear of Lee in Virginia. He was running from another enemy, hunger itself, one far greater and more primordial. Speed alone offered new forage and ever closer relief at the supply depots on the Atlantic.

To read Sherman's own account of the march is not so much to learn of fighting or even of destruction, but of the ingenuity of his men in simply obtaining plentiful food. For Sherman the astonishing achievement of reaching the sea was simply that his army reached it at all, that it was not ruined or even hungry, but in robust heath and well fed on arrival:

> No army could have carried along sufficient food and forage for a march of three hundred miles; so that foraging in some shape was necessary. The country was sparsely settled, with no magistrates or civil authorities who could respond to requisitions, as is done in all the wars of Europe; so that this system of foraging was simply indispensable to our success. By it our men were well supplied with all the essentials of life and health, while the wagons retained enough in case of unexpected delay, and our animals were well fed. Indeed, when we reached Savannah, the trains were pronounced by experts to be the finest in flesh and appearance ever seen with any army.

The overriding concern for food explains Sherman's constant anger, paranoia even, concerning any possible Southern attempts at a scorched-earth retreat—the one strategy that in fact might have stranded the Army of the West. Confederate senator B. H. Hill vainly sought just such a move in his call to arms on November 18: "To the people of Georgia, You have now the best opportunity ever yet presented to destroy the enemy. Put every thing at the disposal of our generals; remove all provisions from the path of the invader, and put all obstructions in his path." The next day the Southern Congress echoed the appeal: "Remove your Negroes, horses, cattle, and provisions from Sherman's army, and burn what you cannot carry." The strategy failed, as the plantation class, whose worth was always self-assessed in material rather than human terms, valued their own tangible world far more than they did the obstruction of Sherman's army.[35]

Armies of marchers, ancient and modern, were overwhelmingly infantry forces, who relied on horsemen mostly for reconnaissance, and skirmishers only as plunderers and ravagers. Implicit to commanders of such forces was the realization that only men marching and with feet on the ground could enter, occupy, and destroy enemy territory—massive columns of foot soldiers alone creating the critical impression to a slave society that it is in fact overrun and impotent. As is true in all great egalitarian infantry armies of the West, beginning with Greek hoplites and Roman legionaries, there was an "Infantry Spirit" that resulted in real disdain for horsemen, who were judged by foot soldiers to be too ostentatious, too aristocratic, or simply too ineffective when the fighting became serious. The prejudice of the yeoman is both cultural and military. Scholars are correct to point out that Sherman did not understand the proper role of cavalry, having no experience with the command of mounted troops himself. It is also true that Sherman's own horsemen were in some sense antithetical to the soul of the Army of the West. Most infantrymen considered Kilpatrick's Union horsemen relatively worthless, who like porters and cooks were afraid of fighting—they, not Sherman's infantry, were the mere raiders.

The infantry was sometimes a veritable moving city of men and animals, but it nevertheless retained an unmistakable deadliness through its firepower, size, and sheer quickness—and it welcomed, rather than shunned, real opposition. Daniel Oakey, a captain of a Massachusetts regiment, summed up the army's resolve to fight when pressed:

> Although we were fully prepared, with our great trains of ammunition, to fight a pitched battle, our mission was not to fight, but to consume and destroy. Our inability to care properly for the wounded, who must necessarily be carried along painfully in jolting ambulances to die on the way from exhaustion and exposure, was an additional and very serious reason for avoiding collision with the enemy. But where he could not be evaded, his very presence across our path increased the velocity of our flying column. We repelled him by a decisive blow and without losing our momentum.[36]

Other similarities abound between the Theban and Union armies of liberation. It is no exaggeration to say that once Sherman left the railroad and telegraph behind at Atlanta, there was not much difference in the way his army foraged and traveled from that of Epaminondas's men some twenty-two centuries earlier—despite the presence of photographers, engineers, and machine workers. The 130-year-old wagon that presently sits outside my house, used by my grandfather to haul raisins as late as 1920, is not really much different in its manner of construction, use of materials, or its source of locomotion from Hesiod's description of such a Boeotian wheeled cart some twenty-seven centuries ago. And the Boeotian campfires that so terrified the Spartans were not unlike the evening blazes of the Army of the West that similarly warmed Sherman's tired men. Leather and wood, with occasional iron and bronze, were what kept both armies together; wood fires warmed and fed Boeotians and Northerners; and ancients and moderns fought, traveled, and got back home on foot. Once they had given up their rail support, except for their firearms and their youth, Sherman's invaders would have appeared scarcely different from Epaminondas's hoplites.

Once the Army of the West left Atlanta, Lincoln knew about as much of Sherman's fate as did the Boeotian assembly of Epaminondas and his men— both forces were completely under the sole control of a general who for all practical purposes was incommunicado with this superiors back home. Even Patton, a captive of the age of radio, conspired for silence, and welcomed rather than feared the interruption of communication with Eisenhower's staff, as he realized that audacious attempts to outflank the enemy on a grand scale would not be approved by a more circumspect and cautious board of planners. The history of the Third Army in Europe is the history of Patton vainly trying to seek the autonomy once granted Epaminondas and Sherman.

A key ingredient for the success of such dramatic forays into the interior of the enemy is that very need for independence of command while on the road. Sherman would have stalled in November and December had he telegraphed for daily permission to advance from Halleck in the War Department. It may be no exaggeration that such marches—the Gulf War is a good example—are in peril in the modern age, when political overseers may monitor hourly the progress or failure of such a daring onslaught—now ordering caution if casualties loom or the visual images of destruction are deemed too harsh for public consumption, then again demanding more ambitious, even rash, action should reports of progress via satellite seem momentarily assuring.

Sherman, who liberated more slaves than any other Union general, and whose reported blustering conversations are at odds with his later reflective essays, was still not sympathetic to the radical abolitionists. But despite what some modern biographers have argued, he was also to become no orthodox racist or even a traditional segregationist. It simply is wrong to think that the spirit of the Army of the West was indifferent to abolition—an ideology that on military grounds alone could only aid Sherman's March to the Sea. Sherman's men made a real distinction between freeing slaves, feeding them, bringing them under the protection of the army, recruiting and training them for front-line military service—a nearly impossible task given the columns' urgency to make it through intact to Savannah—and creating turmoil and destruction in Southern society to provide a fertile ground for escape and liberation. They shot every dog in their path, not because they hated pets or Southerners in general, but because they were furious that such hounds had hunted down runaway slaves and escaping Union prisoners.

On the question of slavery, at first glance, we should not expect real idealism from his Midwesterners. Mid-nineteenth-century America in general was primarily a society of white citizens and immigrants of European extraction who often considered African blacks if not genetically inferior then at least culturally backward. Added to that explicit racism was the idea that Southern Negroes in particular—kept on the plantation in ignorance, illiteracy, and grinding poverty—were far more deprived than the rarer Northern blacks. To the uninformed observer it affirmed the Southern paradox that the more the slave was isolated and kept in ignorance, the more he seemed deserving of his patronizing bondage. Finally, in the Midwest there was a prevailing view that Eastern abolitionists had precipitated the war. Their Army

159

of the Potomac had not won it; and now farmers from Ohio, Illinois, and Indiana were being asked to do the dirty and dangerous work of physically freeing the slaves from Southern whites. Many resented the lectures of New Englanders who either could not or would not field an army courageous—or large—enough to translate their fiery rhetoric into deed. Better they and the plantation class of the South fight it out between themselves and leave the yeomen of the West out of it.

Nowhere was that resentment more manifest than in Sherman's reaction to Secretary of War Stanton's unexpected visit to Savannah in January 1865 at the conclusion of the march. Despite three hundred miles of brilliant marching, and the liberation of the greatest number of slaves by any Union army of the war, Stanton ordered Sherman out of the room to inquire from freed blacks whether they considered the general sympathetic enough to the cause of abolition and racial equality—censure reminiscent of the charges that the uncouth and crude Patton was anti-Semitic even as his closest advisors, friends—and most laudatory biographers—were Jewish. As Sherman indignantly remarked years later:

> It certainly was a strange fact that the great War Secretary should have catechized negroes concerning the character of a general who had commanded a hundred thousand men across four hundred miles of territory, and had just brought tens of thousands of freedmen to a place of security; but because I had not loaded down my army by other hundreds of thousands of poor negroes, I was construed by others as hostile to the black race.[37]

If Sherman was not an abolitionist himself, if there was real uncertainty on his part about the wisdom of granting Southern slaves instant equality to Southern whites, and if his men were sometimes reluctant to bring along the march thousands of freed slaves, whence the overwhelming and clearly ethical zeal of the army? Why as a group had the men voted for Lincoln against the ever popular copperhead, General McClellan, in the elections of November 1864, just days before they set out? And why had the Army of the West enjoyed the highest reenlistment rate of any Union force—nearly 50 percent of its men choosing to keep marching when they could legally return home in safety?

The answer was twofold. First was the understandable notion of self-interest and survival. Rice Bull wrote of the army's realism as it neared Savannah:

> The prevailing feeling among the men was a desire to finish the job; they wanted to get back home. The mass of those in this Army were veterans, nearly all had served three years, many much longer, and all were tired of army life. They had faced the loss of home comforts and loss of business opportunity

and endured privation and danger to maintain the integrity of their country. They were not in the service as soldiers of fortune, they were intelligent and could see that the Rebellion was nearing its end, so were willing and anxious to meet quickly any privation or danger that would bring a speedy end to the war.

Soldiers, in short, realized that the quickest way to return northward to their families was to follow their mad genius into the heart of the Confederacy and very quickly to wreck its economic and spiritual core. Thus wrote a private in Sherman's army of Northerners who wanted a negotiated peace:

> Oh!! those base copperheads. I would like to have them down here in front of our guns and then make them do allegiance to their government or die a traitor's death. Those are my true sentiments, and no doubt it looks hard to you, but to those that have been serving their country for the last three years in trying to crush the Rebels, and now to have those dastardly cowards crying for peace when we have got them so nearly used up. That is the feeling of three-fourths of the army.[38]

There was also another reason for the troops' growing zest in destroying the system of apartheid. At the outset, Midwesterners really knew nothing about either slavery or slaves. Most Northerners in general had never seen a Negro or a plantation; many were, and continued to be, in the abstract, racists. But once Sherman's men learned the character of the slave, the conditions in which he was kept unfree, and the ideology and venom of his master class, there rose among most of them a hatred and repulsion for rich Georgians that only increased as the army daily moved eastward and incurred the petty rebuke of the invaded. Very quickly, Sherman's young troops came to abhor the elite of the society that they overran—a few marchers would even begin to see the black man as the moral superior of the rich Southern white. A soldier from Illinois was only too happy to burn Atlanta; it "and every other Southern city deserve nothing better than general destruction from the Yankees," he wrote, for "buying and selling their betters."[39]

Enlisted men then talked of the exploitation they saw, and their officers nodded in agreement. Given that almost all the regimental commanders of Sherman's forces had been promoted from within the army, and that almost 50 percent of the army's captains and 90 percent of its lieutenants had also served as enlisted men, there was an unmatched familiarly between officer and soldier, creating a volatile populism in the ranks as a whole, as those in command of like class and spirit to the men they led. Egalitarianism, in the absence of aristocratic privilege, helped to create in the army a naturally receptive audience to the cause of servile liberation.[40]

Another Union soldier remarked: "If the negroes on the place told stories of great cruelty they had suffered, or of bitter hostility to the Union, or if there were bloodhounds about, which had been used to run down slaves, the injury was generally avenged by the torch." Presumably, these were not one-time occurrences, but orders issued by officers with the full encouragement of their men. A later witness in South Carolina also wrote of the unanimity of spirit and cause between Sherman's officers and enlisted men:

> The officers and men are on terms of perfect equality socially. Off duty they drink together, go arm in arm about the town, call each other by the first name, in a way that startles an Eastern man. A friend heard a private familiarly addressing a Brig. Gen., as "Jake." Miss Lee saw another General taking hold with his men to help move a lot of barrels on a wharf. He took off his coat and worked three hours, like a common porter. This seems strange to us, accustomed to the aristocratic system adopted in the Eastern regiments.[41]

This ready Union familiarity was in marked contrast not merely to the Eastern armies of the Union, but especially to the Confederate army, which, after all, was more often led by a privileged class for a cause that was based on privilege. Letters from Civil War soldiers reveal patriotic motivations far more varied among Confederate than among Union soldiers. Not only did those from the border states and the upper South show less zeal in the fight for slavery, but there was also a clear contrast by class: the nonplantation recruit was far less eager to fight Northerners than were those who held slaves. As James McPherson points out, of all combatants of the Civil War,

> the prototypical unwilling soldier who expressed no patriotic sentiments and would have preferred to be at home was a nonslaveholding Southern married farmer with small children who was drafted in 1862 or enlisted only to avoid being drafted. . . . Southern nonslaveholding married farmers seemed particularly bitter on this matter [the draft]. They gave substance to the theme of a "rich man's war and a poor man's fight" that is prevalent in modern scholarship on class tensions in both North and South during the Civil War.

When Sherman's men reached Savannah, the signs of hierarchy among the departed Confederates repulsed the Northerners, such as the "Patrician Church" that stipulated: "Officers are requested to occupy the middle and front seats. All other persons are invited as cordially to attend and occupy the remaining seats." Hitchcock wrote of the sheer hatred that the Midwesterner held for the plantationist when he spied Wade Hampton, the millionaire slave-owning Confederate general, at the final armistice between Sherman and Johnston: "Hampton's whole demeanor was marked with the easy 'well-bred' essentially vulgar insolence which is characteristic of *that* type of 'gentleman'; a man of polished manners, scarcely veiling the arrogance and utter selfishness which marks his class, and which I hate with a perfect hatred." Sherman's march really was an ideological crusade; young recruits, like their forty-four-year-old "Uncle Billy," were convinced that they were in a total war with the haughty purveyors of real evil. Sherman's fiery rhetoric and personality had now permeated the entire army.

Southern elites, in the manner of Spartan Similars, at first believed that their Helots would not desert. If they did flee, blacks would probably demonstrate by their cowardice and ignorance why slavery was so necessary in the first place. The exact opposite occurred. A postwar analysis of Sherman's damage recorded:

> The negroes had all along been told that if they fell into the hands of the Yankees they would be worked to death on fortifications, or put into the front of the battle and shot if they did not fight, or sent to Cuba and sold; and that the old women and young children would be drowned like cats and blind puppies. And now the masters showed their affection for these servants by running off the able-bodied ones, who were competent to take care of themselves, and leaving the aged, the infirm, and the children to the "cruelties" of the invaders. The manner in which the great mass of the remaining negro population received the Yankees, showed how little they had been imposed upon by such stories, and how true and strong their faith was in the armed deliverance which Providence had ordained for their race.

Slaves in Sherman's path left the plantations in droves, and those who were employed by the Union army quickly gained a reputation for industry and competence. Many soldiers worried about their eventual fate: "We laugh now at their wild antics and marvelous expectations, but I cannot shut out the thought that the comedy may soon darken into tragedy." Another officer agreed: "The more we become acquainted with the negro character, both as men and Christians, the more we are compelled to respect them."

Not all of Sherman's men professed abolitionist sentiments. Even those that did may have done so for purely practical reasons—the chance to employ cheaply Negro domestics in the army, the idea of spreading the danger of battle among thousands of new recruits, or the simple strategic notion of denying labor resources to the Confederacy. Nevertheless, letters of Union soldiers show that by 1864 a majority clearly knew that their cause was about freeing slaves and they heartily approved of it. Such sentiments grew, rather than diminished, as the war wore on and Northerners entered the South.

If not out of moral ardor, how could thousands of citizen-soldiers have sung abolitionist and republican hymns even as they created an inferno for the defenseless white population in their midst? The answer leads to an understanding of the very essence of democratic armies of liberation: the usual wages of regret and shame that accompany the soldier as arsonist and thief are absent when the immediate, quite visible aim of such terror is to free the oppressed. Sherman may have worried about the wisdom of freeing thousands, and the logistical nightmare of allowing any Negroes but the young and male to accompany his army, but he was quite attuned to the marked psychological effect of liberation on his own men—indeed, on himself as well. In almost biblical terms he describes leading a freed slave to gaze at his own army of liberation:

> I asked him why he trembled so, and he said that he wanted to be sure that we were in fact "Yankees," for on a former occasion some rebel cavalry had put on light-blue overcoats, personating Yankee troops, and many of the negroes were deceived thereby, himself among the number—had shown sympathy, and had in consequence been unmercifully beaten therefore. This time he wanted to be certain before committing himself; so I told him to go out on the porch, from which he could see the whole horizon lit up with camp-fires and he could then judge whether he had ever seen any thing like it before.[42]

Later, and in private letters, Sherman crudely vented his rage about the excesses of the abolitionists and Reconstructionists, but there is no evidence that in practice by 1864 he was anything other than genuinely sympathetic to the slave and had become repulsed by the slave-owner—and that ideology filtered down throughout the army, where the young and impressionable emulated their beloved general. Sherman, remember, signed one of the most radical proposals in American history to aid blacks, in reserving thousands of acres in the Sea Islands and portions of Georgia and South Carolina for some 40,000 freed slaves—an order later overturned by President Johnson. His aide, Henry Hitchcock, once reported a conversation Sherman had with a freed slave: "Those of you who deserve to be free and wish to be, will certainly be free, and will no longer be sold like cattle, nor see their families separated and sold; but we think that any man, black or white, who wants his freedom, and is able to fight for it ought to be willing to do so." In reply to Secretary Stanton's inquiry about Sherman's purported racism, Garrison Frazier, a freed slave, testified in closed session:

> We unanimously feel inexpressible gratitude to him, looking upon him as a man who should be honored for the faithful performance of his duty. Some of us called upon him immediately upon his arrival, and it is probable he did not

meet the secretary with more courtesy than he did us. His conduct and deportment toward us characterized him as a friend and a gentleman. We have confidence in general Sherman, and think that what concerns us could not be under better hands.[43]

If the abolitionists were zealous for a cause that was noble, and the plantationists for an idea that was abhorrent, the pragmatic Sherman at the head of 62,000 cared little—their respective disagreements had led to war, and his Midwesterners were the agents who attacked the latter on behalf of the former, and often died in the process. While he agreed that the Union cause now required the abolition of slavery, Sherman nevertheless felt that the constant calls from the rear for mass enlistments of freed slaves and the resettlement of Negroes were hindrances to the economy and mobility of his army at the front.

In contrast, when his army was occupying Southern capitals and at rest, or later when his Confederate adversaries were unrepentant in their shameful treatment of blacks, Sherman could sound as outraged as any abolitionist. After the war, he hoped that "industrious Negroes" of the North would force the so-called chivalric race of ex-Confederate leaders to "recognize the great proof of virtue in the black race, whom they claim to be inferior in social and political matters." When he paused near Covington, Georgia, Henry Hitchcock recorded a conversation between Sherman and a newly freed slave. The general had just asked the latter what he thought about the war.

> "Well, but you do think something about it—come, now, tell me just what you think—don't be afraid, we are friends." "Well, Sir, what I think about it, is this—it's mighty distressin' this war, but it 'pears to me like *the right thing couldn't be done without it*." The old fellow hit it, exactly. The general has a capital way of talking to these people,—frank, pleasant and unaffected, without being familiar, and they respond with a mingled respect and confidence which shows how well he understands them. He talks in the same simple, clear way to all: tells them the war is because their masters refused to obey the laws, and must be *made to*: that we are their friends, that they are free if they choose, and the able-bodied men among them who *choose* to may go with us, or those who choose may stay with the masters.

In Savannah, Hitchcock also watched Sherman take special care to meet freed slaves. The general, Hitchcock noticed, "has always had them shown in at once, stopping a dispatch or letter or a conversation to greet them in his off-hand—though not undignified way—'Well, boys,—come to see Mr. Sherman, have you? Well, I'm Mr. Sherman—glad to see you'—and shaking hands with them all in a manner highly disgusting, I dare say, to a 'refined Southern gentleman.'" As a senior statesmen in 1888, Sherman wrote, "Let us freely accord to the Negro his fair share of influence and power, trusting the perpetuity of our institutions to the everlasting principles of human nature which tolerate all races and all colors, leaving each human being to seek in his own sphere, the enjoyment of life, liberty, and happiness."

Just as the rank and file in Sherman's army knew that the war was about slavery, so Southerners could admit it too—upon reflection all purported issues of states' rights and suspicions about an all-encompassing Federal government were grounded in the future position of the Negro. A recruit in a South Carolina regiment dismissed the rhetoric of liberty and the rights of Southerners: "I for one am fighting for the maintenance of no such absurdity. . . . We are appealing to chartered rights. . . . It is insulting to the English common sense of race [to say that we] are battling for an abstract right common to all humanity. Every reflecting child will glance at the darkey who waits on him & laugh at the idea of such an 'abstract right.'" Another Confederate soldier in an artillery battery wrote, "A stand must be made for African slavery or it is forever lost." Indeed, one of Mary Todd's brothers-in-law from Alabama confessed, "What would we be without our liberty? We would prefer Death a thousand times to recognizing once a Black Republican ruler altho' he is my brother in law." It is important to remember that, whatever the rhetoric on both sides, Sherman's invaders and Georgia's defenders alike had no doubt that Northerners were in the state because of slavery—their success meant the institution was over; their failure meant the continued bondage of the Negro.[44]

Most astute contemporaries were correct in seeing that the very size, speed, professionalism, and virulence of Sherman's troops were unlike anything that had appeared in any war of the past. What made the army truly unique was not its corporal existence, but its soul. Its own music, the songs written about its mission—there were few memorable hymns written about the Army of the Potomac in late 1864—the mystical nature of its progress, the march's fame that only grew after the war was ended—all are ultimately traced to the ethical nature of this lightning-quick army's freeing the unfree and humiliating the arrogant, all at but nominal cost. How else could Henry Clay Work have sold 500,000 copies of his "Marching Through Georgia" in the first twelve years following the campaign—the equivalent in our own times of selling 5,000,000 record albums?

There was a simmering, terrifying spirit of retribution when the advance guard of this avenging force rode into Madison, Georgia, in a heavy rain during the morning of November 20, 1864. The town was in the richest part of

Georgia, inhabited by the Confederacy's most successful planters and merchants. Rice Bull of the Union army thought Madison was the most beautiful town on the entire march. "The many fine residences were built in the same manner of all the better class of Southern homes, extensive piazzas in front with tall fluted columns reaching almost to the top of the houses. The town boundaries were spread out with many of the residences surrounded by extensive grounds." General Slocum's men, the most "civilized" and Eastern of all Sherman's army, nevertheless quickly looted the stores, burned the courthouse, several of the "better class of Southern homes," and then demolished the slave pens. Once more Rice Bull editorialized:

> The houses were all closed and not a person was seen from window or porch but they sure heard the despised "Yankees" if they did not see them for we marched through the town with all our bands and drum corps playing and the troops shouting themselves hoarse. We felt that the people of these seemingly prosperous cities were more responsible for the war than those whose farms we had overrun since leaving Atlanta. We wanted to impress on them some idea of the power and magnitude of the Army they so hated and despised; so we made all the show we could when we went through Madison.[45]

Such was the spirit of the army that permeated throughout the ranks that General Sherman himself could not have explained Madison's fate any better. But it was only November 20, 1864. The Army of the West, still a mere five days out from Atlanta, was only beginning to learn of the South and its system of slavery—and thus exactly what Mr. Lincoln's war was supposed to have been about all along. There was now to be a day of reckoning that would put to rest more than a half century of legislative compromise and stasis: the beauty of the houses of Madison, the order and tranquility of this Georgia community, the manners of its residents—all were based on a lie and a sin. Now at last both sinner and avenger understood and confronted each other, and so the terrible work began. Theodore Upson, a private from Indiana, captured this spirit of the army later as it neared Savannah:

> We got some Northern papers today. It seems that the good people up there were terribly worried about us. They called us the Lost Army. And some thought we never would show up again. I don't think they know what kind of an Army this is that Uncle Billy has. Why, if Grant can keep Lee and his troops busy we can tramp all over this confederacy; and by the time we were through with that, there would be nothing left but the ground and that would be in a state primeval as the Poet says.

"There is," Sherman wrote, "a soul to an army as well as to the individual man, and no general can accomplish the full work of his army unless he commands the soul of his men, as well as their bodies and legs."[46] The South was about to discover this soul of the Army of the West as it headed to the coast, and so would learn the same terrible lesson that Epaminondas had taught the Spartans so very long ago.

4

WHERE IS THE ENEMY?

GRISWOLDVILLE, GEORGIA

November 22, 1864—Seventh Day Out

SHERMAN'S men on the left horn of the army were now approaching Milledgeville. The right wing under General Howard feinted toward Macon—in line with Sherman's general strategy to have his two wings threaten Augusta and Macon, then bend toward each other, as his entire army passed in between the two cities near the state capital at Milledgeville. Even as Sherman was entering the capital at Milledgeville, outside of Macon some of General Charles Walcutt's men from Osterhaus's 15th Corps had just begun to encamp for their noon meal near Griswoldville, a tiny community recently torched by Kilpatrick's Union cavalry. About 1,500 veterans from Illinois, Iowa, Indiana, and Ohio regiments were relaxing and had put down their new lethal repeating Spencer rifles—seven shots could be fired continuously in ten seconds from such weapons, far more rounds than a traditional musket could discharge in a minute.

Suddenly, a Rebel force at least twice their size came charging across a field, a mere 600 yards away. The Northerners, veterans of dozens of such attacks, methodically formed a line, and begin firing when the Confederates were still 250 yards distant. They kept up a murderous volley until their ammunition nearly ran out, and then prepared to fix bayonets. When the last wave of the enemy had approached to within fifty yards from their position, additional cartridges were brought forward and Sherman's veterans unleashed renewed volleys that slaughtered the last wave of the Confederates. Despite

169

outnumbering the Northern brigade, 600 of the Rebels were killed at the loss of about a hundred Northern casualties. Indeed, Sherman's men were confused about such tyros; why by late 1864 would Confederate soldiers charge seasoned shots with repeating rifles in fixed positions? The Indiana private, Theodore Upson, describes what the Union troops saw when they approached the killing field near dusk:

> We went down on the line where lay the dead of the Confederates. It was a terrible sight. Some one was groaning. We moved a few bodies, and there was a boy with a broken arm and leg—just a boy 14 years old; and beside him, cold in death, lay his Father, two Brothers, and an Uncle. It was a harvest of death. We brought the poor fellow up to the fire. Our surgeons made him as comfortable as they could. Then we marched away leaving him with his own wounded who we could no longer care for.

"We never wanted to fight," another of the survivors told his Union captors. "The cavalry rounded us up and drove us in and made us march." For the most part, the dead were part of some 3,700 Georgia militiamen, forcibly conscripted from farms, all either infirm, far past military age, or mere boys. They were without training, poorly armed, and led by an alcoholic General P. J. Phillips. While the politicians and militia generals—and for the past week there had been dozens fleeing over to the North from Milledgeville—screamed about and threatened Sherman's army, the weakest of Southern society tragically and senselessly—and bravely—died. The mounted and professional Confederate warriors, who harassed the enemy on the wing and rear, forcibly conscripted the amateur and ill prepared to charge ahead. One Illinois soldier sighed of these Griswoldville dead, "I hope we will never have to shoot at such men again"—men variously described by Sherman's soldiers as "old grey-haired and weakly-looking men and little boys not over 15 years old." Such a strange sort of chivalry in the South, Sherman's men were discovering.[47]

Why were boys and old men charging Sherman's veteran corps at all? It was not entirely because there were not other Southerners more hale to stop the Union march. While these brave amateurs were rounded up to be slaughtered, 10,000 regular Confederate troops from South Carolina and Georgia were barricaded in Augusta—these bystanders would remain there safely inside the city with General Braxton Bragg as Sherman's columns passed on by to the coast. If later postbellum Southern critics of Sherman would charge that he had not fought major battles in Georgia, they would still have to confess the complicity of their own troops: Sherman feinted at fortified cities and garrisons, and the Confederates were only too happy to stay fast—and remain alive—in them. Evading Augusta and Macon was at least part of a larger Union strategy that advanced Sherman's material and psychological aims; in contrast, leaving such good troops in isolated pockets was fatal to Southern resistance. Besides Bragg, General William Hardee, a forty-nine-year-old Georgia native and author of a widely acclaimed handbook on military tactics, with some 6,000 to 7,000 Georgia irregulars augmented with survivors from the slaughter at Griswoldville, was assembling a force of over 10,000 defenders to protect Savannah. And throughout Sherman's march, General Joseph Wheeler, with over 3,000 Confederate horsemen, harassed his flanks and sparred with Kilpatrick's Union cavalry. With all these various other contingents, there may have been over 20,000 available mounted and infantry troops under the command of Hardee and Wheeler.

John Bell Hood, with the main Confederate force of some 40,000 who had fought Sherman all the way to Atlanta, was now going in the opposite direction toward Thomas's Army of Tennessee. Unlike Sherman, he was not planning to waste territory and rock the confidence of the North, as much as to fight a decisive battle against an entrenched and superior foe, and seemingly to occupy a vast land with an undermanned army—a doomed proposition on both counts. Hood really was going into a hole he would not come out of. Robert E. Lee was held fast by Grant in Virginia. For all the Northern apprehension, there was little chance that he might break away and hit Sherman unexpectedly somewhere in eastern Georgia or the Carolinas. Sherman felt that if Longstreet or any other of Lee's generals was dispatched southward from Virginia, he would welcome the collision. Scholars, when they review the scant 100 Union dead on the March to the Sea, the near absence of resistance during the monthlong campaign, and Sherman's rapid progress through the Georgian countryside, have sometimes made the mistake of thinking that there was essentially no danger to the Northerners and the success of the march was foreordained. Nothing could be further from the truth.[48]

Had Generals Bragg and Hardee combined forces, and fought in close connection with Wheeler's horsemen, they might have fielded some 20,000 to 30,000 troops who could have entrenched, ambushed, and concentrated on one of Sherman's horns. If they had been successful, even a short delay in his march might have brought Sherman ruin, given the chance of inclement weather and subsequent hunger. Each Union flank, remember, was separated by as much as sixty miles—and, in fact, later at Bentonville, North Carolina, at a stage in the war when it was far too late, Joe Johnston would employ just that strategy of trying to destroy one wing in isolation before turning on the other. During the March to the Sea, Sherman had a smaller army and a more limited amount of ammunition. He was entirely dependent on local supplies.

Unlike the later march through the Carolinas, in mid-Georgia he was now without communications or provisioning from the sea. Because he had no mechanism either to care for or to evacuate his wounded, even a well-planned and concerted Southern fighting withdrawal—in the manner of the great Scythian retreat before the Persian invasion or the Russian scorched-earth evacuation before Napoleon—might have waylaid Sherman's army for days, as local militias, guerrillas, and reinforcements converged to isolate a hungry Union army deep in enemy territory. The Confederates, after all, proclaimed that they had dour mounted raiders in just that grand tradition of the Cossacks and the Scythians.

Just the opposite took place. Bragg timidly kept his 10,000 in Augusta. Hardee evacuated his men to Savannah. Wheeler battled fiercely, but exclusively on the periphery. Hood continued north and was destroyed in Tennessee. Lee could not disengage from Grant. Nor was there to be any serious systematic Confederate effort at destroying food and forage in Sherman's path. The reasons were not merely material—the sheer size or considerable firepower of Sherman's army—but rather psychological as well. As we have seen, the South followed the leadership of a tiny plantation class, men whose influence derived from two properties alone—agricultural land and slaves. To abandon either was in their mind to abandon the South itself.

For all the proclamations about states' rights and the preservation of liberty as envisioned by the Founding Fathers, for all the shrill posturing about a distinctively Southern culture, Sherman had a keen appreciation that the landed wealthy had championed secession mostly for the preservation and expansion of their own vast estates and black Helots—property, not ideas, was the issue. As long as there was the slightest chance that any one Confederate elite's plantation might be missed or spared by Sherman's bummers, a broad consensus for voluntary destruction of Confederate plantations to serve a wider cause was largely impossible. Indeed, sometimes the rich plantationists left their helpless behind as a mechanism to protect their capital in their own absence. The rapidity of the plantation owners' flight amazed Sherman's men. "Soldiers were aghast to find at a plantation only recently evacuated by a Georgia legislator the man's sick wife and newborn infant. At another place, they found two young girls alone in a cabin and were shocked when none of the neighbors was willing to take the small children in."

Yet the more the wealthy of northern Georgia fled, leaving their property intact and their families alone on the land, the bolder the Union army became. Once Sherman left Atlanta and began to cut through Georgia, the entire complexion of the war in the West changed almost overnight. Where before Sherman had in daily fighting sparred with, and had to outflank, Johnston, and pursued Hood endlessly, he now simply dismissed the Confederate army and turned to his own "business down south." Within days the army—itself increasingly veteran and hardened from nearly an entire summer of daily fighting against Johnston—developed a momentum and élan that was nearly unstoppable as word of its sheer destructive power swept through the entire civilian and military fabric of Southern civilization. Sherman's men were now to take it upon themselves to right a great wrong. As Sherman's aide Henry Hitchcock remarked of Georgia, "This is a country which has never before felt the woes which they have long helped inflict on others."

The feebleness of Confederate resistance was clear from the vehemence of the rhetoric. Southern papers railed impotently. The *Savannah Daily Morning News* promised that Sherman's men, "who are not willing to surrender can be beautifully bushwhacked." The *Augusta Constitutionalist* exclaimed: "The opportunity is ours. . . . Let the invader find the desolation he would leave behind, staring him in the face. . . . It is absurdity to talk about his making a winter campaign with no communication with his Government. He is retreating—simply retreating." From generals and politicians the fiery vocabulary masking inaction was to be "defend," "rally," and "fly to arms" for "the native soil" and "patriotic Governor." Sherman chuckled at all this as confirmation that his campaign to bring the war home to the perpetrators was wildly successful, "Of course, we were rather amused than alarmed at these threats, and made light of the feeble opposition offered to our progress."[49]

Sherman posed the question, as Epaminondas had once forced upon a similar slave-owning, chivalric, and military-bound society on the brink of annihilation: who in the South now would be willing to match word with deed, and be the first to die before these frightful Yankees for the home soil of Georgia? Very few indeed, as it turned out, other than conscripted boys and old men like those rotting in the ground of Griswoldville. Major James Connolly of an Illinois regiment remarked of the silence in the Georgia countryside: "Where can the rebels be? Here we are riding rough shod over Georgia and nobody dares to fire a shot at us. We burn their houses, barns, fences, cotton and everything else, yet none of the Southern braves show themselves to punish us for our vandalism." A Texas trooper would write, "General Sherman ought to have been totally defeated and ruined, but the sad fact will be handed down to posterity that while Sherman's minions were devastating the country with fire and committing outrages upon defenseless women, the men of Georgia staid at home, or at least a portion of them, trying to save what they had."[50]

Union soldiers continued to be mystified, more often amused, at the sudden collapse of opposition. A New Yorker wrote home of the anomaly that the closer the army got to the heartland of the enemy, the *less* the resistance: "We think here the rebs are about whipped for they won't wait to give Sherman battle any more." A Wisconsin soldier remarked of the retreating Confederates, "We had a most magnificent view of their coat tails standing out at right angles to a pair of legs that was doing their best to take their owners to a place of safety." Rice Bull noticed the same thing: "The Confederates seemed to have lost their old vigor; they could hardly be induced to make a stand at any place and when they did so it was in a very feeble way. As we advanced many Johnnies deserted and came into our lines. The rank and file of their Army seemed disheartened and those coming in said that they could not hold together much longer." True, there may not have been very many able-bodied residents left in Georgia to create an effective army of resistance. But there *were* Confederate forces in the general vicinity of the central South to have coalesced into a formidable obstacle to Sherman's progress.

The army of Sherman was now exposing one of the great embarrassments of a chivalric, apartheid society: rhetoric, costumes, polite manners, titles, and arcane traditions among a privileged elite hide weakness rather than reflect strength. An egalitarian society of freeholding citizens that can draw on all members of its population, make them feel of equal value to the cause, and sanction their brutality by a true democratic consensus, needs no emblems of ferocity because it is intrinsically ferocious, even scary in war, both numerically and qualitatively. It was no accident that on surrender Grant looked shabby, slouchy, and muddy, Lee resplendent and sworded; Sherman was rumpled, Joe Johnston dapper in his military gray; as a rule, Southern horsemen were more privileged and adroit, Union cavalry workmanlike and more numerous; Southern infantry loud, brave, and bold in their charges, Union troops usually better armed, more plentiful, and in the end far more lethal.[51]

General bickering, class rivalries, and disavowal of the Cause itself were to become the expected dividends of such a mass march into the interior of a hierarchical helot society. Sherman himself, in his infamous "Field Order 120," sought to intensify the now growing rift between Southern rich and poor: "As for horses, mules, wagons, etc., belonging to the inhabitants, the cavalry and artillery may appropriate freely and without limit; discriminating, however, between the rich, who are usually hostile, and the poor and industrious, usually neutral or friendly." A Northern chaplain of the army remarked, "The wealthy people of the South were the very ones to plunge the country into secession, now let them suffer." As Sherman expected from his class war, the poor whites for the first time began to blame those richer. Sometimes, together with freed blacks, they pointed out to Union troops the hidden stores of the long-gone planter. An Indiana officer noticed of their strange succor that "the times were propitious for the 'poor white' to show the arrogant planter that 'one man is as good as another' and for the revengeful who had cherished a grudge to get even with his neighbor." Now the citizenry of Georgia claimed that a few planters all along had been solely responsible for secession—just as shell-shocked German civilians would complain to Patton's men that the Nazi elite were alone responsible for their present catastrophe. Henry Hitchcock once again did not put much faith in such convenient contrition. He sarcastically remarked, "This man Mallory fully confirms all we have heard about the large Union majority in Georgia—that it was *bullied* into rebellion, by a desperate minority,—that they are now "forced" and dragged into the army,—that a vast majority of them long for peace but dare not say so, etc., etc., etc."[52]

Sherman's men were especially fed up with the bold women of the South, whose venom was unconcealed. It was not just the wealthy females of the plantation class who abetted confederate ardor, but rather the entire female ideology of the Confederacy itself that irked Sherman. In the Northern way of thinking, most Southern women were not as brave and boisterous as they seemed, but rather hypocrites. Hiding behind their gender and expecting the Southern traditions of genteel respect usually accorded the "weaker" sex, the wealthy women of the Confederacy felt free to insult and openly berate the invaders. One Savannah matron said of a polite Union soldier, "He walked out like a well bred dog." On the porch of one house another Iowa soldier was lectured by the mistress: "My husband is a captain in the Confederate army and I'm proud of it. You can rob us, you can take everything we have. I can live on pine straw the rest of my days. You can kill us, but you can't conquer us." Of course, they did not kill her, and she was in fact conquered.[53]

Sherman enraged the womenfolk of the South through his quite visible, systematic humiliation of Southern manhood. As he wrote his wife, even before the March to the Sea:

> I doubt if history affords a parallel to the deep and bitter enmity of the women of the South. No one who sees them and hears them but must feel the intensity of their hate. Not a man is seen; nothing but women with houses plundered, fields open to the cattle and horses, pickets lounging on every porch, and desolation broadcast, servants all gone and women and children bred in luxury, beautiful and accomplished, begging with one breath for the soldiers' rations and in another praying that the Almighty or Joe Johnston will come and kill us, the despoilers of their homes and all that is sacred. Why cannot they look back to the day and the hour when I, a stranger in Louisiana, begged and implored them to pause in their career, that secession was everything fatal.

The animosity of Southern women also brought laughs and sneers from Sherman's men, whose anger was born from frustration—proof positive of the enormous chasm between the reality and the avowed ideals of the Confederacy. One plantation mistress describes her terror—and disgust—when some of Sherman's cavalry ransacked her home:

> It is impossible to imagine the horrible uproar and stampede through the house, every room of which was occupied by them, all yelling, cursing, quarreling, and running from one room to another in wild confusion. Such was their blasphemous language, their horrible countenances and appearance, that we realized what must be the association of the lost in the world of eternal woe. Their throats were open sepulchers, their mouths filled with cursing and bitterness and lies. These men belonged to Kilpatrick's cavalry, too terrible to be true.

A few of the more serious of the Union troops tried to illustrate to these women the hypocrisy of Confederate society. An Ohio colonel heard one of his men rebuke a Southern matron, in language which might have come right out of the mouth of Epaminondas had he had the similar opportunity to address the shrieking women on the Spartan acropolis:

> You in wild enthusiasm, urge young men to the battlefield where men are being killed by the thousands, while you stay at home and sing "The Bonnie Blue Flag"; but you set up a howl when you see the Yankees down here getting your chickens. Many of your young men have told us that they are tired of war and would quit, but you women would shame them and drive them back.[54]

The historian Gerald Linderman has characterized these female pressures in the South as "sexual intimidation":

> Those who most imperatively urged enlistment were women. They no less than soldiers expected courageous behavior and anathematized cowardice. Their special weapon might with justice be called sexual intimidation. A Richmond clerk reported in May 1861 that the "ladies are postponing all engagements until their lovers have fought the Yankees."

As Sherman knew, his 62,000 men in Georgia would end such nonsense for good. "I used to feel very brave about the Yankees," one Eliza Andrews wrote in January 1865, "but since I have passed over Sherman's track and seen what devastation they made, I am so afraid of them that I believe I should drop down dead if one of the wretches should come into my presence."

With the advance of the Union army, civilians in general not only blamed the rich, and each other, but also the Confederate army which, faced with the same logistical requirements as Sherman's men in Georgia, plundered the countryside every bit as effectively as the foragers of the Army of the West. The difference between the damage caused by Union troops and by Confederate defenders derived not from differing need, intent, or method so much as simply size. Confederate secretary of state Robert Toombs wrote Vice President of the Confederacy Alexander Stephens of the Southern cavalry depredations, "I hope to God [Wheeler] will never get back to Georgia." Henry Hitchcock saw the same disgust among the civilian population with the Southern military:

> We heard yesterday of Wheeler's "conscripting" an old man of fifty-six and by the way, that preacher yesterday (who did not pretend to be a Union man) abused Wheeler and "his gang of horse-thieves" in the handsomest style, and said they had been going all over these counties, seizing and stealing horses everywhere and taking them into the upper counties and selling them. Lovely fruits this "peaceable secession" bears, truly.

The *Charleston Mercury* later published a similar complaint against Wheeler's foragers in South Carolina: "Private houses are visited, carpets, blankets and other furniture they can lay their hands on are taken by force in the presence of the owner."[55]

Besides the rifts of class, the growing mistrust of civilians toward the Confederate military, and the hypocrisy of gender, Sherman's entry awoke sectarian rivalries from an inherently weak Confederacy—non-Georgians now ridiculed Georgian cowardice; Georgians in turn warned other Confederates that they had never seen anything quite like Sherman's army. South Carolina, which had first ignited the rebellion that had brought such ruin to Georgia, became especially the focus of blame. One devastated farmer begged of Sherman's men, "All I ask is that when you get to South Carolina you will treat them the same way." Others added, "Why don't you go over to South Carolina and serve them this way? They started it." Another Georgian recalled: "Just above Savannah one night while on picket duty about forty men came from South Carolina to enter service. They asked me what in the hell we meant by letting Sherman march through Georgia. I told them; all right, You will have a chance of it in a few days, for he is sure coming, and you will not be able to stop him either."

For all the thousands of Rebels Grant had killed in Virginia, he had been unable to turn poor white against rich plantationist, Georgian against Carolinian, civilian against soldier, or to expose the hypocrisy of the wealthy or female Confederate citizenry in smugly and safely supporting the war from afar. Only a march into the interior led by a firebrand like Sherman could do that. A once proud Georgia soldier wrote home after Sherman's march, "I feel very little inclined to call myself a Georgian any more, and if it were not that you all live in Macon I should disown the state in toto and transfer my allegiance." Just as Epaminondas's entry into Laconia had set Spartiate against Spartiate, Perioikoi against Spartiate, Helot against his master, and Peloponnesian allies against Spartans, so too now Sherman brought out all the contradictions of a similar slave society, whose elite invests its moral capital in rigid delineation between social groups. The states of the Confederacy at large were splitting apart just as easily as had the fractious allies of the old Peloponnesian league that had once centered around the Spartan apartheid state.[56]

The psychological ramifications of the march were immediately felt by Sherman's men, who at last realized the grand plan and strategy of their general, and now knew why they were in the Deep South marching fifteen miles a day. Henry Hitchcock characteristically put the destruction of Georgia in a wider context:

> Evidently it is a material element in this campaign to produce among the *people of Georgia* a thorough conviction of the personal misery which attends war, and of the utter helplessness and inability of their "rulers," State or Confederate, to protect them. And I am bound to say that I believe more and more that only by this means the war can be ended,—and that *by this means it can*. It is a terrible thing to consume and destroy the sustenance of thousands of people, and most sad and distressing in itself to see and hear the terror and grief of these women and children. But personally they are protected and their dwellings are not destroyed; and if that terror and grief and even want shall help to paralyze their husbands and fathers who are fighting and *bringing like terror and grief into more innocent homes* in our Border States, and shall help to break up the terrible despotism which—so they say—"forces them to fight us," even if this can be done only by driving them to despair,—it is mercy in the end.

Another Northerner concluded, "Let the Confederates be assured that they must either whip our armies, or be themselves annihilated unless they give up contest, and many of them will lay down their arms." Jerome Carpenter, an Indiana sergeant, waxed eloquently in a similar vein:

> I wish I could give you something of an idea of the magnitude of this campaign, but I cannot, and can only say that the half will never be told. Suffice it to say that we have seen the Confederacy as it is and feel reassured that a few more decisive blows in the right direction and the Rebellion will be dead; then will justice be meted out to the instigators and they and their sympathiz-

ers branded with eternal disgrace and infamy. The day is already dawning and I trust the sun of Freedom will shine forth in all its fire and blood on many a battle-field, float more proudly in the breeze, then will the Bird of Liberty take a more lofty flight, and peace and prosperity shall again crown this noble Republic.

Typically, Sherman was more blunt. In nine famous brutal words he summed up the destructive capacity of his own army, the pathetic braggadocio of the South, and the real infirmity of the Confederacy: "Pierce the *shell* of the C.S.A. and it's hollow."[57]

In the days after Sherman's departure, no Southern army coalesced to block his success, simply because no army believed it was in its power to do so. Sherman, who had killed few, had now become extrahuman, some terrible biblical avenger that mere human agency could not fathom and who was responsible personally for every single act of devastation the South was to endure. All ruin was to be personified. "Sherman's corkscrews" or "Sherman's neckties" were twisted rails; "Sherman's Sentinels" the chimneys left from torched houses. Southern freed slaves in general were "Sherman's Freedmen," while later a burned city like Columbia, South Carolina, became "Sherman's Brick Yard."

Foreign editorials and domestic proclamations reflected the South's astonishment at the sheer audacity of the onslaught of this Northern army into Georgia. Sometimes Sherman was compared to Napoleon, at other times to Julius Caesar. Those outraged called him Attila or Judas Iscariot; those impressed, Marlborough and Hannibal. His gambit might either end in success rivaling Xenophon's anabasis, or in abject failure like Xerxes' ruin in Greece. In any case, the simile was always to be larger than life. In the space of a few weeks, Sherman was to be ranked not among either the great Northern or Southern generals of the Civil War, but in history's select pantheon of military conquerors. If critics had trouble placing Sherman in the proper context of military history, it is understandable since his military prowess was as unique as the purposes for which it was employed.[58]

Not all the fear of Sherman's army was psychological. His army, after all, possessed more destructive potential than any force its size in history—through the power of its armament, the rapidity of its movement, and its sheer mastery of the art of destroying civilian infrastructure. For all Sherman's efforts at lightening his army's supplies and culling out the infirm, the army nevertheless possessed 62,000 veteran soldiers, a core of crack shots and cool heads matched by none in any other Northern or Southern force—all overseen by a superb veteran staff, skilled logisticians, and ingenious engineers organized by the omnipresent Captain Poe, inventor of various hooks, cranes, and assorted devices to facilitate more rapid destruction of rail tracks, depots, and machine shops. His trek was not a raid, but a methodical sweep by a veritable moving city of avengers. Sherman was not worried about the practicality of moving such huge columns; in fact, had he his choice, he would have brought along even more—when the war ended, his army marching toward Grant was more than 100,000 strong.

Even though Sherman's men on the march had access to only about 200 cartridges each, the army was still capable of shooting over 12,000,000 rounds—if need be all within a few hours from rifled weapons, many of them by fall 1864 repeating Spencers and Henrys that could fire in succession from seven to fifteen shots without reloading. Earlier in the Atlanta campaign during a single day at Kennesaw Mountain, an Ohio regiment of 200 soldiers had fired off 24,000 rounds. If we use accepted figures that between 100 and 200 rounds were usually expended in major battles for each enemy soldier killed or wounded, Sherman's flying columns in Georgia had the potential to inflict somewhere between 60,000 and well over 100,000 casualties from their rifle fire alone. That firepower and the army's quickness explains why Theodore Upson was so confident of his comrades as they marched: "I should think those fool Johnnys would quit. They might as well try to stop a tornado as Uncle Billy and his boys."

The rifles that Sherman's men used during the march through Georgia were a far cry from the assorted obsolete muskets ubiquitous in the army of 1861. In fact, the most modern of them could now fire a rifled bullet of over .50 caliber accurately up to six hundred yards. Unlike the amateur conscripts of the South who had charged at Griswoldville, shooting inaccurately with muskets on the run, Sherman's men were seasoned pros who automatically entrenched, waited, and could often hit from afar what they aimed at. And the science of firearms had far exceeded that of tactics, medical support, and logistics. Sherman's repeating rifles were not all that different from World War Two infantry firearms—yet a Civil War soldier's rations, access to medicine, transportation, and savvy in dealing with the lethal nature of repeating weapons were a world away from the GI's. The result was the bullet wounds that would be quickly and effectively treated a century later, in the Civil War often mean amputation, infection, and death. To attack a force like Sherman's, equipped with modern firearms in an ancient world of medicine and soldier support, could mean the ruination of an entire army. We should keep that in mind when we criticize the absence of a concerted Confederate response.

Similarly, the source of Epaminondas's strategic success in Laconia was not merely its size or audacity, but its tactical battlefield prowess; no Spartan army, as Leuctra demonstrated, could stand up to a Theban mass of fifty shields deep boring down on it. In the same manner, at the heart of Sherman's terror was the realization that by 1864 should any Southern corps arrive in force to meet the Army of the West in pitched battle, it would more than likely be annihilated. At Bentonville, the last major battle of the Civil War, 20,000 Confederate infantrymen, under the capable generalship of Joe Johnston, surprised the left wing of Sherman's army, consisting of about an equal number of troops. After a few initial successes the entire Southern army was cut off and would have been wiped out had Sherman wished to press on with the attack. The Confederacy faced a paradox: its tradition of chivalry demanded a response; the sanctity of Southern soil and womanhood required a defense; militarily a spirited resistance could slow and even harm Sherman's progress—but all such notions ensured the deaths of thousands of Confederate soldiers in the process. Rhetoric increased as action diminished. The sad quandary for the Confederacy was unmistakable: act out the lie and die—or confess to the truth and live.[59]

Even more impressive than the Union army's firepower was its mobility, namely Sherman's proven ability to move between ten and fifteen miles in a single day for weeks on end—a phenomenal rate in the preindustrial age. Should the Confederates ever coalesce and form extensive lines of entrenched defense, there was no guarantee that Sherman's men—as was so characteristic in their unstoppable summer advance from Tennessee to Atlanta—would not simply swing around and march on by. Even the basic strategy on the March to the Sea—two vast groups of nearly 30,000 men each would destroy parallel railroad lines from Atlanta to Charleston and Savannah through the respective Augusta and Macon junctions—was unclear to the Southerners. Given Sherman's speed and mobility, he could feint at any points of concentrated enemy resistance—Augusta and Macon—leaving the enemy trying to defend everything and hence nothing.

To wage a campaign of terror, such a blitzkrieg was essential. Contemporary accounts emphasize that much of Sherman's fearsome reputation derived from his ability to appear seemingly out of nowhere with thousands, when defenders believed only hundreds were still days away. Henry Hitchcock reflected the army's pride in such rapidity when he dismissed Southern claims that Sherman's supply lines had been cut by Hood:

The absurdly desperate stuff in a rebel paper of 20th—viz.: that Hood had completely succeeded in "cutting Sherman's communications," and that S. was thereby forced to his present "desperate retreat through Georgia to the seacoast" with an army *of not over 25,000 men* (!) and that as he could not march over ten miles per day (Howard made twenty miles yesterday) he would inevitably be delayed by burning bridges, etc. till re-inforcements should come to *destroy him*, etc., etc.—How these wretched lies will rebound against their authors! One swing of this army alone is over—yes, much, but no matter how much, *over* 25,000 men. We can march twenty miles a day whenever we choose, and do march over fifteen. It is a magnificent army of *veterans*, brimful of spirit and a deviltry, literally "spoiling for a fight," neither knowing nor caring where they are going, blindly devoted to and confiding in "the old man" in splendid condition, weeded of all sick, etc., and every man fully understanding that there is no return, nor safety but in fighting through.[60]

No wonder Joe Johnston would in the end compare Sherman's men to Julius Caesar's legions—correct in the one sense that no other army before the Industrial Revolution had so mastered the art of *celeritas*. But where Caesar's men were tough pros who fought to overthrow Republican government for a daily wage and a promise of confiscated land upon retirement, Sherman's were ideological warriors. At war's end, most in the Army of the West would have little money, would have suffered years of lost wages, and would never again march with or even see their beloved general, Bill Sherman.

The army had another weapon beside quickness that was also not merely psychological. The troops—who were experts at constructing pontoon bridges and railroad trestles—very quickly mastered the corollary arts of destruction. Devastation of crops and property is not as easy as it looks. Animals can be hidden away; stores concealed; crops if not absolutely dry do not combust readily; bent rails, if not twisted, were reusable; and not all things wooden were flammable. Sherman took special interest in developing not merely a skilled corps of foragers—the infamous bummers who fed the army for over a month from Georgia stores—but experts at fire and ruin. Moreover, his foragers were not merely devastators nor simple agents of logistics and supply, but also a formidable advance guard of the army that could assess enemy resistance, and on occasion clear the way for the main columns, which might not need to halt at the noise of gunfire. General Jacob Cox remarks of their amazing élan and flexibility:

The foragers became the *beau ideal* of partisan troops. Their self-confidence and daring increased to a wonderful pitch, and no organized line of skirmishers could so quickly clear the head of column of the opposing cavalry of the enemy. Nothing short of an entrenched line of battle could stop them, and when they were far scattered on the flank, plying their vocation, if a body of hostile cavalry approached, a singular sight was to be seen. Here and there, from barn, from granary and smokehouse, and from the kitchen gardens of the plantations, isolated foragers would hasten by converging lines, driving before them the laden mule heaped high with vegetables, smoked bacon, fresh meat, and poultry. As soon as two or three of these met, one would drive the animals, and the others, from fence corners or behind trees, would begin a bold skirmish, their Springfield rifles giving them the advantage in range over the carbines of the horsemen. As they were pressed they would continue falling back and assembling, the regimental platoons falling in beside each other till their line of fire would become too hot for their opponents, and these would retire reporting that they had driven in the skirmishers upon the main column which was probably miles away. The work of foraging would then be resumed.

Because the two horns of the army were themselves subdivided, Sherman's force was in reality four independent columns, each responsible for its own supply and area of devastations. For each eastward mile of Georgian countryside, foragers ranged out laterally for about six or seven miles between each column, and cavalry protected the front, flanks, and rear, scouted ahead, and kept communications between the columns constant. Produce and plunder were brought to the wagons where the main infantry marched along without interruption. Sherman describes how the plundering had become a near science:

> Habitually each corps followed some main road, and the foragers, being kept out on the exposed flank, served all the military uses of flankers. The main columns gathered, by the roads traveled, much forage and food, chiefly meat, corn, and sweet potatoes, and it was the duty of each division and brigade quartermaster to fill his wagons fast as the contents were issued to the troops. The wagon-trains had the right to the road always, but each wagon was required to keep closed up, so as to leave no gap in the column. If for any purpose any wagon or group of wagons dropped out of place, they had to wait for the rear. And this was always dreaded, for each brigade commander wanted his train up at camp as soon after reaching it with his men as possible.

While some plundered and destroyed private property, the great majority of the army concentrated on the railroad, determined to cut off Atlanta from the coast for good. Enlistee Rice Bull described the science of rail bed devastation:

> All tools, axes, bars, clamps, etc., were supplied from the wagons. The way we did the work was to line our men along the rack, then with bars made of wood or iron raise the track, with both rails and ties clinging together, push the rails over on the ties where they could then be separated by iron malls. The ties would be gathered and piled up crosswise to a height of four feet with the rails

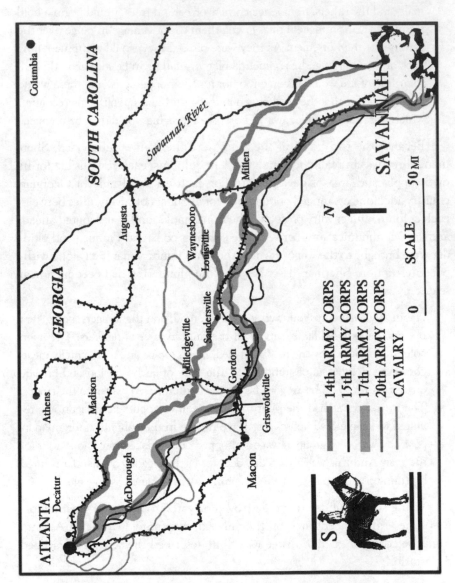

SHERMAN'S ORDER OF ADVANCE

14th ARMY CORPS
15th ARMY CORPS
17th ARMY CORPS
20th ARMY CORPS
CAVALRY

SCALE

0   50 MI

Columbia

SOUTH CAROLINA

Savannah River

GEORGIA

Augusta

Waynesboro
Louisville

Millen

SAVANNAH

Sandersville

Milledgeville

Gordon

Griswoldville

Madison

Athens

McDonough

Macon

ATLANTA
Decatur

N

S

placed on top. When the ties were fired the rails would become red hot and could be twisted and destroyed. The rapidity with which this could be done was surprising. During the day two division of our Corps wrecked ten miles.[61]

It is no exaggeration that by fall 1864 no army in either Europe or America was as mobile, self-supporting, and lethal as Sherman's, which was composed of soldiers in prime physical condition with skilled expertise in the handling of modern firearms. Their general, William Tecumseh Sherman, while he remained at the head of this army, was in some sense not merely the most powerful man in America, but also until the armistice in the spring of 1865 quite literally the most dangerous man in the world. The *Macon Telegraph* warned its readers:

> It would seem as if in him all the attributes of man were merged in the enormities of the demon, as if Heaven intended in him to manifest depths of depravity yet untouched by a fallen race. . . . Unsated still in his demoniac vengeance he sweeps over the country like a simoom of destruction.

Yet the newspaper also assured its readers that Sherman was running away! "Sooner or later his crimes will find their Nemesis. . . . The desolator of our homes, the destroyer of our property, the Attila of the west, seeks sanctuary. His shrine is the sea." Southerners had a poor idea of the Greek deity Nemesis and the Hellenic concept of a just vengeance that slowly claimed its due for crimes of long standing. Had they read their Aeschylus or Sophocles, newspaper editors would have learned that Sherman himself was properly the Nemesis of a rebellious, slave-owning society—the agent, not the target, of a higher retribution. Sherman at least knew this. His depredations in Georgia, in his own later words, were "to be charged up to the account of the rebels who had forced us into the war, and who deserved all they got and more."

The advent of such an army must have been a terrifying experience for an agrarian society. The southern Central Valley of California where I live is similarly about three hundred miles from north to south; the eastern corridor of which between the Sierra Nevada and the state freeway 99 is a belt about forty to sixty miles wide that comprises the richest farmland in the world— Fresno is the wealthiest assessed agricultural county in the nation and the supplier of the majority of America's fresh tree fruit and grapes, as well one of the leaders of dairy and cotton exports. To comprehend anything comparable to Sherman's coming into Georgia is to imagine a huge column of mobile burners, starting out in the state capital to the north at Sacramento, and soon to be descending to torch all the farmland of this valley southward to Bakersfield. Everything to the interior between San Francisco and Los Angeles would be as desolate as the sixty-mile-wide corridor between Atlanta and Savannah.

In my homeland, situated in the exact center, I can imagine continuous columns of marchers from Fresno twenty miles to the north, and east from here to the Sierra Nevada, burning and destroying as they moved through small towns, tearing up the main railroad from San Francisco to Los Angeles, section by section, each day. I can envision that Americans from a different region of the country, with different accents and customs—perhaps Eastern-ers, whom we often automatically distrust and do not fully fathom still—would come onto this farm, lecture and berate us, strip our residence of everything I now gaze upon—furniture, silver, paintings, rugs, ancestral clocks, the sum of the collective acquisition of five generations of previous family members who have lived in this same house. After all, when wagons returned from Georgia's farms to Sherman's columns, they were

> full of pumpkins, chickens, cabbages, guinea fowls, carrots, turkeys, onions, squashes, a shoat, sorghum, a looking glass, an Italian harp, sweet-meats, a peacock, a rocking chair, a gourd, a bass viol, sweet potatoes, a cradle, dried peaches, honey, a baby carriage, peach brandy, and every other imaginable thing a lot of foot soldiers could take in their heads to bring away.

Dour, tough men, more dangerous than any trespassers I have run off on evening walks from this small 120-acre farm, would ride in, camp, sleep, and feast as they saw fit, destroying our pump and water well, and killing our five dogs and assorted pets. To understand Sherman's onslaught would be to see a barn outside my window, constructed by my great-grandfather well over a hundred years ago, torched, trees stripped of fresh fruit, bins of stored raisins, nuts, and dried fruits—the past year's work and the only chance of cash for the future—consumed or simply dumped. Fences and outbuildings, literally everything wooden, would be collected and burned. Machinery in the field would be all wrecked, yard and grounds desecrated—and excavated and redug for buried treasure. Some of the flotsam and jetsam would be the result of gratuitous thievery—my grandmother's silver platter used for target prac-tice, some two thousand books in my study thrown on the dirt and trampled in the alleyway. To imagine Sherman's arrival would be to see flames on every farm of this immediate vicinity, made worse with the realization that heroic defense meant instant death, and worse still that the ravagers were not always the ignorant and illiterate, but occasionally the learned who would hector me about how the destruction of my farm was inevitable, the moral wages of my support for the evil of slavery and the treachery of sedition. In short, our 120-year-old farm, where now five separate family households reside, would resemble the Canning plantation after Sherman's army moved through it on November 28:

> We could hardly believe it was our home. One week before it was one of the most beautiful places in the state. Now it was a vast wreck. Gin-house, packing screws, granary—all lay in ashes. Not a fence was to be seen for miles . . . the army had turned their stock into the fields and destroyed what they had not carried off. Burning cotton and grain filled the air with smoke, and the sun seemed to hide its face.

In my impotence, I would hate the arrogant Eastern Americans who ruined a century of my family's work, destroyed my community, and ended my viability as a farmer—and I would despise more the architect of that desolation, heartless and crazy Bill Sherman. But I would also *never* again think that either my neighbors or I had the right—or power—to hold slaves, much less either the prerogative or ability to declare California and the property of the federal government within it as our region's own. We would have no doubts that we were defeated.

And I would hope that my sixteen-year-old son, Billy Hanson, who like his deceased grandfather and namesake has lived his entire life amid these vineyards and orchards, would not be rotting in some field nearby like Griswoldville, Georgia, after he had armed himself with the assorted obsolete weaponry of this farm to charge bravely into the murderous line of the army of the United States in order to save our property—and along with it the idea of states' rights and thus human bondage itself. And finally, again, I would hope that the commander of such an army of Nemesis was not a man like William T. Sherman, who would say of our ruin and our gallant anger, "Those people made war on us, defied and dared us to come south to their country, where they boasted they would kill us and do all manner of horrible things. We accepted their challenge, and now for them to whine and complain of the natural and necessary results is beneath contempt."[62]

5

AN APARTHEID SOCIETY

MILLEDGEVILLE, GEORGIA

November 24, 1864—Ninth Day Out

A FEW HOURS after the skirmishing to the south at Griswoldville, the north wing of the Army of the West made its way through the Georgia state capital. By the evening of November 24, 30,000 Union troops had marched for two solid days right through an abandoned Milledgeville—by war's end Sherman's army would claim that it had occupied four such state capitals of the Confederacy: Jackson, Mississippi; Milledgeville, Georgia; Columbia, South Carolina; and Raleigh, North Carolina. Now, after the town had been ransacked, Sherman himself was ready to leave the governor's mansion and continue his march in earnest. He was convinced that if he could sleep at ease in the first residence of Georgia, the entire state was surely defenseless before the "second stage" of his advance. Most of the Confederate defenders mistakenly had thought Sherman's northern flank was headed for Augusta. Now completely baffled as to the Northerners' real itinerary, in panic the Southern grandees simply had left their state capital completely undefended.

Most in the Union army were surprised at the ease with which, after three years of Confederate bombast and promises of terrible retribution, Sherman had simply marched hundreds of miles deep into the South and occupied without resistance the capital of Georgia. "It was quiet to all appearance as Madison had been," Rice Bull wrote of the army's entrance. "All the prominent people had fled. The Governor of Georgia, the Legislature that had been in session, the Judges, and all other state officials had left the capital. Not a hand had been raised to defend Milledgeville and the 'Yankees' were in possession without firing a shot." Sherman's entry into Georgia was as easy as Epaminondas's breakthrough at Sellasia—the purportedly fortress garrison that barred the way into Laconia—and Patton's penetration of Hitler's vaunted "West Wall" that guarded the interior of Germany.

Sherman also scoffed at this embarrassing great gulf between Confederate words and deeds:

> The people of Milledgeville remained at home, except the Governor (Brown), the State officers, and Legislature, who had ignominiously fled, in the utmost disorder and confusion; standing not on the order of their going, but going at once—some by rail, some by carriages, and many on foot. Some of the citizens who remained behind described this flight of the "brave and patriotic" Governor Brown. He had occupied a public building known as the "Governor's Mansion," and had hastily stripped it of carpets, curtains, and furniture of all sorts, which were removed to a train of freight-cars, which carried away these things—even the cabbages and vegetables from his kitchen and cellar—leaving behind muskets, ammunition, and the public archives.[63]

The grand plan of the Army of the West was now nearing fruition. Bill Sherman with his 62,000 Union soldiers was camping out on the plantations of Georgia; there were apparently none of the owners about willing to fight him; the Confederate "nation" was shown to be little more than a motley conglomeration of self-interested fiefdoms, the Union now possessed of a moral force that hitherto had not been so manifest. An Indiana quartermaster summed up the Union view of the Confederacy as the army arrived in Savannah:

> This is a new feature in the history of this war and the Rebel government does not know how to meet it. The idea of an invading army running promiscuously over the country, destroying everything that comes within their reach, is to them a terrible affair and I think will do more towards making them tired of war than anything our Government has ever done.

As Sherman now learned when he took over the governor's mansion, Joe Brown, the titular head of the Confederate army in Georgia, would rather eat his vegetables than fight. The Milledgeville papers were long on the rhetoric of resistance to the death, short on men who might charge into Mr. Sherman's army. And if Sherman's agrarians were uncannily similar to Epaminondas's rugged Boeotians, so too now was the Georgian elite as hypocritical as the Spartiate privileged. Just as the old Spartan Antalcidas had sent his own son to safety on the eve of the arrival of Epaminondas, just as King Agesilaus—who once promised the women of Sparta that they would never see the campfires of the enemy—huddled on the Spartan acropolis yelling impotent threats across the Eurotas at Epaminondas, so now the purported white warrior and wealthy classes of Georgia were not present to offer battle with Sherman and his huge Army of the West.

To most in the Northern army the South was unfamiliar territory, and Sherman's marchers were quickly learning that Confederate society—its language, customs, and castes—was a baffling phenomenon, full of contradictions that ultimately could be sorted out and understood only through the South's great pride in, but also embarrassment over, its peculiar institution of chattel slavery. But Sherman, who had lived, worked, and moved extensively throughout the South, knew the Confederate landscape intimately. In his early military career he had traveled more widely in the South than most Southerners, so that now he could assure his baffled young Midwesterners that the unfamiliar countryside was, in fact, quite familiar to their Uncle Billy. Over a year earlier, in September 17, 1863, he had written Chief of Staff General Halleck an astute, albeit sometimes chilling, analysis of Southern social structure. In it Sherman outlined the conditions through which the defeated Confederate states might be forcibly reintegrated into the Union after the war.[64]

At the top of Southern society, Sherman wrote, there was a small elite of large planters who formed the economic and political core of the entire region. These were the owners of hundreds of slaves and the large estates and lovely homes of the kind he had just burnt between Madison and Milledgeville—gentlemen like the Georgia politician Howell Cobb, whose plantation was now to be in ashes a few miles from the ruined capital. The plantation gentry—who had treated Sherman so politely before the war in Georgia, the Carolinas, and Louisiana—possessed most of the slaves, controlled the state governments, and were the catalysts of rebellion. As a general rule, state legislators came from this clique and had voted overwhelmingly to secede from the Union in 1861; in contrast, the few representatives who owned no slaves had vainly cautioned patience and conciliation with the North. Thus the slave-owners, so synonymous with Southern state government officials, high army officers, and former Federal representatives and senators, were *not* truly characteristic of Southern society as a whole. There may have been only 10,000 or so really large slaveholders in the South, whereas 75 percent of the white population had never had any connection with African chattels. Only 385,000 out of some 6,000,000 citizens who lived in the Confederacy or border state counties sympathetic to the South were themselves currently slave-owners.

As of yet, those few who called for war had not paid the human and material wages of that evil gambit; Sherman's march through Georgia would exact punishment from the plantation perpetrators, "the devils" themselves. If less fortunate Southerners suffered as well, then all the better to remind them of the consequences of following blindly those who did not truly care for their interests: "A people who will persevere in war beyond a certain limit ought to know the consequences. Many, many people, with less pertinacity than the South has already shown, have been wiped out of national existence."[65]

The anomaly of the planters' overrepresentation in government and the military, and their inordinate wealth and social prestige called for an extensive apology for slavery, a creative defense that would range beyond their own selfish economic self-interest. Many of the plantation class were highly educated and for half a century had offered to the nation and indeed the Western world at large an array of both pragmatic and moral justifications for slavery that would explain why the vast majority of their Confederate kinsmen should now die for their own cherished idea of holding black people in bondage.

Slavery, they would argue, created wealth for everybody; its value to the nation transcended their own private fortunes. During the cotton boom of the 1850s, the Confederacy earned for the Union over $60 million in yearly exports—at a time of general financial panic in the North. To the Southern plantation owners their immense productive acreage was the natural complement to Northern industry, ensuring that the United States would have a steady abundance of food and fiber to offer resilience should the nation's industrial output slide into recession. Europeans could rival American manufacturers, but they could not grow cotton for their mills, or provide tobacco for their pipes or vast amounts of rice and corn for their children and animals. Slavery, then, which was claimed to be the absolute prerequisite for cotton farming, in economic terms was good even for the North!

The system of cotton latifundia was also passed off as sort of a noble Jeffersonian agrarianism, an honest and natural path of creating real wealth without the exploitation and volatility of free men so inherent in Northern industrial capitalism. Just as many of the Founding Fathers had owned slaves and large estates, so too their few true remaining spiritual descendants in the South were carrying on that agrarian genteel tradition. How, other than through the use of chattel slaves, could Americans farm the vast estates so essential in providing the food and fiber—rice, tobacco, cotton—of the republic? These were crops, the Confederate sophistry went, that were grown in the tropical, muggy climate of the Deep South, where the African Negro was naturally at home and actually at ease in the heat.[66]

At this confident Southern boast of self-importance and pseudo-scientific apology, the pragmatic Sherman would again scoff. He would demonstrate exactly how much he thought cotton was really worth to the Union. When, in South Carolina, General Wheeler, who had dogged him through Georgia at the head of local Confederate cavalry forces, offered to cease burning cotton if Sherman's men would in turn stop torching estates, Sherman replied: "I hope you will burn all cotton and save us the trouble. We don't want it; and it has proven a curse to our country. All you don't burn I will." In his pragmatic way of thinking, the mechanical classes of the North could always create more wealth than could Southern elites. The South, Sherman concluded, would come to need the North far more than the North the South. The North had farmers in the Midwest and West, but did the South have its own industrialists? Sherman set out his views more formally in a brilliantly prescient letter to a colleague in the South before he departed for the North on the eve of the war:

> You mistake, too, the people of the North. They are a peaceable people, but an earnest people and will fight too, and they are not going to let this country be destroyed without a mighty effort to save it.
>
> Besides, where are your men and appliances of war to contend against them? The Northern people not only greatly outnumber the whites of the South, but they are a mechanical people with manufacturers of every kind, while you are only agriculturalists—a sparse population covering a large extent of territory, and in all history no nation of mere agriculturalists ever made successful war against a nation of mechanics. The North can make a steam-engine, locomotive or railway car; hardly a yard of cloth or a pair of shoes can you make. You are rushing into war with one of the most powerful, ingeniously mechanical and determined people on earth—right at your doors. You are bound to fail.[67]

Sherman was dealing in broad generalizations—there were canny capitalists and factory owners in the South, and many a plantation that ran as efficiently and on exactly the same principles as a Northern farm. The large cities of the South had not exactly missed out on the Industrial Revolution, and there were a number of skilled mechanics and engineers throughout the Confederacy. But Sherman's point was one of degree; a war in an industrialized age would now draw on the full resources of a modern society, and in that regard the South—even with its real strengths, such as tradition, honor, and loyalty to family and state—was woefully overmatched. As an Illinois soldier in Sherman's army noticed while on the march, Southern train wheels squeaked from lack of oil; telegraph glass insulators seemed in short supply; and rail iron appeared to be of substandard quality. He summed up the shoddy materials: "In fact, the whole mechanical system of the South was an importation."

The material and cultural impoverishment of the Southern states that accompanied the institution of chattel slavery was unmistakable, and thus Southerners also retorted that they essentially owned slaves for noneconomic reasons! As a moral defense against the abolitionists, the plantation class drew on the classical arguments of servile paternalism. "Slavery is the natural and normal condition of society," wrote the Virginia apologist George Fitzhugh. "The situation of the North is abnormal and anomalous. Capital exercises a more perfect compulsion over free laborers than human master over slaves; for free laborers must at all times work or starve, and slaves are supported whether they work or not." The South, Fitzhugh argued, was in effect offering a social security safety net for over 4,000,000 residents of America at the private expense of the planters. Apparently, slavery was to be properly seen as a costly though noble social burden for Southerners and yet one indispensable to their economic viability: the plantation owners selflessly took care of the black man from cradle to grave at great expense to themselves. Yet they would kill other Americans to retain that charitable responsibility!

It is surprising how astute the rank and file of Sherman's army was concerning such Confederate hypocrisy, and cognizant of the effect of their own march upon Southern hierarchy. "'Tis the educated class of the South caused all this trouble. The poor unlettered masses, and they constitute almost all the population, have been from time immemorial their dupes and instruments . . . they cannot seem to understand they are in reality fighting for the negro and not for themselves." Another agreed: "Each planter was at the head of a little aristocracy in which hardly a law touched him. This didn't content these people; they wanted 'their rights,' and now they are getting them."

Ancient philosophers like Plato and Aristotle long ago had seen the wage bondage of purportedly free men—forced by necessity to work daily in drudgery to another—as not much better than simply owning another human outright. Marx himself embraced similar Aristotelian paradigms, and so made nearly the same argument: capitalism made veritable slaves out of purportedly free laborers even if preserving their rights of citizenship—voting was a meaningless abstraction when millions of "free" citizens nearly starved, slaving in the factories of a few capitalists. So too in the twisted logic of the South, Northern wage-earners only *thought* they were free. In fact, they were no more in control of their destiny than slaves on the plantation—and slaves were at least guaranteed food and shelter. If they should be free, they would become helpless and exploited by Northern industrialists. Theodore Upson quotes a slave who, when visiting in the North with her master, was asked why she did not flee, "Wont I have ter work if I's free?"[68]

The plantation class also embraced another key classical precedent: the notion of natural slavery. Slavery, if the naturally less gifted were enslaved, was beneficial to both master and servant—the former avoided degrading manual labor and could devote the ensuing leisure time to the pursuit of arts, politics, and war for the benefit of the state; while the latter, without worry over his sustenance, welfare, and the future, could do society's mindless labor for which he was most fit and happy. Indeed, slave-owners were subject to an array of customs and protocols designed to protect the slaves' own welfare. That way, the entire agrarian hierarchy in the South could hum on as one well-oiled machine, the properly fitted and interconnected gears and cogs of slaves and poor whites being attended to by a few all-knowing and compassionate skilled plantation engineers.

The plantation apologists went one up on classical thinkers. Aristotle and Plato had worried about slavery per se only because there was no mechanism for determining which Greek should and should not be enslaved. Who could ever figure out who was deservedly the gear and who its operator? Unfortunately, war, as the philosopher Heraclitus lamented, made some free, others slaves—for the Greeks, the terrible randomness that might put the brilliant in the service of fools. Aristotle and Plato particularly found the enslavement of Greeks by Greeks abhorrent. Even the Messenians were Greeks, and thus in the philosophical tradition there was no real reason why the Helots deserved to be enslaved. Persians, Thracians, Cappadocians, and others outside the Greek-speaking world at least might be the more suitable slaves, barbarians who were already half slavish without the culture of the *polis* and exposure to its civilizing institutions.

Most of the classical debate in Epaminondas's time over slavery was not so much about the morality of the institution, but rather was concerned solely how to discover the natural servile profile—a Western dilemma that the Confederacy felt it had at last solved with the importation of the Negro into the Americas. It is true that Southerners were correct in seeing there was nothing in orthodox Christian dogma, as generally embraced, that was antithetical to slavery. Christian theologians from Augustine to Aquinas never expressed precise, detailed moral objections to chattel slavery. If a man was enslaved, much of early Christian writing implied, then the curb on his appetites and the humility of his position might make his efforts at moral perfection easier than those of his haughty and leisured master. For all the abolitionists' stricture that was couched in Christian terms, no New Englander could quote the precise chapter and verse of any Scripture to prove that slavery was amoral. In a spiritual free-for-all that had no real written authority, both Southern and Northern preachers used wide latitude in interpreting the Bible for their own diametrically opposed exegeses.[69]

Southern elites, drawing on both classical support and the complete absence of literal biblical censure, thought that in the African they had at last solved the Greek dilemma of determining who should not be enslaved: natural racial inferiority, not the relative poverty of one's indigenous culture, was the key in determining inherent slavishness. The ancients, who did not believe in racial inferiority—or perhaps even in race itself for that matter—were obsessed with cultural differences, and so did not appreciate fully, as the racialists in the South did, that some humans at birth and as a race were properly servile. But Southerners claimed that they could prove that black Negroes from an impoverished and wild Africa were naturally inferior to white Europeans, and thus their employment as menial laborers would insulate them from the cruel world of capitalism and its rough-and-tumble wage labor—while allowing a natural elite to craft a uniquely Southern genteel culture. Black slaves were better fed and housed in America than their kindred tribesmen in Africa—thus Southerners had done them a favor by bringing them over. Was it not wondrous that a Southerner's slave was safer, fatter, and lived longer than his tribal cousin in Africa?

The planters' apology was not so idiosyncratic as it now seems. Even Enlightenment thinkers as diverse as Hegel and Montesquieu, while opposed in theory to slavery, nevertheless believed that Asiatics and Negroes were naturally more servile peoples. Their benign enslavement by Europeans was at least preferable to enslaving other whites, and might serve as a necessary transitional state—only through such contact with enlightened superiors might Negroes and Asiatics eventually become civilized and free, and hence more blessed than their savage kindred still in Africa and the East. In short, slavery was moral; in a brutal capitalist society it took care of those who could not take care of themselves; it transported poor Negro savages from the horrors of Africa to the humane and stable world of the Southern plantation; it concentrated all of society's exploitation on those who deserved to be exploited, and thus avoided the mess of the North where free whites worked as hard as slaves without benevolent protection and care. General Hood, in his famous exchange of letters with Sherman, before the capture of Atlanta, summed up the Confederacy's generally held views of racial paternalism:

> You came into our country with your army, avowedly for the purpose of subjugating free white men, women, and children, and not only intend to rule over them, but you make negroes your allies, and desire to place over us an inferior

race, which we have raised from barbarism to its present position, which is the highest ever attained by that race, in any country, in all time.[70]

A myriad of contradictions abounded in all such befuddled reasoning, and Sherman intended his "action" in Georgia to be critical in exposing them. In the moral sense, there were disturbing though unacknowledged indications that the South's theory of natural slavery was a lie—opportunity, not race, determined whether one was civilized or not. For example, plantation owners themselves conceded that, once educated, house slaves and craftsmen turned out to be especially valuable. Negroes, as Southerners knew from escaped slaves in the North, could become university educated and successfully employed. Sherman's men in Georgia noticed immediately the marvelous effect of even a little education on purportedly backward slaves. "I do not think, after all I have heard to favor it, that there is any good reason to consider the negro, naturally and essentially, the moral inferior of the white," wrote the prewar observer of Southern plantation culture, Frederick Law Olmsted, "or, that if he is so, it is in those elements of character which should forever prevent us from trusting him with equal social munities with ourselves." Henry Hitchcock remarked of a Negro slave spokesman who came to see Sherman about fleeing the plantation: "Their spokesman was a man over fifty, tall, fine-looking, and really dignified Negro (quite black), remarkably intelligent, and who 'understood himself' very much better than the white man . . . who supped with us last night . . . [he] spoke with quite remarkable clearness and great fluency, and used excellent language."[71]

Nor was it true that slaves themselves were docile and saw their mean tasks as befitting their modest natural talents. The Southern claim that they would not desert to Sherman en masse proved as false as the Spartans' smug assurances that the Helots would not aid Epaminondas; and, again as in the case of the Messenian Helots, its corollary that they would or could not fight for their freedom proved equally erroneous—eventually, 200,000 blacks were to serve in the Union army. As the war progressed, the eagerness of slaves to follow Sherman's army and the industry and the talent that they exhibited were apparent to even the most diehard of Southerner plantationists. Sherman's army would never have made its way through the swamps and forests of the Carolinas without the bravery and initiative of its corps of black pioneers.[72]

Nowhere was the defense of natural slavery more absurd than in the Southern debate over arming blacks for service in the armies. Military necessity increasingly called for their use in the Confederate army on the unspoken assumption that slaves in fact could fight and replace the staggering losses of

1862 and 1863. Yet, should they fight well, the entire ideology of the Negro's natural inferiority was endangered. Faced with Sherman's onslaught, Governor Joseph Brown of Georgia was on the horns of yet another dilemma and now openly confessed the entire paradox of Southern slavery: "Whenever we establish the fact that they are a military race, we destroy our whole theory that they are unfit to be free." Yet, the fact was soon unquestioned that escaped slaves were more eager to join the Army of the North than Governor Brown was to defend his own state capital.[73]

Genetic purity and the preservation of the white race were the most contradictory arguments for slavery. In the Southern view, confinement of blacks on the plantation at least limited their intercourse with the general white population, averting the degradation of America's white stock. Here again Southerners' hypocrisy was most manifest. Their much dreaded nightmare of miscegenation was almost unheard of in a more integrated North, but actually quite commonplace *in the South*, where plantation owners routinely impregnated female Negro slaves—and on rarer occasions white women bore the children of blacks. The class that warned of the mixing of the races to come under Northern paradigms of racial equality was itself about the only body in America that practiced routine miscegenation—albeit often in a particularly brutal and savage fashion. Freed blacks in the North had shown no great eagerness to intermarry with whites; whites in the South had demonstrated an interest in sexual relationships with blacks. Sherman's ideologically driven men pointed this anomaly out again and again. In the first days of the march Henry Hitchcock passed by the estate of a local official: "Judge Harris is a prominent man hereabouts. Nichols had a long talk with his Negro driver and came back full of indignation. The women say that their master, though an elderly man, and with a family, obliges them to submit to him, and *straps* them if they refuse."

Soldiers in Sherman's army made it a point to lecture Southern plantation owners about their hypocrisy whenever possible:

> I stopped at a dwelling on the east side of the river, which the occupants (Merriwether's) dignified with the name of "Airy Mount." Had quite a discussion here with a strong minded elderly woman, on Abolition and Amalgamation: the old lady forced it on me, and as there were three or four very light colored mulatto children running around the house, they furnished me an admirable weapon to use against the old lady's remark that the Northern people were Amalgamationists. She didn't explain to my entire satisfaction how her slaves came to be so much whiter than African Slaves are usually supposed to be.[74]

The final ethical defense of plantation slavery—that self-interest and paternalism guaranteed fair and human treatment for the slave—was proven false by actual events. Well before the war, Frederick Law Olmsted had taken a tour of the Southern states and reported back of slave punishment:

> His drivers are not allowed to carry their whips with them in the field; so that if the overseer wishes a hand punished, it is necessary to call a driver; and the driver has then to go to his cabin, which is, perhaps, a mile or two distant, to get his whip, before it can be applied.
>
> I asked how often the necessity of punishment occurred?
>
> "Sometime, perhaps, not once for two or three weeks; then it will seem as if the devil had got into them all and there is a good deal of it."

Sherman's men now confirmed firsthand the brutal conditions of slavery as they randomly uncovered the equipment of servile torture and punishment. Nothing escaped their eye, from the abandoned slave-owner's whip to the hovels where planters housed their servants. Theodore Upson remarked: "We saw a place today where they used to send the refractory slaves to be punished. There were stocks, iron collars with chains on them, several kinds of whips, and a paddle thing with a lot of holes it. I think that the Darkys did get whipped all right sometimes."[75]

Yet, in economic terms, slavery for the South as a whole caused as much hardship as it created profit. It was clear that for all the temperate climate and rich soil of the Southern states, New England and the Northern seaboard—a cold, often rocky, and relatively confined place—had spawned far more capital and industry, more real wealth, and a greater population. In explication of the vast gulf between Northern and Southern development, economists, in both the nineteenth and twentieth centuries, have attributed the entire state of Southern backwardness to its institution of chattel slavery.

First is the traditional argument that slaves—with no hope of advancement or upward mobility—were simply not as productive workers as free wage laborers. Their use hid intrinsic inefficiencies in production. Northern factories and businesses that paid for labor competed for workers, driving up both productivity and wages. Both the complaints and suggestions of their free employees were valuable in curbing inefficiencies at the plant and in capitalizing on work-saving methods. Without permanent and attached workers, Northern capitalists, taking the constant pulse of the economy, reacted to market pressure immediately by terminating, laying off, or hiring additional laborers. As for as states' versus national rights, the presence of a powerful Federal government that could tax and dispense public largess had been beneficial to Northern commerce. Southerners might damn an all-powerful national government that took away their freedom and interfered with their private lives and property, but they could not deny that such an intrusive system stimulated rather than retarded economic growth.

In this regard, the Southern elites were absolutely right that their paternal system of chattel slavery was antithetical to market capitalism and industrialization itself—and more or less in line with a strain of Western thought beginning with Plato and Aristotle that saw commercialism, materialism, urbanism—and far-reaching unchecked democracy—as far worse for the moral fiber of a community than the existence of chattel slavery. Equally valid was their corollary argument that they had preserved intact the Founding Fathers' dream of a hierarchical agrarian society, run by a small slave-owning elite, immune from Federal interference, whose moral excellence was based on the avoidance of ignoble labor and a paternal regard for the less gifted. The North's nightmares of rampant egalitarianism and materialism fostered by wage labor, free-floating capital, a coercive government, and unchecked immigration were the natural complements to a restless spirit of freedom, equality, and economic progress undreamed of a century earlier even among the most radical of the nation's founders.

The South was also correct in seeing its own economic superstructure and political culture as nearly identical to eighteenth-century America's. But inherent in that boast was the admission that they were now a century behind the times, and thus had sacrificed economic pragmatism and dynamism for the narrow interests of a tiny percentage of the population—all on the dubious notion that the spirit of 1776 was to be a fixed and ethical, rather than an evolving and practical, ethos. To Sherman such Southern reactionary thinking was all well and good, and he tended to be sympathetic to their claims of states' rights, but the Confederate moralists to ensure their survival then must be willing to meet and defeat a massive army such as his own, one that was entirely the product of "a nation of mechanics" that the South purportedly so despised. Such are the contradictions inherent in all self-professed anti-Western societies—the current confusion within the Islamic and Oriental worlds is a good example—which condemn godless industry and amoral consumerism without acknowledging the degree of their own fascination with and often eagerness for just such material bounty.

The South, again like contemporary critics of the West, failed to realize that the Industrial Revolution, market capitalism, a paternalistic, all-powerful government, and radical egalitarianism are not so much evil as insidious, with subtle enticements that are hard to forgo and difficult even to appreciate fully. No nineteenth-century American understood this dilemma—and hypocrisy—of the South better than the prescient William Tecumseh Sherman.[76]

A second paradox of slavery concerned the sheer capital tied up in slave-owning—nearly half the assessed worth of the Confederacy was in Negro slaves, and almost the other half in land itself. Despite the huge profits from the exports of tobacco, rice, and cotton, almost all investment went right back into slaves and farmland—not industry, transportation, education, or social services, much less laborsaving machinery. The creation and maintenance of a permanent, immobile class of uneducated field hands, without labor incentives, and with built-in expenses of sustenance and security, was a brake on the industrialization and mechanization of the South itself—and the sustenance of the aged, young, and infirm slaves was a constant expense in which economy could be found only at the expense of morality. What advantage was it to invest in laborsaving devices when costly slaves of the plantation would simply become idle? And why worry about the growth of a skilled class of free industrial workers and craftsmen when there was a permanent body of unfree laborers? Why be eager for social programs for free citizens when the plantation owner already was responsible for slaves from cradle to grave? Plantationists were more correct than they knew—and for the wrong reasons—when they bragged that they took care of, as well as worked, chattel slaves. The plantation economy aimed at the old classical ideal of *autarcheia*—each estate would be self-sufficient, with its own food, housing, labor, blacksmithing, livestock, and fabrication, ensuring economic inefficiency at the price of political independence and immunity from even state and local government interference. Taxes, as in classical times, might then remain low, or nonexistent. The only reason for state or federal expenditure was to create railroads and canals that might expedite agricultural exports from the servile plantation.[77]

The similarities between the plantation and Spartiate classes were almost eerie—and acknowledged by Southerners themselves, who often defended their own slaveholding and the possibility of using blacks slaves in war by alluding to Sparta's successful relationship with its Helots. But were such racial pundits fully aware of the ramifications of that embarrassing parallelism? Sparta had once claimed that the Helots were naturally inferior, but then felt it still necessary to craft a labyrinth of laws and restrictions to ensure they were not given the opportunity to prove their excellence—and often proceeded to kill them en masse when they did seek manumission in exchange for military service. Sparta had once bragged that the Helots would not desert, but then had witnessed mass defections and the creation of a veritable Helot state from the ground up. Sparta had once bragged that helotage allowed a small natural elite not to do menial labor, but to enjoy a true military egalitarianism that stressed military virtue, not profit. As a result, whereas the thousand other Greek city-states developed market economies, sustained expanding populations, and made unmatched strides in architecture, art, and literature, Sparta essentially missed out on the entire cultural evolution of the polis—and yet still was defeated decisively in battle by the supposedly backward Thebans. Just as Georgia in 1864 more resembled the America of 1776, so too Sparta in 369 was more like the original polis of 700 B.C.—reactionary societies both, nursing yesterday's beliefs, all in the mistaken notion that great ideas are frozen in the time and space of their birth without the ability to transcend the mere material conditions of their creation. Conservative critics, who laudably appreciate stability, continuity, and tradition in society, more so than their liberal counterparts, have a special responsibility to identify an evil legacy, to distinguish what must be preserved from the past and what discarded.

As both Sherman's and Epaminondas's agrarians were to prove, even the one purported truth of the plantation class was entirely false—helot labor really did *not* ensure that their masters could use their leisure to achieve manly bravery and moral excellence. More often the opposite was true. When confronted with a society of freeholding homesteaders, the beneficiaries of apartheid were simply too few, too sheltered, and too impractical—and in the end, possessed of a chivalric ethic that in comparison would not prove to be real courage.

Psychologically, slavery had an insidious effect on plantation owner, free poor white, and black servant alike that ensured a schizophrenia permeating the entire Confederacy. In a culture that put such a premium on ethics, tradition, and values rather than on commerce and mere capital, plantation owners naturally avowed that they were moral and paternal, not exploitive and profit-obsessed. Their increasingly strident protestations confirmed their own deep-seated worries that they were, in fact, amoral; they pronounced Negroes happy and content, but suspected that they might flee—or worse, rebel and kill them—at the first opportunity. Poor whites knew privately that the plantation system left them with little chance of upward mobility, but publicly feigned support to ingratiate themselves with wealthy and influential families. Blacks developed a sophisticated language and behavior of servility to survive bondage, but lived completely different and vibrant lives among their own. This entire charade of the Confederacy would be exposed when 62,000 men swept into Georgia, led by the most keen student of human nature and social pretext of any figure of his generation, a military "prophet" who saw war as the ultimate disclosing agent of hypocrisy.

Sherman, like Epaminondas, was never awed by either plantation or militaristic rhetoric. As early as 1843 during a four-year stay when he was stationed in South Carolina, he had written his brother, John Sherman, the future senator from Ohio: "This state, their aristocracy, their age, their patriarchal chivalry and glory—all trash. No people in America are so poor in reality, no people so poorly provided with the comforts of life." Sherman remarked later in 1859 of Southerners' parochialism, "I would indulge them in their delusion with all the philosophy and complacency of a strong man." The plantation owners were simply pathetic, oblivious to how ridiculous their cries of deprivation sounded to free Northerners. One mistress complained of Sherman's bummers who entered her domain:

> Do the annals of civilized—and I may add savage—warfare afford any record of brutality equaled in extent and duration to that which we have suffered, and which has been inflicted on us by the Yankees? For one month our homes and all we possess on earth have been given to lawless pillage. Officers and men have alike engaged in this work of degradation. I scarcely know how we have stood up under it. . . . Every servant, on pain of having their brains blown out, is forbidden to wait upon us or furnish us food. . . . [78]

Especially bothersome were once more these women of the plantation class—every bit as spirited and bellicose as the estate-owning females of Sparta who once had also shrieked as their slave-worked properties were torched by invading yeomen from the North. Clinging to the tradition of privilege, but now abandoned by their male supporters, the matriarchs of Georgia took it upon themselves to remind Sherman's foragers of their own singular social and racial status:

> I said: "If you are determined to search, begin your work at once." For they were pushing into the rooms, and with them an insolent little mulatto boy, who commenced running about the parlor. I called to the Dutchman and said: "Order that boy out of my house!"

We should assume that some of the strongest voices in the Confederacy in support of slavery came from the women of the plantation who felt the war disrupted their selfless materialism and care for the helpless Negro. One Georgia mistress, Mary Jones, writes about the disruptive presence of Sherman's men and their ruination of the humane institution of slavery:

> The workings of Providence in reference to the African race are truly wonderful. The scourge falls with peculiar weight upon them: with their emancipation must come their extermination. All history, from the first existence,

proves them incapable of self-government; they perish when brought in conflict with the intellectual superiority of the Caucasian race. Northern philanthropy and cant may rave as much as they please; but facts prove that in a state of slavery such as exists in the Southern states have the Negro race increased and thriven most.

In his letter to Chief of Staff General Halleck, Sherman also lamented that the privileged plantation grandees would probably survive the war and eventually reassert their power in the South—such are the unfortunate strong forces of tradition, property, and class that transcend even the upheavals of war. But never again were they to have slaves. Even if they were to retain their estates after the war, "they must adapt themselves to the new order of things"—that is, rebuilding their properties from the ground up in a world of hired labor. It was not by accident that Sherman now allowed his marchers outside Milledgeville to burn and ruin the plantations of the wealthy.

If the Confederacy's investment was not to be in an educated citizenry, a sizable population, or an extensive industrial base, but instead almost exclusively in land and slaves, then all the more easy to burn the former and free the latter. If planters had heretofore escaped service, then bring the war home to their doorstep. If they had sowed the seeds of secession, then let them reap the harvest of their folly. If they had prided themselves on the protection of women and children, then show the world how they had abandoned just these vulnerable dependents to save themselves. To Sherman, the self-avowed agent of the apocalypse, warfare of the new modern age had only one redeeming feature: the bringing of a brutal, immutable truth to the world of hypocrisy and darkness.[79]

On November 22 on the outskirts of Milledgeville, Sherman stumbled onto the estate of Howell Cobb and became particularly incensed when he entered a Negro hut and saw Cobb's name on a candle box. Henry Hitchcock relates:

This plantation is about 600 acres, and worked by 100 hands. They left here the aged, decrepit and young negroes—some forty in all, Nichols says: I did not go to the cabins—too cold and hungry. The chief building is a big log cabin, no hall, divided by mean board partitions into four rooms: one at each end, one rear, and one cut off gallery. No Northern farm owner would allow his agent or farmer to have such. No thrift or neatness about the place: sundry rude log cabins for storehouses, mean rail fences—everything shabby: old negroes wretchedly dressed. H.C. has four or five other plantations, and 500 to 600 negroes in all.[80]

Not that there weren't any yeomen farmers in the South, but even that purportedly middle agrarian class was far smaller than its Northern counterpart. An Illinois farmer in 1861 wrote of them:

The large slaveholders have got all the good land. There can be no schools, and if the son of a poor man rises above his condition there is no earthly chance for him. He can only hope to be slave-driver, for an office is not his, or he must leave and go to a Free State. *Were there no free states, the white people of the South would be slaves* [emphasis in original].[81]

In contrast to the plantationists and small farmers, the great majority of Georgia's whites in the 1860 recorded population of some 1,023,801 total persons—576,719 free, 447,002 slave—were the poor and landless. They comprised most of the 75 percent of the Southern population who possessed *no* slaves at all. In contrast, black slaves owned by the planters constituted 44 percent of the entire Georgia population and comprised 45 percent of its capital wealth! These so-called "crackers" and "white trash" would fight in the hundreds of thousands, to protect the bondage of millions of black slaves to their rear, who were largely the exclusive property of the few thousand who led them from a desk or at best on horseback. Even the governor of Georgia admitted as much. As early as 1863 he confessed to the legislature: "A large proportion of the wealthy class of people have avoided the fevers of camp and the dangers of the battlefield, and remained at home in comparative ease and comfort with their families." Yet before the war it was just this class alone that was deemed worthy to run the South. One planter wrote in 1858:

Thanks to Mr. Jefferson we have made a mistake . . . and pushed the love of democracy too far. . . . A vulgar democracy and licentious "freedom" is rapidly supplanting all the principles of constitutional "liberty"! When shall the American people perceive that all our difficulties arise from the absurdities of deciding that the "pauper" and the "landholder" are alike competent to manage the affairs of a Country, or alike entitled to vote for those who shall?

Most poor whites lived out in the countryside on impoverished farms or rented acreage. In 1860 the taxable land of Georgia was valued at $161,764,000, whereas property in cities and towns was assessed at only $35,139,415. There was essentially no large, urban industrial sector that could employ many free white citizens outside of agriculture—and little chance for a viable freeholding agriculture for white citizens. No surprise that the great mass of foreign immigrants to America, eager for opportunity, voted with their feet and so flowed into the North—and why disenchanted Southerners themselves emigrated westward. Sherman's men again found the families of the white Rebel soldiers both poor and pitiful:

> Notwithstanding the extreme barrenness of these "piney woods," we now and then passed a miserable looking little cabin today, about which we generally found two or three sickly, sallow women, and from five to fifteen children, all looking like persons I have read of called "dirt eaters"; I guess these *are* dirt eaters, and I think they must live on it, for I don't see place for anything except children to grow in these "woods."[82]

By the time Sherman entered Georgia, 106,000 free males of the state had been mobilized into the Confederate army—or an astounding 17 percent of her free white population. Ten thousand more would be called up to serve in the state militia. With nearly a fourth of the entire Georgia population either in the army or already dead, wounded, missing, or prisoners in the North—the number of Georgia planters serving in the ranks was minuscule—there were essentially no able-bodied free men in the state left at home to offer even token popular resistance: most Georgians were in the Confederate army and the Confederate army had no plans to defend the holy soil of Georgia. As Sherman made his way through northern Georgia, the abandoned families at last voiced class resentments, offering the unacceptable though somewhat accurate excuse that the planters had forced war upon them. Henry Hitchcock, like most of Sherman's marchers, had no patience with their apologies:

> Stopped for lunch two hours at house of Mrs. ——— just this side of Murder Creek. Her husband also in the rebel army and like all the rest, "was forced to go." She said "he never was in favor of war." etc. etc.—Pity these men didn't act like men when they might—but they all lay it on their "leading men"—say "they made them do it!" *Delirant reges,—plectuntur Achivi* [the quote from Horace that the Greek people are punished for the mad acts of their kings], but in '61 the poor miserable fools thought it was they who were the kings, and Cotton king of all.[83]

If Sherman's men found the families of the plantation class arrogant, if not evil incarnate, they were just as amazed at the general impoverishment and pathetic condition of these poor whites who were often compared to slaves: "Talk about negro slavery! If we haven't seen white slaves from Atlanta to Goldsboro, I don't know what the word means." Some Northern yeomen felt the soil of the nonplantation farms might account for their shockingly backward condition, "The soil is very poor and the inhabitants, if possible, are poorer than the soil." More often soldiers concluded that the poor diction, illiteracy, and general ignorance of Southern whites were the direct results of the vast inequality in wealth, the absence of good education and jobs—and ultimately due to the pernicious effects of slavery upon the nonslave poor. The free world outside the plantation household, which would produce so many gallant Confederate soldiers, turned out to be a very brutal place indeed.[84]

The Army of the West was ready to show no mercy to any Southern whites if need be, to demonstrate the Confederacy was really not a nation but a motley conglomeration of distrustful factions. Two days after leaving Milledgeville, Major Connolly of an Illinois regiment summed up the army's disgust with the constant Southern threats for a popular mass uprising against the invader:

> Let them do it if they dare. We'll burn every house, barn, church, and everything else we come to; we'll leave their families houseless and without food; their towns will all be destroyed and nothing but the most complete desolation will be found in our track. This army will not be trifled with by citizens. If citizens raise their hands against us to retard our march or play the guerrilla against us, neither youth nor age, nor sex will be respected. Everything must be destroyed. This is the feeling that has settled down over the army in its bivouac tonight. We have gone so far now in our triumphant march that we will not balk. It is a question of life or death with us, and the considerations of mercy and humanity must bow before the inexorable demands of self preservation.[85]

There is no record that wealthy plantation owners ever did much for their poor white brethren. If Southern plantation owners had always labeled Northern yeomen and free laborers "mechanics struggling to be genteel, and small farmers who do their own drudgery, and yet are hardly fit for association with a Southern gentleman's body servant," what did the planters really think of their own far poorer white kinsmen?[86]

Why, then, did the millions of poor whites of the Confederacy fight at all? Before the war in the counties Sherman would later ruin, the top 10 percent of the landowners controlled 40 percent of the assessed wealth, while more than half of those who were lucky enough to own any property at all still possessed less than 15 percent of the area's valuation. Later, in the last dark hours of the war, the poor whites would allege forced conscription. Sherman felt instead that their doggedness was out of sheer ignorance and slavish emulation of the more impressive planters. He asked a freed slave on the march why these poor whites of the South went to war: "Because, Sir, when the war broke out, the rich men told 'em dat when they whipped the Yankees they should have land and niggers too."

The idea of states' rights, the notion of fighting for their home ground, and the common cultural ancestry of the South were strong and understandable incentives as well. But once again behind the entire social fabric of the South lay slavery. If slavery eroded the economic position of the poor free citizen, if slavery encouraged a society of haves and have-nots, if slavery alone drew the hostility of Northern abolitionists, then it alone offered one promise to the free white man—poor, ignorant, and dispirited—that he was at least not black and not a slave. That was often a great comfort to those who otherwise had found very little material or psychological capital under Confederate plantation culture. Governor Brown of Georgia went to great lengths to explain why the poor and exploited white Southerner owed much to slavery: "Among us the poor white laborer is respected as an equal. His family is treated with kindness, consideration, and respect. He does not belong to the menial class. The negro is in no sense his equal. . . . He belongs to the only true aristocracy, the race of white men."[87]

To return to the classical paradigm, slavery is often cited as the reason for the astonishing absence of class conflict in the classical world, in which between the seventh and fourth centuries B.C. the poor almost never arose in mass against the wealthy. Ancient historians, in broad generalizations, attribute this curious absence of class solidarity among the poor to the ubiquity of chattel slavery—whatever the exploitation of the free man, he was one with his betters on at least three counts: there were particular menial tasks, certain "slavish" work (mine work, baggage-carrying, rote agricultural labor, etc.) from which he was exempted; like the wealthy, the poor man could vote; and he was entitled as a free citizen to fight in the militia of the *polis*. In general, the classical example seems a reasonable explanation at least in part for why the poor white of the South felt the slaveholder's cause was also his own—he would fight as if a planter, vote as if a planter, and in exchange receive assurance from the planter that he was not a member of the 44 percent of the Georgia population who really were both legally and naturally "inferior."[88]

There was a far more important group of free whites to take into consideration both during the war and in its aftermath—the very dangerous Spartiates themselves—young zealots, men between eighteen and forty who often formed the cavalry of the South and were led by rabid knights like Nathan Bedford Forrest, Joseph Wheeler, and Jeb Stuart. These fanatics embodied the martial spirit of an apartheid culture and would never surrender unless both the South and its army were in ruins, and the lives of their families at stake. Most in the cavalry corps were the children of the wealthy, excellent horsemen, full of youthful vigor and insolence, and, in their twenties and early thirties, without full cognizance at the great material losses at stake for the South. "The young bloods," Sherman wrote, "never did work and never will. War suits them, and the rascals are brave, fine riders, bold to rashness and dangerous in every sense. They care not a sou for niggers, land or anything . . . they don't bother their brains about the past, present or future." One of the reasons Epaminondas had massed his Thebans on the left wing at the battle of Leuctra was to hit head-on similar recalcitrant Spartiates—and to wipe them out, and all they stood for, in a single blow.

Similarly, on more than one occasion, Sherman stated that for the war to end, and for there ever to be real reconciliation in its aftermath, most of them—he believed they might number 300,000 or so—*would have to be killed off*. To Sheridan, who more than any other Northern general understood the brutalities of war, Sherman wrote, "I was satisfied, and have been all the time, that the problem of war consists in the awful fact that the present class of men who rule the south must be killed outright rather than in the conquest of territory." Even to his wife Ellen, he concluded:

> Still on the whole the Campaign is the best, cleanest and most satisfactory of the war. I have received the most fulsome praise of all from the President down, but I fear the world will jump to the wrong conclusion that because I am in Atlanta the work is done. Far from it. We must kill three hundred thousand I have told you of so often, and the further they run the harder for us to get them.[89]

That admission may explain why both during and after the war Sherman, the advocate of the indirect approach and the attack on the flank, so loathe to send his boys in frontal assaults against Confederate entrenched lines, finally hesitant even to use his army to annihilate Johnston in North Carolina, never openly criticized his friend Grant. Rather, he suspected that Grant's tactic of head-on, brutal assault in Virginia that gobbled up entire regiments, North and South, was a complementary operation to his own. If Sherman was to ruin the material and psychological capital of the South, then Grant, who knew best Lincoln's terrible arithmetic—the "awful fact"—simply was killing off a great number of just that zealous 300,000 who would never be reconciled to the Union. Sherman may have talked barbarically, and promised total war, but it was Grant, not he, who followed Sherman's grim agenda to wipe out an entire class of Southern fanatics. Ironically, after the war, unrepentant zealots in the South might have confirmed Sherman's intuition, though disagreed with him about the relative morality of the purported lost 300,000. The former Confederate general D. H. Hill wrote in dejection to Jubal Early: "Why has the South become so toadyish & sycophantic? I think it is because the best and noblest were killed off during the war and that the scum element is now in the ascendancy."

Sherman was both disgusted by and attracted to these Young Turks of the Confederacy who were often the idle rich—repulsed because they had been, and would continue to be, the original catalyst for so much killing; impressed because they habitually offered up their lives in the effort to kill so effectively as professional soldiers. Indeed, Sherman speculated about the peace, if any of them survived, "when the resources of their country are exhausted, we must employ them." His own later friendship with Confederate zealots like Wheeler and Hood confirmed his earlier admiration of their spirit.[90] The South as a nation was not militarily strong, but it fielded individual warriors who were among the most gallant and deadly in the entire history of warfare.

Finally, and most important, at the bottom of the South's apartheid society were the helots of Georgia, the black slaves who comprised almost half the population and assessed wealth of the state. In the thousands they greeted Sherman, who was overwhelmed both materially and spiritually by their seemingly endless numbers and the heartfelt warmth of their newfound allegiance. A few generalizations about Sherman and the slaves his army met on their march through Georgia can be made and are amplified in all our contemporary sources. First, by 1864 the majority of slaves as a class despised their plantation owners and welcomed the Yankees, about whom they had been told mostly lies. Second, the slaves as a general rule wished to leave the plantation and follow the army, either as combatants, hired servants, or simply refugees; the size of their exodus was limited only by the material constraints of Sherman's army and the slaves' own realistic short-term calculations about their chances of survival away from the housing and food of the plantation. Third, the true wages of slavery—crude hovels, whip scars and permanent injuries, the presence of items of torture and punishment on the plantation, the ubiquity of bloodhounds—put to rest all of the propaganda of Southern benevolence and was absolutely critical to the spirit of nemesis that grew throughout the Union ranks. Thousands of slaves might well have been—and often were—treated humanely in often close paternalistic relationships with relatively humane owners. But far more thousands were simply handled as the property that they were—their degree of care predicated solely on the need to protect monetary investment. Despite avowals that their masters might be honorable men, all slaves either joined Sherman, fled the plantation, or appreciated the Northern army's presence in Georgia as proof of liberation to come and as leverage against their ever more suspicious owners. Fourth, whereas it is true that the vast plantation with two hundred and more slaves was relatively rare, over half of all slaves in the South were, nevertheless, held in groups of from ten to fifty. A very small percentage of the Confederacy's white population typically managed operations where the employment of dozens of slaves was routine—emphasizing the planter's huge capital investment in the unfree and his constant paranoia about protecting his property and indeed his life.

Morally, economically, ideologically, and culturally, the slave was at the center of Southern life and thus at the heart of the Civil War. Even in ways other than race, the system of slavery in the South resembled more the Roman latifundia of the first century B.C. than the yeoman agrarianism of the classical Greek *polis*—in the former, slaves were used in large gangs on a few corporate farms; under the latter, a small farmer and his family usually worked right beside a single slave in the field. Roman agricultural handbooks on estate management, like the elder Cato's extant treatise, reflect the same approach to plantation slave-owning: "Sell worn-out oxen, blemished cattle, blemished sheep, wool, hides, and old wagon, old tools, an old slave, a sickly slave, and whatever else is superfluous." The sick and abandoned blacks that Sherman's men found in Georgia bear out Cato's advice.

The Southern slave's eagerness to be free and willingness not just to leave but to fight, the Union army's embrace of their plight, the physical destruction of the plantation, and the psychological humiliation of the plantation class—all this illustrated that an apartheid state, once cracked, shatters and can never be reconstituted again. From the freeing of the slaves Sherman's men gained the moral imperative to loot and burn and, in turn, from Sherman's men the slaves at last could prove they too were human, even more humane than their masters. Historians—citing Sherman's occasional racial bombast, concerned more with the military aspects of the march, reflecting the modernist assumption that idealism is but the veneer of self-interest, and uncomfortable with absolute notions of good and evil—have downplayed the role of emancipation in the Union army's spirit and success in Georgia. Ultimately, though, the reason why Northern farmers were in Georgia, why Sherman was burning a region he had once grown to love, why the Union soldier found the plantation so abhorrent, and why the army marched to abolitionist anthems is found in slavery and the desire to end it in America for good.

From near Atlanta a forty-three-year-old farmer in a Michigan regiment who had already lost a stepson (the modern mind might wonder what a middle-aged agrarian with numerous children was doing hundreds of miles from home) wrote to his wife, shortly before he was killed in late summer 1864:

The more I learn of the cursed institution of Slavery, the more I feel willing to endure, for its final destruction. . . . After this war is over, this whole country will undergo a change for the better. . . . Abolishing slavery will dignify labor; that fact of itself will revolutionize everything . . . let Christians use all their influence to have justice done to the black man.[91]

A few hours before Sherman entered Milledgeville, ten miles west of the capital, the entire idiotic system of apartheid was laid bare to him as never before when he entered Howell Cobb's plantation. He dined in Cobb's slaves' quarters as he gazed out upon the vast estate. His men were now on Cobb's land, hundreds of miles from their own homes in the North, ready to assault Cobb and his kin. But Cobb—a major general in the Confederate army, the author of fiery decrees and pronouncements calling for secession and the need for die-hard resistance, and now damning Sherman and threatening his destruction—was nowhere to be found, either on the battlefield or protecting his estate. His absence made perfect sense, perfectly illustrative of the vast gap between Southern rhetoric and reality. Sherman, turning to his aide Hitchcock, ordered the soldiers and the slaves to take what they needed, and then barked, "Spare nothing."[92]

6

UNCLE BILLY

MILLEN, GEORGIA

December 3, 1864—Eighteenth Day Out

ABOUT one hundred miles nearer to the Atlantic, Sherman's north wing pulled into Millen, Georgia, the last real city before Savannah on the coast. Sherman was now no longer merely a general, but a veritable mayor of an enormous mobile city that daily grew larger as freed slaves joined the columns and soldiers rounded up livestock and wagons. His hourly concerns were not only strategic or tactical, but rather cultural and logistical—how to feed, house, and protect the thousands whose lives were in his hands alone. There was the incongruity of a vast democratic militia turning absolute power over hundreds of thousands of soldiers and civilians alike to a single man. Contemporary sources reveal that the route of the March to the Sea, its pace, and its ultimate destination were entirely concealed within the mind of William Tecumseh Sherman, whose grand vision unfolded each morning to fit rapidly changing circumstances. General Slocum, commander of the left wing in Georgia, remarked after Sherman's death that the general "never discussed his plans with me to any extent. It was not his habit to discuss them with his subordinates. He preferred saying little about what he intended to do until it became necessary. His self-reliance was remarkable."

Henry Hitchcock, an aide to Sherman, was now becoming worried about the ever increasing responsibilities on Sherman—that the general was becoming too restless, too preoccupied to ensure that all his myriad orders of the march were carefully followed. In some cases his men were not properly twisting heated rails and therefore leaving the enemy the future chance of rebending them back into service; at other times, Sherman's troops were too aggressive, burning residences of the middle classes and stealing private household items, violating the spirit and letter of Field Order 120 that purportedly limited foraging to the collection and acquisition of serviceable matériel and stock for the army. Sherman, thought Hitchcock, needed an executive officer just to ensure that all his orders were followed: "Far-sighted, sagacious, clear, rapid as lightning,—personally indefatigable, but also sometimes too impatient to see always to execution of orders *in detail*. He ought to have a first rate A.A.G. whom he fully sympathized with and trusted and *liked personally*, as well as officially, who would take it on himself sometimes to fill up this deficiency."

The story of Sherman's own life reflected that dichotomy—enemies and friends alike could not decide whether he was too lax or too tough, too frenzied in his efforts to insist on order and punishment, too absentminded or forgiving to follow up on promised threats. Sherman might have countered that the latest inconsistency in his life arose from his own dilemma: he was oathbound to attack his reckless friends in the South who were fighting on behalf of evil, in order to aid those equally impetuous in New England of whom he was not personally fond, but who, he acknowledged, embraced the greater moral and legal right.

In the genteel South he had spent years of steady employment in the army and in the university, while experiencing over a decade of misery and failure amid the sudden prosperity, wild inflation, urbanization, crashes, deflation, and depressions of the boom-and-bust West and North. Sherman was thus a cultural conservative, but also an economic realist and modernist, someone who admired the Southern emphasis on duty, tradition, and honor, but realized that the North, not the Confederacy, embraced real opportunity and technological progress. The former made war gallantly, the latter effectively. For Sherman the pragmatist, a free society might promote a dangerous egalitarianism that approached anarchy, but the greater danger was still a culture of slavery that ensured material regress and technological stagnation. That he felt more comfortable among those he criticized, that he was often out of place with those he admired, was a dilemma he struggled with his entire life.

Sherman often saw an alternative to the tired North-South dichotomy and thus embraced a chauvinism of the West, becoming increasingly proud of his past residence in California, where he, in fact, had had limited success at best. Nevertheless, it was in the West where there might be a real middle ground: economic dynamism among a natural elite of daring risk-takers, without the lies of the aristocratic South that a superior society rested on the

Negro being forever inferior or, he felt, the naïveté of New England that black and white might be instantly equal. Now all those divided sectarian loyalties and mixed emotions were to be played out with the outbreak of civil war. On the eve of hostilities, Sherman wrote to his wife from St. Louis, "I find Southern men, even as well informed as Turner [his employer at the bank], are as big fools as the abolitionists." His wife Ellen agreed: "A Catholic should be governed somewhat by the fact that the Church has always treated slavery as an evil which should be abolished by wise and moderate means. . . . I used to dislike the Abolitionists but their folly sinks in significance when compared with the treason of the South."[93]

When the March to the Sea began, William Tecumseh Sherman was forty-four years old. Until a mere two years earlier Sherman had been acknowledged by both himself and others as an abject failure. Even though his brother was a prominent United States senator from Ohio, although he had met Lincoln personally on two occasions, and although his father-in-law was among the best-known and wealthiest lawyers in America, and at some time or another Sherman himself had either worked among or become friends with the likes of Kit Carson, John C. Frémont, Johann Sutter, and Winfield Scott, the Union had little use for his services by late summer 1861. Since graduating from West Point in 1840 at the age of twenty, he had for the next quarter century held nearly a dozen jobs: itinerant army officer, failed bank official, manager of his father-in-law's properties, road construction administrator, self-taught lawyer, notary public, vegetable peddler and broker, farmer, trader and speculator, military academy superintendent, and railroad company supervisor. His sense of obstinate pride and notion of duty often meant that he stayed in dead-end jobs too long, passed up others that promised profit, and blamed himself, rather than others, for his apparent inability to succeed. When the war broke out, his wife and family were living in his father-in-law's house, he was plagued by continual ill health, mostly asthma and probably clinical depression, and he was for all practical purposes broke and dependent on continual subsidies from his father-in-law. Like Patton, his family's wealth and political connections tended to exaggerate rather than ameliorate his own sense of personal setback. William Tecumseh Sherman's last chance to achieve either prominence or financial security arose with the outbreak of the American Civil War.

Sherman was as unknown to the American public in 1861 as Epaminondas was to the Thebans before the revolution on the Cadmea in 379 B.C. Whereas we know absolutely nothing about Epaminondas's first forty years— whence derived the tactical experience or strategic sense to lead 70,000 into and out of Laconia and Messenia—we can see clearly only in the later light of what he did in Georgia that Sherman had never really failed at all. He unknowingly had been engaged in a quarter-century-long tutorial for his great marches, by 1861 the only American alive who had acquired the technical expertise, temperament, practical know-how, and cultural sense to lead an immense army on a rampage of liberation through the Confederacy.

All that was in the future. When the Civil War broke out, Sherman had no self-confidence and lacked the desire to serve in the Union army as a midlevel clerk or minor officer when former subordinates, incompetents, and politicos were to hold prestigious generalships. A few years earlier, in his late thirties, he would confess to his wife, "I am afraid of my own shadow." His asthma made him feel that "if my lungs are actually diseased one winter will finish me off, which would be infinitely more satisfactory than struggling with trials." His lack of what others would call success had nearly driven him to suicide; a prior two decades of hard work and expertise had led to nothing and had seemingly prepared him for nothing.

These years of dejection also would prove critical later on—prior failure in some sense is vital for a great captain of a democratic march, providing real empathy with the shared setbacks of the soldiers in the ranks (the wealthier and more successful of a society, even in a democracy, usually are *not* in such an army, or at least not as foot soldiers thrust into the heartland of the enemy), as well as liberating him from the career concerns that usually frown on audacity and the unorthodox. Sherman, like Grant, had no psychological investment in a system in which he had found little success. When the Civil War came, he saw warfare as a cruel free-for-all, where anyone with the prerequisite courage, intelligence, and audacity could step forward and change the rules as he pleased—a thought that must have frightened generals like McClellan and Rosecrans who had found both material and professional attainment before the conflict, and who were bothered by war's brutal leveling effect that took no countenance of class, money, reputation, or background. Of Grant, Sherman remarked, "He stood by me when I was crazy and I stood by him when he was drunk; and now, sir, we stand by each other always."

Patton, the wealthy aristocrat, by 1944 was also more or less disgraced, and saw no reason to follow the usual bureaucratic and timid protocols common in the American army—one that, in comparison to its treatment of other generals, had rewarded him little for some forty years of brilliant service. After his demotion and threatened dismissal, he had neither Dwight D. Eisenhower's faith in the wisdom of the Allied coalition, nor Omar Bradley's patience in following the "plan," nor the belief of others that steady, predictable work would lead to victory and eventual recognition. "Men, even so-called great men," Patton concluded, "are wonderfully weak and timid. They are too damned polite. War is very simple, direct, and ruthless. It takes a simple, direct, and ruthless man to wage war."[94]

Sherman had finished West Point sixth in his class in 1840. He might have graduated among the very top, but his 148 demerits in conduct during his senior year placed him 216th in personal behavior out of 233 total cadets enrolled. He was tagged for sloppy and unkempt dress, missed roll calls, not always saluting officers, and in general failing to adopt West Point protocol concerning manners, appearance, and decorum. For an American army at peace, William Tecumseh Sherman would be of little use and an occasional disruption, if not an embarrassment. Yet even as a student he was an especially adept scrounger and forager, rounding up food to bring back to his room for well-prepared dinners far better than those offered at the mess hall.

At West Point the knowledge he gained in the classroom was invaluable—near-perfect marks in engineering, mineralogy, artillery, tactical science, French, and drawing—along with an intimate acquaintance with future colleagues like Halleck, Buell, Thomas, McDowell, Van Vliet, and Rosecrans, and with future adversaries as well, such as Beauregard, Ewell, and Longstreet. If Sherman thought he had learned anything at the military academy, it was the mixed blessing that the acquisition of knowledge itself is indifferent to class and status, but instead is available for anyone and outside of academic protocol. In his simplistic view learning is the product of plain hard work and natural intelligence, and not to be measured necessarily by the approval of superiors or adherence to customs and traditions. During the March to the Sea and later, Sherman was never unduly impressed with the estimation of Southern generals like Bragg, Beauregard, Johnston, Hood, or Hardee, or the warnings of peers, even if they were Grant or Thomas. The reputations of others were of little value in comparison to his own all-night tutorials, constant reading, and continual questioning—what Grant later called Sherman's incessant "boning" that, as in the case of Patton, kept him up way past midnight most nights. Contemporaries remark that it was not unusual to see him still up at two and three in the morning, poring over maps and orders, documents that in his mind became more than mere locations and directions, but immediately were translated into concrete landscapes, industrial capacities, cultural characteristics of local populations, and logistical equations. Education, rather than purely military education, was critical in Sherman's view, and it ranged from art and literature to language and science, always to be tested and refined by the firsthand knowledge of the "man of action."[95]

After graduating in July 1840, for the next fifteen years Sherman saw firsthand most of the Southern and Western United States—frontier campaigning and garrison duty against the Seminole Indians in Florida (1841), artillery service at Mobile Point, Alabama, and Charleston Harbor, South Carolina (1842–43), reconnaissance into the interior of Georgia (1843–44), more artillery posting back in South Carolina (1845–46), a quartermaster stint and constant surveying, occasional real estate and business speculation in his off hours in California (1847–50), commissary duty and purchasing supplies for the army in St. Louis (1851), investigatory work in New Orleans to root out corruption (1852), back again to California to survey the establishment of a bank while on a leave of absence from the army, and finally resignation from the army (1853) and entry into the banking life of San Francisco.

By any standard measure of military success and future promotion, these last fourteen years of active duty in the United States Army had not been especially rewarding. Sherman remained only a captain posted in the commissary. His wife and growing family were being subsidized by his wealthy in-laws. He had missed out on the Mexican War in which men like Pierre Beauregard, George McClellan, Robert E. Lee, Ulysses S. Grant, Winfield Scott Hancock, James Longstreet, John Pemberton, Joe Hooker, Albert Sidney Johnston, Joe Johnston, George Thomas, Braxton Bragg, and George Meade were gaining battle experience and far more notoriety. "These brilliant scenes nearly kill us who are far off, and deprived of such previous pieces of military glory," Sherman wrote of others' success stories in Mexico. He added to his wife, "I have felt tempted to send my resignation to Washington as I really feel ashamed to wear epaulettes after having passed through a war without smelling gunpowder, but God knows I couldn't help it and so I'll let things pass."

All the States-bound Sherman had to show was firsthand geographical acquaintance with Georgia and South Carolina, intimacy with the great southern harbors like New Orleans, Charleston, and Mobile, and a pragmatic familiarity with commercial life up and down the Mississippi from Ohio to New Orleans. Through his travels in Florida, Georgia, and California, he had become a crack shot, expert horseback rider, artillery gunner, camper, surveyor, and explorer. After years of service in the quartermaster corps and commissary, the science of an army's daily consumption of food and matériel had become ingrained knowledge. Through a busy social life in Charleston and New Orleans, Sherman while in his twenties had already developed a deep understanding of the social and cultural life of the elites of the South. Throughout these years of obscurity he was also acquiring insight into the bureaucracy and politics of advancement in the United States Army. Few men knew the culture and geography of the North, Midwest, South, and far West better than Sherman; yet topographical and anthropological insight brought little notice in the peacetime army and translated into even less money in civilian life.

During the California Gold Rush of 1849–50 Sherman had stayed at his post, while dozens deserted; he had tried to keep military garrisons manned and supplied when others had fled into the Sierra. Whereas in theory all that expertise of commanding men, following orders, organizing expeditions to hunt, arrest deserters, survey, and reconnoiter could at some strange future occasion come to fruition for a singular undertaking, in 1853 those army years remained mostly undervalued and ignored by superiors—and gradually acknowledged as of little or no use by Sherman himself. Compared to other junior officers who had seen battle, been attached to the staff of Winfield Scott, or enjoyed lucrative posts in Washington, Sherman had essentially been wasting nearly a decade and half of his life in the army. In California in 1849, he went so far as to send in his resignation, only to have it rejected and not forwarded to Washington: "Self respect compels me therefore to quit the profession, which in time of war and trouble I have failed to merit, and accordingly through you I must respectfully tender my resignation." The only skill with any money-making potential at all that he seemed to have acquired was accounting and finance—in which at least his proven reputation for personal honesty might further bring opportunity. So on September 6, 1853, he permanently resigned from the American army to accept an invitation from his friend and associate Henry S. Turner; he would return to California as a private citizen and open a bank branch office in San Francisco.[96]

The San Francisco years had started out well enough. Gold was brought out of the mountains in huge quantities; thousands were immigrating to California; and the economy of San Francisco was booming as the soon-to-be financial and business center of the entire state. But quickly, wild inflation and speculation nearly ruined Sherman's bank. Gold extraction became more costly and less sure, and commerce in general never returned to its speculatory highs. By 1857, a year of great financial panic nationwide, Turner was to shut down the California office and bring Sherman home. Worse than unemployment, Sherman had himself lost a great deal of his personal capital in the declining real estate market of California. He also now felt himself personally responsible for the sour investments of fellow officers who had eagerly sent their money to a fellow soldier to get in on the Californian profit-making. Although neither legally nor ethically responsible for such losses, he was determined to liquidate everything he owned to make up some $20,000 now lost to his brother officers.

It was a bitter pill to swallow for a stern disciplinarian like Sherman, with a lifelong allegiance to order and stability, to have been wiped out speculating in the most volatile of American investments—Gold Rush real estate in California. Even here we see a side of Sherman not often emphasized by his biographers: beneath the veneer of propriety and sobriety there was a reckless gambler who was not afraid, as the citizens of Georgia would later attest, to stake his entire life and those around him on one enormous gamble that could pay dividends unimaginable.

He wrote to his wife of the failure, "The worst mistake I made was in not succeeding in getting drowned on my first arrival [in San Francisco], or not getting knocked in the head in some of the rows of the country." Now even a return to the army looked good: "I regret I ever left," he admitted. During the winter of 1855–56, Sherman was sleepless and suffered constantly from asthma; he made out a will and arranged for power of attorney, as he expected his health to collapse along with his business interests. A more unbiased observer might have noted that in a volatile boomtown, in the middle of a national depression, Sherman had somehow kept his bank afloat. He had shown unusual integrity in paying back lost capital that he was not responsible for. Despite dubbing himself the "Jonah of banking," he had somehow arrived in a wild city, started a bank from the ground up, purchased and constructed buildings, hired staff, and gained a general reputation for honesty and competence when most others in San Francisco finance were shown to be either deceitful or inept. If there was anyone in 1857 who needed someone to organize an enterprise from scratch, who needed an honest administrator of accounting and finance, and who in addition had sought an intimate knowledge of military science and practical soldiering, Sherman was that man.[97]

Unfortunately, there were no takers. So things got only worse when he returned unemployed to Ohio in 1857. As he put it to his father-in-law during his last trip to California to clean up the mess of the undercapitalized bank, "In the army I know my place, and out here am one of the pioneers and big chiefs. At Lancaster [Ohio] I can only be Cump Sherman." Back in the Midwest he auctioned off horses and mules; fixed government roads; tried to establish a law practice with his brother-in-law; sold produce in Kansas; managed his father-in-law Thomas Ewing's farm near Topeka; and speculated disastrously in corn futures—all as he mostly lived alone, apart from his wife and children in his quest to find a livelihood to support them in the accustomed comfort provided by his in-laws. In his spare time from a home-made cabin in Kansas, he wrote "Notes on the Pacific Railroad" for his brother, Senator John Sherman, about a proposed route for the transcontinental railroad. When the report was published and drew acclaim, Sherman confessed to his brother-in-law: "I did not want John to publish my notes on the Railroad. But it can't now be helped. My reason is I do not occupy any position warranting the publication." One of the most experienced and best-educated men of action in the North was at his prime, restless and full of thought in a hovel in Kansas, while his nation apparently passed him by.

Still, even if his wife was finally embarrassed over the growing family's poverty, once more Sherman was gaining invaluable skills—knowledge of legal matters, agricultural production, horses, road construction and maintenance, and supply trains—information unfortunately far too diverse to coalesce into any one profession in peacetime, but critical prerequisite erudition to move large bodies of men, with horse-drawn wagons, foraging from the countryside, building bridges, corduroying roads, and marching without good maps. Sherman himself now had experience in almost *every* undertaking and profession of the troops he was later to lead to the sea—from the lowliest private to the highest officer. He would know precisely not only how his men were to do their tasks, but also how they would feel about doing their tasks.

Throughout his catabasis, Sherman was never inactive, and even was reckless in his willingness to travel almost anywhere to take up the challenge of supporting his wife and children. During the entire ordeal of joblessness he wrote constantly to family and friends on topics as diverse as banking, the national economy, slavery—and the impending war. The problem was that he was nearing forty, at an age when the absence of capital and steady employment tended to confirm failure and hamper prospects for a profession befitting his education and experience. "I am doomed," he shrugged in 1858, "to be a vagabond, and shall no longer struggle against my fate."[98]

Things would not immediately improve. In late 1859 he accepted a position as the first superintendent of a new military academy in Louisiana, the Louisiana Seminary of Learning, which would one day become Louisiana State University. Sherman was charged with creating a university *ex nihilo*—hiring staff, building classrooms and infrastructure, acquiring books, uniforms, and supplies, and planning a curriculum. By the fall of 1860, on the eve of Lincoln's election, by all accords Sherman was now at last and for a moment at least a success. He was earning $4,500 a year and was provided with a fine house and an immediate social circle of impressed officers and supportive politicians. Somehow he managed to oversee all of the school's finances and the general administration of the new institute, as well as to teach history and geography, as he waited for enough advanced students for planned subsequent classes on drawing and engineering. For the first time in his life, all the previous academic and military training, the years of expertise acquired in accounting and financial organization in California, the firsthand knowledge of both Southern culture and life in the military—all this had come together in one opportunity. Sherman was at last in control of his own fate.

Then it was over as nearly as quickly as it had begun. South Carolina seceded from the Union in December 1860. Sherman, the brother of a Republican senator from Ohio with a quasi-abolitionist record, came under immediate suspicion. For his own part, he was faced with the choice of either supervising a Southern military academy—one that would now expropriate United States military goods and train officers for a secessionary cause—or returning unemployed to the North, broke and without friends back in Ohio, on the eve of war and under some suspicion of having been successful in supervising military education in the nascent Confederacy. His friend and associate, the Southern professor of languages and later Confederate colonel, David Boyd, later wrote to Sherman's daughter of her father's decision to leave:

> I think it was just then—in the Pine Woods of La—from 1859 to 1861—that your Father's character loomed up grandest: he turned his back on his best & truest friends, because he thought we were wrong! Still, his great living heart never ceased to beat warmly for us of the South. And all thro' that terrible struggle, Genl Sherman had more warm devoted friends in the Southern army than any Southern general had![99]

Between Lincoln's inauguration and the outbreak of hostilities, Sherman—his letters range from the pathetic to the near arrogant—tried to arrange some command befitting his experience, education, and family standing as exemplified by the political influence of his brother and father-in-law. To no avail. By early 1861 he was back in St. Louis, supervising a municipal rail line, scarcely able to provide money for his ever expanding family. His letter turning down a low-level appointment in the Union army in April 1861 is full of hurt, ending with "I thank you for the compliment contained in your offer, and assure you that I wish the Administration all success in its almost impossible task of governing this distracted and anarchical people." Finally, in June 1861 he was made a colonel in the regular army in charge of a brigade of about 3,400 recruits, which he trained and led successfully in battle during the first Union disaster at Bull Run in July.

By September 1861, Sherman was a general, given command of all Union forces in Kentucky. But convinced that victory over the South would eventually call for gigantic Union armies of 100,000 soldiers—grandiose and hysterical claims in 1862; more realistic and sensible in light of the war's eventual demands—and appealing for more troops to save the state, Sherman was gradually rumored to have suffered a mental breakdown. After scurrilous attacks in the newspapers alleging insanity—"General William T. Sherman Insane," the *Cincinnati Commercial* blared; "The family and friends of Sherman," the *Cincinnati Gazette* pontificated, "desire to keep his insanity a secret"—Sherman was relieved of command in the fall and given a temporary furlough to find rest and recovery. "I should have committed suicide," he wrote his brother John of his only real absence from four years of war, "if not for my children. I do not think that I can again be entrusted with a command." The *Commercial* concluded its editorial with condescension:

> The harsh criticisms that have been lavished on this gentleman, provoked by his strange conduct, will now give way to feelings of deepest sympathy for him in his great calamity. It seems providential that the country has not to mourn the loss of an army through the loss of mind of a general into whose hands was committed the vast responsibility of the command of Kentucky.

Not until April 1862, when in charge of a division at Shiloh, did Sherman regain his reputation. Few realized that Sherman's dismissal from command would provide the last vital link in his prerequisite education for the March to the Sea: a necessary sense of fatalism and recklessness, and near contempt for the press, conventional wisdom, and the judgment and approval of his peers. In the midst of a near-Northern rout on the first day of Shiloh, Sherman held his troops together, had three horses shot from under him, was slightly wounded twice, and generally credited with saving the Union army from an embarrassing flight. Grant thought Sherman instrumental in the eventual Northern victory.

Shiloh changed Sherman's life—cementing his friendship with Grant, proving his own mettle in battle, and placing him in the center of the most horrific fighting thus far in American history. Before Shiloh, Sherman felt himself afraid of his own shadow; after Shiloh, he never really looked back. By the time he left Atlanta for the Atlantic coast in November 1864, Sherman had behind him over two years of impressive fighting in Tennessee, Mississippi, and Georgia, a string of victories that had confirmed Grant's confidence in him. It was logical that he was made general of all armies in the West after Grant took over in the East in 1863. On the eve of his March to the Sea, this once unsure commander could proclaim with confidence, "I am going into the very bowels of the Confederacy and propose leaving a trail that will be recognized fifty years hence."[100]

The March to the Sea is inseparable from William Tecumseh Sherman. The entire Army of the West—its organization, its mobility, its very ideology—was one with Sherman himself. To investigate the success of the army is to seek out the elements of Sherman's own ability—why on this December 3, outside of Millen, Georgia, 62,000 Union troops were in good health, well fed, high-spirited, safe, and about to capture Savannah. The answer can be found in three areas from Sherman's past: experience, education, and character.

Sherman's knowledge of military science was not singular in the strictly tactical sense. That is, before the war he had little, if any, prior record of expertise in the actual operations of thousands of troops in battle itself—and, like Patton, he was always convinced that his own advance, not the destruction of the enemy per se, would collapse the Confederacy. If anything, Sherman was bored with actual battles that interrupted his larger vision of using marching armies to alter the very fabric of society. Hood escaped from Atlanta, Hardee from Savannah, and Johnston once more from Bentonville. Whereas military historians have not demonstrated that their flights made any substantial difference in the outcome of the war, it is clear that had Sherman destroyed those defeated forces, he would have at least enhanced his reputation as a Great Captain.

His frontal assault at Kennesaw Mountain in June 1864 was a terrible mistake and led to hundreds of needless dead. He was also altogether unsure where the enemy was or what it was doing in the hours before the great Confederate charge at Shiloh. The constant seesaw, drawn-out flanking advance on Atlanta saw a number of missed opportunities. In short, Sherman was workmanlike at tactical operations and brilliant in strategic maneuver, perhaps because he felt that the very need for pitched battles in some sense denoted military failure—that his army had not moved in the proper direction or occupied enough territory so as to make the enemy's direct and frontal resistance impossible or at least foolhardy to the point of being suicidal. In Sherman's way of thinking, a competent general and a good army could march and maneuver themselves into such a position that the enemy forces in the field could not fight without being annihilated and the enemy civilian population not resist without bringing on the end of their very culture. As Liddell Hart remarks:

> He had come to realize that in war all conditions are more calculable, all obstacles more surmountable, than those of human resistance. And having begun the war with an orthodox belief in the sovereign efficacy of battle as a "cure-all" he had learnt that the theoretical ideal of the destruction of the enemy's armed forces on the battlefield is rarely borne out in practice and that

to pursue it single-mindedly is to chase a will-o'-the-wisp. Because of his original orthodoxy it is all the more significant that he reached the conclusion that the way to decide wars and win battles was "more by the movement of troops than by fighting." This was his ultimate theory, constantly expressed.[101]

Sherman also understood, as did no other Union general, the close tie in the Southern mind between pride and property. If he burned Georgia unmercifully, it may have been because he had lived in Georgia, South Carolina, Alabama, and Louisiana and knew exactly what material damage would do to the psyche of the South. "I knew more of Georgia than the rebels did," he quite accurately remarked. Grant and others felt it critical to kill Southern soldiers; Sherman, to kill the spirit of those who fed and encouraged those soldiers. Quite simply, the march through Georgia, the creation of the Army of the West itself, was for Sherman in some sense the final comprehensive examination for whose myriad challenges he had studied continuously for twenty-five years. Sherman wrote to his wife after he reached Savannah of the sense of déjà vu his marches brought, "It seems impossible for us to go anywhere without being where I have been before; every bit of knowledge then acquired is returned, tenfold."[102]

We forget that of all Union generals, Sherman quite literally was present at the first fight at Bull Run and the last major battle of the Civil War at Bentonville. Except for a brief furlough of a few weeks in early 1862, Sherman was constantly in the field from summer 1861 to late spring 1865, and he had fought in nearly every state of the Confederacy, from a few miles outside of Washington to deep inside Mississippi, and against almost every Southern general of the war—Beauregard, Bragg, Johnston, Albert Sidney Johnston, Hardee, and Hood. In short, Sherman knew everyone and was everywhere in the war—this "vagabond" who already had met with the likes of Indian fighters, American explorers, entrepreneurs, and most of the heroes of early California before the war had even begun. No major Civil War commander had more battle experience, had served in more theaters, or had marched farther than William Tecumseh Sherman.

The March to the Sea was considered by observers—and Sherman himself—an easy enterprise. That assessment is only in hindsight and a reflection solely of Sherman's immense preparation and experience, which had now made the impossible seem mundane. It is no accident that no Confederate army could ever attempt a march like Sherman's. It was not simply the Secessionists' lack of abundant manpower, material provisions, or even a professed humanitarian imperative to travel northward to punish the evil of bondage. Rather, the South and the world of the Confederacy simply lacked men with the broad experience and outlook of William Tecumseh Sherman, who so keenly understood the modern world.

In the South there was not the same range of activities open to a man of genius and energy like Sherman—not the degree of financial opportunities, construction, banking, exploration, industry, easy travel and social mobility that had all given Sherman his vast education and keen appreciation of industry and its insidious effect on the populace. Land and roots more likely gave a man prestige in the South—capital and broad experience in the North. The sum of that entire quarter-century experience was now to be turned loose on Georgia. A Union officer concluded of Sherman's ubiquity on the march, "He seemed to forget nothing, to neglect nothing, to foresee everything. . . . An infinitude of detail, instead of wearying him, seemed to stimulate him to new activity."

In contrast, an officer of the Confederacy who had succeeded in the army, agriculture, or politics of the South still lacked the prerequisite training of someone like Sherman who had purportedly failed in almost everything he had attempted in the North. Lee or Early, audacious and courageous generals both, might for a time cross the Mason-Dixon line; but neither had the technical know-how, the political acumen, the intimate familiarity with the Union, or the comprehensive grasp of logistics, rails, and industry to unravel Northern society by a systematic march of terror through Maryland, Pennsylvania, and Ohio. Hood, had he sidestepped Thomas, might for a time have run wild in Tennessee and southern Ohio; that he simply headed for the Union army and made a direct, gallant—and disastrous—frontal assault was more to be expected than it was lunatic. For all of Lee's supposed genius, the North was fortunate that he, not a man of Sherman's mind and ability, led Southern troops into Pennsylvania in 1863. Otherwise the huge Confederate army of 75,000 would have threatened various towns, created a swath of destruction from Pittsburgh to Philadelphia, bypassed Union resistance, and then made a lightning-quick descent on Washington, creating a panic among the citizens and a general loss of confidence among the troops at the front. And the Army of Northern Virginia would have crossed back over the Potomac largely intact, with the Federal capital smoldering in its rear, and the Northern citizenry ready for peace.

Sherman was naturally bright and superbly educated in both the abstract and practical sense while in transit to California, he drilled his soldiers between reading Washington Irving, Shakespeare, and "everything I could get, and yesterday cast about to determine which I should attempt next—the Bible, History of the Reformation or the Wandering Jew." His memoirs—abounding in logistical detail and uncanny calculation of the daily requirements of men and livestock—are beautifully written, reflecting his earlier training in history, English, classical literature, and French, and a lifelong propensity to read and keep up with current academic inquiry and controversy. He had a natural graceful mode of expression similar to Epaminondas's rare ability to produce the pointed and often terrifying statement. This desire to make his own ideas appear in print as startling as the sudden arrival of troops in the field was a particular skill and lifelong obsession. If the Theban could promise to plant the Athenian Propylaea in the Theban agora, turn Attica into a "sheepwalk," destroy Sparta "in a single day," or "crush the head of the serpent," so too Sherman alone of Civil War generals is known for his uncanny ability to express in words the entire strategic and psychological mood of a nation—Georgia would be made "to howl" and war would become simply "hell." The "shell of the confederacy" was "hollow"; his "business was down south," "war and individual ruin are synonymous terms," and he "was going into the very bowels of the Confederacy."

Sherman suspected that to lead great armies required an uncanny ability to capture the proper prose, which must somehow simultaneously appeal to a democratic and at times uncouth citizenry in arms, a more sober, more worried nation at home, and a prickly staff of deskbound overseers. Sherman's phraseology could do all three. His letter to Halleck on the nature of Southern society reads like a scholarly paper presented at an anthropological society. The exchanges with Hood outside Atlanta are really treatises in moral philosophy and the theory of natural and legal right: "In the name of common-sense—I ask you not to appeal to a just God in such a sacrilegious manner. You who, in the midst of peace and prosperity, have plunged a nation into war—dark and cruel war." His report on the transcontinental railroad is a scientific and engineering masterpiece.

Sherman, we forget, really was a professor and college president, just as Epaminondas was a philosopher and Patton both an author and a dynamic lecturer. Sherman quite literally was teaching history in February 1861 and leading men into battle at Bull Run less than six months later. Of all the major Civil War generals in the field, Sherman was the best educated and most voracious reader; that Epaminondas and Patton both were better read than any generals of their respective ages indicates that success for a great march into enemy territory is impossible without a man of genius, experience—and wide learning—at its head. It is no accident that Patton was the last American general that could approximate the range and power of Sherman's aphorisms, from the colloquial to the eloquent: "Hold 'em by the nose and kick 'em in the pants"; "We shall attack and attack and attack until we are exhausted and then we shall attack again. A pint of sweat will save a gallon of blood"; "To conquer, we must destroy our enemies. We must not only die gallantly; we must kill devastatingly."[103]

Like Epaminondas, Sherman also had character, an overused word in the modern age usually employed in contexts of its absence, but in his case specifically a real reluctance to ask of others what he would demand of himself. Rarely, Sherman sought attention at the expense of peers, and he exhibited a ready desire to live, look, and talk like a regular soldier. Like Epaminondas, who fought as a hoplite after the great invasion of 370–369 and who died with a handful of possessions to his name, Sherman was almost indistinguishable in appearance and appetites from his men. A Union major wrote of his first impressions:

> General Sherman is the most American looking man I ever saw, tall and lank, not very erect, with hair like thatch, which he rubs up with his hands, a rusty beard trimmed close, a wrinkled face, sharp prominent red nose, small bright eyes, coarse red hands; black felt hat slouched over the eyes (he says when he wears anything else the soldiers cry out, as he rides along, "Hallo, the old man has got a new hat"), dirty dickey with points wilted down, black old fashioned stack brown field officers coat with high collar and no shoulder stripes, muddy trousers and one spur. He carries his hands in his pockets, is very awkward in his gait and motions, talks continually and with rapidity.

"I never saw General Sherman making for some place in our rear," wrote Rice Bull. "He was on the road going toward the Chattahoochee Crossing accompanied by only three staff officers and a courier. He was very plainly dressed and one not knowing him would never take him to have a rank higher than a Captain or Major, surely not the Commanding General of an Army. He was without sash and sword and wore a common loose blouse; the only thing that would indicate his rank were his ordinary shoulder straps. . . . He seemed to care little for show. . . . Soldiering with him seemed to be a business, not a spectacular entertainment."

Surely his sobriquet "Uncle Billy" came from his ragged appearance that so emboldened his marchers, who were convinced that their general was at heart a bummer like themselves and could be addressed on affectionate if not intimate terms. His aide Henry Hitchcock remarked of his sleeping habits:

> He is proverbially the most restless man in the army at night,—never sleeps a night straight through, and frequently comes out and pokes around in this style, disregarding all remonstrance as to taking cold . . . he always wakes up at 3 or 4 A.M. and can't sleep again till after daylight: and always likes at that hour to be up and about camp—"best time to hear any movement at a distance."

His no-nonsense Ohio upbringing explains Sherman's hatred of pretense—is it any accident that the nondescript appearance and common touch of the Midwesterners Grant, Lincoln, and Sherman reassured the nation in a way that McClellan, Seward, and the Northern abolitionists could not? Ultimately, Sherman worried over his men's pay, because like them he too had been broke; over their food, because he too had been nearly hungry; over their aspirations and ambitions, because he too had seen his own crash. Unlike McClellan the road executive or Lee the aristocrat, but like Grant the grocer from Galena, Illinois, Sherman feared no setback because he had experienced nearly every setback conceivable.

He had been called insane; he had gone broke; he had lost jobs; and he had watched those around him with less talent succeed in war and finance. McClellan, second in his class at West Point, prized student of Professor Dennis Mahan, staff officer to General Winfield Scott in Mexico, member of a United States military commission in 1855–56 to Europe, firsthand observer of the Crimean War—all this while Sherman was bouncing throughout the United States in a series of mostly uninspiring and often humiliating jobs—had all the necessary prerequisites for command other than the sense of desperation and audacity that are about the only valuable dividends from abject failure. McClellan the railroad executive, who was making $10,000 a year on the eve of the outbreak, would never have announced, "Men go to war to kill or to get killed and should expect no tenderness." And he most certainly would have been terrified by Sherman's remark about the South, "Thousands of people may perish, but they now realize that war means something else than vain glory and boasting."

Suicide had been on Sherman's mind. Modern biographers cite Sherman's contemplation of taking his own life as proof that he was either not serious in his avowal or deadly serious and thus insane. True, he may have been posturing in letters or he may have been clinically depressed, but in the Sophoclean sense, such self-realization and readiness to end one's life were not to be seen as jest, weakness, or illness, but rather as strength, if not liberation from one's fears. Once known as mad and suicidal, Sherman could act and speak deliberately in exaggerated, hysterical tones in a way that might terrorize his enemies and embolden his friends: "To secure the safety of the navigation of the Mississippi River I could slay millions. On this point I am not only insane but mad," he wrote.

In the Greek way, once Sherman, like a character of Homeric epic or Athenian drama, could welcome death, then the rest of his life might be considered an unforeseen profit and thus could be lived without fear and at the disposal of others. Great generals of audacious and risky marches are willing, and must be ready, to die at the front of their men—and to let others know of that recklessness. Sherman summed up his own conduct when he finished his *Memoirs* with advice on the role of the general in the future:

> No man can properly command an army from the rear; he must be "at its front"; and when a detachment is made, the commander thereof should be informed of the object to be accomplished, and left as free as possible to execute it in his own way; and when an army is divided up into several parts, the superior should always attend that one which he regards as most important. Some men think that modern armies may be so regulated that a general can sit in an office and play on his several columns as on the keys of a piano; this is a fearful mistake. The directing mind must be at the very head of the army—must be seen there, and the effect of his mind and personal energy must be felt by every officer and man present with it, to secure the best results. Every attempt to make war easy and safe will result in humiliation and disaster.

A single hour in a château to the rear is fatal to the entire enterprise of a great march of retribution into hostile territory.[104]

A dilemma facing all of us as we reconsider Sherman is the status of war and racial sensitivity in the modern world. Most historians have uniformly, and rightly, favored the Union cause and the war for abolition. Yet as most moderns, they have felt that war itself is an aberration, a tragedy—not, as the Greeks believed, something inevitable to the human condition, much less often a necessary tool to destroy evil. A dilemma arises. Slavery is evil and Sherman is brutal. Yet brutality was necessary to end slavery and win the war. What are we to do then with Sherman, whose savagery helped to dismantle a racist South? If Sherman is considered too cruel, if he sounds too "fanatical," then the logical antithesis is that he should have been far easier on those fanatics who promoted slavery. If he is to be blamed for wrecking the plantation class, then he must be praised for his effort in the cause to free the slave.[105]

It is a hard thing for contemporary liberalism to envision war as not always evil, but as sometimes very necessary—and very necessarily brutal if great evil is to disappear. Sherman did not make up out of thin air the "three-hundred thousand" who had to be killed; there really were that many and more courageous Confederates who would kill and die for the reality—though not always the open admission—that black people were to be perpetually enslaved. Some historians often fail to see that a "humane" manner of waging the Civil War gives us someone like McClellan, whose battle incompetence only prolonged the killing, and whose tolerance for slavery might, if Sherman had not taken Atlanta in September 1864, have allowed bondage to continue in North America—under a McClellan presidency.[106]

The real dilemma of Sherman, it seems to me, is rather to understand a man who wrote of the need to slaughter hundreds of thousands but killed very few, and with real reluctance. Sherman, also like Patton, professed his distrust of racial equality; yet he was especially kind to blacks, and very unkind to Southern plantation racists. He wrote of the need to destroy the Confederacy root and branch; yet, he sought to extend the most generous peace and help to a defeated South. As blacks themselves acknowledged, Sherman did more to "cut them loose" than any abolitionist. The man had contradictions aplenty, but the divide between what he said and did reflects mostly positively, not negatively, on his character. Moderns especially fail to appreciate that the visionaries of a conservative society sometimes profess racism to justify their own moderation; they often claim to be hardened war-makers to make their own clemency palatable to self and similarly dour others.[107]

Ultimately, we historians must conclude that William Tecumseh Sherman could do what we could not, what very few Americans, then or now, could envision—this strange mix of abstract genius and pragmatic acumen, infused with a mental and physical energy that seemed immune from the limitations of food and sleep. We must forget his insensitivity in language, forgive his obnoxious bluster, grant that he could be rude, had a tendency to flirt with pretty women, on occasion wrote nonsense about the races, and simply appreciate that he was a great man whose deeds belied his words, a hero whose capture of Atlanta saved Lincoln's administration and the Union itself, and whose march through Georgia and the Carolinas broke the back of the Confederacy at the cost of a remarkably few American lives. "Step by step have I been led deeper and deeper in the game," he wrote his wife Ellen from Savannah, "till I find myself a leader to whom not only my soldiers look but the President and the People, not only our own, but Foreigners and the South now account me one of the Great Leaders of Armies endowed with extraordinary qualities that make me more distrustful than if I were nobody. I cannot now help it and must go on to the end."

In the last analysis, we may yield to the consensus of his men in the field, fellow Westerners who loved—and did not follow blindly out of fear—their "Uncle Billy," this "insane" general, who could confess of his troops, "not a waiver, doubt, or hesitation when I order, and men march to certain death without a murmur if I call on them, because they know I value their lives as much as my own." To a battery on the march, he pronounced, "I would rather be a gunner of this battery than a Major General of the Rebel army." Patton eighty years later would say almost the same thing.

"Don't ride too fast, General," they would warn him of muddy roads, "Pretty slippery going, Uncle Billy; pretty slippery going." "There's our old dad," remarked another. "His shirt is generally bordering on the dirty & he is not the kind of man to put on style," one Ohio soldier wrote. "We all like him for that." Another, nearly illiterate, wrote home, "It is an honor to enney man to have ben on this last campaign with Sherman you se him a riding a long you would think that he was somb oald plow jogger his head bent a little to one side with an oald stub of a sigar in his mouth." A Midwestern private summed up the army's feelings best: "I won't believe he has made a mistake until I know all about it. It can't be. . . . I'd rather fight under him than Grant and if he were Mahomet we'd be devoted Mussulmen." One sergeant remarked, "There was never such a man as Sherman or as they call him Crazy Bill and he has got his men to believe that they cant be whipped." Of his tendency to turn up anywhere during the march, and to be mistaken for a common private, Sherman wrote to his wife, "I must see everything." He was often berated by his men, who did not believe the grungy-looking man scolding them for violations of his orders concerning unlicensed foraging was really the commander in chief of the army itself.[108]

On December 3, this strange and contradictory William Tecumseh Sherman was a few miles away from bringing his huge force unscathed right up to the city limits of Savannah near the sea, coming out of the "hole" into which Grant and Lincoln worried that he had once led so many myriads of their Union troops. As he passed Millen, the lights of Savannah and the applause of the ages were not far off. He later wrote Ellen of his marvelous transformation from the dark days before Shiloh: "After participating in driving the Confederacy down the Mississippi, I have again cut it in twain, and have planned & executed a Campaign which Judges pronounce will be famous among the grand deeds of the World. I can hardly realize it for really it was easy, but like one who has walked a narrow plank I look back and wonder if I really did it."[109]

7

THE END AND THE BEGINNING

SAVANNAH, GEORGIA

December 21, 1864—Thirty-sixth Day Out

T HE ARMY'S last hundred miles from Millen were relatively uneventful. On the twenty-fifth day out from Atlanta, on December 10, the Union troops completed their three-hundred-mile march and approached the Atlantic coast and the Confederate fortifications around Savannah, Georgia. Most of the Westerners had never seen the sea. Given the formidable reputation of Sherman's marchers, this time there was to be no murderous siege as had been the case at Atlanta in August and early September—the Confederate wish was not to die in or even to kill from, but simply to get out of, Savannah. Ten days after surrounding Savannah and at nominal cost, 62,000 Union troops entered and occupied the city as the Confederate garrison stealthily scurried out of town. Sherman wired Lincoln: I BEG TO PRESENT YOU AS A CHRISTMAS GIFT, THE CITY OF SAVANNAH, WITH ONE HUNDRED AND FIFTY HEAVY GUNS AND PLENTY OF AMMUNITION, ALSO ABOUT TWENTY-FIVE THOUSAND BALES OF COTTON. After acknowledging his earlier apprehensions, in his reply to the general the president noted of Sherman's magnificent march: "Now the undertaking being a success, the honor is all yours, for I believe none of us went further than to acquiesce. And taking the work of General Thomas into the count, as it should be taken, it is indeed a great success."

The march now belonged to the world of myth. Former critics of Sherman immediately sang a different tune. The press was ecstatic; the *Times* of London waxed:

232

Since the great Duke of Marlborough turned his back on the Dutch and plunged heroically into Germany to fight the famous battle of Blenheim, military history has recorded no stranger marvel than the mysterious expedition of General Sherman on an unknown route against an undiscoverable enemy.

The *Edinburgh Review* placed the March to the Sea "with the highest achievements that the annals of modern warfare record." To the *Chicago Tribune*, Sherman's march was comparable to "the Anabasis and the best efforts of Marlborough, Napoleon, and Wellington."[110]

When Sherman had left Atlanta over a month earlier, Southern elites had promised his destruction; when he arrived in Savannah, they were now lined up to ask him how Georgia might reenter the Union. Henry Hitchcock, his aide, recalls the general's reaction to this sudden about-face:

"I told them," said the General, "I had no terms or conditions to make—that *we* didn't consider that the *State of Georgia* ever had been out of the Union, and that as for them, we didn't care what they did—that was their business, but the United States was going to put down this rebellion anyhow." I don't give his words, but about the substance. You may think this is a careless and even harsh way of talking, but it is founded, and I think very shrewdly, upon the very character of the men he was addressing. The first step of "reconstruction" is to show these "high-bred Southern gentlemen" accustomed to rule as by birthright, first that they are utterly powerless and then that nobody cares to solicit their obedience—they have *got* to obey, whether or no. Not to obey us—not at all, but the government and the laws which we also obey; and that if they don't they will be crushed like flies on a wheel. This is Gen. Sherman's "policy," and it is the kindest and the *only* one; and he will crush them if need be. Hence this march and its devastation—and the leading ex-rebels of Savannah are bitterly cursing J.D. & Co., and voluntarily abandoning their hopeless cause.

Grant, who had been wary of the enterprise and would not be especially eager for the Army of the West's landward continuance through the Carolinas, now praised Sherman openly as "one of the greatest, purest, and best of men," and helped to organize efforts by the public to raise money for the Sherman household in appreciation of the general's service to the nation. He bragged, "I never had a doubt of the result. . . . I would not have entrusted the expedition to any other living commander." Sherman's men themselves, like their general, could not quite believe they had really made it: "Savannah is ours. Our long campaign is ended. If the world predicted our failure, the world must acknowledge itself mistaken."[111]

It did. Back in the North, people greeted each other on the street simply with "He's made it" or "Sherman's at Savannah." The journey was not to be known as the expedition to the ocean, or the Atlanta-to-Savannah campaign, but rather memorialized as the "March to the Sea"—perhaps deliberately reminiscent of Xenophon's *Anabasis* ("The March Up Country"), a Greek romantic though somewhat similar saga of free men who battled through the interior of Asia to come out unexpectedly and in safety on the Hellenic shores of the Black Sea, exclaiming at their final deliverance, "The Sea! The Sea!"

Whereas Sherman and his superiors agreed that the subsequent Carolinas campaign was to be the far more difficult and important march strategically, the trek to Savannah—being the first and most dramatic—was immediately and alone to be the stuff of song and poetry. Northerners not only rejoiced at his audacious success, but felt that Sherman had crafted a type of lightning war that was moral, economical, and symbolic of the righteous indignation of the Union cause itself. Right after the armistice, Sherman was greeted by the Union League Club of New York: "When you visited upon the absurd and truculent vanity of South Carolina the just vengeance she had provoked we here rejoiced at your array sweeping across the country of that ridiculous chivalry. . . . We talked of you, we praised you, we love you, for the directness and patriotic singleness of duty, with which you made war." Sherman's strategy had not so much destroyed Georgia and precipitated the end of the war as taught the North that it had possessed moral capital all along.

The final tally of material damage of the month in Georgia, however, needed no exaggeration. It was frightening; never before in the history of military conflict had an army wrought such havoc in such a brief period at such small loss to itself. As one Union soldier put it, "The destruction could hardly have been worse if Atlanta had been a volcano in eruption and the molten lava had flowed in a stream 60 miles wide and five times as long." Although only 12 percent of the Georgia countryside had been covered by the Union army, Sherman claimed his troops had inflicted $100,000,000 of damage—$20,000,000 of which, he said, "has inured to our advantage." In the march's aftermath the price of Georgia farmland crashed, losing up to 70 percent of its value; the assessed valuation of slaves who would be eventually liberated in Georgia alone was close to $275,000,000—a figure for which Sherman was greatly responsible. "This may seem a hard species of warfare," Sherman wrote when he finished, "but it brings the sad realities of war home to those who have been directly or indirectly instrumental in involving us in its attendant calamities."

As Sherman gazed out at his men who now walked the streets of Savannah, he observed, "They regard us just as the Romans did the Goths and the parallel is not unjust." Vandals they were, for one calculation put Sherman's

work at 100,000 hogs stolen, 20,000 cattle driven off, 15,000 horses confiscated, and 500,000 bushels of corn and 100,000 bushels of sweet potatoes
consumed—food destined for Confederate armies in the field. The army itself
arrived in Savannah with 200 more wagons than when it started and thousands more in livestock. In actual mileage, given the terrain and variety of
routes, some of his men had marched between 350 and 550 miles, averaging
between 10 and 15 miles a day—a phenomenal rate given the fact that the
army was actively destroying infrastructure as it moved through enemy territory. Modern physical enthusiasts may march 10 miles on a particular Sunday
of strenuous hiking, but the idea that thousands would do so in mass every day
is beyond our comprehension, more so when we appreciate the caliber of the
roads the Union army traversed. "Such roads I've never seen—and still it
rains," wrote one soldier. Another added, "This night's march many will long
recollect, for nearly every man on foot, both officers and men, fell down, some
of them dozens of times."[112]

Besides the booty in Atlanta, the matériel Sherman's men confiscated in
Savannah alone was considerable. Sherman had bragged to Lincoln that he
had found 25,000 bales of cotton and 150 heavy guns. In fact, there were
probably an additional 10,000 to 20,000 bales that were either randomly destroyed or turned up later. The government later sold Sherman's cotton for
$30,000,000, ensuring after the plundering of the Georgia countryside that
the entire march had essentially been self-supporting and cost the Federal
government nothing. The Confederates, in addition, left behind in Savannah nearly 200 railcars, 13 locomotives, nearly 30,000 artillery rounds, and
over 50,000 rifle cartridges.

Sherman's army suffered about 100 dead, a little over 700 wounded or
missing, and another 1,300 captured; in other words, an army of over 60,000
men lost only about 60 men a day from its fighting strength for over a month
as it went through the heart of the Confederacy. In contrast, six months earlier at Cold Harbor, Grant had lost over three times that total number of casualties in less than twenty-four hours.

Most of Sherman's casualties were those caught out of formation and
laden with plunder, who were either summarily executed or taken to horrific
prisoner-of-war camps in rural Georgia or forcibly conscripted into the Confederate army. Few were killed in fights with enemy soldiers. Sherman reported that his army had fired 1,245,000 cartridges—or only about 20 rounds
per man during the entire march. Each soldier on average shot his rifle less
than once a day—mostly at chickens and livestock—and arrived at Savannah with most of his allotted cartridges unfired. In Sherman's new kind of
war, an army was to be in better shape after its campaign than before.[113]

The larger effect on the progression of the war? If Sherman's capture of Atlanta had guaranteed Lincoln his election in November, then the subsequent March to the Sea in the last months of Lincoln's life ensured the newly reelected president soaring popularity and the assurance of the people's lasting faith in his policy. Sherman made Lincoln immortal and his last year as president a tremendous success, as he brought him victory without the costs that Grant had incurred. There would be no more whispers of negotiated settlements, no further talk with the Rebels about anything other than unconditional surrender. All of Sherman's earlier expectations in the late summer had now in winter on the Atlantic coast come to full fruition: his lieutenant Thomas had essentially destroyed Hood's army in Tennessee; Grant was holding Lee firmly in Virginia; and the Southern populace was aghast but also terrified by the ruin that their comrades experienced in Georgia.

Worse still for the Confederacy, now Sherman was poised to march systematically northward through the Carolinas to meet Grant, to destroy the remaining Confederate armies, to occupy more capitals at Columbia, Raleigh—and perhaps Richmond itself—and to punish severely the people of South Carolina, who had inaugurated this murderous war to begin with. As Sherman put it years later, the march through Georgia was all along the beginning, not the end.

> I only regarded the march from Atlanta to Savannah as a "shift of base," as the transfer of a strong army, which had no opponent, and had finished its then work, from the interior to a point on the sea-coast, from which it could achieve other important results. I considered this march as a means to an end, and not as an essential act of war. Still, then, as now the march to the sea was generally regarded as something extraordinary, something anomalous, something out of the usual order of events; whereas, in fact, I simply moved from Atlanta to Savannah, as one step in the direction of Richmond, a movement that had to be met and defeated, or the war was necessarily at an end. Were I to express my measure of the relative importance of the march to the sea, and that from Savannah northward, I would place the former at one, and the latter at ten, or the maximum.

A recently freed slave understood the South's dilemma much better than did its own officials; of Hood's absence and Hardee's flight before Sherman in Georgia, he noted, "Dey got a army behind dat cant catch up with him and de army in front of him cant git out de way." A key to evaluating the success of any democratic march is to appreciate where it ends up: Epaminondas finished in Messenia, creating a Helot nation; Sherman at the Atlantic, in position to march north through the Carolinas; Patton in Bavaria and at the

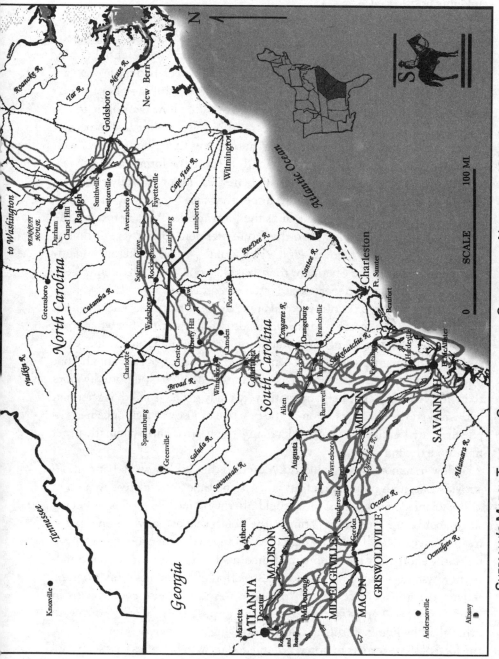

SHERMAN'S MARCH THROUGH GEORGIA AND THE CAROLINAS   NOVEMBER 1864–APRIL 1865

Czech border with a huge army ready to offer resistance if need be against a suddenly hostile Red Army.

In late January, Sherman would begin this other, far more arduous two-month trek of nearly five hundred miles northward through South and North Carolina that would indeed bring matters to a close. Any potential rivalry with Grant—Sherman, at war's end, we should remember, had made one vast circuit through the heart of the South while Grant was still in sight of Washington—remained minor given Sherman's avowal to allow Lee's army to fall to Grant, his promise to eschew politics, and his own willingness to occupy the role of Grant's loyal subordinate. Grant knew that Sherman was well aware that he could tear through the South because the former held Lee fast in Virginia; by the same token, Sherman believed Grant to be fully cognizant that Lee's army and all Confederate forces that faced the Army of the Potomac were crumbling from the rear as the Army of the West ripped out the guts of the Confederacy. It was to the future president Grant's credit that at war's end he was far more loyal—at least for a time—to his boisterous and unpredictable subordinate Sherman, than was the soon-to-be president Eisenhower to an equally obstreperous and often embarrassing Patton.[114]

Critics for the next century would argue over the rectitude, effectiveness, and difficulty of the March to the Sea, paradoxically asserting that what Sherman did in Georgia was either amoral or irrelevant to the Union cause. Others added that Hardee's army had been allowed to escape from Savannah, that Sherman had not been assiduous in collecting freed slaves—purportedly more than 50,000 directly in Sherman's path were ready to flee—and that Sherman had wrecked the entire tradition of the practice of just war that once had expressly spared civilians. Before addressing these criticisms systematically, I must note the irony in each.

How in a moral sense could the March to the Sea be too barbaric in destroying Southern property and yet at the same time not effective enough in killing Confederate soldiers? How could Sherman's men be too lax in freeing slaves, but be the only Union army in the South that actually was engaged in freeing slaves? How could his march be considered either too easy or even militarily effortless, when Grant and Lincoln—both known for neither timidity nor hysteria—feared for the very destruction of Sherman's army when he requested permission to go into "the hole"? And how else could Sherman move his colossal army to the east and be in position to march northward other than by living off the land and destroying property? Was he to pay for the food of slave-owners in prized Federal dollars with promises that such capital would not be forwarded to purchase more bullets for Lee and Johnston?

Were his men to eat hardtack as secessionists fared better? Keep clear of railroads, as locomotives sped by with food, ammunition, and guns to kill Northerners in Virginia? Bypass slave-owning plantationists in a war to end slavery?

As for the charge that Sherman's brand of war was amoral, if we forget for a moment what constitutes "morality" in war, and examine acts of violence per se against Southern civilians, we learn that there were few if any gratuitous murders on the march. There seem to have also been less than half a dozen rapes—a fact acknowledged by both sides. Some Southerners felt the greater damage to property and outrage to the populace came from Confederate cavalry under Wheeler, which was as thievish as Sherman's bummers—one Alabama cavalryman confessed the generally held sentiment that "the citizens of Georgia have more animosity towards Wheeler's Cavalry than they have against the Yankees." Any killing outside of battle was strictly military execution in response to the shooting of Northern prisoners. Southerner irregulars executed and sometimes tortured Union bummers, drawing retaliation from Sherman, who usually shot Confederate prisoners man-for-man for those Union soldiers he found slain. Rather, the real anomaly seems more how Sherman brought over 60,000 young men through one of the richest areas of the enemy South without unchecked killing or mayhem. After the war a Confederate officer remarked of Sherman's swath through Georgia: "The Federal army generally behaved very well in this State. I don't think there was ever an army in the world that would have behaved better, on a similar expedition, in an enemy country. Our army certainly wouldn't."

If civilians were not killed, tortured, or raped, was the march of the army, nonetheless, amoral? John Bennett Walters has argued precisely that, because soldiers traumatized and robbed noncombatants, and wrecked their homes:

> An invading army, without any claim on military necessity, had thrown away every inclination toward mercy for weakness and helplessness. The federal troops resorted to sheer brutality of overpowering strength to despoil a people of their material resources and to injure irreparably their finer sensibilities.

The answer to Walters's charge goes to the very heart of an apartheid society, which has forfeited any collective claim of real humanity. The true moral question is not whether civilians are fair game in war, but whether the property and tranquility of civilians who support chattel slavery and rebellion are fair game in a war precipitated over refusal to end that odious institution—whether, in other words, the supporters of apartheid have abandoned prior claim on the "finer sensibilities." If one believes that slavery is a great evil, and that secession constitutes treason, then Sherman was surely right that the best mechanism to end both, short of killing civilians, was to destroy their property, thereby robbing those fighting on behalf of slaveholding and rebellion of both the material and psychological support of their own citizenry. That seems to me very much a "military necessity."

We must here make a vital distinction between "total" war and a war of "terror." Sherman surely waged the latter, in seeking to shock the enemy through the destruction of their property and the wreckage of their hopes to such a degree that they would desist from supporting the killing of Union troops. But that terror was not total, and he never resorted to any of the barbarity of the modern age—ethnic cleansing, concentration camps, mass killing, indiscriminate bombing, and torture—to achieve his ends. His march has nothing in common with the dirty wars of the twentieth century, wherein revolutions, coups, and ethnic hatreds usually had no moral agenda, and were never part of an effort to stop enslavement. He set up no Andersonvilles to his rear to ship captured soldiers or officials of the Confederate government. Nor did he, as did Southern generals, execute stray soldiers who were captured outside of Confederate lines. When Sherman reached Savannah, Southern generals asked him for the protection of their own families, surely proof positive that they at least did not think they were entrusting their women and children to a terrorist.

> Before I had reached Savannah, and during our stay there, the rebel officers and newspapers represented the conduct of the men of our army as simply infamous; that we respected neither age nor sex; that we burned every thing we came across—barns, stables, cotton-gins, and even dwelling houses; that we ravished the women and killed the men, and perpetrated all manner of outrages on the inhabitants. Therefore it struck me as strange that Generals Hardee and Smith should commit their families to our custody, and even bespeak our personal care and attention. These officers knew well that these reports were exaggerated in the extreme, and yet tacitly assented to these false publications, to arouse the drooping energies of the people of the South.[115]

The late twentieth century has increasingly come to declare *all* war evil. Since peace is considered the natural state of relations, we live in an era of "conflict resolution" and "peace studies" in which some degree of moral guilt is freely assessed equally, both to those who kill to advance evil and those who kill to end it, to those who are aggressive and to those who resist aggrandizement. Regardless of cause or circumstances, we all in the end must become "victims" of those who have the greater power, which transcends national boundaries—politicians, corporations, the military. Indeed, "evil" itself is to be seen as a relative idea—the very thought would have terrified Sherman—a construct whose "truth" is determined by those who hold power for the moment and thus set up courts of inquiry, write our histories, teach our classes, and maintain postwar armies of occupation.

Yet there is always a timeless, absolute difference between slavery and freedom, and those who battle for abolition and those who kill to defend slavery are qualitatively different and can be recognized as such. There would have been a real difference between a Confederate America and a Union America. Sherman's war against property belongs to a particular context, inseparable from the question of slavery. So I am confused when present-day historians write that they are disturbed, for example, to learn that Sherman's men killed bloodhounds in Georgia—as if the gratuitous killing of pets, some of which were accomplished trackers of slaves and Union prisoners, matters very much when half a million blacks in Georgia had been slaves—until Bill Sherman's dog-killers set thousands of them free.

Once the free Southern citizenry—and the apartheid Confederacy was a consensual society of sorts among white people—chose to fight and kill on behalf of human bondage, the destruction of its private property, unlike attacks against Northern farms, took on the logic of retribution and atonement. Was this a fair rationale for Union soldiers when their own Founding Fathers had owned slaves and had seen no reason to bar the practice in either the Constitution or the Bill of Rights? Lincoln grasped perfectly this American dilemma: the cherished protection of local autonomy and the centuries-old presence of chattel slavery on the nation's soil made it hard to justify the notion that the Federal government of 1860 had either the legal right or the moral authority to force the South to give up slaves. Thus Lincoln sought to eradicate the evil of slavery, but, at least in the beginning of his efforts, to do so peaceably without war, with compensation, and over time, as all of American society might slowly evolve to a consensus about the immorality of bondage.

The South, in contrast, wanted no part of that national dialogue, because they knew precisely where it would end up—abolition and a Federal government now strong enough to enforce its moral culture on particular states. Southerners precipitated the war, because they correctly saw Federal policy as leading immutably to the end of their way of life—a way of life whose material riches for a few were to be perpetually supported by the bondage of African blacks, but one which was now generally felt at odds with the natural evolution of American political institutions and cultural values.[116]

Was Sherman's march effective? There seem to be two approaches involved in this answer, and both result in the affirmative. If for a moment we forget the actual material damage done the Confederacy, and consider where

Sherman's army started and where it finished, the march in itself was the definitive act of retribution, against the South, led by a fanatic who saw himself as the reluctant avenging angel of the Union. Sherman's capture of Atlanta saved Lincoln the election. The very fact that he could march unharmed through the South eroded all support in the North for Democrats and copperheads who advocated negotiated peace or surrender under the guise of settlement. If even a true nation cannot afford to have an enemy march unimpeded through its interior without a complete loss of confidence, then no mere conglomeration of rebellious states can fight when an enemy force is running amuck among its populace. Overseas there would be no further talk of recognizing the Confederacy. Henry Hitchcock reported that after only three weeks Sherman's march was having its intended effect, as the general's goals were becoming manifest to all:

> Not we but *their* "leaders" and their own moral and physical cowardice three years ago are responsible. This Union and its Government must be sustained, at any and every cost; to sustain it, we must war upon and destroy the organized rebel forces,—must cut off their supplies, destroy their communications, and show their white *slaves* (these people say themselves that they are so) their utter inability to resist the power of the U.S. To do this implies and requires these very sufferings, and having thus only the choice of evils—war now so terrible and successful that none can dream of rebellion hereafter, or everlasting war with all these evils magnified a hundred fold hereafter,—we have no other course to take.

Moreover, in purely strategic terms, Sherman was now three hundred miles closer to the last major source of Confederate resistance—Lee's army in Virginia. Until Sherman reached Savannah, Grant was holding Lee firmly in his grasp and waging, whether intended or not, a brutal and steady war of annihilation. When Sherman reached the Atlantic—as he had foreseen all along—the complexion of that death lock changed radically: Lee was faced with the prospect of a lethal force marching steadily northward at his rear, devouring the source of supply for his army, and ruining the homes of his soldiers in the trenches. Whereas before, Lee had kept Grant out of Richmond, and had the option either to threaten Washington or just stay still, now he had to move either northward over Grant or southward through Sherman. In fact, whatever Sherman's assurances to Grant, there is every indication that he truly intended to march his marvelous army right into the streets of Richmond and on through the trenches of the Army of Northern Virginia. His men at least believed that Lee and the Southern capital were the Army of the West's final destination. Theodore Upson scoffed at a *New York Tribune* article expressing worry over the whereabouts of Sherman's men in the Carolinas:

> What a lot of faint hearts they must be down there in New York! I wish they would get all of the Johnnys together; we can handle them if Grant will only hold Lee and his Army—don't worry about us, Mr. Tribune; you just cheer up your boys around Richmond and after we get through with our job here we will go and help them and finish things up in a rush. Our boys have become so used to all sorts of dangers and trials that they don't seem to mind anything that comes along.

No Union soldier in any Northern army before the fall of 1864 could have voiced such disdain for the enemy; Sherman in essence through his marching had created an arrogance among Federal troopers that was not present even in the aftermath of victories such as Shiloh and Gettysburg.

Had Sherman not torched one Southern estate, his march would nevertheless have been strategically brilliant for its role in the coordination of the Union armies, and psychologically devastating to the Confederate cause. The artillery officer Thomas Osborne summed it up best when Sherman and his men reached Savannah:

> Thus the immediate object of the campaign is completed. This army has been transferred from the middle of the country to the sea coast, this city captured and the lines for supplies for General Lee's army south of here are destroyed. The Confederacy proper is now southern Virginia and North and South Carolina. It has no other territory now at its disposal for military operations and after this campaign there is not much more left to it, except General Lee's army and the small force in our front.[117]

Damage, of course, Sherman did. As we have seen, it was considerable. Three years after his march, a Freedmen's Bureau agent visited northern Georgia and remarked on "the extreme destitution of this poor poverty stricken and God forsaken country," where one could travel for miles without seeing "a cleared field or a fence rail." Even by 1870 the assessed valuation of farms in Georgia was little more than half of what it had been ten years earlier. The destruction of three hundred miles of railroad lines and bridges tore apart the entire east-west transportation network of the Confederacy; with the additional loss of the Mississippi, the South had essentially been drawn and quartered. Historians have noted that the Confederacy's *Götterdämmerung* was not the losses to Lee's armies, but Sherman's destruction of the heart of the South's rail network. Thousands of acres would now not supply either food or livestock for the Southern armies, not merely because of Union ravagers, but because the railway no longer could transport any food that did survive to Confederate troops in the field.

Unfortunately for the poor of the South, the ripples of Sherman's plunge into the Georgian countryside continued for decades. Long after the Civil War, the majority of Georgians, who did not own slaves and who had never benefited directly from the institution of Southern slavery, would suffer impoverishment as a result of the ruined infrastructure of central Georgia. True, Sherman concentrated on the plantations of the very wealthy and the property of the state, but the result of his depredations was to create years of general economic stagnation that would affect both the free black and white poor. Sherman's apologists—and in the years after the armistice they would continue to shrink as the horror of frontal infantry assault was forgotten— would on various occasions defend his actions on three grounds: first, better that Southerners be poor and alive in Georgia than rotting in the mud of northern Virginia—and the South's only apparent strategy of salvation was the doomed quest to crush Grant's Army of the Potomac; second, the poverty of a few hundred thousand citizens for decades was to be reckoned against the bondage of millions of slaves for centuries; and third, war cannot be "refined": revolutionaries suffer inordinately when they precipitate war, lack the high moral ground, and turn out to be impotent. Again, Sherman would come to be hated in a way Grant never would be because he humiliated and impoverished the South with ease and impunity, rather than killing Southern youth with difficulty and at great cost.

Critics of Sherman's brutality are quite correct about the effects of freeing the slaves—though wrong about its morality. His liberation of blacks did cause millions of dollars of material damage to the South, not merely in lost capital, but in vanished labor, service, and peace of mind. When William Tecumseh Sherman arrived in Georgia, the assurance of servile obedience was ruined forever, and the master's and mistress's eye of suspicion would never leave even the apparently docile slave who chose to stay on the plantation for the final few months of the rebellion. Scholars have rightly emphasized that once Northern armies entered the Deep South, the productivity of slaves fell drastically; that loss of efficiency, coupled with a widespread paranoia, helped to paralyze the rural South—even when slaves themselves stayed on the plantation.

In addition, hundreds of thousands of Confederate civilians, once so critical in encouraging their men at the front, now would have precisely the opposite effect. All our sources stress that through letters, newspapers, and word of mouth, Sherman's wreckage in Georgia reached Confederate troops with Hood, Lee, and Johnston, and as a direct result a great number of them either went home or urged others to cease resistance. Later, when Sherman turned north into the Carolinas, Confederate soldiers wrote their governor:

> It is not in the power of the Yankee Armies to cause us to wish ourselves at home. We can face them, and can hear their shot and shell without being moved; but, Sir, we cannot hear the cries of our little ones and stand.
>
> But it is not for ourselves that we should complain, it is our wives and little ones at home who are necessities. . . . Do something for them and there will be less desertion, and men will go into battles with heartier good will. But it is impossible for us to bear up under our many troubles, the greatest of which is the suffering of our wives and little ones at home.

And this natural reaction, too, had been precisely foreseen by Sherman:

> I attach more importance to these deep incisions into the enemy's country, because this war differs from European wars in this particular: we are not only fighting armies, but a hostile people, and must make old and young, rich and poor, feel the hard hand of war, as well as their organized armies. I know that this recent movement of mine through Georgia has had a wonderful effect in this respect. Thousands who have been deceived by their lying newspapers to believe that we were being whipped all the time now realize the truth, and have no appetite for the repetition of the same experience.[118]

The march through Georgia made all subsequent campaigns by the Army of the West easier. Sherman's yeomen had gained a reputation for frontier ferocity that was worth dozens of traditional battle victories. Sherman himself realized that when he made ready to go northward from Savannah. "It was to me manifest that the soldiers and people of the South entertained an undue fear of our Western men, and, like children, they had invented such ghostlike stories of our prowess in Georgia, that they were scared by their own inventions. Still this was a power, and I intended to utilize it."

Whereas much has been written of the destruction of Southern morale, too little has been devoted to the radically changed spirit in the North brought on by Sherman's march. Lincoln put it best as he summed up the Union effort in his annual message to Congress on December 6—at precisely the time Sherman had passed Millen and was approaching Savannah: "We have more men now than we had when the war began. . . . We are gaining strength, and may, if need be, maintain the contest indefinitely." Grant's army was a force vital to the preservation of the Union and the destruction of the

Confederate soldiers in the field, but neither Grant nor the Army of the Potomac—given the frightful casualties of summer 1864, the absence of movement forward, and the continual obstinacy of Lee—could embolden the American populace to continue the horrific war.[119]

Americans might now sing "Marching Through Georgia" or read poems about "The March to the Sea"; they would never write hymns to celebrate Cold Harbor or read verses about "The Wilderness." Sherman—in light of his army's speed, his preservation of Union lives, his transection of the Confederacy, the sheer hatred he incurred from the South, and his gift for the language of doom—captured the mind of America. In a little over thirty days Sherman had redefined the entire Civil War as a death struggle between yeomen farmers and the privilege of aristocratic plantationists, and the verdict of that ideological contest was plain for all to see in the burning estates of central Georgia. Had he not taken Atlanta, Lincoln would not have been reelected president; had he lost his army in Georgia, a negotiated peace was a real possibility; and had he rested on his laurels in Savannah, Grant would have fought Lee for another six months to a year. It is true that Sherman redefined the American Way of War, but his legacy was not Viet Nam, but rather the great invasions of Europe during World War Two, in which Americans marched right through the homeland of the Axis powers. Sherman, in short, invented the entire notion of American strategic doctrine, one that would appear so frequently in the century to follow—the ideal of a vast moral crusade on foreign soil to restructure a society through sheer force of arms.

It is also true that such rare and brilliantly conceived marches against apartheid result in a situation in which an army of liberation is in far better condition when it finishes than when it began—the liberators' morale soars as the slave-owners' plummets. In the days before the armistice Henry Hitchcock remarked that Sherman's men grew stronger, not weaker, each day.

> We shall move hence with a much larger force than left Atlanta or Savannah, all in splendid condition, and *of course* in first-rate spirits. The *morale* of this army is superb; their confidence alike in Sherman and in themselves, is an immense element of success,—and it is the confidence of veterans, familiar with danger, skillful and wary in encountering it, *not* of rash ignorance.[120]

Was the March to the Sea comparatively easy? The answer is yes, but yes only in light of Sherman's later horrific trek through the Carolinas, in which he traveled not nearly three hundred but almost five hundred miles, not in good weather but through frost and continual rain, not on firm ground but in the middle of swampland, not parallel to great rivers but right across them,

not in a countryside empty of Confederates but in the original home of secession where nearly 40,000 scattered troops had the potential to coalesce to bar
his path, and not toward a city on the coast but directly against the rear of a
veteran enemy army.

Yet ultimately all such assessments of the relative difficulty of Sherman's
two great marches hinge on hindsight. Sherman could conquer the Carolinas
because he had marched through Georgia and created a seasoned army, proficient at carving out roads, building bridges, and destroying track at a phenomenal rate. Much has been written about the horrendous damage done to
Georgia, but we should not forget that the cost to put down slavery was horrendous for the North. By the time of the armistice six months later, the
Union would learn that it had suffered 360,222 dead and spent over
$3,027,791,000 on their armies and navies—a cost, Sherman felt, brought on
entirely by planters like those who theretofore had lived in seclusion and
safety in Georgia.

The only comparable example of such audacity was Sherman's own
prior march against Mississippi and capture of its capital Jackson in the summer of 1863. But before autumn 1864, no general anywhere felt that such a
flying column could leave its rail support entirely and move at so quick a
rate with such a great size. Even had Sherman not been at war, it would still
have been a difficult proposition to take 62,000 men safely through the
countryside—any countryside—without constant and assured sources of
provisions. History is full of great generals—Alexander in the Gedrosian
desert and Hannibal atop the Alps particularly stand out—whose megalomania, poor planning, and general ignorance destroyed their armies in transit when the enemy was never in sight. Moreover, only in retrospect did
Confederate resistance seem feeble. All contemporary sources testify that
Sherman's army had little exact knowledge—albeit numerous threats and
promises enough of destruction—where and how large the enemy was. It
was entirely probable that Southerners would burn or evacuate all their provisions, leaving thousands of Northerners camping in the Georgia winter
without food. For all Sherman knew, once he broke communications,
Longstreet, Hood, perhaps Lee himself were on their way to hit his columns
unseen and at right angles. Not the enemy per se, but Sherman's own sheer
rapidity, his cagey swerves to the north and south of large cities, his mastery
of planning, made the opposition irrelevant. Henry Hitchcock remarked of
Sherman's plans:

> I begin now to understand as never before what a science war is in the hands
> of a master, and what "strategy" means. We have had an easy march, practi-

cally without opposition, because our movements have been so directed as to utterly confound the enemy, and to circumvent him—literally. They have done exactly right in five times abandoning their purpose to stand and fight,—because each time our position gave us great advantage.

Had Thomas or Grant—perhaps the two greatest of Union generals—led their armies through Georgia, they would have either entrenched, fought great battles of annihilation, or arrived in Savannah in the spring. Neither would have paused for a few days, only to continue on foot into the Carolinas.[121]

Did Sherman allow enemy armies to escape? Yes. Did it ultimately matter? No. Students of battle sometimes point out that Sherman not only did not fight a major pitched battle between the Atlanta campaign and Bentonville, but actually took pains to avoid them, even when the odds were in his favor. Hood, Hardee, and Johnston, after all, escaped from Atlanta, Savannah, and Bentonville when they might have been destroyed. Secretary of War Stanton complained to Grant: "It is a sore disappointment that Hardee was able to get off . . . it looks like protracting the war while their armies continue to escape."

Grant probably would not have let that happen. But in Sherman's larger strategic way of thinking, the remnants of demoralized and defeated armies in the eleventh hour of a war did not always regroup into effective forces of resistance, but just as commonly spread their despair as they retreated through their own territory. Hood escaped only to be destroyed soon by Thomas with little Union loss; Hardee's flight allowed his soldiers to fight Sherman at Bentonville, but the Union victory there again was achieved at little real cost. Johnston's own escape from Bentonville simply meant that more Confederates and Union soldiers alike were alive at the armistice a few days later. Unlike the condition of the German armies that escaped in summer 1944, by spring 1865 there was no question of a resurgent Confederate military. Sherman knew that his enemies were escaping, and that their flight was due to his own intention, not always an accident or lapse in judgment.

Sherman, no stranger to brutal slugfests between massive armies, weighed the results of seeking to destroy the enemy outright—the proper goal within limits of any general—against the larger strategic picture. That armies escaped from him but did little future damage, and altered not at all the strategic balance, suggests that Sherman usually knew that their demoralized flight meant little to the final outcome of the war. Although he sometimes offered excuses for not destroying such trapped adversaries, his self-serving explanations that their survival made little difference in the larger strategic picture ring true—and departing and frantic enemies often left without supplies, abandoning millions of dollars' worth of ammunition, heavy guns, and supplies that Sherman confiscated.

We should keep in mind that the timing of the war's close in April 1865 was not fortuitous; the Confederacy collapsed at that particular time not because of Thomas's smashing victory in Tennessee nearly six months earlier, nor because Grant had finally obliterated Lee, but rather because Sherman's gigantic army of Union veterans was now rapidly approaching Lee's rear. The South itself acknowledged this. The obituary for Sherman in the *Americus (Ga.) Daily Times* conceded that. "[Sherman] was the victorious general who really subdued the Confederacy. By his devastations in Georgia the morale of Lee's army was so reduced and his ranks so thinned that Grant's success was possible, so at last Sherman and not Grant was entitled to the credit of Appomattox." The British official historian of the First World War, General James Edmonds, agreed:

> The military genius of the great confederate leaders, Lee and Jackson, the unrivaled fighting capacity of the Army of Northern Virginia, and the close proximity of the rival capitals, have caused a disproportionate attention to be concentrated upon the eastern theatre of war. It was in the west the decisive blows were struck. The capture of Vicksburg and Port Hudson in July 1863 was the real turning point of the war, and it was the operations of Sherman's Grand Army of the West which really led to the collapse of the Confederacy at Appomattox Court House.

Ultimately, the North would have won the war or at least obtained a stalemate; but Sherman's marches precipitated its end in April 1865 at a great savings in lives on both sides. It is no accident that Sherman marched into four capitals of the Confederacy—Jackson, Milledgeville, Columbia, and Raleigh—or that Southerners hated Sherman, not Thomas, not Grant, for the next century. More Southerners deserted, gave up, or simply ceased fighting because of Sherman's march than were killed from Grant's attacks.

All criticisms of Sherman's tactical generalship fail to appreciate the wider context in which Sherman operated, the relatively small costs of his achievement in lives, and the traumatic effect of his presence on the enemy people. But it mattered little whether Thomas had destroyed Hood much earlier in August or later in December; it mattered a great deal that Sherman could at last rip out the vital organs of the enemy as his own army headed for Grant so far away. "Of course I must fight when the time comes," he wrote his daughter, "but wherever a result can be accomplished without Battle I prefer it."[122]

Was Sherman sometimes lax in recruiting slaves into his army on his march? Yes. Did it ultimately matter? No. It is true that Sherman did not welcome the very young, female, or aged freed slaves to join his march. He felt such noncombatants could not aid his army's progress, would drain his supplies, and in some cases would themselves find an itinerant and impoverished freedom no better than a few months more of slavery before the inevitable liberation that armistice would bring. He was interested primarily in hiring on fit young male ex-slaves to serve in his engineering and pioneering corps—the thousands of impressive black troopers who would later carve a path through the Carolinas and march so proudly in review in Washington at war's end.

Moreover, Sherman expressly felt that massive recruitments and the whole-scale arming of slaves in Georgia—Grant's explicit advice—would not materially aid his already massive army, and perhaps would even send an ambiguous message to citizens of the North. There is good reason to believe that Sherman was not so interested in recruiting black soldiers because he was racist—true racists, after all, might prefer black men to white to die in the mud—but to ensure that white recruits did not get off the hook. Sherman felt that the rebellion was an affront to all citizens of the Union and that it was the responsibility of its white citizens to fight and not put the onus of service on black freedmen from the South. It was ironic that Sherman the purported racist had to prevent Federal recruiting officers in Savannah from forcibly conscripting many of his most valuable black pioneers, who were to be rounded up, confined, and shipped north had not Sherman intervened. Employing freed slaves in construction and his devastation corps on the march in the South, rather than sending them northward right into battle against the fortifications of Lee's veterans, does not seem such an inhumane practice. As he pointed out in a letter to his wife Ellen on reaching Savannah, "I have said that slavery is dead and the Negro free, and want him treated as free and not hunted and badgered to make a soldier of, when his family is left back on the plantation."

As events turned out, Sherman still had thousands of blacks in his army at war's end; he had freed thousands more during his march—best estimates put them at over 25,000 or almost a third of the size of his own force—and his efforts at destroying the plantation culture of the South had accelerated the general emancipation at war's end, a mere six months after he cut through Georgia. Later he would put it succinctly:

> My aim then was, to whip the rebels, to humble their pride, to follow them to their inmost recesses, and make them fear and dread us. "Fear of the Lord is the beginning of wisdom." I did not want them to cast in our teeth what General Hood had once done in Atlanta, that we had to call on *their* slaves to help

us to subdue them. But, as regards kindness to the race, encouraging them to patience and forbearance, procuring them food and clothing, and providing them with land whereon to labor, I assert that no army ever did more for that race than the one I commanded in Savannah.

It was no accident that a slave freed in the Civil War was sometimes called a "Sherman Cutloose." One freedman, a Sam Aleckson, wrote of his status, "I am persuaded however that all the Negroes in the slave belt, and some of the white men too, were 'Cutloose' by General Sherman." Over a half century after Sherman's march, local residents of Georgia could assure visitors that Sherman alone "had set the blacks against the whites."

Whatever the modern perceptions and criticisms, contemporaries in the North and South agreed that Sherman was to be both praised and blamed for liberating the slaves. In Herman Melville's poem "The March to the Sea," abolition is a central theme: "The slaves by thousands drew, . . . And they joined the armies blue," as "It was glorious glad marching, . . . For every man was free." In contrast, the Confederate general John Bell Hood felt Sherman had elevated the Negro over the white man—in both the North and the South. It seemed that most on both sides conceded that freeing slaves was inextricable from Sherman's campaign. One could make the argument that the clear hatred the Army of the West displayed for the plantation class, and the bitter example of its destructive power, sent a chilling message to the Southern wealthy well beyond the swath through Georgia—and gave hope and assurance to those slaves aged, young, and infirm who did not immediately join his army that their freedom was now a mere matter of weeks. Sherman's army was seen by Union and Confederate soldiers alike as an ideological force, and that zeal to ruin a slave society spread from its top down.[123]

Finally, and most important, did Sherman ruin the tradition of chivalry in war and bring on the evils of total conflict so well known to the modern age? Yes to the first, no to the second question. The best of the Union generals—Thomas and Grant in particular—were bulldogs, not greyhounds, and had no skill in moving large armies quickly across miles of unknown terrain to the rear of enemy armies. Their forte, in stark contrast to Sherman's sublimation of battle tactics, was in crafting sieges and set, head-on collisions with enemy forces that left the Confederates either materially or at least psychologically worse off after the battle than they were before—and sometimes their own ranks nearly as shattered. Given the North's preponderance in matériel and human resources, such shock battles would eventually defeat the Confederate army. They, not Sherman, had turned war into an anonymous process of an industrial state, where cannon, rifle, and manpower were thrown promiscuously into the inferno, with little regard to past custom or protocol and even less chance that individual achievement or skill in arms in themselves might win the day.

Nevertheless, there were two problems with such an inflexible doctrine. Besides the sheer expenditure in manpower and treasure to ensure its success, even the most brutal of head-to-head frontal assaults were part of a series of such engagements that took years to wear down the enemy, and they gave no guarantee that the enemy's defeat—to occur mostly on battlefields of the northern Confederacy or the Border States—could not be excused, explained away, or simply put out of mind by a still proud and untouched populace far to the rear. Grant in Virginia embraced a brutal simplicity in destroying Confederate armies, one that did not involve the myriad problems of expanding the war beyond the battlefield, and thus he left no assurance that in a decade or two the population of the South, its infrastructure intact, its people still proud, might not once more field armies to champion states' rights.

In contrast, after Sherman's march through Georgia and the Carolinas, every child of the South would come to know that the will of the Confederate people, not merely its army, had been crushed. The hatred of Sherman, the destroyer of the plantations, not of Grant, the devourer of Confederate manhood, is proof enough of that. In short, the South despised Sherman not because he had defeated them, but because he had humiliated them in the process. A Minnesota recruit summed up best the effect of the Army of the West: Southerners were simply "scared out of their wits by the Yanks."

The difference between killing soldiers and destroying the property of those who field them is critical, for it involves the ambiguous notion of what constitutes true morality in war. However inexact the comparison, the difference between World Wars One and Two sheds some light on the respective manner in which Grant and Sherman each fought the South, and the contrast is not, as might be expected, entirely to the detriment of Sherman. From 1914 to 1918, the Allies, Grant-like, waged a horrific war of annihilation in the trenches against the armies of autocracy that ultimately ruined their entire military, but left the populations of the Central Powers largely unscathed—and eager to find scapegoats. World War Two followed a mere two decades later. After World War Two and the savage and systematic demolition of the German and Japanese landscape—far in excess to what even Sherman might have imagined or condoned—neither society warred again, and there has been in Europe and Japan thus far a half century, not twenty years, of peace. No German or Japanese civilians after 1945 could ever underestimate the power of the British and American military, or think that their culture was betrayed rather than conquered, or that their own support for murderous regimes did not have consequences for their own persons and property. Germans in 1945 had far more respect for—and fear of—Patton than they had in 1918 for Pershing.

For Sherman, then, the attack on property and infrastructure was permissible, if the war was an ideological one against anarchy, treason, and slavery, and if it would lead to a permanent peace based on just principles. Those who argue that he was one with the modernist terrorist who indiscriminately attacks civilians fail to note that he did not kill civilians—"I do not war on women and children"—and he did not attack those who had not first attacked his own. Terror, as a weapon to be employed in war by a democratic army, must be proportional, ideological, and rational: proportional—Southerners, who fought to preserve men as mere property, would have their property destroyed; ideological—those who would destroy property would do so as part of a larger effort of abolition that was not merely strategic, but ethical as well; and rational—burning and looting would not be random, nor killing gratuitous, but rather ruin was to have a certain logic, as railways, public buildings, elite plantations—all the visible and often official infrastructure of a slave society—would be torched, but the meager houses of the poor and the persons themselves of the Confederacy would be left relatively untouched.

The issues of age and property are also often forgotten in Sherman's march, but again they are decisive. Sherman constantly stressed his affection for "his boys" and the need to save his army; he showed a shocking lack of concern for those of adult age in the Confederacy who had carried through secession. Yet, it seems to me a far more moral act to make the middle-aged and elderly, male and female alike, who fight wars for property—and that is precisely what the Southern leadership, despite its protestations, did—pay for their folly with their possessions, rather than to exterminate those young and often under twenty, without possessions, and with little real knowledge of the politics that put them in harm's way. It is, after all, a more moral practice to destroy the property of parents who are culpable than the lives of their adolescents who are not—and thousands of Sherman's men and those they opposed, we should remember, were mere teenagers. Liddell Hart best summed up Sherman's view of what constituted real savagery:

It was logical, and due to reasoning that was purely logical, that he should first oppose war; then, conduct it with iron severity; and, finally, seize the first real opportunity to make a peace of complete absolution. He cared little that his name should be execrated by the people of the South if he could only cure them of a taste for war. And to cure them he deliberately aimed at the non-combatant foundation of the hostile war spirit instead of its combatant roof.

He cared as little that this aim might violate a conventional code of war, for so long as war was regarded as a chivalrous pastime, and its baseness obscured by a punctilious code, so long would it be invested with a halo of romance. Such a code and such a halo had helped the duel to survive long after less polite forms of murder had grown offensive to civilized taste and gone out of fashion.[124]

I am also surprised not at the relative assessments made about Grant and Sherman—their differences in strategic thinking, their close friendship, and their shared responsibility for winning the war invite obvious and spirited comparisons that have relative merit on both sides—but rather at the absence of contrasts between Lee and Sherman. The former, who wrecked his army by sending thousands on frontal charges against an entrenched enemy and who himself owned slaves, enjoys the reputation of a reluctant, humane knight who battled for a cause—states' rights and the sanctity of Southern soil—other than slavery. The latter, who was careful to save his soldiers from annihilation and who freed thousands of slaves in Georgia, is too often seen as a murderous warrior who fought for a cause—federalism and the punishment of treason—other than freedom.

Lee, as Sherman noted, crafted the wrong offensive strategy for an outmanned and outproduced South, which led to horrendous casualties; Sherman's marches drew naturally on the material and human surpluses of the North and so cracked the core of the Confederacy, with few killed on either side. Lee wrongly thought the Union soldier would not fight as well as the Confederate; Sherman rightly guessed that the destruction of Southern property would topple the entire Confederacy. The one ordered thousands to their deaths when the cause was clearly lost; the other destroyed millions of dollars of property to hasten the end of bloodshed. Yet Sherman, who fought on the winning side, who promised in the abstract death and terror, who was unkempt, garrulous, and blunt, is usually criticized; Lee, who embodies the Lost Cause, who wrote of honor and sacrifice, and who was dapper, genteel, and mannered, is canonized. Historians would do better to assess each on what they did, not on what they professed. As we shall see, Patton too suffered from a public image at odds with his actual accomplishments.[125]

Sherman's march confirms nearly all of the lessons to be derived from Epaminondas's great trek into Laconia and is the proper precursor to Patton's race across the Rhine. Both ancient and modern armies destroyed the agrarian infrastructure of a culture that was rural, not urban, as a method of humiliating the chivalry of a militaristic society. Both did not kill innocent civilians. It is no accident that women shrieked at Sparta and in Georgia as enemy yeomen soldiers wrecked their estates before their eyes—their respective privilege was based on the bondage of others, and their fathers, husbands, and sons battled in part for just their stern approval. Both armies freed helots, who suffered a worse oppression than the discrimination of the times elsewhere. While Thebans had individual slaves in paternal relationships on their farms, they never sought to enslave an entire race and institutionalize and ritualize murder; so too Northerners in 1860, who had no tolerance for absolute equality with the blacks, would not allow their enslavement either. Epaminondas's and Sherman's armies—like Patton's—whatever the particular politics of their generals, were antiaristocratic to the core.

Neither Epaminondas nor Sherman fought major battles while ruining the countryside of an apartheid state. Both armies proved that marches and an indirect approach to warfare could be particularly effective against a culture whose moral and psychological capital was invested in keeping their homeland pristine, their slaves on the plantation, and their manhood seemingly invincible. Sherman, like Epaminondas, knew how to destroy all three such fantasies; and yet few Spartans or Southerners—and still fewer Thebans or Northerners—died in the process. Sherman's marchers after leaving Tennessee had walked almost two thousand miles, often at clips of fifteen miles and more a day. Like Epaminondas's rapid passage through the isthmus and his dash in and out of Laconia, the sheer quickness of the Army of the West seemed to be the natural expression of the fervor of such a large, rural, and ideological army. It is as difficult to imagine Sherman's army for months on end in the trenches of Virginia, as Epaminondas's Boeotians skirmishing behind wooden stockades against the Spartans in Boeotia during the 370s. Democratic armies are not always mobile, and not always successful when mobile, but when organized for a particular, finite mission and led by a zealot, they draw like no other military operation on the natural restlessness, impatience, and self-righteousness inherent in a democratic culture's war against privilege.

Both Epaminondas and Sherman dressed and lived the same as their men, shared the same hardships, and marched in harm's way, the former dying at Mantinea, the latter coming close at Shiloh. Both men understood perfectly the undeniable strengths and weaknesses of a democracy at war, and thus saw the rapidity and action of a great march, which destroys the psyche of the enemy at little loss to oneself, as the preferable course for a consensual society that is impatient of stasis and intolerant of loss.

What is disturbing about the great marches of Epaminondas and Sherman is that whereas they were democratically inspired and overseen by a board of elected officials—Boeotarchs, and Lincoln and his Cabinet, respectively—the idea itself of slicing through the enemy's heartland and freeing the unfree seems to be entirely the idea of these generals themselves. Lincoln, Grant, and nearly all concerned in the North opposed Sherman's idea in varying degrees, and only with difficulty after his smashing success yielded to his plan for his follow-up drive into the Carolinas—in the same manner as the Boeotarchs never approved Epaminondas's sojourn in Laconia after the first of the year, and put him on trial after his return from his subsequent trek into Messenia. As we shall see with Patton, democratic armies can number in the tens of thousands, but the inspiration and expertise to mobilize and guide such agents of nemesis belong to singular individuals, a very rare few who are usually hated and opposed even as they have led their men to victory.

Neither Sherman, who was nearly dismissed for his generous terms of armistice with Johnston in April 1865, nor Epaminondas, who was tried twice for treason and eventually removed from command, expressed much confidence in democracy itself—Sherman preposterously claimed once that it had almost as deleterious an effect on the North as slavery had upon the South. Both generals were criticized by their governments for being too soft on their enemies, and by their enemies for being too harsh agents of their governments. There was literally not a week in any of Sherman's entire marches when he was not embroiled in some ongoing controversy with his superiors, whether over the recruitment of freedmen, the armistice with Johnston, the censorship of the press, or the wisdom of cutting communications. Patton, in a like enterprise, would come to find all the same enemies.

While the sudden march against apartheid by a militia of free men is the best military expression of a democratic society, it may be that such mobilizations are rare, far too rare, because they require a ruthlessness and a realism of leadership that often bothers progressive politicians, so attuned to the pulse of a powerful electorate that demands victory but wants it cheap and clean. In a democratic culture the very traits necessary to lead a great march in war—eccentricity, audacity, suspicion of rather than disdain for consensus—are precisely those that ensure an individual censure and opprobrium in peace.

Also, such marches are risky; they entrust too much power to one man; and once they begin their terrible course, there is little if any chance for democratic audit, and none for recall. Ostensibly, they are part of a wider co-ordinated plan; in actuality, an army in rapid transit soon develops a will of its own—in Patton's words, making its own plan rather than being made by plans. Sherman, for example, took off through Georgia, though at first told not to by his superiors; from Savannah he plunged headlong into the Carolinas, though Grant wished his forces to come immediately to Virginia by sea.

Democracies understandably do not like to place thousands of their men in the hands of one general to be left loose for weeks on end without control. Should the march fail, thousands in an instant are lost far from home; should the march succeed, the general becomes the most powerful man of the hour, with men far more loyal to him than to the faceless clerks who staff the government and whittle away at their beloved general. Sherman spent his later life, we must remember, turning down repeated offers to run for the presidency, putting either envy, fear, or hope into the heart of every politician for a quarter century to come. Epaminondas later would essentially run the Boeotian confederacy for almost a decade by his personal magnetism and the record earned on the great march into Laconia. By May 1945, Patton was one of the most popular men in America—and rebuffed any attempts to have himself drafted for political office-seeking.

Sherman's rampage through Georgia confirms the great paradox that arose with Epaminondas's maiden march against apartheid: the most impressive weapon in the arsenal of democracy, a rapid-moving mass march into enemy land, is the least likely to be employed, thus this book is about three, not a dozen, great marches of liberation. It is nearly impossible for democratic militias to find themselves in the sole hands of military geniuses who are no threat to democracy itself. What Liddell Hart wrote of Sherman's unique achievement equally describes Epaminondas, and no other general of the ancient world:

> Even above his greatness as a strategist is his greatness as a grand strategist. He perceived that the resisting power of a modern democracy depends more on the strength of the popular will than on the strength of its armies, and that this will in turn depends largely upon economic and social security. To interrupt the ordinary life of the people and quench hope of its resumption is more effective than any military result short of the complete destruction of the armies. The last is an ideal rarely attained in the past, and increasingly difficult since the appearance of nations in arms.

Epic marches can bring no comfort to their generals, who are put in the unenviable position of being criticized after the campaign as being too lenient for attacking the property rather than the lives of the enemy, and yet, as history recedes, as too brutal in leading men on such an audacious enterprise against civilians. Their perceived achievement in democracy's wartime struggle is at the time subject to constant reappraisal by jealous elites and self-proclaimed moralists (Sherman called their postbellum pronouncements "bottled piety")—and assessment always rests as well with the volatile tastes of the assembly who sent them out in the first place. Posterity in a democracy is no better—all too few historians will ever concede that Sherman waged a humane war, which saved thousands of lives and brought an end to human bondage and misery.

He was not merely a "flawed," "complex," or "contradictory" man, but also the most incisive general of his age, who knew precisely what he was doing and why he was doing it. It is hard for us in a free, consensual, and comfortable society to marshal the will to kill evil, and even harder after the sacrifice to agree that the destruction was both just and necessary, much less humane. Sherman realized this years later in a letter to his brother:

> Still in Republics majorities govern, and since only one in sixteen go to war, non-combatants always govern. The soldier who fights must take a back seat and apologize for his vehemence in action. Grant had to apologize, Sheridan to shelter himself behind his most proper orders to devastate the Valley of the Shenandoah, and Sherman to be abused and assailed for the accidental burning of Columbia in the day of Republican rule. . . . In 1861–65 we fought for union and right. Congress surrendered the country to the non-combatants, and now it is questionable whether Lincoln or Jeff Davis was the Union man. Jeff now says he never meant war. He thought that they would be allowed to do as they pleased without war. Lincoln was the assailant, Davis only on the "defensive-offensive."

Patton could have used Sherman's observations verbatim as a defense against his own critics.

As for Sherman himself, the march through Georgia brought both public adulation and continual attacks from the suspicious and envious. Even before the controversial peace agreement with Johnston on April 18, 1865, the press was troubled by Sherman's audacity and his candor. The London *Times* of April 5, 1865, warned that he was "vain, eager, enthusiastic, fanatical, at times gloomy and reticent, at others impulsive and talkative, by some regarded as half mad when the fit is on him"—a man akin to the "great and mysterious actors in history." In short, by spring 1865, Sherman had become a dangerous man—a Cromwell, the *Times* asserted—at the head of the most lethal army in the world, with all his enemies vanquished and his anger now directed at his former friends.

After the swell of public support, the humiliation resulting from Secretary of War Stanton and Chief of Staff Halleck's impugning his honor, and the return of confidence to the military and civilian government, and contrary to silly rumors, Sherman, as planned, simply demobilized his army. He swore off all ambitions for national office, and then for the next twenty-five years accepted the role of senior military statesman and sought-out critic of the national scene. Once it was clear that Sherman had few personal agendas, and as the critical role of his great marches became fully appreciated, the people whom he distrusted worshiped him, even as the politicians and journalists whom he distrusted even more came to enjoy rather than to condemn instinctively his sporadic bombast. Never in history had such a deadly army demobilized so rapidly and quietly; never had such a powerful military leader voluntarily foregone so much political opportunity.

Our next and last march, that of George S. Patton into Germany, raises the question whether such mobilizations are confined to an earlier age, whose essential characteristics—muscular labor, a clear sense of absolute good and evil, freedom from electronic oversight, an audacious and eccentric leader—cannot be a part of a far more complex modern world of machines and less confident notions of what constitutes morality, or indeed if morality is even acknowledged to exist. That there can still be such great marches is a testament to George S. Patton, who in some sense was as out of place in his world as Epaminondas and Sherman were in theirs. If the former were men ahead of their own times, then General Patton in his values and outlook was a century behind his.

Sherman realized that the old chivalrous code and aristocratic gallantry were both outmoded and obscene in a modern war of railroads, repeating rifles, and high-velocity cannon; Patton, in turn, saw that without some sort of soul of battle, the barbarity of contemporary fighting could become meaningless, a simple bureaucratic enterprise—generals as businessmen sending their anonymous troops, in assembly-line fashion, to death. Patton, who had few, if any, friends or admirers among the high command of the British and American armies, would have had to look back centuries to Epaminondas and Sherman for kindred thinkers and men of action, who alone would have understood and approved of what he envisioned. In some ways, it is far more difficult for a gifted man to belong in spirit to a prior rather than to a future age.

Sherman, too, like Epaminondas, was eventually deified by the people, as the voices of envy and criticism faded before the timelessness and magnitude of his achievement; unlike Epaminondas and Patton, he lived a quarter century after his victories, to the grand acclaim of his countrymen. Sherman's most impressive statue, a fifty-foot-high equestrian rendition of the general on the march, still towers today in Washington, D.C., in a beautiful small park at Fifteenth Street and Pennsylvania Avenue, between the Treasury Department and the Ellipse, not far from the White House itself, which he so assiduously shunned. Few Washingtonians know where the statue is; and fewer still of those who lunch in the park seem ever to approach the monument itself. If they did, they would discover that on the north side of the granite base, beneath the mounted general, reads Sherman's own declaration that the proper purpose of battle was to make society right:

"War's Legitimate Object Is More Perfect Peace."[126]

PART III
THE THIRD ARMY

PATTON'S RACE INTO GERMANY

AUGUST 1, 1944–MAY 8, 1945

1

AMERICAN AJAX

HEIDELBERG, GERMANY

December 11, 1945 (Victory in Europe Day Plus 217 Days)

> *It is a contemptible thing to want to live forever*
> *When a man's life gives him no relief from trouble.*
> *What joy is there in a long file of days,*
> *Edging you forward toward the goal of death,*
> *Then back again a little? I wouldn't give much for a man*
> *Who warms himself with the comfort of vain hopes.*
> *Let a man nobly live or nobly die.*
>
> —Sophocles, Ajax

TWO RAZOR-sharp metal fasteners—zygomatic hooks, in the medical parlance of the time—were now affixed to the cheekbones of the nearly lifeless patient. These barbed prongs were in turn attached to a ten-pound weight, part of a traction device designed to pull and extend the general's head and backbone, and thus relieve pressure on his spinal cord. George S. Patton was sixty. A demoted general at the head of a paper army in peacetime, he was now doomed to die a slow death in bed. "This is an ironical thing to have to happen to me," he gasped to his doctor.

It surely was. On December 9, 1945, three days earlier, Patton had suf-

263

fered a broken neck—a fracture of the third neck vertebra, with a partial transection of the spinal cord itself—in a minor traffic accident a few miles outside Heidelberg, Germany. Months after the end of World War Two, he was on his way to do some duck hunting, and had been scheduled to fly *the next day* to London on the first leg of his return to the United States for good. Patton was now in the U.S. Army hospital at Heidelberg, being attended to by American and British neurologists, who were coming to near unanimity that the general's prognosis was hopeless. In fact, he would die in his sleep ten days later on December 21, without gaining any sensation or movement below his shoulders. Intravenous glucose, a catheter, antibiotics, transfusions, sleeping pills, painkillers—the entire arsenal of the new American medicine of the age—were employed to keep the general's motionless body alive and without discomfort. To no avail.

As a man of action, Patton had hoped to be killed in battle: "The proper end for the professional soldier is a quick death inflicted by the last bullet of the last battle," he announced repeatedly, capturing the spirit of melancholy that Sherman likewise felt at the conclusion of peace. Instead, an otherwise unspectacular car crash that seriously injured no one else had left him an invalid. Patton had almost gotten his wish for a nobler end from a gunshot wound in World War One. He had long ago suffered severe head injuries between the wars from horseback-riding accidents, broken nearly every bone in his body at various times, and as general of the Third Army come close to being shot out of midair while reconnoitering in a light plane. He had been repeatedly shelled, and was nearly impaled in a collision with a wagon—all that, only to die in an automobile accident during peacetime eight months after the end of the most murderous war in the history of civilization.

"This is a helluva way to die," Patton remarked seconds after his head was thrown against the steel frame that separated the car's front and rear seats. Scholars, puzzled over some of his more outlandish statements in the last year of his life, still lament the absence of an autopsy. Surely, they have speculated, it would have shown some type of brain damage—perhaps clinical evidence of head injuries in Patton's past might have best explained the general's increasingly bitter outbursts in his last six months of life.[1]

Epaminondas and Sherman, of course, in their respective fates had been far luckier. The Theban died a warrior's death in middle age, at the height of his powers, beneath a barrage of Spartan spear and sword thrusts at the head of his men—gasping, the story goes, in his last moments as the spearhead was pulled out, that the victories at Leuctra and Mantinea were his proud daughters. Sherman became the most sought-after public speaker in late-nineteenth-century America, and for a quarter century after his final march through the Carolinas basked in the glory of his achievements, as he instructed his countrymen why he had led his magnificent Army of the West in the ruthless manner he did. Finally, die-hard Confederates, revisionist historians, jealous rivals, disgraced Southern generals, and puritanical Northern abolitionists alike ceased their attacks, granting by the time of his death that there had been, after all, only one William Tecumseh Sherman, a remarkable man that had saved the Union, avoided the miasma of politics and scandal, and told the truth regardless of the consequences.

Patton, who had commanded a larger army and marched farther than either general, instead would slowly suffocate to death as his sixty-year-old heart and lungs finally collapsed from the trauma and shock to his nervous system. Both his friends and his enemies for different reasons thought that it was time that he should go. Even his stepniece and probable sometime mistress, Jean Gordon, purportedly remarked of his demise, "I think it is better this way for Uncle Georgie. There is no place for him anymore." Whatever his official comments, and despite his later consulting role in the making of the picture *Patton*, few American officers disliked George Patton as much as Omar Bradley. He commented on Patton's sudden death:

> It may be a harsh thing to say, but I believe it was better for George Patton and his professional reputation that he died when he did. The war was won; there were no more wars left for him to fight. He was not a good peacetime soldier; he would not have found a happy place in the postwar Army. He would have gone into retirement hungering for the old limelight, beyond doubt indiscreetly sounding off on any subject any time, any place. In time he probably would have become a boring parody of himself—a decrepit, bitter, pitiful figure, unwittingly debasing the legend.[2]

By December 1945 all German armies were long since demolished. The German people were in their eighth month of Allied occupation and remained fully defeated. Their countryside was in shambles and food was scarce. Nazism was extinct—Hitler long gone, his lieutenants either dead, on trial, or in hiding. In contrast to Patton, other American officers—Douglas MacArthur, Mark Clark, Omar Bradley, Dwight Eisenhower, Courtney Hodges—had either found further glory in the Pacific war, were enjoying prestigious promotions, or were eyeing careers in politics. Why, as Patton slowly suffocated in Heidelberg, had he become the sole victorious American general without a future? MacArthur—or was it Eisenhower himself?—had months earlier vetoed his transfer to the Pacific theater. Eisenhower, embarrassed over Patton's friendship and increasingly bizarre pronouncements that might imperil his future political career, weeks earlier had relieved him of command of the Third Army. Mark Clark made it clear that he did not want that "sonofabitch" near him in Austria. Bradley for the rest of his life would continue to downplay Patton's achievements in Normandy, as he welcomed his own additional promotions and impressive assignments. "God deliver us from our friends," Patton wrote his wife. "We can handle the enemy."

Patton, it seemed, had had more than enough of his own Boeotarchs and Hallecks; but unfortunately his protector was to be a sober, though thoroughly political, man like Eisenhower, not a Pelopidas or Grant. That Patton ever gained command of an army—given his candor and propensity for saying what others felt but by no means wanted articulated—is testament to his considerable reservoir of talent. The envy and embarrassment he provoked finally did recede before the urgent need for the daring he brought to the battlefield. Patton was not exaggerating when he wrote that from his appearance in 1943 in Africa until the end of the war in May 1945 he had been in "continuous battle, and when not in battle had been under the strain of continuous criticism, which I believe is harder to bear."

"Peace," Patton predicted, "is going to be hell on me." It had been for the last eight months, especially the increasing hostility of the Soviets in Eastern Europe. On the day hostilities ended, he announced to correspondents of the Third Army that "tin-soldier politicians in Washington have allowed us to kick hell out of one bastard and at the same time forced us to help establish a second one as evil or more evil than the first. . . . This time we'll need Almighty God's constant help if we're to live in the same world with Stalin and his murdering cutthroats." To the undersecretary of war, Robert Patterson, he wrote: "Let us start training here, keeping our forces intact. Let's keep our boots polished, bayonets sharpened, and present a picture of force and strength to these people. This is the only language they understand. If you fail to do this, then I would like to say to you that we have had a victory over the Germans and have disarmed them, but have lost the war."

Before we dismiss Patton as a lunatic and a dangerous firebrand in charge of a half-million battle-ready troops threatening Soviet allies, we should remember that World War Two originally broke out to keep Poland free and to redress the error of allowing totalitarianism to absorb Czechoslovakia. In Patton's mind, after millions of deaths, we were back to square one: a murderous and nightmarish government now controlled Hitler's first East European annexations—and once again the West sought to placate rather than confront an inhumane military state with territorial ambitions. As Patton saw it, Stalin had murdered millions and taken Eastern Europe in the same way Hitler had; in each case, only an American army could end autocracy and free those enslaved.

Nor were Stalin's nearby hordes the only topic that irked the restless proconsul Patton. His peacetime Third Army was in essence a citizen militia, and he worried that its ongoing demobilization and the end to compulsory military service in the postwar era were the worst courses of action that a democracy could undertake in an increasingly dangerous world of Soviet totalitarianism—especially when free societies looked to the Americans alone for their defense. Typically, he announced his feelings publicly at a time the administration had promised a rapid demobilization and a partnership for peace with the Soviets: "You just wait and see. The lily-livered bastards in Washington will demobilize. They'll say they've made the world safe for democracy again. The Russians are not such damned fools. They'll rebuild; and with modern weapons. But if we have compulsory military service, if we vote for it first at the polls, or in Congress, then in years to come the rest of the world will know we mean what we say." For Patton the march for freedom should continue right through Eastern Europe, to push the Soviets back inside Russia. That the Berlin Airlift was just two years away suggests that Patton's paranoid worries about demobilizing American divisions in Germany were not so paranoid.

Patton, of course, felt it critical that democracy, in view of its traditional reputation for military unpreparedness and complacency, should man up to the new global burden and voluntarily take on a proactive defense. War, after all, was usually a struggle of good against evil. It was brought on when evil perceived that the forces of right were weak and ripe for conquest. War was a continual, not a sporadic, event. So it was natural that a monster like Stalin should follow Hitler; the destruction of both required the constant readiness of forces like his seasoned Third Army. Yet Patton's remarks to that effect only confirmed to a battle-weary nation that he was "a warmonger." Why should still more Americans die to keep Eastern Europeans and Germans— many of whom had fought for Hitler—free from tyranny? Even when he spoke honestly to Americans about the war dead, Patton only made things worse. Of the wounded of the Third Army, he confessed in a Boston speech, "It is a popular idea that a man is a hero just because he was killed in action. Rather I think a man is frequently a fool when he gets killed. These men [the wounded in front of him] are the heroes."

Patton's theatrics confused and outraged his critics, who often themselves showed the same schizophrenia that historians display in the assessment of the equally outspoken Sherman. They sometimes faulted Patton for being bloodthirsty, while at other times thought him not a real fighter for preferring, like Sherman, flanking moves to bloody frontal assaults. As early as 1941 while on maneuvers in the United States, General Lesley McNair had been overtly critical of Patton's propensity for the indirect approach. "This is no way to fight a war" he bellowed, when Patton bypassed resistance. Captain Reuben Jenkins in his *Military Review* radio broadcasts came far closer to reflecting traditional American tactical doctrine in the manner of Grant's Army of the Potomac: "The price of victory is hard fighting and . . . no matter what maneuver is employed, ultimately the fighting is frontal." It was this apparent need for brutal and glorious frontal assault—the age-old Western bugbear that had once fueled the critics of Epaminondas and Sherman—that Patton found so unnecessary.

Upset over Patton's resurgent hagiography at the end of the war, historians and observers would react with the opposite extreme of denigration, forgetting that Patton himself never claimed to be a politician, philosopher, or strategic planner—to be anything other than a general of a rapid-moving army whose furious progress saved American and German lives alike. Eager to prove he alone had not won the war in France, they forget that Patton was given command in Normandy late, that he was subordinate to both Bradley and Eisenhower, and that he was put in a theater farthest away from the strategic center of Germany.

Patton, additional charges go, did not fight a set battle piece, as if his vast flanking victories in August 1944, and his brilliant destruction of two German armies west of the Rhine—won through maneuver rather than sheer firepower—do not really count. Old Blood and Guts, in the end it seems, was simply not bloody and gutsy enough. Charles Whiting illustrates the range of dislike for Patton that lives on to this day:

> But, in essence, Patton was neither a great man nor a great soldier. If he had not lived, it would not have mattered one little bit. His existence did not change the course of human events one iota. He made no contribution to the betterment of man. Nor was he a dreamer of some vast scheme that lived on after his death. Alive or dead, the world would not have missed him greatly.
>
> Nor was he a Great Captain. He initiated no new tactics such as Guderian's and von Manstein's concept of the *Blitzkrieg*. He made no awesome, overwhelming, irrevocable military decision, such as the one Eisenhower made when he decided to go ahead with D-Day, which could decisively affect the course of the war. He fought no decisive battle such as Montgomery did at El Alamein, or the unknown General Alexander Patch in Alsace. If his

Third Army had been defeated during the Battle of the Bulge, it would have been a serious blow for the Allies. But it would not have had a serious influence on the outcome of World War Two. . . . Never once did he fight a set-piece battle successfully.

Lost in all the invective is any mention of American lives—both the numbers saved by Patton's rapid advance in August, and the GIs that might have lived if he had been given permission to advance at critical junctures in 1944.[3]

The last straw for many Americans of the immediate postwar era was a remark made on September 21, 1945. Patton was asked at a press conference about the rumored problems surrounding his increasingly embarrassing postwar administration of Bavaria—specifically, the presence of former Nazis in the reconstructed German government. One reporter egged him on and asked: "Isn't this Nazi thing really just like a Republican-Democratic election fight? The 'outs' calling the 'ins' Nazis?" Patton typically walked right into the trap and replied, "Yes." Later his more lengthy and clumsy explanations of what he really meant—that the sheer number of Germans tainted with either explicit support for or implicit admiration of the Nazis made the idea of weeding them all out nearly impossible, and perhaps not even desirable given the shambles of German infrastructure, the proximity of the Red Army, and the growing Communist movement sweeping Eastern Europe—were to no avail. Eisenhower relieved him of Third Army command on September 28, 1945.[4]

Popular legend had it that Epaminondas killed—rather than slapped—a sleeping sentry, as a warning that such laxness might endanger the safety of his entire army. He was not averse to grabbing a live snake and pounding its brains out before his troops. Not even Old Blood and Guts Patton would have attempted that, although the first thing he promised his men when he landed in Normandy was that "when we get to Berlin, I am going to personally shoot that paper-hanging goddamned son of a bitch just like I would a snake."

Both Epaminondas and Sherman exhibited studied eccentricity and unrepentant moral fervor—traits they felt necessary to lead thousands of men on a march of vengeance, though clearly deeply disturbing to their own democratic societies. Patton was no different. There is another similitude in the words and actions of these battle leaders—repeated praise of their own men, borne out by sharing risk and danger, as well as visibility among the lowliest of infantry soldiers. In addition, these generals' comments, whether directed at foreign nations, war profiteers, or bureaucrats, only emphasized the embattled sense of their own armies: officer and infantry soldier alike were often to feel misunderstood by those at home and hated by those abroad, and thus had only each other for support and comfort. Sherman's staff was every bit as paranoid as Patton's; both felt that they were outsiders and their beloved generals hated by the politicians and high command. Boeotians, Westerners, and Third Army GIs all saw themselves as something apart from both their enemies and allies.

In short, Epaminondas, Sherman, and Patton understood that to create a vast militia and to lead it on a trek into the very interior of an enemy's homeland, it could no longer be merely an anonymous instrument of a democratic society, such as the Peloponnesians' occasional summer musters against Sparta, the ever changing face of the Army of the Potomac, or Hodges's solid First Army. The more that such a general was hated by foreign enemies, and the more he was envied, even vilified, by colleagues and superiors alike, the more his men developed their own necessary sense of a unique and collective personality, one that made them something different from other corps, something strange and eerie even to their very own society.

A half century after World War Two no American veterans would brag "I rolled with Bradley," even though the latter was Ernie Pyle's ideal GI general, who purportedly best understood the mind of the average soldier. Secretary of War Robert Patterson noticed of American soldiers in British hospitals: "When asking a patient what unit he was in, men from other Armies invariably named their regiment or division, very few knowing what Army they were in, or the name of their Commanding General. But a Third Army man always replied: 'I was with the Third Army.' And he not only knew who commanded it, but usually had a personal anecdote about Patton."[5]

Yet Patton faced obstacles undreamed of by the earlier two. Why, after all, did both Epaminondas, who laughed at his tribunal and walked out a free man, and Sherman, who dared his civilian superiors to relieve him, essentially escape lasting censure whereas Patton faced demotion and ridicule? Were they not all three big-mouth products of more or less similar democracies, each man with his own respective rivals, volatile public, and jealous overseers? Were not Epaminondas and Sherman both at times seen to be mad and the target of repeated attack?

The answer, I suggest, is not that Boeotian democracy was radically different from American—although in many ways it was—nor even that the rise of instantaneous communications ensured that Patton's comments were known to millions immediately in a way that Sherman's more disturbing bombast was not. Nor did it matter that Patton was an army, not a theater, commander and thus subject to far closer oversight than either Epaminondas or Sherman.

Rather, Patton, a clearly anachronistic figure who belonged more to the nineteenth century of his birth, functioned in a modern society that he scarcely understood—one that was becoming increasingly imbued with the spirit of psychology and social science, where the purpose of language was not merely to capture a perceived reality, but rather to serve larger social and cultural forces that were to reflect a democratic and egalitarian consensus. Patton never understood those rhetorical responsibilities of a public figure: he was supposed to reassure Americans that their children were not killers, but reluctant policemen in a conflict that might not require too much mayhem; that America's Soviet allies—at least for the time being—were also idealistic antifascists, not past masters of mass extermination; that GIs might be nicked or scraped rather than beheaded, cut in two, or atomized by German artillery. Language itself in the twentieth century was often deemed to be as important as, or even more critical than, events, inasmuch as spontaneous and loose talk in the Freudian sense might better reveal the inner psyche than deliberate acts themselves.

Patton, in the manner of a classical general haranguing his hoplites or a consul hectoring legionaries before battle, thought crude acknowledgment about the need to kill Germans, and honesty about the terror of Stalinism, would create a fighting spirit among his men and respect for his candor—and that, in fact, did happen. But many in the American government, media, military, and intellectual establishment saw these declarations as proof of the general's mental instability, if not his deep inner and unresolved psychoses. "Tomorrow," Patton told his staff in June 1944, "we go to war! I congratulate you. And I prophesy that your names and the name of the Third Army will go down in history—or they will go down in the records of the Graves Registration Bureau. Thank you. Good night!"[6]

That Patton had ruined the Nazis' will to resist in Normandy was deemed not as telling as his later juvenile praise of German cleanliness. The "real" anti-Semite was revealed by the insensitive and boisterous big-mouth who let down his conscious guard, not the disciplined mind that engineered the death of thousands of Nazis and that liberated death camps. In contrast, our two earlier democratic generals functioned in a culture of shame where sleeping on duty, hiding land mines, and profiting from the deaths of others were activities that should incur public rebuke and humiliation, not a private sense of personal guilt. In the moral world of Epaminondas and Sherman there was agreed-on absolute good and evil—the individual, not society, was usually the culprit for failure. Sherman was for a time deemed mad *not* for his promises to kill millions or vowing death and destruction for Confederate "devils," but rather for overestimating the number of troops he would need to crush the South. Americans of his age had no problem with the idea of utterly demolishing the slave-owning plantation class of the South who they felt had started the war. But they did have worries about a general who demanded unimaginable-sized armies and treasure to conduct that crusade.

In contrast, by 1945 a richer, but in some sense more insecure, America gladly offered its capital and manhood in excess to its generals, but worried that they were to kill the enemy as proper, even reluctant, representatives of a humane and enlightened society. A minor incident reflects the times. Patton once spotted a column stalled in Sicily, his men exposed on a bridge due to a local farmer's two stubborn mules. He immediately pulled out his revolver, shot both animals, and had the carcasses thrown over the side. Typically, this incident was seen by critics as proof of his brutal nature, not as evidence that an American general was in the field beside his men, or that Patton had ensured that his GIs were not stopped and rendered vulnerable to strafing by Luftwaffe fighters.

Patton's antiquated efforts at enforcing impeccable personal appearance, shaming the timid, and slapping those who, he thought, openly confessed to battle fatigue belonged to an earlier and far more brutal age, not one in which the individual was deemed inherently blameless and healthy, and faltered mainly due to larger social and economic pathologies. After the horror of World War One, many in America had adopted the radical Enlightenment notion—often rightly and with good reason—that proper education, therapeutic counseling and mediation, or government intervention might prevent wars, depressions, or bad behavior brought on by ignorance, superstition, and stress. By 1941 it was also growing clear to even the most naïve idealist that the Nazis and the imperial Japanese did not share such a charitable view of human nature—thus the American demand for a general and an army that could defeat such savage enemies on the battlefield; and yet do it in such a way that did not partake of their savagery, but rather reflected the values— and even the pretenses—of an enlightened and modern society. There were plenty of generals who would reflect this singularly American optimism and confidence in the nation's idealistic approach to war. But were there any that could take raw troops, teach them to kill, and then lead them against the most highly trained and deadly infantry in the history of warfare?

In fact, Patton was far less blunt than either Epaminondas or Sherman. He was far less ready to inflict corporal punishment, and more careful not to question higher authority. A kindred soul to both, he nevertheless lived under far different protocols than they, ones that appreciated far more the professed empathy of a Bradley, the bureaucratese of an Eisenhower, and the anonymity of a Hodges—the latter all appeared as reluctant warriors who did not enjoy killing fellow human beings, and who envisioned war as a depressing business, a necessary corporate enterprise, or perhaps a proper government task, never as a chivalrous duty in a gory arena where personal courage might at last find its proper role against evil. Theirs was a war of equipment, business organization, and industrial efficiency; Patton's was still one of the soul. "Wars may be fought with weapons," he wrote, "but they are won by men. It is the spirit of the men who follow and the man who leads that gains the victory"—a near direct echo of Sherman's dictum that there was "a soul to an army as well as to the individual man."

That Patton enjoyed killing enemy soldiers because he felt them to be agents of evil and a danger to a democratic society was less important to an increasing number of Americans, who were bothered by his candor and imagery far more than they appreciated the thousands of their sons and husbands that he had saved. Few Americans would have approved of Patton's 1943 Memorial Day speech, when he bellowed: "To conquer, we must destroy our enemies. We must not only die gallantly; we must kill devastatingly. The faster and more effectively you kill, the longer you will live to enjoy the priceless fame of conquerors."

Unlike Patton, Sherman found a receptive audience when he spoke of war as killing, especially when he made the brutal connection between his men destroying plantations and their teaching the South the consequences of their own actions. Yet eighty years later these same Americans took offense at Patton's similar hyperbole about killing far greater enemies of freedom, whether they be Nazis or Stalinist Communists. Millions of deaths in World War One and Two lay between 1864 and 1945. Such seemingly senseless carnage had demanded an explanation, one that would question the very notion of clear-cut evil or good, the traditional values of Western civilization itself, or man's need for horrendous group sacrifices to thwart aggression.[7]

What made George Patton a general so different from—and superior to—other American commanders? First, like Sherman, he was as well educated as any officer in the United States Army and far more intellectually curious than his peers, understanding that education began, rather than ended, upon graduation from West Point. Like Sherman, he obtained at the military academy a first-class education that encompassed a mandatory curriculum now nearly lost from American universities. Patton later recalled:

> Mathematics filled each weekday morning and included geometry, algebra, plane and spherical trigonometry, surveying, and analytical geometry. Afternoons were devoted to French or to ethics and history. Tactical instruction each afternoon consisted of artillery and infantry tactics, fencing, bayonet exercises, and military gymnastics.

Most modern biographers note that Patton suffered from a crippling dyslexia that made even the spelling of the simplest words almost impossible.

He nevertheless managed to graduate in 1909, 46th in a class of 103, without special tutorials or even recognition of his affliction. But his real formal education was not necessarily through class instruction, where his performance was always mediocre at best, but rather through his own disciplined course of reading, which was as impressive as Sherman's and made him every bit as reflective and philosophical as Epaminondas. In his journal of 1906 he was already making systematic and detailed lists of books to read. And he was planning future acquisitions for his own private library that would eventually reach five hundred personally annotated volumes, with titles such as Jomini's *Life of Napoleon*, Oman's *History of the Art of War in the Middle Ages*, Napoleon's *Maxims of War*, and other military classics. Immediately after graduating from West Point, like Sherman, Patton began a lifelong habit of reading constantly, often trying to match his current assignments with germane literary and military masterpieces that might put his own concrete experiences of the moment into a more conceptual context of the ages.[8]

If the Greeks were correct that education is simply the ability to translate everyday observation into abstract ideas and concepts across time and space, then Patton alone of America's generals in Europe was truly educated— Bradley's mistakes, Eisenhower's indecision, Montgomery's vanity, the collapsing German front, all were to be seen by Patton in terms of Shakespeare's plays, Napoleon's axioms, or Alexander the Great's campaigning. Bradley bragged that he taught for years as a formal staff instructor; the profane Patton who publicly played the anti-intellectual was, in fact, the far better read and educated.

During his first assignment with the 15th Cavalry regiment in Illinois, he was reading Guizot's *History of France*, Gibbon's *The Decline and Fall of the Roman Empire*, and Clausewitz's *On War*. In addition to devouring dozens of textbooks on strategy, tactics, armament, logistics, and communications, he made it a point to read biographies and memoirs of the great French and German generals. Even during combat service on the front in World War One, Patton read French histories from 1814 to 1914 late into the night, and often in the original. While on assignment in Hawaii, he devoured texts about non-European wars and imperial garrisons, such as Herbert Sargent's *The Campaign of Santiago de Cuba* and Arthur Conan Doyle's *The Great Boer War*. When Patton was at sea on his way to his first invasion of Morocco, he studied the Koran. While in Normandy, he reread Caesar's Gallic campaigns and secondary literature on William the Conqueror's battles—to correlate their knowledge of the natural passes and routes of passage in France with his own firsthand reconnaissance so many years before. Patton had a real sense that the realm of some knowledge was finite, and thus mastery of French geography and travel through France, whether by foot, horse, or tank—in the first century B.C., the eleventh century A.D., or the twentieth—was more or less the same and could be mastered through concerted study.

Throughout the 1920s, Patton had immersed himself in classical military biography, both primary and secondary—Caesar's *Commentaries*, Xenophon's *Anabasis*, and modern biographies of Alexander the Great, Scipio Africanus, and Charlemagne. On the eve of World War Two he was studying recent translations of tactical manuals by the German generals Guderian and Rommel. In short, as the intellectual historian Roger Nye points out, "By the time Patton went to fight in World War Two he had without doubt read or heard of nearly every significant writing on mobile warfare that had been produced in English since the Great War." Every element of the Third Army's operation in Normandy—tanks, infantry, rifles, machine guns, intelligence, methods of maneuver—he had either read widely on or *himself written about*. Patton was not a passive reader; his copies were fully annotated, and texts were selected precisely to enhance his own understanding of the arts of military command.[9]

For all that formal erudition, Patton nonetheless deprecated the value of book-learning alone, and had made it a point to gain as much practical experience as possible. By 1945 he was completely familiar with the operation of a company, battalion, regiment, brigade, and division, through leadership in World War One, twenty-five years of peacetime drill and maneuvers, and two great campaigns in North Africa and Sicily. Patton was fifty-six when America declared war, and like Sherman he had held almost every type of responsibility in the American army, and had taken on a host of other jobs and careers in addition.

A brief survey of his activity between 1909 and 1944, when he took command of the Third Army in Normandy, reads like fiction, since it is scarcely conceivable that a single individual could have traveled so widely, engaged in so many diverse activities, excelled in all of them—and have survived to the age of almost sixty. Critics forget that behind the foul mouth, sometimes offensive and near-lunatic pronouncements, and showy dress, Patton was without question the best-educated, most-experienced, and most widely read general in the American army.

In 1909, Patton was posted at Fort Sheridan, outside of Chicago, where he learned everything from guarding prisoners to leading cavalry patrols. He honeymooned with his wife in England and traveled to the continent for five weeks during the summer of 1910—the beginning of a lifelong fascination with the history and geography of northern Europe. By 1912 he was at Fort Myer, Virginia, drilling cavalry recruits and serving as quartermaster. Somehow he found time to train for the 1912 Olympic Games, representing the Americans in the modern pentathlon. Out of forty-two contestants, Patton placed fifth in the combined shooting, fencing, running, swimming, and horseback-riding events. The Swedish papers were laudatory of his amazing effort—Patton had passed out on the track after the cross-country run.

Immediately after the games, he went on a tour of Berlin, Dresden, and Nuremberg, and enrolled in a crash course in swordsmanship at Saumur, France, under Monsieur l'adjutant Cléry, master of arms of the French Cavalry School. He would return there the next summer in June 1913 for further fencing instruction, as well as to vacation in general in France—which included a drive through the hedgerows of Normandy. By 1913 he was posted at Fort Riley, Kansas, and was gaining a reputation for the accomplished teaching of cavalry and sword technique; yet even so, at twenty-nine he had not yet made second lieutenant. Bradley in his autobiography would sneer of Patton's surprisingly low rank even as late as 1940: "The outbreak of war in Europe and the creation of the armored command in 1940 saved Patton—then going on fifty-five years old and still only a colonel—from retirement." In 1915–16, on the eve of America's entry into World War One, Patton joined Pershing in his punitive expeditions into Mexico to catch Pancho Villa.

Patton became a lifelong friend of the king of Sweden; while in Mexico, he became the favorite of General Pershing. His sister Nita and Pershing became romantically involved and at one point were to marry. In Mexico he helped kill the notorious Mexican bandit General Julio Cárdenas in a Wild West shoot-out. During the first World War, Captain and later Major Patton was a personal aide to General Pershing and was soon charged with establishing the first American tank school at Langres, France, with the directive of creating a new force of American mechanized armor.

Patton was literally the father of American armored forces, and would turn his instructional base into a major training center for 400 tanks and 5,000 men. On September 8, he led his tankers out as part of the St.-Mihiel offensive. "You must establish the fact," the thirty-three-year-old Patton told his men, "that AMERICAN TANKS DO NOT SURRENDER. . . . As long as one tank is able to move it must go forward. Its presence will save the lives of hundreds of infantry and kill many Germans." Even as a young officer he made the critical though unpopular connection between rapid advance, killing—and saving lives.

Patton was repeatedly on the front lines and almost shot and blown apart on numerous occasions, until becoming wounded from machine-gun fire during the Meuse-Argonne offensive on September 26, 1918. After the armistice, he lectured on tactics and gave demonstrations in France and Luxembourg. During 1919 and 1920 Patton was stationed at Camp Meade, Maryland, and spent nearly every day with Eisenhower, as the two young officers sought to promote the idea of creating independent armored divisions in the peacetime army. He transferred back to the Cavalry Corps, and from 1920 on he became the leading American expert on saber warfare and mounted attack. From 1925 to 1928 he was stationed in Hawaii as an intelligence officer, and during this four-year period he became an even more prodigious reader, annotating hundreds of his volumes with cross references and personal observations. Of his service there his first division commander noted that Patton was "invaluable in war . . . but a disturbing element in time of peace"—an assessment Patton considered a high compliment. From 1928 to 1934 Patton was in the Washington, D.C., area, where he became familiar with the leading military figures of the army and an increasing number of politicians in the Roosevelt administration.

In 1935, Patton returned to Hawaii to take on the assignment of security for the Hawaiian Islands. Back again in the States he was made a full colonel in 1938. But by 1939 it was clear his talents were *not* generally appreciated; he was fifty-four and thinking of retirement, until George Marshall gave him the command of the new 2nd Armored Brigade at Fort Myer. By 1942, Patton had created from the ground up a desert training center in Indio, California, to prepare armored forces for their upcoming invasion of North Africa. In July 1942 he was given charge of the invasion of Morocco, which would lead to an army command in Sicily. After the much reported slapping incidents of two enlisted GIs hospitalized for battle fatigue, Patton was passed over for army leadership in Italy and theater command in Normandy, but studied nevertheless in detail the plans for the upcoming Allied invasion of Europe. When the war had broken out, it was an undisputed fact that no American commander had a more profound knowledge of modern armor and infantry tactics than Patton; surely none had enjoyed a greater variety of assignments. His experience in North Africa and Sicily had proved his mettle in battle. Yet, because of a few proclamations expressing worry about the Soviet alliance, his slapping of two patients, and the graphic nature of his language, the Americans were about to pass over their greatest asset for their greatest military operation in history.

Eisenhower, who had learned much from Patton about armored warfare and himself had no battle experience, wrote to General Marshall, "In no repeat no event will I ever advance Patton beyond Army command." Bradley, his former subordinate and soon-to-be superior, would later remark, "Our roles in North Africa and Sicily were now reversed; I was his boss. Had it been left up to me, I would not have included Patton in Overlord. I did not look forward to having him in my command. He had shown in Sicily that he did not know how to run an army; his legendary reputation (now badly tarnished) was the product of an uncritical media buildup." That Bradley in late July 1944 delayed in making the Third Army operational—with disastrous consequences for those fighting in the hedgerows—and that he sought to confine Patton's operations to the Brittany peninsula and held back his advance on Brest, are all proof that personal animus, not tactical doctrine, often swayed his decisions. George Patton was an easy man to dislike, but inherent in any decision to ostracize Patton out of personal odium was the reality that many GIs would therefore unnecessarily die.

In addition to his constant travel, varied assignments, and vast reading, Patton also became not merely an Olympic athlete but also an accomplished polo player. He learned to pilot airplanes and sailed his own yacht to Hawaii and back. Patton as author published numerous academic articles on tactics, cavalry, and sword use; and he designed the new straight-edged U.S. Cavalry saber. If Sherman had known the most remarkable men of his times—Kit Carson, John C. Frémont, Johann Sutter, and Winfield Scott—Patton had befriended John J. Pershing, Harry Hopkins, George Marshall, Douglas MacArthur, and Dwight Eisenhower, in addition to the king of Sweden, the old Confederate colonel John Mosby, and Mexican generals.[10]

In his late fifties as he was leading the Third Army through Normandy, Patton was better educated, more experienced, and older than either Eisenhower or Bradley. Yet, intellectual curiosity, erudition, and simple age and experience in themselves do not make great leaders of great marches. Rather, like Epaminondas and Sherman, Patton possessed a zeal that bordered on fanaticism and self-destructiveness—something that clearly bothered dependable bureaucrats like Bradley and Eisenhower. He was reckless to the point of being injury-prone: almost fatal heat exhaustion in the Olympic run, severe wounding in World War One, a nearly fatal auto accident and several other serious collisions, grave head lacerations and concussions in polo matches as well as a number of horse falls, facial burns from a gasoline explosion, and a compound leg fracture and embolism that nearly killed him—all were due to his recklessness and impatience. At various times while on duty he contracted jaundice, chicken pox, and ptomaine poisoning, and suffered severe allergic reactions, as well as complications from strep throat—afflictions that sometimes required hospitalization but rarely kept him from work. Given his past record of accidents and his tendency to court danger, Patton felt it was unlikely that he would survive the war.[11]

Like Epaminondas, he believed in reincarnation. Roger Nye notes of Patton's spiritual imagination, "He always suffered horrible deaths. God determined when he would return and fight again." Like Sherman, he was convinced that his peers and superiors were out to ruin him—and they often were. Like both, he exposed himself to enemy attack and showed little, if any, fear when his life was almost taken. We hear that Epaminondas at one point fought as a hoplite and had rescued Pelopidas himself at a skirmish near Mantinea; at his last battle also near Mantinea the middle-aged hoplite was buried beneath Spartan spear thrusts at the head of his army. Sherman nearly perished at Shiloh and deliberately exposed himself to withering enemy fire. So too Patton was almost killed by machine-gun bursts in World War One, and on numerous occasions in France was a few feet from being blown apart by enemy artillery at the front. Several eyewitnesses have written that Patton came close to death a number of times in World War Two—targeted by German artillery, airplanes, tanks, small arms fire, and machine guns while in the air, on foot, and in a jeep. He often, like his spiritual predecessors, deliberately exposed himself to hostile fire to create élan among his troops—and to reassure himself that he had not lost his nerve.

How does this reckless disregard for personal safety, coupled with a fatalism that one's destiny is set and cannot be avoided—together with the sense that one is alone and disliked—translate into superb battle leadership? In such democratic leaders there develops a sense that personal safety is unimportant since it is subject almost entirely to conditions beyond mere human control. That sense of object fearlessness permeates down through an entire army. Patton was not always on the front—what commander of a quarter-million men could be?—but his frequent trips there in the heat of battle reassured his commanders and gave himself a constant firsthand feel for the fighting that usually resulted in yet more emphasis on speed and advance. Patton wrote home about a conversation he had on August 20, 1944, with one of his corps commanders, Manton Eddy: "Unless I get a stop order in the next two hours, we are jumping again. On paper it looks very risky but I don't think it is. Manton Eddy who took over Doc's corps asked me when I told him his job: 'How much shall I have to worry about my flank?' I told him that depended on how nervous he was. He has been thinking that a mile a day was good going. I told him to go fifty and he turned pale."

The Homeric notion of fate, that immortality is achieved solely through deeds of renown, tended to prompt the general to seek daring and the seemingly impossible. Patton, who treasured the acclaim of contemporaries as well as the medals and citations from his peers, nevertheless compared himself mostly to historical figures of the past—Epaminondas, Alexander, Hannibal,

Napoleon, and Sherman. His chief worry was not whether Bradley liked him or even whether Eisenhower or Marshall might decorate him, but rather whether he would lead his men to victory in such a manner that might earn him a lasting place for posterity.

This very Greek approach to immortality would have enormously positive effects on the Third Army at large: the pragmatic Patton would defeat the Germans by ingenious planning and staff organization to permit his armor to career around their flanks; but Patton, the fanatic and romantic, would also balance that academic expertise by instilling his men with his own reckless soul—and he could not earn eternal fame unless he could share that singular zeal with his men at the front. "In acquiring erudition," Patton told an audience in 1926, "we must live on not in our studies. We must guard against becoming so engrossed in the specific nature of the roots and bark of the trees of knowledge as to miss the meaning and grandeur of the forests they compose."[12]

Much of Patton's audacity was, of course, practiced. Whereas he presented a picture of a ruthless warrior, he was, in fact, an often reflective, religious, and philosophical man. "Anything but slapdash," his biographer Martin Blumenson noted, "George Patton was thoughtful and accomplished. He was far more versatile than he is generally regarded, far more perceptive than he is usually given credit for, far more self-controlled than the public image he displayed." The real success in the Third Army lay in Patton's superb staff work and planning, not necessarily in his fiery speeches. Critics might argue that his talents were limited to division or army command, not army group or theater responsibilities. In fact, in both Sicily and North Africa, Patton proved an excellent diplomat and organizer of several divisions. The more wartime responsibility Patton was given, the more careful and systematic became his command procedure.

Patton's entire life was characterized by such contradictions. Highly educated and erudite, he could hardly finish a sentence without gross spelling errors due to his dyslexia. Said to be racist and anti-Semitic, Patton by choice lived intimately all during the war with Jews and blacks on his staff and as his closest aides and colleagues. When he lay dying, black and Jewish organizations sent messages of support. He alone of the major American generals requested more black soldiers; and he was the first American general in the history of the armed forces to integrate rifle companies. He was also the first to employ black tank units, and personally welcomed them into the Third Army, assuring them they were fighting on his own personal request:

> Men, you are the first Negro tankers ever to fight in the American Army. I would never have asked for you if you weren't good. I have nothing but the

best in my army. I don't care what color you are, so long as you go up there and kill those Kraut sonsabitches! Everyone has their eyes on you and is expecting great things from you. Most of all, your race is looking forward to you. Don't let them down and, damn you, don't let me down.

His most sympathetic biographers—Martin Blumenson and Ladislas Farago—were Jewish. Determined to present a tough masculine image, Patton's voice was squeaky and almost feminine. Aristocratic and extremely wealthy, he enjoyed close association in the field with those who were blunt, common, and vulgar. Often cruel in speech to subordinates, in practice he was softhearted and almost remiss in forgiving their mistakes. Promising death to his enemies at all costs, his drive into Germany was characterized by flanking maneuvers and a preference for racing around the rear rather than through the enemy, in order to shorten the fighting and curtail killing on both sides. It was as if William Tecumseh Sherman had been reborn.

Scholars and fellow sympathetic generals who have lamented Patton's unnecessary coarseness and bombast have failed to appreciate the prodigious Patton mind—forgetting that the gifted Patton mind often *concocted* just that coarseness as a vital ingredient in the makeup of a mobile army commander. The hardest task for modern historians is to realize that whereas they might find Patton's staged theatrics personally repulsive, they must concede his achievements changed the direction of the war in Europe, and they must allow that his often vulgar outbursts about killing, war, sex, and race mask the fact that his haste saved thousands of lives. Had his speed been encouraged rather than hindered by more soft-spoken and mild-mannered men, thousands more would have been saved.

The irony is that the larger-than-life Patton, who had a keen sense of his own ability and an archaic faith in his own destiny, was a magnanimous and kindhearted leader. He was a man far more forgiving and adept at command than Bradley, the small-minded, often insecure schemer who consciously projected the proper sense of caring and teamwork, or, Eisenhower, ostensibly the adroit diplomat who ran a coalition army, but who, in fact, at critical phases of the campaign misdirected the Allied attack, rewarding failure and punishing success in the pursuit of harmony and public relations. All of us would have preferred in our living rooms a sober Bradley or a judicious Eisenhower to a Patton—perhaps too as diplomatic representatives of America. But in battle when our lives and those of our friends were at stake, none of us would.

As far as publicity and glory-hunting go, Montgomery crossed the Rhine to a public relations blitz, and required massive use of artillery, smoke, boats, aerial bombardment, and paratroopers—to be watched by Churchill himself.

In contrast, Patton had crossed in silence the night before, "Brad," Patton telephoned Bradley, "don't tell anyone but I'm across. . . . I sneaked a division over last night."

"Sometimes I get desperate over the future," Patton wrote in his private diary while restlessly watching the Americans die in the hedgerows during early July of 1944. "Bradley and Hodges are such nothings. Their one virtue is that they get along by doing nothing. I could break through [the enemy defenses] in three days if I commanded. They try to push all along the front and have no power anywhere." He finished with a prescient forecast of his own dash the next month. "All that is necessary now is to take chances by leading men with armored divisions and covering their advance with air bursts. Such an attack would have to be made on a narrow sector whereas at present we are trying to attack all along the line."

Epaminondas, who likewise massed troops on narrow fronts, knew his success was inseparable from his ascetic and fanatic Pythagoreanism; Sherman welcomed the image of insanity—all the better to terrify his enemies. So too the loudmouth Patton wanted his countrymen, fellow generals, men in the field—and Germans too—either to admire, to be embarrassed over, or simply to fear his promises of reckless audacity to come. Like Sherman, who had been relieved of command in 1862 on charges of insanity, and who had earlier spent twenty years in obscurity, Patton knew that the upcoming great battle in Normandy in the summer of 1944 was his last chance for renown, and so his prior setbacks now gave him a daring unmatched by any other American commander.

Patton was to be to Eisenhower what Sherman had been to Halleck—a rapid-talking, impatient risk-taker whose fearlessness would bring fame to his talented, nit-picking, and often critical deskbound superior. When Eisenhower was deprecating Patton to his fellow generals, General Albert Wedemeyer reportedly scoffed, "Hell, get on to yourself, Ike; you didn't make him, he made you." Eisenhower, who was promoted to a five-star general in the midst of the Battle of the Bulge, when German Panzers had caught his army napping, remarked to Patton, "Funny thing, George, every time I get a new star I get attacked." Patton, who had remembered his role in saving the recently promoted four-star general Eisenhower's haphazard command after the debacle at the Kasserine Pass, retorted, "And every time you get attacked, Ike, I pull you out."

Bradley, typically so, inadvertently stumbled upon the source of Patton's impatience: "I've often wondered how much this nothing-to-lose attitude prodded Patton in his spectacular race across the face of France. For certainly no other commander could have matched him in reckless haste and boldness." Bradley failed to point out two key facts in his condescending assessment of Patton's nothing-to-lose "reckless haste": Patton's "reckless" celerity was always in fact well planned and based on both empirical observation and careful research. Second, the natural antithesis to such a statement was that Bradley's own timidity and worry about the maintenance of his position and prestige amid the American command structure ensured that he himself could never take such risks. And he did not. And thus German armies that could have been trapped—at Brest, at Falaise, on the Seine, and in the Lorraine—would usually escape.

In contrast to Patton, Bradley's was an "everything to lose" attitude in which the chance for a spectacular race was outweighed by worry over an embarrassing and career-ending defeat. Critics, of course, have noted that Patton was an aristocrat, with family money and no need for an army paycheck. True, but GIs who will die are not concerned about the reasons for their unwise deployment; and the joy of command was a more precious commodity for the wealthy Patton than job security was for the middle-class Bradley. In the last analysis, GIs sleeping in the dirt, facing Tiger tanks, and raked by German machine pistols cared little about the personal rivalries among their generals, but they did care a great deal that they be allowed to pursue and kill Germans when they had the rare chance.

As a youth, Patton had been fascinated by Epaminondas, not merely because of his battle victories—especially the Theban's use of the massed oblique attack—but also for his character and aims. At seventeen Patton wrote, "Epaminondas was without doubt the best and one of the greatest Greeks who ever lived, without ambition, with great genius, great goodness, and great patriotism; he was for the age in which he lived almost a perfect man." It is more than likely that there was not a single American general in Normandy who had ever heard of Epaminondas—a figure that had lived with Patton in the forty years before he took command of the Third Army.[13]

Patton quoted Sherman often. He told his men that, of all American generals, he understood best William T. Sherman and his preference for fluidity and rapid marches around the flank of the enemy line. He followed Sherman's dictum that a general should command from the front. Like Sherman, Patton felt that he had been reprimanded for his "misdeeds" but would emerge, like Sherman, spectacularly from the cloud of doubt. Again like Sherman, he promised that he would never run for office and would not serve if elected—Eisenhower said nearly the same thing and was elected president. When he was in England in the days before his assignment to Normandy, the British biographer of Sherman, Liddell Hart, made it a point to meet Patton on two occasions to discuss Sherman's mobile and indirect brand of warfare:

"I think the indirect argument made some impression. At any rate, when I spent another evening with him in June, just before he went over to Normandy, he was no longer talking about the 1918 methods, but on much bolder lines. The way that, after the break-through, he actually carried out his plans, in super-Sherman style, is a matter that all the world knows."

There is a good likelihood that, in Normandy, Patton deliberately emulated the "super-Sherman style" of grand flanking maneuvers to the rear as a result of following Sherman's march firsthand in Georgia. Liddell Hart pointed out in his own memoirs, "It was even more delightful on meeting General George Patton in 1944 to hear from him that some ten years earlier he had spent a month's leave in following Sherman's campaign with my book in hand [Liddell Hart's *Sherman*] and found it 'a very good guide.'" Other historians have also noted the similarities between Uncle Billy and Old Blood and Guts:

> Patton . . . also possessed certain professional and personality similarities to an illustrious military forebearer, General William Tecumseh Sherman—who exactly eighty years earlier had cut the Confederacy in half to precipitate the end of the Civil War even as Patton tore through the heart of Nazidom. Both were dashing, brilliant in often unorthodox tactics such as outrunning supply bases, and both were highly temperamental men. They had commenced their campaigns in the summer, Sherman plunging into Georgia with 100,000 troops, one fifth the number, however needed by Patton to liberate France and conquer central Germany. . . . By VE-day, Patton had fought through more than 1,000 miles of enemy or enemy-held territory. Sherman's march to the sea, then back northward, was slightly short of the 1,000 miles mark when the surrender was consummated at Appomattox.[14]

Patton and Sherman may have shared an identical strategic outlook not simply because they had professional and personality similarities, but because both were deeply devoted to saving the lives of the men they led and ending quickly the war that they fought—and that sense ultimately derived more from their moral than their military character.

Finally, critics have charged that while Patton may have been a great tactical commander, his juvenile outbursts and bizarre political and strategic utterances made him a real danger to the Allied effort in Europe. That he was naïve about the need for prudence and the responsibilities of an occupation administrator are undeniable; that he misunderstood public relations is also true. And that at the end of his life he seemed to suffer nearly uncontrollable bursts of anger, characterized by exaggeration and overdramatic bombast, is a matter of record. Some of his broadsides were anti-Semitic and racist and they belong in the sad category of Sherman's impromptu and sometimes uncouth slurs against blacks and Jews. In many ways, based on what he said and wrote in his diary in the last year of his life—after a year of continuous combat—Patton died a repugnant figure. Yet after saying that, it is difficult to find evidence that in his personal life Patton, the old nineteenth-century paternalistic aristocrat, was either prejudicial or bigoted, or that any of Patton's major political pronouncements were fundamentally wrong—on the brutality needed to combat the German army, the necessity of overwhelming military forces to keep the peace, the danger of an intrinsically evil Soviet Union, the need to save Eastern Europe from communism, and the desire for a strong postwar Germany.

In every tactical crux of the Normandy campaign, Patton alone offered the correct advice—from the rapid follow-up on the breakout in early August 1944, to the need to hurry on to Brest, to the entrapment of the Germans at the Falaise Gap, to the critical goal of sealing off the exits of the German armies once he crossed the Seine, to the idea of approaching and crossing the Rhine rapidly at the end of August, to the notion of enveloping the German counteroffensive in the Ardennes and slicing off the enemy salient at its base, to the desire to trap and destroy two entire German armies *west* of the Rhine, and to the final question of preventing Soviet occupation of Eastern Europe. In each case, had the Americans allowed the Third Army and its seemingly insane general to have his way—profane language, near-lunatic pronouncements, uncontrollable theatrics, and all—thousands of Allied soldiers would have been saved, the war shortened, the horror of the death camps ended months earlier, and the calamity of postwar communism for a few millions perhaps averted.

All this would become clear in the postwar period. But in the last year of the war, Patton was generally ridiculed behind his back and increasingly to his face, kept as much as possible out of the main decision-making involving the Normandy campaign, and at war's end demoted and relieved of command of the army he had created. There is something Shermanesque in Patton in the summer of 1944—directing traffic at key interchanges, appearing unexpectedly at corps headquarters to demand ever more speed from his armored divisions, devising two and three plans at once to be activated by code when his less gifted peers only later would come to similar conclusions, begging for supplies and the chance to press eastward—all the while deliberately ignored by Bradley and to a lesser extent by Eisenhower. As Sophocles' Ajax come alive, the more Patton proved invaluable to the war effort, the more he would become deeply disturbing to his superiors. But approval and praise were inconsequential; what was really at stake in the use of Patton were the lives of thousands of GIs, whose fate was in the hands of a single individual who could keep them moving and alive.

Now on December 21, 1945, Patton was tired. He had had enough. There were blood clots in his lungs; his heart was worn out. The swelling from the crushed vertebra and the accumulation of mucus in his respiratory tract had put him to sleep for good. At ten minutes to six he quit breathing in his sleep, and left it to history, not to his fellow generals and superiors, to sort out what he had really done. "Ignorant men," wrote Sophocles, "don't know what good they hold in their hands until they've flung it away."[15]

2

THE PATTON WAY OF WAR

THE RHINE RIVER, GERMANY

March 22, 1945 (V-E Day Minus 48 Days)

They ran beside these, one escaping, the other after him.
It was a great man who fled, but far better he who pursued him
rapidly, since here was no festal beast, no ox-hide
they strove for, for these are prizes that are given men for their running.
No, they ran for the life of Hektor, breaker of horses.

—Homer, *Iliad*

ONTHS before his accident George Patton had stood over and urinated in the Rhine River, the historical last obstacle to the interior
of old Germany. His own audacity and the bravery of his men had
gotten him there. In the same manner that Sherman was determined to reach
the coast from the instant he departed from Atlanta, so too Patton's entire
obsession since landing in Normandy was to organize an army to cross the
Rhine into the traditional heartland of Germany in as short a time as possible. Speed—reckless car-driving, Olympic sprinting, horse-galloping, low-
level airplane-piloting—was the lifeblood of George S. Patton. In March
1945 the army that was now racing across the Rhine River in pursuit of the
crumbling armies of Adolf Hitler reflected its general's obsession to move
constantly and thereby kill on the run to survive. His letters, diary, and

287

speeches between August 1944 and May 1945 have a single theme: motion. Patton ended a typical letter to his wife on August 21, 1944: "We are going so fast that I am quite safe. My only worries are my relations, not my enemies. Well, I will stop and read the Bible so as to be ready to have celestial help in my argument tomorrow to keep moving."

Patton and many of his Third Army subordinate generals like Robert Grow and John Wood were for the most part old horsemen, professionals from the American peacetime army of the 1920s and 1930s who had originally started out as cavalry commanders trained to sweep in pursuit of broken ranks of infantry. But the advent of motorized armored corps had transformed the traditional image of such mobile corps from raiders into deadly killers. Western infantrymen, unlike both settled and nomadic peoples of the East, have always had an ambivalent relationship with mounted warriors. In Epaminondas's times horsemen were aristocratic dandies, flashy prancers who could not charge the phalanx, in which the real citizen with shield and spear fought in mass. In ancient Athenian comedy, knights were ridiculed as antidemocratic, long-haired snobs. Sherman too, for all his reliance on Kilpatrick's horsemen, never really considered them anything much more than valuable reconnaissance corps and raiders; his men for the most part despised mounted troops as fainthearts who could not stand up to Southern foot soldiers.

Yet, with the advent of tanks and self-propelled guns, the American mobile corps retained the dash and love of speed of the old-time cavalry, all the while adding a new element of firepower that could devastate infantry in minutes. Unlike horse cavalry, armor had no aristocratic connotations. Only the rich could raise horses; but in America almost anyone had experience behind the wheel of a car or truck—more so the muscular classes. Patton realized that it was very American to keep an army constantly on the move, uprooting its headquarters every few days, entering and leaving new landscapes almost simultaneously, always shooting on the run. A colonel in the Third Army remarked that Patton's zest for motion and firepower spread from the division level all the way down to the conduct of the individual soldier:

> That was one of his favorite theories—keep moving forward. He used to tell his divisions not to dig in, but to keep moving forward. He would say: "Dig in and you are dead! You will be a perfect target for the enemy mortars. If you keep moving forward you will be a more difficult target for the enemy and he will be more nervous and unsteady in his aim, because you are getting closer and closer to him for the kill."[16]

Even Eisenhower, who in many ways would turn out to be among Patton's greatest critics, wrote as early as 1943 that the speed of the American army was entirely attributable to its commander. Of the Sicily campaign, which Bradley later claimed was proof of Patton's incompetence, Eisenhower conceded:

> He has conducted a campaign where the brilliant successes scored must be attributed directly to his energy, determination, and unflagging aggressiveness. The operations of the Seventh Army in Sicily are going to be classed as a model of swift conquest by future classes in the War College in Leavenworth. The prodigious marches, the incessant attacks, the refusal to be halted by appalling difficulties in communications and terrain, are really something to enthuse about. This had stemmed mainly from Patton. He has fine division and corps commanders, but it is obvious that had he been willing to seize on an excuse for resting or refitting, these commanders could have done nothing.[17]

On the last night of July 1944, before Patton's army became operational, the general outlined the basic procedure for his men until war's end:

> There's another thing I want you to remember. Forget this goddamn business of worrying about our flanks. . . . Some goddamned fool once said that flanks must be secured and since then sons of bitches all over the world have been going crazy guarding their flanks. We don't want any of that in the Third Army. Flanks are something for the enemy to worry about, not us. I don't want to get any messages saying that, "We are holding our position." We're not holding anything! Let the Hun do that. We are advancing constantly and we're not interested in holding on to anything except the enemy. We're going to hold on to him by the nose and we're going to kick him in the ass; we're going to kick the hell out of him all the time and we're going to go through him like crap through a goose. . . . We have one motto, "*L'audace, l'audace, toujours l'audace!*" Remember that, gentlemen.

Easier said than done for Patton, who was directly subordinate to at least three other American generals—Bradley, Eisenhower, and Marshall—and thus lacked the freedom of both tactical and strategic command enjoyed by both Epaminondas and Sherman. For delays in his progress he would—at times unfairly—come to blame his superiors more than the Germans. Of the rerouting of his supplies to Montgomery in the north and to General Jacob Devers in the south, he wrote in late September 1944, "At the moment I am being attacked on both flanks, but not by the Germans."

There were also other differences in Patton's march from those of his predecessors. Strategic and tactical American airpower now freed him from the need to concentrate on the infrastructure of German society; that is, while he surrounded German armies, raced through occupied countryside, and obliterated recalcitrant villages in his path ("Third Army Memorials"), Patton did not, like Epaminondas or Sherman, attack German infrastructure per se to bring home the consequences of Nazi aggression to the populace. That had been done and brutally so by the American and British strategic and tactical air forces.

Unlike Epaminondas and Sherman, who were not often challenged in decisive battle during their marches, Patton was attacked constantly. His flanking movements around the rear of the enemy were always executed under conditions of extreme enemy resistance, and aimed more immediately at rendering the German army itself incapable of battle, rather than at harming the economic landscape of Germany. Patton did march into the interior of his enemy, and in that sense alone his rapid march put out of commission rail yards, factories, roads, and entire municipalities, but his main efforts were directed at getting behind the German army to encircle and destroy it rapidly and at little cost.

Yet for all these differences, Patton's march shared two key operational similarities with both earlier treks—speed and the desire to outflank, rather than collide with, the main resistance of the Wehrmacht. For Patton, enemy armies, even modern armored forces, could collapse just as easily from panic when they learned that there were enemy tanks to their rear as they might by being fired upon from frontal assaults, "You can't have men retreating for 300 or 400 miles and then hold anything," he scoffed. Patton's haste was a moral quality, in part reflective of the real incongruity of Patton the man: his bluster and profanity were aimed at disguising his real abhorrence for needless killing. For all his vulgar boasts about killing the Hun, he much preferred, like Sherman, to outflank and capture him, and to save his own men in the process. Bradley and Eisenhower, who posed as kinder, gentler men, in their slow and sober approach to battle ironically would—like the equally methodical Grant—wreak more carnage than the crude Patton, who boasted that he loved killing even as he did his best to minimize it. Few historians have grasped that incongruity as insightfully as Martin Blumenson:

> He loved war. But not the death and destruction. The concentration camps and the ruined cities sickened him, and the losses of his soldiers hurt him. Even the bodies of the enemy, no longer an abstraction of warfare, saddened him. He loved the excitement of war, the responsibility of war, the prerogatives of his position, and, most of all, the opportunity that war presented to use the skill, leadership, and courage required by his profession—in the same way that a surgeon loves his calling but not the disease, illness, and injury he treats.[18]

For Patton, student of the great German Panzer attacks in France during the spring of 1940, motion meant life for his men; the stasis of Bradley and Montgomery, defeat and death—"As soon a man gets in a concrete line, he immediately says to himself, 'The other man must be damned good, or I wouldn't have to get behind this concrete.'" Patton also realized, as did Sherman of the Westerner in particular, that movement was the natural mode of the American soldier. As a product both of democracy and the frontier, he was used to moving on, starting anew, forever restless with the status quo. Chester Wilmot notes of the Americans' speed in Normandy:

> Another factor assumed almost equal importance: the survival, or revival, of the frontier spirit. The Americans had in their blood a longing for adventure and an instinct for movement, which they inherited from those pioneers who had broken out across the Alleghenies and opened up the Middle West. To the American troops driving across France, distance meant nothing. They had no qualms about thrusting deep into the military unknown. . . . As soon as the break-out had been achieved, every division, armoured and infantry alike, seemed to be capable of swift and bold exploitation.

More than any other American commander, Patton also understood that the American army fought best when it exploited its inherent mobility as part of a continual allegiance to the indirect approach. When the war began, the inexperience of American infantrymen, the shocking inferiority of American tanks and antitank weaponry, and the relative mediocrity of American divisional firepower when compared to its German counterparts ensured that direct application of military force against German Panzers in the tradition of U. S. Grant's frontal assaults was impossible. Speed, mobility, and envelopment, as we have seen, far better served a zealous though amateur militia—and Patton alone grasped that.

Thus the singular horror of the stricken Patton's last few days in Heidelberg—his neck and head alone capable of only a few painful turns, not unlike his own army's paralysis in September and October 1944, when it too had lost its vigor—its supply of gasoline—and thus its very ability to move when movement might have won the war. But the immobilized Patton's thoughts in his last days also must have raced back to happier times, eight months earlier to February 1944—to the beginning of the last great dash of the Third Army when his men were once more resupplied with gas, ammunition, and provisions for one final roll into Germany. Then for the first time in months he had been more or less left alone to resume offensive operations on his own in the style of August 1944, when the Allies had nearly exterminated the German army and almost brought the entire war in the West to a close—when his men were moving and killing, but not dying.

If other American and British armies were exhausted and now gun-shy after the near collapse from an unforeseen German counteroffensive in the Ardennes, Patton's Third Army this February 1945 would end the war in the same swashbuckling manner that it had begun it on August 1 during the great breakout from Normandy. It would now encircle two German armies west of the Rhine, cut them off, annihilate them, then cross the river and race through the empty German countryside that had been denuded of its defenders.

The prior October through December of 1944 had brought immobility for Patton and nearly all the other American and British armies in France. Supply lines had grown too long; and the Anglo-American armies were spreading hundreds of miles apart over the entire European countryside from the North Sea to the Mediterranean. To the north, General Montgomery, worried about the limitations of British manpower, and wounded by the losses from his Operation Market-Garden fiasco, was hoarding British and American supplies and divisions for a methodical and cautionary single thrust over the Rhine into the heart of Germany. Allied infantry in general was exhausted from some 150 days of constant fighting; much equipment was simply worn-out. All this in the fall of 1944 had conspired to halt Patton and had given breathing room to the enemy, whose inner lines of defense shortened just as the Americans' continued to lengthen. If any Allied armies along the extended front were to move forward in concentration, it was generally agreed that they would do so in loose support of Mongomery's forces.

In the Lorraine region, German divisions offered the Third Army a stubborn defense at Metz, taking advantage of September's sudden and unforeseen window of respite from Patton's attacks. And just when Patton was finally preparing to crack the German resistance in December 1944, he had been suddenly diverted northward to relieve elements of the First Army near Bastogne. That rescue march had occupied most of the latter part of December and early January. As the German counterattack wound down, Patton wrote his wife on February 4, 1945, "You may hear that I am on the defensive but it was not the enemy who put me there. I don't see much future for me in this war. There are too many 'safety first' people running it. However, I have felt this way before and something has always turned up. I will go to church and see what can be done. . . . I feel pretty low to be ending the war on the defensive."[19]

Even as Patton wrote, he did not fully realize that the Battle of the Bulge was largely over, and his Third Army was once again free to drive eastward on their own into Germany. Nor did he fathom that his army had only about a hundred days left in the war, and its greatest successes—the greatest successes

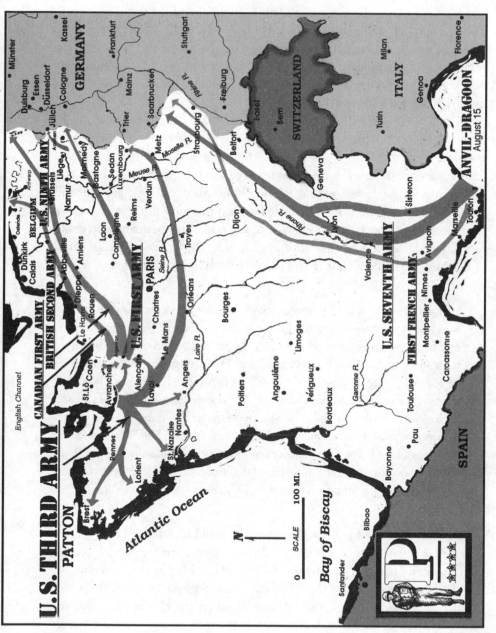

THE LIBERATION OF FRANCE   JUNE 1944–MARCH 1945

of the entire Anglo-American army in Europe—were to come. True, his supplies were to be chronically interrupted, and his official orders were to engage and hold the Germans in the south, while the main Allied thrust was to resume once more under Montgomery in the north. Still, Patton felt that he had finally enough freedom and gas to head for the Rhine and beyond. "I am taking one of the longest chances of my chancy career; in fact, almost disobeying orders in order to attack, my theory being that if I win, nobody will say anything, and I am sure that I will win."

Of the slow, businesslike British plan to approach the Rhine to the north, Patton scoffed, "Let the gentlemen up north learn what we are doing when they see it on their maps." In his way of thinking, the Germans were exhausted after their failed Ardennes offensive, and there were now thousands of German soldiers west of the Rhine River who could be flanked and trapped—the river was not an obstacle for his own army's progression farther into Germany as much as a hindrance for the retreating Germans who could more easily be killed west, rather than east, of it. Hubert Essame has written of Patton's decision in February and March to resume a war of movement and speed:

> Patton's objections to the comparatively passive role now assigned to him were, however, based primarily on more subtle grounds. No American general had a better grasp of the human element in war; no one realized more profoundly that morale is never constant. From his experience in two wars he realized that troops in contact with the enemy should never be allowed to remain quiescent: allow them to sit still and acquiesce in a routine of live and let live with the enemy and they will brood to their own moral undoing; action, and offensive action at that, alone brings release. This, allied with the concept of speed, was the very heart of the Patton approach to battle. With his army already probing the Siegfried defences he had no intention whatever of complying literally with SHAEF's written orders consigning him to the defensive.[20]

As Patton himself put it to his staff, "It would be a foolish and ignoble way for the Americans to end the war by sitting on their asses. And, gentlemen, we aren't going to do anything foolish or ignoble like that—of course." But the Eifel sector and so-called Saar-Palatinate triangle, in which the Third Army now found itself, were difficult terrain, where the idea of a steady holding action seemed far easier than the attempt at an armored breakout. Much of the dirty work required infantry attack, rather than armored thrusts. Small squads of GIs would have to advance village by village through the hilly and forested country and root out concealed pillboxes, artillery, and die-hard SS battalions. The manic dash of summer had been designed precisely to prevent just this sort of fighting.

In approaching the Rhine, first the rivers Moselle, Ourthe, and Sauer had to be crossed by either boat or hastily constructed pontoon bridges—Patton would later call his men's forcing bridgeheads over them "a Homeric feat." It was an extremely wet February and March, and the roads were nearly impassable. Many of the Americans did not have adequate winter gear and were suffering from both trench foot and frostbite. Thousands had been underfed and poorly protected from the continuous December and January fighting in the Ardennes. Patton was thus becoming restless as his men slogged against the Siegfried Line and Germany's last perimeter of fortifications. By February 1945, of all the Allied armies, the Third had the longest distance to go to reach the Rhine; it now faced the greatest concentration of German forces, and confronted the most difficult terrain—and yet Patton was most confident that his army would most likely destroy the German army west of the Rhine.[21]

By February 21, Patton's divisions were in high gear, and on March 1 they captured the ancient Roman city of Trier—Patton said he could smell the sweat of the legions. In the next three weeks the progress of the Third Army was astounding as it sped in an enormous hook toward the Rhine. Stephen Ambrose, the biographer of Eisenhower, describes in obvious admiration Patton in action:

> Through February, Patton attacked, whatever the conditions. He was at his zenith. His nervous energy, his drive, his sense of history, his concentration on details while never losing sight of the larger picture combined to make him the preeminent American army commander of the war. Those qualities, and his professional competence. He was constantly looking for ways to improve.

During the second and third weeks of March, Patton sent his Third Army in various directions against the enemy, determined not to remain static in a holding pattern. Patton's idea once again was to send fast-moving armored columns around points of German resistance in a series of huge enveloping moves designed to dishearten the enemy and to cause him to surrender when he realized Americans were streaking to his rear. Hubert Essame notes of Patton's presence during the February campaign against the Siegfried Line, or West Wall: "Patton personally spent most of the hours of daylight touring his front in an open car: he never had a cold and his face though slightly blistered gave him no trouble. He recorded not without satisfaction that his aides in the back seat suffered more than he did. He was everywhere." Meanwhile, thousands of American foot soldiers were running, crawling, and holed-up throughout the salient, engaging in countless unknown but especially brutal firefights against often fanatical German resistance.[22]

From Trier, Patton's northern divisions barreled through the forests to Koblenz on the Rhine River. Between Patton's northern flank and the southern wing of the American First Army lay thousands of trapped Germans, who often fought furiously when they realized that they would never make it back over the Rhine. Eisenhower and Montgomery, of course, were worried about Patton's progress. "They did not want me to take Trier nor go to the Rhine nor to cross the Moselle southwest of Koblenz, and now, if we don't cross the Rhine, we may be halted again. We have got by due to persistence and on ability to make plans fit circumstances. The other Armies try to make circumstances fit plans." For Patton, the student of military history and the veteran of such armored drives in the first World War and in Africa and on Sicily, the key was once again speed. He had seen in late August 1944 what had happened when the Allies had paused, only to encounter stiff German resistance where just days earlier the Wehrmacht west of the Rhine was nearly in shambles; that delay, to his mind, had inaugurated this entire winter of plodding, dirty warfare in which thousands of Allied and German soldiers were to die.

"The Patton mind," Roger Nye has written, "that emerged from this crucible of private study was capable of creating a kind of warfare that was so fast and so destructive of the enemy that the battle could be won with a minimum of friendly casualties and expenditure of matériel." The way to keep his GIs alive was to encircle the enemy with armor, use artillery to blast hostile concentrations, and thus convince the Germans to give up before being annihilated. In chasing his prey back to its lair, Patton had felt it was far easier to kill him on the run, than root him out of his hole.[23]

As his divisions headed to the north and Koblenz, and to the south of the Moselle River, Patton attempted a simultaneous hook around the German fortifications of the so-called Saar-Palatinate, a huge triangle of seventy-five-mile-long sides, whose base butted up against the Rhine. He would go around the West Wall defenses and take the enemy from the rear. On March 13, Patton unleashed nine divisions from the banks of the Moselle River and turned them loose toward the Rhine. By March 21 the Third Army had reached the river, his armor racing ahead of his infantry at speeds of up to twenty miles a day and more. Within a four-day period 80,000 Germans had surrendered and the Seventh and First German Armies ceased to exist. The entire countryside was left in turmoil, a scene far more tumultuous than what Sherman left behind in Georgia:

Everywhere slave laborers and displaced persons from a dozen different European countries looted the farms and depots of their former masters, taking their revenge of the sufferings they had endured during the long years of captivity. Medieval villages burned by the score, for at the least sign of resistance, Patton's artillery descended upon them and they became instant "Third Army memorials."

On March 23, Patton urinated in the Rhine, after his engineers had ferried thousands of Americans into the heart of Germany. Over 100,000 Germans had now surrendered to Patton in less than a month, and another 25,000 were dead, wounded, or missing. Of the conclusion to the Saar-Palatinate campaign, the sober historian Russell Weigley has concluded:

> The campaign was notable also for its display of the American army's sharpening instinct for the jugular. The campaign's two envelopments, of the German Seventh Army by two columns of Patton's Third Army, and then of the German First Army by both Patton's Third and Patch's Seventh Armies, were models of how not only to gain ground but to destroy enemy forces. . . . The Americans were probably not far wrong in estimating that the enemy had lost 75 to 80 percent of the infantry he had engaged in battle. . . . And the extent of the American victory cannot be attributed merely to German decay . . . [the victory] was in large part the product of mastery at last of a thoroughly mobile form of warfare genuinely aimed at the destruction of the enemy force.[24]

The opportunities for even bigger game loomed across the Rhine. Patton now took Frankfurt and put his armored divisions on the German autobahns and headed them northward and to the east. Thousands of Germans continued to surrender in mass and simply were told to walk west as the Americans drove farther east. The Third Army had now reached its zenith. It consisted of four corps that comprised twelve infantry and six armored divisions. Along with other assorted support forces, there were now nearly a half-million men under Patton's direct command. When the war ended, George Patton was commander in the field of the largest single American army in the nation's history. In contrast, the Third Reich was a shell, and with the arrival of Patton's armor the entire hollow society collapsed:

> Germany had never seen a time like this since the Thirty Years War back in the Seventeenth Century. Millions of slave workers newly liberated, clogging the roads, waving and singing, drunk and mad with hate of the Germans, looting, plundering, raping. These freed bondsmen, uprooted from a dozen different European countries, were now taking their revenge on the fat, pros-

perous German civilians, whose pleasant villages and rich farms had been untouched hitherto by the war. The suffering and humiliation they had endured the last five terrible years now found expression in their terrorization of the German populace.[25]

German civilians were indeed shell-shocked. Patton wrote on March 23, the day after he crossed the Rhine:

The displaced persons is [sic] a problem. They are streaming back utterly forlorn. I saw one woman with a perambulator full of her worldly goods sitting by it on a hill crying. An old man with a wheel barrow and three little children wringing his hands. A woman with five children and tin cup crying. In hundreds of villages there is not a living thing, not even a chicken. Most of the houses are heaps of stones. They brought it on themselves, but these poor peasants are not responsible. I am getting soft? I did most of it.[26]

Like the situation in Laconia and Georgia, the suffering of the civilian population began to sap at the strength of the enemy's military resistance. As Patton's tanks raced through the heart of Germany, the officers of the German army agreed that Patton was indeed responsible for much of the current chaos. A captured Lieutenant Colonel Freiherr von Wangenheim under questioning confessed:

The greatest threat . . . was the whereabouts of the feared U.S. Third Army. General Patton is always the main topic of military discussion. Where is he? When will he attack? Where . . . ? How? With what? Those are the questions which raced through the head of every German general since the famous German counteroffensive last December. . . . General Patton is the most feared general on all fronts. The successes of the U.S. Third Army are still overshadowing all other events of the war, including the campaigns in Russia. . . . The tactics of General Patton are daring and unpredictable. . . . He is the most modern general and the best commander of armored and infantry troops combined.[27]

On April 25, the Third Army arrived at the Czechoslovakian border. Patton was ready to move on Prague when Eisenhower halted his advance to allow the converging Russian armies to occupy the Czech capital. Patton was now aghast that an American army of nearly a half-million men had halted a few miles from Prague, lent no assistance to a popular uprising, allowed the Germans continual occupation of foreign ground, and then sat by while Russian armies had taken control of the country, as the Nazis had done over five years earlier. That there had been prior diplomatic agreements with the Soviets meant little to Patton, who now begged Bradley, "For God's sake, Brad, those patriots in the city need our help. We have no time to lose." Later, Bradley relayed Eisenhower's order to stop Patton—and to allow Prague to be occupied by the Russians to avoid "complications." Patton replied, "For God's sake, Brad, it seems to me that a great nation like America should let others worry about the complications." On the earlier American decision to halt before the Russians in central Germany, Patton himself told Eisenhower, "Ike, I don't see how you figure that out. We had better take Berlin, and quick—and on to the Oder." Eisenhower muttered back, "Well, who would want it?" Patton replied carefully, "I think history will answer that question for you."

Patton, unlike his superiors, felt that the American advance to the Czech capital would present the Russians with a *fait accompli*, and provide a valuable testament of American will in the inevitable postwar tension to come, besides ensuring that Czech civilians would come under Allied, not Russian, occupation. For the *fifth* and last time since the Third Army had become operational in Normandy in August 1944, Patton's sage advice on a critical decision of where to direct his army was overturned, and millions, not thousands, this time paid the consequences—and for a half century to come. Eisenhower, who was a more reasonable man than Patton, and far more able to manage a huge coalition war, and Bradley, a more empathetic and more representative American than Patton, would be repeatedly wrong in almost every decision involving the Third Army. That the former became a good president—his political reputation continues to grow in light of the dénouement of the Cold War and the scandals of recent presidential administrations—and the latter a sober and judicious member of American top brass, while the uncouth Patton died months after the war, in large part has explained our reluctance to criticize both.

The war was over in a few days—on May 9. In the great tradition of American militias, in six months almost all of Patton's veterans were home, and their general was dead in a hospital bed in Heidelberg. The Third Army and its general disappeared almost as abruptly as they had materialized nine months earlier in Normandy—GIs to peacetime America, Patton to five months of ignominious consulship of Bavaria, followed by an embarrassing removal and another three months of humiliation until the automobile accident and slow death.[28]

Epaminondas had once descended into Laconia with a force of 70,000 hoplites and light-armed troops. Sherman's Army of the West comprised over 62,000 soldiers on the March to the Sea. Both forces represented about the largest and most lethal armies of their respective eras—their very size reflective of the great sense of animosity that they held toward their enemies and their desire to annihilate the foundations of contemporary serf and slave culture. Yet each of those armies was smaller than a single one of Patton's six corps. When Patton halted beyond the Czech border in May 1945, he had 437,860 infantrymen under his direct command, an army well over six times larger than his two predecessors'. On average during most of the hard fighting of late 1944 and early 1945, before the sudden stream of new divisions at war's end, the Third Army numbered about 250,000 active troops. If the airplane allowed Patton a bird's-eye view of the battlefield, if the jeep and command car permitted him to reconnoiter along his hundred-mile front at speeds up to seventy miles an hour, if he could communicate directly with both his division commanders and superiors by both radio and phone, nevertheless, the sheer size of his army, and the continental expanse in which it operated, made the challenges of command even greater than that faced by the walking Epaminondas and the mounted Sherman.

Patton's age of warfare was at once both more horrific and civilized than that of either Epaminondas or Sherman. Far more grotesque was the twentieth-century battlefield in which men were not run through by spears or shot down by rifled bullets, but literally blown to bits by mines, tanks, and artillery. In the fourth century B.C., a hoplite at the worst might be stabbed repeatedly and trampled, a Civil War soldier shot a half-dozen times by repeating rifles, or mangled by grapeshot. Yet the soldiers of the Third Army—in large groups at a time—would be atomized by bombs, incinerated by flame, and blown apart by high-explosive artillery shells. By the same token, infantrymen of the Third Army could at times enjoy a level of comfort undreamed of by hoplites or Sherman's bummers. To the rear during leave were warm houses, plentiful food, and rapid transportation and instant communications. While modern soldiers' wounds were far more hideous, medical care in the age of plasma and first-generation antibiotics nevertheless saved the disabled as never before, as amputation became occasional rather than standard practice for injured extremities.

The real great change in warfare from the previous marches—which both relied on foot and horse power—was the sheer anonymity of modern battle. Patton fought engagements that lasted for weeks, involving hundreds of thousands of soldiers on both sides. A hoplite spearmen eyed his prey; even a Confederate marksman was not over a few hundred yards away from a Northern bluecoat. Yet, by World War Two, GIs could kill and be killed miles away from their enemy, who might bomb from over a mile above, shell from across a river, and leave mines that would maim for days after the enemy departed.

Patton, who mastered the technology of the early twentieth century and was keenly aware of the ramifications of the new industrial warfare of the times, was convinced, nevertheless, that there were timeless absolutes in any great march—personal leadership from the front, reckless audacity, the general's personality and unique soul permeating throughout the ranks, and the need for a constant reminder about the ideology of such a great crusade itself. If Patton, who had read both ancient biography and was a keen student of Sherman's memoirs, was to lead a modern army in the ancient style, it entailed a horrendous physical and mental strain on a sixty-year-old man simply to address, visit, and lead such a vast horde. Warfare had ostensibly become too large for generals of the old style like Patton.

Or almost. Hubert Essame reminds us why Patton, alone of the great commanders of the American armies, was nearly always at the front, continuing to hector his men, and confronting his generals:

> His experience in the First War had taught him how men react to enemy fire and convinced him like Montgomery that morale is the most important factor in war—hence his unrelenting efforts to see the battle personally from the front and through the eyes of his staff. Daily he missed no opportunity of emphasizing to regimental officers their personal responsibility for their men. He realized that hot food in battle is often as important as ammunition. He showed himself to the troops as often and as impressively as possible. . . . His addresses to his troops, couched in a vernacular which they understood, read somewhat strangely today: nothing is so outdated as yesterday's slang, which may well have jarred the nerves of intellectuals at the time. It should be borne in mind however that such men are rare at the cutting edge of armies.[29]

Patton's two spiritual predecessors had essentially operated within one or two distinct regions—Epaminondas in Laconia and Messenia, Sherman in Georgia and the Carolinas. Patton, in contrast, would traverse an entire continent, which included six countries—France, Germany, Luxembourg, Belgium, Austria, and Czechoslovakia. While Epaminondas may have been on the road off and on for five months or more, and Sherman marching in his Georgia and Carolina campaigns for perhaps four months, Patton's men fought continually from Normandy to the outskirts of Prague for 281 straight days. How Patton, in the manner of a Great Captain of antiquity, or a dashing Civil War general, was able to lend his own stamp to such a huge monstrosity as the Third Army defies imagination.

Speed, again, was a hallmark of all three marches. But the difference in magnitude of such moving columns is astounding. Epaminondas marched about 160 miles from Thebes to Sparta, a trek that might have taken somewhere around two weeks, given his crossing of passes out of Boeotia and Corinthia, and his stop in Arcadia to join up with his Peloponnesian allies. His army brought along 500 tons of bronze panoplies to arm his hoplites, and perhaps 1,000 pack animals to haul food and water. Sherman, in leading his army at about the same rate of advance as the Boeotians, covered the meandering route of 300 miles from Atlanta to Savannah in a little over a month, bringing along over 40,000 cattle, mules, and horses and 2,500 wagons. In contrast, from the time Patton's army was activated on August 1, 1944, to the end of the war in May 1945, it had consumed 2,186,792 *tons* of supplies, hauled in by 264,606 trucks. By the end of the war it was nearly 1,000 miles to the east of where it had begun. And like both earlier forces, Patton's men foraged liberally from the farms and shops of occupied Germany.[30]

Epaminondas's destructiveness ultimately lay in some 40,000 spears and short swords wielded by his combined hoplite infantry, and the various bows, javelins, and slings of his accompanying 30,000 light-armed troops: the reputation of that iron kept the Spartans pent up in their acropolis while the Boeotians and Peloponnesians plundered their estates. Sherman's 62,000 men had access to 200 rifle cartridges each, giving the army as a whole the ability to fire off 12,000,000 rounds, backed by 65 cannon. In contrast, Patton's army had issued to it 533,825 *tons* of rifle and artillery ammunition alone, besides close tactical air support from hundreds of low-flying fighter-bombers. At any given time there were in the Third Army over 7,581 tanks, self-propelled guns, armed jeeps, and other combat vehicles, augmented by another 4,482 large and small artillery pieces—seventy times more cannon than those much less lethal weapons on Sherman's caissons. Whereas Epaminondas's and Sherman's men had essentially fed themselves from the countryside, and gathered enough loot to pay for much of their own expenses, the Third Army cost the American taxpayer $240,539,569 in military pay alone over its nine-month lifetime. Patton commanded not so much a rolling army as a veritable metropolis, replete with horrendous problems of maintenance, policing, and payroll.

Moreover, the varieties of modern ordnance—ubiquitous land mines, delayed-action bombs, rapid-moving motorized tanks, dive-bombers, grenades, and flamethrowers—meant casualties undreamed of by either Epaminondas or Sherman. Sherman had written Hood sharp letters over the morality of his shelling Atlanta, and he was repelled by Confederate land mines placed in his army's path. Patton's men shelled indiscriminately, and sought to blow up as many Germans by land mines as they themselves lost. While in the past the indirect approach of Epaminondas and Sherman might ensure almost minuscule casualties, in the industrial age battle of any type, whether waged by fast-moving armored columns or not, meant death at unprecedented levels. The Boeotian and Union armies could avoid attrition by hitting the enemy in the rear; the modern American army would take considerable losses in whatever manner it attacked. War by 1944 had become a very lethal enterprise indeed, hence the need as never before for brilliant tactics that could reduce but never eliminate steady casualties. Epaminondas lost a few hundred of his men in Laconia and Messenia, Sherman about 100 dead, a little over 700 wounded or missing, and another 1,300 captured. In contrast, 27,104 Americans were killed from the Third Army, 86,267 wounded, another 18,975 injured, and 28,237 missing for a combined total of 160,692 casualties. More men were lost with Patton than marched with Epaminondas or Sherman. During the lifetime of the Third Army, which more than any other Allied force sought to outflank the enemy and keep constantly moving, there were 258,924 replacement troops—half the total of its net strength at war's end.

Epaminondas liberated nearly a quarter-million Messenians and perhaps thousands more Laconian Helots at minimal costs. Sherman's march freed over 20,000 slaves directly, and was in part responsible for the emancipation of millions more—all at a cost of a little over 2,000 total casualties. Yet, Patton's horrific combined casualties of 160,692 must be weighed against the thousands of occupied cities liberated, the death camps overrun, and the Third Army's sizable contribution to the overall destruction of the Nazi slave state; in that context the ratio of men lost versus others freed was on a par with the prior two ancient marches of liberation.

Whereas the Thebans and Northerners had not killed great numbers of their adversaries, Patton's Third Army, despite its emphasis on envelopment and the resulting capture of territory—81,522 square miles of conquered land, 12,000 cities, towns, and villages taken—inflicted frightening damage on the enemy. The statistical imbalance between German and Patton dead was staggering: the Third Army had killed over 144,500 of the enemy, five times more dead than it had suffered, and wounded nearly four times as many Germans. In total casualties—dead, wounded, and captured—the Third Army caused the enemy ten times the losses that it suffered—by far the greatest ratio of damage inflicted versus losses incurred in the entire Anglo-American force. The astonishing number of enemy captured—over a million Germans—is a testament to Patton's preference for huge enveloping pincer movements. No other Anglo-American army took so many Germans captive.

Nor did all those numbers occur during the final collapse of the Wehrmacht. In the first two months of operations alone, the Third Army took nearly 94,199 Germans prisoners. Even during the brutal months of November, December, and January, Patton somehow had captured nearly another 60,000 Germans. On the average over the entire nine months of Third Army operations, over 2,724 Germans were taken *each day*. By war's end, Patton's army stretched over 200 miles in width; and it usually fought on a front at least

100 miles wide—sometimes twice as broad as Sherman's swath through Georgia. Since August 1, 1944, when the Third Army had officially become operational near Avranches, Normandy, until May 9, 1945, when it ceased operations a little more than 50 miles from Prague, Czechoslovakia, Patton's men had traveled over 1,000 miles in a circuitous route in a little over nine months, a trek contested by German defenders almost every mile of the way. Despite the cut-off of supplies, the autumn rains, and bloody sieges, the Third Army on average advanced about four miles each day of its existence.

As we shall see, Patton proved that the idea of a great democratic march, an ideological trek in which a fiery commander might pour his spirit of vengeance into his citizen soldiers, was not lost, regardless of the sheer magnitude and deadliness of such an undertaking in the murderous new age of mechanized warfare. Oddly, Patton alone of the American generals accomplished that feat not in the bureaucratic and managerial style of the new corporate and governmental age, but precisely because he alone captured the soul of a past age, in which personal displays of courage, daily haranguing, and a constant presence among his troops would assure his men that he would prefer death to immobility. When division commanders halted in fear of depleting reserves, Patton reminded them that Cortes had burned his ships; when subordinates hesitated to attack, he quoted to them General Grant's dictum that victory went to the exhausted army that would be the first to renew the offensive.[31]

The Germans, who put such a premium on heroic leadership and the martial spirit, expected the American armies lifelessly to plod forward with their huge advantages in matériel and manpower; what they did not anticipate was that nearly a half million of their enemy would barrel into Germany led by a frenzied general every bit as fanatic as their most accomplished Panzer leaders. The Germans had felt their men were Teutonic knights of old imbued with the singular ardor of their Führer; in fact, Patton restored the tradition of the great ideological democratic march, in such a deadly and unforgettable way that finally even his adversaries would acknowledge the far superior prowess and spirit of his Third Army.

On the night of March 22, a divison of the Third Army crossed the Rhine River. Two days later Patton walked over on an American-built pontoon bridge near Oppenheim, as the bulk of his army poured over into the heartland of Germany. In less than fifty days his half-million men would be in Czechoslovakia at the end of their thousand-mile dash, and the Nazi slave state would come to an end.

3

A DEADLY ENEMY

THE ARDENNES, BELGIUM

December 22, 1944 (V-E Day Minus 138 Days)

*Hektor, surely you thought as you killed Patrokolos you would be
safe, and since I was far away you thought nothing of me,
O fool, for an avenger was left, far greater than he was,
behind him and away by the hollow ships. And it was I;
and I have broken your strength; on you the dogs and the vultures
shall feed and foully rip you; the Achaians will bury Patrokolos.*

—Homer, *Iliad*

As HE lay suffocating in Heidelberg, Patton must have also remembered another triumph of his Third Army, almost exactly one year earlier and in some ways his most famous and surely his best publicized—the December 22 drive of the Third Army to relieve the Americans trapped at Bastogne by the surprise German offensive in the Ardennes. That rescue march to the north had helped to stop the last German offensive of the Western theater and had led to Patton's subsequent dazzling final hundred days of the war, when he dashed through the Saar-Palatinate triangle, across the Rhine, and into Czechoslovakia. Yet Patton could race across the Rhine through Germany in March and April 1945 only because the final strategic German reserve had been consumed four months earlier in the Ardennes.

305

The German sudden attack had begun on December 16, 1944, about a hundred miles north of Patton's own Third Army, where Hitler had ordered a deadly counteroffensive in a last-ditch effort to reach a negotiated settlement in the war. If German Panzers could break through the American First Army and drive a hundred miles to the coast at Antwerp, perhaps they could proceed to surround and destroy the British army to the north, wrest away control of the Allies' critical port of supply, and seek a negotiated peace with either America or England.

In retrospect, such thinking seems ludicrous. There were not enough supplies in the Third Reich to sustain even a successful reoccupation of Holland; scarce German manpower, fuel, and equipment could have been put to far better use in establishing a huge mobile reserve east of the Rhine, where it could at least be supplied and enjoy the advantages of an entrenched defense. If a quarter-million Germans were pulled from the front and stacked in the Ardennes, very quickly the Allies would learn the location of the resulting German weak points, and might attack on the flanks of the bulging line that gave the battle its name.

But in Hitler's blinkered thinking, Germany was probably doomed anyway without some sort of eleventh-hour mad gamble. Better to terrorize the Allies with an unexpected hammer blow, and, like the 1940 invasion of France, create such a sudden loss of confidence that entire enemy divisions would either capitulate or run, despite their overall own numerical superiority. After all, even if the German attackers were not as numerous as in the past, there were not many more enemy troops facing the German point of attack in 1944 than had been present on the French front in the Ardennes in 1940.[32]

By mid-December 1945, the Germans, without Allied detection, had somehow massed their last reserves into a huge force of a quarter of a million men. At a little past five-thirty in the morning of December 16, almost 200,000 of those troops, supported by nearly 2,000 artillery pieces and 1,000 tanks, attacked the weakest sector of the Allied line in the Ardennes forest; another 200,000 reserves were available to exploit the breakout. At first glance Hitler's thrust made sense, at least tactically. Facing him were under 70,000 American soldiers of Major General Troy Middleton's VIII Corps. They held a seventy-mile front, three times wider than any sector assigned to other corps, resulting in a division of about 16,000 men being responsible for twenty-six miles of territory—far too porous a line to resist any concentration of applied force. Hitler and his generals had done their homework well. The German attackers in this narrow area of the Ardennes now outnumbered the Americans three to one—and over six to one at the initial point of collision.

Worse still, two of Middleton's three American divisions were worn-out from the prior ninety days of constant fighting in the Hürtgen forest; and the third was a replacement division with no combat experience. In the first hours there were only 242 American tanks among these forces to face the Germans' 1,000 Panthers and Tigers. Hitler had also insisted on radio silence and even a hiatus in coded messages; the Allies' great advantage in being able to read German codes through the ULTRA interception of German intelligence was thus now marginalized. In theory, the December snow and ice would make the Belgian countryside passable for tracked vehicles, in a way not possible during the fall and spring mud. The Panzers had gone through the Ardennes once before in May 1940, when they went on to crush the French army in a matter of days. Consequently, the territory was familiar and the method of the German attack had already been tried with great success. Bad weather was forecast, characterized by snowstorms and overcast skies for the last two weeks of December. Such cloud cover ensured that Allied fighters and dive-bombers could not attack the Panzer columns. Hitler had also ordered small bodies of infiltrators, dressed as Americans, to cause havoc and sow panic behind enemy lines.

Finally, Eisenhower and Bradley had increasingly become complacent and were not expecting a resurgence of German power after the Allied August dash across France. They believed that the shortage of supplies, the terrain, and the weather, not a resurgence in German defenses, had stalled their attack. Middleton's Corps was absolutely stationary when it was overwhelmed, without a clue to the deadly German concentrations a mere few miles away. Bradley confessed in his memoirs of the laxity in the thinking of the Supreme Allied Command, "We were all wrong, of course—tragically and stupidly wrong. After the experience of Mortain, it should have occurred to at least one of us that as we pushed Germany to the wall, Hitler might very well do something crazy and desperate again."

Actually, the threat of a counterattack had occurred "to at least one of us." Nearly three weeks before the blow fell, Patton had noted of the Americans' bothersome immobility: "First Army is making a terrible mistake in leaving the VIII Corps static, it is highly probable that the Germans are building up east of them." In fact, his own intelligence officer, Oscar Koch, had sensed from rail movements that the German assault was imminent and was already thinking of ways the Third Army might react to it. Even before the Germans attacked, Patton ordered his staff to draw up provisional plans for a northward march of succor in case of a German assault in the Ardennes.[33]

Patton, having had his supplies curtailed in early September, was meanwhile growing increasingly restless. The Germans in his own theater had had time to regroup in the fall and had forced an autumn of unaccustomed slogging for the Americans, who advanced in rough terrain against an entrenched defender. The August days of racing across France had ended with the interruption of Patton's gasoline supplies, providing the Germans the opportunity to reconstitute their shattered divisions into a deadly last-ditch resistance. The Germans, who had escaped the Falaise envelopment in August, and once more had fled when Patton was halted in the Lorraine in September, were now to kill thousands of Americans in December.

Patton, the veteran of the trench fighting of World War One, and critic of the pacifism of the thirties that put such an emphasis on entrenchment and fortification in France, shuddered to contemplate that his splendidly mobile Third Army would now have to slog it out against German wire and cement. When Bradley withheld the 83rd Division from Patton and so made it unlikely that Patton would break through to Trier and Koblenz, he inadvertently ensured that the Germans would have a quiet staging point for their offensive.

After relentless and brutal fighting in October and November 1944 against the Siegfried Line, the Third Army felt it was now well enough resupplied for another surprise breakout of its own to commence on December 19—scheduled just three days after Hitler's own attack in the Ardennes. In Patton's thinking, one final attack would collapse German resistance and lead to an enormous American envelopment that could at last reach the Rhine and end with his men in Berlin or, better yet, beyond in Prague. As the Third Army prepared to drive east in a great offensive, the Germans to the north were planning to move west in almost equal numbers. Just as Sherman had continued to march east as Hood went north, so Patton now preferred to continue on his own path into Germany and victory. But would Eisenhower allow Patton to race eastward as scheduled, and have the nearby Montgomery drive from the north to chop off the salient as the beleaguered Americans slowly gave ground?[34]

Of course not. In his memoirs, Eisenhower thought Patton's idea scarcely credible:

> We discussed the advisability of attempting to organize a simultaneous attack somewhat farther to the east, against the southern shoulder of the salient. It was concluded that future events might indicate the desirability of such a move but that for the moment we should, in that locality, merely insure the safety of the shoulder and confine our attacks to the sector indicated.

The language of bureaucratese—"we discussed the advisability of attempting to organize"; "It was concluded that future events might indicate the desirability of"; and "to the sector indicated"—were meant to disguise the terrible reality: after a hundred days of entrenched warfare, the Germans were now coming out in the open and would be exposed. A bold counterattack to their flanks and rear offered a good chance of surrounding a quarter of a million German soldiers and collapsing the Wehrmacht before the first of the year.

But on December 17, Bradley called Patton, urgently demanding help for the tottering divisions of General Hodges's First Army. In the first few hours of the Battle of the Bulge, the Germans had wrecked three American divisions. At the current rate they were probably going to protrude fifty miles unchecked in one thrust into Allied lines. There was now, the Allied command felt, a dire need for Patton to come up from the south and strike the Germans from the flank, to deflate the Germans' progress, giving time for the Americans of the First Army to fashion a new line of defense. Then Montgomery's British army might attack simultaneously the other shoulder of the German salient from the north. After all, if the surprised Americans could hold, there were now over 600,000 Allied troops in the general vicinity that within a few weeks could be redirected against the German protrusion.[35]

The problem, however, for the Third Army was that at that very moment it was not idle. After all the unheroic killing and dying of the past fall, the American persistence was about to pay off. Third Army intelligence officers sensed that German divisions at Patton's front were gradually beginning to crumble. A swift Patton pincer movement might trap them west of the Rhine—the Third Army might begin in December what it would later complete in February and March. Cut off from adequate supplies in September, forced to watch Germans regrouping at his static front, Patton was now asked to turn around and head north to rescue his colleagues at the very instant when the last two months of his bitter fighting had finally born fruit. Patton was now ordered to march a hundred miles north in a snowstorm to fight German troops, many of whom had been removed from his own front, which for the first time in months was now vulnerable to immediate attack. No wonder that Bradley, who initially did not realize the severity of the German attack, was worried about Patton's sure-to-be-angry response to yet another dilution of Third Army strength at precisely the moment it was headed east into Germany.

Secondly, Eisenhower and Bradley were asking Patton to cease his penultimate planning for a massive offensive—his final chance to draft a massive assault to his own liking—to make a ninety-degree turn in midwinter, and to enter an entirely separate theater of operations, something even in summer nearly impossible for a huge army to do without weeks of planning.

Suddenly to turn Third Army ninety degrees to the north along icy roads in terrible weather when its supply dumps were located to support the drive to the *Westwall* was a logistician's nightmare. It posed equally daunting challenges to Patton's subordinate commanders. . . . Only a commander with exceptional confidence in his subordinate commanders and in the professional skill of his fighting divisions could dare risk such a venture. Patton not only never hesitated but embraced the opportunity to turn a military debacle into a triumph.[36]

Patton essentially was being ordered to do in a few days what the Germans had taken months to accomplish: to transfer entire armies from their own sectors to another. But he was moving without warning, at greater distances, and while under attack, not stealthily, from the rear, and after weeks of preparation. There was irony here: at the Falaise Gap and along the Seine River, Patton's request for bold operations to encircle the defeated Germans had been overruled, mostly out of the fear that his Third Army would trespass into zones of operations that were not his own, but properly assigned to either the British, the Canadians, or the American First Army. Now, in their hour of peril, Eisenhower and Bradley suddenly envisioned the Allied line as fluid *without* boundaries, one in which entire armies, as Patton had requested for months, might flow freely in response to the German ebb and flow.

Patton's response to the request and his subsequent right-angle turn into the massive German thrust are, of course, now the stuff of history. At an emergency meeting of Allied commanders called on December 19, three days after the beginning of the German offensive, Eisenhower began to formulate the Allied counterattack. The supreme commander at last turned to Patton, asking when his Third Army could begin the relief of the Americans trapped in Bastogne. Patton replied, "The morning of December 21, with three divisions." Eisenhower, sensing Patton's theatrics, realizing the impossibility of turning around nearly 50,000 men in forty-eight hours in near-zero weather, and aware of the rustling in the room at such an audacious promise, turned on him: "Don't be fatuous, George. If you try to go that early, you won't have all three divisions ready and you'll go piecemeal." Later, of course, he would claim Patton's rapid northward turn was proof of "our flexibility."[37]

Little did Eisenhower realize that just hours before Patton had arrived at the Allied emergency meeting in Verdun, he and his staff had met, anticipated the supreme commander's very request, designed the necessary complicated maneuvers for the rescue, and prepared the entire operation for immediate activation—the minute Patton phoned from the Verdun meeting and gave his officers the code to begin moving.

After more than thirty-four years, it was as if destiny had groomed him for this single, defining instant in which the fate of the war rested upon the right decision being made and carried out by the men in that dingy room. While near panic existed elsewhere, in the Third Army there existed a belief in a magnificent opportunity to strike a killing blow. While others debated or waffled, Patton had understood the problem facing the Allies and had created a plan to counterattack the Germans and occupy Bastogne—which, although not yet surrounded, was clearly soon to be besieged.[38]

Patton sped back to his men, turned his army around, and led an impromptu and brutal march through horrific conditions, in snowy subzero weather, to strike the unsuspecting German offensive in full stride. By mid-January the Germans had run out of steam, the bulge gradually receded as the Allied line stiffened, and the respective armies returned to their assault against the Germans all along the nearly thousand-mile front. In this so-called Battle of the Bulge, the Americans had suffered over 80,000 casualties; the Germans' total losses were probably well over 100,000.

David Irving describes Patton at work during the offensive:

He kept cool. The bulge was getting bigger? Then let it get bigger still. He told Middleton, the VIII Corps commander, to give more ground, so that the enemy would become even more extended, and to blow the bridges in such a way as to channel the enemy advance; then he would hit them in the southern flank. This was Patton—hanging onto the telephone, ordering self-propelled guns and headquarters and artillery and replacements moved about the map, cannibalizing antitank units, creating rifle units, shifting ammunition and hospitals and bridging units to the right places for when the fighting began. Since he had no staff officers with him, he ran the whole show through his army staff at Nancy.

Patton, while elated at his finest hour of service in Europe, felt that once more his magnificent army had been denied a great opportunity—since arriving in Normandy, the *fourth* such occasion that he felt might have shortened the war considerably had he been given his freedom. "Hell, let's have the guts to let the sons of bitches go all the way to Paris. Then we'll really cut them off and chew them up," he had roared at the emergency meeting in Verdun. Trevor Dupuy writes of Patton's boast in light of the eventual Allied strategy to contain rather than cut across the bulge:

It is hard to understand why this concept of using the relatively fresh and victorious XII Corps to cut off the German spearheads was not adopted. Bold, yes. Risky, possibly. Foolhardy, no. Had this been done, about fifteen German divisions, including most of the best armored divisions left in the German Army, might have been cut off, and it is hard to see how, even in speculation, they could have avoided destruction. Had this occurred, the Battle of the Bulge would have ended two weeks earlier than it eventually did, thousands of American and German lives would have been saved, and the war probably would have ended in February or March, instead of in May, sparing many thousands more German, British, American, and Russian lives.

Patton's was the classic preference for the indirect approach, so characteristic of Epaminondas and Sherman, who had also bypassed the immediate tactical threat for the larger strategic goal. With obvious bombast, Patton, the student of twenty-five hundred years of military history, was trying to make an essential point that was lost on his terrified associates—on Eisenhower especially, who called him "impulsive." In Patton's mind, the way to cut off an enemy salient was to attack far to the rear against its shoulders, not to butt up against its neck, much less to attempt to crash back into its head. Nursed on classical military doctrine, in which such encirclements at Marathon and Cannae had led to the collapse of entire armies, Patton felt that had the beleaguered First Army gradually and in order backpedaled, his approaching Third Army might have sliced off the entire base of the German inroad much farther to the east. Rather than push the bulge back in head-to-head bloody fighting, better by far to cut it clean out at its source. The day before Patton's army set out he wrote his wife: "Remember how a tarpon always makes one big flop just before he dies. We should get well into the guts of the enemy and cut his supply lines." But, then, Patton, not Bradley, not Montgomery, would be doing the cutting.

Had Patton been given his way this December, he had even more audacious ideas of how to ruin the German offensive. Let the First Army stiffen and withdraw gradually, let Montgomery attack the northern shoulders of the bulge, and he would let his army race on its present course *eastward,* take Trier, then he could circle north and essentially destroy the entire German army west of the Rhine from the rear, a conglomerate of nearly half a million men to be netted. Like Alexander's cavalry, Hodges and Montgomery could then push the Germans right back into Patton's phalanx of waiting tanks. Had Montgomery attacked decisively from the north at the shoulder of the bulge, Patton might have been free to take his third of a million Americans straight on by the Germans and to end up at their rear blocking their retreat to the Rhine. The German effort in the west might have collapsed by the first of the year.

Patton, of course, knew from his initial conversation with Bradley that he would be under orders to go north, not to continue east: "That's too daring for them. My guess is that our offensive will be called off and we will have to go up there and save their hides." Patton was now in a similar situation to that of Sherman in Atlanta, when Lincoln, Grant, Halleck, and Thomas all worried about Hood's army and its offensive move northward at his rear into Tennessee. But unlike Sherman, Patton was not a theater commander, and was subject to far more stringent control by those distant from the actual fighting. He was directed to go *after* the Germans rather than to their rear—the prudent and predictable course that would stop the offensive, but one that would also ensure that there would now be no dramatic collapse of the German army in 1944. It was as if Epaminondas, on orders from the Boeotarchs, had forgone the great trek into Messenia in order to besiege Sparta or to fight the Spartans in continuous battles while in Laconia—or if Sherman had turned around, left Georgia, and marched northward into Tennessee to hit Hood from the flank.

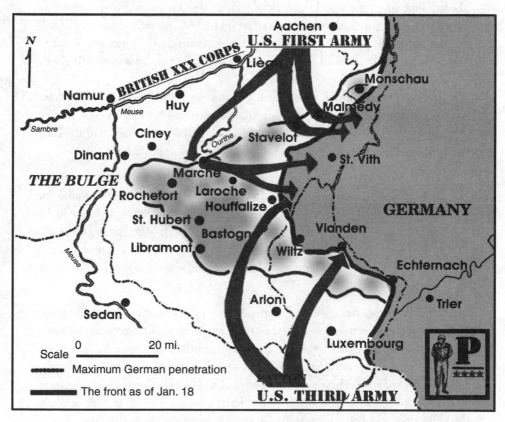

BATTLE OF THE BULGE   JANUARY 1945

In Patton's strategic scenario, Bradley should have been asked to play the role of Thomas—to handle the enemy offensive alone—while his more capable rival made history at the enemy's rear. That was impossible, of course, for two reasons: Bradley had neither the skill nor the nerve of Thomas when faced with a frontal assault, and unlike the latter, he outranked his more flamboyant colleague and thus kept him on a tight leash whenever possible. Eisenhower and Bradley talked grandly of finally getting the Germans out of their fortifications and into the open; but when given the chance to hit such exposed troops in the flank, they passed on the opportunity.[39]

Not that Patton's daring did not also bother all the other American and British commanders, who now for all their optimistic pronouncements about halting the German offensive in effect took counsel of their fears. The key, they felt, to stopping such an immense salient was a conservative attack from all sides, a gradual push, utilizing numerical superiority to restore a linear front. If Patton was late in his proposed encirclement, whether that be his smaller, or preferably larger, hook, then the bulge might become too large to be contained or even burst out at its head. American strategists took the circumspect approach that would guarantee another six months of fighting, rather than the risk of a few more casualties to end the war decisively in December.

Patton, however, and an increasing number of military historians since, felt that such wariness was a grave mistake—but it was neither the first nor, as we have seen, the last error on the side of timidity in the use of the Third Army. Russell Weigley correctly summed up the lost opportunity:

> And Patton certainly recognized the incompleteness of the victory in the Ardennes. He told the same January 1 press conference: "If you get a monkey in a jungle hanging by his tail, it is easier to get him by cutting his tail than kicking him in the face." Kicking him in the face was what Montgomery proposed to do. The First-Third Army convergence on Houffalize was a compromise solution, and cutting the Germans' salient at its tail was never done. The enemy escaped.[40]

The great tragedy of the Bulge was that the Americans suffered the great majority of their dead and wounded in the campaign *after* Bastogne; that is, in late December and January, well after the German momentum had been checked. In horrific conditions of subzero weather, under constant German artillery bombardment, they were now ordered to push the head of the German salient slowly back toward the Rhine. Germans who had been recklessly on the offensive now became even deadlier on the defensive, as GIs were forced to sleep out in the snow and to attack entrenched tanks and machine guns.

Most historians grant that Patton's marvelous race across France, his rescue march at the Battle of the Bulge, and his final onslaught into Germany represented the finest use of American armor and infantry in the Second World War. But Patton's critics also have usually sought to downplay his great march from Normandy to Czechoslovakia on two grounds—that the Americans were fighting a weakened and beaten German army, and the real effort in defeating the Nazis more properly belonged to the Russians, who had waged a much longer and more murderous battle to the east.

Yet despite the undeniable contributions of the Russians, and the horrendous German losses incurred on the Eastern front, the idea that the Western front was somehow a subsidiary theater is simply not true. Patton and the Americans, in fact, destroyed an enormous veteran army and did it far more quickly and efficiently—in time and losses incurred—than did the Russians. The Russians lost millions and killed millions; the Allies lost thousands and had millions of Germans simply surrender. German armies transferred from the Eastern front to the West quickly learned that they could no longer advance with tanks in massed formations as they had against the Russians, inasmuch as American fighter aircraft and mobile artillery—by 1944 in constant radio communications with armored columns—would obliterate Panzers within minutes after they appeared in daylight on major roads.

Second, the Americans were fighting on far more fronts, against far more enemies, at much greater distances from their sources of supply, and were doing it with far greater skill than the Russians, who were engaged on a single linear front, supplied by industries to their immediate rear, and augmented by generous American equipment. American global commitments and the obstacles to their success were far greater than those challenges that confronted either Russia or Germany. These are controversial claims and need to be examined in some detail.

First, what exactly was the nature of the German enemy that Patton faced during his nine months in Europe? It is true that the Germans had been fighting for nearly five years and had taken horrendous casualties, not only in Russia and North Africa where entire armies had vanished, but also just three months earlier in Normandy, with the near destruction of an entire German army group at Falaise. Still, in late 1944 the German economy, under the ruthless direction of Albert Speer, had made astounding gains in the production of armaments, matched by the creation of entire new armies. In a quantitative sense, on the Eastern front the Russians required numerical advantages of from five to even fifteen to one to defeat German divisions. In North Africa, Italy, and Sicily, the British and Americans were also learning that they required at least a two-to-one numerical superiority in fighting troops to defeat the Nazis—given the effectiveness of German command, spirit, and brilliance on the defensive. Past history suggested that a well-equipped German army half the size of its attacking enemy could hold out indefinitely in an entirely defensive role. Hitler and his more fanatic generals envisioned drawing all German divisions back into an iron ring around the fatherland, hoping that the extended Allied supply lines, inevitable bickering between Communist and democratic allies, and the advent of German jets and rockets would force a negotiated settlement in 1946 or beyond.[41]

Yet in particular theaters and at certain loci in the respective battlefronts, such Allied numerical advantages were never assured. Prior to 1944 the German economy had not been on a complete war footing as was true of Russia, England, and to a certain extent America. German industrial potential and manpower reserves before late 1944 had not been fully tapped. This was to change as the eleventh hour arrived. Despite horrendous dislocations caused by bombing, and staggering battlefield losses, the Germans, when the Americans invaded Europe in mid-1944, were fielding armies and equipment at rates unmatched in the past. Even as late as June 1944, the Allies faced nearly 850,000 defenders in the West alone—among the German defenders there had been at least thirty infantry divisions of the highest quality to defend the Normandy beaches—a total that had outnumbered the initial Allied invasion armada. It is often forgotten that in comparison to either the aggregate German or Russian armies fighting in Western and Eastern Europe, the Allies in Normandy were a pitiably small force. As late as September 1944 when Patton was forced to halt when his gas ran out, the Germans were adding 300,000 new troops in August alone, with another 200,000 in both September and October. In August 1944 during the Allies' greatest success, there were roughly 800,000 Germans facing about the same number of American soldiers.

To the north, perhaps even more Germans were pitted against 600,000 Canadian and British troops. These increases more than made up for German losses of nearly a quarter-million dead or wounded, and another quarter-million captured, in Normandy during the summer of 1944. The Allies, not yet realizing that they had won a great victory in Normandy, paused in the pursuit at the moment of their finest success, allowed a desperate Germany a respite, and now essentially had to start over against a new German army larger than the one they had destroyed.

Consequently, in fall 1944 the number of Allied and German combatants in Europe was still roughly equal. While at the end of the year 1944 the Americans would have 2,700,000 troops deployed all over Europe, the majority were in the Air Force or involved in support. Out of that vast figure, only 300,000 were front-line infantry troops in northern Europe. It is a fair generalization to say that the American army simply had too few ground troops in Europe, too many support personnel to the rear, and used those it had on the front without cessation to the point of depletion. Michael Doubler remarks on the exhaustion that finally set in on the American divisions: "Between D-Day and V-E Day stretched 337 days, during which many divisions endured near continuous commitment in battle. Half of the infantry divisions spent over 150 days in combat, and 40 percent spent 200 days or more. Two divisions saw more than 300 days of action."

In contrast to the Americans' tendency to underman their armies, the Germans in their final hour put every able-bodied man into front-line defense. Women and foreign workers replaced German male craftsmen in the factories. Draft call-ups now extended to all those seventeen years of age, as men well in to their late thirties were collected for front-line divisions. Even during January 1945 as the Ardennes campaign wore down, there were still seventy German divisions facing seventy-three Allied. In short, the American army in Europe was operating ever more distant from home at precisely the time the German nation was at last putting its entire manpower reserves forward to resist it.

From September 1939 to April 1945 17,893,200 men passed through the Wehrmacht and Waffen SS; taking 90 million as the population basis, some 3.6 percent of the entire population must have passed through the armed forces each year. At their peak strength in 1943 the armed forces constituted well over 10 percent of this basis; a figure which in all probability has been exceeded only in Israel, and then during a war lasting days or weeks, not five and a half years.

Moreover, the German economy as late as November 1944 on the eve of the Ardennes offensive was still turning out 213,342 rifles a month, 25,741 machine guns, 1,025 tank guns, as well as howitzers and infantry cannon at unprecedented rates. The Allies had entered Europe when German munitions production, for all the losses, was at all-time highs. Yet statistics cannot really capture the horror in store for thousands of GIs who were to go up against hardened German troops, outfitted liberally with the most lethal weapons in the world.[42]

Moreover, the Germans were now fighting on the defensive. In addition to the natural advantage that always falls to entrenched troops, Hitler's divisions were sometimes showing an upswing, not a downturn, in morale—or at least a savage desperation not seen even in the first two triumphant years of the war. A week into the fighting in the Bulge, a German lieutenant could write home to his wife on December 22:

You cannot imagine what glorious hours and days we are experiencing now. It looks as if the Americans cannot withstand our important push. Today we overtook a fleeting column and finished it. . . . It was a glorious bloodbath, vengeance for our destroyed homeland. Our soldiers have the old zip. Always advancing and smashing everything. The snow must turn red with American blood. Victory was never as close as it is now. The decision will soon be reached. We will throw them into the ocean, the arrogant, big-mouthed apes from the New World. They will not get into Germany. We will protect our wives and children from all enemy domination. If we are to preserve all tender and beautiful aspects of our lives, we cannot be too brutal in the deciding moments of this struggle.

Like doomed Spartans and Confederates of the past, the Nazi armies were indeed now fighting for their homes and way of life—a far greater incentive than the conquest of Russia or North Africa. Like those in the uniform of the Confederacy, German soldiers, whatever their own views toward Hitler, rightly feared the image of the postwar Allied occupation, which promised changes in their Nazified society every bit as radical as the Union plans for the defeated South or Epaminondas's liberation of the Messenian Helots.

"When the Führer says that we have the means and the weapons to push the enemy back once more from our borders," wrote one corporal in August 1944, "and that we will ultimately wring victory from him, then I know very well that an unbending trust and a strong and uncompromising belief in the Führer are essential to overcome this momentarily difficult period. . . . Belief gives the strength to bear all hard and difficult sorrow. . . . My belief in the Führer and in victory is unshakable." Even the so-called Volkssturm divisions of recent call-ups had recaptured the German offensive spirit in December. Major General Heinz Kokott remarked of their zeal to fight the Americans: "They were fully conscious of their decisive act, confident in their ability, their strength and the promise of strong air support as well as the effort by the war industries at home. Equipment, organization and armament were up-to-date and good."[43]

True, since the Anglo-American forces did not execute German prisoners or starve them on a massive scale as had been true in Russia, there was not the rationale that fighting to the bitter end was better than surrender. And there was not the specter that defeat meant the massive killing and raping of German civilians as would occur with the Russian capture of Berlin. But Propaganda Minister Goebbels had informed the German people of the so-called Morgenthau Plan, an Allied working paper for postwar German occupation drawn up by the American secretary of the treasury, Henry J. Morgenthau, and endorsed by Roosevelt and Churchill in Quebec on September 15, 1944, that advocated turning Germany into "a country primarily agricultural and pastoral in its character." Germany was to be an impotent nation "stripped of all presently existing industries but so weakened and controlled that it cannot in the foreseeable future become an industrial area. . . . All industrial plans and equipment not destroyed by military action shall either be completely dismantled or removed from the area or completely destroyed."

By late 1944, Morgenthau was real fodder for the German Propaganda Ministry in its daily addresses to German soldiers fighting in the West:

> For once Goebbels did not need to distort the truth. He could rightly claim that the Allies were proposing to turn the Reich into "a potato patch" and the *Völkischer Beobachter* was hardly overstating the case when he declared that the plan would mean "the destruction of German industry to such an extent that fifty per cent of the German population would be faced with starvation or would be forced to emigrate as working slaves. . . . Germany has no illusions about what is in store for her people if they do not fight with all available means against an outcome that would make such plans possible. The Quebec decision will serve only to redouble German resistance." This was indeed its effect, as captured letters written by front-line troops were soon to show.[44]

The Americans, often over British objections, opted for a policy of unconditional surrender, which required the devastation of the German cities, the physical occupation of the German homeland, and the postwar reconstruction of the country—rather than seeking a negotiated peace that asked Germans to renounce Nazism and lay down their arms. America had decided that it must annihilate, not just beat, the German nation. After years of leaflet-dropping on German cities and back-door negotiations through third-party intermediaries, it was clear there was no groundswell of popular German support for replacing Hitler. A German army analysis of letters from 44,948 front-line soldiers in August 1944 after the failed assassination attempt on Hitler bears this out: "The high number of expressions of joy at the Führer's deliverance, presented as a real stroke of good fortune for the German people, prove not only the love and loyalty of the soldiers to the Führer, but also reveal . . . the soldiers' strong determination to fight and win." In truth, all Germans, whatever their views of Hitler, saw the Allied effort as essentially one aimed at crushing and destroying their culture—and they would now fight to the bitter end to prevent their feared extinction. For most of the Ardennes offensive, the German soldier believed both in his cause and in his ability to keep the Americans out of Germany. A German wrote home to his family on Christmas Eve 1944 to just that effect:

It is absolutely certain that the American is going to get something he did not under any circumstances reckon with. For the "Ami," as we call him, expected that he would celebrate Christmas in Berlin, as I gather from his letters. Even I, as a poor private, can easily tell that it won't take much longer until the Ami will throw away his weapons.

Even earlier during widespread retreats of late summer and fall 1944, numerous captured German soldiers gave no hint that loss of morale was sweeping the army—an army that, unlike the American, was recruited and organized in the manner of classical Greek and Roman regiments of old on a regional basis. When Patton's men met such troops in France, they were fighting often against small teams of friends and even relatives, many of whom had known each other for years. An interrogator of the Third Army reported the pronouncements of a German sergeant in October 1944: "He looked us in the eye, and snapped back, 'That is only the fortunes of war. We have been retreating lately, but you have retreated before, and you will again. You will see. In the end we will win.'"

Such bluster and cockiness were not isolated examples. Systematic surveys by Americans of German POWs revealed that more than two-thirds still believed in Adolf Hitler—this as late as November 1944. John Keegan summed up the German will to resist even in the very last days of the war:

> The army's fighting power was legendary. Alone among those of the First World War, it had retained its morale and cohesion almost to the very end, and in the process brought about the disintegration of the Russian army, inflicted something close to breakdown on the French and Italian armies, and visited a severe moral crisis on the British army. In 1945 it was to demonstrate an even greater and more remarkable resolution. In East Prussia, in Silesia, on the Vistula and at Lake Balaton, it was to lose men in the hundreds of thousands. . . . The fighting spirit of the German army derived ultimately from its own character. . . . Like the warriors of the Teutonic tribes of old, they were resolved if necessary to die where they stood.

Or else. We should also remember that, while the Americans executed one GI for failing to advance under fire in World War Two, the Germans tried and shot 50,000 of their own soldiers for either desertion or cowardice. An American private describes a savage local German attack of February 1945, which is reminiscent of the historian Livy's graphic description of the carnage at Cannae:

> Although our artillery and mortar fire was poured into the ranks of the fanatical SS men, it was ultimately rifle fire that stopped them. Some of the Ger-

mans were dropped in their tracks only a dozen feet from the American positions. Bodies of friend and foe were found literally in the same foxholes, so active was the fighting. The Germans were using with extravagance their only remaining source of defense—the bodies of their soldiers.

Among both the Nazis at the top and select soldiers in the front, there was a growing sense that the sheer suffering and barbarism of the war, even the approaching doom of defeat and slaughter, was somehow good for the German *Volk* in at last testing its real spiritual mettle. Germans retreated leaving behind booby traps, and bombs with delayed fuses, and they occasionally executed prisoners and murdered even their own wavering civilians, as they were determined to delay and kill as many Americans as possible if there was really to be a *Götterdämmerung*.[45]

Patton also had to contend with the weather, the terrain, and the question of extended supply lines—all of which increasingly favored the Germans as 1944 wore on and the Third Army neared the Rhine. By November the rains and early snows had turned most roads into quagmires and prevented the easy cross-county movement of heavily armored vehicles, giving the advantage to troops who were dug in and established rather than to those attacking through reliance on mobile tanks and troop carriers. Moreover, the terrain of eastern France and western Germany was mountainous and forested, not flat and clear as had been the case in southern and central France. Small pockets of German soldiers, taking advantage of intimate acquaintance with the local geography, and employing concrete fortifications and pillboxes in ravines, passes, and dense vegetation, could and did bushwhack entire American columns.

Denied open expanses and firm ground, American armor—with narrow tracks poorly suited for cross-country driving—was increasingly confined to winding mountain roads, which were easily defended by camouflaged defenders. On the border between France and Germany was the so-called West Wall, or Siegfried Line—extensive fortifications built during the 1930s that the Germans now manned and improved, giving them a solid line of sheltered defense west of the Rhine. The autumn days were growing shorter and more overcast, cutting drastically the number of hours that American fighters could range over the battlefield and attack the Panzers.

The German supply lines were, of course, no longer global, but increasingly confined to central Europe, allowing divisions to be transferred up and down the Western front—and even from east to west, north and south, as the Russian and Allied offensive ebbed and surged. As Germans retreated from Italy, and their occupied territory in southern Europe was abandoned, more divisions were available to be deployed in the West. The German army might have been overstretched in its occupation of the entirety of Europe, but for purposes of guarding its own borders, it was a relatively huge force—especially against an enemy whose goal, unlike in World War One, was not armistice but rather total victory and the literal occupation of Germany and the capture of the Nazi government. In addition, there was always the suspicion on the part of the uneasy Allies that either Russia or the Anglo-Americans might pause to allow the Germans to concentrate on the other—a paranoia that would only increase as the Reich deflated, Goebbels's propaganda grew more sophisticated, and the once great distance between the Eastern and Western German commands shrunk to a few hundred miles. As the Allies approached along a broad front, German lines retracted and tended to form a circle around the fatherland and in some cases to increase in depth, making it also easier to shift troops to the most pressing breech along a circular perimeter.

In contrast to the German situation, Patton's army was supplied largely by truck, and the distance from the Normandy depots was now reaching six hundred miles and more. Unlike the case of the other North American and British armies, the superb port at Antwerp was hundreds of miles to Patton's immediate rear. Because trucks consumed considerable amounts of fuel, the increasingly longer routes back to the Normandy ports resulted in the law of diminishing returns as more and more of the available stocks were needed simply to power the transport of gasoline.

If the German army was rapid and lethal on the offensive, it was also nearly impossible to defeat when dug in on the defensive. We should remember that while the German army had gone from the Siegfried Line to the Atlantic Ocean in six weeks in 1940, it required four months for the Allies to push them out of France. While the Nazis had nearly reached Moscow in five months after crossing the Russian border in June 1941, it required the Russians nearly forty months to recross the same distance. True, the Germans had attacked unexpectedly and against an unprepared foe in both cases, but the sheer fighting spirit and capability of its men in the field explains much of their lethal record.

The unpredictability of Hitler's overall command of the theater aided the Allies—especially his tendency to refuse requests for German retreats that led to entire armies being cut off and gobbled up. Yet, the Allies were commanded by generals who, while products of excellent military training and education, were nevertheless novices in comparison to the German field commanders. The latter had five years of battle experience and had already played the role of fast-moving attackers in the forests of the Ardennes. Eisenhower and Bradley, for example, had never been in combat before the war started—in marked contrast to the German high command, who from Hitler on down had either fought in World War One or been at the front in France, Russia, or North Africa before 1942.

Much has been written about the Allied superiority in the quantity of military equipment. The virtually endless productive capacity of the United States finally did ensure eventually that along the Allied front as a whole there were far more tanks, heavy artillery, airplanes, and motorized vehicles than on the German side—the Americans produced more Sherman M4 tanks, for example, than all British and German tanks combined. U.S. weaponry, from the Sherman tank to the excellent .30-caliber M1 infantry rifle to the 105-mm howitzer, was plentiful, reliable, and by late 1944 expertly employed. American trucks and tanks needed less maintenance and were better designed for durability than their German counterparts. American artillery was the best in the world, due both to its considerable supply of excellent guns and a masterful system of radio communications and fire direction; the adoption of proximity fuses on artillery shells also increased the danger to German ground troops from American artillery barrages. In general, Americans had access to more artillery ammunition that was of better quality than any other army in the world.

Whereas German divisions still depended on horse-drawn wagons for supplies and equipment, American divisions were powered by three-ton trucks and armored personnel carriers to transport both men and matériel. The German insistence on a multiplicity of weapon designs, laborious craftsmanship, and interference in the arms industry by high-ranking and rather ignorant Nazi officials all tended to produce ingenious weapons that nevertheless had problems in maintenance and were not so easily or quickly mass produced.

All that being said, the Germans enjoyed vast advantages in the lethal quality of individual weaponry in a variety of disturbing areas. If such matchless Wehrmacht armament was not as plentiful, uniform, or reliable as the Americans', it nevertheless was often more deadly. In concentrated thrusts, where the best-equipped German divisions might hit the Americans along a rather narrow front, there was a good chance that even in the last year of the war the German soldier was better armed and equipped man-for-man than the American. In the close fighting in the Ardennes, for example, the faster-firing German machine pistol was more effective than the American .30-caliber M1 rifle. Although a German division might have 1,200 fewer combat infantrymen than its American counterpart, the presence of such automatic weapons in the hands of German infantrymen gave it far more firepower as a whole. Furthermore, German light and heavy machine guns could fire hundreds more rounds *per minute* than their American counterparts. Their mortar and antitank guns—75-mm and 88-mm versus the Americans' 57-mm weapon—were far superior, and the Germans' handheld rocket-launched anti-armor weapons were unlike anything in the American arsenal.

The most embarrassing gulf was in heavy battle tanks. The Sherman M4 was no match for the late models of German Panther, much less the Tiger. Late-model Panthers were faster, better protected, and equipped with far more firepower than even the most up-to-date Shermans. When the Americans landed in Normandy, most Shermans were still armed with the short-barreled, low-velocity 75-mm gun, while German tanks were standardly outfitted with a long-barreled, high-muzzle-velocity 75-mm and the dreaded 88-mm cannon of the Tigers. Hundreds of eyewitness reports record Sherman tank rounds literally bouncing off Tigers and even Panthers, while a single shot from either of the two German tanks could send a Sherman up in flames. One of the great scandals of the war was that all of Patton's armored columns were spearheaded by Sherman tanks that had not a prayer of a chance against their German counterparts in strictly tank-to-tank warfare.

Although there were far more of the reliable Shermans than German Panthers and clanky Tigers, in the Ardennes proper the ratio was about equal, giving the Germans a clear edge due to their superior quality alone. As General Bradley dryly remarked of the American strategy of surrounding Panthers and Tigers with more numerous Shermans, "This willingness to expend Shermans offered little comfort to the crews who were forced to expend themselves as well." In the tradition of its famous Civil War namesake, the Sherman was designed for speed, maneuverability, and to be effective through plenitude not for head-on assault against enemy artillery and heavy armor.[46]

The Americans' strength lay in rapid motorized assaults, in which hordes of Shermans, supported by the tactical airpower, could trap, surround, and overwhelm German armor in flat and exposed terrain. But in the forests and hills of eastern France and western Germany, during winter under overcast clouds, it was an entirely different war—one that Patton had dreaded months earlier, since superior German armor, supported by troops with excellent automatic weapons and antitank guns, could wreak havoc on the Americans. Stephen Ambrose describes Joachim Peiper's SS armored regiment that drove into the Ardennes against the Americans; no comparable American regiment, or even an entire division, possessed such firepower:

Although designated a regiment, Peiper's force contained some 22,000 men and 250 tanks (many of them right off the assembly line and including sixty Tigers), five anti-aircraft half-tracks, a battalion of 20mm guns, twenty-five self-propelled guns, a battalion of 105 howitzers, and two companies of engineers.

Richard Overy summed up well the general German advantages that forestalled earlier Allied victory in France during 1944:

It was by no means preordained. The balance of technology was at best even, though German heavy tanks, the Panthers and Tigers, outgunned those of their opponents. Until well into June the manpower of the 7th Army and von Schweppenburg's Panzer Group outnumbered the invading force; and possessed much greater density of both manpower and firepower than German armies in the east. Moreover the German forces had in general much tougher battle experience than their enemy.[47]

Under no circumstances, Patton believed, should Americans settle down to a war of attrition against better-armed, entrenched, and veteran German divisions. Yet that was precisely the mode of warfare to come from September 1944 to February 1945.

Nor did the respective German, Russian, and American larger strategic situations necessarily favor American troops in Normandy. From September 1939 to June 1944, Germany had *not* fought on two large diverse continental fronts. From late 1939 to mid-1941, Hitler was essentially in control of all the territory from the Atlantic to the Russian border without major resistance— an area comprising the entirety of the modern NATO alliance and recently disbanded Warsaw Pact combined, whose vast industrial base was to be exploited and integrated into the German economy by the Nazis. The German alliance with Italy at least tied down far more American and British troops in the Mediterranean than German ones. Germany had a far more aggressive ally in Japan, which caused the Russians to deploy as insurance from invasion nearly forty divisions on its eastern border, and forced the Americans to fight a huge two-front war. For most of World War Two, America, not Germany, was in the unenviable position of fighting in two theaters thousands of miles from home; indeed Japan had seemed a greater threat to the United States homeland in December 1941 than Russia had been to Germany proper six months earlier.

Similarly, the Russians—who had once signed a nonaggression pact with Hitler that enabled the Germans to concentrate on Britain alone—were fighting a single enemy on their own turf. Their armies were almost exclusively supplied by truck or rail from home industry, without thousands of miles of vulnerable sea-lanes. By 1945 the Germans had shifted great numbers of troops to the West to stop the Allied onslaught, which for the first time allowed rapid Russian advances into Eastern Europe.

Although the Russians had over five times as many divisions as the Allies in Europe—by late 1944 some 500 to 76—half the divisional strength of the

German army *was in the West*. The Germans deployed 2,299 new tanks and assault guns in the last two months of 1944 against the Americans and British, yet shipped eastward only 921 to stop the Russians. In short, the German army, which had been fighting at full strength against the Russian army for three years, in 1944 transferred divisions and created new ones so that half its total infantry and armor was now pitted against a foe one-fifth the size of the Russian army, but whose position, mobility, and dash posed the greater immediate threat to the fatherland.

In large part the huge, though belated, Russian advances of late 1944 and 1945 came against a German army that had withdrawn half its strength to the West. Seventy-six Allied divisions would travel farther and faster in a year than the entire Russian army had in four against a German enemy that was eventually of roughly comparable size. German industry, thousands of its aircraft, and its entire antiaircraft artillery were attacked almost exclusively by American and British bombers, and had little to fear from the strategic Russian air force.[48]

While the American army fought in Europe, it was also conducting an air offensive, not merely against Germany, but increasingly against Japan too. Literally thousands of Americans soldiers—and British as well—were engaged in strategic bombing, fighter escort, and carrier-based attacks, and so were not available to infantry forces in Europe, which increasingly in late 1944 could not count on sizable reinforcements. Neither Germany nor Russia had a real strategic bombing capability, carrier-based air arm, or even much of a surface fleet, much less a large merchant marine. In addition, American industry was sending unheard-of amounts of war matériel to Stalin; thus while Patton's army was short of trucks and gasoline, American industry shipped thousands of tons of supplies to the Red Army. By war's end, for example, the United States would supply the Soviets with over 375,000 six-wheel GMC transport trucks—to Patton's dismay, more than those available to American armies in Europe. For the most part, American industry and its merchant marine and navy organized the supply effort to equip the entire Allied cause.

Neither Germany nor Russia had been involved in a two-front war from the beginning of the hostilities; neither country's army was supplied entirely by distant sea-lanes; both put the majority of their resources into land-based troops in or near their homeland; and both were able to rely on the industrial production of other nations—the Germans through coercion in Western and Eastern Europe, the Russians through American and British largess. By fall 1944, Patton fought with equipment trucked nearly six hundred miles from ports, where it had been unloaded after being shipped—often under constant attack from submarines—across thousands of miles of the Atlantic Ocean.

His adversaries were being supplied from German factories a few hundred miles from the front, whose aggregate production went up, not down, each month that Patton raced through France.

The result of this strategic picture on Patton's Third Army? While American manpower reservoirs were more considerable than Germany's, and while potential American industrial output was far greater, the Americans nevertheless faced commitments both as belligerents and Allies that ensured the Third Army could not be given either material or psychological precedence in the war effort. As Patton fought the Germans near the Rhine, the Americans were beginning a comprehensive strategic-bombing campaign against the Japanese, sending constant convoys to Russia and England, continuing their murderous daylight bombing of Germany, slogging in Italy and advancing through the Pacific islands in a series of bloody assaults.

Patton's army is properly to be seen as an advance force far from home, with tenuous supply lines, driving to the heartland of the enemy as part of one vast American war effort—an effort on land, sea, and in the air far beyond the capabilities of either its German adversary or its Russian ally. As we shall see, Patton's Third Army per se did not even warrant preference in the European theater of Allied ground operations. In the Ardennes, although Patton ostensibly commanded 353,655 men, he came to a point when he had only two battalions in reserve. Such was the radical need for American infantrymen across the globe.[49]

Generals should be content to defeat the armies they face. As architects of military power alone, they are not supposed to collapse entire cultures. When in rare instances through rapid marches into the enemy interior they appear to do so, historians tend to deprecate that achievement, most often by arguing that the caliber of enemy opposition was suspect or perhaps already collapsing. But the Spartan army that was defeated at Leuctra, and the red-cloaked hoplites who the next year watched passively as Epaminondas plundered the Laconian landscape and freed a great many of their Helots were not impotent. Later in 368 in a set battle they defeated an Arcadian army, which was temporarily bereft of its Theban allies. Instead, what made these red-cloaked warriors seem weak was the sheer audacity and mobility of Epaminondas's columns, whose rate of speed, uncertainty of direction, and ultimate intentions completely confused the Spartans.

So too with Sherman. His march, we are told, was made against scant opposition. But, as we have seen, there were up to 30,000 available troops to oppose him in Georgia. That there were not more is due in no large part to his continual fighting the prior summer of 1864 when he wore down Johnston and then Hood. That no real opposition in Georgia materialized against him in November 1864 is a testament both to his past effectiveness in battle and to the rapidity and unpredictability of his advance, which left the Southern army unsure of where he was going or what he would do.

The same situation applies to Patton. He raced through Normandy, charged to Bastogne, and dashed across the Rhine not because the German army was either intrinsically weak or dispirited, but rather because his mobility and tactics left them troubled as to where he was going and what he intended. That he traveled faster, farther, inflicted more casualties, and suffered less harm than other Allied armies bears out this assertion—he certainly had no more advantages than the French army had in 1940, the British army in Egypt, the American army in Italy, or his own associates in Normandy. If the Allied master battle plan had been followed to the letter, Montgomery, not Patton, should have been the real threat to the German heartland.

As the Third Army occupied Bastogne and helped to deflate the German counterassault, Patton on the first day of 1945 praised his men, emphasizing the nature of their long march from Normandy, the caliber of the enemy opposition, and the ideological nature of their struggle:

> From the bloody corridor at Avranches, to Brest, thence across France to the Saar, over the Saar into Germany, and now on to Bastogne, your record has been one of continuous victory. Not only have you invariably defeated a cunning and ruthless enemy, but also you have overcome by indomitable fortitude every aspect of terrain and weather. Neither heat nor dust nor floods nor snow have stayed your progress. The speed and brilliancy of our achievements are unsurpassed in military history. . . . Under the protection of Almighty God and the inspired leadership of our President and the High Command, you will continue your victorious course to the end that tyranny and vice shall be eliminated, our dead comrades avenged, and peace restored to a war weary world.

Driving up behind his 90th Division on January 6 in the Ardennes— trucks bringing GIs into battle in Arctic conditions, ambulances racing in the other direction with Third Army wounded—Patton was startled that at the height of their discomfort and danger, his men let out a cheer at his presence. "It was," Patton recorded, "the most moving experience of my life." In words reminiscent of Sherman, he immediately concluded of Third Army's progress in the Ardennes, "No country can stand against such an army."[50]

4

A COG IN THE WHEEL?

THE LORRAINE, FRANCE

August 29, 1944 (V-E Day Minus 253 Days)

Fate is the same for the man who holds back, the same if he fights hard.
We are all held in a single honor, the brave with the weaklings.
A man dies still if he has done nothing, as one who had done much.

—Homer, *Iliad*

T LEAST Patton had been moving in the bitter December cold of the Ardennes. A few months earlier his supplies had been cut and his tanks stopped—at precisely the moment the Third Army was barreling into the western border of Germany under clear skies and on dry ground. Little did he know that his army would come to rest at the end of August, cut off from sufficient supplies in front of an entrenched enemy for the next hundred days until it was called northward to Bastogne.

Yet tanks, men, generals, and guns in themselves cannot win wars. Even in the modern age of industry and technology, George Patton was convinced that victory still hinged upon the warrior soul of his army. Spirit could prompt soldiers to accomplish things far beyond their apparent material limitations; in turn, the absence of audacity might allow well-equipped and plentiful troops simply to quit in dejection. For a brief moment—an unforgiving minute only—George Patton in the last week of August 1944, as he entered the Lorraine, had a spirited American army of a sort not seen since Sherman's Army of the West entered Georgia, one that might overcome the material limitations of the new warfare and crush the German army for good.

In the latter part of August, Patton had finally been given clearance to continue his advance and for the last few days had been charging full speed from the Seine River to the Lorraine region of eastern France. "Damn it, Brad," Patton screamed to General Bradley on August 31, "just give me 400,000 gallons of gasoline and I'll put you inside Germany in two days." Once across the Rhine, Patton cared little that he would be far ahead of his lines of support, that the strategic prizes of the industrial Ruhr and Berlin were far to the north, that he was not following the original intent of Normandy planners, or that there were still hundreds of thousands of Germans who might circle to his rear. No, once the Third Army was in Germany and in hot pursuit of defeated men, the Germans would collapse as Patton's huge and now arrogant American army chased the Panzers back to their homes. Epaminondas's experience in Laconia and Sherman's in Georgia suggest that Patton was right: advancing victorious democratic armies do have a deleterious effect on the spirit of the enemy that can lead to sudden disintegration— but only if they are allowed by wary overseers to continue on when the enemy is in flight.[51]

As far as Patton was concerned, there should never have been a Battle of the Bulge in December 1944 and January 1945, much less a Rhine crossing in the spring of 1945. The war against Germany in the West should have been settled outright in late August and early September 1944, right here in the Lorraine. A little over three months before the great German December offensive in the Ardennes, Patton had raced from the Seine and across the Meuse River, as thousands of scattered and demoralized Germans trailed back in small groups with scant equipment to the fatherland. For a moment the way to Germany was wide open and the border less than a hundred miles away. Patton was moving his Third Army headquarters sixty to eighty miles forward every three to four days. The summer gallop through southern France had essentially crumbled all German resistance in the West—at least for a few days until retreating units could meet new divisions racing up from Germany to fashion some sort of resistance near the Siegfried Line on the German border.

"With German forces in total disarray at the end of August," Carlo D'Este has written, "a virtually undefended Lorraine beckoned like the Rhine sirens of mythology." Patton was poised on the eastern banks of the Meuse River and now sensed that the Wehrmacht itself was tottering. A final drive over the

Rhine would create such terror among the remnants of the defeated armies that Hitler's resistance would cease. The dreaded West Wall, or Siegfried Line, that constituted Germany's last defense at the end of August was essentially undefended, the doors to the pillboxes rusted, the keys lost. The German chief of staff in the West summed up the state of Nazi resistance at that point: "There were no German forces behind the Rhine," remarked General Günther Blumentritt, "and at the end of August our front was wide open."

Most of France had been liberated in a matter of weeks, and nearly half a million German soldiers had been killed, captured, or were missing. Again the key was *not* to stop, even for a second—"It was a good time to quote Kipling's poem, 'If,'" Patton wrote. "If you can fill the unforgiving minute with sixty seconds' worth of distance run." The backpedaling Germans must not be given even a single day to rest, to reform lines of defense, and to receive new equipment. Since Italy and the Balkans were lost to the Germans, withdrawn Panzer divisions—like the crack 15th Panzer Grenadiers—might hurry back to Germany and be immediately deployed against Patton; the German thin shell must now be smashed before it shrank slowly enough to coalesce and toughen. Patton wrote his wife of just this brief German window of vulnerability, which he felt was already passing away as the Americans paused: "Books will some day be written on that 'pause which did not refresh' any one but the Germans." The cutoff in Patton's supplies during the last week of August and first week of September was the *third* occasion since the inauguration of the Third Army that Patton had been overruled by Bradley and Eisenhower—again with disastrous results for the Allied cause in general. German divisions in shambles at the end of August would be reequipped with armor in the Ardennes in December.[52]

As August wore down, everything in the Third Army came to a grinding halt in the Lorraine area of eastern France—a strategically key, hotly contested borderland of rolling hills, lakes, and streams that had served in most European wars as the historic passageway from France to Germany. Unlike the ability of the Boeotian or Union army to find food and forage, a motorized horde of hundreds of thousands could not easily plunder all the necessary gasoline from the countryside. Patton's men confiscated tons of enemy fuel and captured hordes of food, but in comparison to what was needed on a daily basis, the army was literally starved.

In the Lorraine in late August the Third Army simply ran out of gas and sputtered to a halt. Patton, in fact, needed between 300,000 and 400,000 gallons *a day* to keep his vast mobile army of over a quarter of a million men moving at the rate he felt necessary to pressure the Germans into disintegration. But on August 29, the decision was made by Eisenhower and his subordinates not to meet Patton's fuel requests. By August 31 the Third Army was receiving just 31,000 of its requested allotment of 400,000 gallons. Worse was to come—on September 2, the entire army received only 25,390 gallons of fuel, scarcely enough gas to support a single division. "Give us gasoline," Patton pleaded, "we can eat our belts." At first, Patton's men welcomed the respite and thought it only a momentary lapse in supply, a logical interruption given their Herculean labors of August:

> The tanks of Third Army had stopped and the guns had ceased to fire. The infantry pulled off the road and bivouacked under the trees or in barns. Headquarters moved into châteaux or comfortable farm houses. The mood was still light-hearted: the war would be over in a matter of weeks. Soon petrol would come and all would ride on to further triumphs over the Rhine and beyond.[53]

Patton, the old cavalry commander and veteran of tank warfare in World War One, North Africa, and Sicily, knew better. Like Epaminondas and Sherman, he sensed that respite was terrible for the morale of his army and critical in allowing the Germans to fashion static defenses in the increasingly difficult terrain of eastern France and western Germany. But unlike the former two, he could do nothing about it, impotent either to find fuel on his own or to persuade Eisenhower to order him more supplies. On August 30, Patton sounded desperate and at his wits' end when he again wrote to his wife, "I have to battle for every yard but it is not the enemy who is trying to stop me, it is 'They.' . . . No one else ever tries as hard. But they are learning. Now the infantry rides the tanks, guns, anything that moves, to get forward. It is not pretty, but it works. Look at the map! If I could only steal some gas, I could win this war." Patton now sensed that the sheer audacity of the Third Army—whatever its inferior size in comparison with the German resistance and the vulnerability on its flanks—could end the war while the weather was warm, the landscape dry, and the Germans disorientated—*if* his supplies were just kept at present levels and not curtailed:

> The twenty-ninth of August was, in my opinion, one of the critical days in this war, and hereafter many pages will be written on it—or, rather, on the events which produced it. It was evident at this time that there was no real threat against us as long as we did not allow ourselves to be stopped by imaginary enemies. . . . It was my opinion then that this was the momentous error of the war. So far as the Third Army was concerned, we not only failed to get the back gas due us, but got practically no more, because in consonance with the decision to move north, in which two corps of the First Army also partici-

pated, all supplies—both gasoline and ammunition—had to be thrown in that direction.[54]

Patton added in his diary that the delay would surely mean horrendous American casualties of the type incurred during World War One on the same ground: "Montsec has a huge monument to our dead. I could not help but think our delay in pushing forward would probably result, after due course of time, in the erection of many other such monuments for men who, had we gone faster, would not have died."[55]

Postwar statistics bear out Patton's macabre assessment. Patton, who had driven nearly four hundred miles eastward to the Moselle River in a mere thirty days in August, would now, without adequate supplies and against an entrenched enemy, require a hundred days to crawl a little over twenty to thirty miles farther east of the river. The war would not end in late summer 1944, but go on to spring 1945. Patton's August boast that in "exactly two weeks the Third Army has advanced farther and faster than any Army in the history of war" was probably true; his motorized columns did not depend on horse-drawn wagons like the German's great dashes into France in 1940 and Russia in 1941. Whereas the ocean stopped the former and the winter the latter, Patton's drive came to a halt simply due to lack of fuel—at a time when the weather, the road conditions, and the state of enemy resistance were all conducive to further advance. The fires of Auschwitz and Buchenwald would burn on, as the fastest-moving Allied army now simply halted in the face of nonexistent opposition.

The sober British military historian Hubert Essame concluded of the end to Patton's ride, "Providence had given Eisenhower the greatest cavalry leader and as good an army as his country had ever produced: at the decisive moment he failed to use them." Another British military observer, Ian Hogg, agreed: "There can be little doubt that Eisenhower's decision was wrong in every particular, and if Patton had been given his supplies, and his head, there is every likelihood that the war could have been shortened by six months. It is a matter of record that two-thirds of all the Allied casualties in Europe were suffered after the September check." It was as if after bombing Tokyo on March 11, 1945, Curtis LeMay, flush with victory, ran out of bombs and so ceased his B-29 attacks on the Japanese cities.

Patton, the wounded combat veteran, who often viewed the battle from the front, at once realized that his men would now suffer and die if they could not move freely in rapid armored envelopments. For all Bradley's criticism of Patton's recklessness, he never realized that such audacity grew out of a genuine feeling for just how awful trench warfare could be; in contrast, Bradley's timidity and caution, passed off to the popular press as caring for the GI, would repeatedly—at Falaise, at the Seine, now in the Lorraine, and afterward at the Bulge—bring on the most horrific fighting of the war in the winter of 1944–45.

The change in the comportment of the Third Army from a dashing to a static army in a matter of hours was striking. It was as if Epaminondas had stopped to encamp at the Laconian border, worried about the Spartans' formidable northern forts at Sellasia and troubled over the supply of food in winter, or as if Sherman's men had halted halfway through Georgia to resupply, rest, and worry about their exposed flanks or the Confederates flocking into Savannah.

> Thus it came about at the very moment when the morale of Third Army was at its zenith, when every officer and soldier in it was seized with the desire to reach the Rhine and cross it, when they felt instinctively that provided they pressed on now nothing could stop them, that they pulled up in their tracks.[56]

By September 4, when Patton resumed partial operations and his supplies were restored, if only sporadically, the German army in the Lorraine was in a completely different situation than had been true of the last week of August. By September 7, it was clear the Germans were dug in on the other side of the Moselle River. Whereas ten days earlier the entire German chain of command was in ruins, scattered in retreat throughout France, now von Rundstedt had resumed control of all armies in the West with a momentary freedom from Hitler's interference to do whatever was necessary to restore an orderly defense. The German Army opposing the suddenly stationary Patton now had seven divisions rushed up under the old Russian-front veteran, General Otto von Knobelsdorff.

All across the front, newly assigned German troops were quickly digging in, beefing up the defenses of the ancient fortress at Metz, reequipping the Siegfried Line, and were stocked plentifully with new antitank guns and artillery straight from nearby German factories. Stephen Ambrose sums up the tragedy of Patton's Third Army running out of gas as it reached the Siegfried Line:

> Their fuel tanks were empty. And the Germans had gotten into the Siegfried Line. They had fuel problems, too, but as they were on the defensive they could dig their tanks in and use them as fortified batteries. Their supply lines had grown shorter. . . . They had reached home. Men who saw no point to fighting to retain Hitler's conquests in France were ready to fight to defend the homeland. The German officer corps began taking the terrified survivors of the rout in France and organizing them into squads, platoons, companies, bat-

talions, divisions—and suddenly what had been a chaotic mob became an army. Slave labor, meanwhile, worked on improving the neglected Siegfried Line. The Germans later called the transformation in their army and in the defensive works the Miracle of the West.

A week or two may seem a short time, but in war it is everything, and in that brief period the German army was literally reinvented on the Western front, as Hitler scoured the German countryside and sent every able-bodied man to the front.

In turn, Patton would now need sixteen weeks to clear the Lorraine of Germans, whereas once it would have been possible in a few days—had he kept applying pressure with his huge outflanking movements of late August, when he dreamed of careening across the Rhine far ahead of the other Allied armies. The weather of early fall would now turn bad, unseasonably bad; the days would shorten and flying time for support fighters would diminish; the roads would soon be muddy and booby-trapped; and elaborate systems of ambush would make the conquest of the Lorraine a horrendous battle for the slogging American troops. That the German soldiers who would spearhead the stiff resistance were in great part those veterans who had once been humiliated and defeated—and allowed to escape—during the prior August in the Falaise and Seine envelopments added only further tragic irony. The consequences of a Patton denied were once more becoming apparent. For most of September and October, Patton did not receive adequate supplies to mount a full offensive, and the new German command under von Rundstedt at last sighed relief:

> The overall situation in the West was serious in the extreme. A heavy defeat anywhere along the front, which was so full of gaps that it did deserve the name, might lead to a catastrophe, if the enemy were to exploit his opportunity skillfully. A particular source of danger was that not a single bridge over the Rhine had been prepared for demolition, an omission which it took weeks to repair. . . . Until the middle of October the enemy could have broken through at any point he liked with ease, and would then have been able to cross the Rhine and thrust deep into Germany almost unhindered.[57]

Why Patton's supplies of gasoline and ammunition were cut off at the moment of his greatest success illustrates the entire ambiguous relationship between his Third Army and the overall Allied force in France. His mandated pause was hardly a conspiracy as much as a coalescence of a variety of unfortunate circumstances, ranging from poor judgment bordering on incompetence, to real problems of supply, to petty envy and jealousy on the part of his superiors.

Ostensibly, Patton and the other Allied armies had simply outrun their sources of supplies from the Normandy beachheads and ports. By late August, the Third Army was approaching areas of eastern France that the Allied invasion planners had envisioned would not be reached until late 1945 or perhaps even 1946. Patton was now being supplied by truck convoys—including the famous Red Ball Express—that extended nearly six hundred miles from their points of origin near the Atlantic coast. Yet the problem was not the supply of gasoline, ammunition, food, clothing, and weaponry per se, but rather their transport across France. Allied planners had not foreseen the rapid August progress, and thus by late summer 1944 did not have enough trucks on the roads of France to carry supplies to the ever distant and widening front. Why was this so?

First, there is some credence to the standard apology that, with only the Normandy beaches and Cherbourg operational as sources of supply—the ports of Brest, Le Havre, Dieppe, Boulogne, Calais, and Dunkirk were all to be points of last-ditch German resistance—there was a constant bottleneck in unloading and sending matériel out from the coast. Add to that the problems of the destruction of the French rail system by Allied air and ground attacks, and the Germans' demolition of rail and highway bridges during retreat. In Patton's case, he had none of the advantages enjoyed by the northern and southern Allied armies, which were to employ the soon-to-be-freed nearby ports at Antwerp and Marseille, and whose trajectories into enemy country were far shorter. The army that had traveled the farthest, the fastest, and had established itself as the most lethal, was now the least well supplied to continue into a momentarily naked Germany. Eisenhower, who was more pleased with how far the Allies had already gone rather than concerned that autumn was approaching and the Rhine was not yet crossed, summed up his theory of logistics in his own memoirs:

> Regardless, however, of the extraordinary efforts of the supply system, this remained our most acute difficulty. All along the front the cry was for more gasoline and more ammunition. Every one of our spearheads could have gone farther and faster than they actually did. I believed then and believe now that on Patton's front the city of Metz could have been captured. Nevertheless, we had to supply each force for its basic missions and for basic missions only.[58]

All armies, in Eisenhower's democratic view, were of equal ability; and thus according to the logic of the bureaucracy, all were to be given the same logistical support. Critical in this admission that Patton had lost the opportunity to take Metz in the early fall are three astounding statements. First, blame is *not* assigned to the logistical corps that had stalled Allied armies on the verge of ending the war, but instead praise given to "the extraordinary efforts of the supply system." Second is the banality of the admission that "every one of our spearheads could have gone farther and faster than they actually did." Such a truism meant little when the entire German army was in retreat; the role of the supreme commander, after failing to relieve his logistics officer who had ensured stasis, was to determine *which* army—given its past record and battle leadership—would have gone *considerably* farther and faster if well supplied. Third is Eisenhower's use of language to hide reality. In fact, not all Allied corps were given supplies for "basic missions and for basic missions only": in the latter part of August and early September, Eisenhower had decided to siphon off supplies to Montgomery's disastrous Market-Garden offensive, which was hardly a "basic mission." If Eisenhower's statement had been true—Montgomery confined to a "basic mission"—Patton would have continued farther than he did. Eisenhower, in short, had abruptly decided to back a concentrated thrust into northern Germany but unfortunately chose the *wrong* thrust—with tragic results for the Allied advance in general elsewhere. The irony was unmistakable: he had thrown his logistical reserve behind the precipitate plans of his most conservative general, thereby halting the proven advance of his most audacious subordinate.

The support of the Market-Garden gamble was entirely out of character for Eisenhower's staff. In truth, the Allied logistical planners were also a conservative bunch whose detailed plans of advance called for a broad, creeping offensive from the North Sea to Switzerland. Few logisticians ever envisioned anything like Patton's race across southern France. According to their timetables and figures, the Third Army's advance at forty and fifty miles a day should have been—as Stalin himself acknowledged later—logistically impossible. To some degree Patton was denied support because, when his rapid progress of August demanded radical readjustment in logistical planning, those to the rear instead viewed his startling progress as an *aberration* from the agreed-on agenda! He was terribly ahead of schedule in their eyes and using too many supplies too quickly, which was unfair to other Allied armies. His halt in September, to the more conservative logisticians, was seen not as a tragedy, but rather as a necessary adjustment to put the Allied effort back on a more predictable sequence of events, one which called for the weight of the Allied thrust to be directed toward the Ruhr through Holland. In the words of one historian of logistics, "The Allied advance from Normandy to the Seine, however successful and even spectacular strategically, was an exercise in logistic pusillanimity unparalleled in modern military history."

Had General J. C. Lee, director of all Allied logistical operations, been supportive of Patton, competent, or even subject to control by Eisenhower, then the eventual problem of fall 1944 might have been anticipated far in advance. Under a flexible and skilled logistician, fuel and ammunition could have been rerouted to those points of the Allied line where there was the greatest fluidity and progress. Instead, a near-incompetent logistical staff seemed to welcome rather than lament Patton's halt. As Patton sat idle, Lee gobbled up supplies to establish himself comfortably in liberated Paris, moving "his hugely overstaffed headquarters of 8,000 officers and 21,000 enlisted men to Paris, where he took over 296 hotels, whose beds were still warm from their previous long-term guests, the Germans. In the process, he required the use of an inordinate number of vehicles and consumed more than 25,000 gallons of gas that might have been put to better use than feeding his delusions of grandeur."[59]

Instead of planning for the unforeseen, and rerouting matériel to where armies were most aggressive, the Allied command tended to fault rather than praise Patton's progress. His audacious move had consumed too many supplies and now only Montgomery, the British argued, with the shortest route to the industrial Ruhr region of Germany, could and should be fully supported with fuel and ammunition. Patton had done well and good to draw off German Panzers to the south, but now it was time to stop him and allow the Allied master plan to unfold as originally planned with Montgomery at its helm. Just as had been the case in the blueprint for the invasion of Sicily, Patton was ostensibly to guard the flank, while Montgomery pressed on out ahead.

There was a growing consensus among Allied commanders in France that rather than address the logistical supply head-on, the solution was to halt one wing of the Allied attack to transfer available supplies to others—the well-known dialectic between a single-thrust or broad-front attack against Germany that was never fully resolved as Eisenhower sometimes lavished supplies on Montgomery, only later to distribute them more equitably when American commanders complained. In short, there is no evidence that Eisenhower, Bradley, or Montgomery, in the heady days of the August pursuit, realized, as did Patton, that the clock was ticking on the Allied advance. Like the German's 1941 approach to Moscow, which sputtered the last few miles before the Russian capital when the weather turned bad, so too the Allies were in a race to reach the Siegfried Line before the onset of the autumn rains, muddy roads, cloudy skies, and miserable conditions for soldiers in the field. In all the correspondence of Allied leaders there is little to indicate that any senior commander fully comprehended the need to attack the Siegfried Line in late August and early September—except Patton.

Montgomery, of course, argued that all other Allied armies should be halted, while his thrust was given the utmost priority. The problem in that scenario, however, was twofold. Montgomery had no reputation as a thruster, and thus the British now demanded a Pattonesque role for someone who was not Patton—while Patton to the south was halted to fashion a slow advance more akin to Montgomery's own. Success was to be rewarded with punishment, timidity with greater approbation. Second, while the broad front strung out Allied forces, it also had the even greater effect of dispersing German resistance. Montgomery felt he could charge into the Ruhr on a narrow front precisely because Patton's August romp had drawn formidable German divisions to the south.

Stop Patton, whom the Germans considered the most dangerous of Allied commanders, and the enemy, making use of ever shortening interior lines, could send back its better divisions to the north. Montgomery's linear thrust might—and did—find itself hitting a solid buffer of Germans as they rallied in depth around Berlin and the Ruhr, while Patton's much longer hook to the south might use the German autobahns and open spaces to maneuver and encircle far more freely. Eisenhower and Montgomery looked at maps, Patton to the caliber and nature of his army and his own past record of success in using space to wheel and envelop.[60]

It was not merely the more abstract British idea of a narrow thrust rather than a broad attack that now choked off Patton's gas. Indeed, Patton himself favored a narrow front, with preference of supplies going to any Allied army that might show the greatest potential of reaching Germany the quickest. Instead, Eisenhower's decision in early September to concentrate on Montgomery's needs in organizing the Arnhem offensive through Holland also reflected the supreme commander's own ambiguous relationship with the unpredictable Patton. Due to the slapping incidents in Sicily, and Patton's controversial public announcements, a decision had been made soon after the end of the Sicilian campaign in 1943 that Patton—who had the greatest battlefield experience, was senior in age, at one time outranked other field generals, and remained the best-known American battle leader—was not to be supreme Allied commander, nor senior American battle commander, nor operational head of the Allied armies in Normandy. Nor was he to be instrumental in the actual Normandy landings nor even in the strategic planning of the offensive. Nor was he to be allotted command within the first two months of the theater operations. Nor was he to be transferred either to the Pacific or to Italy.[61]

Rather, Patton was to assume control of a new and untried army, not operational until nearly two months after D-Day, and deliberately assigned the southern flank of the Allied line in Normandy farthest from Germany—with the implicit understanding that his was to be a holding action, a pivot for the British and American armies to the north to swing on shorter routes via Holland and Belgium into Germany. After listening to Bradley's preinvasion plans for the eventual deployment of the Third Army, Patton moaned, "If everything moves as planned there will be nothing left for me to do." At no point in the preparations of the Normandy invasion nor during the first months of the campaign did any Allied planner envision the role that Patton was to carve out for his new Third Army. "The precise mission of the Third Army," Carlo D'Este points out, "had deliberately been left vague and seemingly dependent on the turn of events on the battlefield. While Bradley would never publicly admit it, the evidence suggests that he would not have been unhappy had events unfolded in such a way that Patton's service could have been dispensed with."

In fact, there is good reason to believe Bradley deliberately delayed the operational start-up of the Third Army partly because of his dislike of Patton; and he sought wherever possible in early August to confine him to Brittany rather than have him drive eastward. Other Allied army generals might argue for primacy of supply either by reason of rank, friendship with Eisenhower, proximity to Germany and ports of supply, or original intent of Allied planners. Patton, in contrast, could only demand approval of a thrust of his Third Army into Germany on the basis of its own unforeseen and truly remarkable success. What Patton needed most now at the end of August was the stored capital of friendship and confidence on which he could draw to convince his superiors that his Third Army had truly made the preordained plan of advance in Normandy obsolete—and with a little more support might end the war a year before the hopes of even the most optimistic planners.

Instead, due to his ability, his candor, and his undeniable arrogance, he found envy and disdain in place of succor and encouragement. Had Patton's tanks required fodder rather than gas, then, like the lone wolf Epaminondas or the autonomous Sherman, he might have foraged as he pleased on the French countryside—and not even the most envious Boeotarch or suspicious secretary of war would have managed to stop him. The technological limitations of the modern age, along with a new managerial sense of organizational teamwork, had at least hemmed George Patton in.

In Patton's view, the German army in his front was now collapsing. His army, not Montgomery's forces, had the more impressive record of blitzkrieg. The Americans were providing the vast majority of men and matériel, and thus American public opinion would never tolerate a cessation of American advances while her supplies and men made possible a British spear thrust into Germany. Patton's GIs may have had no training in attacking entrenched positions and street fighting, but if they were allowed to proceed to do what they did best—race around enemy resistance—then such dirty fighting might not even be necessary. If by the end of August the decision was made to concentrate supply to one wing, why not the Third Army? It alone had a record of sustained advance at unprecedented speed. Montgomery's systematic marshaling of forces and his affinity for set-piece battles made him an ideal commander for a steady war of attrition, but if the war was to be ended now in the fall of 1944, then supplies should be given to those who had the best chance of racing into Germany while the forts and pillboxes of the Siegfried Line were still empty.

Moreover, Montgomery would go on to commit some fundamental errors that cast real doubt on his ability to lead the all-out Allied effort into Germany. He hesitated and delayed around Antwerp, allowing the German Fifteenth Army to escape, ensuring that the port could not open fully until late November. His decision to choose the unwise Arnhem corridor for his overly ambitious Market-Garden campaign may have been based on the desire for an all-British theater of operations. During the operation itself, he had paratroopers dropped too far from the bridges they were to conquer; and he did not insist on an aggressive-enough advance by his armored columns once the bridges were captured—all in all, a record that made the idea of giving Montgomery primary preference in material supply extremely unwise.[62]

Critics have argued not that Patton could not have continued on into Germany in September 1944, but that there would have been little point in his doing so, since the real strategic prize was to the north in the Ruhr. In this view, Patton's entrance would only have been a stiletto in the huge German underbelly, unable to carve up much of the Reich's vital organs before it would be liable itself to be absorbed and vanquished through the folds of German reinforcements. The same arguments, of course, were used against Sherman as he proposed to leave Atlanta: his supply lines would be cut; the real prize was Lee's army in Virginia and the Confederate capital at Richmond; he should follow Hood to his rear; and the Northern army would be swallowed up as it blindly marched ahead of its allied force.[63]

Such criticism always assumed that when Patton was at last resupplied and let loose to race through Germany in the spring of 1945, he did little to collapse the German resistance, when in fact the resumption of his accustomed progress destroyed the morale of the German army and set off a chain reaction of enemy defeat. An army that for weeks has continually raced right through the enemy can indeed do damage far out of proportion to its actual numbers when it at least reaches the enemy heartland. Since Patton's armored columns had proven they could move at forty to fifty miles a day, distance meant nothing—good terrain and the room to operate, everything. Because he attacked in depth and on a narrow front in his breakouts, the chance of encirclement on his immediate flanks was less likely than the reality that the enemy would collapse before it could disperse and envelop. The day when the Third Army took its greatest number of casualties—over 3,000 on December 22, 1944—was *not* during Patton's breakneck race across France, but five months after it became operational, in its drive northward to aid the First Army. The latter, like most American forces, had long ago halted and was then fighting a war of attrition along a static front in the weeks before the German counterattack.

In many respects Patton's rapid march from Normandy to Czechoslovakia stands as the more remarkable achievement than either Epaminondas's or Sherman's great trek. The latter two were supreme generals in their own theaters, what we would now call army group commanders; once they set out, they were largely free of control from superiors. Given the difficulty in communications, theirs were autonomous armies that could neither be recalled nor denied supply or support. Their own degree of success or failure was entirely gauged by their skill in bypassing or overcoming enemy resistance. The more self-sufficient nature of human and animal transport, and the ability to pack weapons on the backs of soldiers, meant they were essentially free to live off the land and detach themselves entirely from sources of supply and transport—and thus be freed from the oversight of envious, timid, or blinkered superiors.

In contrast, the moment Patton arrived in Normandy, he alone had a great vision that he would mobilize a quarter-million men, instill them with his own offensive, even reckless spirit, and send them onward at great speed into the bowels of Germany. This was a brilliant and audacious plan, but one that existed solely in the mind of George S. Patton, and one whose execution would draw constant opposition from his immediate superiors—criticism Patton expected as that due to any great innovative thinker: "I am not the first General to catch hell; Wellington had plenty of it, as did Grant, Sherman, and countless others." Epaminondas simply broke off communications from his more timid Boeotarchs and presented them post factum with the destruction of Messenian helotage and the humiliation of the Spartan army. His allies painted Theban clubs on their shield in honor of his army's audacity. Sherman was literally incommunicado for nearly a month, assured that his own success would counter any opposition to either his strategic plan or his tactical manner of operations.

Patton's vision was antithetical to the plans of his immediate superiors, who possessed both the legal authority to stop him and the sole control of the material support essential to sustain his march. While Epaminondas had Pelopidas at his side and Sherman his Grant to the north, Patton in Eisenhower and Bradley had colleagues who sought to limit his achievement—and when he was successful, to incorporate it as their own.

STRUCTURE OF COMMAND

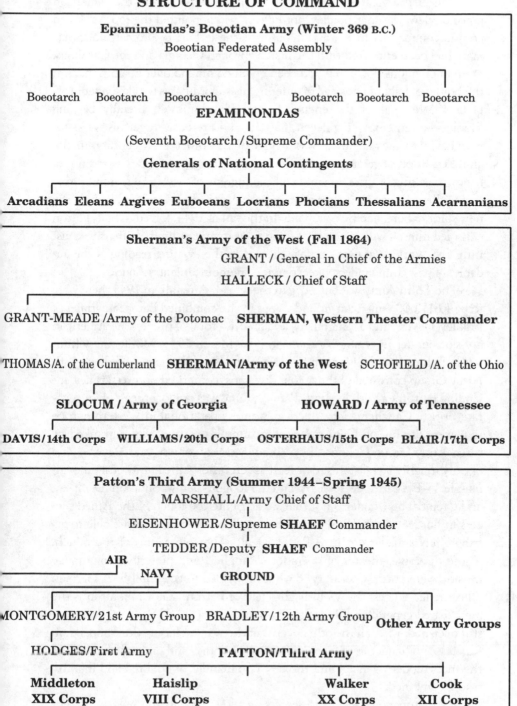

Epaminondas's Boeotian Army (Winter 369 B.C.)

Boeotian Federated Assembly

Boeotarch Boeotarch Boeotarch Boeotarch Boeotarch Boeotarch

EPAMINONDAS

(Seventh Boeotarch / Supreme Commander)

Generals of National Contingents

Arcadians Eleans Argives Euboeans Locrians Phocians Thessalians Acarnanians

Sherman's Army of the West (Fall 1864)

GRANT / General in Chief of the Armies

HALLECK / Chief of Staff

GRANT-MEADE /Army of the Potomac   **SHERMAN, Western Theater Commander**

THOMAS /A. of the Cumberland   **SHERMAN /Army of the West**   SCHOFIELD /A. of the Ohio

SLOCUM / Army of Georgia   **HOWARD / Army of Tennessee**

DAVIS /14th Corps   WILLIAMS /20th Corps   OSTERHAUS /15th Corps   BLAIR /17th Corps

Patton's Third Army (Summer 1944–Spring 1945)

MARSHALL /Army Chief of Staff

EISENHOWER /Supreme **SHAEF** Commander

TEDDER /Deputy **SHAEF** Commander

AIR

NAVY   **GROUND**

MONTGOMERY /21st Army Group   BRADLEY /12th Army Group   **Other Army Groups**

HODGES /First Army   **PATTON /Third Army**

Middleton   **Haislip**   **Walker**   **Cook**
XIX Corps   **VIII Corps**   **XX Corps**   **XII Corps**

One of the greatest tragedies of World War Two, from the American point of view, was that Bradley, not Patton, was appointed the top American ground commander in Europe. It was as if the lethargic Thomas, not Sherman, had been entrusted with the march through Georgia and the Carolinas, or an anonymous Boeotarch had been given command over Epaminondas at the border of Laconia. Instead of ordering his subordinates to take up rapid attacks to the rear of the enemy, Patton found himself literally begging Bradley—often employing deceit, flattery, and pretense to get his way—for permission to move. Patton was a man of the nineteenth century, in the grand tradition of great marshals. But his was a modern military world not of his own making or taste, in which all the ingredients to lead a march of freedom—theatrics, audacity, singular initiative, speed—were at odds with the new spirit of bureaucratic command. In the fall of 1944, forced to halt, Patton consoled himself with scheming to find ways to mount limited offensives, visiting first World War One battlefields, and in the evening reading of the audacity of past commanders, like Rommel's memoirs, *Infantry Attacks*.

The Third Army was but a cog in the wheel. After all, in 1945 there were to be 1,617,000 American ground troops in the combined European armies of Bradley, Devers, and Montgomery, and finally a total of ninety-one American divisions under Eisenhower's command. By March 1945, Montgomery himself had thirty-one divisions in his 21st Army Group, whereas Bradley's 12th Army Group consisted of thirty-four divisions, comprised of three armies, including Patton's Third. In short, Patton's force was one of at least eight separate British, Canadian, and American armies operational in Western Europe that were driving on Germany. Patton himself on paper was outranked by three Army Group Commanders—Bradley, Montgomery, and Devers—and of only roughly equal status to at least seven other Allied army ground commanders—De Lattre de Tassigny, Patch, Hodges, Gerow, Simpson, Dempsey, and Crerar. The wonder is not that we attribute too much of the Allied success in Europe to the Third Army's achievement, but that we are able to attribute *any* singular credit to Patton at all—the sole genius of the bunch, whose directive, theater of operations, supplies, and prescribed long-range mission were entirely contrary to what he wished to accomplish. A German officer reflected best the Wehrmacht's fear of Patton: "General Patton is the most feared general on all fronts. The successes of the U.S. Third Army are still overshadowing all the other events of the war, including the campaign in Russia. . . . The tactics of General Patton are daring and unpredictable. He is the most modern general and the best commander of armored and infantry troops combined."

As Patton now began his depressing plod through the mud of eastern

France for most of the fall of 1944, his rescue march northward during the Battle of the Bulge and his final encirclement of Bavaria lay weeks ahead. But as magnificent as all that subsequent racing would be, he would go to his miserable death thinking it was all so unnecessary. Historians—and their numbers are still growing—tend to agree. If he had had gas, Patton believed, he could have ended it all now in late August of 1944, the Third Army alone doing what the other seven could not. The great majority of America's European battle casualties might have been spared.

Unlike Epaminondas and Sherman, Patton never got his chance to translate such apparent lunacy into history. Of his final drive in late August he quipped right before his gasoline ran out, "It is such a sure thing that I fear someone will stop it."[64]

5

IDEOLOGICAL WARRIORS

THE SEINE RIVER, FRANCE

August 19, 1944 (V-E Day Minus 263 Days)

> *Then glorious Hektor burst in*
> *with dark face like sudden night, but he shone with the ghastly*
> *glitter of bronze that girded his skin, and carried two spears*
> *in his hands. No one could have stood up against him, and stopped him,*
> *except the gods, when he burst in the gates; and his eyes flashed fire.*
>
> —Homer, *Iliad*

THE "sure thing" Patton feared was the Third Army's incredible chase a few days earlier of the German army through Normandy, its intention to envelop German armies in the West, and then start a subsequent thrust across a largely undefended Rhine—all to end inside Germany at the conclusion of September 1944. All these grand designs George Patton envisioned this August 19 as he crossed the Seine River at Mantes, thirty-six miles west of Paris, in an all-out effort to catch those German forces that had escaped from the Allied pincers at the Falaise Gap.

True, he had been temporarily stopped before at Argentan when he wished to close the Argentan-Falaise pocket of retreating Germans. But now his relentless pursuit had given him a nearly identical opportunity—"We should go on," he demanded after the forced halt at Argentan. "There's nothing out there. Nothing between me and the Seine." His men had spirit and his tanks had gas—all that was necessary was approval from Bradley. In these first three weeks that the Third Army had become operational, it had inflicted over 136,000 casualties on the Germans and destroyed over 4,000 tanks, armored carriers, and artillery pieces.

Patton was now at the Seine River, poised on its eastern bank either to double back and help catch all German forces who had survived the early August bloodbath, or to go on ahead of the Germans *before* they got to the Lorraine and found safety within a largely undefended Siegfried Line. In any case, he was at least ready to go down the eastern bank of the Seine and pick off German divisions as they fled from Normandy. Patton speculated on the possible results of his plans for a larger envelopment if he were given the green light to push his entire army far beyond the Seine and trap the Germans as they emerged from the river: "I felt at this time that the great chance of winning the war would be to let the Third Army move with three corps, two up and one back, to the line Metz-Nancy-Epinal." Once he barred the line of German retreat, he would quite simply rip unmolested through the empty Lorraine into an unprotected Germany itself.[65]

Yet shortly later, the German Seventh Army and Fifth Panzer Army with 75,000 men and 250 tanks were somehow allowed to cross the Seine and to head eastward—an exasperated Patton was forced to beg his superiors for the right to press on. He had wanted to trap the Germans on the *east* bank of the Seine, encircling them as they emerged from the river. Instead, the Allied leadership crafted a far more timid strategy of intercepting them on the *west* bank, which more or less failed. "Marveling at the absence of insight among his bosses," Martin Blumenson noted, "Patton regretted their failure to let him reinforce the 79th division across the Seine. A substantial force plowing down the right bank of the river would have dealt the Germans a lethal blow. Montgomery and Bradley were uninterested, and Eisenhower, as usual, was keeping his hands off." Once more the old paranoia about Patton's extended flanks, the supposed lethal fury of trapped Germans, and the specter of exhausted supplies played on the American command. A record of a conversation between Bradley and Patton records the latter's aggravation at being told to halt shortly before reaching the Seine. An observer relates the following:

> About ten minutes after our arrival general B. [Bradley] arrived and he immediately launched into the fact that they had a big conference and decided that the Third Army shouldn't go beyond . . . Dreux. . . . and Chartres . . . and toward the Seine . . . so as to leave an escape route for the Germans in the Falaise

pocket. After Gen. B. had informed Gen. P. [Patton] [that he] was not to advance any further and that was that, Gen. P. told Gen. B. that since he was already to the Seine River, in fact had pissed in the river that morning and had just come from there, what would he want him to—pull back . . . ? After much discussion Gen. B. told him how strong the people [Germans] were in the Falaise pocket and didn't think Gen. P. would be able to contain them, and it was his orders to leave an escape route to the east for them.[66]

The American indecision at the Seine River—when there was as yet still plentiful supplies available—marked the *second* but unfortunately not the last time that Patton's plan either to annihilate a defeated army or to press on ahead for an even wider envelopment had been overruled. The consequences of that failure of nerve were that, when Patton was be denied gasoline ten days later in the Lorraine, there were German troops aplenty nearby to reconstitute a defense. Had he pressed on at top speed from the Seine, or at least been allowed to sweep along the eastern shore of the river to catch retreating German armies, then when his supplies were later cut off, German divisions would still have found themselves surrounded. Such a strange war, Patton thought: root out Germans, chase and scatter them, then stop before trapping them so that they might escape and regroup, then resume the pursuit against a now desperate and savage entrenched foe.

The Germans would now go back east; Patton would start, then pause, then start—only to be denied gas when his full pursuit resumed. Eisenhower had decided, at least for the time being, to promote a single thrust into Germany with Montgomery, who was miles from the Seine River, by holding back Patton who was miles beyond it.[67]

Patton himself wrote on August 20 of the constant temptation to act conservatively, a sense of fear that conquered others, but one that he had long since mastered:

> I always have a funny reaction before a show like this. I think of the plan and am all for it, and then just as I give the order, I get nervous and must say to myself, "Don't take counsel of your fears," and then go ahead. It is like a steeple chase—you want to ride in it, and then when the saddling bugle goes, you are scared, but when the flag is dropped all is well.[68]

Patton and his army had an incredible August, maintaining a drive that had terrified the previously formidable Germans and demoralized almost all formal opposition. The Third Army had advanced over four hundred miles in twenty-six days, liberating 47,829 square miles of French territory in less than a month. It had killed over 16,000 Germans, wounded 55,000, and captured 65,000, and was now poised on the east bank of the Seine to stop any Germans from retreating eastward across the river. In less than a month Patton had fashioned both for himself and for his Third Army a reputation for demolishing the German resistance and in essence allowing for the liberation of Paris—to such a degree that Eisenhower now ordered the press to concentrate more on Hodges's First Army to prevent Patton and his men from unfairly monopolizing the news.

No army in the history of organized warfare had traveled so rapidly through so great an extent of enemy-occupied territory in such a brief time. Yet the ideal conditions offered by the August warmth were transitory. Patton was already worried that he now had a quarter of a million American boys who were sleeping outdoors in comfortable, but soon-to-change, weather. Should he now tarry and allow the war to be prolonged into fall and winter, then his men would be wet, cold, and sick, as the equivalent of a large American city was left to sleep and eat in the November and December cold, unprotected in the snowy French and German mountains.[69]

What had made the Third Army so singularly successful this August?

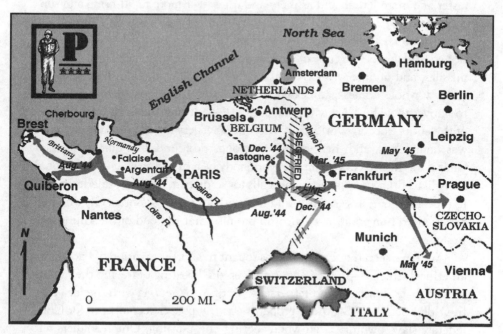

PATTON'S 1,000-MILE DRIVE EASTWARD   AUGUST 1, 1944–MAY 8, 1945

What had brought it to the Seine River relatively unscathed after capturing or killing thousands of German soldiers? After all, the majority of its divisions were without battle experience and fought against German veterans of the Russian front, Italy, and Africa, aided by Waffen SS zealots. The GIs' equipment was not qualitatively superior to the Germans', and they did not yet outnumber their foe. As mobile offensive troops, they were soon to be at a disadvantage against entrenched defenders who enjoyed knowledge of local terrain and shortened supply lines. Victory and forward motion in themselves cannot explain improved morale, since for weeks in June and July the Allies took horrendous casualties among the hedgerows. The presence of overwhelming American tactical airpower cannot entirely account either for the Third Army's wondrous advance; Patton himself, for example, was often under German air bombardment in the Brittany campaign. Nor did Patton receive preference in American supplies of men and matériel, and he certainly was not given a theater of operations closest to either ports of supply or the heartland of industrial Germany.

The war had now been raging for the Germans and British for nearly five years, and nearing three for the Americans. Gone was all the initial bravado about a short patriotic conflict, as tanks became bigger and deadlier, planes faster and more lethal, and artillery and rifles ever more rapid-firing and supplemented by a macabre new generation of self-propelled howitzers, flamethrowers, and sophisticated land mines. Scientists on both sides envisioned still further agents of destruction—jets, sophisticated radar-guided missiles, and atomic weapons. Entire divisions on both sides had been destroyed; whole armies had ceased to exist after continuous fighting. Patton took over the Third Army on August 1, 1944, during the most lethal period of the entire Second World War, when the savagery of weapons on both sides was unmatched, and the cynicism of troops profound. GIs quickly learned what it was like to crawl from the Normandy beachhead against a professional army like Hitler's veterans. Simple calls for soldiers to be good Americans and to repel their nation's enemy would not work for newly seasoned GIs who had experienced human atrocity with no promise that the end of the killing was in sight.

We have seen that Epaminondas sought to cast his invasion of Laconia as an ethical struggle—the epigram on his statue boasting of freeing the Helots proved that. Sherman's Westerners also went into Georgia with the idea that their destruction of Southern property was the proper recompense for Confederate slave-owning. Even when looting and burning, Union soldiers felt that they still occupied the moral high ground as the proper avengers of

Negro slavery. Similarly, the American army in Europe believed that it was fighting to destroy the evil of slavery, in this case National Socialism. Historian Richard Overy concluded that "hatred of Hitler and 'Hitlerism' was the moral cement of the Allied war effort"—a successful mechanism for imbuing the GI with the idea that he was morally superior to his German adversary and present in Europe solely to avenge a great wrong. Such efforts were necessary, since many American soldiers were fighting an enemy that often ostensibly looked like themselves, shared a European heritage, and when captured sometimes claimed the distinction (true enough) between Nazi ideology and the traditional German *Volk*.

In addition, as GIs made their way into Germany, they were sometimes favorably impressed with German communities that often resembled the middle-class landscape of the United States. Similarly, we should remember that Epaminondas fought Greek soldiers who spoke roughly the same language as his Boeotians; Sherman's Westerners in some sense were more akin in background and outlook to rural Confederate troops than to their own New England comrades. In wars against others of a similar Western culture, who shared cultural, linguistic, and at times even racial affinity, it was critical to imbue armies of liberation with an ethical zeal that drew out real ideological differences between adversaries. Our great marches were not driven by religious ardor nor racial hatred nor promises of imperial bounty. What makes these great assaults so rare in the history of warfare is the ethical nature of their mission, and the citizen militias that composed the infantry. Propaganda is necessary for every army, but in the case of Patton's army the dehumanization of the German had at its core fascism, the Wehrmacht's brutality, and Nazi killing.

The American armies in World War Two, unlike either Epaminondas's Thebans or Sherman's Westerners—or even British or German forces—were not organized by regional affiliation. Raw recruits had no sense of belonging to a particular unit, and, of course, there were no lifelong associates or relatives in their immediate locale on the battlefield whose friendship and support they could draw on. All such ties had to be developed in training or on the battlefield between perfect strangers from widely diverse regional backgrounds.

"The effect of such a system on morale, unit cohesion, and fighting power does not have to be imagined," wrote Martin van Creveld, "since direct evidence about it is readily available. According to one official account, some men complained that they had been 'herded like sheep' or 'handled like so many sticks of wood.' Arriving in the theater after weeks of travel by land and sea, the men 'wanted most of all to be identified with a unit,' instead of which they might well spend a few more weeks in various depots." Whatever would make the American soldier fight, it would not be a long record of friendship or blood ties to the man nearby.[70]

Could moral fervor substitute for established ties of kin and friendship? Eisenhower especially grew to feel a deep moral repugnance for all things German. "God I hate the Germans," he wrote to his wife. To his brother Milton, he remarked that "Hitler should beware the fury of an aroused democracy." In his memoirs, *Crusade in Europe*, Ike reflected:

> Daily as it [the war] progressed there grew within me the conviction that as never before in a war between many nations the forces that stood for human good and men's rights were this time confronted by a completely evil conspiracy with which no compromise could be tolerated. Because only by the utter destruction of the Axis was a decent world possible, the war became for me a crusade in the traditional sense of that often misused word.

This view of the need to educate the troops about the larger ethical stakes involved was shared by the entire Allied command.

> British and American propaganda was chiefly concerned to reinforce the positive moral stance from which it argued victory would spring. This was expressed in the conventional language of freedom against tyranny, barbarism crushed by civilization. "We wanted to make the world safe for democracy— and protect the Four Freedoms," wrote the American General Wedemeyer after the war. When the film producer Frank Capra was recruited by General Marshall to produce a series of documentaries on "Why We Fight," to help educate American opinion, Capra took as his working theme the "enormity" of the enemy's cause, "and the justness of ours." The western war was presented as a decent war, as the "good war." This was not difficult to do in the light of Japanese and German atrocity, and the vicious and illiberal regimes that ran the Axis war effort.[71]

In this regard, Patton's constant speeches and written proclamations about the evil of the Germans were entirely consistent with guidelines set out by the Anglo-American high command. Whereas Eisenhower, Bradley, and Montgomery were usually content to remind their soldiers of the global issues at stake, or to express hatred for the Germans in private letters, Patton was far more graphic, crude—and public—insisting that his soldiers in the field, if they were to fight well, must feel exactly as he did about the enemy. As one observer pointed out, "Patton had to harden his troops for battle in a country remote from the actual fighting, with little conception of the realities of war and still enjoying the luxuries of peace. Furthermore, he had to do this in the teeth of lively and at times malicious criticism." Thus Patton's evil Germans became real, living, breathing monsters who wished to kill Americans and to do terrible things to the innocent, not abstractions that threatened world peace and global harmony. Unlike his experience in World War One when his men sought to destroy the German army, Patton's aim now was to lead an army to ruin a very culture. As they neared the German border, Patton reminded his men:

> The friendship and cooperation of the French people will be replaced in Germany by universal hostility, which will require that we regard all Germans, soldiers and civilians, men, women, and even children, as active enemies. It is expected that we shall encounter sniping, guerrilla warfare, sabotage, and treachery. Everyone must be warned of these probabilities and prepared to take all possible protective measures.

Patton was entirely at odds with the colorless managerial style of Eisenhower and Bradley, who viewed as entirely inappropriate his efforts through profanity and harangue to mold the Third Army into a special ideological force in his own image. Much of the high command's dislike of Patton was based not just on his theatrics and headline-grabbing, but because he really did envision this war not, as they did, as a corporate enterprise, but as a horrific contest of the blood spirit, in which the commanding general had a sacred duty to make sure his killers best knew what they were fighting for and why—and to leave tactical details to the individual division commanders. Patton preferred not to micromanage but to inspire. This he could do wonderfully—and his peers simply could not. Colonel Wallace of Patton's staff remarked of Patton's division commanders, "You . . . were never told how to do a thing, only requested in a quiet gentlemanly way to do it. The rest was up to you. Results were all that counted."[72]

As early as March 1944, Patton told his officers that "they were fighting for three reasons—to preserve liberties, to defeat the Nazis who wanted to destroy American liberties and simply to fight—men liked to fight and always would. Only sophists and crackpots denied the latter. They were goddamned fools, cowards, or both. Whoever disliked fighting would do well to ask for a transfer now." At other times Patton pointed out that, while the Nazis were superb fighters, they were also thugs, without the humanity of his own Third Army, which was to advance into Germany as part of a holy crusade to protect American values: "The fact that we are operating in enemy country does not permit us to forget our American tradition of respect for private property, noncombatants, and women," Patton lectured.

Patton's army was thus to be foremost an ideological one, whose brutal fighting was to serve a higher moral purpose—a daunting task of indoctrination in cynical soldiers from a society so highly individualistic and skeptical of authority. He was, after all, fighting an enemy whose government would eventually exterminate a total of 20,000,000 innocent men, women, and children, and envisioned a permanent slave society of over 14,000,000 unfree workers just to realize Hitler's and Himmler's utopian German settlements in the East. Against the architects of that bleak future, strong language seemed appropriate.[73]

There is no reason to believe that Patton's repugnance for the Nazis was not genuine. True, later as proconsul of Bavaria, faced with horrendous problems of food supply, sanitation, and health care, and worn out at sixty years of age after the near-continuous fighting of the past year, he could be criminally lenient toward the employment of former Nazi sympathizers; but during battle he was uniformly contemptuous of them. Patton, for example, ended an interrogation with an SS major general with the following: "I understand German very well, but I will not demean myself by speaking such a language. . . . I think before I turn the General over to the French, I will send him to the Army Group who may question him or have some special investigators question him, and they can do things I can't do. . . . I have great respect for the German soldiers; they are gallant men, but not for the Nazis." Later he wrote that this "Gestapo General" was "the most vicious looking human being I have ever seen, and who, after I got through talking to him, was unquestionably one of the worst scared. He is the first man I have ever brow-beaten, and I must admit I took pleasure in doing it." This animus, again, was in contrast to Patton's view of regular German soldiers, and mirrored Sherman's distinction between Confederate soldiers in the field and the planters who had precipitated the war.[74]

Patton, far better than his fellow commanders, realized the dilemma that faced American troops in Germany—that faced all armies of democracy, which deem that they can field troops capable of engaging those more militaristic in a horrific war:

> Therein lay the heart of the problem facing any military commander, whether Robert E. Lee in the Civil War, George S. Patton in World War II, or Norman Schwarzkopf in the Gulf War of 1991: how to motivate decent young men raised on the precepts of the Bible, the sanctity of human life, and the immorality of killing to become an efficient cog in a gigantic killing machine

such as an armored division. While it was enough to make their mothers cringe, the only method whereby a Patton or a Schwarzkopf could succeed on the battlefield was to trespass on the inherent decency of Americans by training and motivating their men to survive by killing others whose task was to kill *them*. Patton did it as well or better than virtually anyone else.[75]

Most Americans in the Third Army had not fought previously in Sicily and North Africa, but would be pitted against either hardened veterans or recruits who had been for over a decade nursed on a public diet of Nazi propaganda laced with German militarism. American GIs had *not* been under attack at home and had never felt any immediate threat to the safety of their families. Indeed, for the first two years of World War Two, most Americans bitterly resented even the idea of joining in against Hitler; public figures ranging from Charles Lindbergh to Herbert Hoover to students in the universities bitterly resented the notion of compulsory military service or the idea that in the midst of an economic depression the United States would foolishly invest in military rearmament. The incentives to kill would have to be created through rhetoric and ideology, since Americans after Pearl Harbor were not being bombed or invaded, or their children rounded up or starved. Germany, not America, had been the first to declare war; but unlike Japan, it had not attacked the United States. And in the earlier war, their fathers had been asked to defeat German soldiers, not to invade and destroy Germany.[76]

In part, the problem of turning American GIs into ideological warriors was inextricably connected with contemporary American democratic culture itself—not just democracy, but a particular brand of modern American consumer democracy, which had emerged quite differently even from those liberal nations in Europe. Whereas Epaminondas and even Sherman functioned within a consensual society that through popular accord might find slavery in its environs a great evil, and military force thus necessary, Patton now lived in an entirely different world, in which materialism and an expansive idea of individual liberty had created a new democratic citizen reluctant to endanger his own freedom or material comfort. In this new age, danger should be met through machines and technology, without inordinate suffering and personal sacrifice. The death camps of Germany were distant and unknown to most Americans. The war itself in Europe was thousands of miles away, and fought on battlefields that from time immemorial had been the arena for European powers' attempts to destroy one another—a quagmire that most Americans had little desire to reenter.

Even if Americans could understand Nazi Germany as depraved, they also might conclude that the prerequisite force to end its ambitions would be simply too brutal and thus repugnant. Richard Overy describes the initial un-realistic American view of the fighting—both among civilians and soldiers:

> The American censors deliberately played down the theme of death in the first two years of conflict. *Life* magazine did not show a dead American until September 1943. The information Manual produced for Hollywood by the newly created Office of War Information instructed film directors to limit scenes of death or injury: "In crowds unostentatiously show a few wounded men." Between May and November 1942 only five out of sixty-one war films showed deaths in combat. American authorities remained anxious that the reality of war might dent morale. . . . American society was less prepared for the traumas of battlefield violence than the people of Europe and Japan. The first American forces to fight in North Africa suffered a 25 per cent casualty rate from psychological disorders. . . . Unlike the Soviet Union the two west-ern Allies were democracies, whose populations were used to a high standard of living and amenity. They could not be regimented to the extent of Soviet citizens, or their armies terrorized to fight.

The physical conditions of modern warfare, not just the spiritual and psy-chological landscape in which it operated, were far different from those of the prior twenty-three centuries of battle. Despite the recent Depression, most American infantrymen were raised in a society of rising material expectations and entitlements—and yet now they were asked to fight a war simply unimag-inable by more materially deprived hoplites and Civil War soldiers. Patton's GIs, daily and without interruption, saw not hundreds of dead, but often thousands—the rotting corpses in the Falaise Gap, the stiff frozen American bodies in the Bulge, the human debris of attackers and defenders blown apart at Metz. Wounds were not simple penetrations by spearheads nor even the loss of an arm or a leg by rifled bullets, but entire limbs, trunks, and heads taken off by mortar rounds and 88-mm artillery shells.

In short, Patton hectored men who in seconds might be literally pulver-ized into nothingness by high explosives shot from miles away by men they would never see. Like the industrial worker who fabricated on the assembly line endless products for the distant and anonymous consumer, so too the modern soldier shot, bombed, and shelled endlessly and by rote, often against adversaries he would never look upon. The bomber and shooter might never know whether they had missed or, in fact, torn apart their adversaries. In this climate, it was far easier to see warfare as a nameless, faceless horror in which the winner—in the fashion of the modern profitable factory—simply deliv-ered the greater amount of steel and explosive product to the flesh of his enemy. Moreover, under such ghastly conditions, it was understandable to see war itself, rather than the Nazi army per se, as inherently evil.

Cynical and hard-bitten Third Army soldiers knew what awaited them; Bradley and Eisenhower also understood the rules for winning this corporate war far better than Patton. Patton accepted it, functioned within it, but hated it—hated saturation bombing, hated the mechanical killing of the death camps, and hated the barbarity of frontal infantry assault that neutralized the qualities of courage and individual human effort. He tried to train, motivate, and lead soldiers in the manner of a past age of an Epaminondas or Sherman, in which killing would be personal, angry, face-to-face, not anonymous, often even accidental, and sometimes without emotion—killing, above all, for a moral purpose to protect the innocent and weak from the strong and evil. George Patton really did believe, in a manner that either his superiors had forgotten or were ignorant about, that an especially audacious tank driver or a few reckless riflemen could through sheer spirit change the course of a battle—capture a key bridge or take a deadly pillbox—could, in other words, halt the industrial depersonalization of the fighting. If his Third Army was driven on by brave men, the enemy, for all its hardware and efficiency, might crack, and thus the anonymous bombing from the air, the industrial gassing of the multitudes in the camps, the daily slaughter of the shelled, all that might cease, defeated still by the soul of the superior warrior.

Yet, Patton had one advantage of modernity. Its American recruits of the mid twentieth century were extremely well educated in comparison to armies of the past; they possessed as free citizens an innate moral sense that was the real dividend of democracy. Patton felt that with the acquisition of discipline, in concordance with their natural inquisitiveness and independence, such soldiers could be trained to be even more effective soldiers than the Germans.

> Patton's mention of "freedom" and "liberty" in direct context with his blunt reference to "the people we shall kill" was characteristic. He recognized the strange paradox in the two contrasting motivations that had to propel his citizen-soldiers—the subtle ideological impulses dormant within them and an unflinching toughness with which these sheltered American boys had to be imbued. If the two could be fused into a dynamic combination, Patton believed, it would make them invincible.[77]

While Patton drew for this Third Army from the same pool of American recruits as other generals, he almost immediately set to work to make his men different, different in seeing the war in Europe as an ideological contest, of a good democracy at war with a brutal Nazism. If they would not fight for the immediate protection of their families and homeland—like the Soviets did in Russia; if they were not battling for regimental élan and the safety of boyhood friends—like the British army; if they did not kill either out of a fanatical national religion or fear of horrific punishment—like the Nazis, then Patton would tap their latent moral sense in assuring them that no one else but they could stop Nazi Germany, a truly evil country that had made war on American values.

How was Patton able to accomplish this in such a short time? He had nearly a quarter-million men, only a few weeks of training, and the constraint of voluminous regulations and protocols of the American military bureaucracy, which governed everything from the nature of the shoelaces of his soldiers to the type of discipline he could instill. At the most superficial level he turned to rhetoric and profanity-ridden bombast. Patton repeatedly in talks to his officers and enlisted men took care to turn the Allied war effort into a personal contest between evil Nazis and the Third Army proper, not a global struggle between millions of anonymous Americans and Germans. To modern readers these broadsides seem silly; and, in fact, contemporaries like Bradley openly ridiculed Patton's speeches, claiming GIs often laughed at him. In reality, Third Army recruits gradually developed the sense that they were in a personal war with Hitler. Patton yelled at them constantly:

> I want them [the Germans] to look up and scowl, "Ach IT'S THE GOD-DAMN THIRD ARMY AND THAT SON-OF-A-BITCH PATTON AGAIN!" We want to get this thing over and get the hell out of here, and get at those purple-pissin' Japs!!! The shortest road home is through Berlin and Tokyo! We'll win this war, but we'll win it only by showing the enemy we have more guts than they have or will ever have.

Contrary to what his critics argued, there is little evidence that the majority of soldiers in the Third Army ever resented the shrillness of their commander or his idiosyncratic manner; there is instead substantial proof that men who detested the Nazis also soon realized that in Patton's army there was a greater chance that they might move—and thus live—than elsewhere in France:

> Patton left no one in any doubt as to who was in command of the Third Army. As units arrived and were indoctrinated into the Third Army way of doing business, everyone knew who their new army commander was. . . . Patton inspired great loyalty in the troops of the Third Army. They came to identify with and to have confidence in him; they understood that a professional soldier and genuine fighting man was commanding them. And while most ab-

horred the war they were obliged to fight, they understood what it meant to have a commanding general like Patton.

A young officer recorded his first impression of Patton in July 1944 while the Third Army was still in England:

Suddenly the front doors were thrown open and a strange officer walked out and stood in a ray of sunlight, looking them over and at first saying nothing. Everyone stopped talking and looked at him and soon he began to speak, in a high and somewhat unpleasant voice. Their first impressions were of a powerful figure, immaculately and superbly uniformed, shiny boots and insignia, looking every inch the soldier and leader. And before he had talked very long, they knew he was a soldier and a leader. . . . I suppose the performance was carefully staged and that he came to hook us all, but I'll say he did it. As for me, he not only hooked, but landed me, and I will go with him to the ends of the earth.[78]

The outburst and exhibitions of temper were of course both conscious efforts at instilling discipline and élan, and the natural expressions of someone impatient and reckless. Patton insisted on a level of discipline not found in other American armies. Not only were his men to obey orders promptly, but they were also even to salute, dress, and march differently than other GIs—the "chicken-shit" so ridiculed by observers as diverse as Bill Mauldin, Paul Fussell, and Andy Rooney. Stephen Ambrose has suggested Patton's spit-and-polish "obsession sometimes cost dearly. It not only had nothing to do with winning the war; it hurt the war effort." Another detractor wrote similarly, "If you drove in the Third Army sector without steel helmet, sidearms, necktie, dogtags, everything arranged according to some forgotten manual, Patton's fiercely loyal M.P. gorillas would grab you. You could protest, but say one word against their pigheaded general?—I never had the nerve."[79]

If in truth such seemingly trivial protocol aimed only for petty discipline and to gratify the ego of a clerk, perhaps it would be fair to call Patton pigheaded and thus his rules harmful to the war effort. But Patton's intention, of course, was far broader. He reasoned that if Third Army soldiers knew that they were subject to a higher code of discipline than others—even if that meant shaving and wearing ties—they would follow more important orders more promptly and soon see themselves as qualitatively different from other troops—critical in creating any sense of Third Army singularity in an otherwise vast and amorphous American army. The frequent admission that troops from other American armies sometimes dreaded visiting Third Army territory was proof enough of the idiosyncratic nature of Patton's force. Patton himself would argue that because his men looked and acted differently in matters of small importance, then they could more easily execute operations requiring exacting discipline—like the sudden ninety-degree turn into the Ardennes—and of life-and-death significance.

Faced with rivalry with a neat and tidy Army of the Potomac that did not move, Sherman's men prided themselves in their careless frontier dress; faced with casual soldiers in other American armies, Patton's more mobile warriors took on a far neater appearance. While the method was the opposite, both neatness and sloppiness were encouraged by their respective leaders to set their own men off from the regular American soldier. Already by August 1944 an American radio broadcast could end with: "Patton understands the psychology of battle. His pep talks before and after battles are sometimes beautiful enough to be called reverent—sometimes scourging. . . . Yes, Patton will be a legend. To his men he is one of the greatest fighting generals alive."

The problem with American soldiers had never been their unthinking acceptance of orders, or obsession with rote and custom—goose-stepping German and Soviet armies have always maintained ostensibly better-disciplined and more orderly troops. Patton realized that the strength of the GI was his adaptability, independence, and initiative; but to allow those attributes to come into play on the battlefield, the American soldier must, if for a brief time only, come to accept a level of discipline wholly out of his national character. To Patton, rules and protocol would keep his army alive and moving; laxity would lead to disorder and an innate American propensity to criticize authority and question uniformity.[80]

Patton always communicated that his apparently tougher discipline was in the interest of the fighting man, that it would in fact save lives in the long run. He may not have known the full extent of the German atrocities to the east, but he had a good enough acquaintance with Nazi ideology to assure his men that they were in a war of annihilation with a very evil adversary:

> I can assure that the Third United States Army will be the greatest Army in American history. We shall be in Berlin ahead of every one. To gain that end, we must have perfect discipline. I shall drive you until hell won't have it, but a pint of sweat is worth a gallon of blood. We are going to kill German bastards—I would prefer to skin them alive—but, gentlemen, I fear some of our people at home would accuse me of being too rough.[81]

In retrospect, even his worst offense of slapping a soldier who was thought to be suffering from battle stress does not seem as felonious as it did at the time, given the astronomical number of American psychological cases in the ranks compared to other armies, both friend and enemy. A student of combat efficiency in the American army of World War Two has remarked:

> The U.S. Army by contrast put technical and administrative efficiency at the head of its list of priorities, disregarded other considerations, and produced a system that possessed a strong inherent tendency to turn men into nervous wrecks. Perhaps more than any other single factor, it was this system that was responsible for the weaknesses displayed by the U.S. Army during World War II.

Given that reality, Martin van Creveld went on to put Patton's apparent grotesque behavior into some sort of proper disciplinary context:

> Although a historian should avoid hasty generalizations, it is hard to avoid the feeling that something was wrong with an army that first allowed nonbattle casualties to reach epidemic proportions and then failed to utilize its own experience in treating them. These evils were compounded by an extremely permissive attitude on the part of the army, which, possibly based on the widespread acceptance of Freud's theories, was communicated to the troops by semiofficial channels and caused combat fatigue to be regarded as a legitimate, almost normal complaint. While preventing the army from applying the somewhat harsh methods of treatment used by German physicians, this attitude also built "golden bridges" for men who wanted to escape combat. There even exists evidence that, for some soldiers at any rate, going AWOL, deserting and requesting evacuation on psychiatric grounds constituted alternative courses of action. Patton's methods of slapping a soldier who did not fight may not have been so wrong after all.[82]

Beside Patton's rhetorical fireworks—so similar to the practice of the customary prebattle harangues in classical Greek and Roman warfare—and his insistence on discipline to the most minute degree, he also sought to ensure that his Third Army in fact *fought* quite differently than other forces. "Goddamnit, I'm not running for the Shah of Persia," Patton answered his critics. "There are no practice games in life. It's eat or be eaten, kill or be killed. I want my bunch to be in there first, to be the 'fustest with the mostest.' They won't do it if I ask them kindly."

Critics who cite in disdain Patton's constant reference to "killing" and his profanity-ridden bombast should keep in mind what sort of cosmos Normandy was in 1944. Southern France was not a nice place, but a grotesque inferno where hundreds of GIs were dismembered and blown apart each day by opponents who were past masters in the use of horrific machine guns, Tiger and Panther tanks, and antipersonnel mines. The real profanity, it seems to me, is for a general to lecture in measured tones on such killing in language other than killing. When Patton announced to his men on arrival in France, "I'm proud to be here to fight beside you. Now let's cut the guts out of those Krauts and get the hell to Berlin," he was not speaking in fantastic tones, but rather describing a real war in which GIs either were to be disemboweled or would disembowel their German adversaries—an experience that would halt only when the Allies were, in fact, in Berlin. If his men as individuals and in concert were qualitatively superior to their German counterparts, then they could conquer not merely through greater numbers and supplies, but by reason of their own fighting spirit.

Like Sherman, Patton saw no reason to assume that large numbers of his boys had to be sacrificed simply because there were more of them than the Germans. Rather, if man for man they killed more effectively than the Germans, they could advance at a rapid clip that would require few casualties. In short, Patton loathed Grant's idea of the "terrible arithmetic," which lay at the heart of the reasoning of Eisenhower and Bradley. They apparently chose to wage war steadily, conservatively, and soberly, confident that greater American manpower and supplies eventually would ensure that in such barbarous frontal assaults throughout the hedgerows, and the Hürtgen and Ardennes forests, the Germans would crack first. In their memoirs, both Eisenhower and Bradley fell into the classical fallacy of seeing the successful end as proving the wisdom of the prior means; they dismissed criticism of "what might have been" simply on the grounds that the Allies won ahead of projected schedules anyway—as if their conservatism in restraining the impetuous Patton at Falaise, Brest, the Seine, the Lorraine, the Bulge, and near Prague was justified by the Allied victory, as if a careful advance was more prudent than a rapid envelopment.

Patton, the blustering big-mouth, was not merely a realist, but a real humanitarian, for he sensed that in contrast to his superiors he could wage a war so mobile, flexible, and lethal—aiming always for vast encirclements—that the Americans would never need to draw on their human reserves, and, in fact, would lose far fewer casualties than the Germans. Again, the obscenity in Patton's mind was a complacent war of static fronts, huge numbers of men engaged in rear-echelon tasks, commanders ensconced hundreds of miles to the rear, dreary communiqués—war as a daily grind that would inevitably grind the Germans up first. His diary entry on May 17, 1944, notes, "Made a talk. . . . As in all my talks, I stressed fighting and killing." In sum, Patton knew, as Macaulay once wrote, that "the essence of war is violence, and that moderation in war is imbecility."

The need for constant advance and iron-clad discipline ranged from the soldier in the field to the officer in the jeep, and entailed the concept of "moving fire," or constant shooting while advancing. Both contemporary and postwar analysts have suggested that the American army did not always make maximum use of small arms fire, that a great proportion of its infantry troops simply did not discharge their weapons in combat. Patton sought to remedy this by his notion of "marching fire," in which his GIs were taught to shoot away as they walked or trotted forward. He abhorred the usual American emphasis on "dig or die," and the tendency for American troops to stop and dig in at almost any resistance. Soon it became noticeable that Third Army platoons actually had begun to shoot differently than did soldiers in other corps. A contemporary observer of Patton's army remarked:

> Marching fire seemed most popular in Third Army. Patton told his soldiers:
> "The proper way to advance . . . is to utilize marching fire and keep moving. . . . One round should be fired every two or three steps. The whistle of the bullets, the scream of the ricochet . . . have such an effect that . . . small arms fire becomes negligible. . . . The most foolish thing possible is to stop under such fire. Keep working . . . forward. Shooting adds to your self-confidence, because you are doing something."
> One battalion commander said he had never heard of marching fire until he "landed in Third Army." Advancing on the enemy with all guns blazing kept the Germans' heads down and prevented accurate counterfire. Soldiers' morale and confidence increased with the feeling that they were part of an attacking force pumping out "invincible fire" that smothered the enemy. One unit reported that marching fire "paid off 100 percent in diminishing casualties, improving self-confidence of our men, and enabling us to take many difficult objectives," and went on to add that "many men are really sold on this system of battle."

Patton reiterated that all weapons available to the division must be fired constantly. "Our mortars and our artillery are superb weapons," Patton lectured, "when they are firing. When silent, they are junk—see that they fire."[83]

We have discussed earlier Patton's obsession with speed and rapid movement—both as a way to outflank slower-moving and often horse-drawn enemy infantry columns, and as a practical matter of keeping his troops alert, healthy, and battle-ready. In addition, Patton, more than any of the other American military commanders, realized that fluidity matched perfectly the innate American frontier experience, and the American soldier's love affair with the machine. Movement thus could be another tool in Patton's effort to create an ideological army of swarming avengers. Patton realized that young American males liked nothing better than to speed over roads in powerful and deadly tanks, jeeps, and troop carriers—and any army which stressed just that component of mechanized warfare would develop in these same recruits a natural enthusiasm. Patton reminded his men that they were unlike even their own ancestors who had stayed put in Europe, but rather were the off-spring of naturally aggressive and adventurous explorers. "Many of you," he bellowed, "have in your veins German and Italian blood. But remember that these ancestors of yours so loved freedom that they gave up home and country to cross the ocean in search of liberty. The ancestors of the people we shall kill lacked the courage to make such a sacrifice and remained slaves." Such men as his, Patton saw, were naturally drawn to armored and reckless assault:

> The way to prevent the enemy from attacking you is to attack him and keep right on attacking him. This prevents him from getting set. . . . Death in bat-tle is a function of time and effective hostile fire. You reduce the hostile fire by your fire. You reduce the time by rapid movement. We Americans are a com-petitive race. . . . We love to win. In this next fight, you are entering the great-est sporting competition of all times. You are competing with Americans and with Allies for the greatest prize of all—victory.[84]

Closely related to the emphasis on speed was Patton's constant reminder that the aim of the Third Army was Berlin, that the task of the GIs was a fi-nite one, a linear distance to be covered, after which they would be shipped home. The destruction of Germany, not merely Germans, was the ultimate goal of his soldiers. Hence the comment of Douglas Southall Freeman about Patton that "his determination to push straight to the Rhine of course recalls Sherman's march to the sea." Patton may have loved war, but like Epaminon-das and Sherman, he left no doubt in the minds of his soldiers that theirs was an army of a season, with a prescribed and rather short tenure, which strove to outflank the enemy and take him prisoner as part of a larger plan to ruin his culture. On the superficial level, Patton's attempt to excite adolescents with the idea of a wild ride into Germany—one in which they could simultane-ously speed through France, fight evil, become heroic, and go home—seems simplistic and at times grotesque. But beneath the profanity and screaming, Patton wished to create a deadly seriousness among his amateurs about the nature of the murderous professionals they would face.[85]

Besides the theatrical harangues, the emphasis on firing their weapons and moving ahead, Patton also insisted on two other areas in which the Third Army would be distinct from other American armies: its officers from Patton downward would be at the front and its men would have the best of supplies. "There has been a great deal of talk about loyalty from the bottom to the top," Patton reminded his men. "Loyalty from the top to the bottom is much more important and much less prevalent. . . . Each in his appropriate sphere, will lead in person. Any commander who fails to obtain his objective and who is not dead or severely wounded, has not done his duty."

Patton also demanded that his men have better food, plentiful supplies of dry socks, and sufficient ammunition—even when that was not the preference of the Allied high command and sometimes required outright insubordination and stealth on his part to ensure his men were given what he thought they deserved. To combat trench foot, he ordered dry socks to be provided for troops on a daily basis. Commanders who stayed in the rear or were stationary while their men advanced were demoted or sacked. Whatever criticism of Patton was leveled by his later adversaries, it was an indisputable fact that the general of the Third Army had almost been killed a number of times in Europe by enemy fire. If fuel was lacking for his men's tanks, soldiers literally took it from wherever they could—captured German stocks, local French supplies, or even First Army's requisitions. The message soon filtered down throughout the army that Patton's men were the best-fed, -clothed, and -cared-for soldiers in Europe, led by officers from the front, not the rear, who had somehow inculcated in over a quarter-million men the idea that a rapid advance headlong into Germany was the shortest way to end the war and offered them the best chance of survival. To read Patton's memoirs—unlike Eisenhower's, Bradley's, or Montgomery's—is to read constantly of the pragmatics of keeping American soldiers alive: detailed accounts of proper equipment use, infantry technique, and command—and the anguish at not being able to keep his army mobile, which alone offered his men salvation from a deadly enemy.[86]

Patton's men, in fact, were ideological warriors who stormed into Germany with the belief that the Third Army was the best and most lethal force in the American army, and one that believed its crusade was at its core a moral one. Patton himself despised battle cast as a soulless struggle of bureaucracy, technology, and business organization, whether that was manifested in slavish adherence to stale plans, slow progress on the battlefield, dull speeches, reluctance to use honest, graphic language, or failure to visit the front. This animosity on Patton's part arose not just because bureaucracy was antithetical to his own romantic and warrior spirit, but because he felt that such a corporate approach was inefficient, sluggish, and allowed the anonymous clerk to be unaccountable. Worse, corporate war simply got too many of his good men killed. When Eisenhower criticized him for his fiery speeches, Patton replied that he has chosen the wrong target: "My talks make men fight. . . . At the moment all the stress is on unostentatious men who are not criticized because they are colorless."[87]

Stephen Ambrose has observed that despite military sociology's received wisdom that all modern soldiers—Americans particularly—fight only for the immediate safety of a small cadre of friends within their unit, GIs in Normandy really did see themselves on a crusade:

> And yet there is something more. Although the GIs were and are embarrassed to talk or write about the cause they fought for, in marked contrast to their great-grandfathers who fought in the Civil War, they were the children of democracy and they did more to help spread democracy around the world than any other generation in history.[88]

Patton, unlike any other Allied commander, understood this war of ideas and spirit. Of American generals, he sensed best, as did Sherman, that democratic soldiers are not fond of the discipline of militarism. They do not naturally like distant and drawn-out campaigns; they are antiaristocratic, and lack the same degree of blind devotion to a strong man that those defenders of an autocratic society exhibit. If entrenched, they quickly tire of war; if they are kept on the defensive, they lose their spirit; if their commanders are to the rear, they feel the war itself is unfair; and if they are not reminded constantly of the moral stakes of their struggle, they seek simply to survive rather than to kill their enemy.

This August 19, to keep the Americans fighting and moving in the best traditions of the frontier spirit and true to the way they were drilled, Patton could not stop at the Seine. The weather was still warm and dry; the days long; the road ahead to Germany was clear; and he had every intention of crossing the Rhine in a few days and turning his men loose in an undefended fatherland. Impressive Tiger tanks and machine pistols would do the German army little good if it was retreating and demoralized, with hundreds of thousands of Americans chasing the soldiers of the Wehrmacht across France. What a strange war, thought Patton, always to be halted just when the enemy was collapsed and in disarray.[89]

6

THE LABYRINTH OF SLAVERY

ARGENTAN, FRANCE

August 12, 1944 (V-E Day Minus 270 Days)

But it is not so much the pain to come of the Trojans
that troubles me, not even of Priam the king nor Hekabe
not the thought of my brothers who in their numbers and valour
shall drop in the dust under the hands of men who hate them,
as troubles me the thought of you, when some bronze-armoured
Achaian leads you off, taking away your day of liberty,
in tears; and in Argos you must work at the loom of another
and carry water from the spring Messeis or Hypereia,
all unwilling, but strong will be the necessity upon you.

—Homer, *Iliad*

"NOTHING doing," Bradley ordered Patton. "Don't go beyond Argentan. Stop where you are and build up on that shoulder." George Patton's race a week later to the Seine to trap all the German forces in Normandy west of the river should never have been necessary. There was no need for a bitter fall in the Lorraine or an even worse winter in the Bulge. Most of those fleeing enemy troops could have been surrounded and destroyed in early August 1944—hundreds of miles to the west at the small town of Argentan, not far from the Normandy coast.

367

Patton was dumfounded. The next day, August 13, he tried again for permission to press north from Argentan, this time with Bradley's assistant Leven Allen: "Have you talked with Brad?" The answer was the same. "Yes, George. The answer is always no."

Always no? Patton turned to his staff officers and ordered: "The question why XV Corps halted on the east-west line through Argentan is certain to become of historical importance. I want a stenographic record of this conversation included in the History of the Third Army." Patton's Third Army had officially been operational in Normandy for only eleven full days, and this was the *first*—though not the last—time that his armored columns had been ordered to halt, when there was no organized German resistance in their front, and a great chance to envelop and trap thousands of retreating enemy soldiers.

Later Patton recorded Bradley's stop order at Argentan in his diary:

> It was perfectly feasible to continue the operation. Allen repeated the order [from Bradley] to halt on the line and consolidate. I believe that the order emanated from 21st Army Group, and was either due to jealousy of the Americans or to utter ignorance of the situation or to a combination of the two. It is very regrettable that the XV Corps was ordered to halt, because it could have gone on to Falaise and made contact with the Canadians northwest of that point and definitely and positively closed the gap.[90]

It was as if Hannibal had ordered his victorious Carthaginians to cease their final enclosure of the Roman consular armies at Cannae, in fear that the pressure of 50,000 surviving panicky legionaries might break apart his thin lines of envelopment—and thus the trapped Romans would have been allowed to escape through a deliberate hole in his encirclement. So at Argentan, France, on August 12, George Patton was ordered to stop his XV Corps under General Wade Haislip at Argentan, because of the high command's fear that his armor might either meet head-on friendly Canadian troops slowly descending from the north or be steamrolled by desperate Germans heading east. The result of the delay? On the next week of confusion and Allied uncertainty, an enormous force of nearly 175,000 to 200,000 surrounded German troops now had for another week a fifteen-mile corridor of escape between encircling though strangely complacent Allied armies.

Battle commanders always dream of repeating Cannae—a legendary opportunity that rarely is offered on the battlefield. But now with the entire German army in their grasp, the American generals were allowing that singular gift of an entire surrounded army—out of fear or ignorance—to escape. Patton had failed to convince his superior Montgomery in Sicily to trap the Germans on the island before they might cross to Italy, and now once again an entire German army with ostensibly no chance of free exit would not only survive, but would return to fight Americans within a matter of weeks.

Bradley in his memoirs sought to blame Montgomery for the halt, and, extraordinarily, also bragged that he had stopped Patton from a "brash and foolish overextension." He somehow claimed all at once that (1) Patton's advance beyond Argentan would be "a slap in the face" to the Canadians marching from the north; (2) that Patton had infuriated Bradley with his "boastful, supercilious attitude"; (3) that he preferred "a solid shoulder at Argentan to the possibility of a broken neck at Falaise"; (4) that the Germans were already mostly escaping and ready for a counterattack.

We now know, of course, as Bradley must have when he wrote A General's Life, that Montgomery sought to close the gap, but the Canadians were having difficulties and wished, rather than resented, succor; that Patton was frantic and desperate—not boastful—to allow his men to take Argentan; that there was no chance of a broken neck; and that the Germans on August 13, 1944, were *not* mostly gone and *not* planning a counterattack, but disorganized, trapped, and desperate.

Hubert Essame years ago put the tragic decision at Argentan in the proper context of the Allied effort to end the war in 1944:

> Posterity, with its knowledge of the actual plight of the Germans at the time denied to Eisenhower, may justifiably conclude that the complete annihilation of the Germans could have been achieved and a decision reached which might well have enabled the war to be ended in 1944. Patton and Haislip, with the 2nd French Armoured Division, 5th Armored Division and the rest of XV Corps at grips with the battered rump of Panzer Group Eberbach, had it within their power to fight a decisive action at half-price in terms of American life. Argentan might have been as great a battle honor in the annals of the American Army as Second Manassas or Chancellorsville.[91]

Of some 80,000 to 110,000 German soldiers trapped in the actual pocket, at least 50,000 escaped. While there were probably almost nineteen German divisions ruined in or near Falaise, there was lost a good chance to eliminate in one fell swoop at least 100,000 Germans—and perhaps another 150,000 to the north and south. These were the other desperate German armies that would have suddenly lost all their flank support and soon been subject to similar envelopments. But the missed opportunity was not merely one of numbers captured or equipment lost; if an entire German army could be annihilated, the shock of that catastrophe would ripple throughout the Western front, and the Allies could race through an undefended France into a poorly defended and stunned Germany. The Germans would not lose a battle, but rather an entire army group—and that might have been a psychological blow worse to the Wehrmacht than the disaster at Stalingrad, which was far distant, not a few hundred miles, from the German heartland.

Yet Patton alone seemed to grasp the lost opportunity, and thus immediately raced farther east to the Seine River, to attempt to salvage the envelopment, seeking a second chance at an even wider entrapment of the fleeing German Seventh Army and Fifth Panzer Army. By August 16, Third Army corps were in Chartres and Orléans, and on their way to the Seine across a one-hundred-mile front. His Third Army worried not so much about those Germans killed or captured at Falaise, but far more about those alive and retreating, who might well escape across the Seine and so kill his men in eastern France at some not-so-future date.

In contrast, most American commanders were greatly impressed, stunned even, by the undeniable destruction they had wrought at the Falaise Gap. Even though the pocket was not closed until August 19 by the Polish 1st Armored Division and American 90th, the Falaise encirclement had cost the Germans dearly. No accurate figures of their losses are possible, given the chaotic week of retreat and the horrendous confusion inside the salient. Still, German and Allied historians put the number of Germans taken prisoner at about 50,000, and those killed at 10,000—mostly through murderous Allied artillery barrages and constant strafing and bombing of the retreating columns by American fighters. Almost all the Germans' equipment was lost.

Eisenhower visited the battlefield hours after the gap was closed and described the carnage:

> The battlefield at Falaise was unquestionably one of the greatest "killing grounds" of any of the war areas. Roads, highways, and fields were so choked with destroyed equipment and with dead men and animals that passage through the area was extremely difficult. Forty-eight hours after the closing of the gap I was conducted through it on foot, to encounter scenes that could be described only by Dante. It was literally possible to walk for hundreds of yards at a time, stepping on nothing but dead and decaying flesh.

Even as late as 1961 numerous wrecked German tanks still littered the Falaise area, and the partial skeletons of dead and forgotten Germans were exhumed by Normandy farmers yearly for nearly half a century after. Other observers have described in graphic detail the horror of the German carnage, which bears an eerie resemblance to the later "highway of death" in the Gulf War, when American pilots had similarly trapped a retreating Iraqi column speeding back to Baghdad, laden with Kuwaiti loot. James Lucas and James Barker remark of the fate of the trapped Seventh and Fifth German armies:

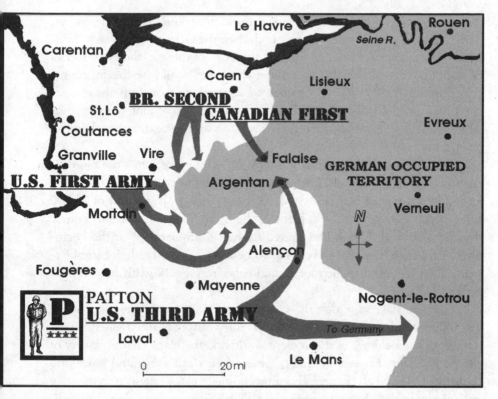

THE FALAISE GAP

Above the battlefield shimmered a miasma of decay and putrefaction; everything was covered with flies and bluebottles. In the hot August sun the cattle which had been killed only days before were masses of crawling maggots, and the unburied Germans, swollen to elephantine grossness by the hot sun inflating the gasses in the stomach, lay with blackened faces in grotesque positions. Here there was no dignity of death. In the worst bombarded areas fragments of bodies festooned the trees . . . some roads were impassable due to the congestion caused by burnt-out trucks, dead horses, smashed tanks and destruction on a scale the Western Allies had never seen.

For thousands of Germans who escaped the actual pocket, along with the other 150,000 troops in Normandy who would make it to the border in safety and the Siegfried Line, the war would now go on into another year. As terrible as this scene of 10,000 dead German combatants was, far worse were the innocent men and women who were being butchered daily in the thousands this August by the Nazis to the rear of these front-line German defenders. The Nazi killing machine could only end when the German army was annihilated or surrendered. In the "terrible arithmetic" of the war, the more scenes of military carnage like this at Falaise, the fewer would be the innocents gassed in Eastern Europe and Germany. Patton alone roared on ahead eastward in search of still more Germans. He preferred to count the Germans who were still alive rather than those dead, to visit the next, rather than the prior, battlefield.

Still, when the Third Army got most of its divisions across the Seine at the end of August, it had killed, wounded, or captured over 100,000 Germans, destroyed over 500 tanks and 700 heavy guns—all at a cost of 16,000 total casualties, less than 13 percent of the total American losses in France thus far. Although Patton had started farthest from Germany at the beginning of the month, at the end of August he was a hundred miles nearer Germany than any other Allied force, and eager to press on with full supplies across the Rhine.[92]

The Nazi slave state that the Germans at Falaise were dying to preserve was unlike anything seen in the long and sorry history of servitude, different from both the helotage of the ancient world and the black chattel slavery of the South. True, Messenian Helots, given their ties to ancestral lands and their identifiable dialect, were also a recognizable class, one seen as separate and inferior to their Spartan overlords. Still, no Spartan could claim Messenians were not Greeks. Much of the moral capital behind Epaminondas's liberation lay in the fact that an entire Greek people had been unjustly enslaved.

Furthermore, what distinguished Spartan helotage from chattel slavery elsewhere in Greece was not so much the conditions of bondage of individual Messenians, but rather the vast perverted apparatus necessary to enslave an entire race. The professional nature of the Spartan army, the creation of a secret police, the institutionalization of torture and random murder—all that was rarely found outside of Sparta and clearly derived from the need to force an entire people to feed a small elite.

In addition, because, unlike chattels, Helots were collectively identifiable by ethnic background and region, the institution of their oppression took on a systematic approach—hence the Spartans' ritual declaration of war each year against the Messenians. The Spartan state, not Spartan individuals, owned the Helots. The further presence of freed Laconian Helots, the Perioikoi, and various categories of disenfranchised Spartans all were a logical result of creating such racial and social categories of exploitation. Much of our current disdain for Sparta arises precisely because of its institutionalized oppression of the Helots; in both its methodology of enslavement and emphasis on ethnicity, Sparta, in fact, shares features with National Socialism.

Nevertheless, although the Spartan state, like the Nazis, took a businesslike approach to servitude, there was still no state policy to eradicate the Helots. To exterminate them *en masse* was against the Hellenic notion of killing other Greek civilians. It made no sense economically given the need for Helot farm produce; and it was perhaps well beyond the physical ability of the Spartan army itself to extinguish a people nearly twenty times more populous. Epaminondas would find no mass graves in Messenia.

The institution of Negro slavery in the Old South shared similar economic—and to a lesser extent ethical—restraints against mass killing. Whereas blacks could be routinely whipped and occasionally murdered, their value as chattels ensured that they were not systematically rounded up and slaughtered. Plantationists were not so much worried about the overabundance of Africans in the South as their growing scarcity—given the end of the slave trade and the increasing Federal restrictions on the spread of slavery to the frontier and newly incorporated territories. Whereas there grew up an accepted theology of racial supremacy that tried to show that blacks were genetically inferior and hence deserving of slavery, even among the worst Southern racists there was never any idea to wipe them out systematically as a people.

Whereas Jews in Germany were often highly educated and had capital, blacks in the South were purposely kept ignorant and without money. Southerners then found little need to blame Negro slaves for the immediate shortcomings of Confederate society and were not jealous of their economic status. As long as blacks were clearly without legal rights and economic hope, the slaves' masters were paternalistic rather than always murderous. The pseudoscience of racial superiority was used defensively, as an apology to outside critics for the horror of chattel slavery in America—not as an aggressive tool for the systematic extermination of blacks. Americans who were tired of the entire question of slavery at most argued that they should be repatriated to Africa or packed off to distant colonies—a brutal and nonsensical enough policy, since most had been on American shores for generations and were more American than many whites, but still a far cry from the notion of murdering men, women, and children *in toto*. Sherman would discover in Georgia slave hovels, instruments of punishment, and plenty of evidence that runaways had been hunted down and shot. Yet the camps at Andersonville and elsewhere were designed mostly for white Union prisoners, not African slaves.

The evil of the Nazi slave state thus eclipsed both ancient and modern slavery in conception and magnitude in a variety of areas. Like the Helots, the Jews were seen as an inferior race. Like the black slave, the non-Aryan was deemed worthy only to work for his master. *Unlike* both prior evils, in Hitler's Germany it was agreed that there should be no economic curbs on killing the unfree, as had been true with both the Spartans and the Confederates. The Nazis were perfectly willing to incur financial hardship through the loss of valuable slave workers and in the use of precious rail and industrial resources to facilitate their mass murder.

National Socialism, which prided itself on protecting the German citizen from the degrading monotony of industrial society, bragged that the spirit and morality of its citizens were as important as their economic well-being. Jews would be killed to ensure the purity of the racial stock of the citizens of Germany, even if it made no economic sense and actually hindered the war effort. There was a real sense in the last months of the war that Germany was in a race of death, a race between the capacity of the ovens to incinerate all Jews and Slavs in Europe and the approach of Allied armies of liberation. In the Nazi mind, if the Wehrmacht were to lose, at least it could hang on long enough to ensure the extinction of European Jewry—an act which future generations might look back on as worth even the sacrifice of the entire Third Reich.

Of that perverted way of thinking, American GIs sensed rightly that the ultimate purpose of the German army was not rationally directed so much to the advancement of Nazi imperialism as to the promotion of a racial and ethnic cleansing on a global scale. German soldiers were ordered to the front not just to kill Americans and to defend Germany, but to ensure that Adolf Hitler would be free to change the racial makeup of Europe. Stephen Ambrose relates the immediate answer of a captured GI to his German guard when asked, "Why are you making war against us?" The American soldier shot back, "We are fighting to free you from the fantastic idea that you are a master race." Patton's men may not have been driving east with the full and exact knowledge that their success meant the end to an intricate labyrinth of death camps and the salvation of millions slated to be gassed, but they had a clear enough idea from Hitler's and Goebbels's speeches, Russian reports of atrocity, rumors from the resistance movements, and interrogations of German officers and Waffen SS troops to surmise that the Nazis were indiscriminate murderers.[93]

The resources of the Spartan and Confederate states had been invested largely in the maintenance and management of slavery—separate laws, special statutes, rules concerning marriage and citizenship—in order to ensure a peaceable and conservative system of *economic* exploitation. In contrast, the religious, scientific, philosophical, and industrial resources of the Third Reich were revolutionary and disruptive, always in service to the previously unheard-of idea that millions of former respectable and prosperous European citizens were systematically to be deemed racially inferior and worthy of immediate extermination. To accomplish a social and cultural revolution of that magnitude in such a short time—helotage had existed for well over three centuries before Epaminondas's invasion, and Negroes had been enslaved in the South for over two hundred years before Sherman's arrival—the level of German involvement in organizing and justifying murder was unlike anything seen in ancient Sparta or the Old South. The Spartans might argue that helotage allowed a small elite to achieve military and political virtue; Southerners might claim that slavery helped the inferior Negro as it aided the Southern economy. Nazis simply desired immediately to start killing Jews and other "inferior" peoples, in and outside of Germany, and devoted their financial, intellectual, and cultural capital to achieve and justify that end in as short a time as possible. If Spartans and Confederates had their way, Helots and black slaves would be ubiquitous; if the Nazi agenda was fulfilled, Jewish slaves would no longer exist.

Consequently, we should keep the issue of urgency in mind. Patton's entrance into Germany meant—whether or not his infantrymen knew the full extent of Nazi atrocity to the east—not merely "the end of the war" and a cessation of killing between Germans and Americans, but rather a halt to the entire Nazi industrial plan of killing innocents. When he stopped, thousands died; when he advanced, the day of salvation was nearer. If successful in their great marches, his two spiritual predecessors could ensure freedom; but Patton's success meant life itself. His superiors monitored and controlled Patton's progress on the basis of overall Allied strategy, logistics, intramural harmony between armies—and occasional jealousy. But that concern does not cloud the real issue that his rapid advance in fall 1944 was about the only chance millions—who would, in fact, be dead by May 1945—had to survive the death camps. More Jews would be gassed from the time Patton closed in on the German border in late summer 1944 until the May 1945 surrender than had been killed during the entire first four years of the war.

There is also the simple question of time and space. Sparta was a preindustrial society of not much more than 30,000 residents, and without cultural or economic influence beyond the southern Peloponnese. The American South possessed not many more than 11 million free and slave citizens, and was hemmed in by the ocean, a hostile North, and an unsympathetic West. In global terms, it had little industrial power. Its importance in international relations was largely due to its production of cotton.

How different was the case of Germany! Soon after the start of World

War Two, the Third Reich stretched from the Atlantic nearly to Moscow, from the Arctic Circle to sub-Saharan Africa, with industrial and population resources unmatched by any single country. Germany was and is the core state of Europe. As late as 1942, Germany produced four times as much steel as Russia. Until well into the war, it dwarfed American military production, which was relatively haphazard before 1942. The presence of an excellent rail system, a skilled workforce, sophisticated electronic communications, and an advanced petrochemical industry meant that for the first time in history a modern state had the means to pursue a holocaust according to the mass-production principles inherent in modern industry. If neither Sparta nor the Confederacy had the ideological zeal or the technological means to kill on a wide scale, Germany most surely did.

There is good reason to believe that anti-Semitism became almost a German religion, permeating far beyond the confines of National Socialism. When reading accounts of the death camps, one is struck not just by the bureaucracy and technology of the death industry, but also by the indiscriminate nature of shootings, stranglings, beatings, and all sorts of torture—and how such barbarity was sometime engaged in by regular German soldiers who were not Nazis and even by German workers outside the camp compounds. True, in World War One, the German army had sent back to Germany as enslaved workers nearly a half-million French and Belgian citizens, and thousands of those captives had perished in transit and at work in German factories. Again, economic exploitation was the driving engine of that earlier inhumanity; thus, while the Kaiser's government might reduce expenditures on food and shelter for indentured servants, it was nevertheless in its interest to keep them alive.

Within five years of the war the Nazi regime would liquidate far more Jews than the entire population of Helots and Confederate slaves put together. Probably over 20,000,000 persons were killed by the Nazi state, apart from the carnage of the Wehrmacht on the battlefield. As many as 16,315,000 of that number were murdered, starved, or worked to death solely on the basis of race, religion, ethnicity, or sexual preference. We must put the evil of the twentieth century into context. Epaminondas freed a quarter million from a degrading serfdom; Sherman burned and plundered the heart of a society that was served by over 4,000,000 slaves. Patton raced toward Germany to dismantle a continental labyrinth of slavery that sought to wipe Jews, Gypsies, Slavs, and a host of other peoples quite literally off the face of the earth.[94]

Finally, Spartan culture was not dynamic—nothing like, for example, classical Athens and its renaissance in drama and art. Other than a few lead figurines, the martial poetry of Tyrtaeus or the choral lyrics of Alcman, and random though impressive hero shrines, there was nothing in Spartan art, literature, or architecture to sweep the popular imagination of Greece. Thucydides remarks that based on Sparta's physical remains, future generations would not understand how it had rivaled the more impressive Athens; it was a pathetic hamlet compared to the majestic Acropolis. Helotage was not merely seen as part of this general Spartan stagnation in cultural life, but by many in Greece as the explanation for the strange militaristic and backward nature of Sparta itself, from its overemphasis on military discipline to the chronic problems of underpopulation to the absence of readily usable coined money.

Similarly, by 1861 the cultural capital of America was clearly in the Northeast, in Boston and New York, with their strong ties to intellectual and artistic life in London and Paris, and their plethora of endowed liberal arts colleges. While there was always a romantic interest in the agrarian life of the South, the growing American intolerance for chattel slavery had cast a shadow over Southern literature and art, which in addition lacked the Northerners' subsidies from plentiful capital and the vibrant commercial life of New England. There was no existing cultural apparatus in the South to spread the idea of either the need for or the morality of Negro servitude beyond its borders.

In contrast, the entire essence of Nazi ideology sought to graft itself onto a long and impressive tradition of German culture and philosophy. Present in Wagner, Hegel, Nietzsche, Spengler, and other distinguished artists and thinkers was the legitimate and often accepted idea of decadence inherent in Western culture, brought on by a leveling democracy and consumer capitalism, a modernism that sought both to make citizens equal when they were not, and to provide them with material comfort that would inevitably blunt their natural aesthetic sense and diminish their very spirit—evils that Nazis now attempted to associate with cosmopolitan and sophisticated Jews. Albert Speer, Hitler's industrial czar, wrote of his youthful attraction toward Nazi thought: "Spengler's *Decline of the West* had convinced me that we were living in a period of decay strongly similar to the late Roman Empire: inflation, decline of morals, impotence of the German Reich. His essay 'Prussianism and Socialism' excited me especially because of the contempt for luxury and comfort it expressed."

Later, as the Nazis killed millions, they looked to the façade of a fertile German philosophic heritage—as well as to a peculiarly aberrant and racialist offshoot of Darwinism. Nazis, like earlier thinkers, argued that they were trying to reintroduce natural hierarchies into Germany, to rediscover the pure German racial essence, and to bring its *Volk* back from a corrupt, urban life into a more natural appreciation for the individual and the need for self-sacrifice.

The worst atrocities of the human spirit were then to be dressed up in pseudo-philosophical terms, designed to appear impressive to the half-educated in Germany and abroad. The Jews, in this line of twisted reasoning, were not Germanic by blood and had no ties to the soil of Germany; their largely non-agricultural wealth was tied to finance and liquid capital—and thus they were purveyors of a capitalism that was profit-oriented and operated outside cultural restraint, slowly eating away at the innate German spirit of which they had no natural claim.

Even the most grotesque orders for Nazi murder were to have a veneer of intellectualism. A brutal SS text in Eastern Europe, full of just such philosophical and scientific pretension, read:

> The sub-human, this apparently fully equal creation of nature, when seen from the biological viewpoint, with hands, feet and a sort of brain, with eyes and a mouth, nevertheless is quite a different, a dreadful creature, is only an imitation of man with man-resembling features, but inferior to any animal as regards intellect and soul. In its interior, this being is a cruel chaos of wild, unrestricted passions, with a nameless will to destruction, with a most primitive lust, and of unmasked depravity. For not everything is alike that has a human face.

Thinkers as diverse as the Nobel Prize–winning Norwegian novelist Knut Hamsun and the German philosopher Martin Heidegger were attracted to some notions of Nazi ideology, whose advocates posed as the protectors of a humane science and civilization, enemies of a crass consumer culture: "Their consciences and humanity protected by a racial *Weltanschauung*, scientifically supported by their interpretation of evolution, and with absolute faith in the rightness of their cause, these murderers could consider themselves cultured and civilized. They really could extol their work at mass murder as a noteworthy contribution to history."

Why, the Nazis insisted, worry about profit, or what was narrowly economically rational, when the removal of the Jews was part of a higher calling that sought to restore the German *Geist*, without the corrupting influence of timid and meek men who flourished in the venal democracies of the liberal West? In short, there had always been in Germanic thought an advocacy for "barbarous utopias," in which a naturally select few were to be immune from the confining effects of democracy and supposedly "civil society." The history of civilization, after all, in this Spenglerian-Hegelian view had been one of an innately racially superior German spirit, safely ensconced beyond the Rhine, seeking to borrow from, but *not* capitulate entirely to, Western civilization.[95]

Because Germany, unlike Sparta and the Confederacy, was neither a cultural nor commercial backwater, its adoption of the politics of slavery made it far more dangerous, far more likely that satellite states abroad—an Italy, Spain, or Eastern Europe—could either be convinced or coerced to adopt similar politics. Germany traditionally may not have been the most anti-Semitic state in Europe and Asia—both Poland and Russia had a more checkered history of Jewish harassment—but since antiquity it had a much stronger heritage of racial awareness, and now a government whose savagery had not been seen in Western civilization for over a millennium. Whereas Epaminondas and Sherman marched into apartheid societies to destroy a local problem, by the time Patton liberated southern France, the slave system of the Third Reich involved millions, most of whom were well beyond the reach of the Third Army. In Italy, Spain, Eastern Europe, even the United Kingdom, and South and North America, there were millions sympathetic to National Socialism—more so, as the victories of the German army by 1940 seemed to validate the racial tenets of Nazi ideology.

We should also remember that Epaminondas's men were not considered deserving of mass enslavement by the Spartans whom they fought; classical Greek hoplites customarily did not seek to enslave each other after the pitched battle was over. Southerners did not think Northern Union soldiers on a par with their own black slaves. Yet many of Patton's GIs—American Jews, Mexicans, Poles, Russians, Blacks—knew that should the Nazis prevail, they and others like them would be slated for death or concentration camps based not on their national but rather racial affiliation. This Patton knew—hence, his constant demonization of the Nazi soldier. Stephen Ambrose relates a typical story of a captured SS sergeant:

> The wounded German, who spoke excellent English, demanded to know if there was any Jewish blood in the plasma. The medic said damned if he knew, in the United States people didn't make such a distinction. The German said if he didn't have a guarantee that there was no Jewish blood he would refuse treatment.
>
> "I had been listening and had heard enough," Norris [an American captain] remembered. "I turned to this SS guy and in very positive terms I told him I really didn't care whether he lived or not, but if he did not take the plasma he would certainly die. He looked at me calmly and said, 'I would rather die than have any Jewish blood in me.'
>
> "So he died."

A fifth difference was that National Socialism, unlike, say, Stalinism, sought to work within the confines of capitalism and the hallowed laws of private property and profit and loss. Free markets had led Germany, unlike Russia, to become a highly affluent and industrialized nation. Its racial policy of exterminating the Jews in some ways was an insidious process, because it existed side by side with a modern and opulent state that had seemingly protected the economic rights of the individual. One could go to work freely, buy and sell property, prosper even right up until 1943 in Germany without worry about or perhaps even direct knowledge of the mass killings—unlike the Soviet terror state, in which private property was always being confiscated and everyone—Russian or not—was liable to be called into special Peoples' Courts. The Nazis were perfectly willing to incur costs in exterminating the Jews, in part because the Holocaust operated quite effectively within capitalism—bids were taken for the ovens, competition was open for superior brands of lethal gas, and labor and infrastructure to create Auschwitz were paid out in budgeted German marks.

In some sense, helotage was antithetical to the growing free market common in most of the Greek city-states; the Southern economy and plantation agriculture were forever altered in mostly deleterious ways by the presence of 4,000,000 chattels. Yet, a highly efficient capitalist Nazi Germany actually used its accruing bounty to pay for the cost of Jewish extermination—and thus the Nazi economy often served the efforts to further slavery, rather than vice versa. It was worse still—there was a literal extermination "business": the private fortunes of the Jews—even their clothes, personal property, and gold fillings in their teeth—would be stolen to pay not for tanks and guns, but for their own execution.

Messenian Helots, "like asses," were impoverished; African slaves in the South destitute. Not so all German Jews. Many were decorated veterans of the First World War. More still were part of elite professions. Assimilation was not uncommon. There were a few European Jewish families of vast fortunes in banking, shipping, commerce, and real estate, and thousands more who were married to non-Jews and employed in key positions in the German economy. In the German mind such influential and successful Jews must be held responsible for the past failings of German society. If some had been rich, now it was their turn to be poor. Envy is a much stronger emotion than paternalism—a bigot and racist of the Old South might be condescending to the poor and uneducated Negro, but the German worker under Hitler would resent and despise the wealthier, better-educated, and more cultured Jew. A dichotomy arose: before Hitler, the Jews of Germany had been treated as near-legal equals with Germans, or at least in no way similar to the slavish condition of the Helots of Sparta or the blacks of the South; after Hitler, unlike the two former groups, they were slated for oblivion.

In short, Patton's GIs were marching into a slave society like none other in the history of civilization. While other countries—the Soviet Union and

Mao's China—would eventually murder more than Hitler's Germany, no country killed so efficiently, so scientifically, so rapidly, and so completely on the basis of race, ethnic background, physical and mental impairment, and sexuality. Never had the moral stakes for a democratic army of a season been so high. Patton stated that explicitly to his men when he outlined why they were in Europe in the first place: they were fighting Germans quite literally out of "hate" for the Nazis and their barbarism. In a letter to all Third Army soldiers, Patton finished with the following:

> We are now entering the final stage of a great war, of a great victory! This victory can only be attained by the maximum use of all weapons, both physical and spiritual. It is the duty of all commanders to see that their men are fully aware of the many vile deeds perpetrated upon civilization by Germans, and that they attack with the utmost determination, ferocity, and hate. I am sure that every man will do his duty, and I am therefore sure that victory is simply a question of when we find the enemy.

Americans today do not like to read of their generals ordering GIs to hate and kill, but then Americans do not like either the idea of an entire system devoted to mass murder—what Patton called "the many vile deeds perpetrated upon civilization by Germans."

The categories of inferiority under Nazi apartheid were even more confusing than those that had existed at Sparta and in the South. At the center of the Nazi's racial cosmology, of course, were the citizens of Germany itself and the satellite German-speaking provinces in eastern France, Switzerland, and Eastern Europe—the only true and chosen "Aryans." While much pseudo-scientific emphasis was put on racial purity—hair and eye color, physique, bone structure—in fact, what constituted the master race was a confused and contradictory idea that simply came down to Caucasian native German-speakers who were not Jewish.

Until March 1945 the Third Army met this so-called master race almost exclusively in the context of the battlefield in France. Most German soldiers in the ranks were ostensibly nonideological. As adolescents, they were not fighting per se to exterminate Jews or to save Aryans, as much out of blind patriotism, natural youthful zeal—and, by 1945, for the defense of their homeland and children. For most soldiers, what animosity there was toward the Jews consisted more of class hatred toward an entire group, one more affluent and influential than their own families. Like a Southern white, a poor German in the army might be uneducated and he might have little capital, but under Hitler he now belonged to a new aristocracy—the Aryan non-Jew.

In addition, it was clear to even the most uneducated German that much of the prosperity of the early war years was due to the presence of slave and concentration camp labor supplied by Jews, Eastern Europeans, and Slavs. As scholars have pointed out:

> The initial successes of the regime on the far-flung battlefields of Europe were enthusiastically acclaimed by virtually all sections of the population. The SD [SS Security Service] reported a "previously unprecedented inner solidarity" and the effective demise of political opposition. The regime's increasing use of concentration camp and foreign forced labour made the working class more or less passive accomplices of Nazi racial policy. The resort to foreign labour, which, of course, contradicted the regime's ideological fixation with racial purity, was largely conditioned by its reluctance to increase the proportion of women in the work force.

Interviews with retired Germans have sometimes confirmed this view that Hitler's slave state had brought average citizens economic security as never before. For many, the recollections of 1935–42 were often characterized as a peaceful and prosperous period—indeed the most enjoyable era of their lives. Interviewers discovered that "the only remarkable thing about this would seem to be that the years between 1935 and 1942 appear as 'quiet' and 'normal' times—and this in the recollections of inhabitants of a working class region where in the first years of dictatorship the labour movement suffered the fiercest persecution."

The general notion that the German citizen profited through the enslavement of others was not lost on the GI. When Americans finally arrived in Germany itself, they had little sympathy for the local citizens and were surprised at their relative comfort:

> First and Third armies were advancing mostly in rural areas untouched by war. The GIs were spending their nights in houses. They would give the inhabitants five minutes or so to clear out. The German families were indignant. The GIs were insistent. As Lt. Max Lake put it in a March 30 letter home, "None of us have any sympathy for them, because we all have been taught to accept the consequences of our actions—these people apparently feel they are the victims of something they had no hand in planning, and they seem to feel they are being mistreated."[96]

Most German soldiers, when they thought of Americans at all in an abstract sense, considered GIs as representative of a motley and mongrel nation, not necessarily evil as much as pathetic. Ours was a country in which gangsters and miscegenation were the logical dividends of unchecked immigration, a nation devoted to excessive individualism and democratic capitalism at any cost. Our troops were spoiled by creature comforts and material bounty, who relied on artillery and air support rather than courage in facing the knights of the Wehrmacht. To the Nazi propagandists we Americans were deluded and distant, rather than inherently evil and familiar. Most of the murderous fanaticism in the war was on the Eastern front—in battles in which the majority of prisoners on both sides perished, and in a theater where the German soldier was indoctrinated that he was a front-line fighter against the Jewish Bolshevism that was creeping ever nearer to Germany's eastern border.

Patton and the Americans had no clear hatred for captured German soldiers on the Western front, who were not members of the Nazi party or the SS; they assumed that front-line troops were simply brainwashed by a childhood of constant indoctrination. But while the killing was going on in France, most Americans still considered soldiers of the Wehrmacht ruthless and dangerous foes on the battlefield, whose skill and tenacity derived in part from the Nazi fanaticism of their nation at large. Patton reminded his men that "Hitler was a paper-hanging son of a bitch," that "Nazis are the enemy," and that they were to "wade into them—spill their blood—Shoot them in the belly!"[97]

It is not true that Patton's rants were directed against a patriotic German army manipulated by the Nazis, with little loyalty for Hitler. The German officer corps was largely devoted to reclaiming both the prestige of a military disgraced by the losses of World War One, and mesmerized by the allure of a world Nazi state that would require a huge, expensive, and modern elite to enforce its will. Their dislike of Hitler—aside from a natural Prussian aristocratic disdain for an Austrian corporal—did not arise from the horrific nature of his policies as much as from his constant interference with military operations—and his frequently disastrous tactical orders that resulted in thousands of needless German army deaths.

Within the high command there were also Nazi zealots, indeed entire SS divisions, and assorted military police and extermination squads who were outside military control, reporting directly to Himmler rather than through the normal chain of army command. All these latter groups were infused with Nazi ideology and claimed that they fought Americans for the ideal of German racial superiority. These zealots were usually at the center of random killing of Jews and Slavs in the field, and they engineered reprisals against local villages and the gratuitous slaughter of Russian, British, and American prisoners of war. Sometimes the distinctions between Nazi fanatics and the traditional German military were completely blurred. Even so-called professional soldiers could not resist the Nazi allure. So, for example, on November 20, 1941 General Erich von Manstein issued his own call to arms to his army in blatantly racist terms:

> Judaism constitutes the mediator between the enemy in the rear and the still fighting remnants of the Red Army and Red leadership. It has a stronger hold than in Europe on all key positions of the political leadership and administration; it occupies commerce and trade and further forms cells for all the disturbances and possible rebellion.
>
> The Jewish-Bolshevik system must be eradicated once and for all. Never again may it interfere in our European living space.
>
> The German soldier is therefore not only charged with the task of destroying the power instrument of this system. He marches forth also as a carrier of a racial conception and as an avenger of all the atrocities which have been committed against him and the German people
>
> The soldier must show understanding for the harsh atonement of Judaism, the spiritual carrier of the Bolshevik terror.[98]

Below the Germans in the hierarchy of the Nazi slave empire were to be the conquered peoples of Western Europe. In general, Dutch, Belgians, Scandinavians, and French were considered branches of a semi-Aryan kindred race, but irrevocably weakened by years of liberal democracy and racial intermingling. Their societies were to be left largely intact, but stripped of political autonomy and personal freedoms, and strictly integrated economically with Germany for the profit of the Third Reich. As long as Frenchmen and others supplied the Germans with war materials and cheap labor, they could go on living in peace under a strict set of Nazi laws that ended any notion of civil rights. That did not mean that thousands of Dutch, Belgians, and French—as in World War One—would not be worked to death inside Germany and thousands more would die from death and disease, given the scarcity of food and medicine brought on by the German occupation and the war in Europe. Hitler simply intended that northern Europeans would get the first scraps left over once Germany had reorganized the European economy for its own benefit. Communists, homosexuals, and religious figures inside occupied Western Europe, whatever their racial affiliation, of course, were given no exemption from the camps.

While for most of the war organized military resistance in the occupied West was relatively minor and has been greatly exaggerated in postwar mythmaking, and whereas Western Europeans were often bombed accidentally by Allied warplanes, in nearly every case the French and Belgians still welcomed the arrival of Patton and his Free French divisions, many of the latter operating with American equipment under the aegis of the Third Army. Each mile Patton headed eastward, he was greeted by relieved Frenchmen who for the most part felt that the disruption and desolation brought on by the American invasion paled in comparison to the years of slow economic and spiritual strangulation that was slated under Nazi occupation. "Every one in this part of the country," Patton wrote of his dash through southern France, "has quit work and stands along the roads cheering, throwing kisses or apples and offering wine, all as presents. I get quite an ovation, but all soldiers get some."[99]

Millions, of course, to the east fared much worse. In general, the *Untermenschen* of the Third Reich to be interned and worked as slave peoples were Poles, Serbs, and various groups of Slavs and Russians, who were felt to be racially inferior to Western Europeans and near savages of uncivilized countries. While not murdered in the same systematic manner as were the Jews, they were worked mercilessly, often murdered gratuitously, and had little if any freedom. In aggregate numbers, probably more Slavs, Gypsies, and East Europeans perished than did Jews. Millions from Poland and occupied Russia late in the war were shipped into the Third Reich proper to work in munitions factories and heavy industry. As the Third Army headed eastward into Germany, it liberated such conscripted workers, whose condition was far worse than those under Nazi occupation to the west in France. Best estimates put the number of Slavs, Poles, Ukrainians, Gypsies, and ethnic Russians who died due to exposure, exhaustion, starvation, shootings, or reprisal executions by the Third Reich at somewhere around 10,547,000. In the last six-year period of the war, somewhere between 8,000,000 and 12,000,000 captives were sent eastward to factories inside Germany. Albert Speer, who reckoned the total was lower—between 7,000,000 and 8,000,000 conscripted—nevertheless calculated that 10 percent of all workers in Germany died every year from simple exhaustion. This was in addition to some 3,000,000 Russian soldiers who perished in captivity out of a total of nearly 6,000,000 taken prisoner.[100]

Worse still was an entirely different class of unfree—those not grouped by race but by perceived disability—all those whose genes should not be passed on to future generations of the Third Reich: the chronically sick, the mentally ill, homosexuals, and the retarded. For the most part, German or not, to the degree they could not work safely in isolation at menial jobs, these were systematically interned and exterminated, often despite the pleas of friends and family. Such policies predated the war, being inaugurated soon after the ascension of Nazi power in the early 1930s. As many as 220,000 homosexuals and 173,500 handicapped may have been eventually executed. German law was quite precise: in addition to the rounding up of alcoholics and homosexuals, there were extensive categories of illness that would mark one for the death camps or local execution. Under Rubric II of the elimination orders was listed the following: "Anyone is hereditarily ill within the meaning of the law who suffers from one of the following illnesses: 1. Congenital feeble-mindedness; 2. Schizophrenia; 3. Manic depression; 4. Epilepsy; 5. Huntington's chorea; 6. Hereditary blindness; 7. Hereditary deafness; 8. Serious physical deformities."[101]

Finally, of course, were the Jews. Scholars cite hundreds of thousands of Eastern Europeans, Slavs, Gypsies, and others who were killed en masse. But it is safe to say that Jews by far comprised the largest numbers of those who were systematically gassed and cremated in the death camps proper. Whenever it was a question of shooting one prisoner and starving another, Nazi commandants selected Jews first for death. Whereas the slave state may have eventually killed more non-Jews through coerced labor and starvation, the Jews were less frequently allowed to work, and hence the percentage of Jewish dead, given their overall numbers in the occupied territories, was quite astronomical. We should never forget that the Nazis' creation of industrial death camps was largely aimed at the Jews.

How many Jews died? Even given the meticulous record-keeping of the Nazi state, the answer is impossible because of the destruction of documents in the last years of the war and the growing realization among camp commanders that Germany would lose the war and her crimes be exposed to postwar tribunals. Most estimates range from 4,000,000 to 6,000,000. Of the nearly 10,000,000 Jews who lived in Nazi-occupied Europe, Hitler may have slaughtered at least 5,291,000—or about 54 percent of them! The Nazi commandant of Auschwitz has left a summary account of a typical day in the life of the camp, which gives some idea of the industrial nature of the macabre enterprise:

> The cremation of about 2,000 people in five ovens took approximately 12 hours. In Auschwitz there were two installations with 5 double ovens each, and 2 installations with 4 larger ovens each. . . . All of the left-over clothing and effects were sorted by a group of prisoners who worked all the time and were quartered in the effects camp. Once a month valuables were sent to the Reichsbank in Berlin. After they had been cleaned, items of clothing were sent to armaments firms for the Eastern labour working there or to repatriates. Gold from the teeth was melted down and likewise sent once a month to the sanitation office of the Waffen SS. . . . The highest number of gassings in one day in Auschwitz was 10,000. That was the most that could be carried out in one day with the equipment available.

As horrific as was the number of the German war dead in the Falaise Gap, this was little more than a day's work at Auschwitz. And we can begin to understand the stakes at hand in even a momentary halt in Patton's progress east: his Third Army by late summer 1944 was the *only* force, on any front, that had a real chance to break into Germany and to stop the horror before the new year.[102]

Months—and millions of deaths—later, in April 1945, the Third Army finally arrived in the heart of the Nazi slave state. They quickly liberated the Ohrdruf Nord forced labor camp, the first such camp to be freed by the Allies. Patton told his stunned division general, Walton Walker, "You'll never believe how bastardly these Krauts can be, until you've seen this pesthole yourself." He later wrote, "Walker and Middleton had very wisely decided to have as many soldiers as possible visit the scene, which I believe will teach our men to look out for the Germans. The mayor of the town, together with his wife, when confronted with the spectacle, went home and hanged themselves. There are several others in the vicinity who I think will be found dead."

Later the next day he wrote to John McCloy: "Yesterday, I saw the most horrible sight I have ever seen. It was a German slave camp. . . . We took all the soldiers we could to see it, as I believe it is one of the best arguments against fraternization that I know." At a press conference the same day, Patton went on: "If any of you haven't visited the charnel house near here, you should go. It is the most horrible sight I have ever seen. We had as many soldiers as possible . . . visit it so as to know what kind of people they are fighting. I think they were duly impressed, and I told them to tell their friends."

Less than a week later the Third Army liberated the even more horrific extermination camp at Buchenwald. Diplomat Robert Murphy described the scene: "The inmates liberated by our forces were skeletons . . . many of the captives had been professional soldiers . . . and they pulled their wasted bodies into gallant salutes as Eisenhower, Patton and their staffs passed them. It was enough to make strong men weep—and some American officers did so unabashedly." Patton wrote of Buchenwald, "This was the camp where we paraded some fifteen hundred citizens of Weimar to give them a first-hand knowledge of the infamy of their own government." His chief of staff, Hobart Gay, remarked:

> The scenes witnessed there are beyond the normal mind to believe. No race except a people dominated by an ideology of sadism could have committed such gruesome crimes. . . . It is a shame that more people cannot see these things, particularly politicians, who, after all, bring on wars, and doubly a shame that they cannot be seen by those people back in our country. . . . No race and no people other than those which are strictly sadists could commit crimes like these.

One of the liberators, James Collins, in an interview decades later, summed up the American soldiers' attitude to the German public once they saw the camps: "They had to almost be physically restrained from attacking them; it certainly made them, shall I say, less friendly towards the populace. . . . It altered their view of the Germans because my men felt the Germans could not live in practically the same town with all that was going on without knowing it . . . therefore they were pretty hard on them."

The gassing of the Jews continued to the very minutes before American and Allied soldiers arrived at the camps. One survivor notes: "The cremations were abruptly interrupted by the arrival of American tank troops in the area, so abruptly, in fact, that the SS did not have time to 'get their act together.' Thus, the various stages of torture (the sequence of operations) were there to be thoroughly examined and understood."[103]

The stakes were high on August 12 at Argentan, for they ultimately involved the unraveling of the entire Nazi slave state—not just the liberation of millions of French, but the reprieve to millions more who would certainly die if not freed. If Patton's warriors could close the Falaise Gap, if they could kill or capture a quarter-million German soldiers west of the Seine, there would be a brief window of opportunity—perhaps a week or two only—in which there would be literally no time for other German armies in France to regroup or for fresh conscripts to rush to the Siegfried Line; thus Patton's boast in early August that he could finish the war in ten days if given gas and the green light. Whatever the improbability of that promise, it is undeniable that had Patton proceeded from Argentan to close the Falaise Gap, and had the war ended a few weeks later, the death camps might have shut down in September 1944—and millions would have survived.

Despite the cynicism of the Third Army soldiers, and the vulgarity of their crazed general, and despite the lack of detailed information concerning the full extent of the Nazi atrocities, the Americans, nevertheless, realized speed was of the essence if millions were to be saved. We might have entered the European war late, and perhaps only because Hitler declared war on us first; Americans also may have gone overseas reluctantly and feared the Russians as much as the Nazis. But by summer 1944 it was clear to even the most cynical GI that American soldiers alone could drive the Nazis out of Western Europe, and that the lives of millions rested on their ability to do so. The destruction of the Nazi slave state, and the entire ideology of a master race itself, were the primary reasons why Patton and his men wished to butcher even more German soldiers this August 12, 1944, at Argentan, France. The Third Army had been operational less than two weeks, and in that time it had turned Bradley's localized

Cobra breakout into a full-scale offensive that could literally destroy all the Germans in Normandy. Surely no one had believed that a single American general in twelve days might now realistically think he could trap the entire German army and perhaps win the war outright.

Did any in the Allied high command other than Patton appreciate the magnitude of the folly in Bradley's order to halt at Argentan? Very few indeed—most certainly not Eisenhower or Bradley himself. Of contemporaries, the French general Paul de Langlade was one of the few who saw the tragedy: "Only General Patton, who has the sense of maneuver, possesses enough ardor and faith to execute the closing. He is an offensive warrior of high class who seems to have no equal among his compatriots for exploitation warfare. One wonders even if he is appreciated or even understood."[104]

One wonders still, a half century later.

7

A DIFFERENT IDEA

KNUTSFORD, ENGLAND

February 3, 1944 (V-E Day Minus 460 Days)

*I for my part
urged you strongly not to, but you, giving way to your proud heart's
anger, dishonoured a great man, one whom the immortals
honour, since you have taken his prize and keep it. But let us
even now think how we can make this good and persuade him
with words of supplication and with the gifts of friendship.*

—Homer, *Iliad*

A T LEAST, Patton had finally managed to get to England, which was much closer to the proposed landing in France than his prior posting in occupied Sicily. After the slapping incident there in the summer of 1943, he was essentially *persona non grata* in the American high command. A man whose tactical brilliance had saved thousands of GIs was now ostracized for slapping two. Despite his stunning operations in North Africa, and his impressive victory in Sicily, he would see no further role in Italy. As Americans died at Anzio, George Patton, the veteran of numerous such amphibious landings, was idling away unwanted a few hundred miles to the south in liberated Sicily. "I have absolutely nothing to do," Patton wrote, "and hours of time in which to do it. From commanding 240,000 men, I have now less than 5,000." [105]

He would not be transferred to the Pacific; and it was even likely Patton might have no command in the upcoming invasion of Europe. "My present status is so confused as to be unexplainable—it is confusion doubly compounded and no one has told me a thing," Patton wrote his wife in January 1944. General Marshall ostensibly left the decision whether to use Patton entirely to Eisenhower—but at least in such language that it was clear he personally wished Patton to be in on the battle for Normandy. General Bradley, Patton's former subordinate and now senior American army group commander in Europe, however, was adamant: he did *not* want Patton anywhere near Normandy. Even after the war, with the Third Army's march a matter of record, Bradley still openly bragged that he had not requested Patton in Europe. "Had it been left up to me, I would not have included Patton in Overlord. I did not look forward to having him in my command. He had shown in Sicily that he did not know how to run an army; his legendary reputation (now badly tarnished) was the product of an uncritical media buildup."[106]

Eisenhower himself was determined not to give Patton command of an entire army group, and wanted to send him home over Patton's offhand remark in Knutsford that after the war the Americans and British would enjoy hegemony. "I have always been fully aware of your habit of dramatizing yourself and of committing indiscretions for no other apparent purpose than of calling attention to yourself," he wrote Patton. "I am thoroughly weary of your failure to control your tongue and have begun to doubt your all-around judgment, so essential to high military position. My decision in the present case will not become final until I have heard from the War Department."

The Allied consensus was that he was not to play any role in the Normandy planning or even the landings in June. Eisenhower was about to send him stateside: "When I came out [of Ike's office]," Patton wrote in his diary, "I don't think anyone could tell that I had just been killed. . . . I feel like death, but I am not out yet. If they will let me fight, I will; but if not, I will resign so as to be able to talk, and then I will tell the truth and possibly do my country more good."

Still, even if left out, Patton with his accustomed prescience could see exactly what would go wrong in Normandy months in advance: "I fear that after we get landed in France, we will be boxed in a beachhead, due to timidity and lack of drive, which is latent in Montgomery. I hope I am wrong." Later, when proved right, he still had auspicious advice—rejected of course—about how the Allies could get out of the hedgerows: "If we play safe and keep on attacking with articulated lines driving in the south, we will die of old age before we finish." Instead, Patton continued:

> It would be better to put one or two armored divisions abreast and go straight down the road [toward Avranches], covering the leading elements with air bursts. I am sure that such a method, while probably expensive in tanks, due primarily to mines, would insure our breaking through to Avranches from our present position in no more than two days. This plan would have the advantage of not requiring setting up an amphibious operation. On the other hand, it is so bold that it would never be approved.[107]

For the time being, Patton was to stay in England, organizing a new army, the Third, which was ostensibly to be the core of some mythical army group to fool the Germans. "Still on the sidelines," he wrote his wife from England two weeks after the Normandy invasion, "still as planned, but it is an awful bore.... I can't tell you how I hate this sitting around." Since Hitler and his generals, unlike the Americans and the British, felt Patton to be the Allies' most gifted commander, the Anglo-American commanders would create an elaborate ruse of having Patton seem to be preparing a second invasion of France at Calais to the north of the June Normandy landing site. Patton, in essence, would—and did—tie down an immense German army to the north, which would wait in vain apprehension for this dashing general to cross from Dover and attempt a characteristically relentless drive through northern Europe on the shortest direct route into Germany. At least that scenario made sense to the veteran German commanders: Calais was directly across the narrow Strait of Dover from England; from there it was the shortest distance from the French coastal sites to the German interior; and the Allies would naturally save their best general for the *coup de main*, consisting of a rumored sixty Allied divisions. All it really meant was that Patton would sit tight on the sidelines as Americans died in the hedgerows of Normandy.

Whereas Patton's continual presence in England did in fact tie up on the French mainland German divisions that were not promptly deployed to stop the Normandy landings, the irony was unmistakable. The Germans feared most an invasion led by Patton in northern France, where his daring might lead to a breakout and a sudden race into Germany; his own superiors, aware of just that reputation, would *not* take concrete advantage of it on the battlefield, but rather make the Germans think that they would. Obviously, Eisenhower and Bradley wished it both ways: to deprecate Patton's ability and to be embarrassed over his theatrics—yet to acknowledge also that the German military was, in fact, deathly afraid of just that ability and theater.

Nor were the Germans alone in believing Patton to be the foremost

American commander. The Free French also considered his Third Army the most deadly of the American forces in Normandy. And after the war Stalin himself purportedly remarked, "The Red Army could not have conceived and certainly not have executed the advance made by the Third Army across France." He was no doubt relieved when Patton was ordered to halt before Prague, and more so when he was stripped of Third Army command in post-war Germany.[108]

General Marshall and hence Eisenhower came to realize that Patton's genius was too valuable simply to waste. They envisioned at some point a real command for Patton, though a clearly secondary role for him with the Third Army in Normandy once the summer wore on, when at last the decoy of a later Patton invasion could no longer tie down German reserves. Patton would arrive with his Third Army weeks after the invasion. As Bradley and Montgomery organized their respective breakouts, Patton would drive not eastward toward Germany like the other Allied armies, but rather in a subsidiary capacity westward and to the south—in the opposite direction of Berlin—to occupy the Brittany peninsula and its port at Brest. Only when that mopping-up operation was achieved—no doubt several months in duration—might he fill in the Allied line to the south, ensuring that the other Allied generals were not outflanked as their main thrusts headed toward Germany. Supplies, gasoline, ammunition—even air support—would be given first to Montgomery and Hodges, who were to command the real advance while Patton came up in support safely to the south. Arriving late into Normandy with an inexperienced and supporting army, he was to work closely with Allied logisticians in obtaining port facilities that would ensure sufficient supplies for other American armies. That at least was the plan.

Inside the brain of George Patton was quite a different idea, one that would now draw on some forty years of intellectual contemplation, training in the field, and combat experience. No command of an army group? Better that way: he could command more directly from the front as leader of a single army. "I think the slapping incident was a good thing," Patton wrote his wife upon arriving in England, "but for it I would probably have had Brad's job, which I certainly would not have liked, certainly not in its present form—the altitude is too great."[109]

A late arrival in Europe? Still preferable. He could survey the battlefield, see where his superiors had erred, and "reconnoiter" his Third Army to the point of enemy weaknesses. Relegated to a southern command and ordered to secure ports? A minor complication. Given the greatest distance from Germany, his advance there would be only the more impressive—he would go the farthest the fastest, and use the bulk of his army to head east into Germany, after clearing out Brittany with a fraction of his armor. Brittany, after all, was a peninsula, and all such salients could be cut off at their base, while the main force of his army continued due east into Germany. Indeed, Patton boasted of his allotted theater far to the south: "I desire [it] as it keeps me on the outside—on the running end."[110]

Uncertainty in supply? No problem: once the Third Army outflanked his adversaries and raced on its way to the Rhine, even the most conservative and blinkered planners would have to adjust and send the ammunition and gasoline to the army that was moving most quickly toward Germany. And his army would attack in a manner quite unlike the Allied forces thus far deployed in France:

> All of Patton's plans were conceived in the light of the cavalry tradition— quick decision, speed in execution, calculated audacity; better a good plan violently executed now than a perfect plan next week. As a matter of general policy he laid it down that in the coming operations the advance guards of every column when they struck opposition would surround and contain the enemy. Meanwhile another advance guard would continue the forward sweep until the next opposition was encountered. The process would then be repeated as in leap-frog. The enemy swept off his feet in this way would thus be given no time to mount a counter-stroke. This, in spirit, was the doctrine which had brought victory to the Germans in Poland, France and North Africa in the early years of the war.

An untried and late-arriving army, without any experience of fighting in Normandy? It mattered little. Patton would so imprint his own personality and discipline on his men that they would be even the more impressive for their drastic change in temperament and acquisition of expertise: the late arrivals into France would turn out to be the best controlled and most aggressive of all the American armies.

Instead of the Allied plan of a gradual, head-on push to evolve over a year or two, George Patton had quite a different, far more audacious idea for his Third Army that would in turn transmogrify the entire Allied battle blueprint. There was no need for the Allies to inch forward, arriving in Germany in 1946 after a series of brutal head-to-head assaults along a thousand-mile front. No, he would immediately seek an opening—any opening in the German lines. Then he would stack his armored divisions and drive thousands of armored troops through a very narrow deep front. Forget about the flanks; speed was the key. "Fear of a flank attack is an obsession," he wrote in the days before his breakout. "As long as you are in depth, there is no danger, and in this congested country, you have to stay in depth. If necessary, Gaffey [his chief of staff] and I will lead the leading companies."

Patton was not merely reckless, but realized that the growing omnipresence of Allied tactical aircraft had instantaneously revolutionized warfare. American Thunderbolts and Mustangs were not slow-moving Stukas of the blitzkrieg practiced five years earlier, but now atrocious engines of destruction, whose four-hundred-mile-per-hour dives, multiple machine guns, rockets, cannon, and bombs might obliterate enemy armor that sought to outflank advancing friendly columns. Patton concluded:

> Whenever air and armor can work together, the results are sure to be excellent. Armor can move fast enough to prevent the enemy having time to deploy off the roads, and so long as he stays on the roads the fighter-bomber is one of his most deadly opponents. To accomplish this happy teamwork, two things are necessary: first, intimate confidence and friendship between air and ground; second, incessant and apparently ruthless driving on the part of the ground commander.

Somewhere near the Normandy beaches Patton would find his initial hole for a breakout. Then he would simply race through it on into the countryside of France, across the familiar territory where he had fought during the First World War, beating the collapsing German army to each new major river—the Seine, the Meuse, the Moselle, the Rhine—as he leapfrogged into Bavaria, outflanking the retreating Nazis. At last he would wheel around and come up from the south to Berlin. After it was all over, he would remark on his rampage through France, "In every case, practically throughout the campaign, I was under wraps from the Higher Command. This may have been a good thing, as perhaps I am too impetuous. However, I do not believe I was, and feel that had I been permitted to go all out, the war would have ended sooner and more lives would have been saved."[111]

His worries? Surely not the veteran Germans whom he had beat before in Sicily and North Africa. "It is funny," Patton wrote in July 1944 on the eve of his assumption of command in France, "that I have never any doubts about licking the Germans any place I meet them. The only question in my mind is being able to survive the lapses between campaigns when I always seem to get myself in trouble." Mostly, he feared his sources of supply and the reprimand of his own superiors, who might not take to the obvious attention that such success would bring the Third Army, and the acknowledgment of obsolescence of the SHAEF master plan. Even should his race ahead of the pack leave more plodding Allied armies vulnerable to German flank attack, as a most loyal subordinate, Patton would simply turn north instantaneously on a given order, and slice any German salient at its shoulder, trapping even more of the enemy. Once he had pushed through Germany, why not head on through Czechoslovakia, freeing the East Europeans from the Nazi yoke and ensuring that the increasingly suspicious and not-to-be-trusted armies of Stalin would not liberate Eastern Europe?

True, in this spring of 1944 in his manorial estate at Knutsford, George Patton was down. He was fifty-nine. Formerly junior officers without battle experience were his superiors. He was ignored at meetings of American generals. And he was soon to wait helplessly while the Americans battled in Normandy and were killed in the hedgerows during all of June and July. But unlike the other American commanders, and unlike the SHAEF master plan, itself the work of thousands of brilliant planners and tacticians, George Patton believed that he knew how to get into Germany in 1944, and he would do so alone and on his own initiative, if turned loose.

That is precisely what Patton did. When he started up the Third Army on August 1, 1944, Allied progress in Normandy was forty-five days *behind* the rather timid Overlord timetable. But in just thirty days of Third Army operations (at D-Day plus seventy-nine days), Patton had not only caught up with the planned schedule, his men were now actually where they were slated to be at D-Day plus ninety days. Ladislas Farago points out the startling transformation in the entire American battle plan:

> But the inescapable realities of the campaign had overridden all the original plans and dispositions. By September 12th (D plus 98) the Third Army stood on a line the forecasts had expected it to reach on approximately D plus 350. . . . Between 25 August and 12 September they [Third Army] had advanced from the D plus 90 to the D plus 350 phase line, thus covering 260 phase-days in 19 days. Coming from far behind, it was the privilege of General Patton and his Third Army to drive the whole campaign swiftly forward and bring the war to the brink of total victory in less than three weeks of ingenious fighting.[112]

In the nearly two months of warring under Bradley and Montgomery, the Allies had advanced not more than twenty miles from the beaches. By the end of the first thirty days of the Third Army's deployment, the Americans were nearly four hundred miles away from the French coast, approaching Verdun and barreling forward less than a hundred miles from Germany itself.

Like Epaminondas's descent into Laconia, and Sherman's March to the Sea, Patton's would be a linear drive of sorts, with a clear beginning and end, from the Atlantic to Berlin. Start in France, end in Germany. End the march,

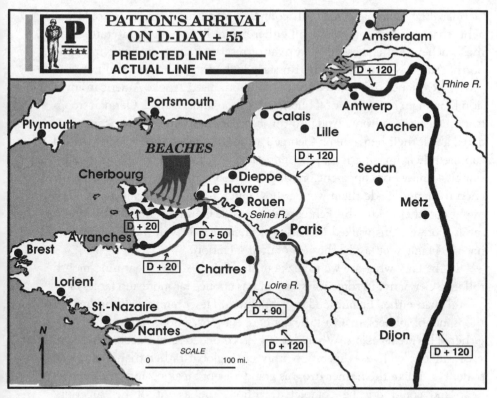

PLAN VERSUS PERFORMANCE

end the war, and go home. Enemy strong points could be quickly bypassed, surrounded, and left to be enveloped by following infantry. Like both his predecessors, Patton realized that whereas the destruction of the enemy's main army in the field is always the objective of battle tactics, strategically such forces could wither through the loss of morale and matériel—once a fast-moving enemy was to their rear, shooting as it went, and driving through their homeland. Little did Patton know that in the last eighteen months of his life that plan and much more still would transpire exactly as he would imagine: his successes as he envisioned them, his setbacks as the predictable wages of working with more timid, less gifted men, who lacked the maturity to overlook the superficial immaturity of George Patton in order to capitalize fully on his rare genius that alone among American commanders could save thousands of lives through his audacity.

This February as the idle Patton paced through the Knutsford estate, the

German high command was still confident that the Americans could not fight, that any invasion would fail either before Rommel's counterattack on the beaches or the subsequent arrival of reserve Panzer divisions from the north. And this February, as the Russians inched steadily westward from the Soviet heartland, they waited for the long-promised Anglo-American invasion that might at last draw off hundreds of thousands of crack German troops from their Eastern front. And also this February millions of Americans wondered about their hero-villain George Patton, the only battle leader who had captured their imaginations, who alone had sliced through the Nazi professionals—and whose apparent brutality and coarse language also had frightened them and made them wonder how much his crusade against the Nazis might cost them. And this February, deep inside Germany, hundreds of thousands more victims walked into the gas chambers, in vain hoping that perhaps 1944 might at last be the year of their salvation.

In the end, what are we to make of the Third Army's great nine-month roll into Germany? In some ways Patton was at once far more and far less successful than either Epaminondas or Sherman. He commanded hundreds of thousands of soldiers, in a vast theater of operations, a horde undreamed of by either of his predecessors. Whereas their efforts ended servitude, his helped to save millions of lives—liberation truly on a global rather than a national scale. But unlike the former two, his grand idea of breaking into the enemy's heartland could not be completed without the assent of his superiors. Whereas Epaminondas simply disobeyed them, and Sherman won them over, Patton did neither, and so repeatedly was reeled in, only to be given slack, as Eisenhower reacted to larger political issues of the high command that were not always attuned to the pulse of the battlefield. Patton offered his assessment of Ike well before the Normandy invasion: "We suffer very much from lack of command. No one is running the show. . . . Ike has no conception of physical command as he has never exercised it. . . . I think that in his heart he knows he is not really commanding anything."

Had Patton reached Germany in the fall of 1944, his three-month, one-thousand-mile trek into Germany would have eclipsed any great democratic march in history. As it was, his audacious nine-month advance, even when it was not commensurably supplied and thus sputtered, had the effect of energizing his rival Allied commanders, and drawing German resistance from other sectors to his own. If Epaminondas and Sherman more consciously led their troops to end apartness, the net effect of Patton's drive was to remove even a greater stain on Western civilization and to collapse a slave society of a size and evil far beyond that of either ancient Sparta or the Confederate South.

Patton's prophetic sense, unlike the prescience of both Epaminondas and

Sherman, was largely manifested concretely on the battlefield. Whereas the former restructured a civilization, and the latter taught an entire society the bitter wages of rebellion and slavery, the lessons of Patton's crusade—given the confining bureaucracy of American political and military officialdom in the mid twentieth century—were far more limited.

Besides his actual tactical brilliance on the battlefield, which even in its abbreviated manifestation helped to shorten the war, Patton must be credited with reintroducing into democratic warfare of the industrial and technological age the notion of spirit. By the outbreak of World War Two, American tactical doctrine increasingly sought to win wars through sheer manpower and material superfluity. Patton, in contrast, reminded Americans that they could only defeat evil when their soldiers were better motivated than those of the enemy—a difficult task, he felt, in a society where uniformity, complacence, and material comfort were at an increasing premium.

If Sherman educated Americans that in the modern era civilians who supported rebellion and slavery would not be exempt from its bitter dividends, then Patton drove home to these same countrymen that in just such an age there was still room for courage and sacrifice on the battlefield, that indeed a moral sense, not mere gasoline and ammunition, was the true fuel of armored advance. Sherman had once demonstrated to the South that martial gallantry would fade before the economic realities of civilian suffering in any conflict of the industrial age; eighty years later Patton countered that gallant men, not machines or mere capital, were still the essence of modern warfare. Sherman was a radical for his times, Patton a reactionary; both were true revolutionaries in their utter disregard for the prevailing orthodoxies of their ages. Critics have begrudgingly conceded that they were realists; in fact, both were humanists whose approaches to war were intended to save lives, not confirm the brutal nature of man.

We have seen that few moderns—so unlike the ancients—have acknowledged Epaminondas as the single greatest democratic general of the ancient world. We praise Pericles; but unlike the Theban, he fought by his own proud admission solely for imperialism, not democracy per se. In the same way as Pericles, not Epaminondas, has inexplicably captured the popular imagination, so too Robert E. Lee—the "Apollo on horseback"—emerged from the Civil War as both a humanitarian and a military genius. He was a good man who was neither. The coarser Sherman was a far better strategist, did far more to end the Civil War, killed fewer of the enemy and lost fewer of his own men—and freed, rather than owned, slaves. And like Epaminondas, he won, rather than lost, a war.[113]

Patton invites similar comparison with popular American icons such as

Bradley and Eisenhower, both of whom were good men. Yet neither saw battle in World War One, in which Patton was nearly killed. At one time or another, both were Patton's juniors in rank and learned most of what little they understood about blitzkrieg from Patton himself. Whereas both were soft-spoken and appeared erudite in public, neither was as well read or as intellectually curious as Patton. If the latter spoke bombastically and at times vulgarly to his men, while the former professionally and in measure, at least Patton did so to create a furor in his men often at cost to his own career, while the rhetoric, if it can be called that, of Bradley and Eisenhower never created an élan, but was often largely measured for their own self-interest. The two often talked of the welfare of the GI, and the obsession with avoiding needless casualties—even as they lost numerous opportunities to use American forces in dramatic advances that alone would have saved American lives, both in the short and long terms. In meetings, as Patton screamed about the need for advance, the necessity of bringing divisions up to full strength, and the horrendous inefficiencies of the American logistical system, he complained bitterly that Bradley kept quiet, worried about offending his superiors: "As usual Bradley said nothing. He does all the getting along and does it to his own advantage. I expect I take a chance because at heart the army is not my living and besides, I am a soldier, a simple soldier."

Patton was as duplicitous and hungry for glory as any American general—indeed, more so. But his point of being a simple soldier, nevertheless, rang true: Eisenhower's career would be preparatory for politics, Bradley's for further promotion within the American military hierarchy. Patton, older and of independent means, had he lived much beyond the armistice, would have neither wished nor found further career advancement or the political spotlight. He scoffed at feelers of political office, and expressed a desire mostly to return to write and travel amid a comfortably aristocratic existence. Like Sherman, whom he quoted in these matters, the capital of his victories would not be transferable outside the sphere of military operations. Since Patton's energy was directed solely to advancing the Third Army as quickly as possible against the enemy in the field, often in a manner that would bother both Americans at home and superiors abroad, he really did remain a simple soldier who would gain the greatest respect among GIs whom he led, former German adversaries whom he fought, and military historians whom he impressed in a way neither Eisenhower nor Bradley ever could.

Should we sympathize with the efforts of Eisenhower and Bradley, who had political responsibilities beyond the battlefield, to bridle the unpredictable Patton and his grandiose plans to determine the nature of the Allied advance to the Rhine? It is difficult to see how, when the lives of hundreds of thousands of soldiers and millions of innocents in the death camps were at stake. In retrospect, Patton's order to close the Falaise Gap would have led to lives saved, not lost. Scholars today argue over who allowed it to stay open, not that it was a wise decision that it was left open, over whether its effect would have ended outright the war in the West, not that its effect was inconsequential. In all such speculations, Patton alone is *not* blamed.

Had Patton been left alone in Brittany, Brest would have been captured far earlier, and American troops released for the drive eastward. I know of no historian who believes Patton should have advanced slower to the French coast, or that he should, as the SHAEF plan mandated, have devoted more of his divisions to clearing the Britanny peninsula. From what we know of German defenses in the Lorraine in late August, and the success of American tactical air forces, it is hard to see how a supplied Patton would have been destroyed crossing the Rhine in late summer 1944; controversy rests solely on how far Patton could have advanced into Germany without being eventually surrounded. We know, of course, the horror that continued in the death camps from September 1944 to May 1945. The Germans themselves thought Patton's idea to cut the bulge off at its base was the preferred course of action; no serious American historian disagrees and none blame Patton for the safe retreat of the Panzers after the offensive to the Rhine. Nearly a half century of Communist suffering in Prague should have settled the argument over the wisdom of stopping Patton's half-million-man army on the outskirts of the Czech capital.

All this is not to deny that problems might not have arisen with a supplied and unleashed Third Army. Eisenhower would have had even greater public relations problems with the British had the Third Army been given the go-ahead at critical junctures. Bradley would have emerged from World War Two an accommodating Halleck, who allowed his headline-grabbing Sherman to march where he pleased; Montgomery and Hodges, fellow Boeotarchs who supported a reckless Epaminondas.

Who knows what a Proconsul Patton would have done in an occupied Germany in late 1944? Eisenhower might have lost chances for his presidency when faced with either relieving the hero of Falaise, Brest, the Seine, Lorraine, and liberator of Prague or allowing his lunatic pronouncements to continue. Can we imagine Patton press releases after bagging an entire German army at Falaise in little more than a week after taking command? As it was, if his superiors' opposition failed to muzzle him fully, what might have their full support and his continual victories done to his rhetoric? Might not British historians today still decry a canceled Market-Garden, claiming that had Montgomery had Patton's supplies, he too would have reached Germany in

1944? Had Patton taken Prague, there might have been shooting with the Russians. As victor of Normandy, Patton, of course, would have been insufferable, and like Sherman, criticized, but probably not relieved, in a postwar Germany.

But these are mostly questions of protocol, fame, ego, and politics, not military decisions that involved the lives of thousands of young men. Quite simply, there were few "what ifs" involved with Montgomery, Bradley, or Hodges, because either they themselves did not create critical situations that could have changed the course of the war, or if they did on rare occasions—such as the Market-Garden operation or the crossing at Remagen—they were then given full material and command support from their superiors. With all other generals in France except Patton, there was usually the issue of "they should have," rather than "they should not have," and the criticism that material supplies—in the hedgerows, at Arnhem, at the Rhine—were not wisely used, not that they were not given.

At a time when the American army of George Marshall was wonderfully organized, trained, and equipped in the image of the modern industrial, bureaucratic state, Eisenhower and Bradley were exemplars of the best of what such an order might produce—sound technicians whose errors might not cost their nation a war. Patton, in contrast, stood in antithesis to the very system in which he operated, not because he deliberately wished to be contrary, but rather because he saw the dangers inherent in a bureaucracy in which men were secondary to machines, individuals to an organization, originality to uniformity. Patton wished to win a war more quickly and economically than his resources justified; his superiors, simply not to lose it as their supplies and manpower inevitably grew. Ideology and zeal the German army also had—but that spirit arose from a source that was evil, in a system that was militarized, and served to enhance the progress of mass murder. Patton sought similar audacity in his own amateurs who were to fight such crack troops, but his fountainhead of emotion was democratic freedom, his society was liberal, and the mission of his army was to free the unfree, not to protect murderers.

There were plenty of gifted and audacious commanders of infantry and armor in World War Two who were of Patton's caliber—Rommel, Guderian, von Manstein, Zhukov, and Koniev come quickly to mind—but all fought for totalitarianism and ultimately for strongmen who had butchered millions of innocents. There were also humane and capable generals in the Second World War—Eisenhower, Montgomery, Bradley, and Clark—whose armies did much to shorten the holocaust. But all of the latter in comparison to Patton were irresolute and let opportunities repeatedly slip when real daring was called for; unlike Patton, they relied on superior Allied matériel and manpower and factored into that strategy that a great number of young men would have to die in a methodical frontal assault against the German army. In the Second World War, as in the annals of military history, it is possible to find firebrands at the head of murderous soldiers, and, similarly, satisfactory leaders of armies of liberation are common. It is nearly impossible to find both at once—fanatical generals who put their unstoppable citizen armies in the service of freedom, not slavery or conquest.[114]

For a few brief months in the winter and spring of 370–369 a single man had created a vast democratic army that changed the course of Greek history. So too in a matter of weeks Sherman fashioned the Army of the West into the most lethal army the world had yet seen. In less than a year George Patton had turned 250,000 amateur American recruits into a mobile and lethal force that could charge ahead at forty miles and more a day through enemy-occupied territory. Superior discipline, pride in accomplishment, unit morale, devotion to an eccentric and brilliant general can all explain much of those remarkable victories. But not all. In the end, Boeotians, Northerners, and American GIs advanced so rapidly and so lethally because they saw themselves as more moral troops than their enemies. As agents of a long-overdue reckoning, they really did believe that they were democracy's ultimate vengeance against a slaveholding society, that they were fighting a culture, not merely an enemy army.

Like the Pythagorean and Uncle Billy, Old Blood and Guts too eventually got his statue. In bronze he stands with binoculars in hand, wearing his four-star infantry helmet, revolvers on his hips. True to his intellectual curiosity, he faces the West Point Military Academy library. Fifty yards away is the likeness of Eisenhower. Fittingly each has his back turned to the other. Beneath the image of Patton are two inscriptions:

"Never take counsel of your fears" is answered by "Pursue the enemy with the utmost audacity."[115]

EPILOGUE
THE END OF THE
DEMOCRATIC MARCHES?

As is the generation of leaves, so is that of humanity.
The wind scatters the leaves on the ground, but the live timber
burgeons with leaves again in the season of spring returning.
So one generation of men will grow while
another dies.

—Homer, *Iliad*

T O ASSOCIATE the names Sherman and Patton with history's marches
for freedom will startle and perhaps anger some; Epaminondas, were
he better known, might be held in as much prejudice. Nonetheless, it
is time to rethink what constitutes real brutality in war and who are the real
peace-makers. All three generals were not realists as much as moralists. True,
they had no delusions about either human nature or war; but this realism
grew out of humanism, not cynicism, as they practiced a brutal war-making in
order to prevent casualties and establish an enduring peace.

Contemporaries assumed that Spartan hoplites, Confederate soldiers,
and Hitler's Panzers were the preeminent warriors of the age—clear proof that
the martial tradition of Sparta, the South, and Germany, buttressed by the co-

erced work of servile Helots, blacks, and Jewish and Slavic gangs, was largely unstoppable. Sparta had attacked and defeated Theban armies for decades. The South had a record of nearly three years of stout resistance to the North. Germany had been invincible for most of World War Two; the thought of landing on the beaches of Normandy and being inside Germany within a year was absurd.

The Spartans thought the Thebans undisciplined rustics; the Confederates dismissed Northerners as motley immigrants and disgruntled wage-earners. So too Hitler and his Nazis dubbed the Americans "cowboys," who were capable of only a few flashes of prowess, before seasoned soldiers of the Wehrmacht butchered them in short order. Within "nine hours" after landing in France, Hitler promised, the Allies would be exterminated. "With this division alone," General Guderian said to the commander of the famous Panzer Lehr division, "you will throw the Anglo-Saxons back into the sea!"

Soon all those armies, which had once boasted they were unconquerable, fought on the defensive, with short supply lines, in or near their own ground, led by a professional military class, and anxious to stop foreign entry onto their soil. They faced democratic armies led by brilliant generals keen on destroying not their forces in pitched battle—that had been done earlier at Leuctra, Gettysburg, and in North Africa and Sicily—but far more ambitiously their very soul. After the terrible marches of retribution into their country, none of these cultures of slavery would field a credible army again. Their entire infrastructure of racial separation would go up in flames. Among the greatest contributions of Western culture were the destruction of Spartan helotage, Confederate slavery, and German fascism by other Western armies.

All three epic marches for freedom—hostilities were to cease immediately after each reached their objectives—were led by eccentrics, considered unbalanced or worse by many of their own superiors. These sometimes repugnant generals kept prodigious amounts of information in their heads, were keen students of history, gifted impromptu orators, devised entire tactical plans alone, and often told few of their ultimate intentions; contemporaries remarked more on their outlandish personal behavior than on their brilliance in battle. All three generals were censured by their own governments, threatened with loss of command, and ridiculed for their belief that a militia could make its way into Sparta, the South, and Germany in a matter of months. But Epaminondas did more than any Athenian to destroy Sparta; no abolitionist did as much as Sherman to dismantle slavery; and the most die-hard antifascist could not match Patton's destruction of Nazi military power. It is tragic that the architects of such humanity still today are either unknown or misunderstood: Epaminondas warrants little in Greek history textbooks; Sherman is mostly remembered as the father of "terror" warfare against civilians; and Patton is caricatured as a dangerous zealot wisely kept on a short leash by a more circumspect Eisenhower or Bradley.

Sherman, both during his March to the Sea and after his agreements with Johnston, was called "insane" by Northern papers, who reminded readers of his nervous breakdown months earlier, and his propensity to talk in apocalyptic images. The historian S. L. A. Marshall once called Patton "half mad;" and Ladislas Farago, his biographer, felt "if he was not actually mad, at least highly neurotic, for reasons (primarily libidinal) that a Freudian psychoanalyst would have no trouble in explaining." Epaminondas remarked, "The most beautiful death is a death in battle"—not much different from Patton's idea that the best death was the last bullet in the last battle of the war. Sherman complained, "The war is over, occupation gone." Ancient anecdotes about Epaminondas range from his nocturnal sentry walks, alone and unwashed, to ensure the safety of others as they enjoyed holiday revelry, to altering statues and faking divine portents to encourage the morale of his faltering troops—similar to Patton's demand that army chaplains pray and force God to give him good weather in the midst of the Battle of the Bulge.

Personal paradoxes abound. Epaminondas freed the Helots, but his own infantrymen brought along their own chattel slave-attendants. Sherman liberated African slaves in his wake, but almost immediately was accused of being unsympathetic to black aspirations. Patton destroyed Nazi Panzers, but his troops who did so were segregated by race. Patton vomited at the death camps he liberated and marched nearby German civilians into the barbed wire to witness what their nation had wrought; but at the end of his life, his anti-Semitic bombast helped to cost him his command. Patton gained a reputation as a breakneck marauder who loved to kill his enemy, and yet, like the infantry of Epaminondas and Sherman, his army's obliteration of the enemy's material and spiritual will to resist did not include gratuitous slaughter. The carpet bombing of German cities and the incineration of civilians by Allied bombers sickened him—"a useless and sadistic form of war," he lamented.

Their armies were designed to overwhelm the enemy in pitched battles, but these generals, for all their saber-rattling, rarely sought to fight the enemy head-on as much as to march around him, destroying his morale and his entire infrastructure in the process. These armies of a season were lethal war-makers, but killed surprisingly few of the enemy, their generals boisterous and melodramatic in word, methodical and economical of their men's lives in deed.

Epaminondas, Sherman, and Patton were the most erudite commanders of their generations, deemed vulgar for the necessary though brutal work they do for the rest of us; they were in fact intellectuals in the true sense of the word. No wonder Liddell Hart, who spent a lifetime in advocacy of fighting evil in ways other than those that had taken place in the trenches of World War One, considered all three masters of the strategy of exhaustion and indirect approach. All three generals agreed that grand envelopment was the proper paradigm for an army that was a reflection of a restless, if not fickle, democratic citizenry ever eager to abandon the fray should the war be prolonged or go bad.

In short, never in human conflict have such vast democratic infantry forces appeared out of nowhere, wrought such havoc, and then dispersed among the consensual culture that fielded them. These marches are not akin to the invasions of history's Great Captains. Alexander's swath to the Indus River killed or displaced over a million people, the vast majority of them innocent civilians. His Macedonians were hired killers keen to loot a corrupt Persian kleptocracy, not to give anyone any freedom. Hannibal too was a mercenary commander of an imperial government who trekked across the Alps for glory and vengeance, not democracy, much less the genuine freedom of Rome's subjects. Caesar crossed the Rubicon to destroy Republican government; his battle-hardened legionaries marched behind him out of personal loyalty to an autocrat and in hopes of a rich retirement and free land. The Crusaders who traversed the Holy Land were not a militia and they did not seek freedom for others as much as forced subservience to their Christian god. Cortes burned his ships and marched inland to destroy a great empire with a band of soldiers for hire, who had hopes of Mexican gold, vast estates, and knighthood at home. There was nothing democratic about Napoleon's march on Moscow—and it led to disaster for both the emperor's and the czar's armies. The Germans who drove into Russia in June 1941 did so as fascists intent on destroying Stalinism, accompanied by the SS, who murdered in the same spirit as the murdering commissars they sought to replace. The Russians in turn who went back from Moscow to Berlin did so as much to enslave Eastern Europe as to free Russia from the Nazis. Marlborough, Frederick the Great, and Wellington—great generals all—won magnificent victories, but their marching armies were not democratic; they fought largely for the supremacy of monarchy or the preservation of empire; and they freed no enslaved. Montgomery chased the Germans back across Africa, but it was a plodding march that could not reach the enemy heartland, and might close out a distant theater, not the war itself. MacArthur nearly drove the Communists out of the Korean peninsula, but he had no authority to go into China, and his United Nations army at its moment of victory was nearly routed. What Epaminondas, Sherman, and Patton did was very rare in military history, for democracy itself is rare in the larger history of civilization, and rarer still its great armies of victory that seek no gold or land, but rather the enemy in its heartland only for the freedom of others.

Yet if history offers only three examples of democratic marches for freedom, the record is at least clear. When a free and consensual society feels its existence threatened, when it has been attacked, when its citizenry at last understands an enemy at odds with the very morality of its culture, when a genius at war leads the army with freedom to do what he wishes, when it is to march to a set place in a set time, then free men can muster, they can fight back well, and they can make war brutally and lethally beyond the wildest nightmares of the brutal military culture they seek to destroy.

The antithesis is equally valid: democratic armies do not fight well when they are not attacked, when they are stationary with nowhere to march, when they fight to preserve privilege or empire, when they are not supported at home, when they are led by careful clerks and bureaucrats who command by consensus—in short, when they are not moving forward with every means at their disposal to destroy the enemy in the cause of freedom. The entire American experience in Southeast Asia, like the Athenian disaster in Sicily, is proof enough of just how mediocre under those conditions—strategic, tactical, spiritual—a democracy at war can become.

Is the age of Epaminondas, Sherman, and Patton long past? In an era of the global village and postmodern relativism, is the idea a linear invasion against clearly defined evil by a democratic nation in arms the stuff of fantasy? Decidedly not. Rather, the study of what these three armies once did holds wisdom for all democracies at the millennium. In the present age we are told that the presence of satellite reconnaissance and nuclear-tipped missiles makes large land armies seem in comparison small and redundant, or that the specter of terrorism, insurrection, and insurgency ensures that they are in fact too big, untrained, and unwieldy. Yet neither proposition is a valid criticism.

Marches for freedom are not frontal assaults but rapid inroads into the enemy's heartland; they are not the horrors of classical Western warfare taken to its logical extreme—set pieces like Antietam, Verdun, or Kursk—but throwbacks to the Hellenic ideal of mustering, invading, conquering, and disbanding. If it comes to a general nuclear exchange—the ultimate apparition of the Western way of war—not just armies, but whole cultures will not matter and it will be the end of us all.

In contrast, if we are to fight with professional commandos perpetually in the jungle and on the street corner against the terrorist or freedom-fighter, then de facto we will not be warring to preserve our existence but our elective influence in places far from our homes. It is precisely when nuclear weapons are ruled out, and yet when our opponents are bellicose nations that field an army in the thousands, that our civilized interests will be imperiled and that an army of a season may well need to arise to battle afar, one that will seek rapid and mobile entry around the enemy to run rampant in its homeland. Defense analysts rightly worry about America's lack of preparedness in the 1990s, but their concern should transcend shrinking defense budgets and the abandonment of vital air wings, divisions, and fleets. Every bit as important as our equipment and organization is the soul of our people, and their willingness to march out in mass against an evil that threatens our safety.

That notion is not as lunatic as it seems. The greatest democratic victory of infantry during the last fifty years was achieved in the Persian Gulf during the nuclear age, where a huge conventional American army and its allies materialized out of nowhere, its combatants convinced that they were fighting far from home for a just cause against an evil aggressor who killed the weak and enslaved the conquered—a regime adept at murder and prone to gas its own people. The Allies were to march forward for a brief season, led by a general who sounded too bellicose, seemed often too unstable for the tastes of the democratic society that produced him. That such an army encircled rather than charged the enemy, that it sought to ruin through the air the infrastructure of its foe without a bloody encounter, that it believed it was fighting for people, not oil, that it lost few of its own combatants as it wrecked the very economy of its enemy, and that within six months it had disappeared as quickly as it emerged was remarkable only to those who did not understand the great strengths of a democratic society and the peculiar and dangerous men who gravitate to its leadership in war.

Critics of such a reactionary infantry expedition to free Kuwait and expel the army of Iraq, who warned of thousands of dead Americans rotting in the sands, of the bellicose record of the Iraqi Republican Guard, of the ruthlessness of Saddam Hussein, knew little of the destructive power of the Theban, Northern, or American militias under Epaminondas, Sherman, and Patton. The real problem for a democratic American army was never defeat by the enemy, but rather the maintenance of a moral high ground—so central to democratic cohesion—in the midst of brutally destroying, on television, the enemy's very will to resist.

By the same token, even some supporters of Desert Storm, who worried about the carnage that their army wrought and the wisdom of invading Baghdad, were equally unaware of the ultimate reason for this sudden muster, ignorant that a great march of a few days or weeks into the heart of Iraq, causing destruction and humiliation in its wake, and then a sudden exit and dispersal were, in fact, entirely consistent with the democratic tradition of war-making. Such a continued march in which Americans finished in Baghdad, destroyed

Iraqi infrastructure, humiliated its army and military culture—and then left—would not "bog" Americans endlessly in an overseas war.

Rather, such an epic march to Baghdad may well have been the only way to rid the world of a great evil, and to justify such an extraordinary muster. Questions of power vacuums and postwar political realities are important, but they pale in comparison with the central mission of destroying evil, of fulfilling the purpose for an ephemeral army in the first place. Epaminondas, Sherman, and Patton were all concerned about the repercussions of their invasions—the resurgence of Macedon or Athens after Sparta's decline, a brutal postwar reconstruction in the South, Soviet divisions in a wrecked Europe—but not concerned enough to halt warring before their central task of overthrowing a slave regime was finished.

Everything in Desert Storm went well until the finale, when planners in the aftermath of Vietnam mistakenly felt that great armies of democracy either cannot destroy the culture of their enemy or cannot, after doing so, with both pride and security, dissolve as quickly as they arose. But as Epaminondas, Sherman, and Patton knew, armies of a season can and do melt away—but only when they have ended the ability of their enemies to make war, when they have ruined enough property not to have to garrison it. Had Epaminondas been content with the plundering of Laconia, thousands in Messenia would have remained Helots for centuries to come; had Sherman ceased operations at Atlanta and negotiated with Southern commanders, McClellan might have won the election on the promise to let slavery survive in the South; had Patton been content with his assigned role in Brittany, the killing of Americans in Europe would have dragged on well into 1946, allowing Hitler's V-2 rockets, long-range submarines, and jet fighters to enter the war in real numbers—and the death camps may have finished their work with the extinction of all European Jewry. The cessation of the American advance in the Gulf War and the negotiated armistice that followed were the greatest American military blunders since Viet Nam.

Had Epaminondas led the Allies in Desert Storm, he would have set up new defensible societies for the Kurds and Shiites, and held off the Iraqi army until both cultures were safe from retribution. Sherman would have preferred to cut a swath through Iraq, leveling every one of Saddam's "palaces," torching his munitions factories and the entire industrial infrastructure of his war-making, and destroying for good measure the homes of the Bath party elite, who should learn the wages of supporting a murderer. Patton, of course, would have headed straight for the Iraqi capital and not left until the Republican Guard was annihilated and Saddam Hussein dead or in chains.

If history is any further guide to democratic warfare, we would have applauded all their efforts during war, and then either put these generals on trial or had them sacked when the danger was past and their reckless bombast made us feel as uncouth as they were. But at least we would not today still have a killer in Iraq and a near decade of constant postbellum vigilance to prevent his missiles and gas from once again murdering the innocent.

The great danger of the present age is that democracy may never again marshal the will to march against and ultimately destroy evil. In the era of television, the image of war's brutality in our living rooms may stop the attack; the education system of the present, with its interest in self-esteem, sensitivity, and the therapeutic, may not turn out sufficiently idiosyncratic, audacious—and well-read—leaders; and instant communications may serve to bridle a mobile column at its moment of victory. But even a greater peril still in present-day democratic society is that we may simply have forgotten that there finally must be a choice between good and evil, that the real immorality is not the use of great force to inflict punishment, but, as the Greeks remind us, the failure to exercise moral authority at all. When men like Epaminondas, Sherman, and Patton go to war to stop evil and to save lives, there is a soul to their battle that lives on well after they are gone.

This tradition of democracy's mustering quickly huge armies, to be led by eccentric fighters, on a moral trek into the heart of slavery, is not the stuff of romance and it is not a fantasy from our past, but rather a rare and hallowed tradition as old as the beginning of the West itself. In the West epic marches for freedom across time and space have liberated us from our own worst enemies. Armies of liberation are the precious dividends of democracy, and we abandon the memory of Epaminondas, Sherman, and Patton and what their hoplites, Westerners, and GIs did only at our great peril.

GLOSSARY

Agesilaus (445–359 B.C.), as Spartan king for nearly forty years campaigned in Asia, Egypt, and on the Greek mainland to extend Spartan hegemony—a mostly failed enterprise since the king had no real understanding of the role of finance, fleets, and siegecraft in a new era of war.

Alexander the Great (356–323 B.C.), through sheer military genius conquered the Persian Empire in little more than a decade. But Alexander's megalomania and desire for divine honors helped to pervert the legacy of Hellenism and left hundreds of thousands of Asians dead and displaced in his murderous wake. Ancient and modern ethical assessments of Alexander vary widely and depend entirely on the particular value one places on military prodigy and conquest.

Allies—nominally all forces in World War Two formally at war against either Nazi Germany, Fascist Italy, or imperial Japan—or against all three combined. In reality, used mostly of the British, American, and Russian forces, and in the context of the West, specifically of the Anglo-American effort.

anabasis—Greek for "the march up," first used of the Greek mercenary 10,000 who marched through the Persian Empire in 401 B.C. as described by Xenophon; thereafter a generic word for any great expedition into the interior of an enemy country.

apartheid—originally an Afrikaans word used to denote segregation from non-European groups in southern Africa; now employed loosely to denote the brutal imposition of "apartness" and "subservience" by any state authority against entire races or ethnic enclaves.

armor—in World War Two refers to tanks, tank destroyers, and other armored mechanized vehicles that were part of a formally organized unit.

army—a group consisting of two or more corps, usually commanded by a lieutenant or full general, such as Patton or Hodges.

army group—a military unit consisting of various individual armies in concert and usually commanded by the equivalent of a full general, such as Bradley or Montgomery.

blitzkrieg—a German word meaning "lightning war"; the bold use of mechanized and air forces to create a sudden rupture in enemy lines, followed by immediate exploitation by infantry, leading to subsequent enemy retreat or capitulation.

Boeotia—the rich agricultural region north of Attica, which often was either in alliance with or at war against its largest city of Thebes.

Boeotarch—one of the seven officials who governed the fourth-century B.C. Boeotian federation and commanded the army.

bummer—originally a pejorative term for Sherman's plunderers who foraged away from the main columns in the Georgia and Carolina countryside; after the war it became a term of approbation for veterans, who were proud of their previous ingenuity and resourcefulness in finding food and booty.

celeritas—literally Latin for "quickness," specifically used in association with Julius Caesar's amazing ability to move legions at a rapid clip, and thereafter of any highly mobile force in general.

chattel slaves—used of slaves who were owned by private citizens and could be transported, employed, or housed wherever their individual masters chose; in opposition to serfdom and helotage, which describe conditions of human dependency in which workers are usually tied to particular plots of land, and often are of ambiguous legal status though occasionally owned by the state.

corps—the largest unit within an individual army, usually comprising two or more divisions, and often commanded by a major general or lieutenant general, such as Haislip, Middleton, or Walker.

D-Day—June 6, 1944, the first day of the Allied invasion of Normandy; the term apparently originated in World War One, and simply meant "the day"—D, the abbreviation for "day," being followed by the word itself spelled out, in the manner of "H-Hour."

division—in the American army, usually consisting of about 16,000 men, designated either infantry or armored, depending on its degree of mechanized armored vehicles, and usually commanded by a brigadier or major general, such as Grow or Wood.

GI—"government issue"; literally, official U.S. military supplies, but the common name for American soldiers, particularly those enlisted men serving in the U.S. Army during World War Two.

Götterdämmerung—German for "Twilight of the Gods," used specifically by the Nazis for the final destruction of the Third Reich, in which the true believers in Wagnerian fashion would exhibit epic courage as they were annihilated by the barbarian invaders.

Helots—Greek for "those taken," a generic term used of peasant serfs in both Messenia and Laconia who were under Spartan subjugation.

hoplite—a Greek heavy infantryman, who fought with body armor, large shield, and spear in a mass formation. The term originally denoted the agrarian class of the Greek city-states, who could afford the necessary panoply, but eventually referred to any soldier who fought in the phalanx.

Laconia—the large valley in the southern Peloponnese that surrounds the city of Sparta, and whose villages were under the political control of the Spartan state.

414

Messenia—the large, southwestern region of the Peloponnese, hereditary home of the Helots, whose free capital city, Messenê, was founded by Epaminondas.

Overlord—the code name for the Anglo-American invasion of Europe in 1944.

Panzers—the German word loosely used for armored troops consisting of tanks, armored carriers, and other motorized guns and vehicles.

Pelopidas (d. 364 B.C.), Theban general and close associate of Epaminondas, commanded the Sacred Band at Leuctra; he played a notable role in a series of Theban victories until killed at Cynoscephalae.

Peloponnese—the large southern peninsula of Greece, connected to the mainland by the Isthmus at Corinth; home to Dorian speakers of Greek, its individual states were either in alliance with or in opposition to Sparta.

Perioikoi—Greek for "those who live around," a loose group of Laconian communities near Sparta, whose residents were subjected to varying degrees of oppression and subservience, but generally fared better than the Helots.

phalanx—a mass formation of hoplites, outside of Boeotia usually eight men deep, sometimes consisting of thousands of infantrymen stretching for a mile or two.

Plato (429–347 B.C.), the great Athenian philosopher, whose devotion to Socrates and involvement in the politics of Sicily left him with keen interests in war and the state, ranging from the tactical and strategic to the cultural and political.

polis—Greek for city-state; over one thousand independent Greek towns and their surrounding farmland that between 700 and 300 B.C. enjoyed political autonomy.

SHAEF—acronym for Supreme Headquarters Allied Expeditionary Force, the organization that coordinated Allied air, naval, and ground operations in northern Europe during World War Two, commanded by Dwight Eisenhower.

Sophocles (496–406 B.C.), the great Athenian playwright, was a general at the Athenian conquest of Samos and served on the Athenian board of audit after the disaster on Sicily. His dramatic career paralleled the high tide of Athenian imperialism.

Spartiate—a more precise adjective than Spartan to denote exclusively those native-born males of the Spartan empire who enjoyed full-citizen status and fought in the phalanx as equals, originally about 10,000 adult male citizens.

theater commander—in World War Two refers to absolute command of several army groups within a large area of operations, commanded by a general of the armies such as Eisenhower.

Thebes—the largest city of Boeotia, which during the time of Epaminondas served as the capital of a federated Boeotian league. For much of the fourth century B.C., Theban and Boeotian were nearly identical adjectives and were used interchangeably to describe the army of Boeotia.

Thucydides (460?–395? B.C.), the brilliant historian of the Peloponnesian War, saw battle firsthand as the Athenian admiral at Amphipolis; for his relative failure there, he was exiled for twenty years by the Athenian Assembly. Thucydides' history reflects a veteran's intimate knowledge of both tactical maneuver and strategic thinking, and the interplay between military operations and civilian audit and control.

Untermenschen—German for "inferior peoples," comprising those in Nazi ideology who were not members of some mythical Aryan and German-speaking race.

V-E Day—"Victory-Europe," the day on which the Third Reich surrendered, May 8, 1945—to be distinguished from V-J Day, the surrender of the Japanese on August 15, 1945, which formally marked the end of hostilities in World War Two.

Volk—German for "folk" or the "people"; used often in a racial context to denote the pristine purity of the Germanic peoples, untouched by both the decadence of Western civilization and the savagery of the East.

Wehrmacht—German for "defense force," a euphemism for the military resources of the Nazi empire.

Weltanschauung—German for "worldview"; in the context of Nazi ideology, appreciation that Aryan supremacy should permeate and transcend all social, economic, political, and cultural questions.

Western—generic adjective for European civilization that grew up west of Greece, and shared core values that originated in classical antiquity, including but not limited to constitutional government, civil liberties, free exchange of ideas, self-critique, private property, capitalism, and separation between religious and political-scientific thought.

Xenophon (428–354 B.C.), Greek historian and antiquarian; his extant work on everything from military history to biography and military science reflects his long and difficult career as an Athenian exile, intimate of Socrates, veteran of the 10,000, and close associate of the Spartan high military command.

ACKNOWLEDGMENTS

I OWE MUCH to other scholars. There is as yet no comprehensive study of the Theban army nor an updated biography in English of Epaminondas. Thus, I have relied largely on primary sources of Xenophon, Plutarch, Pausanias, and Diodorus and have offered my own translations of their narratives. But much of the information in those Greek texts about the life of Epaminondas is discussed with invaluable commentary in Marcello Fortina's *Epaminonda* (Turin, 1958) and Heinrich Swoboda's lengthy article "Epameinondas," published in 1900 in the *Real-Encyclopädie der klassicschen Altertumswissenschaft*. John Buckler's *Theban Hegemony* (Cambridge, Mass., 1980) remains the only modern military narrative of fourth-century Boeotia.

While I have tried to use a variety of published collections of Civil War letters, and especially Sherman's own memoirs, much of the primary information that I cite is found in the work of others. Interest in Sherman is currently in the midst of a renaissance of sorts, and at least five major biographies have appeared in the last five years. In general, the most balanced is Stanley Hirshson, *The White Tecumseh* (New York, 1997), and John Marszalek's *Sherman: A Soldier's Passion for Order* (New York, 1993). Few historians have had such a keen grasp of Sherman's military legacy and his rhetoric as Charles Royster, *The Destructive War: William Tecumseh Sherman, Stonewall Jackson, and the Americans* (New York, 1991). Liddell Hart (*Sherman: Soldier, Realist, American* [New York, 1929]) and Lloyd Lewis (*Sherman, Fighting Prophet* [New York, 1932]) are often now criticized for their laudatory views of Sherman, but no biographies, recent or not, are better written or more instructive. Because there are numerous current and excellent military accounts of the March to the Sea, my interest is not so much in the organization or the actual fighting of Sherman's campaign, as in the army's ideology and relationship with larger ethical issues of the Civil War and democracy at large.

Patton has been the subject of far less vituperation from historians, perhaps because he died at war's close, perhaps because—given his shrill extempore pronouncements—he was taken far less seriously as a reasoned observer of contemporary political and cultural events. Still, we can imagine his place in history had he lived into his seventies, like Sherman, speaking off the cuff at veterans' banquets during the tumultuous Cold War era and nascent civil rights movement. His candor, fierce anticommunism, and disturbing views on race and culture, not his final twelve months of World War Two, might have ensured that he was the

ACKNOWLEDGMENTS

subject of even more critical academic biographies. To some extent, a fuller appreciation of Patton's genius is only now emerging after the deaths of Eisenhower and Bradley, whose long and illustrious postwar careers tended to make contemporary criticism of many of their poor decisions in the European theater difficult for many historians. The degree to which I am indebted to the excellent work of Carlo D'Este (*Patton: A Genius for War* [New York, 1995]), Roger Nye (*The Patton Mind* [Garden City, N.Y., 1993]), and especially Martin Blumenson (six major works on Patton) will become immediately apparent in the Notes.

I have many to thank. My colleague Bruce Thornton of the Classics program at California State University, Fresno, has read the manuscript and offered a number of corrections and sound advice about its form and content. John Health, chairman of the Classics Department at Santa Clara University, and Michelle McKenna of Princeton University Press kindly read the entire manuscript and had numerous suggestions that I have adopted. Katherine A. Becker, a graduate student in military history at California State University, Fresno, was an invaluable research assistant and proofreader. Fred Wiemer greatly improved the manuscript through careful copyediting. The School of Arts and Humanities at California State University, Fresno, provided me a sabbatical leave during the 1997–98 academic year and funds both to cover travel overseas and for preparation of the manuscript. I wish to thank Luis Costa, dean of the school, for his support. Professor M. C. Drake, of the Theater Arts Department at CSU-Fresno, kindly drew the maps and translated my jumbled ideas into visual art. Many classicists and historians gave me sound advice in person or through published literature that I otherwise would not have found, especially Loy Bilderback, Michael Jameson, Donald Kagan, John Keegan, Steven Oberhelman, Paul Rahe, and Barry Strauss. I would also once again like to thank my literary agents, Glen Hartley and Lynn Chu, and my editor at The Free Press, Bruce Nichols, for their trust and continued support.

My greatest debt is to my family. My wife Cara and our three children, Pauli, Billy, and Susannah have for the past year put up with my lectures to them on the unappreciated morality of Epaminondas, the honesty of Sherman, and the sheer military genius and energy of Patton.

NOTES

PART I. YEOMEN OF THEBES. EPAMINONDAS'S DESCENT INTO THE PELOPONNESE, WINTER–SPRING, 370–369 B.C.

(All dates in this section are B.C. unless otherwise indicated.)

Chapter One. "The Dancing Floor of War"

1. For the terrain, size, and geography of Boeotia, see Symeonoglou, *Topography*, 5–13; Fossey, *Topography and Population*, 3–12; Buck, *History*, 1–31; Wallace, *Strabo*, 5–24; Gomme, *Topography*, 189–210; Phillipson and Kirsten, *Landschaften*, I 759–63; and fine ancient accounts in Strabo 9.2.1–42 and Pausanias 9. On the ubiquity of battle in Boeotia, see Hanson, ed., *Hoplites*, 254–55; *The Other Greeks*, 254–56. There is a useful description of many of these earlier battles in Anderson, *Military Theory*, 111–220. The epitaph of the dead of Chaeronea: IG II².5266. Cf. also the *Palantine Anthology* 7.245. The "dancing floor of war" literally in Greek is the more succinct *polemou orchêstra*: Plutarch, *Moralia* 193E18.

2. For a narrative account of the destruction of Thebes, see Bosworth, *Conquest and Empire*, 32–35, 195–96. On the archaeological evidence, see Symeonoglou, *Topography*, 148–50. For the connection of soil fertility and the number of hoplite infantry, see Hanson, *Other Greeks*, 244.

3. Ancient descriptions of the slaughter at Thebes: Arrian, *Anabasis* 1.6–9; Diodorus 17.8–14; Plutarch, *Alexander* 11–13; Justin 11.3.9–10; Aeschines 3.133. Epaminondas's last words at the battle of Mantinea (362): Plutarch, *Moralia* 194C24. A near half century separated the liberation of the Theban Cadmea (379) from the failed attempt to secure freedom from the Macedonians (335).

Chapter Two. "The Boeotian Pig"

4. The dream of Leonidas: Plutarch, *Moralia* 865.F. "Death in war": Plutarch, *Moralia* 192C. Pindar (*Olympian* 6.90) seems the first (ca. 472) to have recorded the swine proverb; the proximity of Attica may account for the wide dissemination of the slur—Boeotians were probably dubbed "swine" in opposition to Athenian aesthetes (e.g., Plutarch, *Moralia*

995A). On the general Boeotian reputation for rusticity, see Roberts, *Ancient Boeotians*, 1–14; Nepos, *Epaminondas* 15.5.2; 7.11.3. See Aristotle, *Rhetoric* 3.4.3, for the quote of Pericles. On the religious shrines of Boeotia, see Demand, *Thebes*, 48–69, 85–105. There is a brief sketch of Theban history from 525 to 404 in Buck, *History*, 107–75; Demand, *Thebes*, 16–47. The "Medism" of the Boeotians is discussed by Hignett, *Xerxes' Invasion*, 18–24; Demand, *Thebes*, 20–27. For the Boeotian plundering of Attica, and the difficulty of ravaging in the ancient world, in general see Hanson, *Warfare and Agriculture*.

5. On the general agrarian tendency to put greater emphasis on social conservatism than economic populism, see Hanson, *Fields*, 213–84. Larsen, *Federal States*, 27–39, points out that the confederacy of the mid fifth century was unusually broad-based, perhaps relying on a liberal hoplite census. The constitution in force from perhaps 447 to 386 is described by the Oxyrhynchus Historian, 11.2–4. The revolution against the Spartan garrison on the Cadmea, and the nature of the Theban revolutionary program, are found in Xenophon, *Hellenica* 5.5.27–31; Diodorus 15.26–27; Plutarch, *Pelopidas* 5–14. Plutarch, over four hundred years later, wrote a curious dialogue, "On the Sign of Socrates," whose dramatic setting is a discussion among the Theban conspirators of 379 (*Moralia* 575B–598F). A review of the primary and secondary sources is provided by Buckler, *Theban Hegemony*, 15–45. Cartledge, *Agesilaos*, 296–99, offers an analysis of the Spartan occupation and defeat from the viewpoint of Spartan foreign policy concerns. The relationship between agrarianism and consensual government is presented in Hanson, *Other Greeks*, 181–219. Aristotle on the best citizen: *Politics* 6.1319a; *Rhetoric* 2.1381a21–24.

6. On the nature of the resurrected democratic confederation in Boeotia, and the nomenclature Boeotian/Theban, see Buckler, *Theban Hegemony*, 15–45; Buck, *Boiotia and the Boiotian League*, 25–99, 105–8; Larsen, *Federal States*, 175–80. For the various demographical calculations concerning Boeotia, see Hanson, *Other Greeks*, 210–12; and see now Hornblower, *Commentary*, 297–99 (on the battle of Delium at Thucydides 4.93–7), who has a review of the secondary literature.

7. Concerning Theban-Spartan enmity, see Cartledge, *Agesilaos*, 274–313; and cf. Plutarch, *Comparison of Agesilaus and Pompey* 3.2–3. On Epaminondas's story about Spartan intentions, see Nepos, *Epaminondas* 1.11.6. There had been a half century of animosity between the two powers since the middle of the Peloponnesian War. Though once ostensibly allies, they had quarreled over the plunder from their fort at Decelea, the fate of Athens after the Peloponnesian War, and support for right-wing revolutionaries at Athens, well before their open hatred in the Corinthian and Boeotian Wars from the mid-390s down to Leuctra. Indeed, almost all of the early fourth-century hoplite battles—Haliartus, Nemea, Coronea, Tegyra, Leuctra, and Mantinea—entailed head-on collisions between Thebans and Spartans.

8. Pelopidas at Tegyra: Plutarch *Pelopidas* 16–17. On the battle of Leuctra, see Lazenby, *Spartan Army*, 151–62; Anderson, *Military Theory*, 192–204; Hanson, "Epameinondas," 190–207; Delbrück, *War*, I, 165–71; Tuplin, "Leuctra Campaign," 84–93. Munn, *Dema Wall*, 129–80, has a synopsis of the Spartan invasions of Boeotia in the 370s.

9. There are keen appraisals of Epaminondas's strategic vision and tactical competence in Roloff, *Probleme*, 11–59; Delbrück, *War*, I, 165–71; Liddell Hart, *Strategy*, 13–16; Grote, *Greece*, 212–15. The Spartan boast: Plutarch, *Agesilaus* 31.6.

Chapter Three. "The Fairest and Most Level Ground"

10. The social and economic forces that led to *polis* formation are nicely summarized in Osborne, *Greece in the Making*, 70–136. Hanson and Heath, *Who Killed Homer?*, 21–80, connect Western values to the early Greek city-state.

11. On the growth of the Greek way of hoplite fighting and its connection to the rise of the *polis*, see Hanson, *Other Greeks*, 221–89.

12. The nature of hoplite fighting is described in Hanson, *Western Way of War*, 135–93, and in a series of essays by scholars in Hanson, ed., *Hoplites*, 15–170; Lloyd, ed., *Battle*, 1–106.

13. The rather unpopular view that Athenian-style radical democracy led to increased war-making in the Greek world, and refuted the old insular—and ethical—system of hoplite warfare is advanced in Hanson, *Other Greeks*, 327–55.

14. For this fourth-century change in Greek warfare, see the ancient consensus at Xenophon, *Ways and Means* 2.3; Demosthenes 4.47; Polybius 13.3.2–4.

Chapter Four. "The Thebans Are Mightier in War"

15. The changing strategic and tactical scenario in fourth-century Greece has been the topic of a vast literature, see the synopsis of secondary work in Hanson, *Other Greeks*, 327–55; 489–92.

16. On the cultural and social effects of establishing democracy without a property qualification in Thebes, see Buck, *Boiotia and the Boiotian League*, 101–22.

17. All ancient sources remark that Theban hoplites had a reputation for physical strength, tough training, and skill in wrestling: Polyaenus, *Stratagems* 2.3.6; Nepos, *Epaminondas* 15.2.4; 5.4; Plutarch, *Moralia* 192C–D; *Pelopidas* 7.3; Xenophon, *Hellenica* 6.5.22–24; Diodorus 15.39.1. On the relationship between depth and width of a Greek phalanx, see Pritchett, *Greek State at War*, I, 135–41; Delbrück, *War*, 53–55; Lazenby, *Spartan Army*, 156–57. For the novelty and wisdom of using a massed phalanx on the left wing, see Hanson, "Epameinondas," 192–201. Anderson, *Military Theory*, 142–44, 160–62, 212–17, and Roloff, *Probleme*, 42–59, review the Theban preference for depth at the expense of breadth and the ensuing ramifications in an allied army. Cartledge, *Agesilaos*, 240–41, points out the subsequent political advantages of sparing the Peloponnesian allies at Leuctra by concentrating on the Spartan elite.

18. On elite units at Thebes and elsewhere, consult Pritchett, *Greek State at War*, II, 221–25; Trittle, "*Epilektoi*," 54–59; Ogden, "Homosexuality and Warfare," 111–14.

19. Theban and Spartan fortunes: Diodorus 15.1.34–35. Theban morale: Diodorus 15.38.2–3; 39.1; 50.5–6; Plutarch, *Pelopidas* 15.3. For the fourth-century monument that was apparently set up in Thebes right after the victory at Leuctra, see Tod, *Greek Historical Inscriptions*, I, 92–94. The inscription on gray limestone is one of the first objects that greets one entering the Theban museum. The seven-line commemoration also claims that three other Thebans "ran not second to Epaminondas."

Chapter Five. "Princeps Graeciae"

20. *Princeps Graeciae*: Cicero, *Tusculan Disputations* 1.2.4, who apparently coined the term from Ephorus's use of "*prôteuô*." For the difficult trail of ancient sources concerning Epaminondas and his laudatory portrayal in surviving literature, see G. Shrimpton's Stanford doctoral dissertation, *The Epaminondas Tradition* (1970)—excerpted in "Theban Supremacy," 310–18. Cf. also Barber, *Historian Ephorus*, 131–33, Westlake, "Sources," 18–22; and Buckler, *Theban Hegemony*, 263–77. In the opinion of the fourth century, Epaminondas had eclipsed Solon, Themistocles, Miltiades, and Pericles—both in military achievement and moral sensibility; see, for example, Diodorus 15.88.

21. On the life of Epaminondas, see Plutarch, *Pelopidas* 3–20; *Moralia* 192C–194C;

Diodorus 15.39ff.; the short sketch in Nepos, *Epaminondas*; Pausanias 9.13–15; Polyaenus, *Stratagems* 2.3. Swoboda ("Geschichte," 460–75; "Epameinondas," 2687–709) has assembled all of the widely diverse ancient testimonia. Much of the modern interest in Epaminondas was shown by German classical scholars at the turn of the century, largely due to his tactical and strategic accomplishments. He was apparently relatively unknown before the age of forty: Plutarch, *Moralia* 1129C.

Fortina's *Epaminonda* is a valuable though curious monograph—it contains a footnote five pages long (on the trial of Epaminondas). Nevertheless, it is an often overlooked storehouse of information, which concludes with a section devoted to the "Prima spedizione di Epaminonda del Peloponneso" (44–49).

22. Freeing captured exiles: Pausanias 9.15.4. Disdain for tyrants: Plutarch, *Pelopidas* 29.5–6. Epaminondas's argument with Agesilaus, the interval to Leuctra, his duty as a regular hoplite, and saving Pelopidas in battle at a siege at Mantinea are found at Diodorus 15.72.1; Plutarch, *Agesilaus* 27.3–4; Pausanias 9.13.1–5; Plutarch, *Pelopidas* 4; cf. Grote, *History*, X, 184, n. 1. On his conduct at his trial in 369, see Buckler, *Theban Hegemony*, 138–42.

23. His "if you want peace, prepare for war" adage is found in Nepos, *Epaminondas* 15.5.3–4, where Epaminondas adds that any who wished Thebes to be the leading city of Greece should vacate the palestra and seek out the military camp. "Iron Gut" (literally, "iron innard"—*sidêroun splangchon*): Plutarch, *Moralia* 1127B. Philosophers on war: Plato, *Laws* 1.626A; Heraclitus frg. 53 (Diels).

24. Not killing or banishing other Greeks: Xenophon, *Hellenica* 7.1.42; anger over the destruction of Orchomenos: Diodorus 15.57.1; Pausanias 9.15.3; Plutarch, *Comparison of Pelopidas and Marcellus* 1.1. Epaminondas's distaste for a sumptuous meal: Plutarch, *Moralia* 192D; one coat only: Aelian, *Varia Historia* 5.5; pride of his parents in the victory at Leuctra: Plutarch, *Moralia* 193A; his "daughters" and solitary life: Diodorus 15.87.6; Plutarch, *Pelopidas* 3.3; lecture about prostitutes: Plutarch, *Moralia* 808D. Frontinus (*Stratagems* 3.2.7) relates a strange story that in Arcadia Epaminondas once had his men dress like women to be admitted to a city in order to open the gates. More at ease with men: Plutarch, *Moralia* 761D; Theopompus frg. 247–49. His call for "one step (*hen bêma*) forward": Polyaenus, *Stratagems* 2.3.2; his death at Mantinea: Diodorus 15.87; Nepos, *Epaminondas* 9; Plutarch, *Moralia* 194C. Epaminondas sacked the obese: Plutarch, *Moralia* 192D; his mastery of arms: Nepos, *Epaminondas* 2.3–5; shunning money and materialism: Nepos, *Epaminondas* 3.3–5; advice for Pelopidas: Aelian, *Varia Historia* 14.14.38; on solitary patrol: Plutarch, *Moralia* 781C–D; advice for servant: Aelian, *Varia Historia* 11.9. For the friendship of Epaminondas and Pelopidas, see Plutarch, *Pelopidas* 3.1

25. The last generation of Pythagoreans (*tôn Pythagorikôn philosopôn hoi teleutaioi*): Diodorus 15.76.4. On why Pythagoreanism was welcome in Thebes, see Demand, *Thebes*, 70–76. "First citizen": Diodorus 10.11.1–2. For Cicero on the Pythagoreans, see his *Tusculation Disputations* 1.17.39. For a review of the main tenets of Pythagorean philosophy, consult the invaluable work of Burkert, *Ancient Pythagoreanism*, 15–119. Also see Demand, *Thebes*, 132–35, for the position of women in Pythagoreanism. For ancient connections between Epaminondas's philosophy and his military and political success, see Nepos, *Epaminondas* 15.2.2; Diodorus 15.39.2–3; 16.2.2–3; Plutarch, *Pelopidas* 3–4. Epaminondas's reluctance to kill other Thebans and reputation as a loner: Plutarch, *Pelopidas* 5.3. His remark about the recently deceased: Plutarch, *Moralia* 136D; his unchanging demeanor: Plutarch, *Moralia* 52F. Cheap wine: Plutarch, *Moralia* 633E. See too, in general, Fortina, *Epaminonda*, 3–7.

26. Dismissal of portents and signs: Diodorus 15.52.5–6; Frontinus, *Stratagems* 1.11.16; "forbidden to sit": Frontinus, *Stratagems* 1.12.7; faked signs: Diodorus 15.53.4–5. For

Pythagoreanism and Epaminondas's tactical doctrine, see P. Vidal-Naquet and P. Lêvêque, "Epaminondas the Pythagorean," 61–82.

27. Thebes ruled by philosophers: Alcidamas (in Aristotle, *Rhetoric* 2.23 [1398b18]). See Aelian, *Varia History* 7.14; 3.17, citing Epaminondas as an example of philosophy's value in war, and also Nonnus, *Commentary on the Speech of St. Gregory Against Julian* 1.119 (*Patrologiae Cursus, series Graecae* 36.993–94).

28. On Xenophon's praise of Epaminondas: *Hellenica* 7.5.19. Cf. Cawkwell "Epaminondas," 255–57. On the various claims by particular cities and individuals for killing Epaminondas at Mantinea, see Plutarch, *Agesilaus* 35.1; Pausanias 8.11.5–6; 9.15.6; Nepos, *Epaminondas* 15.9.

29. Epaminondas insults the Spartans: Nepos, *Epaminondas* 15.4. Nepos fantastically claims that the Theban's open defiance of Sparta in her own hall before her allies did more to ruin her prestige than the subsequent defeat of her army at Leuctra; cf. too Plutarch, *Moralia* 193.D16; *Agesilaus* 27–28. The grabbing of the snake before Leuctra: Polyaenus, *Stratagems* 2.3.15.

Chapter Six. "An Altogether Cruel and Bitter Condition"

30. Theopompus frg. 13. On the differences between chattel slavery and helotage in Messenia and Laconia, see Cartledge, *Sparta*, 165–90; Garlan, *Slavery*, 153–58. "Like asses": Tyrtaeus frg. 6.

31. Plato and Aristotle on slavery and Helots: Plato, *Laws* 776C–777C; Aristotle, *Politics* 1269b7–12; cf. Heraclitus frg. 53 (Diels) on the fate of the vanquished.

32. Slaves of the community: Pausanias 3.20.6; "waiting for the disasters of the Spartans": Aristotle, *Politics* 1269a37–39. On the supposed fear to leave shield bands near Helots, see Critias frg. 88B37 (Diels-Kranz); the Spartan Secret police: Aristotle frg. 538. On Lycurgus and the Lycurgan code of honor, see Xenophon, *Constitution of the Spartans* 8–11.

33. For the military role of the Perioikoi and various inferior groups of Spartiates, see Lazenby, *Spartan Army*, 41–62.

34. For the population of Laconia and Messenia, the size of the Spartan army, and demographic trends within Spartan society, consult Cartledge, *Agesilaos*, 37–40, 160–75; *Sparta*, 175–77, 307–12; Lazenby, *Spartan Army*, 56–62; Sallares, *Ecology*, 170–71, 213–15. Modern scholars have not yet presented exact and reliable figures for the general demography of Messenia, nor for the number of villages that were primarily Helot enclaves or subject to varying other degrees of political subjugation. I assume that Epaminondas's liberation of Messenia did not immediately lead to a cohesive state throughout the entire territory, as some autonomous villages with close ties to the Spartans might have been wary of instant Helot rule. Archaeological field surveys of the Messenian countryside are in the process of being published and may reveal changes in agricultural practice after Messenia was liberated; I would expect that the evidence will show a rise in homestead farms in the Messenian countryside.

35. For Thucydides' remarks on the Helots and the Pylos campaign, see his history 1.101.2; 4.40–41; 4.80.2; Critias 88B37 (Diels-Kranz). Hamilton (*Agesilaus*, 215–51) provides a clear narrative of the resulting weakness to Sparta when the Peloponnesian allies became autonomous.

36. Finley ("Sparta," 161–77) and Cartledge (*Agesilaos*, 160–79) are particularly good on the internal contradictions inherent in Spartan society that arose from the decision to create helotage. Xenophon on the dangers of Helots: Xenophon, *Constitution of the Spartans* 12.4.

37. The murder of 2,000 Helots: Thucydides 4.80.3; the petty humiliation and degradation of Helots: Myron frg. 2; Plutarch, *Lycurgus* 28–29; Cinadon and the general repugnance for the Spartiates: Xenophon, *Hellenica* 3.3.4–11; exiled Messenians flock to Epaminondas: Pausanias 9.26.5; Diodorus 15.66.1; Plutarch, *Pelopidas* 24.5.

Chapter Seven. "An Unravaged and Inviolate Land"

38. For Pericles on imperial democracy, see Thucydides 2.62.2–3; Cleon's similar admission: Thucydides 3.37.2; a defense of Spartan apartheid: Isocrates, *Archidamus* 27–28. The great march into the Peloponnese in winter 370–369 is described in four ancient accounts, which I draw on at various times in the following narrative. Xenophon (*Hellenica* 6.5.25–32) may have been an eyewitness to many of the events, but his hostility to Thebes apparently precluded him from even mentioning the foundation of Messenê or Megalopolis, and often led him to exaggerate the success of Spartan resistance, as well as downplaying the personal role of Epaminondas. His son, we should remember, was said to be killed by the Thebans at the battle of Mantinea. The first-century historian Diodorus (15.63.3–65.5) followed Ephorus, a near contemporary of Xenophon, who wrote a global history up until his own day. But Diodorus often gets some of Ephorus wrong, especially on matters of chronology; and on the other hand, he repeats mostly verbatim much of the former's emphasis of history as moral exempla. Plutarch's life of Epaminondas is lost, but his *Agesilaus* (31–32) and *Pelopidas* (24) contain some information on the invasion, drawing also on the lost fourth-century historians Callisthenes and Ephorus. It is not known precisely how much of these lives represent other sources or Plutarch's own moralizing and editorializing—a native and chauvinistic Boeotian who lived over four hundred years after Epaminondas had died. Pausanias (9.13–15) has anecdotal information about the invasion, mostly drawn from Plutarch's lost *Epaminondas*. In general, the slightly pro-Theban tradition that finds its way into Diodorus, Plutarch, and Pausanias serves as a counterbalance to the more reliable firsthand accounts of the pro-Spartan Xenophon. See Shrimpton, *Epaminondas Tradition*, 32–41, CQ: 45–48; Cartledge, *Agesilaos*, 55–73. There is a brief but lively sketch of the invasion in Cloché, *Thèbes*, 139–44.

39. Mantinea was reconstituted and rebuilt (371–370) after the Theban victory at Leuctra; presumably its fortifications were not completely finished when it called Epaminondas into Arcadia for assistance. And although Xenophon (*Hellenica* 6.5.3–5) does not mention a direct Theban hand in its refounding, both the battle of Leuctra and Epaminondas's appearance in 370–369 surely allowed the idea of a new city to come to fruition. Pausanias (8.8.10; 9.14.4) exaggerates when he says explicitly the city rose through the efforts of Epaminondas. We need not imagine that Epaminondas himself and his architects planned the entire city—which was already rising when he arrived—to see that the ascent of Thebes had given Mantinea the window of opportunity it so eagerly sought. See Grote, *History*, X, 205–6.

On the Boeotian army during the Peloponnesian War and the early fourth century, see Buck, *Boiotia and the Boiotian League*, 115–122. Megalopolis and Messenê in alliance: Polybius 4.32.8–10. A few modern scholars have questioned the ancient tradition (Pausanias 8.52.4; 9.14.4–5) that Epaminondas was responsible for the founding of Megalopolis (e.g., Larsen, *Federal States*, 186–87; Demand, *Urban Relocation*, 115–17). The problem in assessing Epaminondas's role in creating the three new Peloponnesian cities lies in precisely defining the range of meaning captured by the word "founding." We should imagine the following scenario: Leuctra gave impetus for the Mantineans to reconstitute their city and finish the fortifications. Epaminondas's presence in the Peloponnese also allowed the

Arcadians to go ahead with their plans to build Megalopolis with both spiritual and material Theban aid. Epaminondas's liberation of Messenia was entirely responsible for the rise of Messenê. The question of Theban intervention in the founding of these three citadels is one of degree only; none would have survived—or probably even have arisen—had the Thebans not won at Leuctra, and made a subsequent appearance in the Peloponnese. See Buckler, *Theban Hegemony*, 108–9, 239. In antiquity, all three cities were thought to be part of some master plan of Epaminondas (cf. Demand, *Urban Relocation*, 202, n. 7), an idea not always rejected outright by modern scholars, see Roebuck, *Messenia*, 32–33.

40. For the politics of the decision to go south to aid the Arcadians and the intricacies of Boeotian law pertaining to command of the army, see Buckler, *Theban Hegemony*, 70–76; Larsen, *Federal States*, 175–80; Roy, "Arcadia and Boeotia," 569–79. On the ten talents, see Xenophon, *Hellenica* 6.5.19–20. Epaminondas's reticence and keeping secrets: Nepos, *Epaminondas* 3.2–3; Plutarch, *Moralia* 39B. For the enigma of Sherman, see Davis, *Sherman's March*, 9. The idea to fight Sparta by fighting in Laconia: Xenophon, *Hellenica* 4.7.11; Plutarch, *Agesilaus* 30.1; Pausanias 9.14.2.

41. On ancient Greek farming tasks and the nature of winter chores, see Hanson, *Other Greeks*, 127–78; Brumfield, *Attic Festivals*, 11–53.

42. For the provisioning and pay of ancient Greek armies, see Pritchett, *Greek State at War*, I, 3–52; Engels, *Alexander*, 11–25. Six thousand drachmas make a talent, and a drachma represents about the daily wage of a skilled worker. The chilling factor and dormancy for trees and vines are discussed by Sallares, *Ecology*, 306–8.

43. The size of the Boeotian allied army as it left for Arcadia is treated by Lazenby, *Spartan Army*, 166, 203—though he may be too conservative in rejecting outright the notion of 40,000 allied hoplites that eventually gathered at Arcadia. Cf. too Xenophon, *Hellenica* 6.5.23.

44. For the Boeotians' reputation for high spirits and physical prowess in battle, see nn. 17 and 19. On Boeotian hoplite weaponry, see Anderson, *Military Theory*, 14, 22, 27; for the Spartan look, see Lazenby, *Spartan Army*, 30–32. On hoplites' equipment in general, see Hanson, *Western Way of War*, 55–88. There are striking black engraved stelai from Thebes—most likely grave markers commemorating the Boeotian dead from the battle of Delium (424)—that portray idealized Boeotian hoplites at their moments before death. Three examples of these moving limestone reliefs are now on display in the Theban museum; for a line-drawing representation of the warrior Saugenês, see Demand, *Thebes*, 114–16. Boeotians as Dutch: Roberts, *Ancient Boeotians*, 57–65. Scholars sometimes translate the odd Boeotian dialect into English as a Scottish brogue, see B. Rodgers, trans., *Aristophanes, The Acharnians* (Cambridge, Eng., 1924). Perhaps the postclassical army most similar to the Boeotians was the early Swiss phalanx, which also enjoyed a similar reputation for ferocity and was composed of rural democratic contingents.

45. Individual armor in the classical age weighed from fifty to seventy pounds, depending on the type of breastplate and helmet. We should imagine the fourth-century Thebans' armor as lighter, perhaps spear, sword, helmet, greaves, composite breastplate and shield weighing in at around fifty pounds. The complaints of the Corinthians: Xenophon, *Hellenica* 6.5.37. On Xenophon's remarks, see *Hellenica* 6.5.23; 7.5.12. The "puffed-up" Thebans, and the club of Herakles: Xenophon, *Hellenica* 7.5.21.

46. Diodorus says that the army that left Arcadia was "more than 50,000" a figure that presumably meant hoplites and did not include servants and skirmishers. Plutarch (*Pelopidas* 24) says Epaminondas led an army (*stratia*) of 70,000 Greeks south from Arcadia, of which less than a twelfth (ca. 5,800) were Thebans. Plutarch surely means by "Thebans" all the Boeotians, and the 70,000 figure is believable if we imagine that several

thousand light-armed skirmishers and attendants are included in his total. In his *Agesilaus* (31), he says specifically that there were "40,000 hoplites" and "many light-armed and un-armed" (*psiloi kai anoploi*) who followed "for the sake of plunder," making an aggregate "horde" (*ochlos*) of 70,000 that ventured into Laconia. Given what we know of the man-power reserves of the various allies, Plutarch's figures seem about right. See Bauer, "An-griff," 243–46.

47. Epaminondas's prediction that to disband would be "to ruin the army": Nepos, *Epaminondas* 15.7.4–5. "An unravaged and inviolate land": Plutarch, *Agesilaus* 31.2. The six hundred years: Plutarch, *Agesilaus* 31.1. Presumably, the figure—either five hundred or six hundred years, depending on the source—was calibrated in reference to the mythical invasion of the Dorians, the sons of Herakles, which the Greeks thought had occurred sometime around 1000 or so, in the chaos and detritus of the end of the heroic age. See Bauer, "Angriff," 247. "Out of date": Pausanias 9.14.5; Peloponnesians give over command to Pelopidas and Epaminondas: Plutarch, *Pelopidas* 24.2–5.

48. Consult the figures in Engels, *Alexander*, 19–22, who presents logistical calcula-tions for the army of Alexander the Great that may have numbered about 65,000 total personnel when it crossed the Hellespont. Epaminondas's advice in Arcadia: Plutarch, *Moralia* 788A.

49. On the pass from Arcadia to Sparta, and the plan of Epaminondas's descent, see Diodorus 15.63–65. For the problems of armies operating near Sellasia, see Pritchett, *Topography*, I, 59–70; Buckler (*Theban Hegemony*, 78–82) and Cartledge (*Sparta and Lako-nia*, 296–98) discuss the route of the invasion. For Spartan resistance, see Xenophon, *Hel-lenica* 6.5.26; Diodorus 15.62–65.

50. Arrian, *Anabasis* 1.9.4. For agricultural devastation in the ancient world, see in general Hanson, *Warfare and Agriculture*. The situation at Sparta: Xenophon, *Hellenica* 7.1.11; Houses of Sparta: Xenophon, *Hellenica* 6.5.28; Plutarch's quote of Theopompus: *Agesilaus* 31.3.

51. Thebans fought off a Spartan counterattack: Diodorus 15.65.2–3; Xenophon, *Hel-lenica* 6.5.30–32. On the various plots and desertions of Spartiates, Helots, and Perioikoi in Laconia, see Xenophon, *Hellenica* 6.5.25, 30–32; Plutarch, *Agesilaus* 32.7. Scholars con-tinue to argue over whether these plots and rebellions were proof of serious fundamental tensions beneath the veneer of Spartan order, or (hardly likely) less serious insurrections, predictable but tolerable given the magnitude of the crisis. See Cartledge, *Agesilaos*, 384–86 ("Epameinondas did raise the heat under a cauldron of social tensions that had simmering within the Spartan polity"), *contra* Talbert, "Helots," 36–38. See also Liddell Hart, *Strategy*, 340. Agesilaus retires to city center: Plutarch, *Agesilaus* 31.3–4; the oracle about the high ground: Frontinus, *Stratagems* 1.10.3; Antalcidas sends his children away: Plutarch, *Agesi-laus* 32.1. Hysteria of Spartan women: Plutarch, *Agesilaus* 31.5–6; Xenophon, *Hellenica* 6.5.28.

52. Winding streets: Aristotle, *Politics* 7.1330b27–33. Sherman quote: Marszalek, *Sher-man*, 332. Insults to the Spartans: Diodorus 15.65.4–5; Plutarch, *Agesilaus* 31.3–5; nearly inside Sparta: Diodorus 15.65.4; Isocrates, *Philip* 48; Perioikoi joining in: Xenophon, *Hel-lenica* 6.5.31–33; mutinies in Sparta: Plutarch, *Agesilaus* 32.6–7; Polyaenus, *Stratagems* 2.1.14; Aelian, *Varia Historia* 14.27; aid for Sparta: Xenophon, *Hellenica* 6.5.29; multitude of plunder: Diodorus 15.65.5. We need not accept ancient versions in Theopompus (quoted in Plutarch, *Agesilaus* 32.8) and Aelian (*Varia History* 4.8) that Epaminondas refrained from destroying the city either out of fear of upsetting the balance of power or due to bribes from King Agesilaus. During the March to the Sea, similar folktales were rife that Sherman spared certain plantations or villages because of the presence there of former girlfriends.

Real reasons for Thebans leaving Sparta: Plutarch, *Agesilaus* 32.8; Xenophon, *Hellenica* 6.5.50; the sense that the Thebans were more tactically astute and interested in the military aspects of the invasion, the Arcadians more bent on plunder: Xenophon, *Hellenica* 6.5.30. "Pierce the shell of the C.S.A. and it's all hollow inside": Hitchcock, *Marching*, 89.

Chapter Eight. *"Nature Has Made No Man a Slave"*

53. The ambition of Epaminondas: Diodorus 15.66.1. Plutarch's simile of a sick body: Plutarch, *Agesilaus* 33.2

54. Epaminondas's dream and the oracle: Pausanias 4.26–27. On the physical remains of Messenê, see Habicht, *Pausanias* 36–63. Roebuck (*Messenia*, 32–49) has a good discussion about Epaminondas's prominent role in the founding of Messenê and its connection to his larger aims in the Peloponnese. Anger of Isocrates: Isocrates, *Archidamus* 28; Panhellenic nature of Messenê: Diodorus 15.66.1; Lycurgus, *Leocrates* 62; Messenian exiles flock to Epaminondas: Pausanias 4.26.3; cf. Diodorus 15.66; Swoboda, "Epaminondas," 2689–90. Messenê entirely the result of Epaminondas's initiative: Diodorus 15.66.5–6. Spartan fear of Messenê: Plutarch, *Agesilaus* 34.1. We should assume that the original founding of Messenê did not lead automatically to the entire consolidation of the Messenia. Rather, the Helot stronghold allowed a gradual ongoing consolidation of territory and absorption of settlements that were in theory still loyal to Sparta, and had once been enjoying more favorable conditions of tribute than the Helots; see Roebuck, *Messenia*, 38–40.

55. Theban wall builders: Diodorus 14.84.3; Xenophon, *Hellenica* 5.4.38. Difficulty in achieving egalitarianism in already established cities: Aristotle, *Politics* 2.1266a39–1266b6; Grote, *History*, X, 231. Statue of Epaminondas at Messenê: Pausanias 4.31.10–11; Spartan fear of Messenians: Polyaenus, *Stratagems* 2.1.28; fear of the Thebans: Pausanias 4.28.1; timidity of Iphicrates and his Athenians at the isthmus: Xenophon, *Hellenica* 6.5.51–53; cf. 5.33–49; Diodorus 15.63.2–3; "a new flute": Plutarch, *Moralia* 193F. On the Messenian shields, see Anderson, *Military Theory*, 263, n. 28. Alcidamas: his work is lost, but the quote is found in Pseudo-Aristotle, *Rhetorical Speech to Alexandria* 13.1373b. On the context of the quote, see Roebuck, *Messenia*, 43, n. 77.

Controversy surrounds the time and length of the invasion of 370–369. The problem with all ancient accounts is that they disagree with one another and cannot be reconciled, Nor do they calibrate chronologically the distinct phases of Epaminondas's campaign in Laconia and Messenia. Diodorus (15.67.1) says the invasion lasted eighty-five days; Plutarch, *Agesilaus* (32.8), claims "three months." In his *Pelopidas* (24.1; cf. *Moralia* 817F; Aelian, *Varia Historia* 13.42) he remarks that Epaminondas and Pelopidas had "added four entire months" to their commands "as they campaigned in Messenia, Arcadia, and Laconia"—that is, 120 days *after* the first of the Boeotian year when they were to give up command, which must have started somewhere around December 22. See too Nepos, *Epaminondas* 15.7.5.

We should imagine that Epaminondas left Boeotia in late November or early December, was in Arcadia around mid-December (Xenophon, *Hellenica* 6.5.20), ravaged Laconia through late December (Plutarch *Pelopidas* 24.1) and on into early January. Then in later January he headed for Messenia in further disobedience of the law, staying there another three to four months, and returning to Thebes in mid- or late April. Thus he was gone roughly four months after December 22, when his legal tenure expired, and perhaps nearly five months in total from the time he left Boeotia. Appian's (11.41) "six-month" invasion is not so unbelievable (cf. Wiseman, "Epaminondas," 178, n. 3). On the problems of the chronology of the invasion, see Fortina, *Epaminonda*, 51, n. 67; Buckler, *Theban Hegemony*, 233–42; Ryder, *Koine Eirene*, 170–72.

Chapter Nine. "And All of Greece Became Independent and Free"

56. His dog: Aelian, *Varia Historia* 13.42; "overplayed their trumps": Demosthenes, *On the Crown* 18; Isocrates' criticism: Isocrates, *Philip* 53; Epaminondas's proposed public condemnation: Nepos, *Epaminondas* 15.8.3–5. For a complete discussion of the trial of Epaminondas, see Beister, *Untersuchungen*, 75–80; P. Cuff, "The Trials of Epaminondas—a Note," *Athenaeum* 32 (1954), 262–63; M. Cary, "The Trial of Epaminondas," *Classical Quarterly* 18 (1924): 182–84. His weakness as a hegemon: Cartledge, *Agesilaos*, 310–11; Buckler, *Theban Hegemony*, 220–27. Epaminondas, greatest man Greece produced: Diodorus 15.88.4

57. Tearless Battle: Plutarch, *Agesilaus* 33.3–5; Mantineans scared of Thebans and Epaminondas: Diodorus 15.82.4; Philip in Thebes: Plutarch, *Pelopidas* 26.5—a man, Plutarch says, who "neither naturally or by imitation" had any of the "justice, magnanimity, or kindness of Epaminondas."

58. On the wounded in Sherman's army, see Harwell and Racine, *Fiery Trail*, 59. "Splendid legs": Marszalek, *Sherman*, 331; few sick on Sherman's march: Walters, *Merchant of Terror*, 160.

Polyaenus (*Stratagems* 2.3.5) says that Epaminondas changed his mind about attacking and destroying Sparta proper, because he thought his real goal was to bring a rough equivalence of power in the Peloponnese—he did not wish to replace Spartan hegemony with Theban, thus incurring the future enmity of his present Peloponnesian allies. We need not believe that anecdote entirely, but it is evidence that Epaminondas was constantly alternating between direct attack and larger strategic questions of attrition, depending on the immediate status of the enemy before him. See Liddell Hart, *Strategy*, 14–16.

Kromayer (*Antike Schlachtfelder*, I, 79) and Bauer ("Angriff," 270–74) sought to prove that Epaminondas had introduced a new concept of total war against soldier and civilian in Laconia, the model for Alexander and Philip. Roloff (*Probleme*, 38–41) replied that the invasion of 370–369 was largely designed to reduce Spartan material assets and to induce autonomy in Arcadia and Messenia. For criticism of each view, see Delbrück, *War*, I, 170–71; Cartledge, *Agesilaos*, 234–35.

59. Epaminondas worth more than all the Thebans: Nepos, *Epaminondas* 15.10.4. Ruined Sparta in single day: Nepos, *Epaminondas* 15.5.6; "no longer a general left in Thebes": Aelian, *Varia Historia* 12.3; Plutarch, *Moralia* 194C; Demise of the Thebans after Epaminondas: Strabo 9.2.2. The quotation is from Epaminondas's statue at Thebes: Pausanias 9.15.6

PART II. THE ARMY OF THE WEST. SHERMAN'S MARCH TO THE SEA, NOVEMBER 16–DECEMBER 21, 1864

Chapter One. *The Python's Parade*

1. For Sherman's description of the Washington parade, see Sherman, *Memoirs*, II, 377–78; and in general, Royster, *Destructive War*, 405–17. The observations of individual soldiers, the report in the *New York Times*, and the general animosity between the Army of the Potomac and Sherman's Westerners are found in Davis, *Sherman's March*, 293–94; Lewis, *Sherman*, 576–79; Hirshson, *White Tecumseh*, 318–19. Tom Corwin, a former government official in Ohio and at Washington, summed up best the visual impression of Sherman's Westerners, "They march like the lords of the world" (Davis, *Sherman's March*, 295).

2. For the horrendous casualties of the Army of the Potomac between summer 1863 and spring 1865, see Foote, *Civil War*, III, 146–318. Disease rates were usually higher among

Western troops who fought in less healthy climates and were less well equipped, although even in this instance Sherman's soldiers were the exception and remained the most disease-free troops in any theater of the Civil War. In contrast, deaths *in battle* were 23 percent higher among the Easterners than Western armies in general. See McPherson, *Battle Cry*, 472. The number of battle fatalities in the Army of the Potomac was larger than in all the other Union armies combined: McPherson, *Battle Cry*, 472–73. On contemporaries' views of Sherman's sparing of lives, see McDonough and Jones, *War So Terrible*, 311.

3. The remarks of the German ambassador are quoted in various works, among them Davis, *Sherman's March*, 294.

4. On contemporary comparisons of leadership and experience between Grant's Army of the Potomac and Sherman's soldiers, see Liddell Hart, *Sherman*, 382–86; Glatthaar, *March*, 178–82. On the general stereotypes between Westerners and Easterners, see Lewis, *Sherman*, 398:

> In practically every section where there was bold Federal action in the summer of 1864, there was a Westerner in command: Grant in Virginia; Sheridan in the Shenandoah Valley; Sherman in Georgia. . . . The West was in the saddle. . . . Under the gentle Lincoln had arisen informal, rugged, aggressive Westerners to supplant the more technical and suave Easterners who had ruled at the beginning of the war.

There was a growing awareness among troops in the field that, while Northern abolitionists had prompted the war, it would take those in the West and Midwest to defeat the insurrectionists. For the Westerners' dislike of Easterners in the army, see Kennett, *Marching*, 48. There is some statistical support for the notion that Westerners' desertion rates were lower and their reliability in conflict higher—despite a general absence of comparable discipline and grooming.

5. Northern restlessness with the progress of the war was growing even as late as summer 1864, and there were renewed and organized moves to seek a negotiated peace, see McPherson, *Battle Cry*, 742–50, 760–62; Klement, *Copperheads*, 233–35; Klement, *Limits of Dissent*, 265–70. *New York World*: McPherson, *Battle Cry*, 750.

6. For the idea that only a concept of total war would end the hostilities, see Marszalek, *Sherman*, 250–55. The 300,000 is found in a letter to his wife: Hirshson, *White Tecumseh*, 240. For relative manpower of the two sides, see Griffith, *Battle Tactics*, 95.

7. There were tactical advantages for the South as its lines constricted and Northern logistical problems mounted in the quest for the absolute conquest of the Confederacy; see Hagerman, *Civil War*, 276, 282. A negotiated peace based on battlefield superiority was different from the demand for unconditional surrender that was the result of crushing the resources, both material and psychological, of an entire region.

8. For the pacifism in the North, see Catton, *Grant Takes Command*, 338–41. Grant wrote to a personal friend on August 16, 1864: "The rebellion is now fed by the bickering and differences of the North. The hope of a counter-revolution over the draft, or the Presidential election, keeps them together. Then, too, they hope for the election of a 'peace candidate' who would let them go. 'A peace at any price' is fearful to contemplate." (Quoted in Catton, *Grant Takes Command*, 355.)

Chapter Two. The Idea

9. Bauer, ed., *Soldiering*, 174; "a thousand years": Overmyer, *Stupendous Effort*, 155. On the capture of Atlanta, see McDonough and Jones, *War So Terrible*, 269–332.

10. For Grant's letter of November 2, 1864, to Sherman, see Sherman, *Memoirs*, II, 167.

11. Sherman, *Memoirs,* II, 179.

12. Grant's concern and the arguments in favor of following Hood and not cutting loose into Georgia: Sherman, *Memoirs,* II, 164–66; Marszalek, *Sherman,* 294–96. Stanton wired Grant on October 13 that Lincoln was now convinced by his generals that Sherman's plan was too risky: "The objections stated in your telegram of last night impressed him with much force, and a misstep by General Sherman might be fatal to his army." See Lewis, *Sherman,* 429–30.

13. Dismissal of Hood: Lewis, *Sherman,* 430. The differences in logistical and strategic thinking between Hood and Sherman are discussed in Hagerman, *Civil War,* 291–92. Sherman's statements about offensive versus defensive action: Glatthaar, *March,* 4–5; cf. Kennett, *Marching,* 226. The experience at Kennesaw Mountain left Sherman even more convinced of the futility of attacking head-on a fortified and entrenched enemy; see Liddell Hart, *Sherman,* 266–69. Hitchcock quote: *Marching,* 147.

14. Sherman's famous telegraph to Grant: Sherman, *Memoirs,* II, 152. On the differences between camp life and marching cross-country, Sherman remarked, "My marches have demonstrated the great truth that armies even of vast magnitude are not tied to bases. More animals are lost to you whilst standing idle, hitched to their wagons, than during the long and seemingly hard marches into the interior" (Lewis, *Sherman,* 465).

15. On Sherman's strategic and political brilliance, which so resembled that of the modern age, see the encomium of Liddell Hart, *Sherman,* 428–31. Sherman's letter to Halleck: Hirshson, *White Tecumseh,* 247. Army's ideological fervor: Glatthaar, *March,* 134. Pepper's description: Pepper, *Recollections,* 261. Sherman's entire army soon shared their general's dictum that the citizens of the South should know the cruel nature of the war they had supported. On November 20, after a conversation with Sherman concerning his brand of total war, the mild-mannered Henry Hitchcock wrote:

> Either we must acknowledge the "C.S.A." or we must conquer them: to conquer, we must make war, and it must *be* war, it must bring destruction and desolation, it must make the innocent suffer as well as the guilty, it must involve plundering, burning, killing. Else it is worse than a sham.—Shall we then quit and acknowledge the C.S.A.? No, for that is simply to ensure the same thing hereafter, for separation means *ceaseless war.* God help us. (Hitchcock, *Marching,* 77)

16. "Synonymous terms" and related statements: Marszalek, *Sherman,* 296.

17. The horns of a dilemma: Sherman, *Memoirs,* II, 115. In this same letter to Grant of September 20, 1864, Sherman expounded his plans for a march to come sometime in the next two months: "I would not hesitate to cross the State of Georgia with sixty thousand men, hauling some stores, and depending on the country for the balance. Where a million of people find subsistence, my army won't starve."

Connolly: "Diary," 419. Southerners experience Sherman's strategy: Royster, *Destructive War,* 329; cf. Liddell Hart, *Sherman,* 337. In starting out in the Carolinas, Sherman employed the same mastery of bypassing the two obvious objectives of Augusta and Charleston to impose his army in between, and thereby capture Columbia relatively unguarded. See Hughes, *Bentonville,* 3.

18. Cox, *Sherman's March,* 21; for Beauregard's letter of October 17, 1864, see Sherman, *Memoirs,* II, 160.

19. Bill Sherman's raiders: Liddell Hart, *Sherman,* 369. Sherman's professed conservative views on the equality of blacks and his hostility to the abolitionists are often at odds with his behavior in the field, where he bore a real animus to the plantation class and showed freed slaves great kindness. See Hitchcock, *Marching,* 81–85; Hirschson, *White*

Tecumseh, 267–68, 272–73. In that regard, he bears a striking resemblance to Patton, who of all American generals was thought to be the most reactionary and yet felt the most comfortable in the company of black soldiers. For singing and music on the march, see Bauer, ed., *Soldiering*, 174; Kennett, *Marching*, 245.

20. Nowhere can Sherman's unique grasp of the fundamental issues of the war be better illustrated than in this letter to the mayor of Atlanta on September 12, 1864. Sherman additionally pointed out:

> You might as well appeal against the thunder-storms as against these terrible hardships of war. They are inevitable, and the only way the people of Atlanta can hope once more to live in peace and quiet at home, is to stop the war, which can only be done by admitting that it began in error and is perpetuated in pride. We don't want your negroes, or your horses, or your houses, or your lands, or any thing you have, but we do want and will have a just obedience to the laws of the United States. That we will have, and, if it involves the destruction of your improvements, we cannot help it. (Sherman, *Memoirs*, II, 126–27)

21. The Illinois major James Connolly remarked of the march as the troops neared their goal at Savannah, "The whole campaign is an experiment—nothing more; but all the great campaigns of the world were nothing more during their progress, and if this campaign succeeds it will be a successful military experiment, that's all; but it will certainly be entitled to a distinguished position in the military history of the world." Connolly, "Diary," 418. Cf. Sherman, *Memoirs*, II, 170.

22. Logistical monster: Hagerman, *Civil War*, 286–88; cf. 292–93. On supplies and logistics for Sherman's army, see Hirshson, *White Tecumseh*, 18; Liddell Hart, *Sherman*, 330.

23. Cox, *Sherman's March*, 5.

24. For various accounts of contemporary incredulity and dismissal of his idea to head east through Georgia, see Davis, *Sherman's March*, 34–35; Lewis, *Sherman*, 422–37. A review of the argument concerning who originally thought of the March to the Sea is in Hirshson, *White Tecumseh*, 248–49. All major Union officials and generals—Lincoln, Grant, and Thomas—were on record as originally opposing the idea in varying degrees.

25. Sherman, *Memoirs*, II, 179.

26. Merrill, *Sherman*, 266; cf. Cox, *Sherman's March*, 23. So long as Sherman is leading us: Clark, ed., *Downing's Civil War Diary*, 229.

Chapter Three. The Soul of an Army

27. On Sherman's army during the occupation of Atlanta, before the culling process, see McDonough and Jones, *War So Terrible*, 269–332; Marszalek, *Sherman*, 264–65. On Sherman's own characterizations of the nature of his march: Royster, *Destructive War*, 340–41. For the quote about the idealism of the march, and others like it, see Glatthaar, *March*, 44–48.

28. Cortes' image and the problems of the march: Nichols, *Great March*, 37. Poe's letter to his wife is quoted in Kennett, *Marching*, 243. Grant and Lincoln's image of Sherman's army like a mole who burrows stealthily underground with no indication of where it might reappear on the surface: Foote, *Civil War*, 650. Hitchcock's letter to his wife: Hitchcock, *Marching*, 59.

29. Thucydides 7.87.5–6. For the last days of Crassus, see Plutarch, *Crassus* 25–31. Nearly 30,000 legionaries and noncombatants were slaughtered with Varus in the Teutoburg Wald. For a discussion of the battle and its macabre aftermath, see Delbrück, *War*, II,

69–96. On the fate of those Union stragglers who were captured in Georgia and the Carolinas, see Glatthaar, *March*, 152–54. Royster describes how citizens in South Carolina had watched bloodhounds tear apart a Union prisoner and how residents of Columbia asked prisoner guards to release their captives so that they might hang them on the spot; *Destructive War*, 7.

30. Sherman's worry and the size of his army: Sherman, *Memoirs*, II, 172–73; Hagerman, *Civil War*, 340, n. 5. On Sherman's wagons and livestock, see Hagerman, *Civil War*, 284; Davis, *Sherman's March*, 26. Osterhaus's 15th Corps had marched 684 miles between October 14 and December 21, 1864; perhaps as much as 550 miles of that total was spent meandering from Atlanta to Savannah; cf. Hagerman, *Civil War*, 342.

31. The appearance of the army as it set out from Atlanta: Davis, *Sherman's March*, 11; Lewis, *Sherman*, 436. Easterner versus Westerner: Kennett, *Marching*, 48; Sherman's anger at the East: Hirshson, *White Tecumseh*, 318.

32. On the veteran status of Sherman's army and its record prior to fall 1864, and contemporaries' wonder at the army, see Glatthaar, *March*, 15–17, 18–21; Hedley, *Marching Through Georgia*, 259.

33. For the division of the army, cf. Bauer, ed., *Soldiering*, 174–76; Cox, *Sherman's March*, 23–25; Sherman, *Memoirs*, II, 171–72. On the prior experience of the various corps, see Glatthaar, *March*, 15–21.

34. On Sherman's columns, see Marszalek, *Sherman*, 297–98. "Millions": Davis, *Sherman's March*, 45; approach of the 14th Corps: Trowbridge, *Picture of the Desolated States*, 502. Southern onlooker: Kennett, *Marching*, 246. For the various songs Sherman's marches took up, see Hirshson, *White Tecumseh*, 257.

35. For Sherman's concern with provisions and logistics, see Sherman, *Memoirs*, II, 182–85. The Southern appeals are quoted at 189. "Each soldier carried on his person forty rounds of ammunition, and in the wagons were enough cartridges to make up about two hundred rounds per man, and in like manner two hundred rounds of assorted ammunition were carried for each gun" (*Memoirs*, 176).

36. Sherman's limitations as a cavalry tactician: Evans, *Sherman's Horsemen*, 476–77. He complained about his horsemen that it "is hard to get them within 10 miles of the front": Kennett, *Marching*, 32–33; cf. 54, 130–31. On the nature of Sherman's army before and during the march, see Davis, *Sherman's March*, 26–27; Kennett, *Marching*, 38–39. Daniel Oakey's quote: Oakey, "Marching," 921.

37. Stanton and Sherman in Savannah: Fellman, *Citizen Sherman*, 164. Sherman's protestation: Sherman, *Memoirs*, II, 248.

38. Bauer, ed., *Soldiering*, 196. Figures on reenlistment and soldiers' anger at copperheads: Glatthaar, *March*, 45, 40–41. On the direct association among soldiers in 1864 between voting for Lincoln and the cause of abolition, see McPherson, *Cause and Comrades*, 129–30.

39. General attitudes of Sherman's men toward slaves and "Buying and selling their betters": Glatthaar, *March*, 53, 78; Cox, *Sherman's March*, 53. On the changed views of some Northerners once they arrived in the South: McPherson, *Cause and Country*, 118–20. Such attitudes were not so much the product of abstract abolitionist sentiment as much as the soldiers' concrete perceptions of general poverty and reprehensible backwardness of a slave society.

40. That the army was so young, confident, and successful lent a volatility that spread through the ranks. So Henry Hitchcock, an aid to Sherman, writes of his disgust, common to the entire army, with a Southern plantation owner:

The Negroes here say they have been habitually punished by flogging not only with strap, but with hand-saws and paddles with holes—and salt put in the wounds. They also told of a famous "track-hound" (blood-hound) at the next house, nearby, used to hunt runaways. As we went by that house, Nichols had gone there (by General's permission) and had the hound shot by a soldier: he was a large red dog: we heard the shot and the dog's dying howls. (Hitchcock, *Marching*, 78)

41. Burning due to racist attitudes or anti-Union sentiment: Kennett, *Marching*, 278. Reenlistment rates and familiarity between enlisted men and officers: Glatthaar, *March*, 21, 26, 40–41. Sherman's army voted 86 percent for Lincoln in the election of 1864; Glatthaar, *March*, 47.

42. Quote from McPherson, *Cause and Comrades*, 102. On support for abolition among the rank and file, see 116–30. Confederate army hierarchy: Glatthaar, *March*, 67. Hitchcock on Hampton: Hitchcock, *Marching*, 310. Blacks leave the plantation: Trowbridge, *Picture of the Desolated States*, 481. "Into tragedy": Davis, *Sherman's March*, 133; respect for Negroes: Glatthaar, *March*, 65; Sherman and the freedman: *Memoirs*, II, 186.

43. Allotment of land for blacks: Kolchin, *American Slavery*, 213. Hitchcock, *Marching*, 72. The text of Garrison Frazier's comments are found in Sherman's *Memoirs*, II, 244–47.

44. Hitchcock, *Marching*, 71, 202. For Sherman's later support of racial equality, see Royster, *Destructive War*, 352. On a different view of Sherman's treatment of blacks, see the discussion and quotations in Fellman, *Citizen Sherman*, 408–10. For the central position of slavery in the letters of Civil War soldiers on both sides, see McPherson, *Cause and Comrades*, 20–22, 108–10. Of course, most of the protestations about abolition in letters are from slave-owning soldiers. But as McPherson rightly points out:

> Ironically, the proportion of Union soldiers who wrote about the slavery question was great. . . . There is a ready explanation for this apparent paradox. Emancipation was a salient issue for Union soldiers because it was controversial. Slavery was less salient for most Confederate soldiers because it was not controversial. They took slavery for granted as one of the Southern "rights" and institutions for which they fought, and did not feel compelled to discuss it. Although only 20 percent of the soldiers avowed explicit proslavery purposes in their letters and diaries, none at all dissented from that view. (*Cause and Comrades*, 110)

45. On "Marching Through Georgia," see Kennett, *Marching*, 320. On incidents that suggest the march could border on anarchy, see Kennett, *Marching*, 262–87; Davis, *Sherman's March*, 64–65. On the army at Madison: Bauer, ed., *Soldiering*, 186–87. See also Miles, *To the Sea*, 59–62.

46. Upson, *With Sherman*, 141; Sherman, *Memoirs*, II, 387.

Chapter Four. Where Is the Enemy?

47. For the slaughter at Griswoldville, see Upson, *With Sherman*, 138–39; Kennett, *Marching*, 254–55; Davis, *Sherman's March*, 54–56; Sherman, *Memoirs*, II, 187–88. Description of the Griswoldville dead: Glatthaar, *March*, 161. Some put the size of the Southern attacking army at 5,000 to 6,000: Harwell and Racine, *Fiery Trail*, 59.

48. Nature and size of Southern resistance in Georgia: Lewis, *Sherman*, 441. It is not really known how many able-bodied troops were in the various corps of Hardee, Wheeler, and Bragg; see the different figures in Liddell Hart, *Sherman*, 336. Hitchcock quotes Sherman's

dismissal of potential attacks led by Longstreet: "General in fine spirits, and well he may be hereafter. He desires nothing better than for Longstreet (who it is rumored among these people is already at Augusta with large force) to come and fight him" (*Marching*, 104).

49. Noncombatants abandoned: Marszalek, *Sherman*, 305; Hitchcock, *Marching*, 77. For newspaper accounts and public proclamations promising ruin to Sherman's army, see Lewis, *Sherman*, 449–50; Sherman, *Memoirs*, II, 189–90. On the psychology of self-preservation, see Walters, *Merchant of Terror*, 160, who laments:

> There could be no unity of action. Under the pressure of imminent danger, the people of Georgia acted as individuals, each concerned with his own problem, each reluctant to destroy his own property. Perhaps the Federal army would take another road—perhaps the soldiers would take only food and livestock, and supplies of food could be concealed until the army passed. . . . Thus, held in a paralysis of fear, nurturing a spark of hope that he might be fortunate enough to escape, the Georgian, with few exceptions, did nothing. To their sorrow comparatively few of them in Sherman's path escaped serious losses of one kind or another, and countless others lost everything they had. Again terror played its role in General Sherman's remorseless war against noncombatants.

Walters fails to emphasize those same plantations days earlier had supplied Wheeler's cavalry, that their possession of slaves had brought Northern soldiers south, that their loss of property was a preferable circumstance to the thousands who were being butchered in Virginia with Lee and Grant, and that a government that declares its independence from, cultural superiority over, and hatred toward its adversary is responsible to its people to make sure that those claims are both true and sustainable.

50. Connolly, "Diary," 411; Texas soldier: Kennett, *Marching*, 313. On the various numbers of Confederates in Savannah, see Harwell and Racine, *Fiery Trail*, 47: Captain Osborne wrote of Sherman's approach, "When we reached here [Savannah] we had driven 15,000 or 20,000 of the enemy into the city."

51. Observations of Union soldiers on the reluctance of the enemy to fight: Glatthaar, *March*, 162, 163, 70; Bauer, ed., *Soldiering*, 192. On differences in appearance between Grant and Lee, Sherman and Johnston, see Catton, *Grant*, 464. Patton later would seek to adopt a dashing image. But his efforts—polished, bronze-starred GI infantry helmet, dual revolvers on his hips, occasional hand grenades—loudly and ostentatiously emphasized the killing prowess of the average GI, not the genteel traditions of a professional military class. And like Sherman, Patton's vocabulary was a dirty one of killing and slaughter, with no hint of romance or euphemism.

52. Sherman's Field Order: *Memoirs*, II, 175. Chaplain's remarks: Glatthaar, *March*, 78. Class rivalry: Lewis, *Sherman*, 445; Hitchcock, *Marching*, 125.

53. Insults of Southern women: Glatthaar, *March*, 72; Davis, *Sherman's March*, 30.

54. For Sherman's letter about the women of the South, see Coburn, *Terrible Innocence*, 56. Description of Union plundering: Myers, *Children of Pride*, 509. Union rebuke of Southern women: Lewis, *Sherman*, 453.

55. Linderman, *Embattled Courage*, 87. Eliza Andrews: Royster, *Destructive War*, 346. Complaints against Wheeler: Lewis, *Sherman*, 454; Hitchcock, *Marching*, 104; Liddell Hart, *Sherman*, 334.

56. Georgians' criticism of South Carolina: Lewis, *Sherman*, 446; Kennett, *Marching*, 313. Georgia's shame: Kennett, *Marching*, 312.

57. Hitchcock's quote: *Marching*, 125. Carpenter: Overmyer, *Stupendous Effort*, 159. "Pierce the shell" is quoted by Hitchcock in his diary (*Marching*, 89) and variously rendered by other first- and secondhand accounts.

58. For the various epithets, metaphors, and imagery associated with Sherman's march, see Lewis, *Sherman*, 435, 458. For myriad types of destruction named after Sherman, see Royster, *Destructive* War, 346.

59. On rifled weapons: Hagerman, *Civil War*, 15–18; and in general, Griffith, *Battle Tactics*, 84–85. 24,000 rounds: Royster, *Destructive War*, 297; Upson, *With Sherman*, 160. It is often forgotten that the Confederate army of Johnston that surrendered to Sherman in North Carolina was probably larger than Lee's force; for the numbers and casualties at Bentonville, see Hughes, *Bentonville*, 24–26, 218–19.

60. Hitchcock, *Marching*, 108.

61. Foraging techniques: Cox, *Sherman's March*, 39; Hagerman, *Civil War*, 284–85; Sherman, *Memoirs*, II, 183–85. Rice Bull on the destruction of railroads: Bauer, ed., *Soldiering*, 184.

62. *Macon Telegraph*: Lewis, *Sherman*, 435, 441, 442 (Sherman's quote). Canning plantation: Davis, *Sherman's March*, 86. Plunder from foraging: Kennett, *March*, 284–85. Sherman's quote about the South: Marszalek, *Sherman*, 316.

Chapter Five. An Apartheid Society

63. For Rice Bull's comments, see Bauer, ed., *Soldiering*, 187; Sherman, *Memoirs*, II, 188. An onlooker recorded that the Army of the West as it entered Milledgeville was as "thick as pigeons": Trowbridge, *Picture of the Desolated States*, 486.

64. Quartermaster's observation: Overmyer, *Stupendous Effort*, 154–55. For a discussion of Sherman's famous letter to Halleck and his uncanny grasp of Southern class structure, see Kennett, *Marching*, 15–16; Lewis, *Sherman*, 306–7.

65. For the relationship between slaveholding and support for succession among state representatives, see McPherson, *Battle Cry*, 283; "wiped out": Thorndike, *Sherman Letters*, 232. Statistics on slaveholding: Long, *Civil War*, 702–3.

66. For the South's claim that their agricultural output was critical to Northern prosperity, see McPherson, *Battle Cry*, 196–97; general Southern perceptions of the vast social and cultural divide between North and South and their claims to be the true descendants of the American Revolution: Royster, *Destructive War*, 173–78, 182–85.

67. Sherman's answer to Wheeler is quoted in Hirshson, *White Tecumseh*, 279. For Sherman's letter to D. F. Boyd contrasting a nation of mechanics versus a society of farmers, see Lewis, *Sherman*, 138.

68. "An importation": Hedley, *Marching Through Georgia*, 320. Union soldiers and their view of the planters: Glatthaar, *March*, 40. For a discussion of Fitzhugh's *Sociology of the South* and *Cannibals All*, see McPherson, *Battle Cry*, 196–97. A review of ancient ideas of slavery, and their arguments in connection with the South, is discussed by Davis, *Problem of Slavery*, 62–90; Finley, *Ancient Slavery*, 11–66; and cf. 40–46 for a critique of Marx's idea about the slavish conditions of free wage labor in a capitalist society. See too de Ste. Croix, *Class Struggle*, 62–80. Quote of slave in the North: Upson, *With Sherman*, 1.

69. Christianity and its silence in condemning slavery: de Ste. Croix, "Early Christian Attitudes," 3–15; Davis, *Problem of Slavery*, 197–222; Kolchin, *American Slavery*, 15, 86–87; cf. 54–55.

70. For classical support for natural slavery and the use of conquered peoples, see, for example, Plato, *Laws* 6.709a–710a; Aristotle, *Politics* 1.1252a24–b12; Montesquieu, *Spirit of Laws*, passim in bk. 10, bk. 15; Hegel, *Philosophy of Right*, pt. 1, par. 57; pt. 3, par. 351. For Hood's letter, see Sherman, *Memoirs*, II, 123.

71. Olmsted, *Journey*, 446; Hitchcock, *Marching*, 127.

72. Although sometimes a figure from 10,000 to 25,000 freed slaves is mentioned, there are no concise totals of slaves who followed Sherman to Savannah—an impossible number to obtain anyway given the fact that many came and went with his army, others used his presence to flee on their own northward, and still more chose to remain in the South on abandoned plantations in a state of quasi-freedom. For the actual numbers, see Kennett, *Marching*, 238–39. On runaways, see Glatthaar, *March*, 52–65; Kennett, *Marching*, 292–94.

73. For Joe Brown's admission, see Durden, *Gray and Black*, 251.

74. Hitchcock, *Marching*, 72; amalgamationists: Connolly, "Diary," 406.

75. Olmsted, *Journey*, 439; Upson, *With Sherman*, 135.

76. Southern claims of moral superiority, adherence to the spirit of the American revolution, and faith in their patriotism and manhood to overcome Northern material advantages: Royster, *Destructive War*, 144–92.

77. Southern investment: McPherson, *Battle Cry*, 96–101; classical ideals of self-sufficiency: Hanson, *Other Greeks*, 78–79. For an analysis of how slave labor was extremely valuable to the small plantation elite and generally devastating to the economy of the South as a whole, see Ransom, *Conflict and Compromise*, 41–48, 50–81; Phillips, *Slave Economy*, 106–9, 132–35.

78. Southern allusions to the Spartan Helots: Durden, *Gray and Black*, 61. Sherman on "white trash": Fellman, *Citizen Sherman*, 19. Southern "delusion": Royster, *Destructive War*, 127. Complaints of the plantation women: Myers, *Children of Pride*, 525.

79. Plantation woman: Myers, *Children of Pride*, 518. Southern women and slave: Myers, *Children of Pride*, 526. On January 31, 1864, Sherman wrote:

> It is all idle nonsense of these Southern planters to say that they made the South, that they own it, and can do as they please to break up our Government and shut up the natural avenues of trade, intercourse, and commerce. We know, and they know, if they are intelligent beings, that as compared with the whole world they are but as five millions to one thousand millions, that they did not create the land, that the only title to use and usufruct is the deed of the United States, and that if they appeal to war they hold their all by a very insecure tenure. . . . I know the slave-owners, finding themselves in possession of a species of property in opposition to the growing sentiment of the whole civilized world, conceived their property to be in danger and foolishly appealed to war, and that by skillful political handling they involved with themselves the whole South on this result of error and prejudice. I believe that some of the rich and slaveholding are prejudiced to an extent that nothing but death and ruin will ever extinguish. . . . (Thorndike, *Sherman Letters*, 231)

80. Hitchcock, *Marching*, 85.

81. The letter of an Illinois farmer is quoted in Olmsted, *Cotton Kingdom*, 541. For Sherman's comments on the poor whites of the South, see Lewis, *Sherman*, 306–7.

82. Governor's report to Georgia legislature: Kennett, *Marching*, 32; statistics on land-owning and population in prewar Georgia: Kennett, *Marching*, 18–37. Plantation view of democracy: Hahn, *Roots*, 113. Ratios of slave-owning in the South: Stampp, *Peculiar Institution*, 29–33, 67; appearance of poor whites: Connolly, "Diary," 410.

83. Hitchcock, *Marching*, 81.

84. For Sherman's men's attitudes to poor whites, see Glatthaar, *March*, 68–69.

85. Threats to show no mercy to the citizens of Georgia: Connolly, "Diary," 412.

86. The Army of the West saw the plantationists of Georgia as "kings": Glatthaar, *March*, 67; Southern dismissal of Northerners as mechanics: McPherson, *Battle Cry*, 197.

87. Poor whites wished land and slaves too: Hitchcock, *Marching*, 128. For statistics on the antebellum pattern of landowning and distribution of real wealth, see Hahn, *Roots*, 23–26. For analysis of whether the poor served and suffered inordinately in the Southern cause, see McPherson, *Battle Cry*, 614–15. Governor Brown's thoughts: Hahn, *Roots*, 86.

88. On the age-old idea that in a slave society the free poor man might see himself as privileged, and therefore display less class antagonism against the wealthy, see de Ste. Croix, *Class Struggle*, 63–65, 172–75. I have argued elsewhere (*The Other Greeks*) that the absence of class strife is a more complicated phenomenon in the ancient world, and had much to do with the presence of a broad, middling class of yeomen in the city-states of Greece between 700 and 300 B.C.—a class largely absent in the South.

Sherman wrote also of a third very small group of pro-Union whites—either those who had migrated from the North, were married to Northerners, were on moral grounds ashamed of slavery, or were simply independent and astute enough to see in economic terms how slavery had devastated their homeland. He discounted entirely their influence: "I count them as nothing in this great game of war." By the time he marched through Georgia in fall 1864, it made little difference to him whether the plantations he looted and burned housed Unionists or not. In short, it was too late, and he chalked up their newfound affability to the awe his horrendous army inspired. See Lewis, *Sherman*, 306–7.

89. For letter to Sheridan, see Lewis, *Sherman*, 450; for the 300,000 mentioned in Sherman's letter to his wife, see Hirshson, *White Tecumseh*, 240.

90. Lewis, *Sherman*, 306–7. On the "scum" left after the war, see Royster, *Destructive War*, 165. For the 300,000 and Grant's policy, see Royster, *Destructive War*, 338.

91. Slaves and Sherman's army: Kennett, *Marching*, 288–93; Glatthaar, *March*, 52–66. Cato's advice: *De Agri Cultura* 2.7. Letter from farmer: McPherson, *Cause and Comrades*, 130; and cf. 124–30 for the idea that Union soldiers' letters after 1863 showed a fairly wide consensus that they were fighting to end slavery. For the nature and pattern of slave-owning in the South, see Kolchin, *American Slavery*, 93–127.

92. Cobb and his plantation: Hitchcock, *Marching*, 83–85; Sherman, *Memoirs*, 185–86.

Chapter Six. Uncle Billy

93. General Slocum's remarks: Northrop, *General Sherman*, 562–63. Sherman at Macon: Hitchcock, *Marching*, 131; Sherman's letter to his wife: Hirshson, *White Tecumseh*, 64; and Ellen's letter of January 29, 1861, to Sherman: Hirshson, *White Tecumseh*, 77. John Marszalek (*Sherman*, 460–99) correctly saw Sherman's life essentially as an effort to instill order upon the chaos around him. But I think Marszalek would agree that such urges arose out of Sherman's own contradictory character, whose energy, brilliance, and occasional frenzy ensured a very chaotic life of changing jobs, time spent mostly apart from his family, and constant controversy with friends and war against enemies.

94. Sherman's failure and depression: Fellman, *Citizen Sherman*, 63–65; Marszalek, *Sherman*, 66–68, 198–99; Castel, *Decision*, 42–43. On the liberating effect of past failure in wartime operations: Linderman, *Embattled Courage*, 208–10: "Conversely, failure appears to have placed those who were to become the destroyer generals on or beyond the peripheries of many of the conservator's initial precepts. Neither Grant nor Sherman felt any confidence that the individual could master his fate." Sherman on Grant: Glatthaar, *March*, 5. Patton's quote: Nye, *Patton Mind*, 142.

95. Sherman's West Point years are best discussed in Hirshson, *White Tecumseh*, 13–16; Merrill, *Sherman*, 30–42. For Sherman's views on the crucial value of education,

see Marszalek, *Sherman*, 441–43; Royster, *Destructive War*, 384–85. For the hours of academic preparation that went into planning the March to the Sea, see Royster, *Destructive War*, 329; Kennett, *Marching*, 10; cf. 73 for his late night tutorials.

96. For Sherman's various positions and assignments in the prewar army, see Marszalek, *Sherman*, 38–95; Hirshson, *White Tecumseh*, 18–36; Lewis, *Sherman*, 68–97. "These brilliant scenes . . .": Merrill, *Sherman*, 68; and cf. 76 for his letter of resignation from the army. For his general depression about missing the Mexican War and his letter of lamentation to his wife, see Fellman, *Citizen Sherman*, 22–23.

97. Sherman wrote in his memoirs at length of his California years; in the nostalgia of old age and the later success of the Civil War, his long-ago military service and banking career in California had not appeared as terrible as they had seemed in 1857. Cf. *Memoirs*, 11–142; Hirshson, *White Tecumseh*, 37–51; Marszalek, *Sherman*, 93–113.

98. Sherman's report on the proposed rail route: Hirshson, *White Tecumseh*, 60. Letter to his father-in-law: Marszalek, *Sherman*, 114–15; vagabond: Fellman, *Citizen Sherman*, 66.

99. Boyd's letter: Hirshson, *White Tecumseh*, 82. For Sherman's experience as superintendent of the Louisiana Seminary of Learning, see Marszalek, *Sherman*, 123–39; Lewis, *Sherman*, 110–47.

100. Sherman's letter declining military service: Sherman, *Memoirs*, 171. On Sherman's mental state in Kentucky, see Fellman, *Citizen Sherman*, 105–8. And for the newspaper attacks, Hirshson, *White Tecumseh*, 100–101; Lewis, *Sherman*, 195–202. For Sherman at Shiloh, see Lewis, *Sherman*, 120–40. Written comments before departing Atlanta: Hirshson, *White Tecumseh*, 258.

101. For some of Sherman's mistakes, see Hirshson, *White Tecumseh*, 168, 170, 173, 220–21. Quote on Sherman's emphases on marches: Liddell Hart, *Sherman*, 420. For Sherman's practicality: Merrill, *Sherman*, 138. Sherman the intellectual later summed up best his views of what constituted real excellence, "Our country abounds in Scholars. We want men of action" (Marszalek, *Sherman*, 442).

102. Knew more than the Rebels: Davis, *Sherman's March*, 18. Sherman's use of earlier explorations of the South: Hirshson, *White Tecumseh*, 270. We should keep in mind that Epaminondas had traveled to Sparta before his great invasion, and Patton had both fought and traveled in France years before his appearance in 1944.

103. Officer's remark about Sherman's mastery of detail: Kennett, *Marching*, 55. Letter to Hood: *Memoirs*, II, 120–21. Sherman's reading: Hirshson, *White Tecumseh*, 27; his lifelong interest in education and scholarship: Marszalek, *Sherman*, 483–84. Patton's quotes: Nye, *Patton Mind*, 161, 37.

104. Impression of Sherman: Barrett, *Sherman's March*, 34–35; Bauer, ed., *Soldiering*, 163–64. On the similar prewar failures of Grant and Sherman, see Hirshson, *White Tecumseh*, 54. For McClellan's impressive prewar career, see Hagerman, *Civil War*, 31–50. The importance of failure for the destroyer generals, Grant and Sherman, is discussed by Linderman, *Embattled Courage*, 210–12. On various occasions of contemplated suicide, see Fellman, *Citizen Sherman*, 91–109; and the power that the perception of madness gave Sherman: 147–49; Marszalek, *Sherman*, 163, 489; Sherman, *Memoirs*, II, 408.

105. The usual ledger for Sherman: the bad includes burner of cities, terrorist, racist, slaughterer of dogs and horses (see, for example, Coburn, *Terrible Innocence*, 12–14), versus the good Sherman who preferred property destruction to killing and whose dynamism help stop the killing. For a view sympathetic to the South and extremely hostile to Sherman, see Walters, *Merchant of Terror*, 182–83, 205. Sherman, Walters assures us, is guilty of terrorizing innocent Southerners "without any claim on military necessity," not only because he destroyed their property, but because he freed their slaves as well! "The loss of slave labor posed

a problem to women and children left alone on the farms and plantations. Thousands of slaves followed the Federal columns in response to the exhortation of the soldiers, only to be abandoned at Savannah." A Northern general, fighting to end slavery, is to be blamed for destroying property in lieu of lives, as he liberated the unfree and so took away the valuable servants of the Confederacy—"not only a labor force," as Walters reminds us, "but a property investment of several billion dollars." Walters also assures us that Sherman despoiled "a people of their material resources" and injured irreparably "their finer sensibilities." See also Griffith, *Battle Tactics:* "Sherman's doctrine of warfare against civilians I regard as one of the most vicious military theories of modern times" (9).

In general, however, standard outrage against Sherman is expressed by progressives rather than reactionaries. Critics as diverse as Mary McCarthy to Michael Herr have attempted to trace the American pathologies of the postwar period back to the "war crimes" of General Sherman. It may be no accident that the two best of Sherman's biographers, B. H. Liddell Hart and Lloyd Lewis, wrote outside the humanities department, with the clear intention of suggesting that Sherman's intellect and education were impressive, but *inseparable* from and *subordinate* to his military prowess—in their eyes he was a military "prophet" and a "realist" in conflict. His duty was to wage a new, more honest type of war, brutal in its manifestation, but ultimately humane in its emphasis on destroying property, not people, and in bringing terror—but not death—to civilians, to shorten, not lengthen, war. Killing a man ended the disagreement outright, destroying his property at least gave him some chance at resurrection—and comprehension of the wages of his aggression. In the eyes of Lewis and Liddell Hart, Sherman was a great man, who is judged on what he did and not on what he wrote: he saved lives and shortened the war; and he used military science to teach his nation a larger lesson about what war is ultimately for.

106. Michael Fellman (*Citizen Sherman*), for example, believes that Sherman was racist toward blacks (242–43, 255–56, 407), Mexicans (23–25, 79, 154, 410), Indians (260–61, 263–64), as well as being anti-Semitic (63, 153–54) and a womanizer (352–70, 389). But Sherman's rhetoric and bombast aside, what someone says and what someone does are not necessarily synonymous acts; the former provides inference, the latter offers proof; and the nomenclature of racism in 1995 is not identical to that of 1864. Fellman confuses Sherman's empirical observations that blacks, Indians, and Mexicans were in a general state of poverty, ignorance, and illiteracy by white American standards with notions of racial inferiority, rather than cultural deprivation. Sherman is guilty of thinking that Western society was superior to African or indigenous American culture, but he felt that such "civilization"—literacy, technology, sanitation, agriculture, science, education—not only could, but should, be made available to "improve" the lives of the Other, thus his advocacy of voting rights for the Negro and the adoption of yeoman agriculture for the Indian. In practice, Sherman was a cultural chauvinist more than a racist. Fellman has achieved the odd feat of devoting only 147 out of 418 pages to the Civil War, in a biography devoted to a Civil War hero. On Fellman's *Citizen Sherman*, see Hirshson, *White Tecumseh*, x–xi.

James Reston, Jr., offers a bizarre comparison of Sherman to General Westmoreland and thereby condemnation of both, arguing that Sherman was too savage to the plantation owners of the South but not forceful enough in liberating slaves—as if the two are not mutually exclusive, as if Sherman might have peacefully marched his army through the heartland of secession as he politely asked slave owners to allow their blacks thirty days' rations from their plantation's sacrosanct stores and a free pass northward to instant equality of opportunity. All this might occur while Grant and Lee continued to wage a more humane war of the type fought at Cold Harbor. It is no accident that Reston's liberal critique of Sherman must read eerily akin to John Bannett Walters's Southern polemic that Sherman was unnecessarily savage to the planters of Georgia. In general, see Reston, *Sherman's March*, 88–93.

107. See the summation of Sherman's character and achievement by Liddell Hart, *Sherman*, 430.

108. For the notion that Sherman's capture of Atlanta won Lincoln the election and changed the war, see McDonough and Jones, *War So Terrible*, 319–20; Castel, *Decision*, 542–43. For Sherman's prescience that his work would give Lincoln the election, see Marszalek, *Sherman*, 295. His letter to Ellen is quoted in Merrill, *Sherman*, 280. Sherman's love for his men and their remarks on his informality: Glatthaar, *March*, 16, 24–25, 56; Kennett, *Marching*, 46. "Uncle Billy": Merrill, *Sherman*, 288; Barrett, *Sherman's March*, 276; Royster, *Destructive War*, 343. Sherman's ubiquity: Kennett, *Marching*, 73. Sherman cussed out by ordinary soldiers: Hirshson, *White Tecumseh*, 255.

109. Letter to Ellen: Hirshson, *White Tecumseh*, 268; Merrill, *Sherman*, 273.

Chapter Seven. The End and the Beginning

110. Sherman in Savannah and exchange with Lincoln: Lewis, *Sherman*, 470. For the popular and press reaction to Sherman's arrival, see Hirshson, *White Tecumseh*, 265–66; Marszalek, *Sherman*, 311.

111. Sherman and Southern elites: Hitchcock, *Marching*, 208; Union troops' reaction on entering Savannah: Connolly, "Diary," 438. Messages of approval: Davis, *Sherman's March*, 121.

112. Northern public response: Lewis, *Sherman*, 465; Volcano: Miles, *To the Sea*, 244. Union League remarks about Sherman: Royster, *Destructive War*, 361. Damage: Kennett, *Marching*, 310–11; Davis, *Sherman's March*, 122; Hahn, *Roots*, 138–39; Liddell Hart, *Sherman*, 346; Walters, *Merchant of Terror*, 181–82. Like giants: Davis, *Sherman's March*, 119. On the material condition of Sherman's army as it reached the sea: cf. Hagerman, *Civil War*, 286. The poor condition of roads: Kennett, *Marching*, 253.

113. Loot in Savannah: Miles, *To the Sea*, 242–43. "The Confederate property captured," Sherman wrote, "consisted of horses and mules by the thousand, and of quantities of subsistence stores that aggregate very large, but may be measured with sufficient accuracy by assuming that sixty-five thousand men obtained abundant food for about forty days, and thirty-five thousand animals were fed for a like period, so as to reach Savannah in splendid flesh and condition." Cf. *Memoirs*, II, 221. For ammunition expended: Kennett, *Marching*, 309.

114. On the larger political and strategic consequences of Sherman's march, and the complex relationship between Grant's army in Virginia and Sherman's in Georgia, see McDonough and Jones, *War So Terrible*, 314–26; slave's astute observation: Marszalek, *Sherman*, 312. Sherman's plans after the march: *Memoirs*, II, 220.

115. There is a general consensus (*pace* Walters) that there was essentially almost no raping in Georgia. Southerners later charged Sherman with a variety of offenses, but neither the murder of innocent civilians nor the raping of Southern women were among them; see, for example, Kennett, *Marching*, 306–7; Glatthaar, *March*, 72–74; cf. Reston, *Sherman's March*, 71–74. For an isolated case of rape in South Carolina, see Hirshson, *White Tecumseh*, 286. Union authorities executed at least one such rapist: Davis, *Sherman's March*, 246; cf. 151–52. Sherman acknowledged two rapes in Georgia: Davis, *Sherman's March*, 43. By the same token, all primary sources, Southern especially, note that Confederate cavalry was often more destructive of civilian property than Sherman's columns, whether they simply stole provisions and livestock or paid for them in worthless Confeder-

ate currency. At least Sherman was gone in thirty days; Southern horsemen requisitioned continuously for months on end; see Glatthaar, *March*, 152–54; Kennett, *Marching*, 278; Davis, *Sherman's March*, 52–53; Liddell Hart, *Sherman*, 334; Hahn, *Roots*, 138.

Southern officer's assessment of General Sherman's army in Georgia: Trowbridge, *Picture of the Desolated States*, 476. On Sherman as terrorist: Walters, *Merchant of Terror*, 182–83. On the "burnt country": Walter, *Merchant of Terror*, 177. Sherman's protection of Confederate officers' families: *Memoirs*, II, 236.

116. On modernist assumptions that peace, not war, is the natural state of relations between states, see the critique of Kagan, *Causes*, 568–73. Criticism of Sherman and his killing of animals: Coburn, *Terrible Innocence*, 12–14. For modern criticism of Sherman, again see James Reston, Jr., *Sherman's March*, especially 118–21, 171, 184–88. Reston has an array of odd comparisons: Sherman's and McNamara's wives seek charity work to atone for their husband's sins (ignoring that many of Ellen Sherman's letters are *more* bellicose than her husband's and surely more anti-Confederate; her support for Catholic charities was long-standing and established well *before* the war); the burning of Columbia is implicitly part of the "war crimes" of Sherman, different from My Lai "only in their dimensions" (ignoring that the burning was either accidental or largely the result of a Confederate action); Sherman's bummers who stole are the forebears of Viet Nam era grunts who murdered (albeit with Reston's sort-of relativist acknowledgment that "looting differs from killing, but neither time nor morals are static"—and without precise statistics that prove American soldiers in Viet Nam killed indiscriminately at a level greater than any other army). For Reston, Sherman's march "leads conceptually to Dresden [and] Hiroshima" (92). The general whose massive army did not kill civilians is now to be the spiritual forefather of carpet bombing. And, of course, the bombing of Dresden must be seen in a void, not in the context of a long process to stop a murderer like Hitler and to end the death camps; Hiroshima must have nothing to do with either the past unprovoked atrocity of the Japanese army, or saving millions of Japanese and American lives from a horrendous defense of the mainland led by fanatical fascists. The alternatives for the moral relativist are never addressed: the Allies lay off German cities, while hundreds of thousands of soldiers are killed and Jews and Eastern Europeans in the millions are gassed; Hiroshima is spared as the Japanese army tortures and murders the innocent in China and Korea, and hordes its penultimate supplies for a great kamikaze battle for the homeland—and Sherman respects private property in Georgia as thousands are slaughtered in Virginia and millions held in bondage in the South.

A truly accurate comparison between the March to the Sea and Viet Nam would disturb Mr. Reston: A huge American army—led by someone a little more Shermanesque than Westmoreland, with the assent of someone a little more Lincolnesque than Lyndon Johnson—would march into North Viet Nam in the fall, say, of 1964, and then engage in a thirty-day swath from Hanoi to the sea at Haiphong, *not* killing or raping citizens, but its bummers wrecking the military infrastructure, political machinery, and economic fabric of Communist North Viet Nam. Such a mobile column would then declare communism dead and the Vietnamese people free to do what they wished—and after a month's march it would abruptly leave from Haiphong and head home. One can argue whether such a Shermanesque strategy against the Communist heartland that fed and supplied armies that invaded South Viet Nam and enslaved, impoverished, and executed their own people would have been cruel, silly, or impossible, but one should at least concede that such an abrupt, very brief, and vast destructive swath from major city to major city—not a decade of anti-insurgency warfare, search-and-destroy missions, and indiscriminate bombing—is the fair historical comparison to the March to the Sea.

117. Sherman's view of himself as "the angel of wrath": Liddell Hart, *Sherman*, 334.

Postbellum Georgia: Hahn, *Roots*, 140–41; Hitchcock, *Marching*, 169; Upson, *With Sherman*, 156–57; Davis, *Sherman's March*, 79. For the strategic brilliance of Sherman's march, see Liddell Hart, *Strategy*, 149–54; Royster, *Destructive War*, 338–41. Osborne's remarks: Harwell and Racine, *Fiery Trail*, 49–51.

118. Sherman's letter to Halleck of December 24: *Memoirs*, II, 227. Assessed valuation of farms in Georgia: Lane, ed., *Marching*, xxiv. The damage to the rail network: Miles, *To the Sea*, 243. Loss of slave productivity due to Union armies in the South: Kolchin, *American Slavery*, 204–5. On Confederate reaction to Sherman's presence behind their lines, see Barrett, *Sherman's March*, 119.

119. Sherman in Savannah: Lane, ed., *Marching*, 196. Lincoln quoted in McPherson, *Battle Cry*, 816. For the sudden change in Northern morale brought about by Sherman's capture of Atlanta and the subsequent march through Georgia, see McDonough and Jones, *War So Terrible*, 320–21.

120. For the lyrics and music of "Marching Through Georgia," see Lewis, *Sherman*, 614. Herman Melville wrote a poem, "The March to the Sea," of ninety-six lines that ended, "Was it Treason's retribution—/Necessity the plea?/They will long remember Sherman/ And his streaming columns free—/They will long remember Sherman/Marching to the Sea"; *Battle-Pieces*, 132. Hitchcock, *Marching*, 281.

121. For the charge that Sherman's march was relatively simple and unchallenging, see Royster, *Destructive War*, 329, who correctly points out the irony in later critics' charges: the very expanse that Sherman ruined was once claimed by the secessionists at the outset of the war to be so large and so fertile that the very notion of a Union army's invasion and destructive occupation of it was absurd. See also Walters, *Merchant of Terror*, 159–60. On his earlier march to Jackson, and its importance in priming his expertise and confidence for the trek to Savannah, see Hirshson, *White Tecumseh*, 158–62; Walters, *Merchant of Terror*, 87–126. Hitchcock's quote: *Marching*, 149. Union war costs: Long, *Civil War*, 726–27. Albert Castel suggests that "had Thomas's personal relationship with Grant permitted him to command in Georgia in 1864, almost surely the Union victory would have been easier, quicker, and more complete." Perhaps, perhaps not. But then Thomas, not Sherman, would have been in Atlanta, and there is virtually no likelihood that 62,000 Union soldiers would have marched under him on a lightning march through Georgia and the Carolinas. Thomas, we should remember, wrote Sherman in October 1864 of the dangers of setting out in Georgia without support: "I hope you will adopt Grant's idea of turning Wilson loose, rather than undertake the plan of a march with the whole force through Georgia to the sea, inasmuch as General Grant cannot cooperate with you as first arranged." See Castel, *Decision*, 563–65. The letter of Thomas to Sherman is reproduced in Sherman's memoirs (II, 156–67).

122. For post–Civil War appraisals of Sherman in Southern newspapers and interviews, see Kennett, *Marching*, 323. General Edmonds's comments are quoted in Liddell Hart, *Strategy*, 154. On contemporary criticism by Northern officials of Sherman's failure to destroy Hardee in Savannah, see Davis, *Sherman's March*, 130–31. Sherman described Hardee's escape in a letter to Halleck of December 24, 1864; *Memoirs*, II, 228. Liddell Hart felt that Hood's escape out of Atlanta and Hardee's from Savannah were probably not preventable and actually did little to aid the Southern cause; Liddell Hart, *Sherman*, 345–47. On Johnston comparison of Grant's tactics with Sherman's, see Royster, *Destructive War*, 327. Letter to his daughter: Marszalek, *Sherman*, 309. For Sherman's restraint and desire to save lives on both sides at Bentonville, see Hughes, *Bentonville*, 231.

123. The actual number of slaves who left the plantations is controversial. Best estimates put it at over 25,000. Of that number, 6,000 remained in Savannah and the remain-

der either headed northward or returned home. See Miles, *To the Sea*, 242. Sherman's quote: *Memoirs*, II, 249. Sherman's letter to his wife: Lane, ed., *Marching*, 195. Sherman and black pioneers: Liddell Hart, *Sherman*, 353. A Sherman "Cutloose": Royster, *Destructive War*, 346; travelers' observations of Georgia in 1919: Kennett, *Marching*, 323. For Melville's "March to the Sea," cf. *Battle-Pieces*, 130.

124. The fright in the South on Sherman's approach: Glatthaar, *March*, 70; Liddell Hart, *Sherman*, 426. On the age of Sherman's men, see Davis, *Sherman's March*, 10–11.

125. On Lee's limitations, see Nolan, *Lee*, esp. 153–74. On Southern hatred of Sherman and worship of Lee: Marszalek, *Sherman*, 316. Sherman later offered an astute analysis of Lee:

> His sphere of action was, however, local. He never rose to the grand problem which involved a continent and future generations. . . . He stood at the front porch battling with the flames whilst the kitchen and house were burning, sure in the end to consume the whole. . . . As an aggressive soldier Lee was not a success, and in war that is the true and proper test. . . . (Keim, *Sherman*, 72)

126. Vegetius's quote is translated from his *Epitoma rei militaris* (1.3). London *Times*: Hirshson, *White Tecumseh*, 311; Liddell Hart, *Sherman*, 429. Sherman's letter to his brother: Thorndike, *Sherman Letters*, 375–76. For Sherman's statue in Washington, D.C., see again Keim, *Sherman*, esp. 30. On the impressive statue by Saint-Gaudens that still stands in Central Park, see Royster, *Destructive War*, 370–71.

PART III. THE THIRD ARMY. PATTON'S RACE INTO GERMANY, AUGUST 1, 1944–MAY 8, 1945

Chapter One. American Ajax

1. For a description of the injury and final two weeks of Patton's life, see Farago, *Last Days*, 238–94. Patton's various quotes while in the hospital are collated in Blumenson, *Patton Papers*, II, 821–35.

2. For a sketch of Jean Gordon, her comments on Patton's death, and her subsequent suicide, see Blumenson, *Patton Papers*, II, 821–35; Irving, *War Between the Generals*, 412; D'Este, *Patton*, 806–7. Much of Patton's success was due to his loyal wife, Beatrice, whose innate character, political connections, and devotion to her husband were always appreciated by Patton's superiors. In many regards, she is reminiscent of the similarly aristocratic and wealthy Ellen Sherman, who, in her husband's darkest hours, rallied support among politicians and Union officers for his reinstatement. While Sherman and Patton had political connections and family money, their wives were far more politically adroit than they. Both women possessed a keen appreciation of the intricacies of bureaucracies that their husbands often lacked.

For Bradley's assessment of Patton's death, see *General's Life*, 464. It is wrong, as Bradley argued, to envision Patton as ever becoming boring. Had he lived on another twenty years, it is far easier to see him in the role of Sherman—a controversial speaker who nevertheless retained the respect of the nation and his veterans and who, his countrymen could be assured, would speak the truth as he knew it.

3. On efforts to ensure that Patton would have no further command or promotion, see D'Este, *Patton*, 751–72, 739. "Friends and enemies": Blumenson, *Patton*, 238. Patton's statements concerning the Russians, disarmament, and the American war dead in general are

quoted in D'Este, *Patton*, 733–34, 739; Blumenson, *Patton Papers*, II, 760–811. Patton under constant attack: Patton, *War*, 253. The criticism of Patton's indirect approach: Weigley, *Eisenhower's Lieutenants*, 244–45. Quote from Charles Whiting, *Patton's Last Battle*, 22. See also the sharp criticism by Dwight Macdonald, who felt Patton was "brutal and hysterical, coarse and affected, violent and empty. . . . These utterances of Patton are atrocities, atrocities in being communicated not to a psychoanalyst but to a great number of soldiers, civilians and school children; and atrocious as reflections of what war-making has done to the personality of Patton himself" (Farago, *Last Days*, 867). Writing in the *New York Review of Books*, years after Patton's death, John Phillips typified best the intellectual disdain for Patton, "A swaggering bigmouth, a Fascist-minded aristocrat . . . the last of our generals to call the Germans, 'the Hun.' His horizons were limited." It is curious to see in a literary magazine the statement that a man who led a quarter-million GIs through occupied France into Germany to end war had "limited" horizons. Destroying fascism in a transcontinental expedition seems a rather large horizon, whatever Patton's cultural prejudices. For Phillips's remarks, see D'Este, *Patton*, 812. It should be noted that, whatever Patton's bombast, history has borne out his apprehensions. Students of the Holocaust have estimated that over 60,000,000 Russians and foreigners were starved to death or murdered by the Soviets beginning in 1917, and well over 50,000,000 million citizens in China, or roughly double the 20,000,000 or so exterminated by various means by the Nazis (Rummel, *Democide*, 2–3).

4. For contemporary newspaper reactions to Patton's removal, and the politics of his postwar administration, see Farago, *Patton*, 820–26; Whiting, *Patton's Last Battle*, 221–26. Cf. the earlier balanced appraisal of Patton in the *Washington Star*: Blumenson, *Patton Papers*, II, 507–8.

5. "Like I would a snake": Blumenson, *Patton Papers*, II, 476. For the Patton persona that permeated the Third Army's, see Essame, *Patton*, 208:

> No commander in World War Two succeeded more effectively in impressing his own personality on the officers and men under his command than Patton. Indeed many actually developed some of his idiosyncrasies and mannerisms. It was even said that he had created Third Army in his own image. Almost every day he sallied forth to the front to praise, reprimand, and inspire. He was never satisfied with issuing orders: he thought it equally important to see that they were carried out. He sometimes would deliberately take considerable risks: 90 per cent of these however were carefully calculated for the effect of their example on his command from GI to corps commander. He thought it necessary "to show the soldiers that generals can get shot at." By day he would go forward by road to return late in the evening, often at twilight and indeed sometimes after dark in his small liaison plane, his theory being that a commander should always be seen going to the front but never coming away from it.

Soldiers' identification with Patton: Forty, *Armies*, 163.

6. His friend Everett Hughes, on August 2, 1944, wrote to Patton's wife about his recent arrival in Normandy:

> I have insisted for months that George keep his shirt on. For months and months I have stood up for him and his staff against everybody. I have succeeded in getting George into the fight at a time when we needed fighters. . . . I was fearful that he had been cowed by the fools who didn't realize that a fighter couldn't be a saint or a psychiatrist when the job was to kill Germans. Or cowed by those who didn't like pearl-handled pistols, or fancy uniforms, or all the little idiosyncrasies that are George. (Irving, *War Between the Generals*, 233; cf. Blumenson, *Patton Papers*, II, 496)

Patton's speech to his staff: Forty, *Armies*, 63.

7. Patton's inability to judge the prevailing taste of the mid twentieth century and his increasing isolation from modern values: Blumenson, *Patton Papers*, II, 855–59; Farago, *Patton*, 812–26; D'Este, *Patton*, 810–20. For the incident of the mules, cf. D'Este, *Patton*, 530. See Forty, *Armies*, 163, for Patton's emphasis on spirit. His Memorial Day speech is quoted in Nye, *Patton Mind*, 142. Patton himself felt that almost all his public statements were screened and quoted out of context to achieve the desired effect. He told a press conference on September 7, 1944:

> It is rather a disadvantage to be large and florid and profane, because people say all kinds of things about you which are not true. For every man that I have God damned, there has [sic] been a thousand that I have patted on the back. But the patting on the back doesn't ever come out, and so I am considered to be a self-made son-of-bitch that goes around cursing everyone. As a matter of fact, I don't, but it is much better press to say that a man does things like that than to say he goes to the hospital and writes to the mothers, which I do. I have written more damn letters—I suppose a thousand, to the mothers of private soldiers whom I happen to know have been killed, but that never comes out, and I kick some son-of-a-bitch in the ass that doesn't do what he should, and it comes out all over. (Blumenson, *Patton Papers*, II, 542)

8. Patton's West Point years and early education: D'Este, *Patton*, 810–20. To his parents in January 1909, he wrote, "I am different from other men my age. All they want to do is to live happily and die old. I would be willing to live in torture, die tomorrow if for one day I could be truly great" (Nye, *Patton Mind*, 16).

9. On Patton's wide reading and a sample of the hundreds of his annotated texts, see Nye, *Patton Mind*, 13–41, 69, 199, 129, 148.

10. Patton's quote about tank operations: D'Este, *Patton*, 233. His career between World Wars One and Two is discussed in detail by D'Este, *Patton*, 283–427. For a military chronology of Patton's career from 1919 to 1940, see Blumenson, *Patton Papers*, II, 966–70; see also his *Patton*, 128–29. Bradley's deprecation of Patton is thematic throughout his memoir, *General's Life*; see 99–100, 218–22.

11. Patton's illnesses, injuries, and afflictions: D'Este, *Patton*, 131–39, 152–53, 160, 180, 203, 206, 221, 276, 285–86, 313, 358, 532, 362–63, 369, 710, 746. It should be noted that, far from being a malingerer or hypochondriac, Patton usually left hospital stays early and hid his illness and disability to the point where his general health and even survival were on numerous occasions put in real jeopardy.

12. Reincarnation: Nye, *Patton Mind*, 64–66; D'Este, *Patton*, 322–23. His sense of déjà vu: Nye, *Patton Mind*, 5. Letter of August 20, 1944, to Beatrice Patton: Blumenson, *Patton Papers*, II, 522. In that same March 1926, Patton emphasized the timeless communality of the Great Captains:

> Disregarding the personality of Frederick we attribute his victories to a tactical expedient, the oblique order of battle. . . . Yet the history of war is the history of warriors; few in number, mighty in influence. Alexander, not Macedonia conquered the world. Scipio, not Rome destroyed Carthage. Marlborough, not the allies defeated France. Cromwell, not the roundheads dethroned Charles. . . . The secret of victory lies not wholly in knowledge. It lurks invisible in that vitalizing spark, intangible, yet evident as lightning—the warrior soul. (Nye, *Patton Mind*, 77–78)

For Bradley's mostly hostile attitude toward Patton, see D'Este, *Patton*, 643–44.

13. Blumenson's assessment: Blumenson and Stokesbury, *Masters*, 262. Patton and integration: D'Este, *Patton*, 726. Crossing the Rhine: Ambrose, *Citizen Soldiers*, 433. Patton's

wide-ranging comments on the other American commanders: Blumenson, *Patton Papers*, II, 482. Patton and minorities: Blumenson, 293; D'Este, *Patton*, 173, 622. Again for Bradley's quotations in dislike of Patton, see Farago, *Patton*, 439–50. Epaminondas: Blumenson, *Patton Papers*, I, 40–41; Essame, *Patton*, 49. Wedemeyer's comment to Ike, and Patton's retort to Eisenhower: D'Este, *Patton*, 567, 681.

14. Patton and his comments on Sherman: D'Este, *Patton*, 463, 562, 759; Blumenson, *Patton Papers*, II, 245. Liddell Hart's recollections are discussed in Hirshson, *White Tecumseh*, 393. And see also Liddell Hart, *Memoirs*, 169–70. Sherman and Patton: Harkins, *Third Army*, 78–80.

15. Much of Patton's anti-Semitism resulted from a very brief period during his governorship of Bavaria, when he was suffering from exhaustion of the past year in constant combat. His biographers have remarked that much of what he said then he regretted or felt was misinterpreted. See Farago, *Last Days*, 228–33; R. Patton, *The Pattons*, 276–79. For Patton's uncanny ability to see the proper course in the major controversies in Normandy, see Essame, *Patton*, 250–51; Hogg, *Patton*, 156; Sophocles, *Ajax*; 964–66.

Chapter Two. The Patton Way of War

16. Patton to his wife: Blumenson, *Patton Papers*, II, 524. Colonel Wallace, *Third Army*, 204.

17. Eisenhower's letter to General Marshall is quoted in Nye, *Patton Mind*, 137; cf. Blumenson, *Patton*, 213.

18. For Patton's first official speech to his army, see D'Este, *Patton*, 623; Farago, *Patton*, 662–63. "Both flanks": Blumenson, *Patton Papers*, II, 553; Patton on retreats: Blumenson, *Patton Papers*, II, 540. For the quote from Blumenson, see his *Patton Papers*, II, 858.

19. Wilmot quote: *Struggle*, 427. For "concrete" and being on the defensive, see Blumenson, *Patton Papers*, II, 540, 634. For the confusion in American command over the best method of using American troops, see Weigley's perceptive remarks: *Eisenhower's Lieutenants*, 729.

20. Patton's worry that he was taking risks to resume the offensive: Blumenson, *Patton Papers*, II, 636. Montgomery's sluggishness and Patton's quotes on the need for the Americans to end the war on the offensive: D'Este, *Patton*, 710–12; Blumenson, *Patton Papers*, II, 634–36; Essame, *Patton*, 236.

21. On the difficulty of the Eifel and Saar-Palatinate campaigns and Patton's observations, see Blumenson, *Patton Papers*, II, 651; Weigley, *Eisenhower's Lieutenants*, 619–22. For the horrendous conditions under which the GIs fought, see Prefer, *Patton's Ghost Corps*, 205–14. Greatest distance from the Rhine in February: Ambrose, *Citizen Soldiers*, 413.

22. Ambrose on Patton: *Citizen Soldiers*, 411. Sweat of the legions: Blumenson, *Patton Papers*, II, 655. Patton at the front: Essame, *Patton*, 239; D'Este, *Patton*, 706–7. See Blumenson, *Patton*, 233, for Patton's presence in North Africa near the fighting, and the drastic change from his predecessor's command from the rear. He was often nearly killed: Blumenson, *Patton Papers*, II, 566.

23. Patton's observations: Blumenson, *Patton Papers*, II, 658. See also Nye, *Patton Mind*, 161.

24. Whiting, *Patton's Last Battle*, 109; Weigley, *Eisenhower's Lieutenants*, 638. Patton, decades earlier in a lecture "Tank Tactics," had forecast just such rapid breakthroughs of advanced armored columns, spearheaded by tanks coordinated by radio communications (Nye, *Patton Mind*, 47–48).

25. "German civilians": Whiting, *Patton's Last Battle*, 155.

26. Blumenson, *Patton Papers*, II, 660.

27. German reactions to Patton are quoted in Blumenson, *Patton Papers*, II, 654.

28. On the decision to halt Patton before reaching Prague, see Whiting, *Patton's Last Battle*, 171–76, 278–79. On Eisenhower's remarks about the unimportance of Berlin, see D'Este, *Patton*, 721. See especially Essame, *Patton*, 250:

> At the very climax of the war Eisenhower had ready America's finest army nearly half a million strong, superbly equipped and supported by overwhelming air power under the ablest and most dynamic commander in the West, all straining at the leash to reap the fruits of their victories by occupying the strategic centre of Europe. For the fifth time, and at the most crucial moment of all, Eisenhower failed to use it to get a decision. Stalin, who once asked how many divisions had the Pope, would at least have understood the force of an argument such as this.

29. For the size of Patton's army, see Farago, *Patton*, 790; Essame, *Patton*, 250–55; Blumenson, *Patton*, 216–17.

30. For these statistics and others, see Province, *Patton's Third Army*, 289–95; Essame, *Patton*, 252. For the Third Army's capture of territory and damage to the enemy during the Saar campaign, see Patton, *War*, 141.

31. For statistics on Patton's progress, see again, Province, *Patton's Third Army*, 290–91; Forty, *Armies*, 203–42; Wallace, *Third Army*, 194. Patton quotes historical examples to his generals: Patton, *War*, 103–4, 110–11.

Chapter Three. A Deadly Enemy

32. On Hitler's strategy in the Ardennes, see Dupuy, *Hitler's Last Gamble*, 7–20; Wilmot, *Struggle*, 580–602; Morelock, *Generals*, 21–25. Opposition to the Germans in the Ardennes in 1944 was not in a numerical sense greater than in 1940, but qualitatively the British and American armies were battle-hardened after months of campaigning in a manner not true of the French and Allied armies at the beginning of the war. In addition, the now better-equipped Germans attacked with a force about ten divisions smaller than had been the case in 1940.

33. On the numbers involved in the battle: Dupuy, *Hitler's Last Gamble*, 16–19. Bradley's confession: *General's Life*, 351; Patton quote: D'Este, *Patton*, 678. Weigley, *Eisenhower's Lieutenants*, 457–64, points out that Bradley was not entirely to blame for leaving the Ardennes so poorly defended and its troops relatively complacent. Rather, American planners and Eisenhower himself had believed that an enormous front could be manned by ninety Allied divisions, even as the distance from supply bases and the growing encirclement of the German homeland meant an ever greater territory to be covered by ever fewer troops. Patton believed that his forced halt in the fall, and his orders not to take Trier immediately, had given the Germans the opportunity to mount their later counteroffensive in the Ardennes: Patton, *War*, 129. For his anticipation of the German attack, see Weigley, *Eisenhower's Lieutenants*, 498–99.

34. Patton's forced inactivity aided the assembly of forces for the German offensive to the north: Farago, *Patton*, 700. Patton's disdain for fortifications: Patton, *War*, 100–103. For Patton's initial preference to go to the rear of the German offensive, see Dupuy, *Hitler's Last Gamble*, 365–66.

35. Eisenhower, *Crusade in Europe*, 352. On the Allied plans of response, the tardy nature of Montgomery's attack, and the general opposition to Patton's more dramatic suggestions of retaliation, see Weigley, *Eisenhower's Lieutenants*, 546–47. One of Patton's officers

remarked, "Patton would have liked to have seen the Germans drive some forty or fifty miles, then chop them off and destroy them, but he recognized that he would never muster support for that kind of daring": D'Este, *Patton*, 61. For the failure of the Allied leadership to lop off the German salient, see Morelock, *Generals*, 76–80.

36. D'Este, *Patton*, 680–81. Cf. Dupuy, *Hitler's Last Gamble*, 202: "[Patton] had, in fact, accomplished one of the great feats of military history: halting in its tracks an attacking army of 350,000 men and pivoting this massive force ninety degrees to be able to resume the attack in an entirely different direction in less than seventy hours."

37. On the meeting with Eisenhower at Verdun, see Dupuy, *Hitler's Last Gamble*, 141–44; D'Este, *Patton*, 680–81. Eisenhower is especially ungenerous in his memoirs about Patton's bold promise of relief and his entire role in restoring the Allied line. See Essame, *Patton*, 233: "In the faint praise given in *Crusade in Europe* for his [Patton's] part in the battle there is a hint of condescension which comes ill from the pen of one who despite all his talents and virtues was an unbloodied soldier." Compare what Eisenhower himself later wrote in his memoirs about Patton's move:

> Our flexibility was nowhere better illustrated than during the German counteroffensive in the Ardennes when Patton's army ceased its preparations for an eastward attack, changed front, and undertook a movement extending over sixty to seventy miles at right angles to its former direction of advance. In less than seventy-two hours from the time Patton's staff had its orders an entire corps of his army had initiated a new attack. (*Crusade in Europe*, 453)

Somehow Patton's once "fatuous" promise to move immediately had become later proof of the "flexibility" of Eisenhower's forces.

38. Von Rundstedt called the American avoidance of the shoulders of the bulge the "small solution"; cf. Dupuy, *Hitler's Last Gamble*, 32, 365–56. Patton's remarks: Blumenson, *Patton Papers*, II, 599–601.

39. "He kept his cool": Irving, *War Between the Generals*, 351. Patton and the bulge: Dupuy, *Hitler's Last Gamble*, 210. For the casualties of the Battle of the Bulge, see Weigley, *Eisenhower's Lieutenants*, 574. For Patton's bombastic remarks at Verdun, see Eisenhower, *Crusade in Europe*, 350. Eisenhower prefaced Patton's quote with "True to his impulsive nature." "Tarpon": Blumenson, *Patton Papers*, II, 603; cf. 595–600, for alternate plans in dealing with the German offensive. His subordinate, Halley Maddox, reported to Patton that if the First Army would just carry out a fighting withdrawal to lure the Germans farther, the entire enemy army could be annihilated: "If they will roll with the punch up north, we can pinwheel the enemy before he gets very far. In a week we could expose the whole German rear and trap their main forces west of the Rhine."

40. See Patton, *War*, 168–175; Weigley, *Eisenhower's Lieutenants*, 566.

41. On ratios of allied to German forces in Europe in 1944–45, see Weigley, *Eisenhower's Lieutenants*, 28–31; 464: "The American army in Europe fought on too narrow a margin of physical superiority for the favored American broad-front strategy to be anything but a risky gamble." Cf. 356: "Yet in manpower, the Allied advantage was not all that great, especially against enemy soldiers shielded by the pillboxes and dragons' teeth of the West Wall, or by such a fortress complex as encircled Metz." On the amazing restructuring of the German war economy in the face of the increased Allied offensive in the West, see Speer, *Third Reich*, 396–411.

42. For the German recovery, see Wilmot, *Struggle*, 540–61. Allied manpower: Ambrose, *Citizen Soldiers*, 68–69, 290–91; Shulman, *Defeat in the West*, 205–7. Doubler quote:

Closing with the Enemy, 235. The quotation on German manpower is from van Creveld, *Fighting Power*, 65.

43. German letter: Shulman, *Defeat in the West*, 249. Letter of German corporal: Bartov, *Hitler's Army*, 173. Kokott's remarks about the 26th Volkssturm Division are quoted in Ambrose, *Citizen Soldiers*, 190.

44. Possible plans for postwar Germany: Wilmot, *Struggle*, 540–61, 550; cf. 448–49. On the Morgenthau Plan, see Ellis, *Victory*, II, 146–48. There was an increasing German fatalism and fanaticism as prospects grew bleak, most prominently on the part of Hitler himself:

> In the days of Stalingrad, and then more and more often afterwards, Hitler repeated, suggestively and in a gloomy undertone, that we shouldn't have any more illusions. "There is only forward, the bridges are burned behind us. Gentlemen, there is no going back." We all sensed that monstrous things were happening, and that the road to the past would be blocked for each one of us. We never spoke about this, not even among friends." (Speer, *Slave State*, 255)

45. German letters: Bartov, *Hitler's Army*, 172; Shulman, *Defeat in the West*, 249. The interview with a captured German is quoted in Wallace, *Third Army*, 106. For a good discussion of the morale of the German army even late in the war, see Bartov, *Hitler's Army*, 144–46. For the regional basis of Hitler's army, consult van Creveld, *Fighting Power*, 76–78. Keegan's quote: *Six Armies*, 320. 50,000 German soldiers executed: Ambrose, *Citizen Soldiers*, 344; and cf. 411 for his description of fanatical German resistance. Expressions of German fanaticism and philosophical nihilism: Bartov, *Hitler's Army*, 173–74: A young German theologian wrote, "A thousand-year Reich is going to the grave. . . . God will help us. . . . No one in the world is more blessed than our *Volk*, which even today sends its roots deep into the earth." An art historian in the army, Reinhard Becker-Glauch, shortly before his death, echoed that same sentiment:

> War has its greatness and its elevating happiness, more than any other, because it drives us all consciously to the limit of things; the sham-values sink behind and what really occupies the heart, you and the homeland, alone remain strong. These are more than platitudes. Hour by hour we experience the blazing love to you and to the Fatherland as the driving realities.

For German booby traps and delayed fused bombs, see Patton, *War*, 134.

46. For discussion of American and German respective military hardware and the general superiority in most German equipment versus the quantity and reliability of American models, see Weigley, *Eisenhower's Lieutenants*, 8–31; Dupuy, *Hitler's Last Gamble*, 379–423; Morelock, *Generals*, 3–17, 23–25; Ambrose, *Citizen Soldiers*, 61–66; and esp. Forty, *Armies*, 160–81. Bradley's comments on the weakness of the Sherman tank: Weigley, *Eisenhower's Lieutenants*, 21.

47. Peiper's division: Ambrose, *Citizen Soldiers*, 189. Overy, *Why the Allies Won*, 178. For the deadly nature of Tiger and Panther tanks, and the skill necessary for Patton's Shermans to survive encounters with German armor, see Green, *Patton's Tank Drive*, 124–43.

48. On comparisons of the German forces in the East and West and the respective size of the Allied and Russian armies, see Weigley, *Eisenhower's Lieutenants*, 572–73. On the relative accomplishment of the Anglo-American and Russian Allies against the German army, see Keegan, *Six Armies*, 313–33. See also Wilmot, *Struggle*, 621: "The Western Allies were now directly engaging 100 German divisions, 76 in the West and 24 in Italy. A fur-

ther 27 were tied down in the outlying strategic areas, 10 in Yugoslavia and 17 in Scandinavia. Thus on the Eastern Front, where Hitler had been able to commit 157 German divisions when the Normandy invasion began, he now had only 133, barely half the total strength of his ground forces."

49. On the respective strategic problems and resources of the Allies and the Germans, see Overy, *Why the Allies Won*, 7–24; Weinburg, *World at Arms*, 6–48, 722–49. American reserves exhausted: Whiting, *Patton's Last Battle*, 13, and esp. Patton, *War*, 140. By December 1944, many of the Third Army's divisions in the field were at little more than half of their original strength.

50. Patton, *War*, 161. "Against such an army": Farago, *Patton*, 729.

Chapter Four. A Cog in the Wheel?

51. D'Este, *Patton*, 660. Bradley ostensibly supported Patton's request for continued supplies and attributed the entire allied logistical problem on preparations for Montgomery's ill-fated Market-Garden offensive. But see Blumenson, *Generals*, 273–74, for Bradley's long record of hostility to Patton and interference in his operations, with often disastrous results. "Unfortunately," wrote Martin Blumenson, "Patton's authority was limited to his army and subject to the supervision of, in order of ascendance, Bradley, Montgomery, and Eisenhower. However much Patton found his subordinate position galling, he resolved to make the best of the situation and to enjoy the prerogatives and responsibilities of army command. Even Eisenhower's relegation of Patton to anonymity failed to curb Patton's exuberance" (Blumenson, *Generals*, 157).

52. Rapid movement of Patton's headquarters: Wallace, *Third Army*, 55. For Patton's various quotes about the need to press onto the Rhine and the historical significance of his halt, see D'Este, *Patton*, 645–58. German chief of staff Blumentritt's remarks: Essame, *Patton*, 194.

53. Essame, *Patton*, 201. And for the controversy surrounding the cut-off in gasoline, see D'Este, *Patton*, 649–50, 660–63; Weigley, *Eisenhower's Lieutenants*, 266; Eisenhower, *Crusade in Europe*, 302–20. Captured stocks: Wallace, *Third Army*, 66.

54. For Patton's own assessments about his fuel being curtailed, see Blumenson, *Patton Papers*, II, 531; Patton, *War*, 92, 108–9.

55. Patton, *War*, 94. Patton's insistence on movement through France derived in part not merely from his formal training and wide reading, but also from his horrific firsthand knowledge of the stasis of World War One, when tanks, motorized trucks, and audacious planning had at last helped to bring fluidity to the holocaust of trench fighting in late 1918—a ghoulish experience that Eisenhower, in fact, had never undergone.

56. "Farther and faster": Blumenson, *Patton Papers*, II, 510. For the significance of Patton's halt, see Essame, *Patton*, 201–2. On August 30, Patton wrote in his diary:

> We must get a crossing on the Meuse. In the last war I drained ¾ of my tanks to keep the other ¼ going. Eddy can do the same. It is terrible to halt, even on the Meuse. We should cross the Rhine in the vicinity of Worms, and the faster we do it, the less lives and munitions it will take. No one realizes the terrible value of the "unforgiving minute" except me. Some way I will get on yet. (Blumenson, *Patton Papers*, II, 531)

Note in the above quotation Patton's continual emphasis on "less lives." Hogg quote: *Patton*, 115. For Patton's relative progress during August compared to the fall of 1944, see Ambrose, *Citizen Soldiers*, 164–65.

57. For the radical change in German fortunes during the first two weeks of September

throughout Patton's theater of operations, see Weigley, *Eisenhower's Lieutenants*, 344; cf. 295–97. For the quote of General Westphal, the new chief of staff to von Rundstedt, see Essame, *Patton*, 196. Steven Ambrose's assessment is found in *Citizen Soldiers*, 114. See too Wilmot, *Struggle*, 497:

> Thus within three weeks of the fall of Paris and the overwhelming defeat of the German Armies in the Battle of France, the Wehrmacht had almost recovered its balance; at all events, it was no longer "on the run." The Germans were again holding a coherent line—admittedly thin and taut and with meager reserves behind it—but a line nevertheless. And, because of their successful defence and demolition of the channel ports and the approaches to Antwerp, they were denying to Eisenhower the supplies with which to maintain the full momentum of his advance.

For the impotence of the West Wall in August, see Farago, *Patton*, 556–79, esp. the remarks of General Westphal:

> I would like to state unequivocally that we would have been totally incapable of putting up any serious resistance and foiling a drive across the western boundaries of the Reich had General Eisenhower decided upon a truly determined, concentrated and ruthless advance at this point. At that time, headquarters of *OB West* was located in the vicinity of Koblenz. Whenever after sunset we could hear the rattling of chains in the street where the Field Marshal had his quarters, he would ask, "Can this be Patton?" The question was posed in jest, of course, but it did not lack the most serious undertone. (578)

For the strength of the newly reconstructed Siegfried Line by September, see Ambrose, *Citizen Soldiers*, 144.

58. The problem of opening the French ports and the destruction of French rail capability: Weigley, *Eisenhower's Lieutenants*, 277–81; van Creveld, *Supplying War*, 216–25; Shulman, *Defeat in the West*, 187–202. Eisenhower's remarks: *Crusade in Europe*, 310.

59. For the notion that the Allied logistical breakdown was more than simply a problem of transport and port facilities, but rather involved structural rigidity and bureaucracy antithetical to flexibility and tactical innovation, see van Creveld, *Supplying War*, 215. As Patton halted, Lee brought in oranges for his breakfast table from North Africa, and demanded thirteen infantry brigades to guard his huge supply dumps, which he hoarded in the manner of a medieval grandee. For his incompetence, see D'Este, *Patton*, 648–49. Whereas Epaminondas had perhaps a half-dozen Boeotians to organize his assault, and Sherman's staff of twenty or so planned the supply of the Army of the West, thousands of Americans were safely to the rear during World War Two, engaged as clerks in a huge bureaucracy of logistical administration: "The number of—frequently commissioned—pen pushers in the rear was enormous, whereas the fighting arms were starved of high-quality manpower" (van Creveld, *Fighting Power*, 168).

60. Montgomery had preference in Sicily planning as well: Blumenson, *Patton Papers*, II, 240. On the Montgomery-versus-Patton debate about primacy of resources, see Wilmot, *Struggle* 458–76; Weigley, *Eisenhower's Lieutenants*, 260–63. Eisenhower was also concerned that neither a British nor an American general should single-handedly defeat Germany, and thus advocated a broad-front strategy, as he flipped back and forth in priorities of supply; see D'Este, *Decision*, 470–71. On the controversy, see Murray, *Eisenhower Versus Montgomery*, 162–64. For Patton as what the British general Alexander called a "thruster," see Blumenson, *Patton Papers*, II, 415.

61. For the subordination of Patton in the Allied war plans, see Blumenson, *Patton*, 223; Farago, *Patton*, 371–450. Cf. D'Este, *Patton*, 630:

> Patton well understood that he was quite fortunate to find himself again commanding anything, and he was both grateful and wary. More important, Patton was painfully aware that another serious misstep might be his last. What Patton would have done if he had been in Bradley's place and what he did as the Third Army commander were very different indeed, and he was determined to tread lightly. After Bradley turned down one of his proposals (which was often), Patton was occasionally successful in persuading him to adopt his course of action by convincing Bradley that it was *his* idea.

In the vast gulf between Patton's innate ability and the role prescribed for him in Normandy lay the heart of the entire Allied dilemma in Europe: Eisenhower—with urging from Bradley—had put his most audacious and aggressive leader farthest from Germany, with the idea that distance and the tardy activation of the Third Army would preclude a real breakout to the south. Instead, Patton was to mop up Brittany for months. Thus, the shortest corridor into the industrial Ruhr, with the closest supply lines at Antwerp, was to be the theater of Montgomery, who had no history of demanding highly mobile and aggressive operations. Had their theaters been reversed, Patton's aggressive thrust would have fit the preordained Allied agenda to the letter. Cf. Blumenson, *Patton Papers*, II, 435.

62. On the strange agreement between Patton and Montgomery for a single concentrated and well-supplied effort, see Essame, *Patton*, 189–202. For Montgomery's errors, see Weinberg, *World at Arms*, 701–2; Shulman, *Defeat in the West*, 180–81. While each loathed each other in person, both Patton and Montgomery in the abstract had a great deal of mutual respect for each other, each believing quite rightly that the other was the best officer that the respective British and American armies could field. See D'Este, *Patton*, 644; cf. Blumenson, *Generals*, 273:

> For as the American army group commander, as the most experienced American battlefield general, as the most senior American soldier who had proved without a shadow of doubt his combat expertise, Patton could meet Montgomery as an equal. They would have worked closely and effectively together. For they respected each other. Their interests were professional and tied to the operational scene. Their strengths were complementary. The thrust of Patton and the balance of Montgomery would have produced a perfectly matched team.

For the idea that the Normandy campaign was to unfold with a secondary and rather unimportant role for Patton, see D'Este, *Patton*, 670–75; cf. 597. On Bradley's fear of Patton that had negative consequences for the advance of the entire American army in July, see Farago, *Patton*, 501–13.

63. Critics of Patton's idea to smash across the Rhine in August 1944, and his style of generalship in particular: Weigley, *Eisenhower's Lieutenants*, 243–45; D'Este, *Patton*, 670–75. But even Bradley, no friend of Patton, confessed of the lost opportunity: "Three months and many casualties later we were to be forcefully reminded that in war, opportunity once forsaken is opportunity lost forever"; cf. D'Este, *Patton*, 660. The common opinion of military historians (cf., e.g., Murray, *Eisenhower versus Montgomery*, 173–75; cf. 47) remains that Patton could not have ended the war in the fall, because "there were not enough dead Germans by September 1944" and he had but a single army. We should remember that Alexander wrecked an empire of over 70,000,000 people with an army that rarely could bring more than 40,000 infantrymen to the battlefield.

Because it took the Russians 160 divisions and over 100,000 dead finally to destroy

Berlin does not mean that it was impossible for the Americans to win in late 1944. The key is morale and perception, and for a brief few days in late August 1944 there was simply no real defense in front of Patton to stop his progress across the Rhine, and the German resistance even deeper in Germany was completely demoralized—thus the real German fear of a commander like Patton. The Spartan army that huddled on the acropolis before Epaminondas beat the Arcadians decisively a short time later. The Confederacy that cowered before Sherman in Georgia was at the same time slaughtering Union soldiers in Virginia. It is a theme of this book that mobile columns loose in the enemy's heartland can achieve results far beyond their actual numbers or their ability to destroy armies. Armies that are ruined, if left alone, can achieve an amazing degree of recovery within a few days.

64. German assessment of Patton: Blumenson, *Patton*, 298. Criticism of great generals: Blumenson, *Patton Papers*, II, 397. Patton's worries about being stopped: Farago, *Patton*, 581. 3,000 casualties: Whiting, *Patton's Last Battle*, 13. Patton reads Rommel: Patton, *War*, 128. We should remember that no amount of material transferred from Patton to Montgomery for his Market-Garden attack would have ensured success. See Weigley, *Eisenhower's Lieutenants*, 344:

> If Patton's logistical support had been cut back as completely as Montgomery had desired—to immobilize Patton's divisions—it is difficult to conceive how the Third Army could have countered the greater German offensive that Hitler would then have been able to marshal against it—and the effect would have been severe embarrassment to the entire Allied front. Surely no logistical allotment that would have permitted Patton the ammunition and fuel he needed to withstand German counterattacks could have afforded Montgomery enough additional tonnage over what he actually received to have made a decisive difference in the course of his battles.

The Allied order of battle and the growing size of the American armies: Weigley, *Eisenhower's Lieutenants*, 667–69; Eisenhower, *Crusade in Europe*, 511–14.

Chapter Five. Ideological Warriors

65. On to the Seine: Florentin, *Battle*, 157. Patton's grand plans beyond the Seine River: Patton, *War*, 88. Cf. Blumenson, *Generals*, 257:

> What the Germans feared was an immediate and ruthless drive down the right bank of the river, as Patton had wished to initiate. Such an advance would have completely destroyed the German armies that had fought in Normandy. Further resistance in France would have been futile. The path to Germany would have been undefended and open to the invading Allied forces. The Germans were unable to fathom why the Allies failed to pursue this course of action. After the war, Eberbach said, "I still don't understand why the Allies did not crush us at the Seine."

Statistics on August damage done by the Third Army: D'Este, *Patton*, 638.

66. Blumenson, *Generals*, 253. Meeting between Bradley and Patton: Blumenson, *Patton Papers*, II, 521.

67. Of Patton's desire to drive east, Russell Weigley (*Eisenhower's Lieutenants*, 255) notes of the irony:

> None of Montgomery's armored divisions had reached the river, and it would be nearly the end of the month before the British and Canadian armies could close up to the Seine enough to stage their major crossings. By August 23, Patton's Third Army was

already far to the east on the upper Seine. General Eddy's XII Corps spearhead in fact was more than 150 kilometers beyond the longitude of Vernon. Patton was belaboring Bradley for permission, a few more divisions, and the fuel and other supplies he needed to grasp his "greatest chance to win the war ever presented." As Patton saw it, the difficulties of the terrain in front of him mattered little compared to his position far closer to Germany than any other of the Allied armies, with no apparent organized opposition in front of him. If only he could keep on moving, he saw no reason why he should not crash straight through the West Wall fortifications on the German frontier before the enemy could get troops into the pillboxes. But everything depended on speed, keeping the Germans on the run and giving them no chance to regroup.

68. Patton's struggle not to take counsel of his fears: Blumenson, *Patton Papers*, II, 522.

69. Statistics on the Third Army's progress in August: Farago, *Patton*, 458–59.

70. For the Allied effort to cast the Germans as the perpetrators of evil, see Overy, *Why the Allies Won*, 282–313; Weinberg, *World at Arms*, 584. German civilians appearing to GIs much like Americans back home: Ambrose, *Citizen Soldiers*, 449. Problems arose, however, in all such efforts when England and America were allied with a totalitarian state like the Soviet Union, which had butchered as many innocent as Hitler—indeed more. Patton, for example, was nearly relieved of command for unduly emphasizing the Anglo-American alliance and omitting praise of the Russians: Farago, *Patton*, 418–20. For the drawbacks of the American recruitment system, see van Creveld, *Fighting Power*, 77. On Patton's problems with making a killer out of "the civilised, urban-dwelling young American of the 1940s," see Forty, *Armies*, 147.

71. For Eisenhower's moral indignation against the Nazis, see Ambrose, *Citizen Soldiers*, 101, 416. His quote on the need for a crusade: *Crusade in Europe*, 157. On general Allied propaganda efforts against the Nazis: Overy, *Why the Allies Won*, 295. Cf. Essame, *Patton*, 27–28: "Patton had to convince his men that they had a great and noble object, the overthrow of the vile Nazi and Japanese tyrannies which threatened to destroy the liberties which were their birthright and this could only be done by bold offensive action in battle."

72. Patton's warning: Blumenson, *Patton Papers*, II, 590; cf. van Creveld, *Fighting Power*, 58; Wallace, *Third Army*, 17. See Marshall, *Men Against Fire*, 104–5, for the idea that there is a greater, not lesser, need for a commander to visit the front in war of the modern age. All ground commanders in World War Two complained that they received a less well educated, and perhaps less bright enlistee than either the army air corps or the navy, purportedly compounding their task of inculcating a more abstract vision of the difference between Nazi Germany and America.

73. Problems facing Patton in imbuing Americans with the fighting spirit: Essame, *Patton*, 40; Forty, *Armies*, 83. Why Americans fight: Blumenson: *Patton Papers*, II, 429; American values: Farago, *Patton*, 413. On the Nazi dream and the need for millions of slaves to carry it out, see Speer, *Slave State*, 302–4.

74. Patton and the interrogation of German officers: Blumenson: *Patton Papers*, II, 505–6, 577–81. Patton was relieved from postwar command for his disagreements about the role of Russia in postwar Germany and the Allied order to forbid GIs from fraternizing with German citizens. Even critics noted that his crime was abject naïveté, not fondness for National Socialism:

> As he thought about the postwar world and specifically Germany, he felt increasingly out of sympathy with his milieu and particularly with the aims of nonfraternization and denazification. No one had been more zealous than he in working for the defeat of the German military forces. In the process, he came to have great, if grudging ad-

miration for the German military men who had fought bravely, if foolishly, who had maintained the honor of the military profession. Why oppress them? Surely, he began to believe, only a handful had been dyed-in-the-wool Nazis. Party membership, he was certain, had been required in order to survive in Hitler's Germany, and those who had joined had done so to retain their jobs so they could support their families. What, he asked, was wrong with that? (Blumenson, *Patton Papers*, II, 707)

75. See Essame, *Patton*, 34–35. Oddly, given Patton's bombastic Anglophobia, British historians like Essame and Hogg, not to mention British wartime leaders and generals like Churchill, Montgomery, and Alexander, possessed a respect for and an acknowledgment of Patton's talent rarely shared by his American critics, who were far more worried about what he said rather than what he did on the battlefield.

76. For grass-roots American opposition to entering the war, see Hoyt, *GI's War*, 9–10; D'Este, *Patton*, 403. Doubler points out commonalties between U.S. Army practice in World War Two and that during the Gulf War. In both theaters American troops relied on close support of tactical aircraft, sought large enveloping movements, and were indoctrinated with an antityrannical propaganda. In some ways, the entire American approach to infantry battle in the Gulf owes much to George Patton. See Doubler, *Closing with the Enemy*, 295–98.

77. See Overy, *Why the Allies Won*, 293. Problems of discipline and patriotism in modern American society: Marshall, *Men Against Fire*, 211. Patton on the therapeutic view of war: Blumenson, *Patton Papers*, II, 421. Patton's effort to create a free, independent, and disciplined American soldier: Farago, *Patton*, 412. Cf. van Creveld, *Fighting Power*, 173: "The German Army had extremely high fighting power, it is true, but only at the cost of producing troops to whom an order, regardless of its nature, was an order and who could therefore be relied on not only to fight but to commit any kind of atrocity as well. To produce fighting power without paying as high a price, that is the true challenge facing the armies of the West." A central idea of this book is that Epaminondas, Sherman, and Patton accomplished that dual task of democracy as few others have in history.

78. Text of Patton's speech: Blumenson: *Patton Papers*, II, 458. Third Army morale: D'Este, *Patton*, 574. Bradley's dismissal of Patton: Bradley, *General's Life*, 98. He seemed to be especially upset at Patton's use of profanity:

> He was unmercifully hard on his men, demanding the utmost in military efficiency and bearing. Most of them respected but despised him. Although he could be the epitome of grace and charm at social or official functions, he was at the same time the most earthly profane man I ever knew. I sometimes wondered if this macho profanity was unconscious overcompensation for his most serious personal flaw: a voice that was almost comically squeaky and high-pitched, altogether lacking in command authority.

Officer's impression of Patton: Essame, *Patton*, 142–43.

79. For Patton's emotion, see Essame, *Patton*, 256–57. For the animus of Paul Fussell, Andy Rooney, and Bill Mauldin, see Ambrose, *Citizen Soldiers*, 334–36; D'Este, *Patton*, 693–94, 813. Ambrose quote: *Citizen Soldiers*, 335. "I never had the nerve": D'Este, *Patton*, 812.

80. Radio broadcast: Blumenson, *Patton Papers*, II, 524. for the argument that Patton's spit and polish encouraged morale, and his own method of command was, in fact, quite democratic, see Chester Wilmot's quote: *Struggle*, 466.

81. "The greatest army in American history": Blumenson, *Patton Papers*, II, 428. On Patton's sense he was creating an army out of the vast nothingness of raw recruits, see Blumenson, *Patton Papers*, II, 413.

82. See van Creveld, *Fighting Power*, 79, 97.

83. Doubler, *Closing with the Enemy*, 251. Patton's defense of his rhetoric: Forty, *Armies*, 83. For his emphasis in his lectures on killings, see Blumenson, *Patton Papers*, II, 456, 477. See Patton, *War*, 265, for his repugnance for entrenching: "The trick expression, 'Dig or die,' is much overused and much misunderstood. Wars are not won by defensive tactics. Digging is primarily defensive. . . . 'Hit the dirt' is another expression which has done much to increase our casualties. . . . The soldier, obsessed with the idea of hitting the dirt, lies down and waits supinely for the arrival of the shells from the mortars." Cf. Weigley's comments about Patton's preferences: "Patton's aggressiveness was of speed and mobility, not of the application of overwhelming power to crush the enemy. The most aggressive senior American commander remained a soldier of saber and spurs" (*Eisenhower's Lieutenants*, 245). Need to fire: Blumenson, *Patton Papers*, II, 433.

84. For these quotes and others like them, see Farago, *Patton*, 412. For the controversy over just how frequently GIs in battle actually fired their weapons, see Marshall, *Men Against Fire*, 44–63.

85. For the Americans' singular mechanical aptitude, see Wilmot, *Struggle*, 427. The Americans' familiarity with machines helped them to use Shermans to their advantage by keeping far more in service than the more deadly but less reliable Panthers and Tigers:

> For all their shortcomings, the Shermans were a triumph of American mass-produced techniques. First of all, they were wonderfully reliable, in sharp contrast to the Panthers and Tigers. In addition GIs were far more experienced in the workings of the internal combustion engine than were their opposite numbers. The Americans were also infinitely better at recovering damaged tanks and patching them up to go back into actions; the Germans had nothing like the American maintenance battalions. (Ambrose, *Citizen Soldiers*, 64)

86. Freeman's comments: Patton, *War*, xix. On the Third Army's food, its war against trench foot, and Patton's insistence that officers fight at the front, see Hogg, *Patton*, 153–54; Essame, *Patton*, 239–41; D'Este, *Patton*, 689. When the American supply corps could not provide white capes for his men during the Battle of the Bulge, Patton arranged for a French company to make ten thousand a week. Cf. Blumenson, *Patton*, 241: "He made certain that mail deliveries were fast and regular, that food was the best possible, that daily changes of socks were distributed to prevent trench foot. He saw to it that hot showers and clean clothes were available. He rotated units in the line and instituted liberal passes and leaves, providing transportation for troops to visit Nancy and other rear-area towns. Morale remained high despite the almost constant mud, rain, sleet, and snow." On the use of stealth to gain supplies, see Patton, *War*, 95. For the intensely loyal devotion to Patton shown by his soldiers, and years later their boasts that they had fought with Patton, see D'Este, *Patton*, 813.

87. Patton's defense of his speeches: D'Este, *Patton*, 578–79. For the dangers of bureaucratic warfare, see Marshall, *Men Against Fire*, 210. Of course, in the modern age, the notion of chivalry and high-minded patriotism is out of vogue. As early as 1947, S. L. A. Marshall wrote a landmark book arguing that Americans fought simply to survive at the unit level, at most to protect and save their friends on the left and right, not for higher notions of good versus evil. But two things must be remembered about Marshall's often misunderstood study. First, modern soldiers, with the specter of the trenches of World War One in mind, imbued with modernism, exposed to the nihilism of the present age, were far less likely to be so one-dimensionally patriotic in postbattle interviews. GIs tended to adopt a cynical pose to interviewers even when in fact they were quite sure that they were in Europe to fight Nazism. Second, we must not confuse immediate and longer-term incentives: one fights with a machine gun to save his buddy in the same foxhole; one is in the

foxhole in the first place often because one feels it is a very good and necessary thing to do. And it is usually forgotten that spirit and patriotism were precisely Marshall's point about motivation. He was reacting against the postwar notion that an American abundance of industrial might and machines would ensure victory by simply throwing overwhelming human and material capital into battle. Combat discipline, Marshall argued, strong ties of personal loyalties between men, and a common spiritual bond were essential, but they could only emerge if the entire army, indeed the country, understood the moral nature of their larger struggle. See Forty, *Armies*, 163–64, for the Patton emphasis on leading from the front, and esp. Blumenson, *Patton Papers*, II, 422–23: Commanders, Patton wrote, must "visit the front daily . . . to observe, not meddle. . . . Praise is more valuable than blame. . . . Your primary mission as a leader is see to with your own eyes and be seen by your troops while engaged in personal reconnaissance."

88. Ambrose, *Citizen Soldiers*, 473. On the nature and condition of the American army on the eve of the war, see Forty, *Armies*, 145.

89. On contemporaries' observations about the uncanny ability of Patton to create an enormous mobile army of the spirit, see Blumenson, *Patton Papers*, II, 850; Farago, *Patton*, 485. For the contrary mission of American infantry and armored forces in Europe and its own traditions of mobile warfare, see Weigley, *Eisenhower's Lieutenants*, 727–30; cf. Doubler, *Closing with the Enemy*, 282–87. Of all American generals in Normandy, Patton's reputation continues to grow while the others' recede in light of continuing research. See Blumenson, *Generals*, 271–72. If Patton's edited diary entries, collated and published as *War As I Knew It*, were brutal and sometimes repulsive, they were at least honest. Bradley's two memoirs are self-contradictory and characterized by a disturbing disingenuousness throughout. We should also keep in mind that Eisenhower and especially Bradley lived long lives after the war and enjoyed high positions of political and military influence, making overt criticism of their wartime decisions somewhat more difficult than was true of the long-dead and easily caricatured Patton. The recent reappraisal of the generalship of both in Europe is long overdue and will continue. Eisenhower worried about the publication of *War As I Knew It*—especially the case made in it that Eisenhower and SHAEF had prolonged the war in halting Patton. See Murray, *Eisenhower Versus Montgomery*, 40–41.

It takes real circumspection for Americans, who are naturally drawn to the egalitarian persona of Bradley, to appreciate that his natural and understandable irritation with Patton's arrogance had near-disastrous consequences for the American advance into Germany in summer and fall 1944. Moreover, whereas much of Patton's suspicion of others was based on a need for acknowledgment of his genius, Bradley's insecurity grew out of the realization that his own limitations should *not* be known to others.

Chapter Six. The Labyrinth of Slavery

90. For Patton's reaction to Bradley's stop order, see Blumenson, *Generals*, 210–11; *Patton Papers*, II, 598; D'Este, *Decision*, 429–32; Weigley, *Eisenhower's Lieutenants*, 208–11; Florentin, *Battle*, 118. Cf. Ambrose, *Citizen Soldiers*, 89, on what Patton envisioned:

> He had trained and equipped Third Army for just this moment. Straight east to Paris, then northwest along the Seine to seize the crossings, and the Allies would complete an encirclement that would lead to a bag of prisoners bigger than North Africa or Stalingrad. More important, it would leave the Germans defenseless in the west, because Patton could cut off the German divisions in northern France, Belgium, and Holland as he drove for the Rhine.

Patton's complaints about halting at the Seine: Blumenson, *Patton Papers*, II, 519.

91. Bradley, *General's Life*, 298–99. Two things should be noted: (1) Bradley's memoirs were ghost-written; even his speeches were composed by others; (2) the sections of *A General's Life* pertaining to World War Two—in a memoir claiming to be a "An Autobiography by a General of the Army"—were written solely by Clay Blair *after* Bradley had died in 1981 (see *General's Life*, 9–12).

Essame, *Patton*, 172. Cf. the similar assessment of Martin Blumenson, *Generals*, 22–23:

> The fact was, the Allies had the Germans on the ropes in Normandy and had been unable to administer the knockout blow. As the exhilaration of the moment vanished, optimistic intelligence reports foretelling the imminent collapse of Germany quickly changed in tone and substance. . . . Large operations of encirclement are extremely difficult to execute, but the Allies let the chance for the overwhelming victory slip through their fingers. What should have been a finely tuned and well-oiled maneuver was inept and bumbled, displaying contradictory impulses. Hesitation, wrangling, and uncertainty marred the venture. The Germans themselves had foolishly pushed their heads into a noose, and the Allies had been unable to pull the string shut. They closed the Falaise pocket too slowly and then failed to trap the fleeing Germans at the Seine.

92. Eisenhower, *Crusade in Europe*, 279. On the archaeology of the Falaise Gap in later years, see Florentin, *Battle*, 327. A graphic description of the German dead is found in Lucas and Barker, *Killing Ground*, 160. On the numbers lost and killed in the Falaise Gap, see D'Este, *Decision*, 430–31; Florentin, *Battle*, 334–35; Blumenson, *Battle*, 21–23; *Patton*, 235–37. It should be noted that the televised carnage of retreating Iraqis in the Gulf War did much to convince the Americans to allow a cease-fire—even though thousands of Iraqi armored corps were trapped and close to being annihilated. Once freed, they would go on to butcher Shiites and Kurds in the months following the war. For the statistics of the Third Army record at the end of August, see Essame, *Patton*, 187–89.

93. Ambrose, *Citizen Soldiers*, 473. An economic realist like Albert Speer, head of the Third Reich's Arms Ministry, objected to the concentration camps and mass murder of the Jews not so much on moral grounds as on the inherent economic irrationalism of such a policy. He usually opposed views such as those of Otto Ohlendorf's, a self-acclaimed SS expert on National Socialism, who bragged of SS economic ideology:

> We must view and test every economic structure in terms of whether it allows the full development of the basic characteristics of the German. We must be absolutely certain whether we can fully realize in economy the elements of our *Weltanschauung*: honor, freedom, self-responsibility, honesty, and veracity. . . . The goods we produce after the war are not so essential; what *is* essential is that we preserve and develop the substance of our biological values, thus winning the peace. (Speer, *Slave State*, 77)

94. For the advantages in natural resources and industrial output of the Reich before 1942, see Overy, *Why the Allies Won*, 182. For the gratuitous cruelty of those not in the SS toward Jews, see Aroneanu, *Inside the Concentration Camps*, 4–62. On the number of those executed by the Nazis, see, for example, the estimates in Rummel, *Democide*, 100.

95. Speer quote: *Third Reich*, 12. SS text: Rummel, *Democide*, 80; see p. 83 for the Nazi *Weltanschauung*. For the influence of Spengler, Nietzsche, Wagner, and others on Nazi ideology, see Speer, *Third Reich*, 12, 16, 128, 185, 249; Bessel, ed., *Life in the Third Reich*, 27. The idea that Nazi murderers were cultured: Burleigh and Wipperman, *Racial State*, 23–24, 34–36. The general intellectual and cultural basis for anti-Semitism in Germany before Hitler: Goldhagen, *Willing Executioners*, 27–80.

96. Nazi soldier: Ambrose, *Citizen Soldiers*, 441. Reliance on slave labor and perception by Germans of its value: Burleigh and Wipperman, *Racial State*, 295.

> Apart from the nation's foremen, and cases of brutality by, for example, miners in the Ruhr towards the Russian sub-class below them, most German workers seem to have been largely indifferent to the fact that they were working alongside an undernourished army which emerged spectrally from freezing camps but was excluded from public air-raid shelters and swimming baths, and which could be strung up for doing things which the rest of the population took for granted. . . . The Nazis' novel efforts to replace class with a racial society found a ready response in significant section of the populations. (Burleigh and Wipperman, *Racial State*, 303)

For Patton's directive to the Third Army that they were going to wage a war of hatred against the Nazis, see, Green, *Patton's Tank Drive*, 135–36. For the interviews of elderly Germans after the war, see Bessel, ed., *Life in the Third Reich*, 101. German houses: Ambrose, *Citizen Soldiers*, 443.

97. Patton's hatred of Nazis: Forty, *Armies*, 11. For the Nazi perception of America, see Speer's remarks concerning Hitler's ignorance:

> The Americans had not played a very prominent part in the war of 1914–18, he [Hitler] thought, and moreover had not made any great sacrifices of blood. They would certainly not withstand a great trial by fire, for their fighting qualities were low. In general, no such thing as an American people existed as a unit; they were nothing but a mass of immigrants from many nations and races. (*Third Reich*, 121)

Cf. Wilmot, *Struggle*, 427: Hitler reportedly scoffed, "America will never become the Rome of the future. Rome was a state of peasants." He believed Americans to be "rowdies" and "a shocking crowd." More fanaticism on the Eastern front than on the Western: Weinberg, *World at Arms*, 304–5.

98. von Manstein: Bartov, *Hitler's Army*, 130; cf. 168–69. For Nazi ideology within the German ranks, the question of culpability of the German military for Nazi crimes, and the general brutality of the army apart from the battlefield, see Shulman, *Defeat in the West*, 1–13, 313–19; Bartov, *Hitler's Army*, 107–78; cf. Weinberg, *World at Arms*, 302–3. As early as 1936, Hitler had outlined his general plans of conquest and racialism to the German high command. Shulman notes of that lecture:

> Throughout his entire discourse in which the ruthless, aggressive aims of National Socialism were clearly revealed, not a solitary murmur of a moral protest was heard from any of the military personages present. The only matters that worried von Bloomberg and von Fritsch were strategic ones. . . . The minutes of this meeting should decisively destroy any future claims by the German General Staff that they were simple soldiers merely being faithful to their oaths and that they did not realize whither the policy of rearmament was leading them. (29)

For the German army complicity with the Nazis, see also Shirer, *Nightmare Years*, 492–94.

99. Western Europe under occupation, and the attitude of the French people toward Patton's army: Weinburg, *World at Arms*, 509–27; Blumenson, *Liberation*, 57–58, 88–89, 172; Wallace, *Third Army*, 49. Patton's remarks: Blumenson, *Patton Papers*, II, 522–23.

100. For some rough figures of those enslaved and killed from the occupied territories, see Rummel, *Democide*, 64–66; Burleigh and Wipperman, *Racial State*, 113–35; Speer, *Third Reich*, 303. Albert Speer, always the economic pragmatist, saw quickly that the horrific conditions of the SS camps inside Germany made no productive sense, and the hostil-

ity of the forced workers required an enormous investment in guards and police: "Incidentally, it must be noted that according to the figures of January 15, 1945, 36,454 soldiers were employed to guard the 487,000 male prisoners. A newly formed infantry division had an average strength of 11,000 men; thus, over three divisions were tied down because of the prisoners" (*Slave State*, 238).

101. For the unhealthy, homosexuals, and other miscellaneous groups, see Rummel, *Democide*, 18; Bessel, ed., *Life in the Third Reich*, 25–40, and esp. Burleigh and Wipperman, *Racial State*, 137, 295.

102. The literature of the Jewish Holocaust is enormous and beyond the scope of this book; for some general numbers, see Rummel, *Democide*, 5, 30.

> By genocide, the murder of hostages, reprisal raids, forced labor, "euthanasia," starvation, exposure, medical experiments, and terror bombing, and in the concentration and death camps, the Nazis murdered from 15,003,000 to 31,595,000 people, most likely 20,946,000 men, women, handicapped, aged, sick, prisoners of war, forced laborers, camp inmates, critics, homosexuals, Jews, Slavs, Serbs, Germans, Czechs, Italians, Poles, French, Ukrainians and many others. Among them were 1,000,000 children under eighteen years of age. And none of these monstrous figures even include civilian and military combat or war deaths. (*Democide*, 11)

Goldhagen, *Willing Executioners*, 292, points out that Nazi ideologists felt it more valuable to the German state that the Jews were dead than working as slave laborers. See Bessel, ed., *Life in the Third Reich*, 25–82: "Hitler's constant encouragement ensured that the grisly work continued at a time when Germany's military position was deteriorating and it was quite plainly an act of madness to divert precious resources to mass murder. That the Holocaust did continue is the ultimate proof of the irrationality at the heart of National Socialism." On November 19, 1942, Himmler bragged to an assembled group of SS bureaucrats how Germany was at last Jew-free; in euphemistic language he assured the audience that "The Jew has been resettled outside Germany" (Speer, *Slave State*, 251). The description of Auschwitz: Burleigh and Wipperman, *Racial State*, 106.

103. For the reactions of the Third Army when it liberated Orhdruf and Buchenwald, see Patton, *War*, 230–32; Blumenson, *Patton Papers*, II, 684–87; Blumenson, *Patton*, 264; Ambrose, *Citizen Soldiers*, 462; Chamberlin and Feldman, eds., *Liberation*, 5, 76; D'Este, *Patton*, 720–21. Collins's remarks: *Liberation*, 78; "get their act together": Aroneanu, *Inside the Concentration Camps*, 129.

104. "Ten days": Blumenson, *Patton Papers*, II, 504. Langlade: Blumenson, *Battle*, 271. Cf. Essame, *Patton*, 172:

> Eisenhower and Bradley . . . had under their command, eager to take all risks, the most able leader of armoured forces the Allies ever produced in World War Two, at the height of his powers, a man who had devoted the whole of his life for an opportunity such as this, commanding troops whose morale was at its zenith and supported by overwhelming air power. They failed to exploit his talents and in the process took the first of the steps which would ensure the unnecessary prolongation of the war to 1945.

In another context Patton could understand why others fretted. Of Middleton's pause in Brittany he confessed: "I don't know what was the matter with him. Of course, it is a little nerve-wracking to send troops straight into the middle of the enemy front, flanks, and rear open. I had to keep repeating to myself, 'Do not take counsel of your fears'" (Blumenson, *Patton Papers*, II, 495–96).

Chapter Seven. A Different Idea

105. "Nothing to do": Blumenson, *Patton Papers*, II, 372. Much is made of Eisenhower often "saving" Patton from himself; but usually it was vice versa as General Wedemeyer and Patton himself pointed out: Eisenhower sought to deflate unfavorable press accounts about Patton, once it became clear his superiors in Washington wanted Patton to remain. Patton's audacity on the battlefield superseded the SHAEF master plan—and ignored its limitations—in such a way that Eisenhower could later claim such breakouts were part of the master plan all along. The second slapping incident in Sicily and Patton's Knutsford remarks were in retrospect such insignificant occurrences that neither should ever have brought into question Patton's right to command. That Eisenhower saw his determination to support Patton during such manufactured crises as important does not suggest by any means that he "saved" Patton. The more difficult course would have been to come forward immediately and explain to the press and the American people why both incidents had been misinterpreted and blown way out of proportion—and why such vigor and brazenness that Patton had previously displayed was invaluable in leading an American army against the Nazi slave state. The real defenders of Patton—other than his own military brilliance—were, of course, Marshall, Stimson, and Roosevelt, who were not jealous of achievement, but simply wished victory as rapidly as possible. Once Eisenhower sensed that support, he belatedly stepped more forcefully into controversies and claimed Patton to be invaluable. See Farago, *Patton*, 354–56.

106. "Confusing status": Blumenson, *Patton Papers*, II, 397. Bradley, *General's Life*, 218–19. In the revealing comment "did not know how to run an army" concerning the spectacular American victory in Sicily, Bradley exposes his own limitations: operations and "running" an army, not advance on the battlefield, were his definitions of command. I find Bradley's statement—if it is Bradley's real sentiment (see n. 91)—morally reprehensible. Literally thousands of young GIs' lives depended on the excellence in American command to end the war quickly within the parameters of American superiority in manpower and matériel; postwar historical consensus has clearly shown that Patton's requests to advance would have saved American lives. For Bradley to suggest in retrospect that Patton should not have commanded, in light of what he accomplished, is to ignore, either out of personal envy or hurt, the human consequences—here I mean GIs dying in the fall and winter cold on the German border—of the decisions made in France. Much of Bradley's animus, of course, came from Patton's petty and immature derision of him in his diary, excerpts of which were published after Patton's death: "He wears glasses, has a strong jaw, talks profoundly and says little" (Blumenson, *Patton*, 216; cf. Blumenson, *Patton*, 215).

107. Eisenhower's letter: D'Este, *Patton*, 588. Felt "like death": Blumenson, *Patton Papers*, II, 451; "boxed in" at Normandy: Blumenson, *Patton Papers*, II, 419; cf. 450–51. Patton's plans for a breakout: Blumenson, *Patton Papers*, II, 470–71. For Patton's realization that his greatest trouble with superiors—in Morocco, Tunisia, Sicily, and France—came after his greatest battlefield successes, see Patton, *War*, 104–5.

108. On the mythical *Armeegruppe Patton*, see Farago, *Patton*, 407–8; Blumenson, *Patton*, 214. An entry in the official German war diary of the high command of March 20, 1944, noted ominously Patton's presence in England, and followed keenly his movements—through Algiers, Tunis, Corsica, Cairo, Jerusalem, and Malta before arriving in England—which were to signify the approach of his dreaded invasion. Later Hermann Balck, who faced Patton at the Siegfried Line, would remark of his American adversary: "General Patton was the outstanding tactical genius of World War Two. I still consider it a privilege and an unforgettable experience to have had the honor of opposing him"

(Farago, *Patton*, 505). Russian and French respect: Patton, *War*, 86, 138; Blumenson, *Battle of the Generals*, 271.

109. "Altitude too great"—meaning the command was too far removed from the actual fighting: Blumenson, *Patton Papers*, II, 414. Throughout Patton's career, he was willing to be assigned almost anywhere—Sicily, Japan, Europe—if he were guaranteed a chance to fight, even if that meant a substantial reduction from prior responsibility and prestige. Contrast Bradley's attitude about the prospect of going to Japan to command a single army after the victory in Europe—something Patton dreamed of but was denied: "I did not want to go to the Pacific in any job lower than army group commander" (Bradley, *General's Life*, 436).

110. On Patton's own idea for the Third Army once it became operational in France, see Essame, *Patton*, 142–43. The "running end": Blumenson, *Patton Papers*, II, 501. Cf. Ambrose, the biographer of Eisenhower, on the Eisenhower-Bradley attitude toward Patton's audacity at the Falaise Gap: "An entire corps of well-trained, well-equipped tankers, infantrymen and artillery had been wasted at a critical moment. In the boxing analogy, Patton wanted to throw a roundhouse right and get the bout over; his superiors ordered him to throw a short right hook to knock the enemy off balance. But the enemy already was staggering. He should have been knocked out" (*Citizen Soldiers*, 89).

111. Air and armor: Patton, *War*, 84. Patton's leapfrogging: Essame, *Patton*, 142. "Flanks": Blumenson, *Patton Papers*, II, 486; cf. Patton, *War*, 18; Florentin, *Battle*, 18. On July 14, Patton wrote of Bradley and Hodges: "I could break through within three days if I commanded. They try to push all along the front and have no power anywhere. All that is necessary now is to take chances by leading with armored divisions and covering their advance with air bursts. Such an attack would have to be made on a narrow sector, whereas at present we are trying to attack all along the line. I keep worrying for fear the war will be over before I get a chance to fight" (*Patton Papers*, II, 482). "Lives would have been saved": Farago, *Patton*, 790.

112. "Licking the German": Blumenson, *Patton Papers*, II, 472. Patton's transformation of the original Overlord plan and views on his superiors: Farago, *Patton*, 477; cf. 444–45.

113. On the mythmaking concerning Lee and his image as a "Confederate Santa Claus," see Nolan, *Lee Considered*, 153–74.

114. Trevor Dupuy reviewed all commanders active during the Battle of the Bulge, and concluded:

> On the Allied side there were two American Army commanders: Hodges and Patton. Like their German opposite numbers both were skilled professionals, although it is doubtful Hodges was as competent as either [the Germans] Manteuffel or Brandenberger. Patton, on the other hand, was something else. He was probably the most gifted general of any of those being discussed here. He was one of the three or four best American generals of World War II, and perhaps one of the ten best generals of American military history. (*Hitler's Last Gamble*, 370)

It is hard to imagine, however, *which* three or four American generals were Patton's equal in World War Two, much less the other nine that were of similar ability in the pantheon of American war heroes—Washington, Andrew Jackson, Scott, Grant, Sherman, Stonewall Jackson, Pershing, and MacArthur perhaps, but very few others.

115. Timidity of Bradley: Blumenson, *Patton Papers*, II, 434. "Commanding nothing": Blumenson, *Patton Papers*, II, 418. For the significance of the lost opportunities created by stopping Patton, see Hogg, *Patton*, 156, and esp. Essame, *Patton*, 177, 202. The details of Patton's statue, and its relationship with Eisenhower's, are discussed in D'Este, *Patton*, 809.

BIBLIOGRAPHY

(All citations in the Notes refer to one of the titles listed below.)

PART I. YEOMEN OF THEBES.
EPAMINONDAS'S DESCENT INTO THE PELOPONNESE,
WINTER–SPRING, 370–369 B.C.

Anderson, J. K. *Military Theory and Practice in the Age of Xenophon*. Berkeley, 1970.

Barber, G. L. *The Historian Ephorus*. Cambridge, Eng., 1935.

Bauer, A. "Der zweimalige Angriff des Epameinondas auf Sparta." *Historisches Zeitschrift* 65 (1890): 240–74.

Beister, H. *Untersuchungen zu der Zeit der thebanischen Hegemonie*. Munich, 1970.

Bosworth, A. B. *Conquest and Empire: The Reign of Alexander the Great*. Cambridge, Eng., 1988.

Brumfield, A. C. *The Attic Festivals of Demeter and Their Relation to the Agricultural Year*. New York, 1981.

Buck, R. J. *A History of Boeotia*. Edmonton, 1979.

———*Boiotia and the Boiotian League, 432–371 B.C.* Alberta, 1994.

Buckler, J. *The Theban Hegemony, 371–362 B.C.* Cambridge, Mass., 1980.

Burkert, Walter. *Lore and Science in Ancient Pythagoreanism*. Translated by E. L. Minar, Jr., from 1962 German ed. Cambridge, Mass., 1972.

Cartledge, P. A. *Sparta and Lakonia: A Regional History, 1300–362 B.C.* London, 1979.

———*Agesilaos and the Crisis of Sparta*. Baltimore, 1987.

Cawkwell, G. L., "Epaminondas and Thebes." *Classical Quarterly* 66 (1972): 254–78.

Cloché, P. *Thèbes de Béotie*. Namur, Belg., 1952.

Delbrück, H. *History of the Art of War*. Vol. I. English translation of *Geschichte der Kriegskunst im Rahmen der politischen Geschichte* (Berlin, 1920). Westport, Conn., 1975.

Demand, N. *Thebes in the Fifth Century: Heracles Resurgent*. London, 1982.

———*Urban Relocation in Archaic and Classical Greece: Flight and Consolidation*. Norman, Okla., 1990.

Engels, D. *Alexander the Great and the Logistics of the Macedonian Army*. Berkeley, 1978.

Finley, M. I. "Sparta." In *The Use and Abuse of History*. New York, 1975.

Fortina, M. *Epaminonda*. Turin, 1958.

Fossey, J. M. *Topography and Population of Ancient Boeotia*. Chicago, 1986.

Garlan, Y. *Slavery in Ancient Greece*. Translated by J. Lloyd. Ithaca, N.Y., 1988.

Gomme, A. W. "The Topography of Boeotia and the Theories of M. Bérard." *Annual of the British School at Athens* 18 (1911–12): 29–53.

Grote, G. *History of Greece*. Vol. X. London, 1899.

Habicht, C. *Pausanias' Guide to Ancient Greece*. Berkeley, 1985.

Hamilton, C. *Agesilaus and the Failure of Spartan Hegemony*. Ithaca, N.Y., 1991.

Hanson, V. D. "Epameinondas, the Battle of Leuctra, and the 'Revolution' in Greek Battle Tactics." *Classical Antiquity* 7, no. 2 (1988): 190–207.

——*The Western Way of Warfare: Infantry Battle in Classical Greece*. New York, 1989.

——*The Other Greeks: The Agrarian Roots of Western Civilization*. New York, 1995.

——*Fields Without Dreams: Defending the Agrarian Idea*. New York, 1996.

——"Hoplites into Democrats: The Changing Ideology of Athenian Infantry." In *Dēmokratia: A Conversation on Democracies, Ancient and Modern*, edited by J. Ober and C. Hedrick, 289–312. London, 1996.

——*Warfare and Agriculture in Classical Greece*. 2nd rev. ed., Berkeley, 1998.

——, ed. *Hoplites: The Classical Greek Battle Experience*. London, 1991.

Hanson, V. D., and J. Heath. *Who Killed Homer? The Decline of Classical Learning and the Recovery of Greek Wisdom*. New York, 1998.

Hignett, C. *Xerxes' Invasion of Greece*. Oxford, 1963.

Hornblower, S. *A Commentary on Thucydides*. Vols. I and II. Oxford, 1991–96.

Kolchin, P. *American Slavery, 1619–1877*. New York, 1993.

Kromayer, J. *Antike Schlachtfelder in Griechenland*. Vols. I and II. Berlin, 1903–7.

Larsen, J. A. O. *Greek Federal States: Their Institutions and History*. Oxford, 1968.

Lazenby, J. *The Spartan Army*. Warminster, Eng., 1985.

Liddell Hart, B. H. *Strategy*. New York, 1967.

Lloyd, A. B., ed. *Battle in Antiquity*. London, 1996.

McDonough, J. L., and J. P. Jones, *War So Terrible: Sherman and Atlanta*. New York, 1987.

Munn, M. *The Defense of Attica: The Dema Wall and the Boiotian War of 378–375* B.C. Berkeley, 1993.

Ogden, D. "Homosexuality and Warfare." In *Battle in Antiquity*, edited by A. B. Lloyd, 107–68. London, 1996.

Osborne, R. *Greece in the Making, 1200–479* B.C. London, 1996.

Phillipson, A., and E. Kirsten. *Die griechischen Landschaften*. 4 vols. Frankfurt, 1950–59.

Pritchett, W. K. *The Greek State at War*. Vols. I–V. Berkeley, 1971–91.

——*Studies in Ancient Greek Topography*. Pts. 1–8. Berkeley, 1965–93.

Roberts, R. W. *The Ancient Boeotians*. Reprint ed., Chicago, 1974.

Roebuck, C. *A History of Messenia from 369 to 146* B.C. Chicago, 1941.

Roloff, G. *Probleme aus der griechischen Kriegsgeschichte*. Berlin, 1903.

Roy, J. "Arcadia and Boeotia in Peloponnesian Affairs, 370–362 B.C." *Historia* 20 (1971): 569–99.

Ryder, T. *Koine Eirene*. Oxford, 1965.

Sallares, R. *The Ecology of the Ancient Greek World*. Ithaca, N.Y., 1991.

Shrimpton, G. "The Epaminondas Tradition." Ph.D. diss., Stanford University, 1970.

——"The Theban Supremacy in Fourth-Century Literature." *Phoenix* 25 (1971): 310–18.

Swoboda, H. "Zur Geschichte des Epameinondas." *Rheinisches Museum* 55 (1900): 460–75.

————"Epameinondas." In A. Pauly, G. Wissowa, and W. Kroll, *Real-Encyclopädie der klassicschen Altertumswissenschaft*. Berlin, 1893– , col. 2674-26709 (1905).

Symeonoglou, S. *The Topography of Thebes from the Bronze Age to Modern Times*. Princeton, 1985.

Talbert, R. "The Role of the Helots in the Class Struggle at Sparta." *Historia* 38 (1989): 24–40.

Tod, M. N. *A Selection of Greek Historical Inscriptions*. Vol. II. Oxford, 1948.

Trittle, L. "Epilektoi at Athens." *Ancient History Bulletin* 3 (1989): 54–59.

Tuplin, C. "The Leuctra Campaign." *Klio* 69, no. 1 (1987): 84–93.

Vidal-Naquet, P., and P. Lévêque. "Epaminondas the Pythagorean, or the Tactical Problem of Right and Left." In P. Vidal-Naquet, *The Black Hunter*. Baltimore, 1981.

Wallace, P. *Strabo's Description of Boiotia: A Commentary*. Heidelberg, 1979.

Westlake, H. D. "The Sources of Plutarch's Pelopidas." *Classical Quarterly* 33 (1939): 11–22.

————"Xenophon and Epaminondas." *Greek, Roman, and Byzantine Studies* 16 (1975): 23–40.

Wiseman, J. "Epaminondas and the Theban Invasions." *Klio* 51 (1969): 177–99.

PART II. THE ARMY OF THE WEST. SHERMAN'S MARCH TO THE SEA, NOVEMBER 16–DECEMBER 21, 1864

Barrett, J. *Sherman's March Through the Carolinas*. Chapel Hill, 1956.

Bauer, K. J., ed., *Soldiering: The Civil War Diary of Rice C. Bull, 123rd New York Volunteer Infantry*. Novato, Calif., 1977.

Castel, A. *Decision in the West: The Atlanta Campaign of 1864*. Lawrence, Kans., 1992.

Catton, B. *Grant Takes Command*. New York, 1968.

Clark, O., ed., *Downing's Civil War Diary*. Des Moines, 1916.

Coburn, M. *Terrible Innocence: General Sherman at War*. New York, 1993.

Connolly, J. A. "Diary of Major Connolly." *Transactions of the Illinois State Historical Society*. Pub. 35, pt. 3. Springfield, Ill., 1928.

Cox, J. *Sherman's March to the Sea*. New York, 1994.

Davis, B. *Sherman's March*. New York, 1980.

Davis, D. B. *The Problem of Slavery in Western Culture*. Ithaca, N.Y., 1966.

Durden, R. *The Gray and the Black*. Baton Rouge, 1972.

Evans, D. *Sherman's Horsemen*. Bloomington, Ind., 1996.

Fellman, M. *Citizen Sherman*. Lawrence, Kans., 1995.

Finley, M. I. *Ancient Slavery and Modern Ideology*. London, 1980.

Foote, S. *The Civil War: A Narrative: Red River to Appomatox*. New York, 1974.

Glatthaar, J. T. *The March to the Sea and Beyond: Sherman's Troops in the Savannah and Carolinas Campaigns*. New York, 1985.

Griffith, P. *Battle Tactics of the Civil War*. New Haven, 1989.

Hagerman, E. *The American Civil War and the Origins of Modern Warfare: Ideas, Organization, and Field Command*. Bloomington, Ind., 1988.

Hahn, S. *The Roots of Southern Populism: Yeoman Farmers and the Transformation of the Georgia Upcountry, 1850–1890*. New York, 1903.

Harris, J. C. *On the Plantation: A Story of a Georgia Boy's Adventures During the War*. New York, 1892.

Harwell, R., and P. Racine. *The Fiery Trail: A Union Officer's Account of Sherman's Last Campaigns*. Knoxville, 1986.

Hedley, F. Y. *Marching Through Georgia: Pen-Pictures of Everyday Life*. Chicago, 1887.

Helper, H. R., *The Impending Crisis of the South: How to Meet It*. New York, 1963.

Hirshson, S. P. *The White Tecumseh: A Biography of General William T. Sherman*. New York, 1997.

Hitchcock, H. *Marching with Sherman*. Lincoln, Nebr., 1995.

Hughes, N. *Bentonville: The Final Battle of Sherman and Johnston*. Chapel Hill, 1996.

Keim, R. *Sherman: A Memorial in Art, Oratory, and Literature*. Washington, D.C., 1904.

Kennett, L. *Marching Through Georgia: The Story of Soldiers and Civilians During Sherman's Campaign*. New York, 1995.

Klement, F. L. *Copperheads in the Middle West*. Chicago, 1960.

————*The Limits of Dissent: Clement L. Vallandigham and the Civil War*. Lexington, Ky., 1970.

Kolchin, P. *American Slavery: 1619–1877*. New York, 1993.

Lane, M., ed., *Marching Through Georgia: William T. Sherman's Personal Narrative of His March Through Georgia*. New York, 1978.

Lanier, S. *Tiger-Lilies: A Novel*. New York, 1867.

————*Poems of Sidney Lanier*. New York, 1891.

Lewis, L. *Sherman, Fighting Prophet*. New York, 1932.

Liddell Hart, B. H. *Sherman: Soldier, Realist, American*. New York, 1929.

————*Strategy*. New York, 1967.

Linderman, G. F. *Embattled Courage: The Experience of Combat in the American Civil War*. New York, 1987.

Long, E. B. *The Civil War Day by Day: An Almanac, 1861–1865*. New York, 1951.

Marszalek, J. F. *Sherman: A Soldier's Passion for Order*. New York, 1993.

McCormick, E., E. McGehee, and M. Strahl. *Sherman in Georgia*. Boston, 1961.

McDonough, J. L., and J. P. Jones. *War So Terrible: Sherman and Atlanta*. New York, 1987.

McPherson, J. M. *Battle Cry of Freedom: The Civil War Era*. New York, 1988.

————*For Cause and Comrades: Why Men Fought in the Civil War*. New York, 1997.

Melville, H. *Battle-Pieces and Aspects of the War*. New York, 1866.

Merrill, J. M. *William Tecumseh Sherman*. New York, 1971.

Miles, J. *To the Sea: A History and Tour Guide of Sherman's March*. Nashville, 1989.

Myers, R. *The Children of Pride: A True Story of Georgia and the Civil War*. New Haven, 1984.

Nicols, G. W. *The Story of the Great March from the Diary of a Staff Officer*. New York, 1865.

Nolan, A. *Lee Considered*. Chapel Hill, 1991.

Northrop, H. D. *Life and Deeds of General Sherman*. Philadelphia, 1891.

Oakey, D. "Marching Through Georgia and the Carolinas." *Century Monthly Magazine* 34 (October 1887): 917–27.

Olmsted, F. L. *A Journey in the Seaboard Slave States, with Remarks on Their Economy*. New York, 1856.

————*Cotton Kingdom: A Traveller's Observations on Cotton and Slavery in the American Slave States*. New York, 1953.

Overmyer, J. *A Stupendous Effort: The 87th Indiana in the War of Rebellion*. Bloomington, Ind., 1997.

Pepper, G. *Personal Recollections of Sherman's Campaigns in Georgia and the Carolinas*. Zanesville, Ohio, 1866.

Phillips, U. B. *The Slave Economy of the Old South*. Baton Rouge, 1968.

Ransom, R. L. *Conflict and Compromise: The Political Economy of Slavery, Emancipation, and the American Civil War*. Cambridge, Eng., 1989.

Reston, J., Jr. *Sherman's March and Vietnam*. New York, 1984.

Royster, C. *The Destructive War: William Tecumseh Sherman, Stonewall Jackson, and the Americans*. New York, 1991.

Sherman, W. T. *Memoirs of William T. Sherman*. 2 vols. New York, 1875.

Stampp, K. *The Peculiar Institution: Slavery in the Ante-Bellum South*. New York, 1956.

Ste. Croix, G. E. M. de. "Early Christian Attitudes to Property and Slavery." *Studies in Church History* 12 (1975): 1–38.

——The Struggle in the Ancient Greek World. Ithaca, N.Y., 1981.

Thorndike, R. S., ed. *The Sherman Letters*. New York, 1971.

Trowbridge, J. T. *A Picture of the Desolated States and the Work of Restoration, 1865–1868*. Hartford, Conn., 1868.

Upson, F. T. *With Sherman to the Sea: The Civil War Letters, Diaries, and Reminiscences of Theodore F. Upson*. Edited by O. O. Winther. Baton Rouge, 1943.

Walters, J. B., *Merchant of Terror: General Sherman and Total War*. New York, 1973.

PART III. THE THIRD ARMY: PATTON'S RACE INTO GERMANY, AUGUST 1, 1944–MAY 8, 1945

Ambrose, S. *Citizen Soldiers*. New York, 1997.

Aroneanu, E. *Inside the Concentration Camps*. Translated by T. Wissen. Westport, Conn., 1996.

Bartov, O. *Hitler's Army: Soldiers, Nazis, and War in the Third Reich*. New York, 1991.

Bessel, R. *Life in the Third Reich*. Oxford, 1987.

Blumenson, M. *The Patton Papers*. 2 vols. New York, 1972–74.

——Liberation. New York, 1978.

——Patton: The Man Behind the Legend, 1885–1945. New York, 1985.

——The Battle of the Generals. New York, 1993.

Blumenson, M., and J. Stokesbury. *Masters of the Art of Command*. New York, 1975.

Bradley, O., with Clay Blair. *A General's Life*. New York, 1983.

Burleigh, M., and W. Wipperman. *The Racial State: Germany, 1933–1945*. Cambridge, Eng., 1991.

Chamberlin, B., and M. Feldman, eds. *The Liberation of the Nazi Concentration Camps, 1945*. Washington, D.C., 1987.

D'Este, C. *Decision in Normandy*. New York, 1988.

——Patton: A Genius for War. New York, 1995.

Doubler, M. *Closing with the Enemy: How GIs Fought the War in Europe*. Lawrence, Kans., 1994.

Dupuy, T. N. *Hitler's Last Gamble: The Battle of the Bulge, December 1944–January 1945*. New York, 1994.

Eisenhower, D. *Crusade in Europe*. New York, 1948.

Ellis, L. F. *Victory in the West*. 2 vols. London, 1968.

Essame, H. *Patton: The Commander*. London, 1974.

Farago, L. *Patton: Ordeal and Triumph*. New York, 1964.

——The Last Days of Patton. New York, 1981.

Florentin, E. *The Battle of the Falaise Gap*. Translated by M. Savill. New York, 1967.

Forty, G. *The Armies of George S. Patton*. London, 1996.

Goldhagen, D. *Hitler's Willing Executioners: Ordinary Germans and the Holocaust*. New York, 1996.

Green, M. *Patton's Tank Drive: D-Day to Victory*. Osceola, Wis. 1978.

Harkins, P. *When the Third Cracked Europe*. Harrisburg, Pa., 1969.

Hogg, I. V. *Patton*. New York, 1982.

Hoyt, E. P. *The GI's War: The Story of the American Soldiers in Europe in World War II*. New York, 1988.

Irving, D. *The War Between the Generals*. New York, 1981.

Keegan, J. *Six Armies in Normandy*. New York, 1982.

Liddell Hart, B. H. *The Memoirs of Captain Liddell Hart*. London, 1965–67.

Lucas, J., and J. Barker. *The Killing Ground*. London, 1978.

Marshall, S. L. A. *Men Against Fire*. New York, 1947.

Morelock, J. D. *Generals of the Ardennes: American Leadership in the Battle of the Bulge*. Washington, D.C., 1994.

Murray, G. E. *Eisenhower Versus Montgomery: The Continuing Debate*. Westport, Conn., 1996.

Nye, P. *The Patton Mind*. New York, 1993.

Overy, R. *Why the Allies Won*. New York, 1995.

Patton, G. *War as I Knew It*. New York, 1980.

Patton, R. *The Pattons: A Personal History of an American Family*. Washington, D.C., 1994.

Prefer, N. *Patton's Ghost Corps*. Novato, Calif., 1998.

Province, C. *Patton's Third Army*. New York, 1992.

Rummel, R. J. *Democide: Nazi Genocide and Mass Murder*. New Brunswick, N.J., 1992.

Shirer, W. *The Nightmare Years, 1930–1940*. New York, 1984.

Shulman, M. *Defeat in the West*. Westport, Conn., 1948.

Sobel, B. *The Fighting Pattons*. New York, 1997.

Speer, A. *Inside the Third Reich*. New York, 1970.

———*The Slave State: Heinrich Himmler's Masterplan for SS Supremacy*. London, 1981.

van Creveld, M. *Fighting Power: German and U.S. Army Performance, 1939–1945*. Westport, Conn., 1974.

———*Supplying War: Logistics from Wallenstein to Patton*. Cambridge, Eng., 1977.

Wallace, B. *Patton and His Third Army*. Harrisburg, Pa., 1946.

Weigley, R. *Eisenhower's Lieutenants*. Bloomington, Ind., 1981.

Weinberg, G. *A World at Arms*. Cambridge, Eng., 1994.

Whiting, C. *Patton's Last Battle*. New York, 1987.

Wilmot, C. *The Struggle for Europe*. London, 1952.

INDEX